Principles and Practice of Sport Management

Lisa Pike Masteralexis, BS, JD
Associate Professor
University of Massachusetts, Amherst
Amherst, Massachusetts

Carol A. Barr, BS, MS, PhD
Assistant Professor
University of Massachusetts, Amherst
Amherst, Massachusetts

Mary A. Hums, BBA, MBA, MA, PhD
Associate Professor
University of Louisville
Louisville, Kentucky

AN ASPEN PUBLICATION®
Aspen Publishers, Inc.
Gaithersburg, Maryland
1998

Library of Congress Cataloging-in-Publication Data

Principles and practice of sport management / [edited by] Lisa Pike
Masteralexis, Carol A. Barr, Mary A. Hums.
p. cm.
Includes bibliographical references and index.
ISBN 0-8342-1021-5
1. Sports—Management. 2. Sports administration.
I. Masteralexis, Lisa Pike. II. Barr, Carol A. III. Hums, Mary A.
GV713.P75 1998
796´.06´9—dc21
98-12301
CIP

Aspen Publishers, Inc., grants permission for photocopying for limited personal or internal use.
This consent does not extend to other kinds of copying, such as copying for general distribution,
for advertising or promotional purposes, for creating new collective works, or for resale.
For information, address Aspen Publishers, Inc., Permissions Department,
200 Orchard Ridge Drive, Suite 200, Gaithersburg, Maryland 20878.

Orders: (800) 638-8437
Customer Service: (800) 234-1660

About Aspen Publishers • For more than 35 years, Aspen has been a leading professional
publisher in a variety of disciplines. Aspen's vast information resources are available in both
print and electronic formats. We are committed to providing the highest quality information
available in the most appropriate format for our customers. Visit Aspen's Internet site for
more information resources, directories, articles, and a searchable version of Aspen's full
catalog, including the most recent publications: **http://www.aspenpub.com**
Aspen Publishers, Inc. • The hallmark of quality in publishing
Member of the worldwide Wolters Kluwer group.

Editorial Services: Kathleen Ruby
Library of Congress Catalog Card Number: 98-12301
ISBN: 0-8342-1021-5

Printed in the United States of America

1 2 3 4 5

Front cover: Camden Yards and crowd photographs courtesy of Jerry Wachter
Back cover: Courtesy of NBA Properties, Inc.

To all our students, who continue to inspire us to teach and learn

TABLE OF CONTENTS

Lifestyle Sports

Career Preparation

CONTRIBUTORS

Editors

Lisa Pike Masteralexis, JD
Associate Professor
Sport Management Program
University of Massachusetts
Amherst, Massachusetts

Carol A. Barr, PhD
Assistant Professor
Sport Management Program
University of Massachusetts
Amherst, Massachusetts

Mary A. Hums, PhD
Associate Professor
Sport Administration Program
University of Louisville
Louisville, Kentucky

Contributors

Tim Ashwell, PhD
Assistant Professor of Sport
    Management and Sport History
Department of Health and Human
    Performance
Iowa State University
Ames, Iowa

Kevin Barrett
General Manager
Springfield Civic Center and
    Symphony Hall
Springfield, Massachusetts

Adri H. Broeke, PhD
Director
Hanze Service Gamma of the
    Hanzchogeschool
Groningen, The Netherlands

Stephen Bromage, MS
History Department
University of Massachusetts
Amherst, Massachusetts

Dan Covell, MS
Sport Management Program
University of Massachusetts
Amherst, Massachusetts

Todd W. Crossett, PhD
Assistant Professor
Sport Management Program
University of Massachusetts
Amherst, Massachusetts

Howard M. Davis
Assistant Department Head for
    External Affairs
Director of Internships
Sport Management Program
University of Massachusetts
Amherst, Massachusetts

James M. Gladden, PhD
Assistant Professor
Sport Management Program
University of Massachusetts
Amherst, Massachusetts

Virginia R. Goldsbury, MEd
Director of Career Planning
College of Food and Natural
    Resources
University of Massachusetts
Amherst, Massachusetts

Michael J. Graney
President
Springfield Business Development
    Corporation
Springfield, Massachusetts

Laurie Gullion, MS
Outdoor Recreation Specialist
Greenfield Community College
Greenfield, Massachusetts

Dennis R. Howard, PhD
Professor of Sport Marketing
Charles H. Lundquist College of
    Business
University of Oregon
Eugene, Oregon

William C. Howland, Jr.
International Health, Racquet &
    Sportsclub Association
Boston, Massachusetts

Mireia Lizandra, PhD
Sports Management Consultant
Philadelphia, Pennsylvania

Mark McDonald, PhD
Assistant Professor
Sport Management Program
University of Massachusetts
Amherst, Massachusetts

Berend Rubingh, PhD
Director
Manage to Manage, the Sport
    Management Consultancy
Groningen, The Netherlands

William A. Sutton, PhD
Associate Professor
Sport Management Program
University of Massachusetts
Amherst, Massachusetts

Glenn M. Wong, JD
Department Head
Sport Management Program
University of Massachusetts
Amherst, Massachusetts

FOREWORDS

The sport industry is global. It needs leaders to maintain its success and to remain competitive with other industries. Effective sport leaders must have sport management knowledge and preparation. They must learn the intricacies and uniqueness of the global sport industry.

This textbook is a key for the preparation of future sport managers. It is an excellent training manual for understanding the sport industry. It provides a foundation for the preparation of future sport managers. The text provides substantive information on sport management, sport law, sport marketing, sport finance, sport ethics, and sport history. These principles are then applied to all of the segments of the sport industry; from high school, collegiate, and professional sport to international sport and European sport club systems to health, fitness, and recreation. The text also introduces all of the support systems necessary to sustain the sport industry (broadcasting, media relations, and facility and event management).

The authors have done a thorough job addressing the complexities of the sport industry. The text offers a global vision of the sport management field. For those of you in the training process, a book like this can be an excellent resource and a key to your career preparation.

His Excellency Juan Antonio Samaranch
President
International Olympic Committee

It is indeed a privilege and honor to be asked to write a foreword to a text in sport management. It is doubly gratifying when such a request comes from very talented, established, and young scholars in the field. I thank the editors, Lisa Pike Masteralexis, Carol A. Barr, and Mary A. Hums for the honor.

The growth of sport management as a professional field is predicated on a sound body of knowledge unique to the field. One indication of such growth in knowledge base is the publication of scholarly and trade journals. Yet another indication of such growth is the publication of textbooks. It is trite to say that the future of the field depends largely on the current students in sport management programs. Thus, it is critical that we have good textbooks that distill and collate the knowledge for presentation to the students.

The editors must be complimented for bringing out this text and partially filling the void in this area. The nature of the book is best indicated by the title of the book, *Principles and Practice of Sport Management*. The editors have divided the text into broader foci—(a) foundations of sport management which include chapters on the history of sport management, management, marketing, financial, legal, and ethical principles; (b) amateur sport industry chapters on high school and youth sport, college sport, the European club sport system, and international sport; (c) professional sport industry including chapters on sports agency and professional sport; (d) sport industry support segments with chapters on facility management, event management, media relations, sport broadcasting, sporting goods industry; (e) lifestyle sports including chapters on health and fitness industry and recreational sport; and (f) career preparation. The material covers significant aspects of the theory and practice in sport management. As is evident, the text covers most of the topics suggested by the Joint Task Force of the National Association of Sport and Physical Education and the North American Society for Sport Management as imperatives for sport management degree programs, and is best suited for an introductory course in sport management.

The editors have also recruited the right kind of scholars and professionals to write the chapters on specific topics. The authors of various chapters have the necessary expertise and background experience to cover each topic cogently and succinctly. What is remarkable about the authors is that they come from different backgrounds, and they include mostly young writers. Even more remarkable is the fact that the book is not a compilation of previous work; the chapters were expressly written for this text.

In sum, the editors have done a good job of selecting the most relevant topics, enlisting the necessary talent to cover the topics, and compiling an excellent text. While congratulating the editors on completing this arduous task, I am also convinced that teachers and students will find the text quite valuable to their professional preparation programs.

Packinathan "Chella" Chelladurai, PhD
Professor in the Sports Management Program
The Ohio State University

PREFACE

This textbook has been developed for use in introductory sport management courses such as Principles of Sport Administration and Introduction to Sport Management. Directed toward undergraduate students, the textbook has three distinct sections. The first six chapters provide an overview of basic knowledge areas for the successful sport manager, presenting fundamental principles and key skills, as well as information on current issues. Each of Chapters 7 through 19 presents an overview of a major sport industry segment in which a sport manager could work, followed by a case study to spark debate and discussion. Chapter 9, The European Sport Club System, is the only chapter that does not have a case study; however, the chapter's introduction, which gives an American's view of the club sport system, can be used to spark discussion in place of the case study. The last chapter, Chapter 20, provides the reader with the basics of breaking into the highly competitive sport management industry. We have included an international perspective where appropriate throughout to give readers a broad view of sport management in the global context, which they will need as the world grows increasingly "smaller" in the decades to come.

We would like to draw attention to Chapters 9 and 10, which focus on sport in the international setting. Chapter 9, The European Sport Club System, was written by prominent authors from the Netherlands, Drs. Berend Rubingh and Adri Broeke, who are knowledgeable about the historical development of the sport club system and its place in modern sport, especially in Western Europe. The chapter offers the reader unfamiliar with the club sport system a unique insight into its operation. The chapter was written in Dutch and translated into English, so its organization and tone are slightly different from the rest of the text. Chapter 10, International Sport, guides the reader through the global "sportscape" by examining the burgeoning sport industry around the world and the structures of two major international events, the Olympic Games and the Paralympic Games. In this chapter, the reader should pay particular attention to use of the word "football" instead of the word "soccer," to which most Americans are accustomed. This terminology is used purposefully, to remind the reader that in the majority of the world "football" in fact does not mean American football as played by the National Football League and the World League of American Football, but rather the traditional sport played at the much anticipated and celebrated World Cup. The chapter also makes the point that the reader should not confuse "globalization" of sport with the "Americanization" of global sport. Chapters 9 and 10 together offer the perspective that the "American Way" is only one of the many ways successful sport systems operate around the world.

This textbook offers a mix of contributions from scholars and practitioners. Chapter 10, International Sport, was coauthored by a former National Olympic and Local Organizing Committee employee with experience working three Olympic Games and the Pan American Games. Chapter 13, Facility Management, written by two practitioners, provides an insider's perspective into what it takes to work in this high-energy, long-hours profession. Chapter 20, Strategies for Career Success, was coauthored by a longtime university career counselor who is familiar with what organizations look for in successful candidates. These chapters tend to have a somewhat different tone from the others, as they are written by practitioners. In addition, many of the scholars who contributed to the book returned to the classroom after years of working in the industry, so their thoughts offer a unique blend of information from both academic and industry perspectives.

Overall, this textbook allows the reader to learn both the foundations and principles on which sport management operates and an opportunity to apply those foundations and principles to the sport industry. This textbook also offers historical perspectives as well as thoughts about current and future industry issues and trends. For all these reasons, this textbook will prove a valuable resource to those seeking employment in this field, as well as to those whose role it is to educate future sport managers.

ACKNOWLEDGMENTS

We would like to acknowledge the efforts of some individuals without whom this text would not be possible. First and foremost we express our deep appreciation to our contributing authors. Each author contributed his or her valuable expertise and experience to create a work that provides a wealth of knowledge to the sport management student. Through the editorial process, we have gained from them a greater understanding of the sport industry and our curriculum. Finally, we commend their patience and good-natured attitudes as we polished drafts to achieve our goals and present our philosophy.

We are honored that Dr. Packinathan "Chella" Chelladurai, a professor in the Sports Management Program at The Ohio State University, and His Excellency Juan Antonio Samaranch, President of the International Olympic Committee, have agreed to write forewords for our book. Both are internationally respected for their work in sport management. Professor Chelladurai is a highly respected scholar in the sport management field who is clearly a leader in the academic profession. His Excellency is a highly respected leader in the field of sport management who has led the Olympic Movement into the modern sports age. Through His Excellency's leadership skills, negotiating, and diplomacy, the Olympic Games have seen the largest number of nations and participants in their history.

We also thank University of Massachusetts, Amherst, Sport Management Department Head and Professor Glenn M. Wong for his vision of creating an introductory text with contributing authors primarily from one sport management program.

Finally, we thank everyone at Aspen Publishers for their efforts in seeing this project through. Their friendly, patient, and encouraging approach to the publication process made this project an enjoyable experience.

xix

CHAPTER 1

History of Sport Management

Todd W. Crosset, Stephen Bromage, and Mary A. Hums

Key words: clubs, The Jockey Club, league, William Hulbert, professional tournaments, Fred Corcoran, James G. Mason, Walter O'Malley, Ohio University, North American Society for Sport Management (NASSM)

INTRODUCTION

The contemporary sport industry is complex and has unique legal, business, and management practices and imperatives. The complexity of contemporary sport management is a product of history. Sport management structures that have developed in the past several hundred years organize sporting events in different ways to meet the particular needs of participants, spectators, and sponsors at a particular juncture of history. The club system, the league system, and tournaments each evolved in response to broad social changes and to address specific issues within a segment of the sport industry. The evolution of each of these three management structures illustrates that managers need to be creative in the ways they run sports and need to understand that a particular management structure won't work in all situations. The evolution of these structures also shows that managers who are flexible and adaptable to changes in the broader society can play a significant role in determining the viability of their sport.

THE ENGLISH CLUB SYSTEM: SPORTS AND COMMUNITY

England was the birthplace of modern sport and sport management (Mandell, 1984). Almost all western sports played today, including track and field, all the variations of football, and the stick-and-bat games like baseball, field hockey, and

1

cricket, can be traced to England. To an extent, the broad influence of England's sporting culture is the result of the British Empire's imperial power in the eighteenth and nineteenth centuries. Britain had colonies all over the world and took her sports to all of them. Even so, the continuing influence of the British sports tradition after the empire's demise has as much to do with how the English organized sport as the country's political and cultural domination does with imperialism. Even sports that originated outside of England—including basketball, gymnastics, and golf—employ English sport organization and management principles.

In the eighteenth century, the English aristocracy, made up of nobles and the landed gentry, began to develop sports **clubs** to provide sporting activities for club members. Membership in these clubs was limited to the politically and economically powerful of English society. The earliest clubs simply organized one-time events or annual competitions and brought members together for social events. By the nineteenth century, clubs standardized rules, settled disputes between clubs, and organized seasons of competitions. Thoroughbred racing was one of the first sports transformed by the club management system. **The Jockey Club**, based in Newmarket, originated in the mid-1700s and became the regulatory body and management center for the sport for over a century. Other English sports like cricket, rugby union, and soccer adopted a similar club management structure. Thoroughbred racing is focused on here simply because it is the earliest example of club management.

THOROUGHBRED RACING

During the feudal era (1100–1650) the English aristocracy used horses to demonstrate their power over their serfs. After the collapse of the feudal system, the horse retained its symbolic power, becoming a sign of wealth and economic power as well as a symbol of military might.

Early races were local events, often associated with holidays or horse sales. By the mid-eighteenth century, thoroughbred racing had established a broad following among the elite. Local groups of breeders organized races. Despite the extreme stratification of eighteenth-century English society, horse races drew a broad and diverse audience. All levels of society attended races. Horse owners arranged the events and put up purses to show off their best horses and to demonstrate their prestige. The owners, the elite of the community, keeping with tradition and meeting their social obligation to entertain the masses, did not charge admission.

At this point horse racing was locally managed by a local club. The organization was essentially a volunteer system of management and was controlled by the same wealthy men who owned the horses and estates. This system gave horse racing the appearance of fairness. The public believed that the aristocracy—men of breeding, culture, and wealth—would not be tempted by bribes, influenced by petty feuds, or swayed to make unfair decisions. In addition, even though horse races were important for demonstrating prestige, they were rarely the primary business interest of the horse owners who controlled the sport. Consequently, seventeenth-century horse racing and sport remained largely separate from the growing capitalist system. Horse racing at this time existed primarily for the entertainment of wealthy club members and did not have to be an independent, self-supporting financial entity.

The local club system governed the sport successfully as long as racing remained local. Soon, however, three factors combined to create a need for more systematic management: the desire of owners to breed and train the fastest horse, the increasing complexity of gambling, and the expansion of the sport.

As the elite gained prestige for owning the fastest horses, horses were bred for no other purpose but to win races. Races usually consisted of a series of four-mile heats. The ideal horse combined speed with endurance. Speed, for the first time, was appreciated for its own sake, distinct from its religious, military, or economic purpose—a uniquely modern phenomenon (Mandell, 1984). The thoroughbred horse was the product of this search for speed. The breed was so closely connected to the English sense of identity and prestige, in fact, that for many years it was illegal to sell a thoroughbred to foreigners.

Gambling on thoroughbred horse races was common among all classes. In earlier times, those who wagered had believed that successful bets were evidence of God's favor. However, much as speed became appreciated for its own merits, betting on thoroughbred races began to be appreciated for its own, secular value. Gambling provided exciting entertainment and allowed bettors to demonstrate their ability to calculate rationally who would win (Mandell, 1984).

Before horse racing was organized formally, gambling actually ensured fair competition. Horse racing had generally been a head-to-head competition between two horses. If the crowd suspected that a jockey had allowed another contestant to win, they would punish that jockey themselves, often physically. By the eighteenth century, innovations to the sport that had been made to draw larger audiences and enhance the ways spectators could wager had also made the system of gambling more complex. The English created handicapping, tip sheets, and sweepstakes; used the stopwatch to time races; standardized race distances; and added weights to horses. However, as the influence and importance of gambling grew, so did the opportunity to cheat and fix the outcome of races. The increased complexity of the sport made it difficult for the audience to detect when and how races were fixed. As a result, conventional methods could not be counted on to police the sport (Henriches, 1991).

In the 1830s rail transportation enabled owners to compete nationally. Local management governing area breeders, owners, and jockeys had worked well because of the familiarity between all involved, but national competition meant that race organizers now managed participants they did not know very well, if at all. Thus, the management of thoroughbred racing needed to become more systematic.

THE JOCKEY CLUB

The roots of this management system can be traced to around 1750 when a group of noble patrons in Newmarket established The Jockey Club. This group's responsibility was to settle disputes, establish rules, determine eligibility, designate officials, regulate breeding, and punish unscrupulous participants. The club organized, sponsored, and promoted local events (Vamplew, 1989). Club members put up the purse money and restricted entries to thoroughbreds owned by club members. The effective organization and management of thoroughbred racing in Newmarket made it a national hub for the sport. Local champions faced challenges from owners outside their region. The Jockey Club sponsored prestigious races that attracted horse owners from across England. As the need grew for a strong national governing body to establish rules and standards and to create a mechanism for resolving disputes, The Jockey Club from Newmarket emerged to serve that function (Henriches, 1991).

Some of the lasting contributions The Jockey Club made to racing included sponsorsing a stud book listing the lineage of thoroughbreds, to help ensure the purity of the breed; promoting a series of race schedules; announcing, regulating, and reporting on sales of horses; and restricting the people involved with thoroughbred breeding and racing to the English elite. Beyond horse racing, The Jockey Club served as a model for wider sport management practices in England. Cricket, boxing, and other English sports adopted the management and organizational structure developed in thoroughbred horse racing. In each case, one club emerged, not out of a formal process, but by collective prominence, as the coordinating and controlling body of the sport (Henriches, 1991). The Marylebone Cricket Club, for example, revised the rules of cricket in 1788 and became the international governing club for the entire sport (J. Williams, 1989). In 1814, the Pugilist Society was formed by a group of gentlemen to regulate bare-knuckle boxing and guarantee purses. This group governed boxing until the late 1860s, when it was challenged by the Amateur Athletic Club, the organization behind the creation and promotion of Marquis of Queensbury rules for gloved competitions (Sugden, 1996; Shipley, 1989). Even sports like association football (soccer) and rugby, which were organized much later, adopted the club organizational structure (Henriches, 1991). Local school sports, including rugby, were organized by alumni into clubs. As the clubs arranged competitions, disputes over rules emerged. Collectives like Rugby Football Union (1863) were created to standardize the rules. But even here, in its formative years, Rugby Football Union was dominated by men associated with the Rugby School (G. Williams, 1989).

The club structure was a highly successful way to organize sport in eighteenth- and nineteenth-century England. Club structure depended on the appearance of fairness, loyal support, and volunteer management for its success. The aristocrats who managed and sponsored sport were presumed to be honest and disinterested and gave spectators the sense that competition was fair. Fairness was cultivated through the reputation of sport organizers and their nonprofit motives. Loyalty to specific teams was cultivated through membership. Clubs, to this day, are committed to serving their broad membership and not simply managing an elite sports enterprise. European football clubs, for example, offer programs and facilities intended to build community and provide recreation for members in addition to patronizing their high-profile teams. Clubs organize youth teams and adult recreational leagues and hold social events like dinners and dances for their memberships. Some club sports, like association football in Europe, have large built-in memberships and loyal fan bases and consequently rarely have a problem attracting crowds for their matches.

Many contemporary sports have their organizational roots in the club sport system. These include American college athletics, the National Olympic Federations, rugby, and European football. These organizations are characterized by their nonprofit status and inclusive membership. Once the dominant management structure of elite sport in Europe, the club system is being replaced by a profit-oriented league system. Even European football, once the prime example of the club system, is changing. Elite European club teams are increasingly being controlled by wealthy individuals and run like businesses (King, 1997). The emerging European sport management system has its roots in the American professional sport league system that appeared in the nineteenth century. Ironically, the American league system developed when the English club system proved poorly suited to the social atmosphere in the United States in the nineteenth century.

THE AMERICAN LEAGUE STRUCTURE: SPORT GROWS INTO A BUSINESS

In the early 1800s, upper-class sports enthusiasts in the United States attempted to develop American sports along the lines of the English club system but found limited success. Young men formed clubs throughout the nineteenth century, complete with volunteer management, but these clubs were not able to establish a place in American culture the way clubs had in England and Europe. The greatest obstacle to the club system in the United States was probably the country's lack of the aristocratic tradition that had given the club system both its means of support and its legitimacy in Europe. While European clubs emphasized sport to attract large and broad memberships, the most prestigious clubs in the United States were primarily social clubs that did not sponsor sporting events. Athletic clubs, like the New York Athletic Club, did not gain prestige until late in the century when the profit-oriented league system had already established a foothold on the American cultural landscape (Gorn & Goldstein, 1993). The league structure grew out of the success of harness racing in the 1830s and 1840s.

THE FAILURE OF THE JOCKEY CLUB IN THE UNITED STATES

The problems faced by an early nineteenth-century jockey club in New York City illustrate why the club system was poorly suited to the United States and why a new sport management system arose. Attempts by the New York Association for the Improvement of the Breed (NYAIB) to overcome the managerial limitations of the club system were the first steps toward a league system. In the 1820s and 1830s, the NYAIB regulated and promoted thoroughbred horse racing in New York and on Long Island and operated the Union Race Course. The NYAIB's membership consisted of wealthy businessmen who pursued horse racing as a hobby. The NYAIB struggled with finances and found itself in debt to racetrack owners and unable to put up sufficient purses to attract the best horses (Adelman, 1986). In 1828, Caldwalder Colden, a member of the club, proposed an entrepreneurial solution. He suggested that the club sell $10,000 worth of stock in the club and charge spectators admission. The membership, wanting to maintain their exclusiveness, balked at the idea of selling stock in the club but agreed to allow Colden to manage the track like a business for the 1829 season. It was an innovative but uneasy mix of commerce and patronage. The NYAIB continued to put up prize money and regulate racing at the course while Colden ran the track as a profit-driven business (Adelman, 1986).

Colden managed the track to appeal to spectators instead of strictly for the entertainment of the owners. He extended the racing season to attract better horses and more fans. He also charged *all* spectators admission, something previously unheard of. In the past, only grandstand spectators might have been asked to pay admission. Colden was ahead of his time. English racing fans would not witness the enclosure of tracks and admission fees for another 50 years (Vamplew, 1989). The general public resisted the new admission policy, feeling that as long as the upper class promoted and profited from the sport, the upper class had an obligation to provide the sport free as entertainment to the masses (Adelman, 1986).

The experiment in professional management ultimately failed. The members of the NYAIB thought that Colden's business strategy undercut their patronage and control of the sport. They resented having to contribute to the purse without sharing in the financial return. Hence, Colden's experiment remained undercapitalized and only partially supported. In 1830, a Union Race Course event was canceled because of insufficient purse money. The crowd, most of whom had paid the large sum of $1 for the half-day ferry and train travel to the track, and then paid 50¢ admission, rioted. The NYAIB blamed Colden. Colden blamed the NYAIB. Colden was fired and his effort to run horse racing as a joint partnership between patronage and capitalism was dropped (Adelman, 1986).

HARNESS RACING: THE FIRST NATIONAL PASTIME AND PROFESSIONAL SPORT

While horse racing languished, a uniquely American sport developed: harness racing. Harness racing was the sport of the common person, an early precursor of stock car racing. In the 1820s, the horse and buggy was commonplace and the preferred transportation of a growing middle class. Many early harness races took place on the hard-packed streets of cities, and anyone with a horse and buggy could participate. The sport was not exclusive. The horses that pulled the buggies were of no particular breeding. It was relatively inexpensive to own and maintain a horse, and horses that worked and pulled a wagon by day raced in the evening (Adelman, 1986).

As the popularity of informal harness races grew, enterprising racing enthusiasts staged races on horse racing tracks. Track owners—whose business was suffering from the mismanagement and elitism of thoroughbred racing—were eager to rent their tracks to harness racers. Promoters began to offer participants purse money raised through modest entry fees and paid track owners rent by charging admission (Adelman, 1986).

The middle class, which included artisans, shopkeepers, dockworkers, clerks, and the like, were far more likely to participate than were wealthy merchants. Because harness racing lacked the elitist tradition of horse racing, the public was more willing to pay admission to subsidize the event. The sport was their own. Promoters could count on spectator interest, and participation grew. By the 1830s harness racing was America's most popular sport (Adelman, 1986).

Although harness racing was not always as dramatic as thoroughbred racing, it was a better spectator sport. A traditional horse racing event consisted of a single four-mile race. Often only two horses were in the field. The races were so grueling that horses raced only once or twice a year. Consequently, it was difficult for individual horses to develop a reputation or following among fans. In contrast, harness racing was a sprint. Horses recovered quickly and could compete almost daily. Promoters offered spectators as many as a dozen races in an afternoon. Horses of any breed could race, ensuring a large field of competitors. These dynamics gave the public more races, excitement, and opportunities to gamble (Adelman, 1986).

The management structure of harness racing was also distinct from that of horse racing. The sport was managed by track owners and race promoters instead of wealthy clubmen. These entrepreneurs' livelihood depended on the gate for revenues, and therefore they catered to spectators. Ideally, promoters tried to match the best horses against each other to build spectator interest. Competition created problems for harness racing promoters, though. Potential contestants often tried to increase their chances of victory by avoiding races with highly touted trotters. However, without being able to offer the fastest trotters competing against each other, promoters had difficulty promoting races. In order to ensure a high level of competition, innovative promoters began to offer the owners of the best and most famous trotters a percentage of the gate (Adelman, 1986).

The desire to improve gate revenues and increase profits led some participants and promoters to fix races in order to promote and create demand for future races. Highly regarded trotters traded victories in an effort to maintain spectator interest. Harness races were sometimes choreographed dramas. Unlike those involved with The Jockey Club, harness racing promoters and participants lacked the reputation to convince the public that races were legitimate, and ultimately spectators lost faith in the integrity of the sport. By the Civil War harness racing had lost its appeal and its audience (Adelman, 1986).

WILLIAM HULBERT'S NATIONAL LEAGUE

Harness racing's popularity and the commercial promise it showed led sports enthusiasts and managers to further refine and develop a sport management system that would work in the United States. The solution proved to be the profit-oriented **league**, which baseball organizers pioneered in the 1870s. Baseball was the first sport to successfully employ the league structure.

Baseball surpassed cricket in popularity in the United States after the Civil War. Baseball required less skill to play than cricket. America lacked a stick-and-ball tradition, so a game that required less skill was more attractive. Individual games could be played and completed in several hours, rather than requiring days of play, like a cricket match. A shorter game fit better with the American middle-class work routine. As a result, the game was gaining popularity prior to the Civil War. Then the war brought thousands of young men from different parts of the country together, each with his own version of baseball, and gave them ample idle time to play between battles. As a result, the best characteristics of the game were standardized. In short, the war focused the attention of young men on the game. At the conclusion of the Civil War, baseball was America's most popular stick-and-ball game (Adelman, 1986).

At first, baseball too was organized according to the club system. Club leaders organized practices, rented field time, and invited other clubs to meet and play.

Loosely organized leagues formed, encouraged parity of competition, and regulated competition between social equals. In 1871, a group of professional baseball teams formed the National Association. Any club that was willing to pay its elite players could join. The league, like horse racing before it, depended on the patronage of its well-off members and consequently lacked stability. It was not uncommon for teams to form, fall apart, and reform within a season (Adelman, 1986; Leifer, 1995; Seymour, 1960). Only the best teams, like the Cincinnati Red Stockings of 1869–1870, were able to sustain fan interest. The Red Stockings' road trips to play eastern teams drew thousands of fans and earned enough to pay the team's travel expenses and player salaries. Then after two seasons of flawless play, the team lost three games at the end of the 1870 season. Despite the Red Stockings' impressive record, they were no longer considered champions, and their popularity fell along with revenue. The team disbanded prior to the next season (Seymour, 1960).

In 1876, **William Hulbert** took over management of the National Association. Hulbert would become known as "the Czar of Baseball" for his strong leadership of the game and his role as a major figure in the development of American sport management. He believed baseball teams would only become stable and profitable if they were owned and run like businesses. With clubs, members managed and participated in sporting activities haphazardly, and the financial interests of individual clubs carried more authority than any association of clubs. Hulbert realized that to build a sports league that would last, authority needed to rest with the league, not with the teams. Hulbert revamped the management of baseball to center around a league structure and created strong rules to enforce teams' allegiance. Appropriately, he changed the name of the league from the National Association to the National League (Leifer, 1995; Seymour, 1960).

Profit-oriented baseball gained legitimacy with the public when the owners assumed financial risk. Strict enforcement of the league schedule guaranteed that owners faced financial risk and fielded competitive teams. Learning from earlier experiences in American sport when owners and supporters were able to abandon a team or season when it began to lose money, Hulbert structured the National League to withstand losses and forced teams to comply with his rules. Regardless of profit or loss, teams were expected to complete their schedules. Previously, teams had simply stopped playing when they began to lose money, much like a Broadway show. Hulbert understood that ending a season early to decrease short-term costs eroded the long-term faith of the public. By tying owners to a schedule, Hulbert hoped fans would see that teams were in earnest competition with each other and would have faith that owners needed to win to increase their profits.

Hulbert established the league's credibility by strictly enforcing these rules. In the first year of National League play, two struggling teams, Philadelphia and New York, did not play their final series. Even though the games would not have had an impact on league standings, Hulbert banned the two teams from the league

(Leifer, 1995; Seymour, 1960; Vincent 1994). The message was clear: The long-term success of the league would not be compromised by the short-term financial interests of individual teams.

Hulbert also understood that the integrity of baseball was suspect as long as gambling was commonplace. To reduce the influence of gambling, league rules prohibited betting at ballparks. Hulbert tried to clean up the atmosphere at ballparks further by banning unwholesome groups and activities from the game. He raised ticket prices to decrease the number of working-class patrons and make the games more appealing to the "better" classes. He also prohibited playing games on Sunday and selling beer at ballparks, and players caught gambling were banned from the league for life (Leifer, 1995; Seymour, 1960; Vincent, 1994).

Once the league established fair play and a solid league structure, Hulbert still needed to create a market for the game. It was relatively easy to attract spectators to championships and other big games between rival clubs, but team owners needed to find a way to attract audiences to regular-season games. Hulbert's dilemma was complicated by the fact that many of the independent clubs not affiliated with his league fielded superior teams. In the late 1870s, National League teams lost more often than they won in nonleague play (Leifer, 1995). Hulbert's solution was to create the pennant race, a revolutionary idea in 1876. The success of the National League depended on spectators' viewing baseball as a series of games and not a single event. A genuine pennant race requires fairly even competition. In other words, for the league to be a successful business even the best teams had to lose a substantial portion of their games (Leifer, 1995).

League rules were designed to cultivate pennant fever. Hulbert kept his league small by limiting it to eight teams, even though other leagues accepted all teams willing to put up a membership fee. The National League was small enough to ensure that no team was so far out of first place that winning the pennant seemed impossible. Hulbert instituted rules to distribute the talent between teams to further encourage competition. To protect their teams from being raided by other National League teams during the season, owners agreed to respect each other's contracts with players for one year. Other leagues could pay the National League a fee to participate in this "reservation" system and protect themselves from raids by National League teams. The practice not only helped distribute talent more evenly but also kept player salaries down. Further, National League teams were required to share their gate revenues with the visiting team. This practice allowed even the least talented teams to draw revenue when they played away from home. Gate sharing redistributed wealth around the National League and enabled teams to compete financially for players (Leifer, 1995).

The National League also appealed to fans' loyalty and pride in their towns and cities. League rules prohibited placing more than one National League team in or near any current National League city and prohibited teams from playing non-

League teams within the same territory as a National League team (Seymour, 1960). The prohibition required discipline on the part of team owners because non-League games, especially against local non-League rivals, generated strong short-term profits. By avoiding independent clubs in National League cities, the League promoted the notion that National League teams represented the community exclusively. Independent teams, languishing from this National League prohibition, moved on to non-League cities, and spectators increasingly identified the National League teams with their cities (Leifer, 1995).

The league structure got a significant boost from newspapers, another rapidly expanding American institution. While the initial response to the National League by the media was generally unfavorable (Vincent, 1994), newspapers with teams in the League warmed to the idea of a pennant race. In the 1870s most major cities supported a dozen or more newspapers. One effective way to attract readers was to cover local sporting events. Newspapers played up the concept of the home-town team in a pennant race to hold the attention of sports fans between games. Reports on injuries, other teams' records, players' attitudes, and coaching strategies were given considerable coverage before and after games. Presenting baseball in terms of an ongoing pennant race sold newspapers and underscored Hulbert's desire to promote continuing attention to regular-season games (White, 1996).

Major League Baseball teams became important local institutions in their own right, and supporting the local major league team became synonymous with civic pride. Consciously or unconsciously owners expressed and promoted the tie between teams and local communities through the stadiums they built. In the 1920s baseball's owners built steel and concrete stadiums to replace old wooden parks. More than just functional facilities, these stadiums and their majestic architecture paid tribute to the permanence of the community and the sport of baseball. Stadiums were monuments to the symbiotic relationship between teams and their cities, preeminent, visible expressions of the place owners wanted baseball and their teams to take in the psyche of urban citizens (White, 1996).

The National League's successful strategy seems fairly straightforward when compared to the strategies used by today's professional sports leagues. The success of contemporary commercial sports leagues also depends on consolidated league play with strong centralized control and regulation. By managing leagues closely and assiduously, sport managers promote the belief that competition is honest and that owners' financial successes are tied to the on-field successes of their teams. League play is in large part designed to encourage the fans' faith that teams operate on equal footing, both on the field and off, and that there is a relatively equal distribution of talent and resources. Finally, allegiance to specific teams is fostered through marketing campaigns and the media, and sport managers work closely with both to promote the game and each others' interests (Leifer, 1995).

PROFESSIONAL TOURNAMENT SPORTS: BUSINESS AND CHARITY

While teams and leagues are less dependent on gate revenue now than at the turn of the century due to the development of other revenue streams, including corporate sponsorship, spectator attendance remains the foundation of the league system. However, another sport system, the **professional tournament,** is highly dependent on the relationship between corporate sponsorship and sport.

Tournament sports like tennis and golf also have their roots in the club system. Early tournaments were usually sponsored by private clubs for the benefit of their membership. Professionals, usually employees of the clubs, were often excluded from these tournaments. Without wealthy patrons to sponsor tournaments or control facilities, professional athletes in some sports needed other alternatives if they were going to participate.

PROFESSIONAL GOLF

Many early golf professionals were European men brought to the United States from Europe by country clubs to help design, build, and care for golf courses and teach the finer points of the game to the club owners. Some golf professionals made extra money by giving exhibitions, and golf manufacturers hired the most talented professionals as representatives to help publicize the game and their brands of clubs at exhibitions and clinics.

Although these golfers were technically professionals, they were much different from the tournament professionals of the contemporary Ladies Professional Golf Association (LPGA) and Professional Golfers' Association (PGA). There were numerous attempts to organize golf leagues prior to the 1930s, but the leagues failed both to capture public interest and to attract golf professionals. Professionals shunned these risky tournaments in favor of the stability of exhibitions and clinics, and when they competed they vied for prize money they had put up themselves. It was not until the professionals found someone else—in the form of community and corporate sponsors—to put up the prize money that professional tournaments stabilized.

One entrepreneurial type of tournament, which ultimately failed, was that used in the 1940s and 1950s to generate a profit from gate revenue for private owners of country clubs. Following the proven approach of baseball, club owners produced events themselves and kept the principal profit from the gate and concessions. Owning and operating the facility was the key to success. The failure of the privately owned tournaments to catch on had less to do with the energy and creativity owners put into the events than with the nature of the sport. Individually owned golf courses were rare, and even if there were a consortium of course owners, players operated independently—they did not need teams, managers, or promoters—and therefore were difficult to control.

Fred Corcoran, the architect of the professional golf tournament, understood the unique qualities of golf. Golf "operates upside down" in comparison to other sports, he wrote. "The players have to pay to tee off, and they use facilities constructed for the use of the amateur owners who, occasionally, agree to open the gates" to professionals (Corcoran, 1965, p. 246). Corcoran took his lead from Hollywood and advertising executives. Corcoran used athletes and golf tournaments the same way that newspapers use news—to sell advertising space to the public. Corcoran never promoted golf strictly as entertainment. The golf tournament, for Corcoran, was the medium through which a celebrity, a local politician, a manufacturer, a charity, a town, or a product gained exposure. He sold the *event*.

CORCORAN'S TOURNAMENTS

In 1937, a consortium of golf manufacturers hired Fred Corcoran as tournament director for the men's PGA circuit. He served in that capacity for over a decade. Then, in 1949, the manufacturers hired him again to organize the women's tour (Corcoran, 1965; Hicks, 1956). For many decades golf manufacturers had understood the value of retaining professional golfers to use and endorse their golf products. For manufacturers of golfing equipment, a tournament circuit was ultimately a better value than retaining players as manufacturer representatives. The cost of tournaments was minimal because many tournaments were sponsored by local chambers of commerce or benevolent organizations. With a solid tournament circuit in place, the cost of retaining a player representative was reduced because better players earned their salaries through prize money. Successful tournament players began to see themselves as independent operators, and manufacturers were soon relieved of having to pay travel costs and per diem expenses.

One of Corcoran's first contributions to the professional golf tour was the creation of the financially self-sufficient tournament. Prior to 1937, the PGA had guaranteed to pay the players' purse to entice communities to sponsor tournaments. Corcoran, who had spent a decade organizing amateur tournaments in Massachusetts, understood the potential revenue a tournament produced for a community. Corcoran was able to convince communities to take responsibility for providing the purse by demonstrating to them that the revenue generated by 70 professional golfers eating in restaurants and sleeping in hotels would generate three times the minimum $3,000 purse (Corcoran, 1965).

Corcoran witnessed the tremendous boost competitive golf received by sharing status with Bing Crosby. In addition to being a famous movie star and singer,

Crosby was a sports entrepreneur associated with horse racing and golf. In 1934, Crosby orchestrated the first celebrity pro-am tournament preceding a men's golf tournament to raise money for charity. The combination of a celebrity and pro playing together on a team in a mock tournament was extremely successful. Amateur golfers, celebrities, and community leaders paid exorbitant fees to participate in the tournament. Although these funds were directed toward charity, there were also spinoff professional golf benefits. The appearance of celebrities not only enhanced the athletes' status but also increased attendance, which increased the proceeds for charity and the exposure for professional golf. The celebrity pro-am has been the financial core around which most professional golf tournaments have been built (Graffis, 1975).

The financial power of this type of charity event became clear during World War II. During the war, golf was used to raise money for the Red Cross. Using a celebrity pro-am format, Bing Crosby teamed up with movie costar Bob Hope, professional golfers, and various other celebrities, including Fred Corcoran, to raise millions of dollars for the war effort and the Red Cross (Graffis, 1975). At the end of the war, Corcoran kept the pro-am tournament format and used civic pride and charities like hospitals and youth programs to draw crowds.

Turning professional golf into a charity was good business in addition to being good for the community. Donations to charitable organizations were fully tax-deductible. Local businesspeople not likely to benefit directly from a golf tournament were more easily persuaded to contribute to the tournaments with tax deductions as incentives. In addition, a good charity attracted the hundreds of volunteers and essential in-kind donations needed to run a tournament. Further, a charity with broad reach and many volunteers acted as a promotional vehicle for the tournament. Thus, Corcoran transformed a potentially costly labor-intensive event into a no-cost operation. By appealing to the altruism of a community to put on a tournament, Corcoran obtained a tournament site, capital, and event management for no cost.

It was clear to Corcoran that if manufacturers could use their association with tournaments to sell golf products, and celebrities could use it to add to their status, and local community groups could use it to raise funds or gain political influence, then tournaments could also be sold as an advertising medium for non-golf-related merchandise. As tournament director of the PGA and the LPGA, Corcoran orchestrated the first non-golf-related corporate sponsorship of professional golf tournaments. For the men's tournament, Corcoran arranged for Palm Beach Clothing to sponsor tournaments. A few years later he orchestrated a transcontinental series of women's tournaments sponsored by Weathervane Ladies Sports Apparel (Corcoran, 1965).

Corcoran's adaptation of Crosby's celebrity tournaments to tournaments funded by advertising for clothing foreshadowed the immense corporate involvement in contemporary professional tournaments. Still, professional golf was not able to take full advantage of corporate interest in athletes until the late 1950s. Until that time, the major media wire services, Associated Press and United Press International, followed a policy of using the name of the city or town to distinguish a tournament. They argued that using the name of the corporate sponsor was a cheap way to avoid paying for newspaper advertising. In the late 1950s, the newspaper industry reversed its policy and agreed to call tournaments by the name of their corporate sponsors. This change meant that by sponsoring a national sporting event, a corporation gained tax-free exposure to a target market in the name of charity (Graffis, 1975). In the end, professional golf, the charities, and the corporations all benefited from this arrangement.

Corcoran did not sell golf solely as entertainment. Instead, he sold the golf tournament as a medium through which a person, community, or corporation could buy exposure. Gallery seats, pro-am tournaments, and the pre- and post-tournament festivities were the focuses of interaction, access to which could be sold. While politicians and radio and movie personalities have found tournaments a worthwhile investment, it is the corporate community that has benefited most handsomely from golf. The golf tournament, as an event, has evolved into a corporate celebration of itself and its products (Crosset, 1995). Variations of the tournament structure described above can be found in tennis, in track and field, and in multisport events like the Olympic Games.

Sport clubs, leagues, and tournaments are three of the more important structures currently used to manage and organize sport. Management systems, like amateur bodies such as the National Collegiate Athletic Association and the United States Track and Field Association and professional organizations like the World Boxing Association and the National Basketball Association, employ some variation of these structures to produce sporting events. But contemporary sport management is far more complex than its historical antecedents. Furthermore, the growing popularity of new sports like mountain biking, snowboarding, and rock climbing is encouraging the evolution of new management structures. The continuing growth of the sport industry and its importance to numerous sponsors and institutions have created demand in the last several decades for systematic study of sport management practices. Since the late 1960s, the academic field of sport management has focused on the unique and special issues facing the people who conduct the business of sport.

THE BIRTH OF SPORT MANAGEMENT AS AN ACADEMIC FIELD

As the sport management profession began to grow and prosper, it became apparent that while similarities existed between running a general business and running a sport organization, there were also intricacies peculiar to the sport industry that managers needed to know. Early on, sport managers learned from hands-on experiences gained in the industry. However, as the sport industry became more complex, there was a need to train sport managers in a more formal fashion. From this need emerged the formal study of sport management.

The concept of a sport management curriculum is generally credited to two people: **James G. Mason**, a physical educator at the University of Miami (Florida), and **Walter O'Malley** of the Brooklyn (now Los Angeles) Dodgers, who discussed the idea in 1957 (Mason, Higgins, & Owen, 1981). The first university sport management program was the master's program established at **Ohio University** in 1966, which was based on Mason and O'Malley's ideas (Parkhouse, 1996). Shortly after the Ohio University graduate program began, Biscayne College (now St. Thomas University) and St. John's University founded undergraduate sport management programs (Parkhouse, 1996). The University of Massachusetts, Amherst, started the second master's program in 1971.

The number of colleges and universities in the United States offering sport management majors grew rapidly. By 1985 the National Association for Sport and Physical Education (NASPE) indicated there were over 50 undergraduate programs and over 40 graduate programs offering sport management degrees (Parkhouse, 1987). By 1996, the total number of sport management programs was just over 200. In Canada, the number of programs has remained at approximately 10 programs (Parkhouse, 1996).

The growth of sport management as an academic field was prompted by the sport industry's need for well-trained managers, but it was also pushed by universities' and colleges' need to attract students. Some schools wishing to increase enrollments in a highly competitive market added sport management programs to their curriculum in the 1980s. Given the rapid growth of the academic field, concern developed among sport management educators over what constituted a solid sport management curriculum capable of producing students qualified to work as managers in the sport industry. The first group of scholars to examine this issue formed an organization called the Sport Management Arts and Science Society (SMARTS), which was initiated by the faculty at the University of Massachusetts, Amherst. This group laid the groundwork for the present scholarly organization, the **North American Society for Sport Management (NASSM)** (Parkhouse, 1996). NASSM and NASPE, which is a subgroup of the American Alliance for Health, Physical Education, Recreation and Dance (AAHPERD), are the organizations that monitor curricula in sport management. The purpose of NASSM is to promote, stimulate, and encourage study, research, scholarly writing, and professional development in the area of sport management, both the theoretical and applied aspects (NASSM, 1997). Sport management professional organizations also exist in a number of countries outside of North America. Two of these organizations are the Sport Management Association of Australia and New Zealand (SMAANZ), and the European Association of Sport Management (EASM) (Global Sport Management News, 1995).

In consultation with educators, practitioners, and professional associations, the NASPE/NASSM Joint Task Force on Sport Management Curriculum and Accreditation set standards for curricula in 1993 (NASPE/NASSM Joint Task Force, 1993). This task force recognized the importance of a set of core content areas that undergraduate, master's, and doctoral programs should embrace. For undergraduate students, the core content areas determined by the task force* are:

Area 1. Behavioral dimensions of sport
Area 2. Management and organizational skills in sport
Area 3. Ethics in sport management
Area 4. Marketing in sport
Area 5. Communication in sport
Area 6. Finance in sport
Area 7. Economics in sport
Area 8. Legal aspects of sport
Area 9. Governance in sport
Area 10. Field experience in sport management

The master's students' core curriculum set by the task force* contains some of the same elements:

Area 1. Management leadership and organization in sport
Area 2. Research in sport
Area 3. Legal aspects of sport
Area 4. Marketing in sport
Area 5. Sport business in the social context
Area 6. Financial management in sport
Area 7. Ethics in sport management
Area 8. Field experience in sport management

These guidelines represent a North American model for sport management curriculum. By following these guidelines, North American sport management academic programs ensure consistency of curricula and ensure that their graduates are getting a truly well-grounded sport management education. As sport management becomes more global in nature, successful country-specific curricula outside of North America are producing successful sport managers as well. Universities in Australia, China, Czechoslovakia, Germany, Greece, Italy, and South Africa, for example, are preparing future sport managers (Baker, Cao, Pan, & Lin, 1993; Caslavova, 1996; Deakin University, 1996; Gouws, 1993; Horch, personal communication, 1996; Laios, Tzetzis, & Costa, 1996; Manno, Beccarini, Carbonaro, & Madella, 1994). As the sport industry evolves, sport management curricula will continue to change to meet the needs of the industry.

Source: Data from NASSM Joint Task Force (1993), Standards for Curriculum and Voluntary Accreditation of Sport Management Education Programs, *Journal of Sport Management*, Vol. 7, pp. 159–170.

SUMMARY

This chapter discusses the historical origins of three sport management structures: clubs, leagues, and tournaments. Sport management structures that developed over the past several hundred years organized sporting events in different ways to meet the particular needs of participants, spectators, and sponsors at a particular point in history. The club structure, the league structure, and the tournament structure each arose in response to changes in broad social structures and addressed specific issues within a segment of the sport industry. The evolution of each of these three management structures illustrates that managers need to be creative in the ways they mange sports and to understand that one management structure will not work in all situations.

In contemporary sport these three structures operate as highly complex organizational systems. As a result, the sport industry demands highly trained managers. Sport management has developed as an academic field to meet this demand. In order to maintain quality control in this fast-emerging field of study, the NASSM/ NASPE curriculum guidelines have been established. As the sport industry continues to evolve globally, the academic field of sport management will evolve as well in order to produce the future leaders in the industry.

REFERENCES

Adelman, M. (1986). *A sporting time: New York City and the rise of modern athletics, 1820– 70*. Urbana, IL: University of Illinois Press.

Baker, J.A.W., Cao, X.J., Pan, D.W., & Lin, W. (1993). Sport administration in the People's Republic of China. *Journal of Sport Management, 7*, 71–77.

Caslavova, E. (1996). Contemporary conception of teaching future professionals in the subject of "Sport Management" at the faculty of physical education and sport, Charles University, Prague. *Official proceedings of the Fourth European Congress on Sport Management*. Montpellier, France: European Association for Sport Management.

Corcoran, F. (1965). *Unplayable lies*. New York: Meredith Press.

Crosset, T.W. (1995). *Outsiders in the clubhouse: The world of women's professional golf*. Albany, NY: SUNY Press.

Deakin University. (1996). *Deakin University curriculum materials*.

Global Sport Management News. (1995). Regional sport management association news. *Global Sport Management News, 1*, 1–2.

Gorn, E., & Goldstein, W. (1993). *A brief history of American sport*. New York: Wang and Hill.

Gouws, J. (1993). Sport management curricula in Rand Afrikaans University, South Africa. *Journal of Sport Management, 7*, 243–248.

Graffis, H. (1975). *The PGA: The official history of the Professional Golfers' Association of America*. New York: Crowell.

Henriches, T. (1991). *Disputed pleasures: Sport and society in preindustrial England.* New York: Greenwood Press.

Hicks, B. (1956). Personal correspondence, LPGA Archives.

King, A. (1997). New directors, customers and fans: The transformation of English football in the 1990s. *Sociology of Sport Journal, 14,* 224–240.

Laios, A., Tzetzis, G., & Costa, G. (1996). Sports management and the role of the department of physical education in Greece. *Official proceedings of the Fourth European Congress on sport management.* Montpellier, France: European Association for Sport Management.

Leifer, E.M. (1995). *Making the majors: The transformation of team sports in America.* Cambridge, MA: Harvard University Press.

Mandell, R. (1984). *Sport: A cultural history.* New York: Columbia University Press.

Manno, R., Beccarini, C., Carbonaro, G., & Madella, A. (1994). Criteria and aims of the educational programs for sport managers run by the Divisione Attivitá Didattica of the Scuola Dello Sport in Italy. *Official proceedings of the Second European Congress on sport management.* Florence, Italy: European Association for Sport Management.

Mason, J.G., Higgins, C., & Owen, J. (1981, January). Sport administration education 15 years later. *Athletic Purchasing and Facilities,* 44–45.

NASSM. (1997). http://www.unb.ca/web/SportManagement/nassm.htm.

NASPE/NASSM Joint Task Force on Sport Management Curriculum and Accreditation. (1993). Standards for curriculum and voluntary accreditation of sport management education programs. *Journal of Sport Management, 7,* 159–170.

Parkhouse, B.L. (1987). Sport management curricula: Current status and design implications for future development. *Journal of Sport Management, 1,* 93–115.

Parkhouse, B.L. (1996). *The management of sport: Its foundation and application* (2d ed.). St. Louis, MO: Mosby.

Seymour, H. (1960). *Baseball: The early years.* Oxford: Oxford University Press.

Shipley, S. (1989). Boxing. In T. Mason (Ed.), *Sport in Britain: A social history.* Cambridge, England: Cambridge University Press.

Sugden, J. (1996). *Boxing and society: An international analysis.* Manchester, England: Manchester University Press.

Vamplew, W. (1989). *Pay up and play the game: Professional sport in Britain, 1875–1914.* Cambridge, England: Cambridge University Press.

Vincent, T. (1994). *The rise and fall of American sport.* Lincoln, NE: Nebraska University Press.

White, G.E. (1996). *Creating the national pastime: Baseball transforms itself: 1903–1953.* Princeton, NJ: Princeton University Press.

Williams, G. (1989). Rugby Union. In T. Mason (Ed.), *Sport in Britain: A social history.* Cambridge, England: Cambridge University Press.

Williams, J. (1989). Cricket. In T. Mason (Ed.), *Sport in Britain: A social history.* Cambridge, England: Cambridge University Press.

CHAPTER 2

Management Principles Applied to Sport Management

Carol A. Barr and Mary A. Hums

Key words: scientific management, human relations movement, organizational behavior, planning, organizing, staffing, directing, delegation, controlling, people skills, communication skills, managing diversity, managing technology, decision making, organizational politics, managing change, motivation

INTRODUCTION

It has recently been said that sport today is too much of a game to be a business and too much of a business to be a game. The sport industry in the United States is growing at an incredible rate. Current estimates by *Financial World* magazine of individual professional team sport franchises list the average National Football League (NFL) team's value at $174 million, the average National Basketball Association (NBA) franchise at $127 million, the average Major League Baseball (MLB) franchise at $115 million, and the average National Hockey League (NHL) franchise at $74 million (Atre et al., 1996). Total retail sales of licensed products in 1995 for the NFL, the NBA, MLB, and the NHL combined totaled approximately $8.5 billion (TLB 1996 Annual Industry Report, 1996). Last year, the National Collegiate Athletic Association (NCAA) signed a contract to broadcast the Final Four basketball tournament that is worth $1.75 billion over eight years, and the NFL is in the middle of a four-year deal worth $4.38 billion (TV Sports, 1996). The health and sports club industry reported a 1994 total annual dollar volume of $7.75 billion (IHRSA, 1995). As the sport industry has grown, there has been a shift in focus toward a more profit-oriented approach to doing business (Hums, Barr, & Gullion, 1996).

While keeping the financial scope of the sport industry in mind, it is important to note that in whatever segment of the sport industry they work, sport managers need to be able to organize and work with the most important asset in their organization: *people*. This chapter on management will help the future sport manager recognize how essential the utilization of this most important asset is to the success of a sport organization. Every *sport* manager needs to understand the basics of being a *manager* in the twenty-first century. A manager in a sport organization can go by many different titles—athletic director, general manager, director of ticket sales, coach, health club manager, ski resort owner—and the purpose of this chapter is to introduce the reader to basic management knowledge areas and skills that can be applied by sport managers in *any* segment of the industry.

DEFINITION AND HISTORY OF MANAGEMENT PRINCIPLES

Management can be defined as the process of working with and through others to achieve organizational objectives in an efficient manner (Kreitner & Kinicki, 1995). The goal of managerial work and the role the manager plays within an organization is to get the workers to do what the manager wants them to do. The process of management is performed through the use of numerous knowledge areas including planning, organizing, staffing, directing, and controlling. These knowledge areas will be discussed in the next section of this chapter.

The development of management theory has gone through a number of distinct phases. Two of these phases are scientific management and the human relations movement. Management theory was epitomized by the work of Frederick Taylor during the **scientific management** movement in the early 1900s (Gray & Starke, 1988). Taylor worked as an industrial engineer at a steel company and was concerned with the way workers performed their jobs. Taylor believed that through scientific study of the specific motions making up a total job, a more rational and efficient method of performing that job could be developed. In other words, workers should not be doing the same job different ways, but instead there exists "one best way" to perform a job in the most efficient way. In Taylor's view, the manager could get the workers to perform the job this "best way" by enticing them with economic rewards.

The second major phase in management theory is known as the **human relations movement**, which occurred from the 1930s through the 1950s (Gray & Starke, 1988). The human relations movement concerned itself with the behavior of people rather than the scientific approach to performing a task. The human relations movement was popularized by the work and writings of Elton Mayo and Mary Parker Follett. Mayo was an Australian who led the Hawthorne studies, in which he concluded that social factors, such as supervisory methods, social interactions, incentive systems, and worker autonomy, were more important to worker productivity than physical variables such as lighting, rest periods, length of work, or length of workweek. Follett was a pioneer as a female management consultant in the male-dominated industrial world of the 1920s. Follett saw workers as complex combinations of attitudes, beliefs, and needs, and she noted that managers needed to motivate job performance rather than merely demanding it (Kreitner & Kinicki, 1995).

Today, it is common to view the study of human behavior within organizations as a combination of the scientific management and human relations approaches. **Organizational behavior**, or "OB" as it is commonly referred to, characterizes the modern approach to management. The field of organizational behavior is used to describe human behavior within the organization and the activities of managers as they try to understand and manage people at work. Current management theory stresses the concepts of employee involvement, employee empowerment, and managers' concern with the human components of employees. Command-and-control management is giving way to participative management and empowerment, while ego-centered leaders are being replaced by customer-centered leaders who view employees as internal customers (Kreitner & Kinicki, 1995). However, the essence of organizations is productivity, and thus managers need to also be concerned with getting the job done. In looking at the study of management theory, we can see how the approaches to management have moved from the simple to the complex, from a job orientation to a people (worker) orientation, from the manager as a dictator and giver of orders to the manager as a facilitator and team member. Humans beings, though, are complex and sometimes illogical, and therefore no one method of management can be seen as a sure success. The role of managers can be challenging as they try to assess the needs of their employees and utilize appropriate skills to meet the needs of the employees, all the while also getting the job done.

FUNCTIONAL AREAS

Sport managers must perform in a number of "functional areas" and execute various activities in fulfilling the demands of their jobs. Some of the functional areas used to describe what managers do include planning, organizing, staffing, directing, and controlling. Although these functional areas may be helpful in providing a general idea as to what a manager does, these terms and their descriptions do not provide a comprehensive list. Organizations are constantly evolving, as are managers and the activities they perform. The functional areas used here will describe an overall picture of what a manager does, but keep in mind that it is impossible to reduce a manager's activities to the level of a robot following a set pattern of activities.

Planning

The **planning** function includes defining organizational goals and determining the appropriate means by which to achieve these desired goals (Gibson, Ivancevich, & Donnelly, 1997). Planning involves setting a course of action for the sport organization. VanderZwaag (1984) defines the planning process as involving forecasting, establishing objectives, formulating strategies to reach the objectives, and designing the budget to put into concrete terms what the planning process is trying to accomplish. It is important to keep in mind that the planning process is a continuous one. Organizational plans should change and evolve and not be viewed as set in stone. In case of problems or if situations arise that cause the goals of the organization to change, the sport manager must be ready to adjust or change the organizational plan to make it more appropriate to what the organization is trying to accomplish.

The planning process consists of both short-term and long-term planning. Short-term planning involves goals the organization wants to accomplish soon, say within the next couple of months to a year. For example, an athletic shoe company may want to order enough inventory of a particular type of shoe so that its sales representatives can stock the vendors with enough shoes to meet consumer demands for the upcoming year. Long-term planning involves goals the organization may want to try to reach over a longer period of time, perhaps five to ten years into the future. That same shoe company may have long-term goals of becoming the number one athletic shoe company in the country within five years, so the company's long-term planning will include activities the company will participate in to try to reach that goal. Managers must participate in both short-term and long-term planning.

Organizing

After performing the planning function, the sport manager next undertakes the organizing function. The **organizing** function is all about putting plans into action. As part of the organizing function, the manager determines what types of jobs need to be performed and who will be responsible for doing these jobs. From this information, an organizational chart is developed. An organizational chart shows the various positions within the organization as well as the reporting schemes for these positions (Figure 2–1). In addition, an organizational chart may also contain information about the people who will be filling the various positions.

After an organizational chart has been put together, the next step is to develop position descriptions for the various positions within the organizational chart. These position descriptions are important in defining the tasks for which each

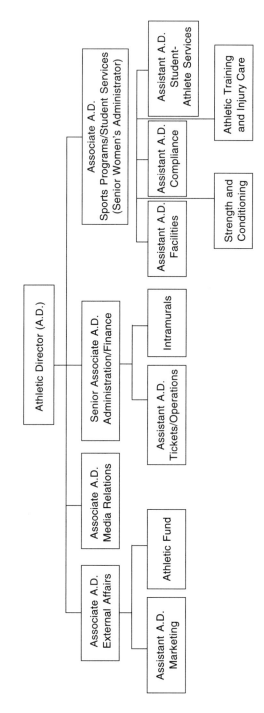

Figure 2–1 Athletic Department Organizational Chart.

position is responsible. The position descriptions define responsibilities and indicate the authority accompanying each position. For example, the position description of the assistant athletic director for marketing may include soliciting corporate sponsors, promoting teams or special events, and selling stadium signage. Finally, position qualifications must be developed. Position qualifications define what is needed in the person filling a particular position. Position qualifications will depend on the organizational chart, the responsibilities of a particular position, and the authority that is given to a particular position. Thus, the position qualifications for the assistant athletic director for marketing may include a master's degree, three to five years' athletic department experience, and good written and oral communication skills.

The need for a well-developed and well-communicated organizational chart cannot be overemphasized. On numerous occasions organizations may find that problems start occurring because one person does not know what another person in the organization is doing. The organizational chart can be extremely beneficial in showing employees the various positions within the organization, who fills those positions, the responsibilities of each position, and who reports to whom.

Staffing

Once the organizational chart has been developed and the position qualifications established, the next managerial function, staffing, can take place. **Staffing** involves the effective recruitment and selection of people to fill the positions within an organization. The position qualifications developed during the organizing function come into play here. Recruiting and selecting employees is all about finding the right person, with the appropriate qualifications, to get the job done. In order to find that person, managers must do their homework and go through the proper steps to really get to know and understand the people they interview. These steps include appropriate advertising of the position, reviewing applications that are submitted, choosing qualified people for the interview process, checking references, and selecting the "best fit" person for the job.

In addition to the selection process, staffing also includes the orientation, training, and development of staff members (VanderZwaag, 1984). Orientation introduces the new person to the nature of the organization, to organizational goals and policies, and to his or her fellow employees. Training focuses on the actual job and teaching the employee how to do the job. For example, new ushers may be involved in a half-day training seminar to learn seating arrangements, locations of first aid stations and uniformed security, and procedures for checking in and out of work. Development involves a commitment to improving the employees' knowledge, skills, and attitudes, which allows them the opportunity to grow and become better employees. For example, sending athletic department employees to a week-long seminar on new technology used in the workplace is one way that development can occur. Unfortunately, many sport organizations are so busy trying to do the day-to-day work that they ignore the development of their employees. Development can help lead to more efficient and productive workers.

Directing

The **directing** function has often been referred to as the "action" point of the management process. This is where it all happens. The sport manager is involved in directing the activities of employees as he or she attempts to accomplish organizational goals. In carrying out the directing function, the manager participates in a variety of activities, including leading, delegating, managing differences, managing change, and motivating employees. In carrying out these activities, the manager utilizes numerous skills, which will be discussed in the next section of this chapter.

The directing function begins with the process of **delegation**, which involves assigning responsibility and accountability for results to employees. Effective communication is key to the delegation process. Employees need to know what they are being asked to do and need to be assigned the appropriate authority to get the job done.

The directing function also requires the manager to take on a leadership role and manage any differences or changes that may take place within the organization. Ultimately, the manager is responsible for the employees and how they are performing their duties. Any type of conflict, work problems, or communication difficulties that arise must be handled by the manager so the employees can achieve their goals. The manager also must be ready to stimulate creativity and motivate the employees if needed. Thus, the manager takes on a very active role in the operations of the organization when performing the directing function.

Controlling

The manager performs the **controlling** function by ensuring progress toward organizational objectives. This progress is accomplished through the employees effectively carrying out their duties. The manager oversees, or controls, the workers through the establishment of reporting systems, the development of performance standards, the evaluation of the employees in fulfilling the performance standards, and reward systems designed to acknowledge successful work on the part of the employees. Position descriptions, described earlier in this chapter, are important in the controlling function as well, for they set criteria by which employee performance is evaluated.

The reporting system involves the collection of data and information regarding how a job is being performed. For example, the director of corporate sponsorship for an event would collect information on how many sponsorship packages the local corporate sponsorship representative has sold. This information would be reported to the event director. Development of performance standards sets the conditions or expectations for the employee. In the previous example, the local corporate sponsorship representative, in conjunction with the director, would determine how many local sponsorship packages should be sold. Employee performance can then be evaluated based on how well (or poorly) the employee did in meeting these performance standards. Finally, a reward system should be put in place so that employees feel their work is noticed and appreciated. Recognition for good performance and accomplishments helps motivate employees to reach job expectations. Employees will not be motivated to reach the performance standard placed before them if they feel they will not be rewarded or recognized in some way.

As mentioned previously, the managerial functions involve the manager's performing a number of activities requiring various skills. The next section discusses the skills managers use when fulfilling their job responsibilities.

KEY SKILLS

People Skills

As mentioned earlier, the most important resources in any sport organization are the human resources—the people. The sport management industry could be called a "people-intensive" industry. Sport managers deal with all kinds of people everyday. For example, on a given morning a ticket manager for a minor league baseball team may have the task of meeting with chief executive officers or chief financial officers of local businesses to arrange the sale of stadium luxury boxes. That afternoon, he or she may be talking with the local Girl Scouts, arranging a special promotion night. The next morning may bring a meeting with the general manager of the "big club" to discuss ticket sales. Before a game, a season ticket holder may call to complain about his or her seats. The sport manager must be able to respond appropriately to each of these situations, to each of these different constituencies. Without proper **people skills**, the sport manager is destined to fail. Learning to treat all people fairly, ethically, and with respect is essential for the sport manager's success.

Communication Skills, Oral and Written

The importance of mastering both oral and written **communication skills** cannot be overstated. Sport managers deal with all kinds of people on a daily basis, and knowing *how* to say something to another person is equally as important as knowing *what* to say to another person. Communication may take place one-on-one with employees or customers, or in a large group setting. When problems arise, people will call wanting help, such as someone who loses his or her tickets. Sometimes people just need general information, such as when the next home event takes place. To sport managers, sometimes these types of questions begin to seem mundane and repetitive. However, the sport manager must remember that for the person asking the question, this may be the first time he or she has asked it, and this instance may also be the first personal contact the person has had with anyone in the organization. Answering each question professionally and courteously wins a lifelong fan. Being rude or uncooperative only ensures an empty seat in your arena or stadium. And remember that people who have had bad experiences talk to others, which may result in the loss of other existing or potential fans.

Being representatives of sport organizations, sport managers are often asked to give speeches to community groups, schools, and business leaders. Sport managers need to learn how to give a proper oral presentation to a group. According to Roger Ailes, President of CNBC and media advisor in three winning presidential campaigns, the four essentials of being a great communicator in an oral presentation are to (1) be prepared, (2) make others feel comfortable, (3) be committed, and (4) be interesting (Ailes, 1988, p. 63). In further explaining the area of being prepared, Ailes states that there is a preparation checklist that managers, or anyone giving an oral presentation, can follow. This preparation checklist consists of the following points:

1. Evaluate your audience (be aware, in advance, of their special interests, expertise, etc.).
2. Consider the occasion.
3. Determine the length of your talk.
4. Determine the purpose of your presentation (to entertain, to inform, to inspire, or to persuade).
5. Decide on a central theme.
6. Develop background knowledge in the area of your presentation to aid your confidence.
7. Gather facts.
8. Consider the makeup of the audience (their attitudes, whether hostile or supportive).
9. Find a good opening line or story that relates to the presentation.

10. Use a presentation structure to prepare the delivery of the material (Ailes, 1988, pp. 67–68).

Successful sport managers have excellent written communication skills. Beyond that, sport managers must be able to write in many different styles. For example, a sports information director needs to know how to write press releases, media guides, season ticket information brochures, interoffice memos, and business letters to other professionals, as well as lengthy reports that may be requested by the athletic director or university faculty. Coaches need to be able to write solid practice plans, letters to parents or athletes, and year-end reports on a team's status. A marketing researcher for a footwear company has to write extensive reports on sales, consumer preferences, and product awareness. Knowing how to communicate facts and information in an organized, readable fashion is truly an art, one a sport manager must master to be successful.

Managing Diversity

A major issue facing sport managers today is the issue of diversity in the workplace and the need to include more women, people of color, and people with disabilities at the managerial level in the sport industry. According to Thomas (1993), **managing diversity** can be described as the process of creating and maintaining an environment that naturally enables all organizational participants to reach their full potential in pursuit of the enterprise's objectives. The employment process, from hiring through retention through the exiting of employees from an organization, has become a much more complex process than in the past.

The face of the American work force is changing rapidly. One of the biggest challenges is the inclusion of people of diverse cultures into all segments of the workplace (Denton, 1992). Today minorities account for 23% of the work force compared to 10.7% in 1964, and women make up nearly half the managerial and professional ranks (Jones, 1995). Information from the 1990 census indicates there are 49 million Americans with disabilities. The employment rate for people with disabilities is approximately 39%, and a 1994 Harris Poll indicated that 79% of the 61% not working in fact want to work (President's Commission on Employment of People with Disabilities, 1995).

As a part of the greater business community, the sport industry must keep pace with this diversification in the workplace and encourage the inclusion of people of diverse cultures into the management of sport. However, there has been increasing discussion about how well the sport industry is doing in that regard. Concern over the lack of women, minorities, and people with disabilities in administrative positions in sport has been well-documented in several areas, including professional sport (Ashe, 1992; Lapchick, 1996; Lyons, 1992; Major League Baseball,

1992; Shropshire, 1996), intercollegiate athletics (Blum, 1993; Carpenter & Acosta, 1994; Farrell, 1992; Whitaker, 1992; Weiberg, 1994), the sporting goods and retail industry (Williams, 1993), facility management (Weinstein & Hums, 1997), and athlete representation (Clay, 1992; Norment, 1992; Shropshire, 1996). The underrepresentation of women, minorities, and people with disabilities in the sport industry is an important issue for sport managers who value diversity in the workplace.

When examining ethical considerations for including all qualified individuals in the employment process, each phase of the employment process should be examined. These stages include recruitment, screening, selection, retention, promotion, and ending employment. Given the low number of women, minorities, and people with disabilities in leadership positions in the sport industry, steps must be taken to increase opportunities for access to the industry. The following suggestions offer concrete steps sport managers can take to successfully manage diversity in the sport industry:

1. Be knowledgeable about existing labor laws related to discriminatory work practices.
2. Be knowledgeable about existing Affirmative Action guidelines for the employment process.
3. Increase knowledge and awareness of multiculturalism.
4. Be knowledgeable and supportive of issues of importance to all groups in the workplace.
5. Write statements about valuing diversity into the organization's code of ethics.
6. Expand personal and professional networks to include those of different races, genders, physical abilities, and social classes.
7. Act as a mentor to people of diverse cultures in one's sport organization.
8. Be courageous enough to "buck the system" if necessary. This is indeed a personal challenge and choice. A sport manager who perceives discrimination or discriminatory practices within a sport organization should speak out against these practices (Hums, 1996).

The American work force is rapidly changing and diversifying. Sport leaders must be aware of the impact this trend will have on their sport organizations. By being proactive and inclusive, sport leaders can ensure that all qualified individuals will have an opportunity to work in the sport industry, allowing for the free exchange of new and diverse ideas and viewpoints and resulting in organizational growth and success. Sport leaders advocating this proactive approach will have organizations that are responsive to modern American society and will be the leaders of the sport industry into the next century.

Managing Technology

Technology is evolving more and more rapidly every day and **managing technology**—that is, being familiar with it and using it to advantage—is something every manager should strive for. The computer that produced this book was considered state-of-the-art at the time this book was written, but by the time you read these words, that computer will have been replaced by a newer, faster model, capable of processing words and data with ever-increasing complexity. The Internet and the World Wide Web have become pivotal sources of information on a variety of subjects. Computerized ticketing systems such as PACIOLAN and PROLOGUE are used on a daily basis by professional sport teams, major college athletic departments, theme parks, and museums. With the current explosion of the Internet and other multimedia interactive technologies, sport managers and sport management educators are now facing a new challenge: how to examine the impact of ever-expanding technologies on the sport industry and how to educate future sport managers to enter into this exciting high-tech world. The ongoing continuous developments of these technologies will impact both the sport industry and the sport management curriculum (Hums & Stephens, 1995).

Decision Making

People make decisions every day that range from simple to complex. Any decision we make consists of two basic steps—gathering information and then analyzing that information. For example, when you got up this morning, why did you choose the clothes you have on? Because they matched? Because they were clean? Because they were on the top of the clothes pile? Because you had a presentation to give in class? While this is a relatively simple decision (for most people), other decisions are more complex. Think about choosing a major. What made you decide to major in sport management, as opposed to management or accounting or theater management? A decision like that involves **decision making** on a much deeper level.

Sport managers have to make decisions on how to solve problems every day. The types of problems sport managers face generally fall into two categories: common or unique (Railey & Tschauner, 1993). An example of a common problem a facility manager may face is what to do if a sink plugs up in a restroom during an event. The manager knows to call maintenance to get a plumber to fix the problem. This is a common problem, solved with a simple decision to call the right person. An example of a unique problem for a facility manager might involve theft of pyrotechnic materials to be used during a concert or halftime show. Now the facility manager must make decisions about who is allowed to speak with investigative authorities such as the FBI or ATF, how to handle the media coverage of the incident, and how to prevent future similar incidents. A unique problem such as this involves decision making on a much higher level.

When making decisions, sport managers must follow an organized step-by-step process. A suggested decision-making process is presented by Railey and Tschauner (1993):

Step 1. Define and clarify the problem.
Step 2. Identify the decision objectives.
Step 3. List, categorize, and analyze all relevant information.
Step 4. Identify any hurdles that may hinder a solution to the problem.
Step 5. Brainstorm for alternatives.
Step 6. Narrow choices to two or three acceptable alternatives.
Step 7. Make your decision.
Step 8. Evaluate the decision after it has been implemented.

Following an organized decision-making process helps ensure consistent decision making throughout the sport organization and makes sure that no piece of important information is overlooked.

There is one other consideration for sport managers when making decisions: When is it necessary to include group input and feedback into the decision-making process? According to Chalip (1996), groups can be used in a number of decision-making situations, including planning, idea generation, problem solving, agenda setting, governance, and policy making. He suggests that group decision making should be used when more ideas need to be generated, when there is a great deal of information to share, when alternative perspectives are needed, and when the fairness of the decision is highly valued. Another consideration is that the more an individual's job may be affected by the decision, the more outside input that person should seek before making the decision.

Organizational Politics

What is meant by the term **organizational politics**? Gray and Starke (1988) note that political behavior occurs when people use power or some other resource outside of the formal definition of their jobs to get a preferred outcome. Although it is somewhat intangible and hard to measure, politics pervades all sport organizations (Slack, 1997). Organizational politics and political behavior are met with mixed results. Some people feel that political behavior is demeaning and possibly destructive to an organization, while others view politics as a way of accomplishing goals and objectives. Whatever their beliefs on the subject, sport managers must be aware of the presence of politics within their organization and the different types of political tactics that may be used. Four generally accepted types of political tactics used in organizations include (Slack, 1997):

1. The building of coalitions with others in order to increase a person's political power.
2. The use of outside experts to support or legitimize a person's position.
3. Building links or creating a network of contacts with people inside and outside the organization.
4. Controlling information, thus influencing decisions and the outcomes of decisions within the organization.

What is most important for future sport managers is that they learn to be aware of the political environment around them. Who is truly the most "powerful" person in a sport organization? Sport organizations, like all organizations, have two different types of leaders—formal and informal. The formal leader is the leader because of title, such as athletic director, director of community relations, or store manager. Informal leaders, on the other hand, are leaders because of the power they possess, from knowledge, association, or length of time with an organization. For example, if the coaches in an organization are trying to convince the athletic director to make some sort of change, the coaches may seek out an associate athletic director who has been there for many years, knows the ins and outs of the organization, and knows how to persuade the athletic director. The coaches would ask this associate athletic director to mediate on their behalf with the athletic director. Learning who the informal leaders are in an organization can help new sport managers understand the politics of a sport organization.

Managing Change

Sport organizations change on a daily basis. New general managers are hired, teams move into new facilities, league policies and rules change, health clubs purchase new fitness equipment, and environmental use laws affect state or national park recreation areas. Just as life is all about adapting to change, so, too, is the sport industry all about adapting to change. Changes happen at basically three different levels in a sport organization: the individual level, the group level, and the organizational level (Gray & Starke, 1988). For example, on the individual level, a sales rep for a footwear company may be assigned a new geographic region. On the group level, a team may decide to downsize its front office staff. Finally, at the organizational level, a professional league may add expansion teams, which would result in organization-wide changes for league management.

While most change happens without *major* resistance, sport managers have to be aware that people tend to resist change for a number reasons. Some people resist for emotional reasons, economic reasons, social reasons, status reasons, security reasons, skill and competence reasons, and "path of least resistance" reasons (Gray & Starke, 1988). For example, the sales rep assigned to the new geographic area may resist because he or she is scared about getting a new territory (emotional), may be concerned that the potential for sales and commissions is lower in the new territory (economic), may have had friends in the old territory (social), may now have a territory not as highly thought of in the company (status), may feel unsafe in the new territory (security), may wonder if he or she will be able to establish new contacts (skill and competence), or may just see the change as another hassle (path of least resistance). While not all of these reasons may be present, sport managers need to be aware of what employees may be feeling.

How then should sport managers respond to resistance if it occurs? Kotter and Schlesinger (1979) suggest trying a continuum of possible responses: (1) education and communication; (2) participation and involvement; (3) facilitation and support, (4) manipulation and co-optation; or (5) explicit and implicit coercion. Each of these suggestions has positives and negatives and may only be successful under certain conditions. Sport managers need to be keenly tuned in to how employees are responding to change so that any resistance can be dealt with fairly and honestly.

Motivation

The ability to motivate employees to strive to achieve organizational goals and objectives as well as their personal goals and objectives is an art form. For example, both a head coach and a player for an NBA team want their team to win. However, the player also knows that his personal game statistics will determine his salary. As a head coach, how do you motivate a player to be a "team player" (organizational goal) while still allowing him to maximize his personal statistics (personal goal)?

Theories of **motivation** abound, with works including Maslow's hierarchy of needs, Herzberg's two factor ideas, McClelland's achievement motivation theory, as well as equity theory and expectancy theory (Gray & Starke, 1988). After reviewing these and other theories, Katzell and Thompson (1990) point out seven practices that can raise the level of employee motivation:

1. Ensure that workers' motives and values are appropriate for the jobs in which they are placed.
2. Make jobs attractive to and consistent with workers' motives and values.
3. Define work goals that are clear, challenging, attractive, and attainable.
4. Provide workers with the personal and material resources that will facilitate their effectiveness.

5. Create supportive social environments.
6. Reinforce performance.
7. Harmonize all of these elements into a consistent socio-technical system.

Motivating employees on a daily basis is a constant challenge to any sport manager. In order for any sport organization to be successful, it is critical for everyone to be "on the same page" when it comes to working to accomplish organizational goals and objectives.

CURRENT ISSUES AND FUTURE TRENDS

Diversity in the Work Force

As mentioned in the previous section, the demographics of the American work force are ever-changing. Sport management professionals need to stay abreast of these changes. The sport organization that embraces diversity will be seen as the leader into the next century. Sport managers need to stay on top of the latest legislation and managerial theories in their efforts to help their organizations become truly multicultural.

Managing Technology

As mentioned earlier, the technology sport managers work with is changing every day. Sport managers need to be aware of how these changes impact the segment of the sport industry in which they work and how new technology can be incorporated into the workplace. It is imperative for sport managers to understand how expanding technology will improve customer relations and service. Just as the computer replaced the typewriter and e-mail is replacing phone correspondence, so the next wave of technology will affect how sport managers run their daily business operations.

International Sport Management

Sport management is not unique to the United States. Sport, and with it the field of sport management, has grown in popularity throughout the world. For example, Europe has a number of successful major professional soccer and basketball leagues. Sport managers from the United States working abroad must be aware that they cannot unilaterally impose American models of sport governance on other cultures. Differences exist in terms of language, culture, etiquette, management, and communication styles. Sport managers need to learn, understand, and respect these differences when dealing in the international sport marketplace.

New Management Theories

Management theory and approaches to management are constantly changing with new thoughts and ideas taking hold on a regular basis. Two of the more recent approaches to management include transformational leadership and horizontal organization (HO). Transformational leadership is about motivating followers to work for personal reward, experience, achievement, and self-actualization instead of short-term self-interest and security (Bass, 1990). The transformational leader encourages employees to become internally motivated to work hard to achieve the organization's goals. The HO introduces a new structure to job activities. Instead of workers working within specific departments with particular job responsibilities, teams of workers work on core processes. Rather than focusing on functional goals or financial objectives, the HO focuses on customer satisfaction (Gibson, Ivancevich, & Donnelly, 1997).

SUMMARY

Sport managers today face ever-changing environments. One constant, however, is the necessity to successfully manage the sport organization's most valuable resource—its people. The work force of the twenty-first century will be vastly different from the work force of even the recent past. The influence of people of different cultures, rapidly changing technology, and the globalization of the marketplace all make it necessary for tomorrow's sport managers to adapt. The measures of a good sport manager are flexibility and the ability to move with modern changes so that the sport organization and, more importantly, the people within that sport organization continue to grow and move forward into the future.

Functional areas of management have been used to explain and prepare managers for the various activities they get involved in as a result of their management role. These functional areas include planning, organizing, staffing, directing, and controlling. In fulfilling these functional activities of management, managers employ a variety of skills essential to success as a manager. The skills discussed within this chapter include people skills, communication skills (oral and written), the ability to manage diversity, managing technology, decision-making skills, awareness of organizational politics, managing change, and motivating employees.

Sport managers in today's sport organizations need to be aware of ever-changing management thought and ideas, learn from these theories, and incorporate what works best within their organizations. Management is all about finding the best way to work with the employees to get the job done. The fact that there is no one best way to manage underscores the excitement and challenge facing managers today.

REFERENCES

Ailes, R. (1988). *You are the message*. New York: Doubleday.

Ashe, A. (1992, August). What does the future hold for blacks in sport? *Ebony*, 132–133.

Atre, T., Auns, K., Badenhausen, K., McAuliffe, K., Nikolov, C., & Ozanian, M. (1996, May 20). Sports: The high stakes game of team ownership. *Financial World*, 53–70.

Bass, B.M. (1990). *Bass & Stogdill's handbook of leadership* (3rd ed.). New York: Free Press.

Blum, D.E. (1993, April 21). Forum examines discrimination against black women in sport. *Chronical of Higher Education*, A39–A40.

Carpenter, L.J., & Acosta, R.V. (1994). *Women in intercollegiate sport: A longitudinal study—Seventeen year update 1977–1994*. Brooklyn, NY: Department of Physical Education, Brooklyn College.

Chalip, L. (1996). Group decision making and problem solving. In B. Parkhouse (Ed.), *The management of sport* (2d ed.). St. Louis, MO: Mosby.

Clay, B. (1992, July). Black agents compete for blue chip athletes. *Black Enterprise*, 48–55.

Denton, W. (1992, Sept./Oct.). Workforce 2000. *Credit World*, 14–18.

Farrell, C.S. (1992). NCAA details lack of minority opportunities, sets long range plan. *Black issues in higher education, 8*, 20.

Gibson, J.L., Ivancevich, J.M., & Donnelly, J.H. (1997). *Organizations* (9th ed.). Chicago: Richard D. Irwin, Inc.

Gray, J.L., & Starke, F.A. (1988). *Organizational behavior: Concepts and applications* (4th ed.). Columbus, OH: Merrill Publishing Company.

Hums, M.A. (1996). Increasing employment opportunities for people with disabilities through sports and adapted physical activity. *Proceedings from the Second European Conference on Adapted Physical Activity and Sports: Health, well-being and employment*. Leuven, Belgium: ACCO.

Hums, M.A., Barr, C.A., & Gullion, L. (1996). Ethical issues confronting managers in the sport industry. Manuscript submitted for publication.

Hums, M.A., & Stephens, K. (1995). Sport management enters the high-tech arena. Presentation at the North American Society for Sport Management Conference, Fredericton, NB.

International Health, Racquet and Sportsclub Association. (1995). *The 1995 IHRSA report on the state of the health club industry*. Boston, MA: Author.

Jones, D. (1995, May 15). The changing face of the workforce/Companies won't derail diversity. *USA Today*, p. 1B.

Katzell, R.A., & Thompson, D.E. (1990). Work motivation: Theory and practice. *American Psychologist, 45,* 144–153.

Kotter, J.P., & Schlesinger, L.A. (1979, March-April). Choosing strategies for change. *Harvard Business Review*, 102–112.

Kreitner, R., & Kinicki, A. (1995). *Organizational behavior* (3rd ed.). Chicago: Richard D. Irwin, Inc.

Lapchick, R. (1996). *1996 racial report card*. Boston, MA: Northeastern University Center for the Study of Sport in Society.

Lyons, D.C. (1992, August). Why black coaches and executives are still second class citizens. *Ebony*, 116–118.

Major League Baseball. (1992). Baseball minority employment increases. Press release, Office of the Commissioner.

Norment, L. (1992, August). Scoring with multi-million dollar contracts. *Ebony*, 120–122.

President's Commission on Employment of People with Disabilities. (1995). *Profit from our experience*. Washington, DC: Author.

Railey, J.H., & Tschauner, R.R. (1993). *Managing physical education, fitness and sports programs*. Mountain View, CA: Mayfield Publishing Company.

Shropshire, K.L. (1996). *In black and white: Race and sports in America*. New York: New York University Press.

Slack, T. (1997). *Understanding sport organizations*. Champaign, IL: Human Kinetics.

Thomas, R.R. (1993). Managing diversity: Utilizing the talents of the new work force. In A.R. Cohen (Ed.), *The portable MBA in management*. New York: John Wiley & Sons.

TLB 1996 Annual Industry Report. (1996). *Team Licensing Business, 8,* 20–27.

TV Sports: The 3.5 Billion Ticket. (1996, May 13). *Broadcasting and Cable*, 34–39.

VanderZwaag, H.J. (1984). *Sport management in schools and colleges*. New York: John Wiley & Sons.

Weinstein, H.Z., & Hums, M.A. (1997). *Inclusion of people with disabilities in facility management*. Unpublished manuscript.

Whitaker, C.E. (1992, Dec. 11). Minority women in short supply as head coaches. *Atlanta Journal Constitution*, p. F5.

Weiberg, S. (1994, August 18). Study faults colleges on minority hiring. *USA Today*, p. 1C.

Williams, R. (1993). Sporting goods industry survey. Unpublished document.

CHAPTER 3

Marketing Principles Applied to Sport Management

William A. Sutton

Key Words: target market, demographic, psychographic, pass-by interviews, marketing mix, Fan Cost Index, fan identification, database marketing, relationship marketing, aftermarketing, ambush marketing, affinity marketing

INTRODUCTION

The Marketing Concept

As defined by Kotler (1997), "The marketing concept holds that the key to achieving organizational goals consists of being more effective than competitors in integrating marketing activities toward determining and satisfying the needs and wants of target markets" (p. 19). This effectiveness can be in the form of a better product, better service, better distribution system, or simply a better perception of the wants and needs of the consumer. According to Ries and Trout (1993), "Brilliant marketers have the ability to think like a prospect thinks. They put themselves in the shoes of the consumer" (p. 106). However, not all marketers have this talent, and those who don't must devote their attention to effectively identifying the target market, recognizing customer needs, and creating an effective delivery system to reach the consumer.

Consumer needs and wants can usually be categorized as either products or services. In terms of the sport industry, a product can be tangible, like a set of golf clubs, or intangible such as attending a baseball game—when its over, it's gone, and the consumer only has a memory. Examples of sport services are golf lessons, hospitality at an event, fitness instruction from a personal trainer, or the work of a guide leading a rafting trip.

Sport, because of its broad appeal, has a much larger target market than most traditional products. A **target market** is a segment of the overall market that has certain desirable traits or characteristics and is coveted by the marketer. These traits or characteristics can be (1) **demographic**, such as age, income, gender, or educational background; (2) geographic, including ZIP code or postal code; or (3) **psychographic**, that is, related to the preferences or behavior of the individual or group. Psychographic characteristics may include beliefs, lifestyles, activities, or habits. Collegiate athletic departments have several target markets, such as alumni or past letter winners, which can be viewed as having either specific demographic characteristics or psychographic characteristics. These target markets are often approached on the basis of their geographic proximity to the campus.

The target market for sport is similar to the target markets of other segments of the entertainment industry (such as music, film, and literature) in that there are actually multiple target markets according to the nature and presentation of the product. For example, when considering the broad category of film, there are films such as Disney's 1997 animated release "Hercules," for which the target market is children and families. Jane Austen films are targeted primarily to women, while Bruce Willis action films such as the "Die Hard" series may be primarily aimed at a male target audience. Turning back to sport, the target markets for a sport like basketball may be based upon age for participation or income for spectatorship.

Sport Marketing Defined

As defined by Mullin, Hardy, and Sutton (1993), "Sport marketing consists of all activities designed to meet the needs and wants of sports consumers through exchange processes. Sport marketing has developed two major thrusts: the marketing of sport products and services directly to consumers of sport, and marketing of other consumer and industrial products or services through the use of sport promotions" (p. 6). In marketing sport products and services directly to the consumer, the sport marketer faces certain unique challenges, limitations, and in some cases advantages that are not experienced by the marketer of traditional products and services. These differences are listed and described in Table 3–1.

How the sport marketer deals with these unique aspects may vary greatly from organization to organization. This issue is discussed more fully in the section of this chapter that highlights the sport marketing mix. However, in general, the sport industry, which is slower to change than other industries, usually follows the trends in other industries as executives from these industries move into the sport environment. These new approaches are quite evident in the approaches of two large corporate entities that are relatively new to sport, Disney and Rupert Murdoch. Disney's impact on professional sport, in the form of Major League

Table 3–1 Contrasts between Sport Marketing and Traditional Marketing

Sport Marketing	*Traditional Marketing*
In many cases, sport organizations must simultaneously compete and cooperate.	In mainstream business, the success of any entity may depend on defeating and eliminating the competition. In sport, particularly in the case of professional leagues, it is in the best interest of all owners and franchises for all teams to prosper and survive. This is particularly true with regard to revenue sharing and the all-for-one, one-for-all theory of "League Think" as developed in the NFL (Harris, 1986).
Due to the preponderance of information and the likelihood of personal experience and strong personal identification, sport consumers often consider themselves experts.	In mainstream business, very few consumers consider themselves experts and instead rely on trained professionals for information and assistance.
Consumer demand tends to fluctuate widely.	While products such as Coca-Cola can anticipate consistent demand and annual growth, performance in the sport industry can drastically alter consumer interest and demand within the same calendar year.
The sport product is invariably intangible, subjective, and heavily experiential.	In mainstream marketing, when a customer purchases a sweater, it is tangible and can be seen and felt and used on more than one occasion. What each sport consumer sees and feels is quite subjective and occasionally even irrational, and thus it is extremely difficult for the sport marketer to ensure a high degree of consumer satisfaction. Often the consumer leaves with only a memory.
The basic sport product is simultaneously produced and consumed; there is no inventory.	Mainstream products have an inventory and a shelf life, and supplies can be replenished. However, once the game or event has taken place, it is gone and cannot be sold. This condition places an intense emphasis on the need to presell the product.

continues

Table 3–1 continued

Sport Marketing	Traditional Marketing
Sport is generally publicly consumed, and consumer satisfaction is invariably affected by social facilitation.	In mainstream marketing, while other people can enjoy the purchase of a car, the enjoyment or satisfaction of the purchaser does not depend upon it. The sport product (games, events) is usually consumed in public and in the company of others, and thus a consumer's ability to enjoy the activity frequently depends upon others' enjoyment or at least is a function of interaction with other people.
The sport product is inconsistent and unpredictable.	In mainstream marketing, inconsistency and unpredictability are considered unacceptable—for example, if a particular car occasionally went backward when the gear indicated forward, consumers would be up in arms. However, this is not the case for sport, because people produce sport and people are inconsistent. Numerous intangibles such as weather, individual ability and performance, injuries, location, momentum, and crowd support can all affect the outcome of the sport product. This unpredictability is accepted by the consumer.
The sport marketer has little or no control over the core product and often has limited control over the product extensions.	The mainstream marketer works with research and design to create the perceived perfect product. However, in sport, the product core, rules, players, and so on are not within the locus of control of the marketer. The marketer must thus focus on extensions such as promotions, food, music, and entertainment-related options, which he or she can control.
Sport is both a consumer product and an industrial product.	Sport is produced as an end product for mass consumer appeal for both spectators and participants, and thus it can be considered a consumer good. At the same time, spectator and participant sports are also used by businesses and industry, which sponsor events and broadcasts and advertise in conjunction with events and

continues

Table 3–1 continued

Sport Marketing	Traditional Marketing
	organizations as a means of reaching their target markets. Businesses also use sport personalities for endorsements and events for client entertainment and rewards. Thus, sport can also be considered an industrial good because it promotes the sale of other products or services. There is no such duality in traditional marketing.
Sport has an almost universal appeal and pervades all elements of life.	Sport is international, appeals to and is consumed by all demographic segments, and is associated with sociocultural facets of everyday life such as motivations, needs, desires, and so on. Only religion and politics, which in and of themselves are not viewed as products or services but rather as beliefs, are as widespread as sport.

Baseball's (MLB's) Anaheim Angels and the National Hockey League's (NHL's) Mighty Ducks of Anaheim, has been accomplished primarily through merchandising and hospitality management, which increased emphasis on in-park entertainment. Disney has also shown the ability to convert sport entertainment to the big screen in the form of feature films. Murdoch, on the other hand, has been very aggressive in using sport to link and promote his communication empire through his acquisition of Fox Television and his pending purchase of the Los Angeles Dodgers. His Fox Sports Net cable empire, which encompasses more than 30 regional sports networks, will offer a strong challenge to the ESPN/ABC/Disney team in the balance of this decade.

Sport marketing includes the marketing of (1) products, such as equipment, apparel, and footwear; (2) services, such as skill lessons or club memberships; and (3) entities, such as leagues as teams or individuals. There are a number of similarities involved in marketing a multiple entity such as a league or team and marketing an individual such as Michael Jordan, Rebecca Lobo, or Tiger Woods. First of all, an individual athlete, much like an organization, can be marketed to create an affinity for the fan. For example, an individual athlete like Rebecca Lobo can be marketed to create an affinity for the new league in which she competes, the Women's National Basketball Association (WNBA), and also for products for which she serves as an endorser, such as Chevrolet. An athlete just embarking upon a career is similar to a new league or team entering its first year of operation in that the marketer must market the hope or the promise of the future because there is no past or other intangible asset that can be sold to the consumer.

Yet at the same time, an athlete is an individual, and a human being. Because of this element of human nature, there is a risk in marketing an individual. Mike Tyson, Tonya Harding, Lawrence Taylor, Lawrence Phillips, and Will Cordero provide telling examples of the risk element involved in marketing an individual athlete either as an endorser or as a representative of a team or organization.

HISTORICAL DEVELOPMENT

A number of key concepts in sport marketing have evolved over time. These concepts developed to help solve problems or were instituted to more effectively communicate with the target market. In some cases these concepts were utilized as the result of experimentation, in other cases because of the intuitive nature of the sport marketer, and in still other cases because they were found to be successful in mainstream business marketing. This section examines a number of these key concepts, along with the innovators responsible for sport marketing's growth and acceptance.

The Acceptance and Growth of Sport Sponsorship

Considering that the very first collegiate athletic event, an 1852 rowing contest between Harvard and Yale, was held in New Hampshire and sponsored by a railroad company, it is easy to understand how corporate sponsorship has become a dominant part of the American sport marketing environment. There have been and continue to be many pioneers in sport sponsorship and corporate involvement related to sport. One of the earliest pioneers was Albert G. Spalding, a former professional baseball player who parlayed his fame into one of the largest sporting goods manufacturing companies in the world. Spalding was the first marketer to capitalize on the term "official" as it relates to a sport product, when his baseball became the "official baseball" of the National League in 1880 (Levine, 1985). Having secured the "official" status, Spalding then marketed his baseball as the best because it had been adopted for use in the National League, the highest level of play at that particular time. In the consumer's mind, this translated to: *Why choose anything but Spalding? If it is good enough for the National League, it must be superior to any other product in the market.* Spalding also carried over this theme when he began producing baseball uniforms for the National League in 1882.

Spalding was not alone in recognizing the opportunity for corporate involvement in sport. Bert Sugar (1978) has documented the early roles of such companies as Coca-Cola, Bull Durham Tobacco, Curtiss Candy Company, Chalmers

Motor Car Company, Purity Oats, American Tobacco Company, and Gillette in exploiting the country's interest in sport through sport promotions, contests, advertising, and the use of sport personalities as endorsers. While the money involved may seem insignificant by today's standards, these early activities set the tone for what is perceived to be acceptable and advantageous in today's marketplace.

In today's marketplace, however, one company stands high above the rest in terms of its corporate influence and power in the sports world: Nike. From its beginning as Blue Ribbon Sports in 1964 (an American offshoot of the Asian-based Tiger), to its emergence as a brand in 1972, to its dominant role in the industry in 1997, Nike has faced numerous challenges and emerged victorious on every front. Utilizing a creative and visionary management team, headed by founder Phil Knight, Nike has evolved from a corporation utilizing celebrity endorsers to sell its products to an entity capable of creating and marketing celebrities to dominate the footwear and apparel industries. As most people are aware, one of the key elements in the history of Nike and its role in the world today was the packaging of the Nike brand, product, advertising, and athlete into one personality. This was achieved when Nike and Michael Jordan created "Air Jordan" (Strasser & Becklund, 1991). Understanding the impact of an athlete on footwear sales, and having experienced disloyalty among some of its past endorsers, Nike sought to create a win-win situation by involving the athlete, in this case Jordan, in the fortunes of the product. Nike looked long term and created a package that provided royalties for Jordan not only for shoes but for apparel and accessories as well. It was Nike's opinion that if a player had an incentive to promote the product, he or she became a member of the "team." The result of this strategy was the most successful athlete endorsement in history, with over $100 million of Air Jordan products sold in a single year (Strasser & Becklund, 1991).

Since the advent of Air Jordan, Nike has increased its market share and now dominates sport in a way no other company can hope to do. Nike advertising is the standard by which other sport-related advertising is measured. Nike has expanded its role and formed a strategic alliance with the NBA in creating a grass-roots marketing approach with Hoop-It-Up, a national three-on-three basketball tournament. Nike has claimed other sport opportunities, too, purchasing companies such as Bauer with expertise in the hockey industry and NHL licenses.

Nike initially became involved in the National Football League (NFL) through an exclusive licensing arrangement with one of the NFL's premier franchises, the Dallas Cowboys, prior to actually becoming an NFL licensee. Nike attempted to sign a major licensing deal with Major League Baseball, but the leadership and ownership of the league were unable to agree upon terms. Nike also initiated and has signed university-wide athletic sponsorship agreements with major athletic programs such as the University of Michigan and Penn State University. These exclusive college licensing agreements have proven to be very lucrative for the schools involved and have been of great value in achieving better gender equity at these particular institutions.

Nike has recently signed an agreement that could prove to be the most significant and lucrative agreement since the famed Air Jordan agreement, namely their agreement with projected golf superstar Tiger Woods. Nike's agreement with Tiger Woods, whose impact upon the sport of golf, particularly in the youth and minority markets, could be astounding, is a once-in-a-lifetime opportunity. Only time will tell if the agreement and Nike's packaging of Woods will have a global impact. Based upon Nike's track record and influence at this time, this agreement could revolutionize golf in terms of participation, spectatorship, viewership, and yes, the purchase of golf equipment and apparel.

Emphasis on Product Extensions and Development of Promotional Strategies

The emphasis on product extensions and the development of sport promotional strategies can be attributed to the late Bill Veeck (1914–1986), a sport marketing pioneer in professional baseball for almost 40 years. At various times from the 1940s through the 1970s, Veeck was the owner and chief operating officer of the Cleveland Indians, the St. Louis Browns, and the Chicago White Sox (on two different occasions). Veeck was one of the first leaders in sport to recognize that to operate a successful and profitable franchise, one could not totally depend upon fan attendance and support. In other words, a team must provide reasons other than the game itself for people to attend and support the franchise.

Often called "the Barnum of Baseball," Veeck was firm in his belief that fans came to the ballpark to be entertained (Holtzman, 1986). Prior to Veeck, sporting events were not staged for the masses but rather for the enjoyment of sports fans. Through Veeck's efforts, sport marketers broadened their perspectives and actively marketed and promoted events to a much broader and more diverse universe. Promotions and innovations attributed to Veeck include giveaway days like Bat Day, exploding scoreboards, fireworks, and the organizing of special theme nights for students, scouts, and church groups (Veeck & Linn, 1962). Much like Disney, Veeck emphasized cleanliness, hospitality, and entertainment. He carried out this philosophy by enlarging bathrooms, adding day-care facilities, greeting his "guests" and thanking them for coming, providing roving entertainment, and creating a spectacle whenever possible.

The rationale behind Veeck's promotional strategy was based upon several facts he ascertained through his experiences. First, according to Veeck, "In baseball, you are surprisingly dependent upon repeat business. The average customer comes to the park no more than two or three times a year. If you can put on a good-enough show to get him to come five or six times, he has become a source of pride and a source of revenue" (Veeck & Linn, 1965, p. 20). Secondly, "It isn't enough for a promotion to be entertaining or even amusing; it must create conversation. When the fan goes home and talks about what he has seen, he is getting an additional kick out of being able to say he was there. Do not deny him that simple pleasure, especially since he is giving you valuable word-of-mouth advertising to add to the newspaper reports" (Veeck & Linn, 1965, p. 13). Finally, Veeck recognized early on that one has to have something more to sell than the win–loss record of the team, and thus Veeck's promotional philosophy embraced the goal of "creating the greatest enjoyment for the greatest number of people . . . not by detracting from the game, but by adding a few moments of fairly simple pleasure" (Veeck & Linn, 1962, p. 119). While Veeck was often criticized for his practices, they are commonplace today, and in baseball's efforts to regain its audience, his approaches are being widely utilized throughout both major and minor league baseball.

The Evolution of Broadcasting

One of the most dynamic changes in sport marketing was the evolution of sport broadcasting from pure, factual reporting aimed at sports fans to sport entertainment aimed at the masses. This was achieved most notably through the efforts of ABC's Monday Night Football and a man named Roone Arledge. Similar to Bill Veeck, Arledge understood that sports in prime time had to be more than sport— they had to be entertainment, too. He incorporated that philosophy into Monday Night Football through the use of three broadcast personalities (initially sports journalist Howard Cosell, the voice of college football; Keith Jackson, who would be replaced the next year by Frank Gifford; and former NFL star Don Meredith), more cameras and more varied camera angles, video highlights of the preceding day, commentary and criticism, humor and wit. As a result, Monday Night Football has become a sports institution.

Premiering in the fall of 1970, Monday Night Football was "a television phenomenon, a sensation in television ratings and in financial terms, the most successful sports package in history" (Cosell, 1973, pp. 273–274). In the view of Roone Arledge, who had witnessed the failure of CBS in prime time, Monday Night Football required a different approach. Arledge wanted an approach that:

> would excite the press. One that would draw enormous attention to the package. He wanted three men in the broadcast booth. It was his conviction that the play-by-play announcer should really serve as a public address announcer, that he should be on quickly with the basic information, and then quickly be off, as Dandy (Meredith) and I (Cosell) were to pick up with color and analysis, and hopefully some candor,

some humor and some human insight into the athletes so that they would become more than face masks, shoulder pads and numbers. (Cosell, 1973, p. 276)

Arledge sought to do what many thought was impossible: to take a game where the players, because of the helmets and masks, were rarely identified or singled out as individuals, and make them personalities through the use of commentary, humor, and video replays chronicling their exploits the previous day. Arledge encouraged "personalities"—actors, actresses, politicians, and the like—to "stop by the booth" on a Monday night where they would be interviewed by Cosell, thus contributing to the evening's entertainment.

When asked about his approach and view that sport was entertainment, Arledge responded that his job was "taking the fan to the game not taking the game to the fan" (Roberts & Olson, 1989, p. 113). Arledge wanted the viewer sitting in his or her living room to see, hear, and experience the game as if he or she were actually in the stadium. "What we set out to do in our programming (College Football, Monday Night Football, Wide World of Sports, and The Superstars to name a few), was to get the audience involved emotionally. If they didn't give a damn about the game, they might still enjoy the program" (Roberts & Olson, 1989, p. 113). Arledge's innovations, most notably instant replay, multiple cameras, crowd and rifle mikes, and sideline interviewers, added to the enjoyment of the program.

The manner in which Monday Night Football, Wide World of Sports, and The Superstars successfully married sport and entertainment paved the way for the success of other sports in prime time, most notably the NBA, as well as proving there was enough interest in sport to support a 24-hour-a-day sport network, ESPN. ESPN was quick to capitalize on the entertainment aspects of sport by encouraging its broadcasters and on-air talent to be personalities, not just reporters. From the zany nicknames and commentary offered by Chris "Boomer" Berman to the "Big Show" on Sunday night's SportsCenter hosted by Keith Olberman and Dan Patrick, ESPN grew and provided expanded coverage through ESPN2 and ESPNNews, along with being the inspiration for CNNSI, a joint effort of CNN and Sports Illustrated designed to compete with the ESPN offerings.

To support the notion that ESPN emulated ABC's initial marriage of sport and entertainment, two examples clearly stand out. First of all, ESPN created an awards show similar to the Academy Awards called the ESPYs, which it televises annually in prime time. Secondly, Keith Olberman and Dan Patrick placed ninth in the 1995 *TV Guide* list of top performers and were selected for the 1996 *People* magazine's "TV's 40 Most Fascinating Stars" (Olberman & Patrick, 1997). As defined earlier in this chapter, if sport marketing includes all of the activities designed to meet the wants and needs of a market, sports broadcasting has clearly identified these wants and needs and created the products (programming) and delivery systems (broadcasters/entertainers) the market dictates.

The Birth of Research in Sport Marketing To Improve Performance and Acceptance

Although some early pioneers like Bill Veeck communicated well with their customers through informal contacts, letters, and speaking engagements, Matt Levine is the individual most often credited with formalizing customer research in the sport industry. Like Veeck, Levine was well aware that there were other marketing variables in addition to winning and losing. Employed as a consultant by the Golden State Warriors in 1974 and given the goal of increasing attendance, Levine developed what he termed an "audience audit" to capture the demographic and psychographic information from the fans attending the games (Hardy, 1996). Levine was also a pioneer in using intercepts (one-on-one on-site interviews) and focus groups (discussion groups involving 8 to 12 individuals with similar characteristics discussing a predetermined agenda) to gather marketing information for professional sport franchises. The purposes of Levine's research, and for that matter, most research in sport marketing, are as follows:

- To profile the sport consumer demographically, geographically, or psychographically.
- To categorize attendance behavior and segment attendance by user groups related to potential ticket packages.
- To analyze purchasing behavior as it relates to product extensions such as merchandise, concessions, and so on.
- To evaluate operational aspects of the sport product such as parking, customer service, entertainment aspects, and employee courtesy and efficiency.
- To measure interest in new concepts that may be under consideration.
- To document viewing and listenership behavior.
- To understand the consumer's information network so as to determine efficient methods of future communication to that consumer and like consumers.
- To offer two-way communication with the target market.

One of the most successful applications of Levine's market research techniques involved his current employer, the NHL's San Jose Sharks. Levine used a series of what he calls "pass-by interviews." **Pass-by interviews** are on-site interviews in heavy traffic areas like malls. These interviews utilize one or more visual aids and assess the interviewee's reaction to the visual aid. The visual aid is usually a sample or interpretation of a product (style, color, or logo) under consideration. Levine's pass-by interviews were used to determine the reaction of people who had submitted ticket deposits for the expansion San Jose Sharks to a series of proposed logo and uniform designs. The results of Levine's research efforts?

Based upon the research results, the color scheme under consideration was eliminated and the graphic logo of the shark was changed. In 1992, the new logo and colors resulted in estimated retail sales of Sharks' merchandise in the United States and Europe of $125 million (Hardy, 1996). As a result of Levine's approach and success with his clients and their acceptance of his methods and findings, market research in the sport industry has become common practice rather than the exception.

KEY CONCEPTS: THE SPORT MARKETING MIX

As defined by McCarthy and Perreault (1988), **marketing mix** refers to the controllable variables the company puts together to satisfy a target group. The marketing mix then is the recipe for creating a successful marketing campaign. The elements of the marketing mix most commonly associated with sport are often referred to as the "5P's": product, price, place, promotion, and public relations (Mullin, Hardy, & Sutton, 1993). All elements of the marketing mix, while they can be considered individually, must be considered as interdependent variables and viewed in a combination with each of the others to determine if and how the target market needs can best be satisfied. In the paragraphs below the 5P's are examined in pairs to help demonstrate their ultimate impact.

Product and Price

There is an impact of price upon the product available. For example, escalating ticket prices in the NHL, NBA, and MLB, as documented annually in the *Team Marketing Report's* Fan Cost Index, have led to the reemergence of minor leagues such as the International Hockey League and baseball's Class A Midwest League. Both of these leagues operate franchises within major league markets and position their product as major league entertainment at minor league prices—or, simply, affordable family entertainment. (Fan Cost Index is discussed in more detail later in this chapter under the heading Price and Public Relations.)

Product and Place

Sport consumers develop perceptions of the place where a sport event is marketed, namely a facility image that influences the perception of the quality, and often the credibility, of the product (Mullin, Hardy, & Sutton, 1993). For example, for the Continental Basketball Association (CBA), whose teams are often housed in small college arenas or second-tier facilities in the market, the perception that the venue is not first-class often confers a minor league image on the teams involved.

In women's collegiate athletics, particularly basketball, even though in the majority of markets attendance is less for women's games than men's games and even though smaller facilities may be available for use on an appropriate campus, women's teams are electing to play before seemingly smaller crowds in larger venues. They elect to do this because the image the larger facilities present positions the program as first-class and also helps in recruiting.

Product and Promotion

In the majority of situations, the product defines the appropriate media through which the promotional mix will be communicated. For example, the promotion of an aerobics class at a local YMCA will most likely involve direct marketing— mailings or telemarketing to past participants and current members—and may also involve fliers and posters in key locations. Television and radio, because of the cost and the mass direction, would not be appropriate. In the summer of 1997, the WNBA began marketing its product. To ensure its credibility, the WNBA was heavily promoted on NBA telecasts and through the local NBA teams that were to serve as the home sites for WNBA teams. For example, the Cleveland Rockers, marketed by the NBA's Cleveland Cavaliers, mailed information to all Cavs ticket plan holders, utilized local television and radio, promoted the WNBA using in-game PA announcements during Cavs' games in April and May, and utilized press conferences and special events to introduce the team logo, coach, and players. In many cases, the WNBA related a particular team's colors and/or nickname to the NBA host team.

Product and Public Relations

Public relations, which includes community relations, plays a critical role in the marketing mix because of its long-term focus and direction and because of its limited organizational control and reliance on public perception and interpretation. The sport marketer must realize that essentially he or she is positioning the product in the mind of the consumer through an image-building/enhancement program and that there is no guarantee the consumer will accept the positioning of the product as presented by the sport marketer. The current negative perception of professional boxing, arising in part from the heinous incident in which Mike Tyson bit part of Evander Holyfield's ear off in a highly hyped championship rematch, may prove to be a difficult obstacle to overcome, despite the astute use of professional public and community relations campaigns and personnel.

Price and Place

There are two major impacts of the relationship between price and place. The first is the willingness of sport consumers to pay higher prices for better facilities and amenities. This is especially true in the health and fitness industry, but it is also evident in the construction of new stadiums and arenas, the growth of the concept of club seating, and the continued utilization of luxury suites. The second impact is the willingness of consumers to pay more for convenience. This is demonstrated by the consumers' willingness to pay premium prices for parking locations and even valet service and is quite evident in the wide usage of ticket distribution networks such as Ticketmaster, which charge consumers an additional cost above the regular ticket price in exchange for the convenience of purchasing tickets for sporting and entertainment events by telephone.

Price and Promotion

The price of the product most often dictates the type of media used to promote the product. Since price dictates profit margin and the cost of advertising is of course rolled into price, electronic advertising through a medium such as television might be out of the question for some products. The Internet offers a cost-effective method of promotion in the form of websites, which may also contain cyberstores providing worldwide advertisement as well as a place where tickets, apparel, and souvenirs may be promoted and purchased electronically. Professional sport franchises use the Internet to promote their schedules, merchandise, and promotional dates and often include stadium diagrams to promote ticket locations and special opportunities.

Price and Public Relations

Price is the most visible of all of the marketing mix variables and thus must be managed carefully. As previously described, Chicago-based *Team Marketing Report* publishes an annual Fan Cost Index for each of the major league sports (NBA, NFL, NHL, and MLB). The **Fan Cost Index** is the total cost of four tickets, four soft drinks, four hot dogs, a game program, and four souvenirs. The list ranges from the highest cost to the lowest cost and illustrates where teams rank in regard to their competitors in other markets. This information is published not only nationally but also in each of the individual markets. In many cases, publication of such information is not in the best interests of the "home team," but as it is newsworthy information, the team cannot control its use. Changes in price can often quickly impact the image of an organization, and thus great efforts must be made to explain (and in some cases, justify) price increases to the target market.

Place and Promotion

A fortunate organization can capitalize on and promote a good location or facility (for example, Camden Yards, Jacobs Field, the Ballpark at Arlington); on the other hand, it is difficult, if not impossible, to overcome negative facility or location images. For example, Jacobs Field, home of the Cleveland Indians, is much easier to promote (the venue sold out for all games in both the 1996 and 1997 baseball seasons) than was the previous facility, Municipal Stadium, an antiquated, oversized facility often referred to as the "Mistake on the Lake."

Promotional vehicles such as publicity and advertising are usually only effective once a negative situation regarding location or facility has been rectified. When Gund Arena, home of the Cleveland CAVS, opened in 1994, floor seat holders (the first 15 rows) discovered they had great difficulty seeing the court because of the lack of pitch in their seats. This minimal pitch was designed by the architects to provide the best possible view for the luxury suite holders located immediately above the fifteenth row. The media seized on this situation and it became an ongoing news story—first the problem, then the attempts to rectify the problem, and finally the reaction of the ticket holders to the final solution. It was a story the CAVS would have been happy for the media to ignore instead of promote.

Place and Public Relations

No other organization in the world realizes the importance of the relationship between place and public relations better than the Disney organization. Disney capitalizes on the public relations and publicity associated with a friendly, clean, and hospitable environment. Disney training programs in hospitality management are legendary and attract personnel from other amusement entertainment venues, sport franchises, and other public venues throughout the world. Word-of-mouth to new customers and repeat business from previous visitors are the results of a well-publicized campaign built around the venue and the hospitality at that venue.

Industry recognition of outstanding sport facilities appears in *Athletic Business* magazine's annual "Facilities of Merit" issue. Facilities receive awards based upon design, space utilization, cost, energy use, and access. One notable facility, Oriole Park at Camden Yards in Baltimore, receives a lot of attention and recognition because its design and features greatly enhance the experience of those who attend Orioles games. The success of this facility, which is sometimes referred to as a "retro-park" because of its links to the past, inspired the design of Jacobs Field in Cleveland and the Ball Park at Arlington, home of the Texas Rangers.

Promotion and Public Relations

As previously stated, publicity in many cases produces an image (of a team, a facility, a product, etc.) in the mind of the consumer. The job of public relations is to make this image as favorable as possible, or, if necessary, to minimize or counter the effects of publicity that causes the public to have a negative image. Recently, athletic shoe manufacturers, and Nike in particular, have been portrayed as exploiting laborers in Third World countries by paying substandard wages or in some cases employing children. This negative image is in stark contrast to the advertising image of graceful NBA athletes promoting these same shoes on the court and performing incredible acrobatic feats. Which image is more powerful? Which lasts longer in the mind of the consumer? Which will generate more attention in the media?

Each of these elements of the marketing mix is interdependent and may positively or negatively influence the others. For that reason, the marketer must develop a strategic plan to account for and control all of these elements in order to ensure marketing effectiveness. This strategic marketing plan should be a component of the overall organizational business plan.

KEY SKILLS

As marketing is a form of communication, the key skills involved in sport marketing are communication-based and are in many ways similar to the key skills outlined in Chapter 2, Management Principles Applied to Sport Management.

- Oral communication—the ability to speak in public, speak to large groups, and make persuasive presentations demonstrating knowledge about the product and its potential benefit to the consumer.
- Written communication—the competence to prepare sales presentations, reports, analyses, and general correspondence.
- Computer capabilities—in addition to basic word processing skills, expertise in all types of software, including databases, spreadsheets, desktop publishing, ticketing systems, and Web page design and utilization.

- Personnel management—the skills to develop, motivate, and manage a diverse group of people to achieve organizational goals and objectives.
- Sales—the ability to recognize an opportunity in the marketplace and convince potential consumers of the value and benefits of that opportunity.
- Education—a minimum of a bachelor's degree in sport management or a bachelor's degree in business with an internship in a sport setting. A master's degree in sport management or an MBA degree, while not essential in some positions, is desirable for advancement and promotion.

Finally, the successful marketer must also understand the sport product. It is not essential for the marketer to be a dedicated follower of the sport; however, the marketer must comprehend the sport product and know its strengths and limitations.

CURRENT ISSUES AND FUTURE TRENDS

As noted earlier in this chapter, innovation in sport marketing practices usually lags behind innovation in other service industries, in mainstream marketing, and in business in general. However, in recent years, certain innovative approaches and philosophies have begun to be accepted and have become widespread in the sport industry. Some of these approaches and philosophies came from marketing practices in industries external to sport, while some have evolved internally as the sport industry has researched and examined both its core and its constituency. This section briefly identifies some of these practices and philosophies and why they are of value in the sport industry. These programs may exist in and of themselves, but in many cases they are integrated in the marketing mix and strategic market planning of the organization.

Fan Identification

Fan identification is defined as the personal commitment and emotional involvement customers have with a sport organization (Sutton, McDonald, Milne, & Cimperman, 1997). In theory, the more a fan identifies with a team or organization, the greater the likelihood the fan will build a broad and long-term relationship with that team and attach his or her loyalty and lifetime value to the organization. This lifetime value can take the form of annual ticket or merchandise purchases.

College and university athletic programs have various booster and alumni organizations that illustrate the concept of fan identification. Booster clubs may have certain levels of membership related to the amount of giving. Athletic programs may institute priority seating and points programs whereby the purchaser of seats located in certain sections must become a donor to the athletic program.

The fan may also demonstrate his or her degree of identification emotionally and outwardly through actions at games or by purchasing and wearing team logo clothing. Buying and wearing team uniform replicas, often with a name of a player, is a way that a fan can demonstrate support and identification with a player, team, or organization.

This interest in and in some cases need to identify with a player, team, or organization has not escaped the savvy sport marketer. Professional sport teams, particularly the Baltimore Orioles, have capitalized on this interest/need to identify by creating volunteer sales organizations such as the Orioles' Designated Hitters Program. The Designated Hitters Program affords interested fans the opportunity to identify with the Orioles by becoming part of their volunteer sales force. The reward for success in the Designated Hitters Program and similar programs is targeted to those fans with a high interest or need for identification. Rewards usually take the form of exclusive opportunities such as taking a road trip with the team or attending a special event such as an autograph party. This exclusivity is a major attraction for identification because it provides the fan an opportunity that is not available to the general fan base and thus increases his or her personal identification with the team.

Database and Relationship Marketing

Database marketing involves creating a database, usually consisting of names, addresses, and other demographic information related to consumers, and then managing that database. Managing the database usually involves developing and delivering integrated marketing programs, including promotions and sales offers, to the database universe or to appropriate segments or target markets of that database.

Relationship marketing begins with the customer and in essence encourages the organization to integrate the customer into the company; to build a relationship with the customer based upon communication, satisfaction, and service; and to work to continue to expand and broaden the involvement of the customer with the organization. In effect, this integration, communication, service, and satisfaction combine to create a relationship between the consumer and the organization (McKenna, 1991).

The San Diego Padres organization, through its Compadres Program, has created a relationship marketing program that begins with creating a database of the fans attending Padres games and involves using this database to provide offers and opportunities to these fans to increase the breadth and depth of their relationship with the Padres through opportunities to purchase additional tickets, merchandise, and sponsor products. According to Don Johnson, vice president of marketing for the Padres, "The Compadres Program is an exciting example of how relationship marketing can pay significant dividends to a franchise" (Sutton, 1997, p. 5). Membership is free to all fans who complete an application, which in reality is a 10-question survey. This information becomes part of the Padres' database, and the fan receives a bar-coded membership card that functions as a tracking device. When Compadre members attend a game, they "swipe" their membership cards at an electronic kiosk. Upon swiping the card they are greeted electronically by name and given a coupon for offers good at that day's game and points similar to a frequent flyer program that can be renewed for prizes such as meals, merchandise, or autographs as the member attains a certain level of points. Johnson notes the benefit of such a database/relationship marketing program as "creating a sense of privilege and exclusivity that has allowed us to develop relationships with *all* of our fans—individual ticket buyers as well as ticket plan purchasers" (Sutton, 1997, p. 6).

Aftermarketing/Service Quality

As competition for customers intensifies and the emphasis shifts from acquiring customers to retaining customers, the ability to provide consistent high-quality service is becoming a source of competitive advantage for firms (McDonald, 1996). Terry Vavra, a successful marketing consultant, coined the term **aftermarketing** to describe customer retention activities demonstrating the care and concern of the marketer for the customer after the purchase has been made (Vavra, 1992).

Aftermarketing is a critical consideration because of the significant competition for the sport consumer's entertainment dollar. To illustrate this competition let us examine the sport landscape of the New York metropolitan area. In this specific marketplace, the consumer is provided the opportunity to purchase tickets for the following professional sport franchises: New York Liberty (WNBA), New York Knicks (NBA), New Jersey Nets (NBA), New York/New Jersey Metro Stars (MLS), New York Yankees (MLB), New York Mets (MLB), New York Giants (NFL), New York Jets (NFL), New York Rangers (NHL), New York Islanders (NHL), and New Jersey Devils (NHL). These 11 "major" league teams include neither the minor league teams operating in the area nor the collegiate athletic programs that also provide entertainment opportunities. Given the competition, it is critical that each team has an aggressive plan for retaining its market share of fans.

The best plan for retention is to ensure that the fans become *raving fans*—ambassadors who speak highly of their relationship with the organization to others while continuing or expanding their own relationship with the organization (Blanchard & Bowles, 1993). This goal can best be accomplished by providing the highest levels of customer service to each consumer regardless of his or her current level of involvement with the organization. This customer service should include the following elements:

- regular and meaningful communication
- personal service whenever possible
- a readily identifiable procedure to address problems
- a hospitality management program for all personnel interacting with customers
- a knowledgeable staff that assumes responsibility
- a quality product or service at a reasonable price in which the customer perceives a value

The Orlando Magic and Cleveland CAVS of the NBA are organizations with a high commitment to service quality. The CAVS offer personal account representatives to enable customers to build a relationship with one member of the organization whom they can contact at any time and for any reason. The Orlando Magic is one of the premier franchises in all of professional sport, maintaining a season ticket renewal rate of over 95%. Contrary to the majority of professional franchises, the season ticket is the only ticket plan offered by the Orlando Magic. Thus, the Magic must concentrate the majority of its marketing effort on retaining customers rather than seeking new customers. This has resulted in the development of a special survey instrument called TEAMQual, which was developed to assist the Magic in assessing their level of service quality to their customers. The Magic has discovered that the quality of service is directly related to renewal, whether it be ticket plans, sponsorship, or licensing agreements. Dissatisfied customers who feel they are not receiving service commensurate with their investment will not renew their relationship with the organization (McDonald, Sutton, & Milne, 1995).

Ambush Marketing

Ambush marketing refers to activities such as advertising, promotions, and publicity by companies that, although they are not official sponsors, attempt to capitalize on the popularity of certain events by inferring to the consumer or general public that some type of relationship exists between the event or product and the company, when in fact no official relationship exists. *The Wall Street Journal* ("Ambush Marketing," 1988) described the practice as it related to the Winter Olympics: "Companies ambush the official sponsors by associating themselves with the Games indirectly; they buy commercial time during Olympic broadcasts or support individual teams or athletes—all at a fraction of the official sponsors' costs" (p. 25). During the 1994 Winter Olympics in Lillehammer, McDonald's paid $40 million for the rights to be an official Olympic sponsor. Wendy's "ambushed" McDonald's by designing an advertising campaign featuring founder and spokesperson Dave Thomas with Olympic performers such as Kristi Yamaguchi. Wendy's capitalized on the fact that Yamaguchi, a widely known Olympic performer, would create a perception in the consumer's mind that Wendy's was an official Olympic sponsor. Research conducted following the commercials found that 57% of respondents incorrectly identified Wendy's as the official sponsor instead of McDonald's ("Wendy's Ambush," 1994).

Affinity Marketing

Affinity marketing refers to an individual's level of cohesiveness, social bonding, identification, and conformity to the norms and standards of a particular reference group with an expectation of benefits for both the provider and the consumer (Macchiette & Roy, 1992). Affinity marketing in sport is dependent upon the level of fan identification present in the consumer. The most successful affinity marketing programs in sport are programs involving credit cards featuring a person, team, or institution that is the source of some level of preference and identification. The premise is very simple and usually involves either a charitable cause or personal benefit. For example, the consumer may accept the credit card because a percentage of the annual charges (in most cases 1%) will be provided to the cause pictured on the card. The National Museum and Baseball Hall of Fame offers such an affinity card and receives the "donation" from fans with an affinity for baseball. Collegiate athletic departments are also capitalizing on the affinity program to generate funds from past letter winners, alumni, and other fans of their athletic programs. The second inducement, personal benefits, provides some type of personal reward or benefit to be earned by the consumer as he or she spends at certain levels. For golfers, Citibank has just unveiled the Jack Nicklaus Platinum Visa card, which enables the card user to earn points that can be redeemed for golf equipment, golf travel, lessons, and even the opportunity to play with the Golden Bear. The key to successful affinity marketing is a cause or opportunity that will not only attract a large number of participants but that will also encourage them to spend using the affinity card in lieu of another card, cash, or check.

SUMMARY

The marketing of sport includes unique advantages and disadvantages when compared with the marketing of more traditional products and services. Sport benefits from the immense media coverage afforded the industry, often at no cost, while simultaneously it can suffer from the scrutiny imposed by the same media. Besides sport, there is probably no other industry in which the majority of the consumers consider themselves experts. Finally, the sport marketer's control over the core product offered to the consumer is often significantly less than that of his or her counterparts in other industries.

Sport marketers must not only understand the unique aspects of their own product but must also be well informed and knowledgeable about marketing innovations and practices in the more traditional business industries and be able to adapt or modify these practices to fit the situations they encounter in sport.

REFERENCES

Ambush marketing is becoming popular event at Olympic games. (1988, February). *The Wall Street Journal*, p. 25.

Blanchard, K., & Bowles, S. (1993). *Raving fans: A revolutionary approach to customer service*. New York: William Morrow & Co.

Cosell, H. (1973). *Cosell by Cosell*. Chicago: Playboy Press.

Hardy, S. (1996). Matt Levine: The "Father" of modern sport marketing. *Sport Marketing Quarterly, 5*, 5–7.

Harris, D. (1986). *The league: The rise and decline of the NFL*. New York: Bantam Books.

Holtzman, J. (1986, January 3). Barnum of baseball made sure fans were entertained. *Chicago Tribune*, pp. D-1, D-3.

Kotler, P. (1997). *Marketing management: Analysis, planning, implementation and control*. Upper Saddle River, NJ: Prentice Hall.

Levine, P. (1985). *A.G. Spalding and the rise of baseball*. New York: Oxford University Press.

Macchiette, B., & Roy, A. (1992). Affinity marketing: What is it and how does it work? *The Journal of Services Marketing, 6*, 47.

McCarthy, E.J., & Perreault, W.D. (1988). *Essentials of marketing*. Homewood, IL: Richard D. Irwin.

McDonald, M.A. (1996). *Service quality and customer lifetime value in professional sport franchises*. Unpublished doctoral dissertation, University of Massachusetts, Amherst.

McDonald, M.A., Sutton, W.A., & Milne, G.R. (1995). TEAMQual: Measuring service quality in professional sports. *Sport Marketing Quarterly, 4*, 9–15.

McKenna, R. (1991). *Relationship marketing*. Reading, MA: Addison-Wesley Publishers.

Mullin, B., Hardy, S., & Sutton, W.A. (1993). *Sport marketing*. Champaign, IL: Human Kinetics.

Olberman, K., & Patrick, D. (1997). *The big show: Inside ESPN's SportsCenter*. New York: Pocket Books.

Ries, A., & Trout, J. (1993). *The 22 immutable laws of marketing.* New York: Harper Business.

Roberts, R., & Olson, J. (1989). *Winning is the only thing: Sports in American society since 1945.* Baltimore: Johns Hopkins University Press.

Strasser, J.B., & Becklund, L. (1991). *Swoosh: The unauthorized story of Nike and the men who played there.* New York: Harcourt Brace Jovanovich.

Sugar, B. (1978). *Hit the sign and win a free suit of clothes from Harry Finklestein.* Chicago: Contemporary Books Inc.

Sutton, W.A. (1997). SMQ profile/interview, Don Johnson. *Sport Marketing Quarterly, 6,* 5–8.

Sutton, W.A., McDonald, M.A., Milne, G.R., & Cimperman, J. (1997). Creating and fostering fan identification in professional sports. *Sport Marketing Quarterly, 6,* 15–22.

Vavra, T.G. (1992). *Aftermarketing.* New York: Richard D. Irwin.

Veeck, B., & Linn, E. (1962). *Veeck—as in wreck.* New York: G.P. Putnam's Sons.

Veeck, B., & Linn, E. (1965). *The hustler's handbook.* New York: G.P. Putnam's Sons.

"Wendy's ambush of McDonald's snatched away official glow." (1994, March). *The Sports Marketing Letter, 6*(1), S-2.

CHAPTER 4

Financial Principles Applied to Sport Management

Dennis R. Howard

Key words: debt service, ticket sales, concession sales, per cap, luxury seating, luxury suites, club seats, permanent seat licenses (PSLs), naming rights, corporate sponsorship, licensed sport merchandise, chief financial officer, business manager, balance sheet, income statement, statement of cash flows

INTRODUCTION

The popular media remind us daily about the connection between sport and money. From the recent headline story in *USA Today* (Bodley, 1997) about Major League Baseball's billion-dollar payroll to the feature story in *U.S. News & World Report* (Rainie, 1997) about sport gambling's topping $100 Billion, the press continues to "show us the money," the vast amounts of money tied to the production and consumption of sport. Various attempts have been made to quantify or measure the economic magnitude of the sport industry. Unfortunately, no single standard exists, and estimates range from $152 billion in direct spending on sport products and services, a figure provided by Georgia Tech's Economic Development Institute (Hiestand, 1997), to $369.9 billion for sport and entertainment (from the U.S. Bureau of Economic Analysis; see Figure 4–1). The substantial discrepancy is a function of the different measurement standards used in defining sport. The U.S. government incorporates sport into a larger category, leisure (discretionary) spending. Although personal consumption on sport products and services makes up a sizable chunk of this category, the category also includes a number of activities that may touch sport only indirectly, such as the purchase of photographic equipment, or not at all, such as membership in clubs and fraternal organizations. The $152 billion estimate of sport product and services spending provided by the Georgia Tech economists is the most recent,

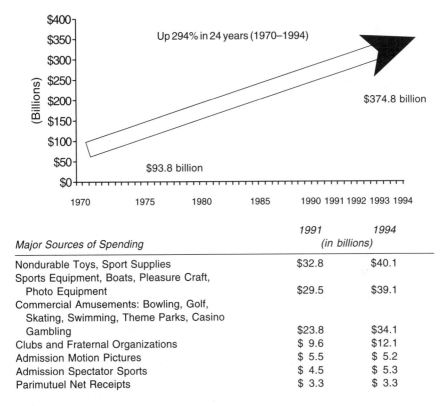

Major Sources of Spending	1991	1994
	(in billions)	
Nondurable Toys, Sport Supplies	$32.8	$40.1
Sports Equipment, Boats, Pleasure Craft, Photo Equipment	$29.5	$39.1
Commercial Amusements: Bowling, Golf, Skating, Swimming, Theme Parks, Casino Gambling	$23.8	$34.1
Clubs and Fraternal Organizations	$ 9.6	$12.1
Admission Motion Pictures	$ 5.5	$ 5.2
Admission Spectator Sports	$ 4.5	$ 5.3
Parimutuel Net Receipts	$ 3.3	$ 3.3

Figure 4–1 Sport/Entertainment Dollars Pile Up. *Source:* U.S. Bureau of Economic Analysis, Survey of Current Business, January/February 1996.

and arguably the most accurate, estimate of spending based strictly on spectator and participatory sport. Significantly, this $152 billion estimate ranked the sports industry as the eleventh largest in the United States, ahead of industries such as chemicals, electronics, and food (Hiestand, 1997). Even that figure may be conservative. According to the report's head researcher, "Because sports isn't a well-defined industry, total spending could be actually higher" (Hiestand, 1997).

Spending on sport and leisure is also significant outside of the United States. Berrett (1996) shows that the economic impact of sport has grown substantially in both the United Kingdom and Canada. From 1985 to 1990, spending on sport in Great Britain almost doubled, to $8.3 billion. Although a summary statistic on sport and leisure spending in Canada is not available, evidence suggests the magnitude of consumer expenditures on various sport goods and services by Canadians is comparable on a per capita basis with that of Americans, with families in both countries spending about $400 per year per family on sport equipment and apparel in 1989 and 1990.

By any measure, Americans spend a great deal of money on sport, and their already considerable investment is growing. The U.S. Department of Commerce's Bureau of Economic Analysis projects spending on sport and entertainment to eclipse $400 billion by the year 2000. Roughly translated, this means that about $1 out of every $8 spent by Americans is devoted to sports and entertainment, "a larger share than for housing construction or even national defense" (Jensen, 1995, p. 145).

From this broad perspective, then, it would seem that managers of sport teams at all levels and of sport service businesses such as golf courses and fitness clubs would be operating in an economic environment in which they simply could not fail. And, in fact, the great majority of sport organizations do succeed financially. The most recent data on the financial health of multipurpose sport clubs in the United States indicate that the operators of a broad range of fitness, racquet, and sport clubs enjoyed steady increases in membership revenues and profit margins (International Health, Racquet and Sportsclub Association, 1996).

According to the most recent National Collegiate Athletic Association (NCAA) data, the financial condition of college athletics has improved steadily over the past decade (Fulks, 1996). Whereas in 1985 the average "big school" or Division I-A program ran in the red, with close to a $100,000 annual deficit by 1995 these same programs reported profits on average exceeding $1 million. Despite the labor disputes that plagued Major League Baseball (MLB), the National Hockey League (NHL), and the National Basketball Association (NBA) as recently as 1994 and 1995, according to *Financial World*, almost 80% of the 113 major league teams in North America's four premier professional leagues (NFL [National Football League], MLB, NBA, NHL) made a profit in 1996 (Badenhausen, Nikolov, Alkin, & Ozanian, 1997).

Facing the Financial Challenge

Although the general financial health of sport in North America is good and improving, serious challenges face managers of sport organizations. Increasingly, managers must cope with situations in which traditional sources of revenue like gate receipts and government support have stagnated or declined at the same time costs have continued to climb. Everything costs more. An 18,000-seat arena that on average required $30 million to build in 1975 cost $100 million to $120 million in 1995. The citizens of Cincinnati spent $44 million in 1970 to build 60,000-seat Riverfront Stadium to house the Reds (MLB) and Bengals (NFL). In 1996, Cincinnati residents voted to spend $500 million to replace the "old" stadium (actually to raze it) with two venues, one 42,500-seat baseball-only stadium and one 70,000-seat football stadium (Howard, 1997). Ironically, it is possible that the annual **debt service** alone—the cost of paying back a portion of the principal amount borrowed plus interest—could in any given year be as high as $40 million, or almost what it cost to build Riverfront Stadium in its entirety just over 25 years ago.

The costs associated with funding the teams that play in these sport venues, new or old, have skyrocketed over the past decade. Player costs in the NFL increased from 41% of total league revenues in 1990 to 68% in 1995. In 1996, the average player in the NFL made $795,000, up 260% from 1986. And in baseball, player costs have almost doubled, to 63% in 1997, up from 33% in 1990 (Brady, 1997). At the start of the 1997 season, the average salary of a player in major league baseball was $1.3 million, an increase of 21% from just the previous season. While not as dramatic, roster costs in both the NHL and NBA have climbed steadily over the past decade.

Soaring player costs are not unique to professional sport in North America. Player salaries ("wage bills," as they're called in England) have increased as much as 20% per year over the last few years in English soccer. Fortunately, at least for British soccer's elite teams, much of the increased player costs have been absorbed through a massive television deal. English soccer's FA Premier League recently signed an agreement with BskyB, which will pay the league $261 million a year for the rights to telecast live league games through the year 2002 (Irvine, 1997).

Spiraling costs have placed intercollegiate sport programs under severe financial pressure as well. According to the U.S. Department of Education, tuition at the average public university will rise 70 to 80% between 1990 and 2000 (Krupa & Dunnavant, 1989). In real terms this means athletic departments spent on average $1 million more on scholarships and grants-in-aid in just the first half of the 1990s. In 1989, at an average of $8,201 per scholarship, the typical Division I-A college sports program spent $1.68 million on "free rides" for its athletes. By 1995, for the same number of scholarships (on average about 210), athletic departments were spending $2.68 million at an average cost of $12,738 per scholarship (Fulks, 1996). In addition to scholarships, salaries, and equipment costs, as well as costs associated with Title IX compliance, are all financial issues facing intercollegiate athletic administrators. Chapter 8, Collegiate Sport, considers these issues in greater detail.

In addition to rising costs, sport managers also face the challenge of increased competition from both inside and outside of the sport industry. The proliferation of sport and entertainment opportunities over the past few decades has been unprecedented. Sport consumers have never had so many options for spending their discretionary dollars. In 1975, there were 73 teams in the "major" professional leagues in North America. Given its early success, it may be appropriate to add Major League Soccer (MLS) to the inventory of major league sports, which includes MLB, the NFL, the NBA, and the NHL. By 2000, accounting for announced expansion plans for each of the leagues, the number of teams in the five preeminent leagues will total 131. While the "big league" sport teams have almost doubled over the last quarter century, the real explosion has occurred at the minor league level. According to the 1997 issue of *The Sport Market Place*, there are almost 800 professional sport teams in North America.

Since 1990, minor league hockey expansion has exploded, particularly in the Sun Belt states. Minor league baseball has enjoyed unprecedented growth and prosperity over the past decade. And, in 1996–1997, with the formation of two women's professional basketball leagues and a women's fastpitch professional softball league, 20 new teams were added to a growing number of teams vying for spectator loyalty, advertising dollars, and corporate support. Add to this mix of professional sport teams the numerous collegiate sport programs affiliated with the NCAA and the National Association for Intercollegiate Athletics (NAIA), plus the thousands of high schools offering a full range of boys' and girls' sport teams, and the total arena of organized sport across professional and amateur levels is truly staggering. Of course, to fully account for the many other commercial sport spectating opportunities available to consumers, it would be necessary to include $3.3 billion spent by Americans at parimutuel dog and horse racing tracks in 1995; the enormous popularity of motor sports, which attracted 160 million viewers to NASCAR events alone in 1995; and the emergence of sports like beach volleyball and roller hockey.

What does all this mean for a fan in a given local market? In a mid-size city like Columbus, Ohio, fans have a myriad of options, including the following:

• The Ohio State University Athletic Department, offering 34 varsity sports that play 476 games, matches, and/or competitions year-round
• The Major League Soccer team, the Crew, which plays 18 home games
• The East Coast Hockey League, the Chill, which plays 41 home games
• The National Professional Soccer League indoor soccer team, the Invaders, which plays 16 home dates
• The American Basketball League women's basketball team, the Quest, which plays 20 home games
• The Columbus Clippers AAA baseball franchise, which plays 70+ home dates

In addition, four Division III colleges provide comprehensive sport programs within the Columbus market area. Including the numerous special events booked at the State Fairgrounds (e.g., the annual Quarter Horse Congress) and the Columbus Convention Center (e.g., BMX Motocross Championships), it is evident that the competition for fan support from local residents in the Columbus market is very intense. And as in all markets, there are a finite number of fans, just so many potential season ticket holders, and only a limited number of dollars available among corporations to sponsor the various teams and events.

Extending beyond direct consumption (actual attendance) to encompass opportunities for passive consumption of sport via television viewing, the competition for sport spectators' time and money becomes even more heated. In 1997, sports programming on television in the United States will exceed 37,000 hours, with four major networks allotting over 2,000 hours and four cable network programs devoting 24 hours per day to sport (Bandyopadhyay & Buttone, 1997). In 1988, the three major networks and one sports cable channel (ESPN) devoted 8,760 total hours to sports programming (Wenner & Gantz, 1989). All of these numbers illustrate the reality facing contemporary sport managers. Yes, people are spending more on sport, but they have many more choices than ever before. Finding sufficient dollars to meet payroll, to retire debt on expensive new facilities, or to pay for athletic scholarships at an average of $12,738 (in 1995) is placing great pressure on managers in all segments of the sport industry to squeeze more from existing resources and, at the same time, seek new sources of revenue. Increasingly, financial success results from innovations such as luxury seating, licensing, and corporate sponsorships.

Doing More with Less

Over the past decade, traditional sources of revenue, including tax support, broadcast revenues, and gate receipts, have not kept up with rapidly escalating costs. For many intercollegiate and interscholastic sport programs this has necessitated budget cuts and changes in traditional patterns of operation. For the approximately half (52%) of the largest (Division I-A) collegiate athletic programs and the vast majority of smaller (Division II) departments that do not make as much as they spend, this has meant increased reliance on institutional support and fund-raising (Fulks, 1996). Faced with declining tax support while at the same time striving to accommodate increased demands for girls' sports, many local school districts have turned to participant fees, booster clubs, and corporate support to sustain middle and senior high sport programs. And, as shown earlier, the spiraling costs of operating professional sport franchises has made it increasingly difficult for teams to turn a profit.

Maintaining programs at even current levels has often meant that sport managers have had to learn to do more with less. The most successful administrators have recognized in the face of this "double whammy"—stable or declining revenue coupled with growing costs—the need to aggressively secure new sources of revenue. Increasingly, effectiveness in the sport industry will be measured by the ability of managers to seek out resources for their organizations.

KEY CONCEPTS

Costs associated with sport seem to be rising all the time: ticket prices increase, salaries increase, and the cost of equipment continues to climb. With increased pressure to meet rising costs, sport managers must answer the question, where do the dollars come from? In this section, the many methods and strategies for revenue acquisition, both old and new, will be described.

The first portion of this section examines the current status and future prospects of traditional sources of revenue, those income-generating options that have provided the financial foundation for sport organizations for many decades. These income sources include ticket sales, concession sales, and the sale of radio and television broadcast rights. The remaining portion of this section focuses on the latest strategies and methods for raising revenues, many of which have been broadly used within the sport industry only within the last 5 to 10 years. These "new" revenue sources include permanent seat licenses (PSLs), corporate sponsorships, sale of licensed merchandise, and luxury seating.

Since 1990, *Financial World* magazine has provided an annual estimate of the profitability of every major league sport franchise. Table 4–1 combines the data provided for each of the 113 teams in 1996 into an overall summary of revenues and expenses for the four major professional sport leagues. Revenues are separated into four major categories: (1) gate receipts—revenues realized from admission ticket sales; (2) media revenues—national, local, and cable TV and radio broadcasting fees; (3) venue revenues—income derived from luxury suites, concessions, and parking; and (4) miscellaneous—largely revenue from the national sale of licensed league goods and apparel.

Since 1985, the NCAA has provided a detailed breakdown of the revenues and expenses of intercollegiate athletic programs at each classification level. Table 4–2 provides a summary of the major sources of revenue for collegiate athletic

---

Table 4–1 The Economic Structure of Professional Sport

	MLB	NFL	NBA	NHL
Revenues:				
Gate receipts	38.9%	29.1%	40.6%	60.5%
Media rights	38.2%	55.4%	36.9%	14.9%
Venue revenues	19.1%	9.8%	13.1%	18.9%
Miscellaneous	3.8%	5.7%	9.4%	5.7%
Expenses:				
Player salaries	60.3%	72.6%	58.2%	55.7%

Source: Data from T. Badenhausen et al., More Than a Game, *Financial World*, pp. 40–50, © 1997.

Table 4–2 Principal Revenues and Expenses of Large and Medium Intercollegiate Athletic Programs: Percentage of Total Revenues and Expenses by Size of Athletic Program

	Division IA		Division II	
	Public	Private	Public	Private
Revenues:				
Ticket sales	30%	23%	6%	2%
Postseason	4%	4%	0%	0%
Institutional support	8%	17%	38%	78%
Donor contributions	15%	15%	7%	12%
Student fees	7%	2%	27%	1%
Direct government support	2%	1%	10%	0%
Radio/TV	7%	8%	0%	0%
Signage/sponsorship	3%	2%	1%	0%
Concessions	2%	4%	1%	0%
Expenses:				
Grants-in-aid	16%	25%	22%	51%
Salaries	32%	26%	40%	26%
Team travel	7%	6%	9%	6%

Source: Fulks, D. (1996). *Revenues and expenses of intercollegiate athletic programs.* Overland Park, KS: National Collegiate Athletic Association.

departments across the spectrum, from "big time" programs (Division I-A) to smaller school programs (Division II).

Tapping Traditional Revenue Sources

Ticket Sales

The relative importance of gate receipts or income from the sale of admission tickets varies greatly from one professional league to another. For all but teams in the media-rich NFL, charged admissions are the single most prominent revenue source for professional sport franchises. The importance of **ticket sales** is most evident for the NHL, where over half of the franchises rely on gate receipts for more than two-thirds of their total annual income. The NFL, due to lucrative long-term contracts with three major networks (ABC, Fox, NBC) and cable television companies (ESPN, TNT), which combined pay each team a total of $40.5 million per year, is much less dependent on live gate receipts. The amount of ticket revenue generated by sport organizations is dependent on two interrelated factors: (1) the number of tickets sold, and (2) the unit cost or price of each ticket sold. In recent years, when the NBA, NFL, and NHL have achieved near-capacity attendance—on average, teams sell more than 90% of the available seats—teams have steadily increased ticket prices in an effort to further increase gate receipts.

Not surprisingly, the greatest increase in the average admission costs have occurred in the two leagues that are most dependent on ticket sales, the NHL and the NBA. In the five-year period from 1991 to 1996, the average cost of an NHL ticket has gone from $23.04 to $38.34—the highest in all of professional sport— which works out to an increase of 66.4%. The NBA has followed close behind with an average ticket price during the 1996–1997 season of $34.08. Major League Baseball, struggling to win back fan support after the costly strike that prematurely ended the 1995 season, has increased prices only modestly over the past couple of years, with an average ticket costing around $12 (Howard, 1997).

As Table 4–2 indicates, the relative contribution of ticket sales in collegiate sport varies according to the size and prominence of the collegiate athletic program. Reliance on ticket sales is particularly heavy for the largest athletic departments, where on average 30% of annual revenues are derived from ticket sales. At major Division I schools such as Michigan and Ohio State, ticket sales for football games in 1996 alone earned each athletic program $16.9 million and $13.2 million, respectively (Girard, 1997). However, football is not the only collegiate sport to generate revenue through ticket sales. Men's and women's basketball, as well as ice hockey and baseball in some parts of the country, also produce gate revenues.

Concessions

Concession sales have long been an integral part of sporting events and venues. Harry Stevens was reputed to be hawking soda pop and hot dogs in New York's Polo Grounds as far back as the 1890s (Howard & Crompton, 1995). Food service and souvenir merchandise sales now account for a significant share of a sport facility's revenues. Bigelow (1995) estimates that concession sales can amount to 10 to 28% of a stadium's or arena's total income. In minor league baseball parks, where the players' salaries are paid by the "parent" major league club and ticket prices are relatively low, concession sales may determine the team's profitability.

According to Bigelow, in amateur sport, food service plays a smaller financial role than it does in professional sport for two primary reasons: the lower disposable income of the fan and the lack of beer sales. Beer sales often account for 35 to 55% of a concessionaire's sales. Because most colleges do not allow beer sales at their facilities, and no high schools allow alcoholic beverage sales, concession volumes for amateur sport are at least 35% less than for professional sport.

While the sale of alcoholic beverages, particularly beer, makes sense from a revenue perspective, the heightened awareness in recent years of the negative consequences of drinking, such as traffic deaths, underage consumption, and unruly fan behavior, has led many sport organizations to evaluate both the benefits and costs associated with the promotion and sale of alcohol at sporting events. Some facilities now have designated "family sections" where alcoholic beverages are prohibited. It is common practice to stop selling alcohol after the seventh inning at baseball games, after the third quarter at football games, and after the second period in hockey games. It is very likely that control of alcohol sales and consumption at athletic events will continue to be a serious concern for sport managers well into the future.

The measurement standard used to gauge the effectiveness of concession operations is per capita sales—the average expenditure per customer or fan—also called the **per cap**. In Table 4–3, the per caps compiled by the Bigelow companies, the leading concession consulting firm in the United States, show the great range of per capita expenditures on food service and merchandise concessions from one sport to another.

Managers in team and club settings are expected to maintain or boost per capita spending on food and souvenir merchandise. In recent years, a trend toward providing more diverse and higher-quality food and beverage options in stadiums and arenas is based on the recognition that fans will pay more if offered appealing choices. Expanded menus, food courts, upscale menus, and waitstaff services, now common in new sport venues, have increased per capita spending by as much as 50 to 100% over traditional in-stadium concession operations.

Tapping New Revenue Sources

While sport managers must continually work to sustain the revenue building blocks of their organization by attracting and holding fans and members at optimal prices and by inducing them to spend on a growing array of concession options while in attendance, effectiveness in amateur and professional sports and sport club operations depends more and more on managers who are adept at implementing recent innovations in sport financing.

Table 4–3 Food Service and Souvenir per Capita Spending by Event or League

Event	Low	High
High school basketball and football	$.25	$2.00
College basketball (without beer)	.85	2.00
College football (without beer)	1.25	3.25
Minor league baseball	3.00	7.00
NBA	4.25	8.50
NHL	4.50	8.25
MLB	5.00	10.50
NFL	5.50	12.50

Source: Data compiled by the Bigelow Companies, Independence, MO.

Luxury Seating

Since 1990, **luxury seating** has been the fastest growing source of income for professional sport teams. Originally called skyboxes, but now more commonly referred to as **luxury suites** and **club seats**, luxury seating involves selling preferred seating for a premium price. The yield from the sale or lease of suites and/or club seats is immense. Funk (1997) estimates that teams in the four major leagues realized $894 million from luxury seating income during 1996. Although the size and amenities may vary from one venue to another, most luxury suites include the same basic features, such as a wet bar, carpeting, TV monitors, catered food, often a private bath, and seating for 12 to 24 people. Generally a suite package will include VIP parking passes and access to restaurants and other special amenities provided at the venue.

For the most part, suites are purchased or leased by corporations for entertaining business clients and/or rewarding company employees. Currently, tax laws provide incentives to corporations buying or leasing suites by allowing companies to deduct 50% of the cost as a business entertainment expense. This combination of benefits has stimulated thousands of corporations to invest in luxury suites. The price of suite occupancy varies by location and size of suite, amenities provided, popularity of the team, and market conditions. In 1996, the cost of suites per year ranged from $21,600 to $23,600 at Three Rivers Stadium in Pittsburgh (110 suites) to $40,000 to $290,000 at the Carolina Panthers' new Ericsson Stadium (137 suites). The New York Knicks in Madison Square Garden command the overall highest priced suites, with annual leases for their 89 suites ranging from $250,000 to $300,000. The NBA Knicks receive 50% of their total revenues from suite sales—an estimated $12.4 million per season.

Club seats represent a less extravagant option for individual fans seeking premium seating. Typically, club seats provide fans with wide-bottomed, cushioned seats with chairbacks, having immediate access to a variety of services, including in-seat wait service, wide-screen TVs, and an enclosed lounge area. The majority of club seats are sold to individual fans seeking priority seating enhanced by VIP treatment. Fans must pay a premium for these special privileges. In 1996, fans paid close to $400 million to occupy the approximately 145,000 club seats available in major sport venues in the United States and Canada. The cost of club seats varies tremendously from one league and venue to another. Having no luxury seats to sell in the Forum, the Los Angeles Lakers charge an average of $9,500 per club seat per season. In 1996, the Lakers generated over $32 million in club seat sales alone. Down the road from Los Angeles, the San Diego Padres sell their club seats on a single game basis, at an average price of $27 per game, offering potential revenues of $369,000 per season.

Although skyboxes have been around since the mid-1960s, when they were first introduced in the Houston Astrodome, it was not until the Palace at Auburn

Hills was built in 1988 that the income potential of luxury seating was fully demonstrated. The $70 million arena built to house the NBA Detroit Pistons was completely financed by the presale of 180 luxury suites. The $12 million-a-year income from suite rentals (leasing for up to $120,000 per season) allowed the team to retire all of its construction debt within six years. That income stream now flows directly into the Pistons' coffers each year. When other team owners saw the success of the Palace, many venues around the country were declared economically obsolete. The Charlotte Coliseum, built during the same year as the Palace, included only 12 suites and no club seating. As a result, the NBA Charlotte Hornets, even though playing in a venue with greater overall seating capacity, realized almost $15 million less in overall facility revenues in 1996 than did their league-rival Pistons. This disparity and many others like it throughout professional sports has created a new lineup of "haves" and "have nots." The economic gap between teams, once determined by market size—big-market versus small-market teams—is now largely a function of the "newness" of the venue. Since 1990, 31 major league teams have moved into new stadiums or arenas. Many team owners, using the threat of relocation (the NFL Cleveland Browns actually moved to Baltimore, acting on their relocation threat), were able to extract the most favorable terms possible for new venues for their teams. This generally means the lease agreements provide that the majority of luxury seating revenues are retained by the team. For example, the Baltimore Orioles retain 90% of luxury suite rentals and 93% of club seat annual fees. The Orioles' share of gross revenues from Oriole Park at Camden Yards is $12 million, $4.9 million from suites and $7.1 million from club seats (Badenhausen et al., 1997).

Given the enormous income-generating capability of luxury seating, interest in the sale of suites and club seats has recently been extended to many segments of the managed sport industry, including college and high school sports and motor sports. There is not a major track in the country without a full range of luxury suites to accommodate corporate sponsors of National Hot Rod Association (NHRA), National Association of Stock Care Auto Racing (NASCAR), and Indy car events. A number of colleges have also reaped great financial benefit from the sale of luxury seating. In the last several years, new stadiums and arenas on the campuses of Louisville, Ohio State, Wisconsin, Tennessee-Chattanooga, and many others have been financed largely from the proceeds of luxury suite sales.

Seat Licenses

Seat licenses, most commonly referred to as **permanent seat licenses** or "PSLs," are the most recent innovation in sport facility financing. PSLs give fans the right to purchase season tickets, often for the life of the venue, in return for an upfront payment. In many cases, fans are offered the opportunity to actually choose the seat for which they buy the PSL. The purchase of the seat license, then, entitles the license holder the right to buy tickets to that seat. Max Muhleman, a sport marketing consultant credited with pioneering the concept, refers to PSLs as simply "user fees" that ensure rabid fans access to their favorite sport teams. The price of seat licenses varies from $250 to $16,000 depending on the location of the seat and the team's determination of fans' willingness to pay. Typically, PSLs sell for between $750 and $4,000, averaging from $1,028 apiece in Baltimore's new stadium for the NFL Ravens to $2,234 apiece in Charlotte's Ericsson Stadium. In those cities where PSLs have been successfully marketed, the amount of money raised through the sale of seat licenses has been impressive. In Charlotte, the expansion Carolina Panthers of the NFL sold over 50,000 licenses for a total of almost $140 million in PSL revenues. In St. Louis in 1995, over 72,000 fans placed orders for the 46,000 PSLs available in the new Transworld Dome, home of the NFL Rams. The PSL offering raised $74 million for the Rams organization, much of which was later shared with other league members. The St. Louis example raises an interesting issue concerning PSLs: the fact that they result in disparities in financing between teams. Los Angeles Rams owner Georgia LaFrontiere was "forced" to share PSL revenues with owners to avoid a lawsuit by the NFL. Raiders owner Al Davis is currently being sued by the NFL to share revenues from PSLs. Davis contends there is no NFL rule requiring him to share PSL revenues with other teams (Howard, 1997).

To date, PSLs have done well in those markets in which teams have either a strong existing fan base (Washington Redskins, Cincinnati Bengals) or in which fans have a strong (often pent-up) demand for attracting new teams, as was the case in Charlotte, Baltimore, and Cleveland. In each of these cities, PSL sales have been very strong. However, even in those cities where a team has a strong following, PSL sales may face some difficulties. The Oakland Raiders, when they returned to the Bay Area from Los Angeles in 1994, expected to raise $100 million from PSL sales to finance an expansion of the Oakland Coliseum. Their seat license campaign, despite an avid fan base, fell far short of expectations, selling only 37,000 of the 52,000 seats offered. Although the over $60 million raised by the Raiders was a significant amount, the almost $40 million shortfall meant that taxpayers in the City of Oakland and Alameda County had to make up the difference.

Critics of the Raiders' seat license program attribute its disappointing results to the fact that the seat licenses sold were good for only 10 years, not for an extended time or on a permanent basis as in every other seat license program. As Muhleman (1996) points out, three features are essential to the successful sale of seat licenses. First, they must be sold on a permanent basis so that fans actually own the rights for the life of the stadium. Extended ownership then provides fans with the second benefit, which is the right to transfer or sell the license to any other family member. Finally, Muhleman advocates "equity maintenance" as the third essential ingredient. This provision provides PSL purchasers with, in effect, a money-back guarantee. Under this arrangement, a team agrees to buy back a fan's seat license for current market value or for no less than 70 to 85% of its original price. It is clear that seat licenses will become a permanent feature of sport financing. College athletic programs around the United States have begun to adopt the concept. The Ohio State University Athletic Department raised approximately $20 million from the sale of 5,100 seat licenses in its new 20,000-seat arena. PSLs have also recently been successfully extended to motor racing. The new Texas Motor Speedway offered 30,000 seat licenses at $1,000 apiece in order to finance a quarter of the track's $110 million construction costs. It is probable that future sport managers will see the PSL concept extended to even more segments of the sport industry. Certainly, seat licenses will continue to be a prominent consideration in new sport facility construction.

Naming Rights

Since the early 1990s, an increasing number of corporations like United Airlines, Coors, and BancOne have bought the rights to put their names on stadiums and arenas. The going rate at major league venues ranges from $1 million to $2 million per year. Pacific Telesis Corporation struck a $50 million, 24-year deal with the San Francisco Giants for the **naming rights** to the Giants' new downtown stadium. The baseball-only facility will be called Pacific Bell Park.

The naming rights "rage," as recently characterized by *The Sporting News* ("NFC Report," 1995), is not confined to major league venues. All across North America, small and medium cities have found corporate sponsors for new community arenas and ballparks. In Greenville, South Carolina, Bi-Lo, a leading regional supermarket chain, committed $3.5 million over 15 years to have its name placed on the city's new 15,000-seat arena. In three cities—Buffalo, New York; Edmonton, Alberta; and Lansing, Michigan—minor league baseball teams play in North AmeriCare Park, TELUS Field, and Olds Park, respectively. Recently, college athletic programs have begun to aggressively pursue naming rights sponsors as a way to raise monies to build new facilities. Rather than naming a stadium or arena after a prominent former athlete or coach, as has been the tradition on many campuses, athletic departments have begun to recognize the substantial investment corporations are willing to make to align their company's name with a university's reputation and athletic tradition. Faced with the need to raise at least one-third of the $80 million cost of their new arena, the Ohio State University Athletic Department struck a $12.5 million naming rights deal over five years with Schottenstein Stores, a private retail discount chain. The naming rights agreement along with the successful sale of seat licenses resulted in the Ohio State Athletic Department raising close to $30 million toward the construction of its new facility, the Schottenstein Center.

Corporations see their considerable investment as a cost-effective way for their companies or brands to receive extensive public exposure. For a company like Marine Midland Bank, which paid $15 million over 20 years to have its name associated with the new home of the NHL Buffalo Sabres, the naming rights agreement package, which included broadcast exposure, news coverage, and team-generated publicity, was seen as a great investment opportunity. In addition to providing national exposure for this financial institution, typical of most naming rights agreements the Sabres agreed to provide the following benefits: the name of the arena in 16-foot letters, the logo on the roof and ceiling, the name and logo on street signs leading to the arena, one luxury suite, the right to install automatic teller machines (ATMs) in the arena, a mini-bank branch near the ticket counters, a nameplate on each row of seats, dasherboard signage, and name and logo at center ice. As with luxury seating and PSLs, there is no doubt that the next generation of managers in many segments of the sport industry will be involved with the sale and marketing of naming rights agreements.

Corporate Sponsorships

It is evident from previous sections that corporations have assumed an increasingly prominent role in financing both professional and amateur sport organizations and the venues in which they perform. The purchase of luxury suites and naming rights by the corporate sector has been instrumental in fueling the sport facility construction boom of the 1990s. It is quite possible, however, that the business sector's greatest contribution to sport is through **corporate sponsorship** of teams and events. In 1996, over 4,500 North American companies spent close to $4 billion for the rights to sponsor sporting events (e.g., teams, leagues, and championship events/tournaments). According to the *IEG's Complete Guide to Sponsorship* (International Events Group, 1996), worldwide spending on sponsorship approached $10 billion in 1996, and these figures represent just the tip of the iceberg. According to Eisenhart (1988), for every dollar paid for sponsorship rights (i.e., the right to be the "title sponsor" of a Professional Golfers' Association [PGA] Tour event such as the Kemper Open, or a NASCAR race series, like the Winston Cup), another $5 is spent on promoting the company's association with that event, including TV, radio, print advertising, and event signage.

Corporate sponsorship in sport is not strictly a North American phenomenon. In fact, perhaps the greatest growth in corporate investment in sport has occurred in Europe and South America in the past decade. A significant amount of international sponsorship activity has been initiated recently by American-based multinational firms such as Nike and Coca-Cola. For example, recently Pepsi-Cola, in an effort to increase its market presence in Argentina, paid $2 million to sponsor two soccer tournaments organized by the Argentinean Soccer Association. Pepsi linked its sponsorship investment to a nationwide ad campaign featuring Argentinean soccer players wearing Pepsi T-shirts with the slogan, "More soccer, more Pepsi." The campaign is intended to capture market share from Coke, which currently monopolizes soft drink sales in Argentina. On a much grander scale, Nike recently signed a 10-year, $200-million deal with the Brazilian national soccer team. The agreement provides Nike with the right to stage five international matches per year with full broadcast and merchandising rights for each event. Nike's link with Brazilian soccer is just one example of the apparel giant's increasing commitment to global sponsorship. Nike expects international sales will account for 50% of the company's total revenue by 2000 (Himelstein, 1997).

Corporate sponsorship has grown to be an integral part of almost every segment of the managed sport industry. Sponsored events, or "properties," include everything from the Olympic Games, for which top sponsors paid $40 million to become Olympic Partners for the 1996 Games in Atlanta, to the Women's National Basketball Association (WNBA), with corporations paying $4 million per season to become major sponsors of the new women's summer professional basketball league. Recently, Georgia Tech invited sponsors to pay $75,000 per game for five football games at Bobby Dodd Stadium. In return for the fee, each corporate sponsor received 100 regional TV spots during the game, full-page ads in Atlanta's leading newspapers and game-day program, a corporate hospitality tent on game day, a fully catered luxury suite, priority seating for 250, and the corporate logo posted at the stadium and on all season football posters (Howard & Crompton, 1995).

The Georgia Tech agreement illustrates the central concept underlying sponsorships: the exchange of mutual benefits between the sport organization and the corporate sponsor. For a sponsorship to succeed, both parties must gain from the relationship. A sport organization offers a variety of potentially valuable benefits to business organizations. Some of these benefits include (1) *heightened visibility*—the opportunity to increase awareness of a new or existing brand or product with a desirable target audience; (2) *image enhancement*—the ability to create or reinforce an image for a product or to counter a negative public perception by aligning the company's name with a team or event that has great prestige and/or fan appeal; (3) *product trial or sale opportunities*—the opportunity for manufacturers to showcase product benefits (think of tire manufacturers' sponsorship of auto racing) or to induce incremental sales through promotional giveaways, coupon tie-ins, and point-of-purchase displays; and (4) *hospitality opportunities*—the opportunity for companies to entertain key clients at sporting events. For example, golf tournament sponsors offer prime customers the chance to play in pro-am events and to be hosted in VIP tents, providing the corporation with a great setting for solidifying business relationships.

As sponsorship has grown in prominence, two sport marketing firms have emerged as important resources for sport managers involved in soliciting and servicing corporate sponsors. Since 1980, International Events Group, Inc. (IEG), has served as the single most comprehensive source of up-to-date information on effective professional practice and emerging trends related to sponsorship. IEG produces a bimonthly publication, the *IEG Sponsorship Report*, which presents case studies and quantitative analyses of the latest sponsorship agreements. Readers are provided with in-depth descriptions and commentaries on prominent features of each agreement, including how and why the deal was made and how much the sponsor is paying. The sponsorship report allows sport managers to keep abreast of the latest developments in sponsorship packaging and implementation. Team Marketing Report, which like IEG is based in Chicago, produces a monthly sports marketing newsletter that devotes considerable attention to summarizing key features of current sponsorship agreements, specifically as they relate to major and minor league sports. Team Marketing Report also publishes the *Sport Sponsor FactBook*, which annually profiles the sport marketing activities and names of decision makers for over 2,200 companies involved in sport sponsorship. Sport managers whose jobs include selling corporate sponsorship agreements should take advantage of the beneficial resources provided by these two sport marketing firms.

Licensing

Revenues received from the sale of **licensed sport merchandise** have become an important source of income for many professional sport franchises and an increasing number of amateur sport organizations. In 1996, the retail sales of products bearing the trademark or logo of the 113 teams in the four major professional leagues in North America totaled $8.8 billion (National Sporting Goods Association, 1996). A breakdown of gross sales by league is provided in Table 4–4.

The more fans spend on merchandise licensed by sport teams, the greater the return to the teams themselves. For the right to sell merchandise with a team name or logo, the clothing manufacturer (e.g., Champion or Nike) must pay a royalty fee, generally calculated as a percentage of the net or wholesale selling price of

Table 4–4 Licensed Sports Products Retail Sales—United States

	1993	1994	1995	1996
	(in Millions)			
NFL	$2,600	$3,000	$3,150	n/a
MLB	2,400	2,500	1,700	$1,800
NBA	2,100	2,500	2,600	2,600
NHL	800	1,000	1,000	1,000

Source: Reprinted with permission from 1997 Annual Industry Report, *Team Licensing Business*, Vol. 9, No. 4, pp. 23–26, © 1997, Virgo Publishing.

goods bearing logos. The standard royalty fee charged by the four professional leagues is 8.5%. Applying that fee on total net sales, the total amount of royalty revenues received by the four leagues exceeded $700 million in 1996. In each league, proceeds from the sale of team merchandise are pooled and divided evenly among the league teams. According to Zimbalist (1992), this meant that each Major League Baseball team's share amounted to $3.7 million in 1992. It would be reasonable to estimate that in 1996, each NFL team received a share of about $6 million from the league's royalty pool. Minor league baseball and hockey have recently followed the lead of the major leagues. Now, over 200 minor league teams participate in licensing programs intended to market and protect the use of their trademarks and logos.

The four established professional leagues and the more recently formed Major League Soccer have all established highly centralized licensing programs. In 1987, professional baseball established Major League Baseball Properties (MLBP) as the league's licensing arm. Up to that point, the sale of baseball merchandise consisted primarily of baseball cards, T-shirts, caps, and pennants sold at stadium concession stands and in selected sporting goods stores. By the early 1990s, MLBP had introduced a new line of high-quality products, including authentic reproductions of team jerseys, men's ties, silk scarves, and boxer shorts, with prints of team logos in shopping outlets in every major mall in the United States and Canada. This same kind of merchandise program, coordinated by a central "properties" division, exists for each of the major leagues. Professional football's licensing branch, NFL Properties (NFLP), has taken the most aggressive approach to merchandising licensed league products. They have successfully developed more than 30 merchandise programs, such as "NFL Throwbacks," which featured clothing items from original or classic league teams such as the Canton Bulldogs and the 1946 San Francisco 49ers. These and many other specialty apparel lines are available in a number of NFL stores owned and operated by NFLP. In this case, the majority of sale proceeds—well beyond the standard royalty fee—goes directly into the NFL coffers. Total sales of NFL team and league-related products could reach $3.5 billion in 1997.

Colleges and universities have also become actively involved in licensing. The Association of Collegiate Licensing Administrators (ACLA) estimates that between 275 and 300 institutions have established formal licensing programs (R. Van Brimmer, personal interview, May 24, 1997). By 1996 the total sales of licensed collegiate products exceeded $2.0 billion. Universities that have established formal licensing programs have taken one of two alternate approaches. Slightly over half have procured the services of an outside licensing management firm to oversee all aspects of their licensing programs. This "contracting out" approach has been most common among smaller institutions lacking the necessary staff expertise to manage a full-service program. Typically, licensing management firms provide their services for a fixed percentage of the royalty revenues, generally around 20% of the gross income. Rather than contract out these services, an increasing number of universities have decided to establish their own "in-house" staff to recruit and/or approve those companies that can use the institution's name or logo, to enforce appropriate use of all trademarks and logos, and to collect royalties. For many "big time" athletic programs, annual royalty income exceeds $1 million a year. The University of Michigan Athletic Department was estimated to have received over $3 million in 1996 from its in-house licensing program (R. Van Brimmer, personal interview, May 24, 1997). It is important to note that while a growing number of collegiate athletic programs are tapping licensing royalties as a new and expanding source of revenue, a recent survey found that one out of every four athletic departments on those campuses where licensing programs had been established received no funds from the annual licensing revenues. In most all of these instances, authority for the licensing program is located outside of the athletic department, generally within the university's central administration. On these campuses, it is important that athletic departments strive to have their interests represented.

Unfortunately, many amateur and interscholastic sport organizations have yet to explore the potential of licensing. It is conceivable in many instances that prominent local multipurpose sport clubs and high school sport programs could generate substantial revenues through the adoption of a licensing program to protect and promote their names and logos.

Given the existing prominence of licensing revenues and the potential for further development and expansion to almost all segments of professional and amateur sport, it is likely that most sport managers will become involved in making decisions related to the administration and promotion of licensed products for their organizations. Highly specialized career opportunities related to the licensing and merchandising of sporting goods and products exist throughout professional and collegiate sport. Successful models for selling and promoting team logo apparel and souvenirs exist in each major professional league through their respective properties offices. It is highly probable that licensing opportunities will continue to grow in collegiate and interscholastic sport as well.

KEY SKILLS

It appears that financial challenges facing sport managers are universal, cutting across all segments of the industry, including recreational, youth, interscholastic, intercollegiate, and professional sport. No matter what the setting, those managers most likely to succeed will have some financial management knowledge and expertise. The extent to which sport managers need specialized training in finance and accounting depends, to some degree, on the size and complexity of the sport organization for which they work. Generally, the larger and/or the more complicated the organization, the greater the likelihood that the organization will utilize specialized financial management expertise. For example, the norm for major league teams and Division I collegiate athletic departments is to appoint a senior staff member as the **chief financial officer** (CFO) or **business manager.** This individual assumes primary responsibility for coordinating the organization's cash and credit, financial planning, accounting, budgeting, and management information services. Despite the increased presence of trained financial specialists in sport organizations, it is important to understand that almost all decisions made by sport managers—no matter what their role in the organization—have financial implications. Even in those organizations in which staff take on specialized roles in marketing, stadium operations, or concessions, it is critical for these individuals to understand how their decisions affect and are affected by available funds and cash flow considerations, projected revenue streams, and budget constraints. Therefore, it is extremely important for any student aspiring to become the manager of a sport organization to develop skills in basic accounting, financial analysis and planning, and budgeting.

At the minimum, a well-prepared sport executive should have the ability to interpret three basic financial documents—the balance sheet, the income statement, and the statement of cash flows. The **balance sheet** shows what an organization owns and how it is financed. The **income statement** measures the financial performance of the organization over a specified time period, typically a year. Finally, the **statement of cash flows** shows how the organization's operations have affected its cash position. The effective interpretation of these three documents is crucial to making sound business decisions. These documents equip managers with information essential to analyzing, controlling, and improving the organization's day-to-day operations and long-term financial prospects. In addition to acquiring basic skills in financial and managerial accounting, students contemplating senior executive roles in sport organizations should also gain knowledge of the fundamental concepts of corporate and public sector finance. Exposure to managerial finance will provide sport managers with an understanding of such basics as how to make effective capital investment decisions, how to manage and control inventory, and how to successfully manage credit.

Gaining an understanding of the budgeting process is also an indispensable skill for sport managers. Creating and overseeing a budget is an almost universal responsibility of senior sport executives. Budgeting is a method for allocating available funds among the many, sometimes competing, purposes of an organization. The historic purpose of budgeting has been to keep spending within fixed boundaries and to exert financial control over organizational staff. More recently, however, rather than viewing the budget as strictly an instrument for controlling spending, effective managers see budgeting as a strategic plan for achieving organizational goals. Proposed expenditures are linked to organizational aspirations. While there is considerable literature on the principles of budgeting and the "dos and don'ts" of budget preparation, there is no substitute for actual exposure to the budgeting process. Students interested in gaining firsthand experience should take every opportunity during visits to sport organizations or while on internship assignments to talk with knowledgeable staff about the budget process and, whenever possible, examine past and current budget documents and attend actual budget hearings. Given the many challenges facing sport managers, there is no doubt that individuals adept at applying fundamental concepts of accounting and finance will have a significant advantage in advancing their careers as sport executives.

CURRENT ISSUES

Ticket Sales

A challenge facing sport managers in the future is determining optimal ticket prices. Some evidence suggests that the continuous increase in ticket prices is discouraging substantial numbers of sport fans from attending professional league games (Brown, 1993). It appears that for many fans, a definite ceiling exists, what marketers call the "price threshold," beyond which fans will resist payment. Unfortunately, when it comes to establishing prices, Quirk and Fort (1992) concluded that "ticket prices for professional teams are the best informed *guesses* of management" (p. 144). In the future, successful sport managers must establish ticket prices based on market research, which provides an understanding of sport consumers' expected price threshold, that is, their willingness to pay. Finding the "right" price of admission will be an increasingly important responsibility of sport managers.

While the managers of sport teams will spend considerable energy designing ticket programs to maximize total cash flow per seat, managers in club settings, such as private golf, racquet, or multipurpose sport and health clubs, will focus much of their attention on developing optimal membership programs. Selling and retaining memberships is the lifeblood of the sport club sector. The key challenge facing sport club managers will be to sustain membership levels in the face of growing competition. In 1995, sport and fitness clubs in the United States had, on average, 1.25 more competitors—in the form of other clubs—in their marketplace than the previous year (International Health, Racquet and Sportsclub Association, 1996). Increasingly, success in the club industry will be measured by the extent to which managers will be able to hold or retain existing members (current annual membership retention rates average only 65%) and by their ability to increase revenues per membership. In the future, sport club performance will be based on how effectively clubs recruit and retain members as well as their ability to maximize income return from each member. Additional financial issues confronting sport managers in this segment of the industry are discussed in Chapter 18, Health and Fitness Industry.

Luxury Seating

Although luxury seat revenues have fueled an unprecedented boom in sport facility construction and have provided many teams with a major source of new income, the future of suite and club seat sales is not without some serious concerns. The next generation of sport managers faces some serious challenges. A concern already evident in several market areas is that suite construction may have exceeded demand. For example, the Washington, D.C.–Baltimore area has experienced unprecedented growth in arena and stadium development. Since 1992, the Orioles have built a new ballpark, the Redskins and Ravens have created separate football-only stadiums, and the Bullets and Capitals occupy a new arena in downtown Washington, D.C. By 1998, the area could be saturated with over 600 luxury suites. The New York market, by comparison, with more teams, more annual events, and a much larger business community to support the purchase of suites, has a total of 328 luxury suites (Hilsenrath, 1996). The key question, which to date remains unanswered, is whether there will be enough corporations to support the sale of all the suites being built. That question was raised recently in South Florida, in the San Francisco Bay Area, and in Atlanta, where substantial facility development has filled each of these markets with hundreds of new suites. In every market there are only a finite number of businesses with both the economic capability and the willingness to spend $100,000 to $200,000 a year to lease a suite. Faced with increased competition and a continued trend toward corporate downsizing, sport managers may find it increasingly challenging to convince companies to commit significant corporate resources to lease suites for extended periods of time.

Sponsorship

As the sport industry moves into the next millennium, it is clear that corporations have become more savvy and sophisticated about what benefits they expect to receive from sport sponsorships and about how much they are willing to pay for those benefits. It is not uncommon for large corporations with a history of sport sponsorship (e.g., Miller Brewing, Wendy's) to receive thousands of sponsorship proposals per year. Therefore, sport managers would be most likely to succeed in soliciting sponsors for their teams or events if they adopt a marketing approach. The extent to which sport managers are able to see their opportunities through the eyes of potential sponsors and tailor proposals to meet the needs of businesses is likely to determine the managers' success. The marketing approach requires a sport organization to identify what companies are likely to want in return for investing their resources. Chapter 3, Marketing Principles Applied to Sport Management, contains information relevant to this point. This information forms the basis for developing a presentation for each prospect. Too often, sport organizations spend too much time thinking about their own needs and not enough time considering what their prospect, the potential corporate investor, wants. Sport managers should perceive themselves as brokers who are concerned with furthering the welfare of potential sponsor companies by offering opportunities in which both the business and organization win.

SUMMARY

The next generation of sport managers faces some exciting financial challenges. It is evident that traditional sources of revenue will be increasingly hard pressed to meet the growing expenses of most professional and amateur sport organizations. Skyrocketing costs in all professional sports and in collegiate athletics have made it increasingly difficult for a growing number of teams and athletic departments to break even financially. During 1996–1997, about one of every four major league franchises reported it was losing money (Badenhausen et al., 1997). A recent NCAA report (Fulks, 1996) found that slightly less than half of all Division I-A and a relative handful (16%) of Division II athletic programs were able to pay their own way, with schools at both levels increasingly dependent on institutional support or subsidies to meet growing budget needs.

Player costs in all four major professional leagues have doubled or tripled just within the last decade. The *average* player in both the NBA and MLB now makes more than $1 million per year. Collegiate athletic managers face a similar squeeze with respect to supporting team rosters. In the 1990s, the cost of supporting the average student-athlete on a grant-in-aid is expected to increase as much as 80%. At the same time the cost per scholarship is rising sharply, athletic directors must also deal with the substantial financial obligations related to complying with Title IX, a comprehensive statute aimed at eliminating gender discrimination in federally funded educational institutions. It is critical that sport managers recognize, plan for, and accommodate the soaring interest in sport among women. (This topic is considered at length in Chapter 5, Legal Principles Applied to Sport Management.)

What all of this means to those contemplating careers in intercollegiate athletics is that college athletics is far from its popular perception as a "cash cow." Spiraling costs associated with rising tuition and Title IX compliance, increased competition, and flat or declining traditional revenues have combined to place collegiate athletic programs under substantial financial pressure. While the circumstances or pressure points may be different in other segments of the sport industry, sport managers of all kinds face similar fiscal strains. Increasingly, administrators in professional and amateur sport settings are finding it hard to keep up with rapidly escalating costs by relying only on traditional revenue sources like gate or membership receipts, concessions, and, in some cases, media revenues.

The era of unparalleled growth that characterized much of the late 1970s and the 1980s has been replaced with a future that is much more challenging. The most successful managers will find ways not only to do more with less, but to create and expand opportunities for their organizations to secure additional funding. Although ticket and concession sales will continue to be important sources of revenue, financial success will increasingly be determined by more recent innovations such as PSLs, luxury seating, and sponsorship agreements. Garnering corporate support will be a key measure of success. While sport teams have stretched the individual fan's ticket price tolerance almost to the limit, with average prices from $30 to $50 per game in many venues, corporations in growing numbers have demonstrated a willingness to pay $150,000 to $250,000 per year to lease a luxury suite. An important future challenge will be to not only establish a high level of business support but also sustain it. Sport managers entering the industry over the next few years will be faced with the task of renewing thousands of luxury suite leases, originally signed on average for three to six years, which will expire around the turn of the century. The financial future for most sport managers will be largely about carefully preparing and presenting marketing-oriented sponsorship proposals to targeted corporations, administering licensing programs, and creating innovative facility development programs around the sale of PSLs and luxury seating.

REFERENCES

Badenhausen, K., Nikolov, C., Alkin, M., & Ozanian, M. (1997, June 17). More than a game. *Financial World*, 40–50.

Bandyopadhyay, S., & Buttone, M. (Spring 1997). Playing to win. *Marketing Management*, 9–19.

Berrett, T. (1996). Economics of sport management. In B. Parkhouse (Ed.), *The management of sport*. New York: Mosby.

Bigelow, C. (1995). Sale of foodservice and souvenir concessions. In D. Howard & J. Crompton (Eds.), *Financing sport*. Morgantown, WV: Fitness Information Technology, Inc.

Bodley, H. (1997, May 7). Baseball salaries soar to $1.06 billion. *USA Today*, p. 1A.

Brady, E. (1997, April 3). Just how high can salaries go? *USA Today*, p. 1C.

Brown, B. (1993, May 11). Supply and demand set ticket prices. *USA Today*, p. 8C.

Eisenhart, T. (1988, January). Sporting chances zap competitors. *Business Marketing*, 92–97.

Fulks, D. (1996). *Revenues and expenses of Division I and II intercollegiate athletic programs: Financial trends and relationships—1995*. Overland Park, KS: National Collegiate Athletic Association.

Funk, D. (1997). The economics of professional sport franchises. *Proceedings from the 12th Annual North American Society for Sport Management Conference* [Abstract], San Antonio, TX, May 28–31.

Girard, F. (1997, March 2). MAC schools dripping red ink. *The Detroit News*, p. 9D.

Hiestand, M. (1997, February 14). How big's the big? *USA Today*, p. 2C.

Hilsenrath, J. (1996, April 7). The cost of luxury could blow sky high. *New York Times*, p. Y21.

Himelstein, L. (1997, May 12). The corporation: The swoosh heard 'round the world. *Business Week*, 76–78, 80.

Howard D.R. (1997, June). *The changing economics of professional sports: Implications for sport managers*. Paper presented at the North American Society for Sport Management Conference, San Antonio, TX.

Howard, D., & Crompton, J. (Eds.). (1995). *Financing sport*. Morgantown, WV: Fitness Information Technology, Inc.

International Events Group. (1996). *IEG's complete guide to sponsorship*. Chicago: Author.

International Health, Racquet and Sportsclub Association. (1996). *Profiles of success*. Boston: Author.

Irvine, A. (1997, April). A share in the spoils. *Sport Business*, 9, 21.

Jensen, C. (1995). *Outdoor recreation* (5th ed.). Champaign, IL: Human Kinetics.

Krupa, G., & Dunnavant, K. (1989, January 2). The struggle with the downside. *Sports Inc.*, 33–38.

Muhleman, M. (1996, Sept. 8). *Essential elements in financing today's sports facilities*. Paper presented at the Bond Buyer Conference on Stadium and Arena Finance, San Francisco, CA.

National Sporting Goods Association. (1996). *The sporting goods market in 1996*. Mt. Prospect, IL: Author.

NFC report. (1995, June 5). *The Sporting News*, 49.

Quirk, J., & Fort, R. (1992). *Pay dirt: The business of professional team sports*. Princeton, NJ: Princeton University Press.

Rainie, H. (1997, April 7). The boom and bust in sport gambling. *U.S. News & World Report*, 6.

Wenner, L.A., & Gantz, W. (1989). The audience experience with sports on television. In L.A. Wenner (Ed.), *Media, sports, & society* (pp. 241–269). Newbury Park, CA: Sage.

Zimbalist, A. (1992). *Baseball and billions*. New York: Basic Books.

CHAPTER 5

Legal Principles Applied to Sport Management

Glenn M. Wong and Lisa Pike Masteralexis

Key words: sport law, administrative law, risk management, plaintiff, defendant, judicial review, injunction, tort, negligence, duty of care, agency, principal, agent, fiduciary duties, vicarious liability, independent contractor, contract, consideration, capacity, disaffirm, breach, waivers and releases of liability, constitutional law, state actor, due process, equal protection, unreasonable searches and seizures, invasion of privacy, collective bargaining agreement, Title IX, antitrust law, National Labor Relations Act, Equal Pay Act, Title VII of the Civil Rights Act, bonafide occupational qualification, Age Discrimination in Employment Act, Americans with Disabilities Act, trademark, secondary meaning, Lanham Act, service mark, ambush marketing

INTRODUCTION

The term **sport law** signifies the application of existing laws to the sport setting more than it represents the creation of a new area of law. There are, however, a few instances in which state or federal governments have enacted new laws to regulate the sport industry. For instance, 26 states currently have specific laws to regulate the activities of sport agents. A few examples of sport-related laws on the federal level are laws that regulate the boxing and the sport broadcasting industries; Title IX, a law enacted in 1972 that prohibits discrimination in education including athletics; and the Amateur Sports Act, a law enacted in 1978 that governs Olympic and other amateur sport. Sport law also includes the governance of sport organizations. Rules and regulations in sport often model laws and legislation. Sport governing bodies operate much like federal and state administrative bodies. As a result, this aspect of sport law mirrors the administrative law followed by state and federal governments. **Administrative law** describes the body of law created by the rules, regulations, orders, and decisions of administrative bodies. Often when a dispute arises over the interpretation of a rule or regulation, sport lawyers work representing both the governing body and the participant or participants to resolve the dispute through the administrative process established by the sport organization. One reason for the involvement of sport lawyers is that many sport organizations hire lawyers to draft their rules and regulations. If lawyers draft the legislation, when a dispute arises it is often thought that lawyers can best interpret, challenge, or defend the legislation.

Over the past three decades the sport industry has evolved into a complex multimillion-dollar global entity. Because of its growth, there is often much at stake for those involved in the business and the participation segments of the industry when sport managers make decisions. When these decisions cause disputes, those working and participating in sport are now relying more heavily on the legal system for a resolution. Thus, sport law has become increasingly important for sport managers. Sport managers must have a basic understanding of legal principles to manage risk in their daily activities and to know when to seek legal assistance to resolve disputes.

HISTORY

This chapter focuses on the application of law to the sport industry in the twentieth century. There have been, however, many tort law cases involving participation in sport and games dating from the early evolution of tort law in the United States and Great Britain. For instance, a treatise published in 1635 in Britain and a landmark torts case, *Vosburg v. Putney* (Wis. 1891), both discuss tort liability for participation in games and horseplay (Yasser, McCurdy, & Goplerud, 1997).

Many of the earliest U.S. lawsuits in the sport industry involve baseball. Professional baseball has the greatest amount of litigation of all the professional sports, due in part to the fact that it is the oldest organized professional sport league but also due to its arduous labor history. Early cases in professional sport involved baseball players challenging the reserve system adopted by owners to keep players from achieving any form of free agency (*Metropolitan Exhibition Co. v. Ewing*, 1890; *Metropolitan Exhibition Co. v. Ward*, 1890). Interestingly, a player involved in the case, John Montgomery Ward, led the first union efforts in baseball in the late 1800s and went on to become a lawyer (Berry, Gould, & Staudohar, 1986). Throughout the early to mid-twentieth century most cases in the sport industry were based in contract, antitrust, and labor law applied to professional sport.

At the time of these early cases there was not a formally recognized specialty called "sport law." Sport law was first recognized in 1972 when Professor Robert

Berry of Boston College Law School offered the first course addressing sport law, entitled "Regulation of the Professional Sport Industry," which focused on legal issues in the professional sport industry (Wong & Masteralexis, 1996). There are many reasons for the considerable growth in the field of sport law over the past 25 years. First, the legal profession as a whole has moved toward a greater degree of specialization. Second, the amount of litigation and the diversity of law cases in the sport industry have increased as more people turn to the courts to resolve their disputes. Third, many athletic associations have adopted their own governance systems with rules, regulations, and procedures that are based on the U.S. legal system. Challenges to these governing bodies have provided lawyers with specialties in the sport industry. For instance, a specialty has developed for lawyers specializing in representing schools and athletes in investigations by and hearings before the National Collegiate Athletic Association (NCAA) (Haworth, 1996).

As a result of this growth, the number of sport law textbooks has increased from the first one, published in 1978 by John Weistart and Cym Lowell and titled *The Law of Sports*, to the over one dozen published today. Numerous law schools and sport management programs now include one or more sport law courses in their curricula. Lawyers and law firms have developed specialties in sport law. While there is no available data as to the number of sport lawyers working in the field, four professional associations devoted to sport law exist in North America, and there are others in Europe, Australia, and New Zealand. The North American associations are the American Bar Association's (ABA) Forum Committee on Sport and Entertainment Law, the Sport Lawyers Association, the Marquette University Law School's National Sports Law Institute, and the Society for the Study of the Legal Aspects of Sport and Physical Activity (SSLASPA). All of the associations publish their own journals and newsletters. There are approximately 385 members in the ABA Forum Committee on Sport and Entertainment Law's Sports Division (ABA, 1992), 1,200 members in the Sport Lawyers Association (Sport Lawyers Association, 1996–1997), and 175 members in SSLASPA (SSLASPA, 1997) (note that an individual may belong to more than one organization). In addition, there are at least four law school or university-based institutes dedicated to studying sport law in the United States.

Possessing a law degree is not necessary for a sport manager, but the skills a legal education provides are beneficial to many positions in the industry. A legal education establishes skills in written and oral communication, analytical reasoning, critical thinking, problem solving, and negotiating. Many in the sport industry possess law degrees but work in sport management rather than practicing law. For instance, the current commissioners of the National Football League (NFL; Paul Tagliabue), the National Hockey League (NHL; Gary Bettman), and the National Basketball Association (NBA; David Stern) are lawyers, as were some previous Major League Baseball (MLB) commissioners (Fay Vincent, Bowie Kuhn, Judge Kennesaw Mountain Landis). In addition, many professional league commissioners' office staff, professional team general managers, players' association executive directors and staff, National Collegiate Athletic Association (NCAA) officials, college conference commissioners, college and university athletic directors and compliance staff, International and U.S. Olympic Committee members and staff, national governing body members and staff, player representatives, and facility managers possess law degrees but do not practice law in the traditional sense. Their knowledge of law often allows them to make wise decisions and may save their organizations the expense of hiring outside counsel. For example, a facility manager may need to understand such law-related topics as local ordinances and codes, labor and employment laws, and the Americans with Disabilities Act, just to name a few. A facility manager may also be responsible for negotiating many contracts, including leases with sport teams, contracts with shows or events, collective bargaining agreements with labor unions, contracts for concessionaires, sponsorship agreements, facility naming rights agreements, and pourage rights for the beverages sold in the facility.

KEY CONCEPTS

Legal disputes have been occurring more frequently in the sport industry than they did years ago. Litigation has increased because more people turn to the legal system to resolve their disputes. One reason for this is the rising financial interests in amateur and professional sport. On the amateur side, gender discrimination, constitutional rights violations, recruiting violations, the use of ineligible players, and rule violations by athletes, coaches, and educational institutions are all sources of litigation (Wong, 1994). On the professional side, labor disputes, broken contracts, misconduct by athletes and owners, and the enforcement of and challenges to rules are the primary sources of litigation. Personal injury and product liability cases filed by recreational sport participants have increased. In order to make legally sound decisions, it is important for sport managers to have a basic understanding of these legal issues.

Risk Management

The concept of **risk management** is a key lesson a sport manager can learn by studying sport law. Risk management requires developing a management strategy to maintain greater control over the legal uncertainty that may wreak havoc on a sport business. Whatever the type of sport business, risk management plans contain the same goals. The two key goals of a risk management plan are prevention and intervention. Prevention involves keeping problems from arising, while intervention involves having a plan of action to follow when problems do occur. Risk management is a strategy that encourages sport managers to develop a plan to prevent legal disputes from occurring and a plan for intervening when a legal problem does arise. Through such risk management, sport managers may limit their losses by avoiding becoming defendants in court actions. Note that a **plaintiff** is the person or organization who initiates a lawsuit, and a **defendant** is the person or organization whom the lawsuit is brought against.

The D.I.M. Process is one method used to establish a risk management program. The D.I.M. Process consists of three steps: (1) *d*eveloping the risk management plan, (2) *i*mplementing the risk management plan, and (3) *m*anaging the risk management plan (Ammon, 1997). It is important that a sport organization use these steps to create a risk management program specifically tailored to its operation. The risk management plan should address all potential legal liability. Many people think of risk management plans as addressing the potential for tort liability, in particular, negligence. The plan should not be so limited but should include the many areas of law discussed in the following sections. For instance, adopting a risk management philosophy for a sport business may also keep a sport manager from losing an employment discrimination suit, an arbitration proceeding, or a challenge to an athletic association's rule. A key to a successful risk management strategy is to have all the organization's employees involved in the three stages of the process. This way, employees will have "ownership" in the plan (Ammon, 1997). They will know why the plan is in existence and what its goals are and thus will be more likely to follow it.

Judicial Review

Athletic administrators make decisions regarding athletic rules and regulations daily, often over areas such as eligibility or recruiting. As decision makers, athletic administrators must realize they do not possess complete control over athletes. Courts may review their decisions. **Judicial review** occurs when a plaintiff challenges a rule and the court evaluates it to determine whether it should apply. Historically, courts have declined to overturn the rules of voluntary athletic organizations, except where the rule meets *one* of the following conditions:

1. The rule violates public policy because it is fraudulent or unreasonable.
2. The rule exceeds the scope of the athletic association's authority.
3. The athletic association breaks one of its own rules.
4. The rule is applied in an arbitrary and/or capricious manner.
5. The rule violates an individual's constitutional rights.

A court will not review the merits of the rule but will simply grant a remedy only if one of these conditions exists. Judicial review is not limited to amateur athletics, but it occurs more frequently there than in professional sport. In professional sport judicial review is used most often by owners or players challenging a rule or decision made by a commissioner or ownership committee.

When a plaintiff seeks judicial review, the plaintiff will also request an **injunction,** that is, an order from the court to do or not do a particular action. Courts have the power to grant two types of remedies: monetary damages and injunctive relief. Monetary damages compensate a plaintiff or punish a defendant. Money, however, is not always the best remedy. A student ruled ineligible for a tournament simply wants to play. In cases involving a challenge to an athletic association's rule, the plaintiff's interest is to keep the rule from applying or to force the athletic association to apply it differently. Injunctive relief is a better remedy because it provides a court order, usually an injunction. Court orders prevent future wrongs and can only be used to prevent an irreparable injury. An injury is considered irreparable when it involves the risk of physical harm or death, the loss of a special opportunity, or the deprivation of unique, irreplaceable property (Wong, 1994). Money does not provide adequate compensation for an irreparable injury such as being barred from participation in sport. For instance, assume a high school provided a boys' soccer team but no girls' soccer team. A girl tried out and made the boys' team. Her play impressed the coach, and he gave her a starting position after the first game of the season. Her team went undefeated in the regular season. The night before the first playoff game the league commissioner called the coach to tell him that the other coaches in the league launched a complaint against the team for having a girl on its roster when they were competing in a boys' league. The commissioner further stated that if the girl showed up to play in the tournament, the team would have to forfeit those games. In such a case, the coach and the female student-athlete might seek an injunction to compete in the tournament. They are not interested in money. Besides, there is no way to determine how much participating in the soccer game is worth. She will argue that she will face irreparable harm by the fact that she is being kept from the opportunity to play with her teammates. She may never have the opportunity to participate in this type of tournament again, and even if she were to have another opportunity, it would not be the same for she has worked hard with this team. In addition, the other coaches had all season to complain and they waited until the playoffs in an attempt to damage an undefeated team. No amount of money can compensate her for this opportunity. Besides the court order, the plaintiff here will file suit against the league and the commissioner's action for gender discrimination.

Tort Liability

A **tort** is a personal injury suffered by an individual because of another's improper conduct. Tort law provides money damages to compensate an injured person (plaintiff). Tort law is also used to deter defendants and others in society from engaging in similar conduct in the future. The sport industry is susceptible to tort claims because people participating in sport may hurt themselves or others and tort law allows people to allocate loss.

To determine the tort committed and to aid in assessing damages available to a plaintiff, the court focuses on the intent of the defendant when committing the tortious act. Intentional torts allow for punitive damages to punish the defendant. Intentional torts occur when one person purposely causes harm to another or engages in an activity that is substantially certain to cause harm. Assault, battery, defamation, intentional infliction of emotional distress, intentional interference with contractual relations, invasion of privacy, and gross negligence are all intentional torts. **Negligence** is an unintentional tort and will likely be the most common tort faced by sport managers. Therefore, the focus in this introductory chapter will be on negligence and not intentional torts.

Sport managers are negligent when they commit an act or omission that causes injury to a person to whom they owe a duty to act with care. To determine whether a sport manager has been negligent, a court will focus on the relationship between the plaintiff (injured) and the defendant (sport manager). Before a sport manager is liable for negligence, the plaintiff must show that the sport manager owed the plaintiff a **duty of care**. A legal duty of care is more than simply one's moral obligation. According to van der Smissen (1997), a legal duty arises from one of three origins: (1) from a relationship inherent in a particular situation, (2) from a voluntary assumption of the duty of care, or (3) from a duty mandated by a law. For instance, assume a college track-and-field coach was conducting a private training session with her top athlete. After running 500 meters, the athlete collapsed. Because of her special relationship with the runner, the coach has a duty to provide the athlete with prompt medical assistance. Assume further that a citizen of the community who has no connection to the team is exercising at the facility. The citizen may be under a moral obligation to help the athlete, but the citizen has no relationship to the athlete, and thus, no legal duty to render assistance. However, if the citizen ran over to the collapsed athlete to help the coach administer cardiopulmonary resuscitation (CPR), the citizen would then voluntarily assume a duty of care toward the athlete. Finally, the law may impose a duty of care on certain individuals due to their special training or skills. Assume further that the citizen is an off-duty emergency medical technician (EMT) and the state where the incident occurs requires all licensed EMTs to respond to emergencies. Such a law would create a relationship between the collapsed athlete and the EMT who is working out. In such a case, if the EMT did not respond, the athlete could argue that the EMT was negligent.

To be negligent, a defendant must also be the actual cause of the injury and the injury must be a reasonable, foreseeable consequence of the defendant's action. Negligence imposes a duty to refrain from careless acts. A good risk management plan, then, can help a sport manager avoid lawsuits based on negligence. Risk management involves developing a plan to avoid liability. To develop the plan, sport managers must brainstorm about the potential problems the business may face and contemplate what is reasonable and foreseeable. If the sport manager then implements a plan to avoid reasonable and foreseeable injuries, the risk manager is working to establish an environment free from negligence. This way the sport manager will also reduce the risk of a successful tort claim.

Agency Law

The law of **agency** impacts all businesses, including those in sport. The term "agency" describes a relationship in which two parties agree that one will act on behalf of the other (Howell, Allison, & Henley, 1984), and all businesses rely on people to work on behalf of others. In the agency relationship, the **principal** is the person who wishes to have something accomplished and the **agent** is the one who will act on the principal's behalf to achieve it (Howell et al., 1984).

One purpose of agency law is to establish the duties that the principal and agent owe to each other. The agency relationship is consensual, and although often the principal and agent have an underlying contract to establish the relationship's parameters, agency law is not concerned with promises established by contract. **Fiduciary duties** are inherent in the principal–agent relationship and are imposed on the parties under agency law regardless of what a contract between the parties does or does not specify. A second purpose of agency law is to hold the principal responsible to others for the actions of the agent, provided the agent is acting under the authority granted to the agent by the principal.

Under agency law the principal owes the agent three duties:

1. The duty to comply with a contract if one exists.
2. The duty to compensate the agent for his or her services.
3. The duty to reimburse the agent for any expenses incurred while acting on the principal's behalf.

The agent owes the principal five fiduciary duties:

1. The duty to obey.
2. The duty to remain loyal.
3. The duty to exercise reasonable care.
4. The duty to notify.
5. The duty to account (Howell et al., 1984).

The first duty is to obey the wishes and requests of the principal. The second duty is to be loyal by avoiding conflicts of interest. Since conflicts of interest arise so frequently, an agent can continue representing a principal when a conflict of interest is present, provided the agent fully discloses the conflict to the principal and gives the principal the option to work with a neutral party in place of the agent. For instance, assume a sport agent is representing two all-star shortstops who are free agents. Both have similar defensive skills and are consistent hitters. Assume that the Toronto Blue Jays are in need of a topshelf shortstop. The agent may be in a position of favoring the interest of one free agent over another, as the Blue Jays will need just one of the two players. The agent and shortstops need not end their relationship. The agent should disclose the conflict to the shortstops and give one the option of finding another negotiator for that contract negotiation. An agent's third fiduciary duty owed to the principal is to exercise reasonable care when acting on the agent's behalf. The agent's fourth duty is to notify the principal of all information important to the principal, and the agent's fifth duty is to account for finances to the principal on a reasonable basis (usually every six months to a year).

Under agency law the principal will be liable for any torts committed by the agent, provided the agent was acting within the scope of employment. The discussion of vicarious liability below addresses this issue in greater detail. The principal is also liable for any contracts the agent has entered into on the principal's behalf, provided the principal gave the agent authority to enter into contracts.

Agency law is also an important component to the player representation industry. A player representative or sports agent works as an agent for an athlete who acts as a principal. These relationships are often based in contract law, but they are also governed by the law of agency and its imposition of fiduciary duties. When lawsuits do occur, they may involve claims under contract, tort, and agency law (*Zinn v. Parrish*, 1981; *Brown v. Woolf*, 1983; *Detroit Lions, Inc. and Sims v. Argovitz*, 1984). Player and coach representation is discussed in greater detail in Chapter 11, Sports Agency.

Vicarious Liability

Vicarious liability allows a plaintiff to sue a superior for the negligent acts of the subordinate. Often lawsuits arise when a tort is committed by an employee and the plaintiff seeks to hold the employer (who generally has more money, and thus, a greater ability to pay damages) liable. Under vicarious liability the employer need not be negligent to be liable. The employer will be legally responsible provided the employee is in fact an employee and the employee committed a tort while acting in the scope of his or her employment. If, however, the employer is negligent for hiring an unqualified individual or not providing the proper training, the employer's negligence may also provide a basis for an additional claim by the plaintiff.

Three defenses are available to an employer faced with a vicarious liability claim. First, if the employee was not negligent, the employer cannot be held vicariously liable. Second, the employer may argue that the employee was not acting within the scope of employment, as is the case if an employee is out doing something on his or her own. Third, the employer may argue that the employee is an independent contractor. An **independent contractor** is an employee who is not under the employer's supervision and control. Examples of employees who could be independent contractors are freelance sportswriters or photographers, sport officials, part-time instructors or personal trainers at health and fitness centers, or sport team physicians or athletic trainers (if the physicians or trainers do not work primarily for the college, university, or professional team).

Contract Law

A **contract** is a written or oral agreement between two or more parties that creates a legal obligation to fulfill the promises made by the agreement. Every aspect of the sport industry uses contracts. Sport managers use contracts for the following: hiring players, officials, and other employees; television and radio broadcasting deals; merchandise sales agreements; facility leases; sponsorship deals; concession arrangements; ticket sales; membership agreements; awarding scholarships; enforcing rules and codes; purchasing equipment, uniforms, and other goods and services; and scheduling games, events, and appearances. Many sport managers negotiate and enter into contracts regularly with or without help from a lawyer. It is essential that sport managers have a basic understanding of contract law to limit their contract liability. Sound contract drafting should be part of the sport manager's risk management plan.

For a contract to be valid there must be an offer by one party and an acceptance by another. A contract also requires that something of value, called **consideration**, be given by both parties. Consideration may be money, property, or something intangible. For instance, if Big State University (BSU) hires a men's football coach for five years at a salary of $200,000 per year, the consideration BSU gives is the $200,000 plus any fringe benefits that go along with being an employee. The consideration the coach gives is his skill, talent, time, effort, and the promise not to coach anywhere else for five years. The value the coach gives is intangible and worth $200,000 annually to BSU.

People entering into contracts must also have the **capacity** to understand the nature and effects of their actions. Generally, individuals over the age of 18 possess capacity. Under contract law, minors and mentally incompetent people may enter contracts, but they may opt out of them any time. Thus, sport managers agreeing to appearances or endorsements with athletes under age 18 should enter into those contracts at their own risk, knowing that minors may **disaffirm** (opt out of) the contracts any time provided they return anything of value that they have not earned.

Once a contract is made, if a promise is broken it is considered a **breach**. A full breach occurs when the contract has been entirely broken, and a partial breach occurs when one or more, but not all, of the provisions in the contract have been broken. The remedy for a breach is usually money damages to compensate the injured party for the breach, for money will usually enable the individual to fulfill his or her expectations elsewhere. In rare cases an injunction is available as a remedy to force a party to comply with a contract. Most often this remedy is available only when the subject matter of the contract is so rare that no amount of money will provide an adequate remedy. For instance, if a sports memorabilia collector entered into a contract to purchase the last mint-condition Honus Wagner rookie baseball card in existence and the seller backed out of the deal after the contract was made, then the collector may go to court to obtain a court order to force the seller to comply with the contract.

Waivers and releases of liability are contracts that may form an important component of a manager's risk management plan. Through waivers, parties agree contractually to give up their right to sue for negligence. Waivers cannot be used to waive a right to sue for gross negligence or intentional torts. Waivers are signed before people participate in the activity for which they are waiving their right to sue. A release of liability is similar to a waiver, but it is a contract that a party signs *after* an injury occurs, by which the injured party gives up the right to sue later, usually in exchange for a financial settlement.

Jurisdictions vary as to whether waivers will be upheld against a plaintiff. When using waivers sport managers should be concerned with drafting them in such a manner that the court will enforce them. Many courts will invalidate a waiver if there is a flaw in the language used in the waiver. Flawed language may lead a court to conclude that the individual signing the waiver did not knowingly and voluntarily agree to waive his or her right to sue. Therefore, a waiver should be drafted with clear, unambiguous, and precise language that is easily understood by nonlawyers. Waivers should also be printed in large, readable print, preferably 10- or 12-point type. Some courts have ruled waivers invalid as a matter of public policy. Generally, a waiver violates public policy if (1) it pertains to a service important to the public, (2) the parties are not of equal bargaining power, (3) there is an employer–employee relationship between the parties entering into the waiver contract, or (4) it attempts to preclude liability for extreme forms of conduct, such as gross negligence or intentional acts (Cotten, 1997). At least one case has also invalidated the mandatory use of waivers to bar negligence claims by high school athletes on public policy grounds (*Wagenblast v. Odessa School District*, 1988). Another important issue regarding waivers is the use of them for minors. Since waivers are contracts and minors may disaffirm contracts, it is advisable to have parents of a minor also sign a waiver involving a minor. Three state courts have indicated that under some circumstances, waivers signed by parents for children or signed by both parents and children will stand (Cotten, 1997).

Constitutional Law

Constitutional law is a body of law developed from precedents established by courts applying the language of the U.S. Constitution and state constitutions to the actions and policies of governmental entities. State constitutions vary. Some appear to be models of the U.S. Constitution, whereas others have language granting even greater rights to their citizens. Many rights are guaranteed by the U.S. Constitution, but there are four challenges that tend to arise in the sport industry relatively frequently: due process, equal protection, the right to be free from unreasonable searches and seizures, and invasion of privacy. There are also occasional challenges on the First Amendment grounds of the right to freedom of religion, the right to assemble peaceably, and freedom of speech.

State Action

As a rule, the U.S. Constitution and individual state constitutions do not apply to private entities such as professional teams, athletic associations, private high schools or colleges, and private golf or health and fitness clubs. However, in some cases it can be argued that the private entity is so enmeshed with the public entity that the two are dependent upon one another. When a private entity meets this standard it is called a **state actor** and the court may apply the Constitution to that private entity. For instance, Major League Baseball is a privately operated sport league. In April 1975, Major League Baseball Commissioner Bowie Kuhn enacted a rule that banned female reporters from baseball clubhouses. Despite the contrary wishes of Yankee players, Kuhn insisted that Melissa Ludtke, a female *Sports Illustrated* sportswriter covering the 1977 World Series, be banned from the Yankees' clubhouse (Weiler & Roberts, 1993). Ludtke challenged the rule because it discriminated against her on the basis of her gender and kept her from pursuing her profession, a liberty protected by the Fourteenth Amendment's Equal Protection and Due Process clauses. Central to her argument was the determination of whether the U.S. Constitution applied to Major League Baseball and the New York Yankees, both private entities. Ludtke successfully argued that the discrimination took place in a publicly owned facility, Yankee Stadium, which was leased to a private organization, the New York Yankees, for the benefit of the Yankees and Major League Baseball (*Ludtke and Time, Inc. v. Kuhn*, 1978). The court found that Yankee Stadium was maintained and improved with public money. It also found that the lease agreement stated that annual rent owed to New York City by the Yankees was calculated by the number of fans the Yankees and the city drew to the stadium. These two factors made the city and the Yankees "so entwined" that Major League Baseball was considered a state actor and its rules were therefore subject to constitutional scrutiny (Weiler & Roberts, 1993).

Due Process

Athletic associations adopt many rules and regulations that they enforce through their own administrative processes. If the athletic association is a state actor, then its own administrative process must provide constitutional procedural **due process** as well. Procedural due process is the right to notice and hearing before life, liberty, or property may be taken away. Obviously, no athletic association makes decisions to take away someone's life. Some do, however, impact on the liberty and property interests protected by the due process clauses in the Fifth and Fourteenth Amendments. Liberty interests are such things as the right to be free from stigma, to be free from damage to one's reputation, and to pursue one's livelihood. Property interests involve the taking away of anything of value. The U.S. Supreme Court has stated that property interests arise from explicit understandings that can support a claim of entitlement (*Perry v. Sindermann,* 1972). For instance, college scholarships have long been held to be property interests (*Gulf South Conference v. Boyd,* 1979), as have been tenured positions of employment (*Perry v. Sindermann,* 1972).

Equal Protection

The **equal protection** clause of the Fourteenth Amendment guarantees that no person shall be discriminated against unless a constitutionally permissible reason for the discrimination exists. Discrimination occurs when two similarly situated individuals are treated differently on the basis of a status or classification. The Equal Protection clause often applies in sport when there are allegations of discrimination on the basis of race, gender, or alienage in eligibility or employment decisions. The court uses different standards of review depending upon the status or classification of the party alleging discrimination to decide whether a rule or regulation in sport discriminates. The first standard of review, strict scrutiny, applies to situations where one discriminates on the basis of race, religion, or national origin. To withstand a constitutional challenge, a defendant must convince the court it has a compelling need to violate a fundamental right or discriminate. This standard is the most difficult to meet, so defendants usually lose these challenges.

The second standard of review applies to discrimination on the basis of gender. A defendant may discriminate on the basis of gender only if a legitimate interest for doing so exists. The court in *Ludtke v. Kuhn*, discussed above, found that Major League Baseball's legitimate reason of protecting the privacy of the players and the family image of the game could not withstand judicial scrutiny when the league allowed television cameras in the clubhouses at the end of the game to get interviews from scantily clad players. In intermediate scrutiny cases in amateur athletics, courts have found two legitimate reasons for upholding the use of separate-gender teams. The first reason is to protect the health and safety of the athletes, for example when a girl is attempting to participate on a boys' football or hockey team in which a high degree of contact and injuries are prevalent. The second reason for which the court has found that separate-gender teams are necessary is to avoid existing discrimination or to make up for past discrimination. Typically, such a case arises when a boy is seeking to participate on a girls' team in a sport not offered for boys, such as field hockey or volleyball.

The third standard of review applies to discrimination based on any other status or classification. Some discriminatory actions have been challenged on the basis of economic or social background, sexual orientation, physical or mental disability, or athletic team membership. The court will only allow the discrimination to exist if the defendant convinces the court there is a rational basis for the discriminatory rule. This standard is the easiest for defendants to meet.

Unreasonable Search and Seizure

The Fourth Amendment provides that people have the right "to be secure in their persons, houses, papers and effects against **unreasonable searches and seizures.**" Applying this to a drug testing program, the act of taking the athlete's urine or blood, for example, may constitute a seizure and the testing may constitute a search within the meaning of the Fourth Amendment. These searches may be deemed reasonable by the courts if the defendant can show a compelling need for the search. Recently the U.S. Supreme Court has upheld drug testing of high school athletes on the grounds that the school has a compelling interest in deterring drug use by children to ensure their health and safety and in keeping the school environment free from the disciplinary problems created by drug use (*Vernonia School District 47J v. Acton*, 1995).

Invasion of Privacy

The U.S. Constitution does not specifically state that there is a fundamental right to be free from an **invasion of privacy**; however, the U.S. Supreme Court has implied one from the Constitutional Amendments. To bring an action for invasion of privacy, a plaintiff must establish that the invasion is substantial and is in an area for which there is an expectation of privacy. In the sport industry these cases most often arise as challenges to drug testing programs. In *Vernonia School District 47J v. Acton*, James Acton challenged Vernonia School District's drug testing program as an invasion of privacy. The Supreme Court found that school children had a reduced expectation of privacy when they entered school. Those who participated in athletics had an even lesser expectation of privacy, for participating on an athletic team subjected one to a locker room environment, physical examinations, and the need for medical attention. Therefore, the Supreme Court held the drug testing of high school athletes was not an invasion of privacy.

It is not likely the *Acton* ruling will apply to collegiate athletes. In the *Acton* opinion, Justice Antonin Scalia went to great lengths to state that the high school students had a lower expectation of privacy due to the fact they were minors who were under the school's care while away from their parents and in such a situation the teachers had to have discipline in the school (*Vernonia School District 47J v. Acton*, 1995). Collegiate athletes are adults under considerably less supervision from the administration of their colleges and universities. Additionally, just over a year before the *Acton* decision the U.S. Supreme Court refused to hear an appeal of the Supreme Court of Colorado's decision that found that drug testing of football players at the University of Colorado was an invasion of privacy (*University of Colorado v. Derdeyn*, 1993). In *Derdeyn*, the Supreme Court of Colorado held that despite the University of Colorado's interest in protecting the health and welfare of student-athletes and although student-athletes do consent to restrictions on their private lives by participating in collegiate athletics, it is not enough to justify the intrusion on privacy interests of the nature and extent involved in the random, suspicionless testing for drugs.

Finally, no constitutional challenge to drug testing has been effective on the professional level. Recently, the federal district court for the Western District of Pennsylvania ruled that the National Football League's drug testing program was not subject to a constitutional challenge as it did not involve state action *(Long v. National Football League*, 1994). The court found that neither the business relationship between the City of Pittsburgh and the Steelers nor the city's acquiescence to testing by the NFL in Pittsburgh were enough to establish the interdependent relationship necessary for the NFL to be considered a state actor. Drug testing challenges on the professional level are most effectively brought through the administrative or arbitration process set up under each league's rules, or collective bargaining agreement. The **collective bargaining agreement** is the contract agreed to by the players' association and the owners. It covers all issues related to hours, wages, and terms and conditions of employment that are common to all players. The concept of collective bargaining is discussed in greater detail in Chapter 12, Professional Sport.

Title IX of the Educational Amendments of 1972

Enacted in 1972, **Title IX** is a comprehensive statute aimed at eliminating gender discrimination in educational institutions that receive federal funding. Therefore, Title IX cases only involve interscholastic and intercollegiate athletics. In athletics, Title IX applies to employment discrimination and participation opportunities. When applying Title IX to employment discrimination, courts have relied on the standards set forth in Title VII, discussed later in this chapter in a section called Labor and Employment Laws (*Bowers v. Baylor University*, 1994; *Pitts v. University of Oklahoma*, 1994; *Stanley v. University of Southern California*, 1994).

The U.S. Department of Education's Office of Civil Rights (OCR) has set forth policies for applying Title IX to athletics. To decide whether an educational institution is in compliance, the OCR focuses on three areas. First, the OCR assesses whether an institution's athletic scholarships are awarded on a substantially proportionate basis (male versus female). Second, the OCR assesses the degree to which an educational institution has given equal treatment, benefits, and opportunities in specific athletic program areas. The OCR examines such benefits as the provision of publicity, promotions, facilities, equipment and supplies, the opportunity to receive quality coaching and support staff, and the scheduling of games and practices. Third, the OCR assesses the degree to which an educational institution has equally and effectively accommodated the interests and abilities of male and female students. Most cases have been brought under this third factor. It has been an area of growing litigation since the U.S. Supreme Court ruled that nothing in Title IX precluded a plaintiff from receiving compensatory damages and attorneys' fees (*Franklin v. Gwinnett County Public Schools*, 1992). As a result, athletes and attorneys can better afford the cost of bringing Title IX lawsuits.

Antitrust Laws

A capitalist economy such as that of the United States depends on competition between businesses. Competition in this sense refers to economic rivalry among firms, such that they are engaged in a contest for customers (Howell, Allison, & Henley, 1984). To promote competition in the free market, Congress enacted the Sherman Antitrust Act of 1890 (the **antitrust law**). The Sherman Act's goal was to break up business trusts and monopolies and prohibit restraints of trade. In the sport industry, antitrust challenges have primarily occurred in professional sport in which monopolization of the market and restrictive policies are common. For instance, there is only one major professional league for each sport. These leagues' dominations of the market for each sport have been challenged as monopolies in violation of the Sherman Act (*Federal Baseball Club of Baltimore v. National League of Professional Baseball Clubs*, 1922; *American Football League v. National Football League*, 1963; *Philadelphia World Hockey, Inc. v. Philadelphia Hockey Club, Inc.*, 1972 ; *United States Football League v. National Football League*, 1986). All of the professional sport leagues and organizations are subject to antitrust laws except Major League Baseball. In 1922 the U.S. Supreme Court found that baseball was not engaged in interstate commerce and thus was not a business Congress intended to be subject to the Sherman Act (*Federal Baseball Club of Baltimore v. National League of Professional Baseball Clubs*). The judicially granted antitrust exemption has since survived congressional hearings and has been affirmed by the U.S. Supreme Court (*Toolson v. New York Yankees*, 1953; *Flood v. Kuhn*, 1972). Antitrust law violations carry a penalty of tripling the damage award. Since professional teams are worth millions and athletes' salaries total millions, an anticompetitive practice that injures a competitor league, a team owner, or a player's ability to make use of a free market may create a financially crippling damage award for a league.

In the past, amateur athletic associations were free from antitrust scrutiny. As amateur athletics has increased in prominence and in its capability to bring in money, organizations such as the NCAA have increasingly become targets of antitrust scrutiny. Member institutions, coaches, athletes, and alumni have challenged NCAA rules on antitrust grounds. Before subjecting amateur association rules and regulations to antitrust scrutiny, the court will decide if the rule is one that regulates a commercial or noncommercial activity. Courts have ruled that eligibility rules are noncommercial (*McCormack v. National Collegiate Athletic Association*, 1988; *Banks v. National Collegiate Athletic Association*, 1992), but rules restricting coaches' earnings (*Law v. National Collegiate Athletic Association*, 1995) and limitations on NCAA members' television contracts (*National Collegiate Athletic Association v. Board of Regents of the University of Oklahoma and the University of Georgia Athletic Association*, 1982) are commercial and subject to antitrust laws.

Labor and Employment Laws

The sport industry is people-intensive, so sport managers must have a good understanding of how the law affects human resource management. To effectively manage personnel, a manager must have a basic knowledge of labor and employment laws. There are both state and federal labor and employment laws. Since state laws vary by jurisdiction, the focus for this chapter will be on the following federal laws: the National Labor Relations Act, the Equal Pay Act of 1963, Title VII of the Civil Rights Act of 1964, the Age Discrimination in Employment Act, and the Americans with Disabilities Act.

The National Labor Relations Act

Enacted in 1935, the **National Labor Relations Act** (NLRA) applies to sport organizations that are unionized. This law establishes the procedures for union certification and decertification and sets forth the rights and obligations of union and management once a union is certified. The law also established the National Labor Relations Board as the federal agency administering labor laws in the United States. The primary areas of the sport industry in which the NLRA applies are in facility management, interscholastic athletics, and the professional sport industry. Facility managers may employ various unionized employees, all with different collective bargaining agreements. In some cases, interscholastic coaches may be covered by a teachers union. In collegiate athletics, coaches are not unionized but staff members may be. Currently, the four major professional sport leagues (MLB, NBA, NFL, NHL) and the minor league hockey players in the East Coast Hockey League and the International Hockey League are unionized. The Major Indoor Lacrosse League recently unionized, as did the Major League Soccer players and women athletes in the National Soccer Alliance and Women's Professional Fastpitch (softball).

Labor relations in professional sports are unique for many reasons. First, professional athletes have individual bargaining power derived from their unique talent that is unmatched in other industries. This bargaining power creates a great deal of leverage for players in the major leagues. As a result, professional leagues have adopted restrictive practices for the efficient management of their players (Masteralexis, 1997). Restrictive practices are practices that limit a player's ability to make money or to move throughout the free market and include such practices as the draft, salary cap or luxury tax, and restrictions on free agency that may violate antitrust laws (*Mackey v. National Football League*, 1976; *Smith v. Pro-Football, Inc.*, 1978). However, under labor laws, practices that normally violate players' antitrust rights that are agreed to through the collective bargaining process may be exempt from antitrust laws (*McCourt v. California Sports*, 1979; *Zimmerman v. National Football League*, 1986). Therefore, it is in the leagues' best interests to have unions and negotiate restrictive practices through the collective bargaining process. This approach is unique to sports, as most management groups either prefer not to deal with unions or simply tolerate them. Generally, management in other industries tends to perceive that unions take power and control from them. A good example of the irony of the professional sport situation arose in 1996 when some star NBA players sought an election to decertify their players association and NBA Commissioner David Stern publicly supported the players who favored keeping the players association.

Second, players associations differ from unions in other industries. For one thing, job security is limited. The turnover rate for sport union members is much higher than for other union members because athletes' careers are far shorter than those of employees in other industries. This forces players associations to constantly spread their message to new members. In spreading the message, the players associations also face the logistical challenges of being a bargaining unit with employees on different teams spread throughout the United States and Canada. In addition, there is a great disparity between players' skills and thus their need for the union. A player such as Michael Jordan does not need the services of the union as much as a late second-round draft pick or a recently released free agent trying to make his way back onto an NBA roster. When negotiating for the collective interests of the players, unions must struggle to keep the superstars and the players on the bench equally satisfied. Without the solidarity of all players, the players association loses its strength (Masteralexis, 1997).

The Equal Pay Act

Enacted in 1963, the **Equal Pay Act** (EPA) prohibits an employer from paying one employee less than another on the basis of gender when the two are performing jobs of equal skill, effort, and responsibility and are working under similar conditions. EPA only applies to sex-based discrimination on the basis of compensation. In order to qualify, the plaintiff and comparable employee must be of opposite genders. For instance, the statute would not apply if a man coached a women's team and argued under the EPA that he should be paid a sum equal to the male coach of the men's team. Trivial differences between two jobs will not prevent them from being considered equal in terms of the EPA . Note that the idea of comparable worth is not an issue under the EPA. Recently, EPA lawsuits have been filed by female coaches whose salaries are not equal to those of their male counterparts. *Stanley v. University of Southern California* (1994) involved U.S.C. women's basketball coach Marianne Stanley's complaint that she was not paid equally to the male basketball coach, George Raveling. In finding that their jobs were not equal, the court focused on the additional pressure and responsibility it said Raveling had due to the fact that the men's team had a larger season ticket base and a greater national presence. The court found that such responsibility created more media pressure and a greater time investment in dealing with fans and the media. Interestingly, the court never considered whether Stanley actually could have had *more* responsibilities and pressure than Raveling because she had to constantly work to get a larger season ticket base and get more media attention for her team and herself.

If an employee proves the elements of an EPA violation, the four defenses available to the employer are that the disparity in pay is due to the presence of (1) a seniority system, (2) a merit system that is being followed in good faith, (3) a system measuring pay on the basis of quality/quantity production, or (4) a factor other than gender.

Title VII of the Civil Rights Act of 1964

The Civil Rights Act of 1964 is a federal law prohibiting discrimination in many settings, including housing, education, and public accommodations. **Title VII** covers employers with 15 or more employees. Title VII, however, excludes "Indian Tribes" and "bonafide membership clubs" (such as country clubs) from its definition of employer. Title VII specifically prohibits any employment decision, practice, or policy that treats individuals unequally due to race, color, national origin, gender, or religion.

Although much of the U.S. civil rights movement focused on discrimination against African-Americans, Title VII's definition of race is not that limited. It protects all classes of people from dissimilar treatment, including, but not limited to, Hispanics, Native Americans, and Asian-Americans. The focus for color under Title VII is on skin pigment or the physical characteristics of one's race. Regarding national origin, the court focuses on one's ancestry. Title VII does not prohibit employment discrimination solely based on a lack of U.S. citizenship; however, the lack of U.S. citizenship may not be used to disguise discrimination that is actually based on race or national origin. In other words, an employer may follow a policy of employing only U.S. citizens but may not give unequal treatment to different noncitizens based on their country of origin. In addition, rules that require communication in "English only" are allowed only if the employer can prove the rule is a business necessity. As for gender, Title VII is self-explanatory, but it also includes sexual harassment. Title VII does not yet include discrimination on the basis of sexual orientation, although California, Connecticut, Hawaii, Massachusetts, New York, New Jersey, Vermont, and Wisconsin prohibit such discrimination under state law. Finally, Title VII prohibits religious discrimination against all well-recognized faiths, and also those considered unorthodox, provided the court is convinced that the belief is sincere and genuinely held and not simply adopted for an ulterior motive. Employers must make *reasonable accommodations* to religious practices and observances, unless it would place an *undue hardship* on them.

It is not illegal to discriminate based on religion, gender, or national origin if the classification is a **bonafide occupational qualification** (BFOQ). Race and color are never BFOQs. The BFOQ must be reasonably necessary to the normal operation of the business. The BFOQ defense requires the employer to prove that members of the excluded class could not safely and effectively perform essential job duties, and the employer must present a factual basis for this belief. An example of a BFOQ might be that an all-male boarding school may make it a requirement that resident directors in the school's dormitories also be male. The school may justify the requirement with such reasons as the comfort and security of the male students living in all-male dormitories and for the school to establish male role models in the school's social settings.

Affirmative action policies involve giving preference to those underrepresented in the workplace. These policies often contain goals and timetables for increasing the percentage of the underrepresented to rectify past discrimination. The affirmative action policy may be voluntary, or it may be court-ordered due to a discrimination suit. Affirmative action policies may result in discrimination against the overrepresented classes—this is termed "reverse discrimination."

Age Discrimination in Employment Act

Enacted in 1967, the **Age Discrimination in Employment Act** (ADEA) prohibits employment discrimination on the basis of age. Currently there is no age limit to protection, but the ADEA exempts several classes of workers, such as public safety personnel and certain top-level managers. It applies to employers who engage in commerce and hire over 20 workers for 20 or more calendar weeks, as well as labor unions and state and federal governments. Proving discrimination under ADEA is very similar to doing so under Title VII. ADEA also contains a BFOQ exception that is almost identical to Title VII's. An employer can also defend a claim by proving the decision was made due to reasonable factors other than age.

Americans with Disabilities Act

Enacted in 1992, **Americans with Disabilities Act** (ADA) protects employees with disabilities from discrimination at all stages of the employment relationship. An applicant or employee who is disabled must be able to perform all the essential functions of a position in order to challenge discrimination in employment on the basis of disability. Therefore, an employer must assess the responsibilities required for a position and assess the individual's ability to perform the position. When interviewing, an employer cannot question an applicant about the specific nature of his or her disability or require medical records or exams as part of the screening process. An employer may, however, prepare a list of essential functions and ask if the applicant can perform those tasks. While the ADA promotes the removal of barriers, it does not relieve employees with disabilities from carrying out the same job responsibilities as their able-bodied coworkers. If the individual can perform the job with or without a *reasonable accommodation*, the employer cannot refuse the employee based on disability. An employer must attempt to *reasonably accommodate* employees with disabilities, *unless doing so will cause undue hardship* to the employer.

The ADA reaches beyond employment law to ensure that people with disabilities have access to places of public accommodation. Thus, the ADA requires public assembly facilities, stadiums, theaters, and health and fitness centers to be barrier-free. Sport managers working in facilities that are open to the public must be sure that their facilities comply with the ADA regulations for such areas as entrances and exits, seating, walkways, parking, locker room, and bathroom facilities. The ADA should continue to positively impact the ability for those people with disabilities to be sport spectators and participants. This aspect of the ADA is discussed in greater detail in Chapter 14, Facility Management; Chapter 18, The Health and Fitness Industry; and Chapter 19, Recreation Sport.

Trademark, Service Mark, and Licensing Law

A **trademark** is a word, name, or symbol used by a manufacturer or merchant to identify and distinguish its goods from those manufactured and sold by others (Reed, 1989). The trademark performs a variety of functions: it designates the source of origin of a product or service, it denotes a particular standard of quality that the customer comes to expect from the owner, it symbolizes the goodwill of its owner, it represents a substantial advertising investment, it protects the public from confusion and deception, and it enables courts to fashion a standard of acceptable business conduct from mark holders (Wilde, 1997). Trademarks can be strong, entitled to a wide scope of protection, or weak, entitled to limited protection in only a narrow field (Reed, 1989). Strong trademarks are those that are completely distinguishable, such as Exxon, Polaroid, and Kleenex. Haigis Hoopla and Hoop-D-Do (outdoor 3-on-3 basketball tournaments) are good examples of fanciful, distinguishable event names. On the other end of the spectrum are the weak names, like Musicfest, Food Fest, and Art Expo, which use common words in their ordinary meanings and would be difficult, although not impossible, to protect (Reed, 1989). Such names may be protected if they possess "secondary meaning." **Secondary meaning** exists if the public distinguishes one product or event from another by the trademark. Reed (1989) uses World's Fair as an example of this. Although the words are common and used in their ordinary meaning, the trademark is descriptive due to the amount of advertising and public exposure it receives. Since there is only one World's Fair, use of this trademark by others without permission may lead consumers to confuse the secondary use with the original trademark. Helping to protect against such consumer confusion is the **Lanham Act**, which governs trademarks and service marks, gives protection to the owner of a name or logo, and keeps others from selling goods as the goods of the original source (Wilde, 1997). A **service mark** differs from a trademark in that a service mark is used to identify the source of an intangible service. Professional sports franchises' marks are registered as service marks that identify and represent the entertainment value of sports events (Wilde, 1997). The Lanham Act is a federal law that does not preempt state laws. State laws are useful for businesses that are not engaged in interstate commerce, such as an organization operating a purely local event (Reed, 1989).

The Lanham Act has become increasingly important for sport managers who are involved with licensed products, sports events, and exhibitions. As colleges, professional teams, and the Olympic Movement seek to maximize revenues from names, logos, and goodwill, the Lanham Act is the source of protection of their property. The law in this area is somewhat complex, and those sport managers involved with licensed products should rely on legal counsel who are experts in trademark law to handle registering trademarks and pursuing claims against those who misappropriate them.

The preceeding discussion of legal concepts is not all-inclusive. It should, however, serve as a place to start for a future sport manager to begin to build a legal knowledge base to manage risk and limit liability.

KEY SKILLS

Rather than focusing on those skills necessary for becoming a practicing sport lawyer, this section examines the skills that studying law will bring to a sport manager. The study of law involves a great deal of problem solving. By practicing problem solving, sport managers can improve their logical and analytical reasoning skills. Such skills will make it more likely that a sport manager facing a crisis will resolve it in a logical, thoughtful manner.

For most people, analysis of case and statutory law will lead to more persuasive and clear written and oral communication skills. The study of law involves studying the language used in cases and statutes and making arguments to apply it to various situations. Practice in this area will aid the student in developing clearly stated written policies and procedures. Such clearly stated rules and regulations are an important part of a sound risk management plan. Good communication is also a key to good leadership, and good verbal communication skills can lead to good relations with staff, peer and superior administrators, the public, and clients. Verbal communication skills can also enhance negotiating skills, and negotiation is something that all sport managers do on a daily basis, even if they do not realize it. Managers negotiate for everything they need, whether it is in a formal setting, such as negotiating with a television network to broadcast games, or on a more informal scale, such as negotiating with a staff member to cover a shift for someone who has called in sick.

The study of law, particularly in areas such as negotiation and client interviewing, also focuses on good listening skills. A successful sport manager should be prepared to invest time listening to staff and clients. A good listener will be a better judge of people and will know what it takes to motivate staff and to keep staff and clients satisfied.

Law and ethics are entwined. In setting parameters for acceptable conduct, the law establishes codes of ethical conduct. Studying law may not change a sport manager's behavior, for values may already be instilled, but it may help sport managers to better establish codes of ethical conduct in their workplaces. Sport law may also guide sport managers in how to best pursue resolutions of disputes and violations of ethical codes without a violation of individual rights.

CURRENT ISSUES

The challenge for sport managers is to know and understand potential legal problems, to manage legal problems, and to reduce the likelihood of legal problems arising. A sport manager can effectively manage legal problems by knowing and understanding law and sport law. By knowing legal pitfalls, managers can avoid, prevent, or reduce many kinds of problems. A well-written and well-administered risk management plan can help a sport manager avoid legal liability. For example, a health and fitness club manager may be faced with the option of adding wall-climbing equipment at his or her club. The manager must make this decision based on consumer interest and also financial benefits, costs, and potential legal liability. When considering legal liability, a club manager should consider all of the potential problems that may arise with the wall-climbing equipment. This analysis should involve creating a list of issues to consider, such as the following:

1. Who should be allowed to use this equipment?
2. Should training be required before use?
3. Who is qualified to train users? What additional training will staff need?
4. Should participants be required to provide medical approval?
5. Should participants be required to sign a waiver of liability?
6. Should minors be required to sign a waiver of liability?
7. What if someone refuses to sign a waiver of liability?
8. If used, how should a waiver of liability be drafted?
9. Is a waiver of liability likely to hold up in court?
10. What type of signs and/or warnings should be posted on or near the equipment?
11. What if a physically challenged member wants to participate in the activity?
12. What emergency procedures and services are in place in the event a participant is injured while using the equipment?
13. Should an individual injured while using the equipment be allowed to participate again? When?

While this list was compiled for a health and fitness club manager, similar lists can be created for other programmatic and policy decisions made by sport managers in other segments of the industry. A second example might be helpful here.

The job of a general manager of a professional sport team was once a job primarily consisting of evaluating talent, drafting amateur players, and making trades. Today a general manager has many other responsibilities, often arising from provisions negotiated in the league's collective bargaining agreement or the players' individual contracts. As such, the general manager may find a law degree helpful in doing his or her job. As a result of the more complex nature of a general manager's job, some other factors that must be considered when making decisions are:

- Factors affecting the cost of acquiring a new player:
  1. For an MLB or NHL player: What impact will signing a player who is eligible for salary arbitration have on the team's budget?
  2. For an MLB player: How will his salary affect the team's luxury tax? For an NBA or NFL player: How will his salary affect the salary cap?
- Factors affecting the ability to keep a player:
  1. When will the player become a free agent?
  2. Are there any rights of first refusal?
  3. Is there any compensation due to the club in the event the free agent player signs with another club?
  4. Is the player one who is highly sought after by other clubs?
- Insurance issues:
  1. Can the club reduce its risk when agreeing to a long-term guaranteed contract by purchasing temporary or permanent disability insurance to pay the club in the event the player is seriously injured?

The challenge for sport managers is to understand the legal implications, if any, of the decisions they make. Sport managers must know or obtain the answers to these questions, either alone or with the advice of in-house or outside counsel. Sport managers who can anticipate potential problems can then reduce risk. For example, the health club manager who allows only trained and healthy adults who have signed a waiver of liability to participate in the activity has established parameters that reduce the club's risk. People who meet the conditions can then participate in a carefully and adequately supervised activity, with medical procedures in place. (Note that the sport manager has decided to eliminate part of the risk by not allowing minors to participate.)

A professional team's general manager may decide against acquiring a particular player because the potential salary of the player, either through salary arbitration or through leverage from free agency, will be too expensive. Or the general manager may take the approach of reducing the risk of this expense by signing a multiyear contract. In the NFL, the general manager can structure the contract to be "salary cap friendly." For instance, the contract can be negotiated so that the salary cap impact is spread evenly over the years, or it can be structured so that the impact can be made in the early or late years of the contract. Thus, a general manager whose team currently has room under the salary cap can structure the contract so that the salary cap impact is in the early years. This reduces the salary cap cost of the player in later years and gives the club more money and freedom to sign other players. Finally, the general manager may also decide to reduce the club's risk by purchasing insurance to "cover a serious injury to a player." If a player suffers a career-ending injury, the team is provided the insurance proceeds to pay some or all of the player's salary. A team may then be in a position to acquire a replacement player.

FUTURE ISSUES

The impact of the law on sport organizations is more likely to increase rather than decrease in the future. Sport business is becoming ever more complex. For instance, in 1988 the NBA collective bargaining agreement was 138 pages in length. The most recent agreement is now 236 pages. The NCAA Manual, too, has grown in the number of pages and complexity. Due to restructuring in 1997–1998, the NCAA now publishes three manuals (one for each division). Division I's manual is now 482 pages. In each manual are numerous provisions, rules, and regulations that require interpretations, all resulting in more legal considerations for sport managers.

Amateur Sport Industry

In the amateur sport industry, there are a growing number of challenges over rules and regulations imposed on participants. Sport managers working in the Olympic arena are facing legal challenges resulting from ambush marketing, the rights of individual athletes to market themselves, and the imposition of codes of conduct for athletes. **Ambush marketing** occurs when an organization misappropriates the trademarks, logos, and goodwill of the events or organization (Reed, 1989). For example, a company that has not paid to be a sponsor but confuses the public into thinking it is a sponsor by indirectly associating itself with the events or organizations by buying commercial airtime during broadcasts or sponsoring individual athletes or teams at a fraction of the cost is engaging in ambush marketing ("Ambush Marketing," 1988). Nike's relationship with the 1996 Olympics in Atlanta provides a specific case: While Nike did not pay the $40 million to be a major sponsor of the Olympics, it set up a massive display, Nike Park, just outside Centennial Park; individually sponsored some of the biggest-name athletes; and invested a great deal in advertising around the site of the Olympics and during Olympic broadcasts and media coverage. As a result, an overwhelming majority of Americans believed Nike was a major sponsor of the 1996 Olympics (Thomas, 1996).

On the collegiate level, challenges may arise regarding NCAA amateurism rules. For instance, problems will likely continue to arise regarding restrictions on athletes' involvement with sport agents and restrictions on athletes' abilities to market themselves. The protection and licensing of collegiate trademarks and logos are of growing concern for college athletic directors and lawyers. Gender equity continues to be a legal and financial challenge for athletic administrators on the high school and collegiate levels. The U.S. Supreme Court recently let the current Title IX guidelines stand, which may encourage more athletes to pursue gender discrimination claims against athletic departments.

Professional Sport Industry

In the professional sport industry there may be a period of labor peace in the four major sports, since all have for the first time entered into collective bargaining agreements with longer terms. There are, however, pending negotiations between the players association and management in Major League Soccer, in women's soccer, and in women's fast-pitch softball. In addition, there are more disputes arising between owners in the professional leagues. Many of the disputes arise as owners attempt to challenge the restrictive rules and regulations they have agreed to as owners. The disputes usually center on whether an owner can circumvent league restrictions to benefit his or her investment or team. Two recent legal problems illustrate this. First, the Chicago Bulls and WGN have challenged the NBA's limitation on the number of games teams can broadcast on cable superstations (*Chicago Bulls and WGN v. National Basketball Association*, 1992). The NBA wants to limit the games to benefit the entire league's agreement with TBS, but the Bulls want to sell their games to WGN now while the team is extremely popular and marketable to bring in more revenue for the Bulls. Second, Dallas Cowboys owner Jerry Jones recently settled a dispute with the NFL over the marketing of the Dallas Cowboys (*Dallas Cowboys v. National Football League Trust*, 1995). Jones felt that he should no longer give NFL Properties the power to control the marketing of his team, because he felt he could do a better job. In addition, Jones began entering into sponsorship agreements with competitors of the NFL official sponsors by entering into agreements with Texas Stadium rather than the Dallas Cowboys. Thus, Nike and Pepsi became the official sponsors of Texas Stadium, home of the Dallas Cowboys. The antitrust suits brought by Jones and the NFL against each other settled out of court. However, Yankees owner George Steinbrenner is attempting similar moves with Adidas.

While Major League Baseball does not currently have an official footwear sponsor, it has attempted to conduct negotiations with Nike and does not want the Adidas deal having an impact on the value of a leaguewide deal. In response, Major League Baseball removed Steinbrenner from his post on the Executive Council ("Steinbrenner Is Suspended," 1997).

There has been a steady increase in governmental scrutiny and regulation of the sport industry. For example, state regulation of player agents has increased from 2 statutes in 1986 to 24 statutes in 1997. State regulation has also increased in the boxing industry, particularly because of the onset of HIV and AIDS. On the federal level, there have been numerous congressional hearings on Major League Baseball's antitrust exemption, on the Department of Education's Title IX policies to prohibit gender discrimination in intercollegiate athletics, and on the Federal Trade Commission's review of the College Football Association and Congress' review of the college bowl alliance for potential antitrust violations.

There is no evidence of a slowdown in the tort and contract litigation in the sport industry. However, in the contract area many disputes are being resolved through the commercial and labor arbitration processes. There has also been a more widespread use of buyout provisions to release parties from their agreements when a better opportunity arises. This practice is particularly evident in coaching contracts and is becoming more common in lease agreements with professional sports franchises.

SUMMARY

As the sport industry has evolved into a complex multimillion-dollar global entity, law has played a more dominant role in carrying out management functions in sport organizations. When sport managers make decisions and disagreements arise, those working and participating in sport are relying more heavily on the legal system for a resolution. Thus, a knowledge of key aspects of sport law has become increasingly important to the sport manager's ability to manage risk and to know when to seek legal assistance to aid in decision making and dispute resolution.

REFERENCES

Age Discrimination in Employment Act of 1990, 29 U.S.C. §§ 621–634. Minneapolis, MN: West Publishing.

Ambush marketing is becoming a popular event at Olympic games. (1988, February 8). *The Wall Street Journal*, p. A25.

American Bar Association Forum Committee on the Entertainment and Sport Industries. (1992). *Membership directory*. Chicago: ABA Publishing.

American Football League v. National Football League, 323 F.2d 124 (4th Cir. 1963).

Americans with Disabilities Act of 1990, 42 U.S.C. §§ 151–169. Minneapolis, MN: West Publishing.

Ammon, R. (1997). Risk management process. In D.J. Cotten & T.J. Wilde (Eds.), *Sport law for sport managers* (pp. 174–180). Dubuque, IA: Kendall/Hunt Publishers.

Banks v. National Collegiate Athletic Association, 977 F.2d 1081 (7th Cir. 1992).

Berry, R.C., Gould, W.B., & Staudohar, P.D. (1986). *Labor relations in professional sports.* Dover, MA: Auburn House Publishing Co.

Bowers v. Baylor University, 862 F. Supp. 142 (W.D. Tex. 1994).

Brown v. Woolf, 554 F. Supp. 1206 (S.D. Ind. 1983).

Chicago Bulls and WGN v. National Basketball Association, 961 F.2d 667 (7th Cir. 1992).

Cotten, D.J. (1997). Exculpatory agreements or waivers. In D.J. Cotten & T.J. Wilde (Eds.), *Sport law for sport managers* (pp. 63–69). Dubuque, IA: Kendall/Hunt Publishers.

Dallas Cowboys v. National Football League Trust, 94-C-9426 (N.D. Cal. 1995).

Detroit Lions, Inc. and Sims v. Argovitz, 580 F. Supp. 542 (1984).

Equal Pay Act of 1964, 29 U.S.C. § 206 (d)(1) (1990). Minneapolis, MN: West Publishing.

Federal Baseball Club of Baltimore v. National League of Professional Baseball Clubs, et al., 259 U.S. 200 (1922).

Flood v. Kuhn, 407 U.S. 258 (1972).

Franklin v. Gwinnett County Public Schools, 112 S. Ct. 1028 (1992).

Gulf South Conference v. Boyd, 369 So.2d 553 (Sup. Ct. Ala. 1979).

Haworth, K. (1996, December 20). A cottage industry helps sports programs in trouble. *Chronicle of Higher Education*, A35.

Howell, R.A., Allison, J.R., & Henley, N.T. (1984). *The legal environment of business.* New York: Dryden Press.

Law v. National Collegiate Athletic Association, 902 F. Supp. 1394 (D. Kan. 1995).

Long v. National Football League, 870 F. Supp. 101 (W.D. Pa. 1994).

Ludtke and Time, Inc. v. Kuhn, 461 F. Supp. 86 (S.D. N.Y. 1978).

Mackey v. National Football League, 543 F.2d 606 (8th Cir. 1976).

Masteralexis, L.P. (1997). Antitrust and labor law: Professional sport applications. In D.J. Cotten & T.J. Wilde (Eds.), *Sport law for sport managers* (pp. 394–407). Dubuque, IA: Kendall/Hunt Publishers.

McCormack v. National Collegiate Athletic Association, 845 F.2d 1338 (5th Cir. 1988).

McCourt v. California Sports, 600 F.2d 1193 (6th Cir. 1979).

Metropolitan Exhibition Co. v. Ewing, 42 F. 1989 (S.D. N.Y. 1890).

Metropolitan Exhibition Co. v. Ward, 9 N.Y.S. 779 (Sup. Ct. 1890).

National Collegiate Athletic Association v. Board of Regents of the University of Oklahoma and the University of Georgia Athletic Association, 468 U.S. 85 (1982).

National Labor Relations Act, 29 U.S.C. §§ 151–69 (1990). Minneapolis, MN: West Publishing.

Perry v. Sindermann, 408 U.S. 593 (1972).

Philadelphia World Hockey, Inc. v. Philadelphia Hockey Club, Inc., 351 F. Supp. 462 (1972).

Pitts v. University of Oklahoma, No. Civ. 93-1341-A (W.D. Okla. 1994).

Reed, M.H. (1989). *IEG legal guide to sponsorship*. Chicago: International Events Group.

Society for the Study of the Legal Aspects of Sport and Physical Activity. (1997). *Membership directory*. Terre Haute, IN: Author.

Sport Lawyers Association. (1996–1997). *Membership directory*. Reston, VA: Author.

Stanley v. University of Southern California, 13 F.3d 1313 (1994).

Steinbrenner is suspended from baseball's council. (1997, May 11). *The Wall Street Journal*, p. B9.

Thomas, E., Jr. (1996, July 19). The bottom line. *The Wall Street Journal*, p. A14.

Title VII of the Civil Rights Act of 1964, 42 U.S.C. § 2002 (a)(1)(2) (1990). Minneapolis, MN: West Publishing.

Title IX of the Educational Amendments of 1972, 20 U.S.C. §§ 1681–88 (1990). Minneapolis, MN: West Publishing.

Toolson v. New York Yankees, 346 U.S. 356 (1953).

United States Football League v. National Football League, 634 F. Supp. 1155 (S.D. N.Y. 1986).

University of Colorado v. Derdeyn, 863 P.2d 929 (1993).

Van der Smissen, B. (1997). Elements of negligence. In D.J. Cotten & T.J. Wilde (Eds.), *Sport law for sport managers* (pp. 26–32). Dubuque, IA: Kendall/Hunt Publishers.

Vernonia School District 47J v. Acton, 115 S.Ct. 2386 (1995).

Wagenblast v. Odessa School District, 758 P.2d 968 (Wash. Sup. Ct., 1988).

Weiler, P.C., & Roberts, G.R. (1993). *Cases, materials, and problems on sports and the law*. St. Paul, MN: West Publishing.

Wilde, T.J. (1997). Trademark law: General principles. In D.J. Cotten & T.J. Wilde (Eds.), *Sport law for sport managers* (pp. 423–434). Dubuque, IA: Kendall/Hunt Publishers.

Wong, G.M. (1994). *Essentials of amateur sports law* (2d ed.). Westport, CT: Praeger Publishers.

Wong, G.M., & Masteralexis, L.P. (1996). Legal aspects of sport administration. In F.L. Bridges and L.L. Roquemore (Eds.), *Management for athletic/sport administration: Theory and practice* (2d ed.) (pp. 85–132). Decatur, GA: ESM Books.

Yasser, R., McCurdy, J., & Goplerud, P. (1997). *Sports law* (3rd ed.). Cincinnati, OH: Anderson Publishing.

Zimmerman v. National Football League, 632 F. Supp. 398 (D.D.C. 1986).

Zinn v. Parrish, 644 F.2d 360 (7th Cir. 1981).

CHAPTER 6

Ethical Principles Applied to Sport Management

Todd W. Crosset and Mary A. Hums

Key Words: ethics, ethical dilemma, ethical reasoning, morality, morals, moral principles, codes of conduct/codes of ethics, ethical decision making

INTRODUCTION

Ethics

Ethics is the systematic study of values that guide individual decision making. Ethical reasoning depends on our values or the values of the organizations for which we work and reflects how we believe people should behave. For example, in recreational softball leagues, teams are faced with the decision of whether to play only their best players or to play everybody. The decision is based on the relative value team members place on winning versus the value they place on participation.

The question of whether to play everyone or to play only the best players is an ethical dilemma. An **ethical dilemma** is a practical conflict of more or less equally compelling obligations (Solomon, 1992). In the recreational softball example, the obligation to participate is in conflict with the equally compelling obligation to try to win. To solve the ethical dilemma, decision makers try to make a rational argument. They weigh the pros and cons of two or more seemingly valid choices that reflect equally cherished values. The argument could be made that the primary purpose of a recreational softball league is for participants to play and have fun. Recreational leagues provide camaraderie and emphasize team spirit that grows out of cheering for each other, playing, and going out together after games. However, an equally compelling argument could be made that competition and winning are central to the enjoyment of sport, even on the recreational level, and that teams should field their best players so that competition and victory are more intense and therefore more satisfying. Both outlooks make sense.

Sport managers are faced with ethical dilemmas on a daily basis. How does a sport manager know when he or she is facing such a dilemma? Zinn (1993) suggests that managers ask the following questions to ascertain if they are facing an ethical dilemma:

1. When talking about the matter at hand, do people use words or expressions such as "right or wrong," "black or white," "bottom line," "conflict," or "values"?
2. Will anyone be harmed because of my action/inaction or decision?
3. Am I concerned about my decision's being equally fair to all parties?
4. Do I feel a conflict between my personal values and my professional interest?
5. Is there controversy or strong opposition regarding this decision?
6. Do I have a feeling something is "just not right" about the situation?
7. Will I be hesitant to reveal my decision to others?

If a sport manager answers "yes" to any of these questions, he or she is most likely facing an ethical dilemma.

Ethical values should not be confused with personal preferences. Ethical decisions impact *other people* in a way that personal preferences do not. Ethical dilemmas have social implications. As such, ethics requires decision makers to consider how their actions will affect different groups of people and individuals. In the example of the softball league, the decision makers have to put themselves in the shoes of both the "bench warmers" and the "starters" and consider how both will be affected. They also have to think about what type of values they want to emphasize through their team. Finally, ethical decisions are complicated further because they cannot be made outside of their specific social context. In the case of the softball league, the decision makers on one team cannot realistically decide to give all of their players equal playing time if every other team in the league is playing their best players all the time and focusing on winning. While the team's desire to include all of their players is commendable, the decision about which players to play needs to be appropriate to the league.

Moral and Ethical Reasoning for Sport Managers

Few areas of sport management present managers more difficulty than ethical dilemmas. Consider, for example, the following ethical dilemmas sport managers may face:

* changing the start time of a contest to accommodate television programming at the expense of class time for college athletes
* use of painkillers by injured athletes to enable them to play hurt

- the extent to which an organization should help an athlete with a drug/alcohol/ marital problem
- making stadiums accessible to people with disabilities
- relocation of professional teams from a profitable site to another city that promises even more revenue
- cutting nonrevenue sport teams

Decision making is complicated because decisions impact diverse groups of people (athletes, fans, the community, businesses, the press) whose interests are often in conflict. While weighing decisions regarding these issues, sport managers may consider financial costs, the affect on the team and league's reputation, the law, and the impact on winning games. Sport managers may also try to determine what the "right thing" to do is. The process of making a correct and fair decision is called **ethical reasoning**. This chapter provides a framework to help future sport managers think about moral and ethical decision making as it applies to the sport industry.

Part of the reason ethical dilemmas are so difficult to resolve is that most people do not approach the process of making ethical decisions systematically. The complexity of issues and interests involved can easily overwhelm a person's judgment, especially when conflicting options seem to make equally good sense and are being argued emotionally by opposing parties. Confusion may result from not being clear about what is meant by the terms used when discussing ethics. For example, people tend to use the terms "morals" and "ethics" interchangeably. Some people confuse what is legal with what is moral. Distinctions between morality, ethics, and the law can help sport managers make better ethical choices.

Morality, like ethics, is concerned with values that guide behavior. Morality is a specific *type* of ethics. **Morals** are the fundamental baseline values that dictate appropriate behavior within a society (Solomon, 1992). The belief that stealing and murder are wrong, for example, is a moral value in most societies.

A distinctive feature of moral values is that they are grounded in the practical affairs of social life, while other ethical decisions are based on broader abstract principles (DeSensi & Rosenberg, 1996). In sport, a moral principle is that all athletes will give their honest effort whenever they compete. If athletes stopped giving honest efforts in sports, the essence of sport would be threatened. In business, the expectation is that everyone who enters an agreement or contract will honor that contract. For businesses and the economy to function, everyone needs to be able to trust that other parties will deliver the agreed-to goods and services. Shared morality cultivates trust between strangers and enables individuals to function in a society.

Moral values are generally accepted so broadly within a community that they are considered self-evident and largely go unquestioned. Because people perceive that moral values are basic and inalienable, it is often assumed they derive from a "higher order" or from common sense. For example, if people are asked why they oppose murder, they will likely simply respond "because it is wrong." If pushed, they might refer to a higher principle like religion or the sanctity of human life. Similarly, if an athlete is asked why he or she strives to win, a common response would be "because that's what sports are about."

Moral rules that prescribe "correct" behavior in one situation can generally be applied to similar situations within similar specific social contexts. For example, people believe it is always wrong for an elite athlete not to give his or her honest effort, especially when playing for money. It is always wrong to violate a business agreement made voluntarily in good faith. Our social practices depend on people's upholding these baseline values. When people act morally—according to generally acceptable standards of behavior—they contribute to the maintenance and smooth functioning of society.

Moral decisions are complicated by the fact that moral principles are often applied and valued differently in different social contexts. Family life, for example, is distinct from business life. The values guiding our behavior within our families may not be the same values that guide our behavior at work. Decision making is made more difficult given the variety of roles each of us fills; one collection of moral rules does not necessarily apply to all situations. Honesty, for example, means different things in the family, in athletics, and in the business world.

Consider the example of the famous "Rumble in the Jungle," the heavyweight fight between Muhammad Ali and George Foreman. Before the fight, Ali repeated again and again that his strategy would be to dance around Foreman and avoid close contact. But during the fight Ali did not dance. He stood toe to toe with Foreman and exchanged blows. Boxing commentators considered Ali's deception one of the greatest strategic moves in sport, enabling Ali to defeat the bigger, stronger, and heavily favored Foreman. Technically, Ali was dishonest, but his actions were not immoral in the context of sport.

Consequently, the process of making a moral choice, of deciding what is right and wrong, involves understanding the parameters of acceptable behavior within the context of one's role(s) within society. To judge Ali's morality, his actions must be placed in the context of his position as an athlete. The expectation is that athletes are loyal to their team, obedient to and disciplined by the coach, and never compromise the integrity of the game. Athletes are trusted not to cheat, gamble, or misuse the celebrity their athletic prowess gives them. Within limits imposed by the rules of the game, athletes are expected to try to win the game by any means available to them. Many sport strategies depend on forms of deception. Feints and setting up opponents to believe you intend to do one thing when you plan to do another are fundamental sport strategies.

Understanding the Unique Qualities of Moral Choices

One of the biggest distinctions between moral decision making and other ethical decisions is the extensive ramification of immoral choices. An immoral decision can lead to systemic corruption that can destroy a sport enterprise. Other ethical decisions (e.g., the decision whether to play everyone or only the best players) may be difficult to make and have serious implications for others but do not corrupt the entire enterprise. The following examples of two dilemmas facing a boxing judge illustrate the differences between moral dilemmas and ethical dilemmas.

A boxing judge is approached by a gambler who is intent on fixing a fight and is forcefully offered money to help the underdog win an upcoming fight. The correct moral decision is fairly clear. The judge's objectivity is a basic principle of judging. If the judge's objectivity is compromised, the fight becomes corrupt, and the integrity of the sport is jeopardized as long as the judge's transgression remains undiscovered. Participation and complicity in corruption even once usually leads to further compromise. Once a judge or other manager makes a corrupt or immoral decision, having crossed a moral line and being susceptible to blackmail, he or she is much more likely to repeat the transgression and escalate the corruption. Single corrupt acts can quickly lead to systemwide corruption.

The issues involved in ethical dilemmas present themselves differently. A boxing judge finds out that one of the boxers she is to judge in an upcoming fight is a distant relative through marriage. She has never met the fighter, is not in contact with his family, and thinks she can judge the fight fairly. The backup judge who would take her place is a rookie, and she is worried about his judging abilities. Should she remove herself from the fight in an effort to retain the appearance of impartiality? Should she stay on for the sake of the quality of the judging? The correct decision is not immediately clear. Either choice could be the right decision and neither threatens to destroy the integrity of the sport itself.

Morality versus the Law

Many of the moral values in a society are codified in laws. For example, theft is not only immoral but it is also against the law. Occasionally, someone may justify distasteful behavior by saying, "It's not against the law, is it?" Such an argument does not justify the behavior. Laws and morality are not the same.

Laws are created and enforced to maintain order and to help society function smoothly. Even so, at times immoral laws are instituted. For much of this century in the United States, laws in some states prohibited interracial competitive sports. Teams with both white and black players complied with these laws and at times left their black players at home. The long history of legal segregation in this country was clearly immoral and yet it was protected by law.

Likewise, moral behavior cannot always be legislated and people cannot be forced to act morally. It is generally accepted that people should try to help others in need or distress, but laws cannot and do not require people to do so. If we see someone who is injured or the victim of a crime, our moral sensibility directs us to come to his or her aid, but in most cases laws do not punish us for failing to do so. Our personal moral sensibility creates a stronger obligation than the law.

Similarly, laws cannot enforce morality, and often people are able to comply with the law without achieving its spirit or its stated goals. Recent legislation required stadium managers to make their facilities accessible to people with disabilities. In a number of cases, stadium managers drew criticism for obeying the letter of the law but failing to actually make their stadiums welcoming to fans with disabilities. Space was created for wheelchairs, but often the view from the spaces was obscured when other fans rose to cheer. When such laws are passed, managers make conscious decisions how to respond. They can decide to do the minimum required by law to save money and effort, or they can act innovatively to truly change how people can experience sport.

Morality and Corruption

Immoral behavior like cheating in sports violates our basic assumptions and corrupts our social institutions. Immoral practices can easily become institutionalized. Many times people justify immoral behavior by pointing out that others are doing the same thing and that they, too, must do certain things to maintain their competitiveness. Both players and managers face these kinds of moral decisions. The use of steroids is a good example. A player and team can both benefit from an individual athlete's use of steroids in the short term, but both are facilitating decreased standards of behavior. Likewise, agents pursue younger and younger athletes; in fact, agents are actually tracking the development of athletes as young as 12 years old. Even though some agents may at first be hesitant to do this, many come to believe that they have to follow suit to be competitive. When a society or organization's immoral actions become standard practice, moral reasoning becomes muddled and the rationale for behavior unclear.

Acting morally, then, is not just about following norms and common practices. Nor is morality simply about following the law. Moral and ethical reasoning focus on the process through which decisions are made in accord with socially esteemed values.

Moral Reasoning and Work

Sound moral reasoning is the basis of a healthy sport organization. Some **moral principles** are universal and esteemed in all aspects of life. Such principles include cooperation, courage, perseverance, foresight, and wisdom. Virtues such as these are esteemed across the board. Other moral principles are tied to particular situations. For example, a moral value like competition is esteemed in business but not in family relations. Honesty is essential in scientific research, but in sport the very notion of a game is dependent on feinting an opponent. Moral principles are tied to a social situation.

Further, contemporary society is characterized by innovation, which is forever presenting us with new ethical dilemmas. Consider, for example, how computer technology forces us to consider privacy and intellectual property in new perspectives. As society changes, we periodically need to assess whether our current practices are in keeping with the values that underlay a just society. Moral and ethical principles evolve over time.

In order to make moral decisions in the sport industry, managers are required to understand the responsibilities and duties of their jobs. According to Jane Jacobs (1992), work life consists of two types of work, commercial and noncommercial. The moral rules that guide each type of work are distinct from each other.

Moral rules that govern commercial work, like sales and marketing, have their roots in the rules of the marketplace. Honesty is a linchpin of commercial trading. Honesty ensures fair trading practices and allows individuals to trust that they will receive agreed-upon goods or services. In commercial occupations, insider trading, fraudulent accounting, and deceiving customers are all forms of dishonesty and are condemned.

Noncommercial moral values guide other kinds of occupations, including the medical and legal professions, civil servants, police, and building inspectors. In sport, officials, league commissioners, athletes, and coaches most likely operate according to noncommercial principles. The most important value in noncommercial endeavors is loyalty. These occupations demand loyalty to an oath of office or professional standards to guard against "selling out." In these occupations, it may be all right to deceive others for the sake of the overall task (e.g., undercover police work). It is not all right to commit acts like treason, bribery, or failing to uphold an oath, such as the medical profession's Hippocratic Oath.

Morality and Multiple Roles

Specific jobs do not actually reside completely within either the commercial or the noncommercial sphere. For example, even marketing and sales people working on commission need to demonstrate loyalty to an organization and observe some respect for authority. Professional athletes who demonstrate team loyalty throughout the season become commercially minded when renegotiating their contracts. It is unrealistic to suggest that any occupation is completely commercial or completely noncommercial.

Making moral decisions is not always easy in the contemporary sport world. Occupations in sport management often focus on the protection, promotion, and regulation of sport while at the same time emphasizing selling the sport. However, that does not mean people can arbitrarily choose which values will guide their behavior. Specific situations and roles in our society demand specific moral values. Sometimes an action that is moral in one setting is immoral in another setting.

Consider, for example, the case of Brad Smith, a reporter for the *Springfield Union News*. Through a confidential source, Smith received the academic transcripts of University of Massachusetts athletes. According to Smith, the transcripts indicated that many of the basketball players were not performing well academically. The information suggested that the high-profile UMass basketball program was having a debilitating effect on athletes' academic lives. Although the situation presented Smith with a number of ethical issues (e.g., weighing the embarrassment the individual students might feel against the need to expose an unjust system), ultimately Smith's responsibility as a reporter led him to publish the information.

A few months after the story ran in the paper, Smith was invited to a University of Massachusetts journalism class to discuss the ethics behind the decision to run the story. As part of his presentation, he passed out copies of the actual transcripts he had received to students in the class. The information included the transcripts of the basketball team and student-athletes from other teams. In his effort to simulate ethical decision making, Smith violated a fundamental value that governs student-teacher relationships—respect for a student's privacy.

Smith was acting as a teacher when he entered the classroom, not a reporter. The moral principles that guided his behavior should have changed as well. Smith acted unethically because he was still guided by the values of reporting (giving people all of the information) and not the moral principles of education (to create a safe learning environment). Students in the class complained, and Smith and his employer apologized to the university community for his error.

The Smith case illustrates that moral rules are tied to a person's current social position. People never hold just one position in society and therefore cannot simply adopt one set of moral guidelines. Managers have to assess their responsibilities and choose virtues that help them to complete their work fairly and morally.

KEY SKILLS

Ensuring Morality in the Workplace

The complexity of competing interests in sport makes moral and ethical dilemmas especially difficult to resolve. In theory, athletic competition is a straightforward contest of skill, strategy, and physical prowess; however, the industries and management structures that have grown around sport have complicated the roles played by athletes, coaches, management, and league officials. Increasingly, each has to operate under commercial and noncommercial principles simultaneously, and it is easy for distinctions between the two to become blurred. Sometimes athletes are simple participants in an athletic competition, while at other times they are businesspeople who have to reconcile how endorsements or salaries relate to the game and their willingness to play. Rules designed to protect the integrity of sport operate uncomfortably alongside the business structure that underwrites it.

This complexity makes decision making more difficult—and more critical—for sport managers, but there are ways to simplify the decision-making process and to ensure that decisions are made as intelligently and conscientiously as possible. One way to encourage morality in society or the workplace is to make the requirements and standards of behavior of a job or institution clear and to involve employees in a dialogue about organizational expectations and goals. Sport management employees need to know that the organization they work for—whether a team, league, or university—is committed to certain standards of behavior and that the organization will work with employees to make them clear.

Moral reasoning at work requires flexibility and effective communication. Organizations can help employees make moral choices by doing four things to promote and support moral reasoning: (1) establish clear standards of moral behavior (such as codes of conduct) and publicize them within the organization, (2) encourage employees to periodically examine and review their individual moral judgments through self-examinations, (3) provide support structures through which employees can consult each other *during* and after the decision-making process, and (4) make clear that violations of the code will not be tolerated, and publicize a process for enforcing codes within the organization.

Codes of Conduct

Codes of conduct (also called **codes of ethics**) explicitly outline and explain the principles under which an organization or profession operates. Codes of conduct provide employees with guidelines for their behavior. Codes should be clear and straightforward. They should not be needlessly long or complex, and they should encourage employees to understand the goals they are trying to accomplish instead of just outlining rules and punishments.

In today's society, corporations are under increasing public scrutiny to act in an ethical manner and to establish ethical climates within their corporate cultures. As a multibillion dollar industry, the sport industry is under the same scrutiny. According to Sims (1992), the ethical climate of an organization establishes the shared set of understandings that determine correct behavior and how ethical issues will be handled. One way to establish this climate is through what are known as codes of conduct or codes of ethics. Codes of conduct are probably the most visible statements of a company's, a business's, or an organization's ethical philosophy and beliefs (DeSensi & Rosenberg, 1996).

Codes of conduct and codes of ethics are not a twentieth-century invention. In fact, they are as old as the earliest religious oral traditions and writings, such as the Torah and the Koran. While the development of modern codes in the United States was initiated in the medical, accounting, and legal professions, these are not the only professional areas to have codes of ethics. Codes are also found in such institutions as health care facilities, energy companies, marketing firms, social work agencies, the computer industry, and school administration. Professional organizations are not alone in having codes of ethics for their members. Individual corporations and businesses are adopting codes in increasing numbers. A "Survey of Corporate Values" sent to corporations on the Fortune 1000 list of industrial and service corporations indicated that in 1991–1992, 93% of respondents had written codes of ethics (Center for Business Ethics, 1992).

In the sport world, codes have been adopted or are being considered by a number of sport organizations. The United States Olympic Committee; the Izaak Walton League; the New York State Youth Sports Coaches Association; the International Health, Racquet and Sportsclub Association; the American Camping Association; and the Ogden Corporation are just a few examples of sport organizations that have codes of conduct.

Codes of conduct are not unique to the American sport industry. In England, the Institute for Professional Sport has devised a code of conduct for professional athletes. In Ireland, the Minister of State for Sport requested the National Sports Council to prepare a code of ethics and practice in sport (McNally & Cusak, 1994). The Scottish Sports Council endorses accepted and agreed-upon codes of behavior to be applied by national governing bodies (Alstead, 1994). The Australian Rugby Football League National Coaching Scheme has developed codes of conduct as well (Corcoran, 1990). In Canada, the Mountain Biking Committee of the Ontario Cycling Association has issued a code of mountain biking ethics (Lebrecht, 1993).

While rules can help people understand the moral guidelines of a job, they do not promote active moral reasoning by themselves. According to Bowie and Duska (1990), codes of conduct make the following contributions to ethical reasoning:

1. Provide clear guides to right and wrong actions.
2. Can provide guidance in ambiguous situations.
3. Can motivate ethical action through peer pressure.

4. Control the autocratic power of employers.
5. Specify the social responsibilities of an organization.
6. Serve the long-term interests of an organization or business by reiterating the baseline values necessary to maintain public trust and smooth operation.

An example of a code of conduct for a sport organization is given below. This code of conduct is from the International Health, Racquet and Sportsclub Association, or IHRSA, and is intended to guide organizational behavior at health and fitness clubs. The IHRSA Associate Member Code of Conduct reads as follows:

As an Associate member of IHRSA, we consider it our mission to enhance the quality of life through physical fitness and sports. To this end, we endeavor to provide quality products and services. We further strive to instill in those we serve an understanding of the value of physical fitness and sports in their lives.

In order to fulfill our mission, we pledge the following:

- That we produce quality products and services.
- That we deliver on our commitments.
- That we are an equal-opportunity employer.
- That we will cooperate with our customers toward the continual expansion of the club and fitness industries.
- That we will utilize our benefits of IHRSA membership solely for the purposes and under the guidelines for which they were established.
- That we agree to conduct our business in a manner which commands the respect of those we serve.
- That customer satisfaction will be the determining factor in all our business dealings. (IHRSA, 1997)

Codes of conduct are not the "be all and end all" of organizational ethics. In fact, some codes of conduct might actually discourage moral reasoning. If the codes of conduct are too long or complex to understand easily, if they try to intimidate employees into acting morally, or if the organization does not demonstrate a commitment to them, codes of conduct can be counterproductive. Sport ethicist Russell Gough has noted that the large volume of National Collegiate Athletic Association (NCAA) rules forces coaches and administrators to ask if behavior is against the rules instead of whether the behavior is morally just. "NCAA policy has become so rule dependent, so comprehensive and so situation-specific that athletic administrators, coaches and support staff are increasingly not required to make ethical judgments. . . . A myopic emphasis on rule conformity has displaced a more circumspect emphasis on personal integrity and considered ethical judgment" (Gough, 1994, p. 5).

Self-Examinations

One way to promote moral reasoning is to ask employees to think about hypothetical ethical dilemmas. This strategy assumes that most people want to make the correct and moral decision. More people will do the right thing if they have thought about ethical behavior prior to making important decisions and/or if they think people in their organization care about their behavior. Self-examinations are an effective tool to remind people of ethical actions and to express institutional concern for ethical issues.

Self-examinations do not have to be reviewed by management to be effective, nor is it necessary to take severe punitive measures against those who do poorly. The NCAA, for example, requires that all coaches involved in recruiting take and pass a test. The exercise tests the coaches' knowledge of recruiting rules. It is not a difficult test, and most coaches pass it with little trouble. Coaches who fail the test can retake it until they pass. The test is not designed to keep immoral coaches from recruiting but to remind coaches of "right" actions. The simple act of reviewing the rules reminds coaches of the rules and reinforces the view that abiding by these rules matters. Serious recruiting violations by coaches have dramatically decreased since the NCAA mandated this self-examination (D. Schultz, personal communication, April 11, 1995).

Self-examinations can be performed on the organizational level as well. The NCAA has recently instituted an accreditation process mandating athletic departments to review their organizational practices. A review committee, made up of outsider experts, judges the athletic department and makes recommendations as to how the department might better fulfill the mission of the NCAA. The real benefit of the accreditation program is the process of preparing for the review. The accreditation process forces department administrators to examine their day-to-day practices in light of institutional goals. Such reflection might not happen otherwise given the demands of most sport management positions.

Forum for Moral Discourse

A great contributor to immoral behavior is isolation. Because morality is tied to social situations, communication is a key to decreasing corruption and resolving ethical dilemmas. Employees should be encouraged to get together to discuss where and how they faced specific problems. By doing so, employees understand they are not alone in making difficult choices and that their colleagues can provide significant insight, perspective, and help. The process takes the pressure off individuals and clarifies the issues at stake. It also brings employees together in the resolution of problems. Ethical discussions can be incorporated into the normal management systems, such as staff meetings or sales meetings.

Decisions should not be reviewed only *after* they have been made. Employees should be encouraged to consult with each other and their supervisors *during* the decision-making process. This helps employees avoid making wrong choices, leaving out important parts of the decision, or being overwhelmed by the weight and complexity of issues.

Forums for discussion should not be confined to individual organizations. This is especially true for managers. Because management is often the smallest branch of an organization, there may not be an effective forum for the exchange of ideas. Conventions, executive education, or management training may be employed as forums for ethical discourse. So might informal settings like lunches between friends, a confidential call to colleagues with similar responsibilities, or a casual conversation at a golf outing.

Ethical Decision Making

How then should a sport manager use ethical discourse to help solve problems? **Ethical decision making** is not a random process where the sport manager just reacts from his or her "gut" feeling. Ethical analysis involves a systematic process of reasoning. It is not a haphazard procedure where one guesses at the best solution (Cooke, 1991). Ethical decision making is similar to the regular decision-making process in business situations in that there is a given structure to follow when making an ethical decision. An adaptation of a model suggested by Zinn (1993) outlines the following steps in the ethical decision-making process:

1. Identify the correct problem to be solved.
2. Gather all the pertinent information.
3. Explore codes of conduct relevant to your profession or to this particular dilemma.
4. Examine your own personal values and beliefs.
5. Consult with your peers or other individuals in the industry who may have experience in similar situations.
6. List your options.
7. Look for a "win-win" situation if at all possible.
8. Ask yourself this question: "How would my family feel if my decision and how I arrived at my decision were printed in the newspaper tomorrow?"
9. Sleep on it. Do not rush to a decision.
10. Make your best decision, knowing it may not be perfect.
11. Evaluate your decision.

While this may seem like a complicated decision-making process, remember that ethical decisions and ethical dilemmas involve complicated problems. It is essential for sport managers to fully think through any ethical decisions they have to make.

Consequences

Finally, employees need to know there are consequences for immoral behavior. Even in the best organizations, some people will be motivated solely by self-interest. However, if people understand that corruption comes with certain risks, they are less likely to engage in immoral acts. A good deal of poor judgment can be eliminated simply by making consequences clearly understood. People need to understand that they will lose their jobs, customers, or eligibility if they are caught violating rules. By making consequences of immoral acts clear, organizations help to promote ethical actions.

To be effective, discipline must meet two criteria: they must be meaningful and they must be enforceable. One of the complaints about rules imposing fines on professional athletes is that some professional athletes make so much money that fines of thousands of dollars are of little consequence to these players. Sometimes an athlete's team will pay a fine imposed on the athlete. Thus, fines have limited impact on behavior and are not meaningful in some cases. All the rules in the world will be ineffective if they are not enforceable, which is the second criterion of punishments. For example, prior to the 1980s the NCAA enforcement staff was woefully inadequate to investigate charges of corruption, so schools and coaches had little fear they would be punished by the NCAA.

CREATING ETHICAL ORGANIZATIONS

How an Individual Influences the Sport Organization

While a sport organization tends to operate as a whole, sport managers must remember that all sport organizations are made up of individuals, all of whom bring something unique to the workplace. Each and every individual in a sport organization has the ability to "make a difference" within that sport organization. People sometimes ask, "What difference does it make if I act ethically or not?" It makes a *significant* difference, because each individual *can and does* influence her or his sport organization. The following equation illustrates how this happens:

Individual Values ⇨ Leadership Style ⇨ Managerial Functions ⇨ Organizational Success

Each person brings to the organization a unique set of personal values that determines how he or she acts. Because the sport industry does not operate in a vacuum separate from the rest of society, individuals manage sport using their personal values, beliefs, and backgrounds (DeSensi & Rosenberg, 1996). A person's values are related to his or her religion, socioeconomic class, and ancestry, and values continually evolve through interaction with peers, family, teachers, coaches, and the media. Values are at the center of who people are and determine many of the basic decisions they make and preferences they have. Individual values directly affect choice of leadership style, the way managers work, and how they communicate with people. Inventories such as the Myers-Briggs Type Indicator reveal to us our preferences in leadership style, but these preferences are influenced by the individual values each of us holds.

The leadership style a sport manager adopts affects how that manager carries out the basic management functions mentioned in Chapter 2, Management Principles Applied to Sport Management: planning, organizing, staffing, directing, and controlling. Since each of these functions shapes the overall organization, it is obvious that they influence "organizational success," as determined by different sport organizations individually. For example, a Major League Baseball (MLB) team might consider itself successful if it maximizes profits, an NCAA institution if it graduates 90 percent of its student-athletes, a facility if it minimizes "dark days," and a camp for inner-city children if it maximizes the number of campers funded by camperships. Each of these sport organizations would consider itself successful but for very different reasons.

No matter which segment of the sport industry is examined, the fact is that overall organizational success can be traced directly back to individual decision making within that sport organization. The following are two examples of leadership, ethical decision making, and organizational success. The first case, which involves the World Basketball League and the retail giant Phar-Mor, illustrates how unethical decision making can have dire results. This case is based on an exposé by the television program *Frontline*. The second case demonstrates how decision makers' will to invest in right actions paid off at the University of Massachusetts. This case is based on conversations with University of Massachusetts employees and consultants.

The World Basketball League: How To Keep a Struggling League Afloat

When attendance began to fall at WBL games, the professional men's basketball league for players under 6 feet 5 inches tall, the league found itself in a difficult position with some tough decisions to make. The league, founded in 1989 with teams in nine small-market Midwestern cities, had met with brief early success, attracting both fans and sponsors. The teams and league had been placed

well: cities with franchises had little or no direct competition from other professional sport teams, and the communities seemed eager to have their own teams and
games to attend.

The league had been the brainchild and passion of Mickey Monus. He was also
the WBL's major financial backer. Monus had built a substantial fortune over the
previous decade through the success of his primary business, Phar-Mor, a rapidly
expanding chain of discount stores. Because of his wealth, he could write the
league's losses off for a short time when attendance began to slip, but eventually
he needed to find a way to bring the league around and make it solvent. The
decisions he made led to the collapse of the league and, ultimately, to the
discovery of substantial illegal business practices.

Facing the loss of profits and revenues from fans and sponsors, the WBL had to
decide between two general approaches to reviving the league. One approach was
to study the reasons fans and sponsors were no longer interested in the league and
make changes to address these reasons. Earning back the interest of the fans would
in turn attract sponsors. Such an approach would make the league solid and stable,
but it would be labor-intensive, would require patience, and might take a great
deal of time—time Monus did not have. The other approach, which Monus
favored, was to find ways to prop up the league more immediately, by winning
sponsors back quickly to generate the cash flow necessary to cover the league's
operating expenses. With the support of the sponsors, Monus and league officials
could sustain the league until it "caught on" with sports fans. However, it would
be difficult to attract sponsors to a product that seemed to lack excitement and fan
interest.

Monus did several things. First, he used the leverage of his Phar-Mor business
to pressure sponsors into continuing to support the league. Because Phar-Mor was
such a large purchaser, supplier, and employer in the communities where the
league played, Monus threatened to withhold Phar-Mor business from sponsors
who backed out of the league. If, for example, Coca-Cola decided it did not want
to support the WBL any longer, Monus would threaten to stop selling Coke
products at Phar-Mor. Phar-Mor controlled a significant enough percentage of the
market that such a loss could mean millions of dollars to a vendor. In comparison,
it was relatively inexpensive for companies to underwrite the WBL according to
Monus's wishes and ultimately would cost them less than losing Phar-Mor
business. Thus, instead of working to improve the league itself, Monus tried to
maintain cash flow by strong-arming the sponsors.

Sponsorship money was a short-term solution to a systemic problem. The
league continued to lose money. Monus made other bad decisions when he was no
longer able to or no longer wanted to cover the league's costs out of his personal
resources and money from sponsors. He began to pay the league's operating
expenses out of Phar-Mor's bank accounts, which was illegal and also violated the
trust of his employees and investors in Phar-Mor. Eventually, and only by

coincidence, a Phar-Mor investor stumbled across a canceled Phar-Mor check that had been used to pay WBL travel expenses. The investigation that followed led to the demise of the WBL, Phar-Mor, and Monus's wealth and power.

While Monus was the mastermind and guiding hand behind the Phar-Mor and WBL corruption, it was made possible by the complicity of the employees who performed the actual accounting at his behest. As in many companies, Monus hired a number of young employees who were eager to establish themselves and rise quickly in their careers. By giving them significant responsibility and autonomy, he encouraged their loyalty and faith in him. In the eyes of these employees, Monus had seen their potential, placed faith in them, and they owed him something in return. Hence, when he asked them to bend and then break their personal and professional moral and ethical values, the decision to go along was not a simple or clear case of right or wrong. Instead, they hoped that their "creative accounting" would be only temporary and that they would soon have the opportunity to make things right. They found, however, that bad decisions led to worse decisions and quickly spun out of control.

As is often the case with unethical behavior, one bad decision put the entire organization on a path toward corruption. It is not surprising that given the corporate culture of Phar-Mor and the WBL, none of the employees in the know stepped forward to challenge Monus and redirect the organization. What began as a bad business practice evolved into unethical behavior and then illegal actions. Ultimately, the league collapsed, many of the employees were fired for allowing the illegal activity, and some went to jail (Frontline, 1994).

The University of Massachusetts Athletics: How To Comply with Title IX

In 1993, Bob Marcum was hired as the athletic director at the University of Massachusetts. Despite the success of the basketball team and a new arena, Marcum faced a major problem. Three years earlier, during the 1990 and 1991 academic years, the State of Massachusetts had cut funding for higher education. The administration's response was to impose across-the-board cuts. The athletic department had thus come to the unenviable conclusion that five sport programs—women's volleyball, women's lacrosse, men's soccer, and men's and women's tennis—needed to be eliminated in order to operate within the budgetary decreases.

The elimination of the five sport programs left the department open to a Title IX complaint. Title IX is federal legislation, enacted in 1972, which prohibits discrimination based on gender in any program in any educational institution receiving federal funds. The university, including the athletic department, was required to comply with Title IX since it was an educational institution receiving federal funds. The athletic department was made up of 69% male student-athletes and 31% female student-athletes. In addition, athletic scholarship aid was being allocated on a basis of 63% going to the male student-athletes and 37% going to the female student-athletes. The female student-athletes collected information on Title IX requirements, obtained legal counsel, and threatened a lawsuit against the athletic department alleging discrimination against female student-athletes.

An interim athletic director held off the court case by agreeing to reinstate the women's programs and increase scholarship funding for women athletes. These steps may have placated the offended athletes, but it did not solve the university's overall problem—that the athletic department was in violation of Title IX. So in addition, the university agreed to develop a five-year Title IX compliance plan.

One of Marcum's first acts as the new athletic director was hiring a consultant to perform a Title IX review to determine all areas where changes could be made in order to come into compliance with Title IX. The athletic department and university administration could have selected from a number of different options. For example, one option adopted by other schools has been to cut men's sport programs and scholarship funding to existing men's sport programs in order to bring the percentages of men's funding more in line with the funding for women's programs. But Marcum, in discussions with the university president and chancellor, decided that the intent of Title IX and the right approach was to increase sport participation opportunities and funding to female student-athletes, not decrease the opportunities and funding being provided to the men.

A five-year plan was adopted shortly thereafter that committed the university to investing in women's athletics. The university added two new women's sports, water polo and crew. While water polo was not too difficult to add, women's crew was a monumental undertaking demanding a huge investment. The university also made investments in facilities (including an artificial turf field for field hockey), per diem allowances, coaches' salaries, and scholarships to bring the department into compliance with Title IX. In addition, keeping with the university's vision of the meaning of Title IX, the investment in women's sport enabled the university to reinstate the previously eliminated men's sport programs.

Marcum could have complied with the letter of the law in ways that were more cost-effective, but he decided to increase women's sport participation opportunities and funding without eliminating or decreasing participation opportunities or funding for the men's sport programs because, as he put it at the time, "This is the right thing to do!" Twenty-five years after the passage of Title IX, the University of Massachusetts is one of only a handful of Division I athletic departments in compliance with the federal law. And the University of Massachusetts women's crew team? Well, it finished second at the 1997 NCAA Nationals, and two team members were chosen for the U.S. National Team (C.A. Barr, personal communication, April 17, 1997).

SUMMARY

Sport managers need to be aware of the importance of morality and ethics in the sport workplace. Sport managers make decisions on a daily basis that have an impact on large numbers of people, ranging from athletes to team owners to fans. Therefore, sport managers need to understand the far-reaching effects of their decisions, and how management structures, and personal values shape those decisions. Incorporating codes of ethics, self-examinations, forums for moral disclosure, and statements of consequences for ethical violations into the organizational priorities will help ensure that sport managers and employees make the "right" decisions.

REFERENCES

Alstead, A. (1994, Aug. 7). Good sport requires constant vigilance. *The Scotsman Publications Ltd.,* Scotland on Sunday section.

Bowie, N.E., & Duska, R.F. (1990) *Business ethics* (2d ed.). Englewood Cliffs, NJ: Prentice Hall.

Center for Business Ethics. (1992). Instilling ethical values in large corporations. *Journal of Business Ethics, 11,* 863–867.

Cooke, R.A. (1991). Danger signs of unethical behavior: How to determine if your firm is at ethical risk. *Journal of Business Ethics, 10,* 249–253.

Corcoran, P.D. (1990). *Illustrated codes of conduct.* Sydney: Australian Rugby Football League.

DeSensi, J.T., & Rosenberg, D. (1996). *Ethics in sport management.* Morgantown, WV: Fitness Information Technology.

Frontline. (1994). *How to steal 500 million dollars.* Alexandria, VA: PBS Video.

Gough, R. (1994, June/July). NCAA policy's strangling effect on ethics. In *For the record* (pp. 3–5). Milwaukee, WI: National Sports Law Institute.

International Health, Racquet and Sportsclub Association (1997). Associate member code of conduct. http://www.ihrsa.org.

Jacobs, J. (1992). *Systems of survival: A dialogue on the moral foundations of commerce and politics.* New York: Random House.

Lebrecht, S. (1993, April 17). Seeing Ontario from the seat of a bike. *The Toronto Star,* p. 67.

McNally, F., & Cusak, J. (1994, Dec. 7). Minister seeks report from IASA on sex abuse claims. *The Irish Times,* p. 3.

Sims, R.R. (1992). The challenge of ethical behavior in organizations. *Journal of Business Ethics, 11,* 505–513.

Solomon, R.C. (1992). *Above the bottom line: An introduction to business ethics*. Fort Worth, TX: Harcourt, Brace.

Zinn, L.M. (1993). Do the right thing: Ethical decision making in professional & business practice. *Adult Learning, 5,* 7–8, 27.

CHAPTER 7

High School and Youth Sport

Dan Covell

Key words: National Federation of State High School Associations (NFSHSA), state high school activity associations, public school, secondary schools, non-school agencies, settlement houses, governing body, Progressive movement, youth league directors, athletic directors, national youth league organizations, coaching certification, home schooling, charter/magnet schools

INTRODUCTION

Consider the following statistics as reported in 1997:

- Over 500,000 boys and girls ages 7 through 18 participated on 42,563 teams run by the American Youth Soccer Organization (American Youth Soccer Organization, 1997).
- 250,000 boys and girls ages 5 through 16 participated on 4,500 tackle, 600 flag, and 3,900 cheer squads overseen by Pop Warner Little Scholars, Inc. (*The Pop Warner Story*, 1997).
- Nearly 200,000 boys and girls ages 7 through 18 competed on basketball teams, and over 60,000 competed on swimming, wrestling, gymnastics, and track teams administered under the auspices of the Amateur Athletic Union (AAU).
- Membership in USA Hockey, the national governing body for ice hockey in the United States, includes approximately 294,000 boys and girls 17 years old and younger who participate on 21,000 teams (*This Is USA Hockey*, 1997).
- Nearly 6 million young men and women participated in high school athletics during the 1995–1996 school year. Somewhere between 20 and 35 million

youths participate annually in non-school-sponsored sports ("The Case," 1997).

Table 7–1 shows the most popular high school sports by participant, as surveyed by the **National Federation of State High School Associations (NFSHSA)** (see the Governing Bodies section of this chapter) in 1996 and participation totals over the previous 25 years.

The following studies, as reported to the NFSHSA, indicate that athletics provides positive influences in the lives of adolescents at a crucial juncture of their lives:

- Research conducted by **state high school activity associations** in Colorado, Iowa, Minnesota, and New Mexico as recently as 1992 found that activity participants had higher grade point averages, had higher reading and math scores, and were absent from school less often than nonparticipants.
- In 1991, Hardiness Research of Casper, Wyoming, determined that by a 2-to-1 ratio for boys and a 3-to-1 ratio for girls, those who participate in high school sports are more successful academically in school, drop out less, are

Table 7–1 High School Sports with Greatest Number of Participants, 1996, and Total Participants in 1971, 1976, 1986, and 1996

Boys		Girls	
Sport	Number of Participants	Sport	Number of Participants
1. Football	957,573	1. Basketball	445,869
2. Basketball	545,569	2. Track and field	379,060
3. Track and field	454,645	3. Volleyball	357,576
4. Baseball	444,476	4. Softball	305,217
5. Soccer	283,728	5. Soccer	209,287
Year	Total Number of Participants	Year	Total Number of Participants
1971	3,666,917	1971	294,015
1976	4,109,021	1976	1,645,039
1986	3,344,275	1986	1,807,121
1996	3,634,052*	1996	2,367,936*

*Exclusive of 17,901 coeducational sport participants.

Source: Compiled from data presented in *The Case for High School Activities* (1997), Kansas City, MO.

more apt to be successful in college, and focus not on cars and money but rather on life accomplishments for career goals.

- Data from a national sample of the high school Class of 1992 showed that students who are more involved in high school competitive sports have higher grades, higher educational aspirations, and fewer discipline problems.
- The testing services that administer the ACT and SAT concluded that achievements gained through participation in high school activities were a better predictor for later success than their standardized examinations.

Although professionals working in high school and youth league sports may not garner the limelight and national prominence shared by other sport management professionals, such job opportunities offer significant challenges and substantial personal rewards. A coach, official, or administrator at this level never lacks for responsibilities, and every day brings a fresh set of issues to tackle to ensure that the educative framework of youth athletics is maintained.

HISTORY

The recognition of the positive educatory and developmental aspects of athletic participation is not a recent phenomenon. The history of athletic participation by precollege youth predates the signing of the Constitution and the formation of the United States. As long as there have been children, native and immigrant, there has existed the need and desire for play. Native Americans played a game that French Jesuit priests called "lacrosse" because players used a stick that resembled a bishop's cross-shaped crosier. European settlers brought tennis, cricket, and several early versions of what would become baseball, and Africans brought to America as slaves threw the javelin, boxed, and wrestled. Despite all this, formally organized athletic participation, particularly those programs run under the auspices of secondary educational institutions, only began to emerge in the mid-nineteenth century.

High School Athletics in the Nineteenth Century

In 1838, educator Horace Mann noted that in an increasingly urbanized America, outdoor recreation space was becoming scarce and children were at risk of physical deterioration. Urban populations were doubling every 10 years due to the steady country-to-city migration, as well as immigration from Europe. In response to the common popular appeal of baseball in the nineteenth century, schools and other agencies began to promote the sport to aid in solving broad social problems such as ill health and juvenile delinquency (Seymour, 1990).

The first free school, or **public school,** in the United States opened in 1821 (Swanson & Spears, 1995). By 1850, the principle of state-supported schools for all children, not just the affluent, was still not fully realized. For example, only half the children in the New England region, where public schools were relatively more available, were able to access this education. Educators at established public schools did not fully embrace the value of exercise and play. In contrast, the values of athletics were recognized much earlier by private schools. The Round Hill School, founded in Northampton, Massachusetts, in 1823, introduced athletics as early as 1825 (Swanson & Spears, 1995). Wallkill Academy in New York and St. Paul's in New Hampshire established baseball teams that competed against outside competition in the 1860s (Seymour, 1990), and in 1862, students from Boston's Dixwell Private Latin School formed the nation's first organized football club, the Oneida Football Club (Hardy, 1982). As at the collegiate level, secondary students organized the games. In the public schools, male students at Worcester (Massachusetts) High School formed a baseball club sanctioned by the school in 1859, and school-sanctioned baseball teams were formed at both Central School and Heathcote School in Buffalo, New York, in 1868 (Seymour, 1990). The University of Michigan baseball team played high school squads from the nearby towns of Ann Arbor and Ypsilanti in 1866 (Forsythe, 1950). Interscholastic athletics, much as with the collegiate system after which they were patterned, were seen by students as not only an outlet for physical activity but also a vehicle through which to develop communal ties with classmates and alumni.

The establishment of free **secondary schools** accelerated in the 1860s and 1870s, eventually numbering 6,000 institutions by 1900, with over 15 million children enrolled (Swanson & Spears, 1995). The acceptance of University of Chicago educator John Dewey's theories encouraging games helped to hasten the incorporation of athletics into school curricula. The State of New York required every public school to include an adjacent playground (Wilson, 1994), citywide school baseball tournaments were held in the 1890s in Boston and in Cook County, Illinois, and students from several Boston and Boston area public and private schools formed the Interscholastic Football Association in 1888 (Hardy, 1982). Concurrently, statewide high school athletic associations in Illinois and Wisconsin were formed to coordinate interscholastic competition. The most popular school sport for women was basketball. Girls' teams were playing in high schools in Lansing and Detroit in Michigan in the late 1890s, and girls began to play in New York City's Public School Athletic League (PSAL) in 1905. Illinois formed a separate girls' state association in 1917 (Cahn, 1994).

Private Athletic Organizations in the Nineteenth Century

Athletics promoted by **non-school agencies** emerged in various locations in the United States nearly simultaneously. The most prominent private agency to promote youth athletics was the Young Men's Christian Association (YMCA). The YMCA, founded in England in 1844 by Protestant clergyman George Williams, was established in the United States in 1851 to attract urban youth to Christianity through athletics. The first YMCA gymnasiums were built in New York and San Francisco in 1869. By 1900, the YMCA had grown to include 250,000 members (this number would double by 1915) at 1,400 branches, with a national athletic league under the direction of Dr. Luther H. Gulick. Gulick is credited with the development of the New York City's Public School Athletic League in 1903, and he may have suggested in 1891 that James Naismith, then an instructor at the YMCA's physical education training school in Springfield, Massachusetts, devise the game that would become basketball. In 1909, the YMCA also initiated the first national program to teach swimming and diving (Putney, 1993). The Young Women's Christian Association (YWCA), established concurrently with the YMCA, began offering calisthenics in its Boston branch in 1877 and opened a new gym there in 1884. By 1916, 65,000 women attended gym classes and 32,000 attended swimming classes sponsored by the YWCA nationwide (Cahn, 1994).

From the 1930s through the 1950s, YMCA branches were opened in suburban areas, which allowed female members to join as determined by local policies. Family memberships were made available in an effort to retain and attract members. In the 1960s, the organization's leadership faced the issue of whether to reestablish its Christian evangelical elements and drift away from promoting its athletic programs, even as the exercise-seeking membership grew to over 5.5 million in 1969. The YMCA chose to emphasize individual values and growth, which dovetailed nicely with individual personal fitness goals (Putney, 1993).

Other private entities that developed sports programs included **settlement houses**, established by social workers who moved into urban slums in the Northeast and Midwest to set up programs, including athletics, designed to help the poor. Other Christian denominations followed the lead of the YMCA in the early part of the century by using athletics, primarily baseball, to promote male youth membership, with church athletic leagues formed in Baltimore, Chicago, Kansas City, and New York (Seymour, 1990).

Another agency, the Amateur Athletic Union (AAU), a privately administered **governing body,** was formed by 15 amateur "gentlemen's" athletic clubs in 1888 to organize track-and-field championships. The AAU attempted to assume the role of national ruling body for amateur sports, and by 1893, it claimed jurisdiction over 23 sports, including the YMCA and collegiate athletics. Member athletes paid dues of 25¢ to join, and member teams participated in AAU-sponsored national tournaments and competitions in basketball, gymnastics, swimming, and track and field. The colleges left the AAU in 1905 to form an early version of what would become the National Collegiate Athletic Association (NCAA), partly over conflicts regarding AAU basketball playing rules that banned dribbling. The AAU added formal competition for women in swimming in 1915 and in track and field in 1923. Nine years later, a 19-year-old woman from Beaumont, Texas, Mildred "Babe" Didrickson, single-handedly won the team competition of the National Women's AAU Track Meet. By the 1940s, the AAU had asserted control over boxing and wrestling. Except for swimming, track, and boxing, the AAU's influence over amateur sport declined as the NCAA and the Olympic Movement emerged. Continued eligibility and membership conflicts with the NCAA, combined with the Amateur Sports Act of 1978, which designated the U.S. Olympic Committee as the coordinator for Olympic competition, diminished the AAU to its current status as a national coordinator of amateur adult and non-school-based youth athletics in a wide variety of sports (Noonkester, 1982).

The Twentieth Century

During the first two decades of the twentieth century, youth athletics were popular vehicles through which newly formed secular government organizations sought to combat the proliferating ills of urban life. The social and political efforts of educators aligned with the **Progressive Movement**, such as John Dewey, G. Stanley Hall, and William James, touted athletics as a tool to prepare for the rigors of modern life and democracy and to assimilate immigrants into American culture. They promoted child welfare by advocating for increased playground space, such as the development of year-round play spaces in Los Angeles in 1904 and in Chicago's congested South Side in 1905.

Progressives also promoted a longer school year, stricter attendance laws, and formalized public school athletics as an antidote to child labor exploitation and regimented physical education curricula based on the German tradition of body building through repetitive exercise (Dyreson, 1989). Emerging city, state, and parochial school athletic associations coordinated competitions in baseball, track, and rifle shooting and emphasized sportsmanship and academic integrity. In 1896, in an effort "to preserve the physical benefits of these games and the higher interests of the schools from the abuses which are wont to threaten athletic contests," the Michigan State Teachers' Association's Committee on High School Athletics proposed a minimum course load, satisfactory progress, and semester residency requirements, as well as administrative certification of athlete eligibility and a five-year participation limit (Forsythe, 1950). Also, in 1909, 75 Nebraska high schools opted to deny athletic participation to boys whose grades were too low. As a result of the movement promoting athletics as a critical part of the educational experience, government-funded educational institutions eventually assumed the administration and provision of the vast majority of athletic participation opportunities for American youth (Vincent, 1994).

Post–World War I

In the period during and immediately after World War I (1914–1918), the nation began to recognize the health benefits of athletics for male youths and adults alike. School sports for males were promoted as a source of physical training for the armed forces without directly encouraging militarism and as a means to develop social skills such as cooperation and discipline valued by an increasingly ethnically diverse and industrial society. Sports also boosted student retention and graduation rates—an important consideration, because in 1918 only one-third of grade school students entered high school, and only one in nine graduated (O'Hanlon, 1982).

During this period, athletics became entrenched in schools, and educators took control of athletics from students. But concerns from educators about their ability to administer and teach in an athletic capacity had been voiced since the 1890s. Individuals such as Dr. Dudley Sargent of Harvard University's Hemenway Gymnasium and instructors groomed at the YMCA's training school (now Springfield College) such as James Naismith and Amos Alonzo Stagg made significant contributions toward meeting the burgeoning instructional and curricular development needs. Sargent began his career as director of the gymnasium while an undergraduate at Bowdoin College in his home state of Maine, and he was instrumental in instituting a program of gymnastics and physical education at Harvard (Swanson & Spears, 1995). While most teams were initiated by students, by 1924 athletics in all but three states were managed by state associations.

Emerging school physical education (P.E.) and intramural programs were also developed on the competitive interscholastic model, although programs for girls were not encouraged. In 1915 only Idaho, Ohio, and North Dakota had laws requiring school P.E.; by 1930, 36 states had passed laws pertaining to it. By 1931, 47 states had athletic associations that monitored and controlled boys' high school athletics and conducted state championships in baseball, basketball, football, and track (Swanson & Spears, 1995). In contrast, only 21 states had some form of organization for girls' sports; 12 states combined governance with boys' sports, and 5 had separate organizations. State associations in 7 states (Colorado, Illinois, Iowa, Kansas, Nebraska, North Carolina, Oklahoma) constructed special game rules for girls' athletics to foster a less competitive atmosphere for fear that girls might be injured or made to be less feminine. The popularity of basketball and softball grew nonetheless. Girls at Western High School in Washington, D.C., played basketball as early as 1899, eight years after the game's inception. Interscholastic girls' basketball grew dramatically in Florida in the 1920s to include a state tournament, as school populations were too small in the then mostly rural state to conduct intramural programs and in addition, such teams could supplant more costly P.E. programs (Welch, 1978). In Iowa and Oklahoma, six-player girls' basketball (three restricted to each half of the court, with limited dribbling) thrived. By the mid-1950s, attendance figures in Iowa for the five-day state tournament approached 87,000 (Beran, 1979). Basketball was not the only game enjoyed by early participants in girls' athletics. Girls were playing a school-organized "indoor baseball" (the game that would develop into softball) at Chicago's West Division High School in 1895; by 1920, 91% of girls in Cleveland area schools played modified versions of baseball (Welch, 1978).

The financial calamities of the Great Depression of the 1930s launched unprecedented governmental involvement in recreation. Private companies and businesses cut back on the athletic participation opportunities they had sponsored before the economic downturn, and government agencies were asked to fill the void. The Works Progress Administration (WPA) provided funds ($500 million by 1937) and labor for field and playground construction, and city recreation departments provided "schools" for athletic skill instruction and league coordination. The WPA helped build 3,600 baseball fields, 8,000 softball fields, and 6,000 athletic fields. A total of 344 public buildings, including gymnasiums and swimming pools, were built at this time in the state of Kansas alone (Seymour, 1990).

Government fostered participation as well. In 1931, 107 teams entered Cincinnati's boys' baseball tournament, and 75 teams of boys under age 16 played in a municipal baseball league in Oakland, California, in 1935 (Seymour, 1990). The Crawford Bath House, maintained by the City of Pittsburgh's Bureau of Recreation, first sponsored a baseball club that would become one of the most renowned in the professional Negro Leagues: the Pittsburgh Crawfords (Ruck, 1993). Many significant private and parochial youth sport organizations were also initiated during this period, including American Legion Junior Baseball in 1925, Pop Warner Football in 1929, the Catholic Youth Organization (basketball, boxing, and softball) in 1930, the Amateur Softball Association in 1933, and Little League Baseball in 1939.

Little League Baseball

Little League Baseball may be the best known youth athletic organization in the United States. Founded in 1939 as a three-team league in Williamsport, Pennsylvania, by factory worker Carl Stotz, the organization for boys ages 9 through 12 grew to 867 teams in 12 states over the next decade. By 1963, Little League boasted 30,000 teams in 6,000 leagues on four continents and even licensed its trademark and name to Random House Books to publish "The Little League Library," a series of baseball-related nonfiction books for adolescent boys. Currently it involves over 2.5 million participants in 40 countries; requires strict adherence to administrative guidelines, including standardized field size and use of uniforms; formalizes rosters composed via the draft system; and promotes its ability to provide adult supervision and safe play. Little League also requires each player to pledge: "I trust in God. I love my country and will respect its laws. I will play fair and strive to win but win or lose I will always do my best" (Davies, 1994, p. 119).

In the period from 1968 to 1975, Little League Baseball was subjected to 22 class action sex segregation suits, highlighted by the 1974 case involving Maria Pepe, when all the Little League–affiliated programs in New Jersey chose to shut down rather than accept a state court ruling allowing girls to play (Michener, 1976). Little League chose to accept female players who wished to participate under the threat of amendments to its charter via federal legislation proposed by Michigan Congresswoman Martha Griffith in 1984. In response, Little League began softball league play for girls. American Legion baseball had its initial gender conflict in 1928, when Margaret Gisolo played for the Blanford, Indiana, team. Girls were explicitly barred through league bylaws the following year, and Gisolo never played again (Ladd, 1978).

KEY CONCEPTS

Critics of highly organized youth athletics often cite that such leagues create an increased pressure to win, and rob children of the opportunity to create and initiate their own play and competition. Professional physical educators and organizations such as the American Alliance for Health, Physical Education and Recreation (AAHPER) decried the "win at all costs" approach as early as the 1930s (Berryman, 1978). In response to these claims, some private groups began to emphasize participation. The American Youth Soccer Organization (AYSO), founded in 1965, promotes soccer and emphasizes that all participants play, that all teams are competitively balanced, that children "sign up" rather than "try out," and that all coaching is positive.

Through the first 75 years of this century, only white males on team sports enjoyed full participation opportunities in high school athletics. The passage of the Education Amendments of 1972 (Public Law 92-318), contained language under Title IX of the law specifically forbidding discrimination based on sex in educational programs that received federal funding. In 1975, the Department of Health, Education, and Welfare specifically cited the applicability of the law to athletics. Participation numbers for girls grew dramatically, from 294,015 in 1971, to 1,300,169 in 1974, to 2,083,040 in 1978, up to 2.3 million in 1996, even though the National Federation of State High School Associations initially decried the passage and mandates of the gender equity legislation as an "unwarranted intrusion by the Federal government" (National Federation, 1974).

Racial segregation played a significant role in restricting high school athletic participation opportunities for African-Americans. For example, Luberto (1994) details that the Constitution and Rules of the University Interscholastic League (UIL; the association formed in 1913 for Texas high school activities, administered by the University of Texas at Austin) was changed in 1919 to read that membership was open only to "any white public school." In response, the State Association of Colored Teachers formed the Texas Interscholastic League of Colored Schools (TILCS) in 1920, with the hope of eventually uniting with the white association. The TILCS, eventually maintained by Prairie View State College and renamed the Prairie View Interscholastic League (PVIL) in 1963, held boys' championships in football, basketball, baseball, and track, and reached a total membership of 500 schools by the mid-1960s.

The U.S. Supreme Court's ruling in *Brown v. Board of Education of Topeka, Kansas* (1954), that segregation of public schools violated the Fourteenth Amendment of the Constitution made segregated schools and associations illegal, but the changeover was slow due to white resistance and, in some cases, violence. In Texas, the El Paso Independent School District, a UIL member and one of the first state schools to desegregate (primarily due to a large percentage of resident Latino students), was allowed to remain in the UIL in 1955 when the UIL determined that membership could be retained by a member school that had "previously limited its enrollment to white students, but which has modified its rule so as to admit the Negro race." Previous nonmember (African-American) schools were not invited to join until 1965 and did not participate in UIL football and basketball until 1967. The PVIL ceased operation in 1969 after many of the smaller, formerly African-American schools were absorbed by larger, formerly all-white schools. School desegregation plans and forced student busing in the 1960s and 1970s brought about more balanced educational and participatory opportunities, but some cities, such as Odessa, Texas, were cited by federal courts for maintaining segregated schools as recently as 1982 (Luberto, 1994, p. 151).

The 1980s and 1990s have seen overall proportional participation numbers fall as participation opportunities are lost due to increasingly restricted local tax revenues and reduced state tax allotments. Junior varsity teams and sport programs have been cut, and many states now require user fees for students who wish to participate. School administrators have increasingly been forced to seek auxiliary funding to maintain programs. The remainder of this chapter focuses on job opportunities and current trends and issues in high school and youth sports.

CAREER OPPORTUNITIES

There are many similarities in the employment opportunities in high school and youth league sports. What follows is a brief listing of the roles critical to the operation of high school and youth league sports, including major job functions and responsibilities.

High School Athletic Director/League Director

As outlined in Chapter 2 the general duties of an administrator are planning, organizing, staffing, directing, and controlling (Jensen, 1992). Specifically, supervising a high school athletic department or youth league includes, but is not restricted to, hiring, supervising, and evaluating coaches; coordinating nearly all facets of contest management, including the hiring and paying of officials and event staff; setting departmental/league training and disciplinary policies; determining departmental/league budgets; overseeing all associated fund-raising; determining and verifying game scheduling and athlete eligibility; transmitting relevant publicity; and handling public relations. In addition, most school athletic directors do not have the luxury of devoting their whole working day to this job. Most must also coach, teach, perform other administrative roles, or do some combination of all three. **Youth league directors** must sometimes perform their duties on a completely voluntary basis, without compensation or work release time. Compared to coaches, **athletic directors** have less direct involvement with athletes and perform their duties less publicly, but these administrators have by no means a less important role in successfully managing an athletic program. Some of their major responsibilities and concerns are risk management, insurance, employment issues, sexual harassment, gender equity, and fund-raising.

Risk Management

The primary responsibility for any administrator is to inform his or her staff of the risks and dangers inherent in their profession. Some risks, like injury, cannot be eliminated from athletic activities. In these cases, waivers and releases of liability are used by schools to ask student-athletes and their parents to release schools from a potential lawsuit or liability in the event an injury is sustained during athletic activity. A waiver and release of liability will not be enforceable if it attempts to insulate the school district from wanton, intentional, or reckless misconduct. Only liability for negligent actions can be waived. The terms of the waiver and release of liability must be presented clearly and conspicuously and must not be forced upon a student-athlete (Wong & Covell, 1995c). Student-athletes who are minors can disaffirm waivers, and some courts have found that parents lack the legal standing to waive the right of their children. Other court decisions have found waivers in general to be contrary to public policy (Cotten, 1997).

Insurance

Liability and medical insurance are crucial components of risk managment plans in high school athletics. Administrators are responsible for maintaining an adequate insurance program for participants and coaches. School districts, athletic departments, and youth leagues carry insurance to pay for losses resulting from lawsuits brought against them for negligent behavior. Common subjects for liability insurance are risk from use of the school premises and school vehicles and risk from the practice of professions (e.g., the actions of employees). Many school districts require student-athletes to carry some level of medical insurance. If a student-athlete has no insurance through his or her family, the school district usually provides school activity medical insurance through a commercial carrier for a small fee. The National Federation of State High School Associations, many state associations, and member school districts have adopted a liability/lifetime catastrophe medical plan. The plan covers member schools, school districts, administrators, and coaches. The philosophy behind the insurance plan is to provide needed benefits to injured parties without the time, costs, and risks that accompany litigation (Wong & Covell, 1995c).

Employment Issues

Administrators are responsible for hiring, supervising, and evaluating athletic personnel. Hiring processes vary, with some schools and leagues favoring a committee approach involving teachers, students, parents, and school/league board members. The specific duties and expectations of a particular position are outlined in the employment contract. The contract is the agreement between the employee and the employer regarding the terms of the job, and it is enforceable under law. Employees promise to perform the duties outlined in the contract, and the employer high school or school district promises to compensate them for their efforts. If the conditions of the contract are not met by either party, the other party is discharged of its contractual duties. Often such cases are not resolved simply, and breach of contract lawsuits result (Wong & Covell, 1995c). Administrators also need to be aware of whether the school district has entered into union collective bargaining agreements, as often such agreements mandate coaches' pay scales and working conditions.

Sexual Harassment

Administrators must be particularly attuned to situations involving sexual harassment claims against staff members. Concerns over adequate supervision and potential harassment situations are indeed important. Claims of improper use of language, improper conduct regarding locker room supervision, medical treatment, and student privacy have increased in recent years. All administrators and coaches, despite their gender or the gender composition of their teams, should make every effort to eliminate situations from which harassment claims could arise. Coaches of either gender, no matter the gender composition of their team, should have an assistant or monitor with them to aid with duties in these and other areas. Administrators should also look to implement an educatory component that defines sexual harassment and instructs staff members how to avoid potentially problematic situations.

Gender Equity

Most sex discrimination challenges in high school athletics have been based on state or U.S. Constitution equal protection clauses, state equal rights amendments, Title IX of the Education Amendments of 1972, or a combination thereof. Gender equity is a flashpoint of controversy for schools but is less so for youth leagues, unless they depend on municipal funding or utilize public facilities. Administrators are responsible for ensuring that athletic programs treat boys and girls equally. The National Federation of State High School Associations states as one of its legal foundations for the administration of high school athletics that interscholastic athletic programs must demonstrate equity or substantive and continuous progress toward equity in all facets of men's and women's athletics. Areas of concern include providing uniforms and equipment, scheduling practices and games, budgeting funds, and travel. Obviously, sports such as football and ice hockey will always have higher equipment costs than sports such as volleyball and soccer, but administrators still need to show that the needs of all male and female sports are being met. One such way is to institute a rotating schedule to replace such things as game uniforms. This will ensure that over a given period of time, every sport will be provided with new uniforms. A similar rotation schedule can be implemented to equitably assign practice times in facilities that are shared by boys' and girls' teams. For example, for swim teams that must share the same pool, one week the boys team can practice from 3 PM to 5 PM, and the girls can swim from 5 PM to 7 PM, and the next week, the teams can switch time slots. The scheduling of game times and game opponents is also an area of concern. Both girls' and boys' teams should have the opportunity to play at a time when as many parents, students, and fans can attend. This means that if the boys' basketball team plays at 7 PM, a time at which the greatest number of spectators can attend, then the girls' teams must also have the opportunity to play at 7 PM.

Another important facet of gender equity is pay equity. Such claims are based on the Equal Pay Act of 1963, Title VII of the Civil Rights Act of 1964, Title IX of the Education Amendments of 1972, and possibly state statutes relative to equal pay. The Equal Pay Act deals solely with wages paid to men and women within the same company. The basic theme underlying the act is "equal pay for equal work." Title VII focuses on discriminatory hiring and firing practices and advancement policies within companies. Title VII forbids discriminatory employment practices based on the race, color, religion, sex, or national origin of the applicant, and it contains a "nonretaliation" provision that prohibits all employers defined in the act from discriminating against any employee or applicant who has invoked his or her rights under the law. Title VII also prohibits sexual harassment in the workplace. Both acts are enforced by the Equal Employment Opportunity Commission (EEOC) (Wong & Covell, 1995b).

Fund-Raising

As stated previously, as financial circumstances for schools and leagues have become more strained, administrators are often expected to be fund-raisers or to supervise the fund-raising efforts of individual teams. Administrators should have final approval on all fund-raising efforts, take care to ensure fund-raising programs are run with reputable companies, coordinate campaigns so individual team fund-raising efforts are staggered throughout the year to avoid overlap, and ensure that all funds raised are given to the school or league and are accounted for and disbursed.

Coach

The job description for a high school or youth league coach is indeed demanding. Coaches must face complex human resource management issues, deal with constant and extreme pressure to perform successfully, and work long and irregular hours for low (or no) pay. Significant knowledge of injury and physical training, equipment knowledge, and bus-driving skills are also highly recommended. The job of the high school and youth league coach is probably the most challenging, most underappreciated, and yet most rewarding role in all of sport. The role of coach can become that of teacher, parent, confidant, friend, and leader, and a successful coach knows that he or she cannot overlook any facet of these duties and perform the job adequately. The responsibilities are substantial: coaches are entrusted with protecting and promoting the physical, emotional, and social health and safety of girls and boys in physically precarious situations and are expected to take every reasonable precaution to ensure that their players are not at risk. The pressures are great, as the coach is evaluated by many who have a strong interest in the sport and an artificial sense of expertise concerning the execution of the job. Sage (1987) found that the complexity of duties and high job expectations led to significant stress for coaches, but a greater opportunity to have a positive impact on students, a school, and a community can be found nowhere else. Someone seeking the challenges and rewards inherent in this career should be aware of the significant issues and specific areas of responsibility facing coaches, most of which have little to do with game strategies and motivational speeches.

Supervision

Coaches are the principal supervisors of the athletic activities of their teams, and it is their responsibility to provide and ensure a reasonably safe environment for all participants. A coach's responsibilities in this area are diverse and may include issuing proper equipment, maintaining issued equipment, ensuring that all student-athletes have had physical examinations and have been found fit to participate, and maintaining the various necessary forms of documentation (confirmation of physical status, confirmation of eligibility, proof of insurance, parent permission to participate). In terms of the actual play of participants, coaches are responsible for organizing drills, ensuring that physical mismatches are minimized, maintaining safe practice and playing grounds, suspending practice or play during dangerous weather conditions, and monitoring locker rooms during the time preceding and following activities. In play situations, coaches must monitor activities to be sure that student-athletes are not performing in an improper and dangerous manner that might harm themselves and/or other student-athletes (Wong & Covell, 1995a).

It is advisable for coaches to have a demonstrated proficiency in dealing with injuries, such as an active first aid and cardiopulmonary resuscitation (CPR) certification. Coaches are held to the "reasonable care" standard when rendering medical assistance to an injured student-athlete. They are not expected to provide the medical assistance of a doctor or one with medical training. The main responsibilities of coaches are twofold. First, they may have to render medical assistance before other medical personnel arrive. When an athlete sustains an injury during practice or games, a coach is usually the first to administer care. Second, coaches must determine the nature and extent of the injury, what treatment is necessary, and whether additional medical assistance is required. The nature of the injury may require the student-athlete to be treated immediately or to seek medical attention as a precautionary measure (Wong & Covell, 1995a).

Fund-Raising

As financial circumstances for schools and leagues become more strained, coaches are frequently expected to act as fundraisers in addition to their other myriad duties. To pay for items formerly included in budgets, such as long-distance team and scouting trips and special practice and playing equipment, coaches must create methods to raise funds. Such methods may include direct sponsorships donated by local businesses and individuals, the sale of items such as candy bars or other novelties, or selling advertising space within school publications or facilities.

Trainer/Physical Therapist

Injuries inevitably occur in athletic activities, and the nature of injuries can range from the superficial to the severe. Most school districts and state associations require medical personnel and emergency medical transportation to be present at football games or other high-risk contact sports, while the dictates of youth leagues vary. Most schools and leagues do not have the personnel or monetary resources to provide trainers or medical personnel (paramedic, certified athletic trainer, emergency medical technician, physician) for all contests, and such personnel are almost never provided for practices. According to the National Athletic Trainers Association (NATA), only 12% (2,142) of their membership work full time at the approximately 20,000 U.S. high schools, while another 2,520 work part time as contracted through local sports medicine clinics (Cohen, 1995c).

The presence of such personnel drastically reduces the potential for coaches or other unqualified personnel to be placed in a situation where they have to react to a medical emergency they cannot treat. Providing adequate medical treatment for injured athletes significantly reduces the risk of litigation against coaches, schools, and leagues and can reduce injury rates by 41%. However, because 80% of injuries occur during practices and training (Cohen, 1995c), some schools are looking to contract trainers or medical personnel to be present at all times and to set up year-round training and fitness programs. Trainers can be contracted by a school or league from a local hospital, physical therapy center, or fitness club, or the position can be linked to internal jobs such as classroom or physical education teacher, school doctor or nurse, or athletic administrator. Such programs benefit the school athletic program and can provide a student-trainer with an educational opportunity. Salaries for this position vary widely, depending on the employment status (part-time or full-time) and the other job responsibilities linked to the post.

Officials/Judges

Officials are vital to the proper administration of high school and youth athletics, and they share much of the public scrutiny associated with coaches and administrators. Officials are employed by schools and leagues but are considered independent contractors because the school or league exhibits no supervisory capacity over the official. Depending on the locale, officials may require certification from national, state, and local sanctioning organizations to gain the approval to work in interscholastic events. Most youth leagues rely on volunteers with such accreditation to officiate contests. While this aids in the logistical operations, the use of such unprofessional personnel can leave a league liable for litigation for the actions of these individuals.

Officials possess a significant amount of control over game administration and supervision. In game situations, officials usually have the responsibility and authority to postpone and cancel games due to inclement and dangerous weather situations, and they are responsible for controlling rough and violent play.

At this level, officials work on a part-time basis, as compensation is not sufficient to cover full-time employment. Administrators are responsible for keeping tax information on officials and for submitting to the Internal Revenue Service (IRS) records on individuals who earn over a certain amount from the school. Officials are also responsible for submitting their income figures to the IRS for tax purposes.

Governing Bodies

The administration of high school and youth sports is primarily a local affair, with most policy and procedural decisions made at the district, school, or youth league level. However, the existence of local, state, and national governing bodies ensures the running of championships, coordination of athlete eligibility, dissemination of instructional information, and implementation of certain coach and administrative certification programs. Governing bodies also create and maintain stated rules and guidelines and apply them to all affiliated athletic programs equitably and consistently.

The National Federation of State High School Associations

The National Federation of State High School Associations, or NFSHSA, is a nonprofit organization headquartered in Kansas City, Missouri, that serves as the national coordinator for high school sports, as well as activities such as student council, debate, and drama. The NFSHSA encompasses all 50 individual state high school athletics and activity associations, as well as similar governing bodies operating in the District of Columbia, Bermuda, Guam, St. Croix, St. Thomas, St. John, and 10 Canadian provinces. NFSHSA represents over 10 million students in over 17,000 high schools, as well as coaches, officials, and judges through the individual state, provincial, and territorial organizations. In addition to compiling national records in sports and national sport participation rates, the NFSHSA coordinates official certification; issues playing rules for 16 boys' and 16 girls' sports; prints 8 million publications annually, including officials' manuals and case books, magazines, supplemental books, and teaching aids; holds national conferences and competitions; and acts as an advocate and lobbying agent for school-based youth sports. The NFSHSA also maintains a high school Hall of Fame, which currently has 180 inductees ("What Is," 1997).

The organizational structure of the NFSHSA comprises three facets. The legislative body, the National Council, is made up of one representative from each member state, provincial, or territorial association. Each council member has one vote, and the council meets to conduct business twice each year. The administrative responsibilities are handled by the 12-member board of directors, elected by the National Council from professional staffs of member associations. Eight board members are elected to represent one of eight geographic regions, with the remaining four chosen on an at-large basis. The board of directors approves the annual budget, appoints an executive director, and establishes committees for conducting association business. The NFSHSA has a paid administrative and professional staff of 50, including the current executive director, Robert F. Kanaby ("What Is," 1997).

Other professional organizations and services offered by the NFSHSA include:

- The National Interscholastic Athletic Administrators Association (NIAAA), made up of 5,000 individuals responsible for the administration of high school athletics
- The National Federation Interscholastic Coaches Association (NFICA), made up of 40,000 member high school coaches
- The National Federation Interscholastic Officials Association (NFIOA), which includes 130,000 member officials who benefit from liability insurance and skills instruction
- The National Federation Interscholastic Spirit Association (NFISA), formed in 1988 to assist members and coaches of cheerleading, pompom, and spirit groups ("What Is," 1997).

State Associations

The NFSHSA model is typically replicated at the state level by state associations. State associations, which are also nonprofit, have a direct role in organizing state championships and competitions in athletics and activities and are the final authority in determining athlete eligibility. The scope of activities, size of full-time administrative and support staff, and number of schools represented vary from state to state and are proportionally related to that state's population.

The legislative business of state associations is administered in much the same manner as the NFSHSA, with several general meetings each year attended by one voting representative from each member institution. While championships and competitions are administered by the associations, committees consisting of coaches and administrators perform most of the actual duties associated with the

events, including determining criteria for selection of event participants, event management, and the general rules pertaining to regular season competition.

National Youth League Organizations

National youth league organizations focus administrative efforts on promoting participation in a particular sport among children. The activities and duties of these organizations are illustrated by examining one such association, USA Hockey. USA Hockey, located in Colorado Springs, Colorado, is the official representative to the United States Olympic Committee and the International Ice Hockey Federation and is responsible for organizing and training men's and women's teams for international competition in ice and in-line skating. USA Hockey organizes competition at the grassroots and adult levels in 11 districts across the country; registers teams and officials; organizes player, official, and coaches' clinics; promotes risk management and safety programs; and facilitates participant and parent educational and instructional programs to further ice and in-line hockey participation. USA Hockey also conducts annual regional championships in five different age and gender classifications and publishes informational magazines, guides, and bylaws. Through these efforts, total team registration in USA Hockey programs has grown from 4,255 in 1969 to 26,902 in 1996 (*This Is USA Hockey*, 1997).

CURRENT ISSUES

Part-Time and Volunteer Personnel and Mandatory Coaching Certification

Due to budgetary and staffing limitations, more and more schools and virtually all youth leagues are forced to rely on insufficiently trained personnel. The expansion of girls' sports has also increased the demand for coaches (Chambers, 1992). As coaches decide to step down from coaching but keep their full-time teaching positions, schools are forced to look outside the school to hire part-time coaches. While these individuals may have some of the necessary qualifications, they often lack knowledge of the basic principles of child development and adolescent growth and development, as well as information concerning proper training and conditioning (Seefeldt, 1996). Bob Scharbert, regional manager of the Miami Metro-Dade Park and Recreation Department, underscores concerns over the training of volunteer coaches: "Would you think of enrolling your children in a school if you knew their teachers had not one bit of training in education? This is what you're doing with your young athletes" ("Kids' Programs," 1997, p. 25A). As such, more and more schools and youth leagues are looking toward independent organizations to provide **coaching certification** to ensure competency in basic coaching and educational skills. As of August 1997, 28 states required some form of mandatory coaching certification program for high school coaches. Most states require certification only for those coaches who are not also full-time faculty members (White, 1997). One such organization, the American Sport Education Program (ASEP), offers courses intended to help coaches, administrators, and parents develop expertise in training, conditioning, and motivation. ASEP programs are used by 25 state associations (White, 1997). NFSHSA also offers similar certification programs for administrators.

Sexual Abuse

The problem of sexual abuse is a serious concern in youth and high school sport. For example, USA Gymnastics expelled 11 coaches between 1990 and 1996 for sexually abusing approximately 20 girls and boys (Freid, 1996). With all personnel, including part-time and volunteer staff, administrators should check all references when hiring and ask specific questions about candidates' past involvement with criminal activities. Other techniques to defuse potential abuse, as illustrated by Freid (1996), include conducting criminal background checks, educating current personnel about proper behavior, implementing a sexual abuse prevention program and explaining the program to parents and participants, and securing facilities from access by nonapproved personnel. Such questions and procedures will serve to screen out potentially dangerous candidates.

Opportunities for People with Physical and Emotional Disabilities

Although some schools, school districts, and leagues set policies prohibiting participation by athletes with physical disabilities, the 1990 passage of the Americans with Disabilities Act (ADA) has led to increased opportunities for athletes like Chris Bittinger, a swimmer with spina bifida who competed (and scored) in the 500-yard freestyle for South Western High School in Hanover, Pennsylvania, in 1996 and also holds National Wheelchair Games records ("Pennsylvania Swimmer," 1997). Policies restricting participation are based on American Medical Association (AMA) guidelines, which state that the physical requirements of certain athletic activities pose a significant degree of physical risk to the student-athlete's safety. The ADA has, however, overturned many of these guidelines. The ADA stipulates that methods of organized sports will be sought to integrate students with disabilities into regular programs and that special athletic opportunities will be provided for those unable to participate in regular athletic programs (Wong & Covell, 1995c), but the vague definitions of the ADA have sometimes made compliance with the law difficult and open to significant interpretation. Most state antidiscrimination laws also disallow the exclusion of any participant unless the participation would radically alter the nature of the activity (Cohen, 1995b). Programs and leagues that either receive federal funding or utilize public facilities are all subject to ADA application.

Home Schooling

The increase in **home schooling**, where parents choose to educate their children at home rather than utilizing the local public school system for educatory or religious reasons, has had an impact on school athletics. The number of home-schooled students has grown to approximately 1.2 million in the United States, with more than 19,000 in Florida alone (Hums, 1996). This increase has led to a similar rise in requests to participate in local school athletics. There is very little consensus at the national, state, or local level as to how these requests should be accommodated, if at all. Requests for access by home-schooled students have been perceived as a threat to the authority of the NFSHSA, state associations, and local schools and school districts and have gained the attention of state and local legislators looking to address the concerns of constituents on both sides of the issue. The major concern of administrators, according to Helen Upton of the NFSHSA, is "that the first time a player is suspended because he hasn't maintained his grades, I believe he is going to declare himself a home schooler" (Cohen, 1995a, p. 16) and gain total access to school athletics and circumvent school eligibility rules enacted to promote academic progress (Cohen, 1995a).

When home-schooled students have sought access to athletic participation through the courts, they have been mostly unsuccessful, with many courts citing the fact that schools and associations have the right to set their own participation regulations that require athletic participants to attend a certain number of classes and that athletic participation is not a constitutionally protected right (Wong & Hums, 1996). However, some decisions have favored the home-schooled. In *Davis v. Massachusetts Interscholastic Athletic Association* (1994), the Supreme Court of Massachusetts ruled that the plaintiff, Melissa Davis, had been illegally barred from playing on the Norton High School (her local public high school) softball team because the only difference between her and the other team members was that she was home-schooled and that her disqualification from participation did not relate to a legitimate state purpose (Hums, 1996).

Many state legislatures, including those in Arizona, Florida, Idaho, North Dakota, Oregon, Texas, and Utah, have begun to address the issue of home schooling. For example, the North Dakota statute (N.D. Cent. Code section 15-34.1-06) defines home-based instruction as that which is based in the child's home and is supervised by the child's parent or parents. The supervising parent must keep an annual record of courses taken, track the child's progress, including standardized test scores, and file an annual report with the local public school superintendent listing the parent's teaching qualifications and the courses or extracurricular activities, including athletics, in which a child hopes to participate (Hums, 1996).

Recruiting

The increase in municipalities allowing students to choose from among a number of local high schools and to attend **charter, or magnet schools** (schools founded to create specific or advanced academic programs) rather than restricting them to attend their local high school has led to increased concerns about recruiting. Even though such schools and rules are created for academic reasons, concerns have risen that they will be exploited for athletic reasons. While many administrators laud the rationale behind the formation of magnet schools and school choice, there is unease concerning potential abuse.

In response to school choice, state associations are having to relax eligibility codes formerly instituted to discourage recruiting transfers and school jumping for athletic reasons (Trichka, 1995) or to institute waiver systems whereby students can seek an exemption to transfer rules. These rules generally mandated that a student sit out a proscribed period of time (anywhere from a month to a school year) after transferring from one school to another without a change of residence. These issues are complicated by the presence of private schools that compete against public schools for wins as well as for students. Some private schools are not members of state associations and therefore not subject to the same bylaws that regularly restrict recruitment efforts by public schools.

Drug Testing

As society looks increasingly to schools to fill social and parental, as well as academic, educatory roles, some schools have adopted drug testing to combat the use of illegal drugs by athletes. Generally, substances are banned because they illegally enhance performance and are potentially harmful to the student-athlete's health. Drug testing raises several legal concerns, including an athlete's constitutional rights to due process, equal protection, privacy, protection against illegal search and seizure, and self-incrimination. Public institutions are held to a greater scrutiny due to the necessary adherence to state and federal constitutional law requirements. In 1995 the U.S. Supreme Court determined that schools had a legal right to conduct random drug tests of athletes, as athletes have a diminished expectation of privacy, and that schools have a legitimate right to conduct such tests to curtail drug use (*Vernonia School District 47J v. Acton*, 1995). However, some state constitutions have stricter privacy laws than that of the U.S. Constitution, laws that may impact the applicability of drug testing programs.

Academic Eligibility

Since educators and adults have taken over the responsibility of administering school and youth sport, eligibility rules have been a major source of discussion and controversy. Eligibility rules are instituted to protect student-athletes and institutions and to promote and protect high school athletics. Documentation that confirms student-athlete eligibility ensures against using an ineligible player or a physically unfit student-athlete and guards against any potential associated lawsuits. A wide variance exists in school and state association rules regarding voluntary transfers, academic eligibility, behavior in and out of uniform, waivers for extra years of competition, and age limitations. Many state associations set statewide guidelines for schools and coaches to follow, while some associations allow individual schools and school districts to determine the elements of their interscholastic competition policies. Most state associations have set governing standards for minimum academic eligibility. Many have adopted the "no pass, no play" rule, which deems a student-athlete ineligible if he or she fails a course in a specified grading period. Some states, including Arkansas, California, Louisiana, New Mexico, and West Virginia, also require that students meet a minimum grade point average (GPA) requirement to be eligible to participate (Sawyer, 1995). Only Maryland, Minnesota, and Vermont have no set statewide academic standards, instead delegating that authority to local school districts (Wong & Covell, 1995b). But as Ness (1995) points out, administrators must formulate policies to avoid publicizing academic and conduct records that may violate the privacy of student-athletes.

SUMMARY

High school and youth sport has evolved from its modest beginning in New England private schools in the early 1800s to incorporate boys and girls of all ages in a multitude of sports and activities. These participation opportunities have expanded as administrators, coaches, and other associated personnel have developed the skills and expertise to deal with the challenges and issues that have accompanied this booming expansion. Although some contemporary issues have served to complicate today's high school and youth sport landscape, the need and demand for well-run sport programs have never been greater. As long as there are boys and girls, the need for play and competition will exist, as well as the need for professionals well trained to ensure that these needs will be met.

CASE STUDY: BALANCING THE HIGH SCHOOL ATHLETIC DEPARTMENT BUDGET

Derron Damone turned off his calculator and tossed it into the top drawer of his desk. It was one o'clock in the morning, and he had never felt so tired. He was at a loss. However he ran the numbers for the upcoming year's budget, he was still $17,000 short. The school board had been very explicit in their instructions: cut $30,000. Berwick Falls, Mount Hiram, Orinoka, Pittston, and Waterford, the five small, rural towns that comprised State School Administrative District (SSAD) #12, had been going through some tough economic times as of late. The recent economic upturn the rest of the nation had been enjoying hadn't reached these little towns yet, and the community residents were looking to reduce their tax burden by slashing the budgets of all local services, including police, fire, road repair, and schools. The school board members were looking to avoid a messy fight at the annual budget meeting, so they were pushing to present a reduced budget rather than go through a long rancorous evening of public outcry about overpaid teachers and undereducated students.

Derron had cut his budget last year by $10,000 after just such a meeting. He had been the athletic director at Green Valley District High School (GVDHS), the high school in SSAD #12, since 1988, and the financial situation had never been this bleak. He had started his career as an educator at GVDHS in 1981, teaching two sections of geometry and two sections of algebra and serving as head coach for varsity football and junior varsity girls' basketball. When he became the athletic director, his teaching load was reduced to one section of algebra, but he had to give up coaching football—it took too much time, and most people thought that football got the lion's share of funds, so he quit to avoid any perceptions of conflict of interest. He still coached girls' basketball because he liked the contact with students coaching gave him that administration did not. Derron liked having control over, and forming the educational direction of, the 15-sport athletic program, which was substantial for a school with an enrollment of only 450, grades 9 through 12. But it was times like these that made him long for his former duties. He knew how important athletics were to the students; in fact, involvement in the athletic program was the only thing that kept some kids going to class. He also knew that athletics were a focal point of community interest, one of the few things left that these dwindling towns could look to with pride. The last thing he wanted to do was cut programs.

Terri Fletcher, the school principal, had already told Derron that three full-time teaching positions had been cut, so it seemed unrealistic for him to plead with the school board to reinstate the athletic funds when the whole school was facing deep cuts. He also considered trying to drum up community support to raise money to make up the difference in the budget, or to come to the annual budget meeting and propose that money be allocated to keep the programs intact, but he doubted that money was available and wondered whether significant monetary community support really existed. Another option was to implement activity fees, which required students to pay to play—up to $200 per season, depending on the sport. Many local states had instituted these fees long ago, but his had not. Derron didn't want to be the first athletic director in the state to propose such fees, nor did he relish the idea of a student's not going out for sports if he or she couldn't afford the fee.

Derron looked at his watch again—it was now 1:30 AM. He had put off the decision long enough. He turned to his computer and pulled up the spreadsheet he had been working on. Coaches' salaries couldn't be touched, as they were negotiated on a pay scale as part of the teachers' collective bargaining agreement. He had already put a freeze on all purchases of new uniforms. Some new equipment purchases, like balls, medical supplies, and equipment reconditioning, were unavoidable, as were transportation costs and officials' fees. So it was clear; Derron had to cut sports to make his budget figure. He had two options: the outright cutting of three programs (wrestling and girls' and boys' tennis) or the cutting of all existing freshman and junior varsity programs. Neither choice made Derron comfortable. Wrestling served a different type of athlete in a low-participation season, and tennis was a sport from which many students could develop good lifetime fitness skills. But the frosh and JV programs gave a greater number of younger kids the chance to participate and improve, and they provided feeder teams for the more competitive varsity teams.

Derron tapped in the final figures, saved the changes, and turned off the monitor. "Damned if you do, damned if you don't," he muttered as he locked his office and walked down the hall toward the back parking lot.

Questions for Discussion

1. Which option should Derron choose—or is there another option?
2. Should the athletics department look to raise money? If so, how?
3. Should activities fees be instated? What are the potential implications?

RESOURCES

Amateur Athletic Union of the United States, Inc. (AAU)
The Walt Disney World Resort
P.O. Box 10000
Lake Buena Vista, FL 32830-6171
407-363-6170; fax: 407-363-6171

American Sport Education Program (ASEP)
Division of Human Kinetics Publishers
1607 North Market Street
Champaign, IL 61820
800-747-5698; fax: 217-351-2674
home page: http://www.humankinetics.com

National Association for Girls and Women in Sport
1900 Association Drive
Reston, VA 22091
703-476-3452; fax: 703-476-9527
NRGWS@AAPHERD.org

National Association of Sports Officials
2017 Lathrop Avenue
Racine, WI 53405
414-632-5448; fax: 414-632-5460

National Federation Interscholastic Coaches Association (NFICA)
11724 N.W. Plaza Circle
Kansas City, MO 64153
816-464-5400; fax: 816-464-5571

National Federation Interscholastic Officials Association (NFIOA)
11724 N.W. Plaza Circle
Kansas City, MO 64153
816-464-5400; fax: 816-464-5571

National Federation of State High School Associations
11724 N.W. Plaza Circle
Kansas City, MO 64153
816-464-5400; fax: 816-464-5571

National High School Athletic Coaches Association
One Purlieu Place, Suite 128
Winter Park, FL 32792
407-679-1414; fax: 407-679-6621

National Interscholastic Athletic Administrators Association (NIAAA)
11724 N.W. Plaza Circle
Kansas City, MO 64153
816-464-5400; fax: 816-464-5571

Each state, Canadian province, and U.S. territory also has a high school athletic and activity association.

REFERENCES

American Youth Soccer Organization. (1997). *Everyone Plays!* Hawthorne, CA: American Youth Soccer Organization.

Beran, J. (1979). *The story of six-player girls' basketball in Iowa.* Austin, TX: North American Society for Sport History Annual Conference.

Berryman, J.W. (1978, Spring). From the cradle to the playing field: America's emphasis on highly organized competitive sports for preadolescent boys. *Journal of Sport History, 5*(1), 112.

Brown v. Board of Education, Topeka, KS, 345 S.Ct. 294 (1954).

Cahn, S.K. (1994). *Coming on strong: Gender and sexuality in twentieth century women's sport.* New York: The Free Press.

The case for high school activities. (1997). Kansas City, MO: National Federation of State High School Associations.

Chambers, R.L. (1992, Spring). New administrative concerns: Hiring off-the-street coaches—staffing salvation or legal liability? *Journal of Legal Aspects of Sport, 2*(1), 83.

Cohen, A. (1995a, August). Leaving home. *Athletic Business, 19*(8), 16.

Cohen, A. (1995b, March). Running risks. *Athletic Business, 19*(3), 16.

Cohen, A. (1995c, January). Triple indemnity. *Athletic Business, 19*(1), 16.

Cotten, D.J. (1997). Exculpatory agreements or waivers. In D.J. Cotten & T.J. Wilde (Eds.), *Sport law for sport managers* (pp. 63–69). Dubuque, IA: Kendall/Hunt Publishers.

Davies, R.O. (1994). *America's obsession: Sports and society since 1945.* New York: Harcourt, Brace.

Dyreson, M. (1989). The emergence of consumer culture and the transformation of physical culture: American sport in the 1920s. *Journal of Sport History, 16*(5), 3.

Forsythe, L.L. (1950). *Athletics in Michigan high schools: The first hundred years.* New York: Prentice Hall.

Freid, G.B. (1996, Fall). Unsportsmanlike conduct: Strategies for reducing sexual assaults in youth sports. *Journal of Legal Aspects of Sport, 6*(3), 155.

Hardy, S. (1982). *How Boston played: Sport, recreation, and community.* Boston: Northeastern University Press.

Hums, M.A. (1996). Home schooled students' opportunities to participate in interscholastic sport: Legal issues and policy interpretations for secondary education. *Journal of Legal Aspects of Sport, 6*(3), 169.

Jensen, C.R. (1992). *Administrative management of physical education and athletic programs* (3rd ed.). Philadelphia: Lea & Febiger.

Kids' programs look for volunteers who are both competent and caring. (1997, January 12). *The Miami Herald,* p. 25A.

Ladd, T. (1978). *Sexual discrimination in youth sport: The case of Margaret Gisolo.* College Park, MD: North American Society for Sport History Annual Convention.

Luberto, D.K. (1994, May). The integration movement: Texas high school athletic and academic contests. *Journal of Sport and Social Issues, 18*(2), 151.

Michener, J.A. (1976). *Sports in America.* New York: Random House.

National Federation of State High School Associations. (1974, August 15). Guest editorial: High schools denounce Title IX. *The NCAA News, 11*(9), 2.

Ness, R.G. (1995, Spring). Family Education Rights and Privacy Act and athletics. *Journal of Legal Aspects of Sport, 5*(1), 45–51.

Noonkester, B.N. (1982). The American sportswoman from 1900–1920. In B.N. Noonkester (Ed.), *Her story in sport: A historical anthology of women in sport.* West Point, NY: Leisure Press.

O'Hanlon, T.P. (1982, Spring). School sports as social training: The case of athletics and the crisis of World War I. *Journal of Sport History, 9*(1), 5.

Pennsylvania swimmer, wrestler defy the odds. (1997, January 10). *USA Today,* p. 13C.

The Pop Warner story. (1997). Langorne, PA: Pop Warner Little Scholars, Inc.

Putney, C.W. (1993, Summer). Going upscale: The YMCA and postwar America, 1950–1990. *Journal of Sport History, 20*(2), 151.

Ruck, R. (1993). *Sandlot seasons: Sport in black Pittsburgh.* Urbana, IL: University of Illinois Press.

Sage, G.H. (1987). The social world of high school coaches: Multiple role demands and their consequences. *Sociology of Sport Journal, 4,* 213–225.

Sawyer, T.H. (1995, Fall). The new academic requirements for amateur sports: 'No pass, no play.' *Journal of Legal Aspects of Sport, 5*(2), 34–56.

Seefeldt, V. (1996). The future of youth sports in America. In F.L. Smoll & R.E. Smith (Eds.), *Children in sport: A biopsychosocial perspective* (pp. 423–435). Indianapolis: Brown & Benchmark.

Seymour, H. (1990). *Baseball: The people's game.* New York: Oxford University Press.

Swanson, R.A., & Spears, B. (1995). *Sport and physical education in the United States* (4th ed.). Dubuque, IA: Brown & Benchmark.

This is USA Hockey. (1997). Colorado Springs, CO: USA Hockey.

Trichka, R.E. (1995, Fall). State high school athletic associations' rules and regulations pertaining to transfers and recruiting. *Journal of Legal Aspects of Sport, 5*(2), 89–94.

Vernonia School District 47J v. Acton, 115 S. Ct. 2386 (1995).

Vincent, T. (1994). *The rise of American sport: Mudville's revenge.* Lincoln, NE: University of Nebraska Press.

Welch, P. (1978). *Interscholastic basketball: Bane of collegiate physical educators.* College Park, MD: North American Society for Sport History Annual Convention.

What is the National Federation? (1997). Kansas City, MO: National Federation of State High School Associations.

White, C. (1997, August 5). Massachusetts latest to make nonteaching coaches pass course. *USA Today, 15*(227), 13C.

Wilson, J. (1994). *Playing by the rules: Sport, society, and the state.* Detroit: Wayne State University Press.

Wong, G.M., & Covell, D. (1995a, March). Duty bound. *Athletic Business, 19*(3), 10.

Wong, G.M., & Covell, D. (1995b, May). Legal procedure. *Athletic Business, 19*(5), 10.

Wong, G.M., & Covell, D. (1995c, April). The rights thing. *Athletic Business, 19*(4), 10.

Wong, G.M., & Hums, M.A. (1996, April). Homecoming. *Athletic Business, 20*(4), 10.

CHAPTER 8

Collegiate Sport

Carol A. Barr

Key words: Intercollegiate Football Association, Intercollegiate Conference of Faculty Representatives, Big Ten Conference, Intercollegiate Athletic Association of the United States (IAAUS), National Collegiate Athletic Association (NCAA), Carnegie Reports of 1929, Knight Commission, Commission on Intercollegiate Athletics for Women (CIAW), Association for Intercollegiate Athletics for Women (AIAW), National Association of Intercollegiate Athletics (NAIA), National Junior College Athletic Association (NJCAA), Division I, Division II, Division III, one-school, one-vote, Restructuring, NCAA National Office, Legislative Services, Enforcement and Eligibility Appeals, institutional control, Division I-A, Division I-AA, member conferences, independent schools, student-athlete services, fund development, compliance, senior women's administrator (SWA), faculty athletics representative (FAR), Title IX, institutional support, NCAA Initial-Eligibility Clearinghouse

INTRODUCTION

Intercollegiate athletics is a major segment of the sport industry. It garners increasingly more television air time as network and cable companies increase coverage of sporting events, receives substantial coverage within the sport section of local and national newspapers, and attracts attention from corporations seeking potential sponsorship opportunities. The business aspect of collegiate athletics has grown immensely as administrators and coaches at all levels have become more involved in budgeting, finding revenue sources, controlling expense items, and participating in fund development activities. The administrative aspects of collegiate athletics have changed as well. With more rules and regulations to be followed, there is more paperwork in such areas as recruiting and academics.

166

These changes in the business and administrative aspects of collegiate athletics have created more job opportunities for sport managers. While the number of personnel and specialization of positions in collegiate athletic departments has increased, jobs can still be hard to come by as the popularity of working in this segment of the sport industry continues to rise.

The international aspect of this sport industry segment has grown tremendously through the participation of international student-athletes. Coaches are more aware of international "talent" when recruiting. The number of international student-athletes competing on U.S. college sports teams has grown from an average of 8.55 international student-athletes per institution in 1993 to 10.52 international student-athletes per institution in 1996 (NCAA Olympic Sports Liaison Committee, 1996). Athletic teams are taking overseas trips for practice and competitions at increasing rates. It is not unusual to stroll down a street in Munich, Germany or Montpellier, France, and see a Michigan basketball jersey or a Notre Dame football jersey with the number and name of the "big name" collegiate athlete at the time displayed in a store window.

HISTORY

On August 3, 1852, on Lake Winnepesaukee in New Hampshire, a crew race between Harvard and Yale was the very first intercollegiate athletic event in the United States (Dealy, 1990). What was unusual about this contest was that Harvard University is located in Cambridge, Massachusetts, and Yale University is located in New Haven, Connecticut, yet the crew race took place on a lake north of these two cities, in New Hampshire. Why? Because the first intercollegiate athletic contest was sponsored by the Boston, Concord & Montreal Railroad Company, which wanted to host the race in New Hampshire so both teams, their fans, and other spectators would have to ride the railroad to get to the event (Dealy, 1990). Thus, the first intercollegiate athletic contest involved sponsorship by a company external to sports that used the competition to enhance the company's business.

The next sport to hold intercollegiate competitions was baseball. The first collegiate baseball contest was held in 1859 between Amherst and Williams (Davenport, 1985), two of today's more athletically successful Division III institutions. In this game, Amherst defeated Williams by the lopsided score of 73–32 (Rader, 1990). On November 6, 1869, the first intercollegiate football game was held between Rutgers and Princeton (Davenport, 1985). This "football" contest was far from the game of football known today. The competitors were allowed to kick and dribble the ball, similar to soccer, with Rutgers "out-dribbling" their opponents and winning the game six goals to four (Rader, 1990). By the early 1900s, football on college campuses had become immensely popular, receiving a tremendous amount of attention from the students, alumni, and collegiate administrators.

The initial collegiate athletic contests taking place during the 1800s were student-run events. Students organized the practices and corresponded with their peers at other institutions to arrange competitions. There were no coaches or athletic administrators assisting with the organization of collegiate athletics. The Ivy League schools became the "power" schools in athletic competition, and football became the premier sport. Fierce rivalries developed, attracting numerous spectators. Thus, collegiate athletics evolved from games being played for student enjoyment and participation to fierce competitions involving bragging rights for individual institutions. Colleges and universities began to realize that these intercollegiate competitions had grown in popularity and prestige and thus could bring increased publicity, student applications, and alumni donations.

As the pressure to win increased, the students began to realize they needed external help. Thus, the first "coach" was hired in 1864 by the Yale crew team to help it win, especially against its rival, Harvard University. This coach, William Wood, a physical therapist by trade, introduced a rigorous training program as well as a training table (Dealy, 1990). College and university administrators also began to take a closer look at intercollegiate athletics competitions. The predominant theme at the time was still nonacceptance of these activities within the educational sphere of the institution. With no governing organization and virtually nonexistent playing and eligibility rules, mayhem often resulted. Once again the students took charge, especially in football, forming the **Intercollegiate Football Association** in 1876. This association was made up of students from Harvard, Yale, Princeton, and Columbia who agreed on consistent playing and eligibility rules (Dealy, 1990). Nevertheless, football continued to be dangerous, with many injuries occurring at virtually every contest, and sometimes even deaths.

The dangerous nature of football pushed faculty and administrators to get involved in governing intercollegiate athletics. In 1881, Princeton University became the first college to form a faculty athletics committee (Dealy, 1990). This faculty athletics committee was formed to review football. The committee's choices were to either make football safer to play or ban the sport all together. In 1887, Harvard's Board of Overseers instructed the Harvard Faculty Athletics Committee to ban football. However, aided by many influential alumni, the Faculty Athletics Committee chose to keep the game intact (Dealy, 1990). In 1895, the **Intercollegiate Conference of Faculty Representatives**, better known as the **Big Ten Conference**, was formed to create student eligibility rules (Davenport, 1985). Nevertheless, the number of injuries and deaths occurring in football continued to increase, and it was evident that more legislative action was needed.

In 1905 during a football game involving Union College and New York University, Harold Moore, a halfback for Union College, was crushed to death.

Moore was just one of 18 football players who died that year. An additional 149 serious injuries occurred as well (Yaeger, 1991). The chancellor of New York University, Henry Mitchell MacCracken, witnessed this incident and took it upon himself to do something about it. MacCracken sent a letter of invitation to presidents of other schools to join him for a meeting to discuss the reform or abolition of football. In December of 1905, 13 presidents met and declared their intent to reform the game of football. When this group met three weeks later, 62 colleges and universities sent representatives. This group formed the **Intercollegiate Athletic Association of the United States (IAAUS)** to formulate rules making football safer and more exciting to play. Seven years later, in 1912, this group took the name **National Collegiate Athletic Association (NCAA)** (Yaeger, 1991).

Finally, in the 1920s, college and university administrators began recognizing intercollegiate athletics as a part of higher education and placed athletics under the purview of the physical education department (Davenport, 1985). Coaches were given academic appointments within the physical education department, and schools began to provide institutional funding for athletics.

The **Carnegie Reports of 1929** painted a bleak picture of intercollegiate athletics, identifying many academic abuses, recruiting abuses, payments to student-athletes, and commercialization of athletics. The Carnegie Foundation visited 112 colleges and universities. One of the disturbing findings from this study was that although the NCAA "recommended against" both recruiting and subsidization of student-athletes, these practices were widespread among colleges and universities (Lawrence, 1987). The Carnegie Reports stated that the responsibility for control over collegiate athletics rested with the president of the college or university and with the faculty (Savage, 1929). The NCAA was pressured to change from an organization responsible for developing playing rules used in competitions to an organization that would oversee academic standards for student-athletes, monitor recruiting activities of coaches and administrators, and establish principles governing amateurism, thus alleviating the paying of student-athletes by alumni and booster groups (Lawrence, 1987).

Intercollegiate athletics experienced a number of peaks and valleys over the next 60 or so years as budgetary constraints during certain periods, such as the Great Depression and World War II, limited expenditures and growth among athletic departments and sport programs. In looking at the history of intercollegiate athletics, though, the major trends during these years were increased spectator appeal, commercialism, media coverage, alumni involvement, and funding. As these changes occurred, the majority of intercollegiate athletic departments moved from a unit within the physical education department to a recognized, funded department on campus.

Increased commercialism and the potential for monetary gain in collegiate athletics led to increased pressure on coaches to win. As a result, collegiate athletics experienced various problems with rule violations and academic abuses involving student-athletes. As these abuses increased, the public began to perceive that the integrity of higher education was being threatened. In 1989, pollster Louis Harris found that 78% of Americans thought collegiate athletics were out of hand. This same poll found that nearly two-thirds of Americans believed that state or national legislation was needed to control college sports (Knight Foundation, 1993). In response, on October 19, 1989, the Trustees of the Knight Foundation created the **Knight Commission**, directing it to propose a reform agenda for intercollegiate athletics (Knight Foundation, 1991). The Knight Commission was composed of university presidents, CEOs and presidents from corporations, and a congressional representative. The reform agenda recommended by the Knight Commission played a major role in supporting legislation to alleviate improper activities and emphasized institutional control in an attempt to restore the integrity of collegiate sports. The Knight Commission's work and recommendations prompted the NCAA membership to pass numerous rules and regulations regarding recruiting activities, academic standards, and financial practices.

Women in Intercollegiate Athletics

Initially, intercollegiate sport competitions were run *by* men *for* men. Sports were viewed as male-oriented activities, and women's sport participation was relegated to physical education classes. Prevailing social attitudes mandated that women should not perspire and should not be physically active, so as not to injure themselves. Women also had dress codes that limited the type of activities in which they could physically participate. The first women's intercollegiate sport contest was a basketball game between the University of California, Berkeley, and Stanford University in 1896 (Hult, 1994). Senda Berenson of Smith College introduced basketball to collegiate women in 1892, but she first made sure that appropriate modifications were made to the game developed by James Naismith to make it more suitable for women (Paul, 1993). According to Berenson, "the selfish display of a star by dribbling and playing the entire court, and roughhousing by snatching the ball could not be tolerated" (Hult, 1994, p. 86).

The predominant theme of women's involvement in athletics was participation. Women physical educators, who controlled women's athletics from the 1890s to 1920s, believed that all girls and women, and not just a few outstanding athletes, should experience the joy of sport. Playdays, or sportsdays, were the norm from the 1920s until the 1960s (Hult, 1994). By 1960, more positive attitudes toward women's competition in sport were set in motion. No governance organization for women similar to the NCAA's all-encompassing control over the men existed until the creation of the **Commission on Intercollegiate Athletics for Women (CIAW)** in 1966, the forerunner of the **Association for Intercollegiate Athletics**

for Women (AIAW), which was established in 1971 (Acosta and Carpenter, 1985).

The AIAW endorsed an alternative athletic model for women, emphasizing the educational needs of students and rejecting the commercialized men's model (Hult, 1994). The AIAW and NCAA soon became engaged in a power struggle over the governance of women's collegiate athletics. In 1981, the NCAA membership voted to add championships for women in Division I. By passing this legislation, the NCAA took its first step toward controlling women's collegiate athletics. The NCAA convinced women's athletic programs to vote to join the NCAA by offering to:

- subsidize team expenses for national championships
- not charge additional membership dues for the women's program
- allow women to use the same financial aid, eligibility, and recruitment rules as men
- provide more television coverage of women's championships (Hult, 1994)

Colleges and universities, provided with these incentives from the NCAA, began to switch from AIAW membership for their women's teams to full NCAA membership. The AIAW immediately experienced a 20% decrease in membership, a 32% drop in championship participation in all divisions, and a 48% drop in Division I championship participation. In the fall of 1981, NBC notified the AIAW that it would not televise any AIAW championships and would not pay the monies due under its contract (a substantial percentage of the AIAW budget). Consequently, in 1982, the AIAW Executive Board voted to dissolve the association (Morrison, 1993). The AIAW filed a lawsuit against the NCAA, *Association for Intercollegiate Athletics for Women v. National Collegiate Athletic Association*, 558 F. Supp. 487 (D.D.C. 1983), claiming that the NCAA interfered with its commercial relationship with NBC and exhibited monopolistic practices in violation of antitrust laws. The court found that the AIAW could not support its monopoly claim, effectively ending the AIAW's existence.

ORGANIZATIONAL STRUCTURE AND GOVERNANCE

The NCAA

The primary rule-making body for college athletics in the United States is the NCAA. Other college athletic organizations include the **National Association of Intercollegiate Athletics (NAIA)**, founded in 1940 and having approximately 280 member institutions, and the **National Junior College Athletic Association**

(NJCAA), founded in 1937 and having approximately 550 member institutions (*1997 Sports Market Place*). The NCAA is a voluntary association with more than 1,000 institutions, conferences, organizations, and individual members. All collegiate athletics teams, conferences, coaches, administrators, and athletes participating in NCAA-sponsored sports must abide by its rules. The basic purpose of the NCAA as dictated in its constitution is to "maintain intercollegiate athletics as an integral part of the educational program and the athlete as an integral part of the student body and, by so doing, retain a clear line of demarcation between intercollegiate athletics and professional sports" (Article 1.3.1, *1996–97 NCAA Manual*, p. 1). Important to this basic purpose are the cornerstones of the NCAA's philosophy that college athletics are amateur competitions and athletics are an important component of the institution's educational mission.

The NCAA has undergone organizational changes throughout its history in an attempt to improve the efficiency of its service to member institutions. In 1956, the NCAA split its membership into a University Division, for larger schools, and a College Division, for smaller schools, in an effort to address competitive inequities. In 1973, the current three-division system, made up of **Division I, Division II,** and **Division III,** was created to increase the flexibility of the NCAA in addressing the needs and interests of schools of varying size ("Study: Typical I-A Program," 1996). This NCAA organizational structure involved all member schools and conferences voting on legislation once every year at the NCAA Annual Convention. Every member school and conference had one vote assigned to the institution's president or CEO, a structure called "**one-school, one-vote.**" The NCAA established support groups and committees made up of member school presidents, athletic directors, and NCAA staff members to handle business affairs and policy between conventions (see Figure 8–1).

In 1995, the NCAA recognized that Divisions I, II, and III still faced "issues and needs unique to its member institutions," leading the NCAA to pass Proposal 7, "**Restructuring,**" at the 1996 NCAA Convention (Crowley, 1995). The restructuring plan, which gives the NCAA divisions more responsibility for conduct within their division, took effect in August 1997. Restructuring includes the elimination of the "one-school, one-vote" structure. The annual convention was replaced by division-specific mini-conventions, or meetings. In addition, each division has an overseeing body called either the Board of Directors or Presidents Council, as well as a Management Council made up of presidents, CEOs, and athletic directors from member schools who meet and dictate policy and legislation within that division (see Figure 8–2). The NCAA Executive Committee, consisting of representatives from each division as well as the NCAA Executive Director and chairs of each divisional Management Council, oversees the Presidential Boards and Management Councils for each division.

The unique governance of the NCAA involves the membership's overseeing legislation regarding the conduct of intercollegiate athletics. Member institutions

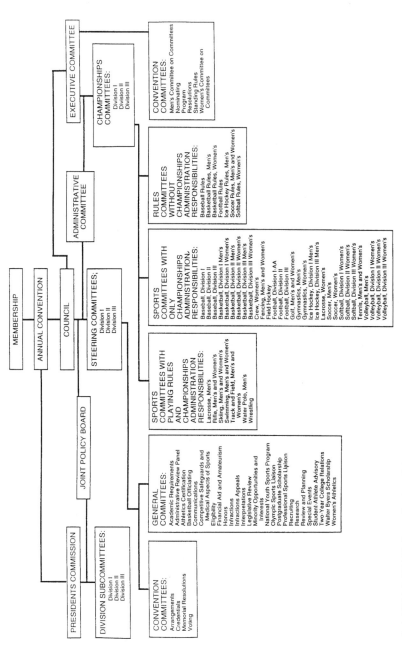

Figure 8–1 NCAA "Old" Organizational Structure. *Source: 1996–97 NCAA Manual.* Overland Park, KS: National Collegiate Athletic Association, p. 41.

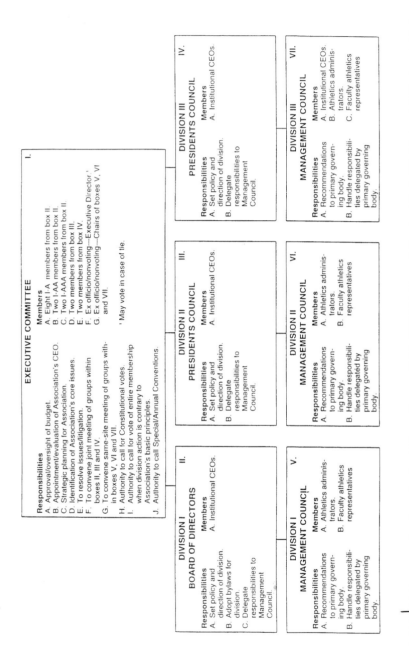

Figure 8–2 NCAA Restructuring Organizational Chart. *Source: 1996–97 NCAA Manual.* Overland Park, KS: National Collegiate Athletic Association, p. 42.

and conferences vote on proposed legislation, thus dictating the rules they need to follow. The **NCAA National Office**, located in Overland Park, Kansas, merely enforces the rules the membership passes. The office is scheduled to move to Indianapolis by the year 2000 ("Indianapolis Lands," 1997). The NCAA National Office currently employs approximately 250 people who administer the policies, decisions, and legislation passed by the membership, as well as providing administrative services to all NCAA committees, member institutions, and conferences. The NCAA National Office is organized into departments, including administration, business, championships, communications, compliance, enforcement, educational resources, publishing, legislative services, and visitors center/special projects.

Two of the more prominent departments within the NCAA administrative structure are **Legislative Services** and **Enforcement and Eligibility Appeals**. These two departments are pivotal because they deal with interpreting and enforcing NCAA rules and regulations. The Legislative Services department has 18 legislative assistants responsible for answering inquiries from member institutions and conferences regarding the interpretation of particular rules (Rushin, 1997). The majority of legislative assistants have a legal background. A member school or conference office can contact the Legislative Services department and speak to a legislative assistant, who provides an interpretation regarding a particular rule. The Enforcement and Eligibility Appeals department staff members are responsible for investigating possible rule violations by member institutions and restoring eligibility to student-athletes who may have been involved in possible NCAA rules violations. It is important to note that although the NCAA National Office staff members collect information and conduct investigations on possible rule violations, the matter still goes before the Committee on Infractions, a committee of peers (representatives of member institutions), which determines responsibility and assesses penalties.

Institutions are taking a more proactive approach regarding potential violations by conducting their own investigations rather than waiting for the NCAA enforcement staff members to perform an investigation and uncover the facts. In 1996, the NCAA estimated that of 1,200 cases involving secondary or minor violations, 90% were self-reported by the institution. Schools also initiate 30% to 40% of the 15 to 20 cases that arise during the year that involve major violations (Wieberg, 1996). This proactive approach is encouraged by the NCAA through the endorsement of **institutional control**, the concept that the individual college or university is responsible for conduct within its athletic department. Through this principle of institutional control the institution's administrators must oversee and monitor the activities of the athletic department, making sure that NCAA and conference rules and regulations are being followed.

Divisions I, II, and III

As the latest NCAA restructuring calls for divisions to take more responsibility and control over their activities, it is important to look at similarities and differences among these divisions. A few of the more prominent differences among divisions are highlighted in this section. The sport management student interested in pursuing a career in intercollegiate coaching or athletic administration should be knowledgeable about the differences in legislation and philosophies among the divisions in order to choose a career within the division most suited to his or her interests. Students should be aware that each institution has its own philosophy regarding the structure and governance of its athletic department. This section concentrates on the differences between Division I and Division III philosophies as these two divisions represent the two extremes. Division II institutions can be categorized as a hybrid of the other two, with some Division II institutions following a Division I philosophy and some following a Division III philosophy. Keep in mind, though, that some Division III institutions, although not offering any athletic scholarships, can be described as following a nationally competitive, revenue-producing philosophy that is more in line with a Division I philosophy. Thus, generalizations regarding divisions are not applicable to all institutions within that division. The student should thoroughly research an athletic department to determine the philosophy that the school and administration embrace.

Division I of the NCAA is further divided into two subdivisions: **Division I-A** is the category for institutions that are the somewhat larger football-playing schools in Division I, and **Division I-AA** is the category for institutions playing football at the next level down from I-A. In order to be a member of the NCAA within Division I, II, or III, an institution must sponsor a minimum number of sport programs and is held to certain restrictions in terms of athletic scholarship funding to student-athletes. Additional membership requirements include football stadium size, attendance at home football contests, and scheduling of competitions against other division member schools, to name a few. Each division also has its own philosophy statement providing operational guidelines to the member institutions within that division (see Figure 8–3).

It is important to note some of the differences that exist among the divisions. Division I athletic departments are usually larger in terms of number of sport programs sponsored, number of coaches, and number of administrators. Division I athletic departments also have larger budgets due to the number of athletic scholarships allowed, the operational budgets needed for the larger number of sport programs sponsored, and the salary costs associated with the larger number of coaches and administrators. The philosophy statements of the divisions further define some differences that exist. For example, Division I institutions (1) strive for regional and national prominence, (2) sponsor at the highest feasible level the spectator-oriented, income-producing sports of football and basketball, and (3)

DIVISION I PHILOSOPHY STATEMENT

In addition to the purposes and fundamental policy of the National Collegiate Athletic Association, as set forth in Constitution 1, members of Division I support the following principles in the belief that these statements assist in defining the nature and purposes of the division. These statements are not binding on member institutions but serve as a guide for the preparation of legislation by the division and for planning and implementation of programs by institutions and conferences. A member of Division I:

(a) Subscribes to high standards of academic quality, as well as breadth of academic opportunity;

(b) Strives in its athletics program for regional and national excellence and prominence. Accordingly, its recruitment of student-athletes and its emphasis on and support of its athletics program are, in most cases, regional and national in scope;

(c) Recognizes the dual objective in its athletics program of serving both the university or college community (participants, student body, faculty-staff, alumni) and the general public (community, area, state, nation);

(d) Believes in offering extensive opportunities for participation in varsity intercollegiate athletics for both men and women;

(e) Sponsors at the highest feasible level of intercollegiate competition one or both of the traditional spectator-oriented, income-producing sports of football and basketball. In doing so, members of Division I recognize the differences in institutional objectives in support of football; therefore, the division provides competition in that sport in Division I-A and Division I-AA;

(f) Believes in scheduling its athletics contests primarily with other members of Division I, especially in the emphasized, spectator-oriented sports, as a reflection of its goal of maintaining an appropriate competitive level in its sports program;

(g) Strives to finance its athletics program insofar as possible from revenues generated by the program itself. All funds supporting athletics should be controlled by the institution; and

(h) Understands, respects, and supports the programs and philosophies of other divisions. Occasionally, institutions from other divisions or athletics associations will seek membership in Division I. In such cases, the applicants should be required to meet, over a period of time, prescribed criteria for Division I membership in order to assure that such institutions agree and comply with the principles and program objectives embodied in this statement.

DIVISION II PHILOSOPHY STATEMENT

In addition to the purposes and fundamental policy of the National Collegiate Athletic Association, as set forth in Constitution 1, members of Division II believe that a well-conducted intercollegiate athletics progam, based on sound educational principles and practices, is a proper part of the educational mission of a university or college and that the educational welfare of the participating student-athlete is of primary concern.

continues

Figure 8–3 continued

Members of Division II support the following principles in the belief that these objectives assist in defining the division and the possible differences between it and other divisions of the Association. This statement is not binding on member institutions but shall serve as a guide for the preparation of legislation by the division and for planning and implementation of programs by institutions and conferences. A member of Division II:

(a) Believes in offering a maximum amount of intercollegiate athletics participation to as many of its students as possible, whether or not these students are athletically recruited or financially assisted;

(b) Believes in striving for broad participation and competitive excellence, encouraging sportsmanship, and developing positive societal attitudes in all of its athletics endeavors;

(c) Believes in scheduling the majority of its athletics competition with other members of Division II, insofar as geographical location and traditional or conference scheduling patterns permit;

(d) Recognizes the dual objectives of its athletics program of serving both the campus (participants, student body, faculty-staff) and the general public (community, area, state);

(e) Believes in permitting athletically related financial aid for its student-athletes, but on a more modest basis than that permitted in Division I; and

(f) Believes that all members of Division II, including those institutions aspiring to membership in some other division or those unable to subscribe to all of the aspects of the Division II philosophy, should commit themselves to that philosophy and to the regulations and programs of Division II.

DIVISION III PHILOSOPHY STATEMENT

Colleges and universities in Division III place highest priority on the overall quality of the educational experience and on the successful completion of all students' academic programs. They seek to establish and maintain an environment in which a student-athlete's athletics activities are conducted as an integral part of the student-athlete's educational experience. They also seek to establish and maintain an environment that values cultural diversity and gender equity among their student-athletes and athletics staff. *(Revised: 1/10/95)*

To achieve this end, Division III institutions:

(a) Place special importance on the impact of athletics on the participants rather than on the spectators and place greater emphasis on the internal constituency (students, alumni, institutional personnel) than on the general public and its entertainment needs.

(b) Award no athletically related financial aid to any student;

(c) Encourage the development of sportsmanship and positive social attitudes in all constituents, including student-athletes, coaches, administrative personnel, and spectators;

continues

Figure 8–3 continued

(d) Encourage participation by maximizing the number and variety of athletics opportunities for their students;

(e) Assure that the actions of coaches and administrators exhibit fairness, openness, and honesty in their relationships with student-athletes;

(f) Assure that athletics participants are not treated differently from other members of the student body;

(g) Assure that athletics programs support the institution's educational mission by financing, staffing, and controlling the programs through the same general procedures as other departments of the institution;

(h) Provide equitable athletics opportunities for males and females and give equal emphasis to men's and women's sports;

(i) Give primary emphasis to regional in-season competition and conference championships; and

(j) Support student-athletes in their efforts to reach high levels of athletics performance, which may include opportunities for participation in national championships, by providing all teams with adequate facilities, competent coaching and appropriate competitive opportunities.

The purpose of the NCAA is to assist its members in developing the basis for consistent, equitable competition while minimizing infringement on the freedom of individual institutions to determine their own special objectives and programs. The above statement articulates principles that represent a commitment to Division III membership and shall serve as a guide for the preparation of legislation by the division and for planning and implementation of programs by institutions and conferences.

Figure 8–3 NCAA Division Philosophy Statements. *Source: 1996–1997 NCAA Manual.* Overland Park, KS: National Collegiate Athletic Association, pp. 421, 430, 434.

strive to finance their athletics program from revenues generated by the program itself. Division II and, to a greater extent, Division III institutions (1) strive and encourage broad participation, (2) serve the participants rather than the spectators or general public, and (3) do not mention revenue at all within their philosophy statements.

Conferences

The organizational structure of intercollegiate athletics also involves **member conferences** of the NCAA. Member conferences must have a minimum of six member institutions within a single division in order to be recognized as a voting member conference of the NCAA (National Collegiate Athletic Association, *1996–97 NCAA Manual*, Bylaw 3.3.2.2.2.1). Conferences provide many benefits and services to their member institutions. For example, conferences run seminars regarding NCAA rules and regulations in an effort to better educate member schools' coaches and administrators. Many conferences also have specific staff members identified to assist member institutions with questions regarding NCAA rules. Thus, the member school can contact the conference office for a rule interpretation rather than contacting the NCAA National Office. The conference staff member is in contact with the NCAA National Office through usage of a computer database that assists the conference with NCAA rule questions.

Conferences also have legislative power over their member institutions in the running of championship events and the formulation of conference rules and regulations. Conferences sponsor championships in sports sponsored by the member institutions within the conference. The conference member institutions vote on the conference guidelines to determine the organization of these conference championships. Member institutions of a particular conference must adhere to conference rules in addition to NCAA rules. It is important to note, though, that while a conference rule can never be less restrictive than an NCAA rule, many conferences maintain additional rules that hold member institutions to stricter standards. For example, the Ivy League is a Division I NCAA member conference, but it prohibits its member institutions from providing athletic scholarships to student-athletes. Therefore, the Ivy League schools, while competing against other Division I schools that allow athletic scholarships, do not allow their athletic departments to award athletic scholarships.

Conference realignment is one of the current issues affecting collegiate athletic departments. In 1997, there were 32 Division I conferences and only three **independent schools**, that is, schools with no conference affiliation (NCAA Membership Services, personal communication, August 11, 1997). Some of the reasons for a school's wanting to join a conference or change conference affiliation are (1) exposure from television contracts with existing conferences, (2) potential for more revenue from television and corporate sponsorships through conference revenue sharing, (3) the difficulty independent schools were experiencing in scheduling games and generating revenue, and (4) the ability of a conference to hold a championship game in football, which can generate millions of dollars in revenue for the conference schools if the conference possesses at least 12 member institutions.

Probably the biggest conference realignment that has taken place to date involved the demise of the 80-year-old Southwest Conference. In 1990, the Southwest Conference (SWC) comprised nine member schools (Mott, 1994). In August 1990, the University of Arkansas accepted a bid to leave the Southwest Conference and join the Southeast Conference (SEC). The University stated that the SEC gave them bigger crowds in revenue-producing sports and gave them more national exposure ("Broyles Hopes," 1990). In 1994, four Southwest Conference schools, Texas, Texas A&M, Baylor, and Texas Tech, announced they were leaving to join the Big Eight Conference (Mott, 1994). In April 1994, three other SWC schools, Rice, Texas Christian University, and Southern Methodist University, joined the Western Athletic Conference (WAC) ("Western Athletic," 1994). Thus, the Southwest Conference had lost all of its member schools except Houston. This led to the demise of the Southwest Conference as it dropped below the six-member school minimum required by the NCAA for recognition as a member conference. Houston, the sole remaining SWC school, joined Conference USA in 1995.

CAREER OPPORTUNITIES

For many decades, the traditional route followed for a career in collegiate athletics was to be an athlete, then a coach, and then an athletic administrator. It was a very closed system, with college athletic administrators selecting from among their own who would coach teams and then move into administrative positions. Much has changed with this apprentice system, although within the collegiate coaching and administrative ranks there is still a predominance of athletic and coaching experience. A study of Division I and Division III athletic directors (Barr, 1992) found that 86% of the athletic directors in both divisions had been athletes at the collegiate level, while 78% in Division I and 90% in Division III had collegiate coaching experience. Yet, when asked in the hiring process whether more emphasis is placed on the athletic participation and coaching experience or the educational background of the applicant, the athletic directors in both Division I and Division III emphasized the importance of educational background over athletic participation and coaching experience (Barr, 1992).

Differences exist among the divisions in terms of coaching and administrative duties and responsibilities. When moving from the smaller Division III institutions to the larger Division I-A institutions, the responsibilities and profiles of coaches within these athletic departments change. At the smaller Division III institutions the coaches are usually part-time, or if full-time they serve as coach to numerous sport programs. These coaches may also hold an academic appointment within a department or teach activities classes. The Division III coach's budget on average is smaller than that of a Division I coach because most competition is regional and recruiting is not as extensive. There are no athletic scholarships allowed in Division III. Division III athletic directors may sometimes also coach or hold an academic appointment. Depending on the size of the athletic department, the Division III athletic director may wear many hats, acting as manager of the athletic department and coaches, business manager of the athletic department budget, media relations staff person, fund-raiser, and compliance officer; some Division III athletic directors have one or two assistant athletic directors providing administrative help in these various areas.

Athletic department budgets at the Division I, and especially I-A, level are in the millions of dollars. It is common at this level to find coaches employed full-time coaching one sport program. It is also common at this level to find assistant coaches, in at least the higher-profile sport programs, employed full-time. Athletic scholarships are allowed, increasing the importance of recruiting, travel, and other activities geared toward signing the blue-chip athlete. Individual sport program budgets are larger, providing more resources for recruiting and competitive travel opportunities. Division I athletic departments are larger with more numerous and specialized staff positions. The athletic director is usually seen as the figurehead who attends public relations and fund-raising events, participates in negotiating television contracts, and looks out for the interests of the athletic department in the development of institutional policies and financial affairs. Under the athletic director are associate and assistant athletic director positions functioning in specialized areas such as business manager, media relations director, ticket sales manager, fund development coordinator, sport programs administrator, facilities and events coordinator, academic affairs director, or compliance coordinator. Depending on the student's interest, various educational course work will be helpful in preparing for a position in this area. For example, business courses will prepare the student for positions working within the business aspect of an athletic department, communications courses will prepare the student for a position working with public relations and the media, educational counseling course work is beneficial for positions within academic affairs, and a legal background will be helpful to administrators overseeing the compliance area.

Areas of growth where increased attention is being directed within collegiate athletic departments are student-athlete services, fund development, and compliance. **Student-athlete services** addresses the academic concerns and welfare of student-athletes, overseeing such areas as academic advising, tutoring, and counseling. **Fund development** has increased in importance as athletic departments seek new ways to increase revenues. Fund development coordinators oversee alumni donations to the athletic department and also oversee fund-raising events. **Compliance** is the term used to describe adherence to NCAA and conference rules and regulations. The compliance coordinator works closely with the coaches to make sure they are knowledgeable about NCAA and conference rules. The compliance coordinator also oversees the initial and continuing eligibility of the student-athletes, as well as being directly involved in preventing or investigating any violations that take place within the athletic department.

Two other positions important to the collegiate athletic department are the **senior women's administrator (SWA)** and the **faculty athletics representative (FAR)**. The senior women's administrator is the highest-ranking female administrator involved with the conduct of an NCAA member institution's intercollegiate athletics program (*1996–97 NCAA Manual*, Bylaw 4.02.4). The faculty athletics representative is a member of an institution's faculty or administrative staff who is designated to represent the institution and its faculty in the institution's relationships with the NCAA and its conference (*1996–97 NCAA Manual*, Bylaw 4.02.2).

The ever-changing world of collegiate athletics is demanding new skills of the men and women administrating and directing these programs. Marketing expertise, financial knowledge, and effective human resource talents have become the desired skills for athletic directors (Huggins, 1996). This range of talents means that emphasis has switched from hiring the college athletic star or successful coach to hiring the person who has educational training and experience in marketing, financial, managerial, and even legal areas. An informal study of Division I-A college presidents in 1996 found that presidents look for the following characteristics when hiring athletic directors:

- strategic thinking—the ability to develop, evaluate, and implement short- and long-term plans
- knowledge of and sensitivity to gender-equity issues and regulatory procedures
- ability to manage complex financial issues and budgets
- capability to direct a large and diverse staff, including coaches
- marketing expertise
- strong public speaking, writing, and media relations skills
- creativity and problem-solving abilities
- effective human resource talents for dealing with parents, students, faculty, alumni, booster groups, and sponsors
- loyalty to the college president (Huggins, 1996)

For the student interested in pursuing a career in collegiate athletic administration it is important to keep these qualifications in mind and prepare for this position by taking appropriate academic course work and obtaining work experience in these areas.

Although only 24 out of 107 Division I-A athletic directors since 1990 have retained their jobs, a turnover rate of more than 80% (Huggins, 1996), the availability of collegiate athletic director positions should not be interpreted as overwhelming. The average age of athletic directors within both Division I and Division III was found to be between 46 and 55 years old (Barr, 1992). This statistic reveals that people "pay their dues," working their way up the ranks before becoming an athletic director. And the fact that there are 305 Division I institutions, 246 Division II institutions, and 351 Division III institutions (NCAA Membership Services, 1997) also points out that the number of athletic director positions is not immense, leading to great competition to obtain these positions.

For women and minorities the statistics are even worse, as is discussed later in this chapter in the section called Minority Hiring and Pay Equity.

CURRENT ISSUES

As is true for the other segments of the sport industry addressed throughout this text, there are current issues affecting collegiate athletics. Coaches and athletic administrators must be aware of the financial, legal, managerial, and ethical impact of these issues.

Title IX/Gender Equity

Perhaps no greater issue has affected collegiate athletic departments in the 1990s than **Title IX** or gender equity. As discussed in Chapter 5, Legal Principles Applied to Sport Management, Title IX is a federal law passed in 1972 that gained its enforcement power among college athletic departments with the passage of the 1988 Civil Rights Restoration Act. Title IX prohibits sex discrimination in any educational activity or program receiving federal financial assistance. The enforcement of Title IX, therefore, includes collegiate athletic departments. In 1991, the NCAA released the results of a gender-equity study that found that although the undergraduate enrollment on college campuses was roughly 50% male and 50% female, collegiate athletic departments on average were made up of 70% male and 30% female student-athletes. In addition, this NCAA study found that the male student-athletes were receiving 70% of the athletic scholarship money, 77% of the operational budget, and 83% of the recruiting dollars available (NCAA Gender Equity Task Force, 1991). In response to statistics such as these, female student-athletes, coaches, and administrators have started a movement for equal treatment, resulting in increased numbers of sex discrimination lawsuits, with the courts often ruling in favor of the female student-athletes.

Collegiate athletic administrators have started to realize that Title IX is being enforced and they are required to provide equity within their athletic departments. The struggle athletic administrators are faced with is how to comply with Title IX given institutional financial limitations. In order to bring male and female participation numbers closer, numerous institutions are choosing to eliminate sport programs for men, thereby reducing the participation and funding numbers on the men's side. Another method selected by some institutions is capping roster sizes for men's teams, thus keeping the men's numbers in check while trying to increase the women's numbers. A third, and most appropriate, option under Title IX is increasing participation and funding opportunities for the female student-athletes. Of course, in selecting this option, the athletic administrator must be able to come up with the funds necessary to add sport programs, hire new coaches, and provide uniforms for the new sport programs.

The University of Massachusetts, Amherst, is one example of an institution that selected this option in complying with Title IX. After performing a Title IX Self-Review of its athletic department, the university found that in order to comply with Title IX it was necessary to add two women's sport programs, increase athletic scholarships to female student-athletes, increase coaches' salaries and operational budgets for the women's sport teams, and upgrade athletic facilities. To generate the funds necessary to implement these Title IX changes it took a commitment by the university administration, which increased **institutional support** (the college or university's general operating funds provided to departments on campus for their operations) to the athletic department; a commitment by the state legislature, which passed a bill providing funding to the state institutions to be used for Title IX purposes; and an increase in athletic fund development activities.

A study by *The Chronicle of Higher Education* in 1995–1996 found that undergraduate enrollment on college campuses was 53% women, yet athletic departments were made up of 63% male student-athletes and 37% female student-athletes, with the women student-athletes receiving 38% of athletic scholarship funding (Naughton, 1997c). While these recent statistics do indicate improvements with Title IX/Gender Equity, there is still much work to be done. Collegiate athletic administrators must continue to address this issue and develop strategies within their athletic departments to comply with Title IX and achieve gender equity.

Minority Hiring and Pay Equity

Minority hiring and pay equity have long been issues of concern and debate within collegiate athletics. In 1993–1994, the NCAA's Minority Opportunity and Interests Committee found that African-Americans accounted for fewer than 10% of athletics directors and 8% of head coaches, and when predominantly African-American institutions were eliminated from the study, the results dropped to 4% representation in both categories (Wieberg, 1994). In 1996, women represented 17 of the 305 Division I athletic director positions, with only 6 of these 17 female athletic directors at Division I-A institutions (Blauvelt, 1996). In Division II, 36 of the 246 athletic directors were female, and in Division III 84 of the 351 athletic directors were female (NCAA Membership Services, 1997). A study by *The Chronicle of Higher Education* found that universities pay substantially higher salaries to the head coaches of men's athletics teams than to the head coaches of women's teams. The study found that at the Division I institution, on average the head coach of a men's team was paid 44% more than the head coach of a women's team (Naughton, 1997b). Some athletic directors argue that the market drives coaches' salaries or that the coach of a men's team has more responsibilities or pressures, thus justifying the pay differential. According to Title IX and the Equal Pay Act, it is the responsibility of the athletic director and institutional administrators to ensure that coaches performing similar duties and having similar job responsibilities are paid equitably.

The NCAA as an organization has taken a stand regarding appropriate female and minority representation within the new restructuring organization. Legislation passed at the January 1997 Annual Convention requires that at least one member of the 15-member Division I Board of Directors be an ethnic minority and one other member be a woman and also that at least 20% of the 34-member Division I Management Council be ethnic minorities and that 35% be members of the underrepresented gender (women) ("Summaries of," 1997).

Finances

Coaches across all divisions face the challenge of accomplishing their goals while making the most of the money in their budgets. Athletic administrators are also under increased pressure to provide coaches with appropriate funding while working within budgetary limitations placed upon them by the college or university administration. The financial picture within college athletics has become "big business," with coaches and administrators having to be more creative in generating revenue. Although the financial picture of collegiate athletic departments across divisions is better than it used to be, there is still cause for concern as athletic departments are not the "cash cows" that many people believe them to be.

The 1996 NCAA Revenue and Expense Report shows that Division I-A is the only division in which the average member operates at a profit (on average, $1.2 million per year). However, this statistic includes institutional support. If institutional support is removed as a revenue source, the average Division I-A program operates at a deficit (on average, $237,000 per year) ("Study: Typical I-A," 1996). On average, athletic departments in other divisions, even with the inclusion of institutional support, operated at deficits (see Table 8–1).

One of the more recent funding trends within collegiate athletics, especially at the Division I level, is the involvement of corporate sponsors. The advent of corporate sponsorship has provided a creative means for athletic departments to generate revenue, or at the very least provide budget relief for their sport programs. One example of corporate sponsorship involvement is the seven-year, $7 million contract between the University of Michigan and Nike. As part of this contract, Nike agreed to equip every varsity team (22 teams) with shoes and apparel, including team uniforms and practice gear; provide a cash payment of $75,000 to the athletic department; fund a year-long fellowship in sport journal-

Table 8–1 Average Deficits of Athletic Departments by Division

Division	Average Deficit
Division I-AA	$469,000
Division II (with football)	$221,000
Division II (without football)	$177,000

Source: "Study: Typical I-A Program Is $1.2 Million in the Black," *The Chronicle of Higher Education,* Jan. 24, 1997, pp. A35–A36.

ism; pay $15,000 a year for three years to a scholarship endowment begun by former basketball star Chris Webber; and establish an endowment for two scholarships in women's athletics. In addition, Nike has already built an outdoor court facility in Ann Arbor (Falls & Girard, 1994). Corporate sponsorship involvement in collegiate athletics is not limited to sport-related companies; McDonald's signed a $5.5 million contract with Georgia Tech that included the operation of two McDonald's restaurants on campus and renaming the area of campus containing the basketball arena and other athletic facilities to the "McDonald's Center at Alexander Memorial Coliseum" (Blumenstyk, 1995).

Paying Student-Athletes

As the NCAA membership had long been opposed to "paying" student-athletes because of amateurism concerns, maintenance of the "level playing field" concept, and increased involvement and violations by booster group members, the NCAA took a step in allowing additional monies for student-athletes by approving legislation at the January 1997 Annual Convention allowing student-athletes to work and earn up to the amount of the cost of attending their institution (Naughton, 1997a). This issue has long been supported by student-athletes, who spend an enormous amount of time with their athletic activities but were prohibited from obtaining additional monies during the school year beyond the amount of an athletic scholarship. Although the athletic scholarship provides much-appreciated financial support for student-athletes, such scholarship money covers only tuition, room and board, and books and fees, but not additional monies to pay for transportation, clothing, and meals beyond the dining halls.

This new legislation, though, causes concerns for athletic administrators such as ensuring that valid employment positions are being provided for student-athletes, ensuring that the student-athletes earn only up to the cost of attendance, and overseeing the administration of the legislation. In addition, there is concern among athletic administrators and coaches that the student-athlete, because of the time demanded by athletic activities and academic courses, experiences tremendous time constraints. If the student-athlete is allowed to work, the time devoted to academics will suffer, impacting the academic progress and graduation rates of student-athletes. This new legislation was to take effect in August 1997, but it was put on hold for one year while coaches and administrators studied how to monitor the employment of student-athletes.

Academic Eligibility: Student-Athletes with Learning Disabilities

The NCAA has been struggling with the issue of the eligibility of student-athletes with learning disabilities competing in intercollegiate athletics. This issue was brought to light when Chad Ganden was denied initial eligibility certification by the **NCAA Initial-Eligibility Clearinghouse** in July 1996. The NCAA Initial-Eligibility Clearinghouse reviews the academic transcripts and standardized test scores of incoming student-athletes and determines whether they are eligible to practice and compete their freshman year. Ganden was not certified because he lacked the 13 core courses the NCAA requires for eligibility. Ganden took special classes in high school for students with learning disabilities and consequently did not take enough of the core courses required by the NCAA. In August 1996 the NCAA granted Ganden a partial waiver, which allowed him to practice and receive an athletic scholarship but prohibited him from competing. Ganden filed a lawsuit (*Ganden v. NCAA*, 1996) requesting to be allowed to compete, but a federal judge denied his request for a preliminary injunction ("Judge Denies," 1996).

At the 1997 January Convention, the NCAA membership addressed the issue of student-athletes with learning disabilities and took action to accommodate these student-athletes. Although initial eligibility standards will continue to be the same for all student-athletes, including those with learning disabilities, the NCAA developed accommodations that include:

- use of nonstandard test scores for meeting initial-eligibility standards when approved by the NCAA
- acceptance by the NCAA Initial-Eligibility Clearinghouse of approved core courses designed specifically for students with learning disabilities
- use of core courses taken after the eighth semester of high school
- a case-by-case review of students with learning disabilities ("Accommodations for," 1997).

The NCAA has addressed this issue to accommodate student-athletes with learning disabilities who wish to participate and compete in collegiate athletics. Concern exists, though, that this legislation may become a loophole student-athletes and coaches could abuse in obtaining initial eligibility status.

Medical Concerns and Athletes' Right To Compete

Coaches and athletic administrators are sometimes placed in the position of deciding whether to allow a student-athlete with a medical condition to practice and compete. One prominent case involved Nicholas Knapp, a basketball player at Northwestern University. In 1994, Nick Knapp suffered full cardiac arrest while playing in a pickup game at his high school. Knapp had to be resuscitated and a defibrillator was implanted inside his body to regulate his heart beat. Knapp had already made an oral commitment to attend Northwestern on an athletic scholarship. Upon arrival for his freshman year at Northwestern, the university barred him from practicing and competing with the basketball team. Knapp sued the university (*Knapp v. Northwestern University*, 1996a), claiming that the university was discriminating under the Rehabilitation Act of 1973 against disabled, but otherwise qualified, people. In September 1996 the U.S. District Court ruled in favor of Knapp stating that Knapp should be allowed to decide for himself whether to play varsity basketball. This decision, though, was overturned by the U.S. Court of Appeals for the Seventh Circuit, which stated that playing Big Ten basketball was not a "major life activity" protected by the Rehabilitation Act of 1973 (*Knapp v. Northwestern University*, 1996b). Therefore, the Northwestern University team physician had the power to declare Knapp medically ineligible. Since medical opinions vary, this decision is limited to Northwestern University, so Knapp may participate at another institution if cleared by that institution's medical staff (Masteralexis, 1997).

This issue is one that places coaches and athletic administrators in a difficult position. The student-athlete wants to practice and compete, but if this is allowed to take place then the coach and athletic administrator may be opening themselves up to a potential lawsuit should an injury or death occur.

SUMMARY

Sport management students and future athletic department employees need to be aware that intercollegiate athletics, as a major segment of the sport industry, is experiencing numerous organizational, managerial, financial, and legal issues. The NCAA, first organized in 1905, has undergone organizational changes throughout its history, including the recent restructuring legislation, to accommodate the needs of the member institutions. The new NCAA organizational structure is important because it provides information about the power and communication structures within the organization. College athletic administrators and coaches need to be aware of this new structure so they can be knowledgeable about how future rules and policies will be developed within the NCAA.

It is also important for students to know the differences that exist among the various divisions within the NCAA membership structure. These differences involve the allowance of athletic scholarships, budget and funding opportunities, and competitive philosophies. Distinct differences exist between and even among divisional schools. Students, future collegiate athletic administrators, and coaches must become informed of these differences in order to better select a career within a school or NCAA membership division that best fits their interests and philosophies.

In pursuing an administrative job within collegiate athletics, the sport management student should be aware of and work on developing skills that current athletic directors have identified as important. These skills include marketing expertise, strong public speaking and writing skills, creative and problem-solving abilities, the ability to manage complex financial issues, and the ability to manage and work with parents, students, faculty, alumni, booster groups, and sponsors. Appropriate course work and preparation in these areas can better prepare the student interested in a career in collegiate athletic administration.

Probably the most important quality a coach or administrator needs to possess is being informed and knowledgeable about issues currently affecting this sport industry segment. Perhaps the most prominent issue affecting collegiate athletic departments is Title IX/Gender Equity. Coaches and administrators must educate themselves in understanding what the law requires and how to comply. Another current issue foremost in collegiate athletic administrators' minds is finances. Today, athletic department budgets are in the millions of dollars, and television contracts play a large role in the operation and scheduling of intercollegiate athletic competitions. Staying on top of these and other issues affecting college athletics is important for all coaches, administrators, and people involved in the governance and operation of this sport industry segment.

CASE STUDY: TITLE IX AND THE COLLEGIATE ATHLETIC DEPARTMENT

David Kaplan, athletic director at a Division I-A institution, came into work one fall Monday morning and found three female student-athletes waiting outside his office. David has always employed an open-door philosophy encouraging any coach, student-athlete, or undergraduate student at the university to stop by and talk to him whenever he or she had a question or concern. David could tell by the faces of these three women that they were quite upset. As he welcomed them into his office and they introduced themselves, David found out that these three women were former student-athletes on the women's gymnastics and softball teams. Their sports had been eliminated last spring, along with the men's gymnastics and baseball teams, due to budgetary cutbacks at the university. These three women were upset because they had chosen to attend the university because it offered these two varsity sport programs. Now, with the elimination of these sport programs, the three women were not sure they wanted to continue to go to school here. David explained to the three women that an athletic director never wants to eliminate a sport program, especially one like the men's baseball team that had been at the school for over 100 years or the women's gymnastics team that qualified for the NCAA championships the previous year, but the budgetary problems provided him with no other choice and he had to make the difficult decision. David assured these female student-athletes, though, that they would continue to receive their athletic scholarships as long as they were enrolled as students at the university.

Finally, Linda (a former softball player) looked at David and said that she knew that Title IX was passed to prevent discrimination in athletics by requiring institutions to provide equitable opportunities and funding to female student-athletes. Linda went on to say that she had already contacted a lawyer and was going to pursue a Title IX lawsuit against the University. David immediately became concerned. He had heard about Title IX, but really did not know what the law said and what was required. The NCAA had sponsored a number of Title IX seminars for institutions across the country over the past couple of years, but they had always coincided with another trip or meeting so David never went. He realized he was out of touch and needed to do something about this situation right away.

Questions for Discussion

1. Put yourself in David's position. What is the first thing that you should do?
2. What types of information and data does David need to collect in order to determine the athletic department's current compliance with Title IX?
3. What are some potential solutions to bring the athletic department into compliance with Title IX?
4. What solution would you choose, and what would you need to do to get your solution accepted and implemented?

RESOURCES

National Association for Intercollegiate Athletics (NAIA)
6120 S. Yale Ave., Suite 1450
Tulsa, OK 74136
918-494-8828
home page: http://www.naia.org

National Association of Collegiate Directors of Athletics (NACDA)
24651 Detroit Road
Westlake, OH 44145
216-892-4000
home page: http://www.nacda.com

National Association of Collegiate Women's Athletic Administrators (NACWAA)
4701 Wrightsville Avenue
Oak Park D-1
Wilmington, NC 28403
910-793-8244
email: nacwaa@wilmington.net

National Collegiate Athletic Association (NCAA)
6201 College Boulevard
Overland Park, KS 66211-2422
913-339-1906
home page: http://www.ncaa.org

National Junior College Athletic Association (NJCAA)
1825 Austin Bluffs Pkwy.
Colorado Springs, CO 80918
719-590-9788
home page: http://www.njcaa.org

The NCAA provides a number of resources helpful to collegiate athletic administrators and coaches, including the *NCAA Manual* and *The NCAA News*.

REFERENCES

1997 Sports Market Place. Phoenix, AZ: Franklin Quest Sports.

Accommodations for learning disabilities explained in mailing. (1997, March 3). *The NCAA News*, 1.

Acosta, R.V., & Carpenter, L.J. (1985). Women in sport. In D. Chu, J.O. Segrave, & B.J. Becker (Eds.), *Sport and higher education* (pp. 313–325). Champaign, IL: Human Kinetics.

Association for Intercollegiate Athletics for Women v. National Collegiate Athletic Association, 558 F. Supp. 487 (D.D.C. 1983).

Barr, C.A. (1992). *A comparative study of Division I and Division III athletic directors: Their profiles and the necessary qualifications they deem as essential in their positions*, Unpublished master's thesis, University of Massachusetts, Amherst.

Blauvelt, H. (1996, October 2). Women slowly crack athletic director ranks. *USA Today*, p. 1C.

Blumenstyk, G. (1995, February 3). Georgia Tech and McDonald's sign $5.5-million deal. *The Chronicle of Higher Education*, A43–A44.

Broyles hopes a move won't end Arkansas' SWC rivalries. (1990, August 1). *The NCAA News*, 20.

Crowley, J.N. (1995, December 18). History demonstrates that change is good. *The NCAA News*, 4.

Davenport, J. (1985). From crew to commercialism—the paradox of sport in higher education. In D. Chu, J.O. Segrave, & B.J. Becker (Eds.), *Sport and higher education* (pp. 5–16). Champaign, IL: Human Kinetics.

Dealy, F.X. (1990). *Win at any cost*. New York: Carol Publishing Group.

Falls, J. and Girard, F. (1994, October 21). Michigan-Nike endorsement deal includes scholarships, new court. *USA Today*, p. 6C.

Ganden v. NCAA, 1996 Westlaw 680000 (Northern District of Illinois 1996).

Huggins, S. (1996, November 4). Broad range of talents required for today's athletics directors. *The NCAA News*, 1.

Hult, J.S. (1994). The story of women's athletics: Manipulating a dream 1890–1985. In D.M. Costa, & S.R. Guthrie (Eds.), *Women and sport: Interdisciplinary perspectives* (pp. 83–106). Champaign, IL: Human Kinetics.

Indianapolis lands NCAA headquarters. (1997, June 9). *The NCAA News*, 1.

Judge denies injunction in Ganden case. (1996, December 2) *The NCAA News*, 24.

Knapp v. Northwestern University. (1996a). (Civ. No. 95-C-6454) 1996 U.S. Dist. LEXIS 13580.

Knapp v. Northwestern University. (1996b). 101 F.3d 473 (7th Cir. 1996).

Knight Foundation. (1991, March). Keeping faith with the student-athlete. *Report of the Knight Foundation Commission on Intercollegiate Athletics*, Charlotte, NC.

Knight Foundation. (1993, March). A new beginning for a new century. *Report of the Knight Foundation Commission on Intercollegiate Athletics*, Charlotte, NC.

Lawrence, P.R. (1987). *Unsportsmanlike conduct*. New York: Praeger Publishers.

Masteralexis, L.P. (1997, March). Doctor, doctor. *Athletic Business, 21*(3), 10–14.

Morrison, L.L. (1993). The AIAW: Governance by women for women. In G.L. Cohen (Ed.), *Women in sport: Issues and controversies* (pp. 59–66). Newbury Park, CA: Sage Publications.

Mott, R.D. (1994, March 2). Big Eight growth brings a new look to Division I-A. *The NCAA News*, 1.

National Collegiate Athletic Association. (1996–1997). *1996–97 NCAA Manual*. Overland Park, KS: Author.

Naughton, J. (1997a, January 24). NCAA completes action on its new structure and approves academic-year jobs for athletes. *The Chronicle of Higher Education*, A33–A34.

Naughton, J. (1997b, May 16). A new debate over disparities in coaches' salaries. *The Chronicle of Higher Education*, A35.

Naughton, J. (1997c, April 11). Women in Division I sport programs: 'The glass is half empty and half full.' *The Chronicle of Higher Education*, A39–A40.

NCAA Gender Equity Task Force (1991). *NCAA Gender Equity Report.* Overland Park, KS: National Collegiate Athletic Association.

NCAA Olympic Sports Liaison Committee (1996). *NCAA Olympic Sports Liaison Committee foreign student-athlete study.* Overland Park, KS: National Collegiate Athletic Association.

Paul, J. (1993). Heroines: Paving the way. In G.L. Cohen (Ed.), *Women in sport: Issues and controversies* (pp. 27–37). Newbury Park, CA: Sage Publications.

Rader, B.G. (1990). *American sports* (2d ed.). Englewood Cliffs, NJ: Prentice Hall.

Rushin, S. (1997, March 3). Inside the moat. *Sports Illustrated,* 68–83.

Savage, H.J. (1929). *American college athletics.* New York: The Carnegie Foundation.

Study: Typical I-A program is $1.2 million in the black. (1996, November 18). *The NCAA News,* 1.

Summaries of rules adopted at the annual convention of the NCAA. (1997, January 24). *The Chronicle of Higher Education,* A35–A36.

Western Athletic Conference to become biggest in I-A. (1994, April 27). *The NCAA News,* 3.

Wieberg, S. (1994, August 18). Study faults colleges on minority hiring. *USA Today,* p. 1C.

Wieberg, S. (1996, November 7). Schools no longer wait for NCAA to make a move. *USA Today,* p. 18C.

Yaeger, D. (1991). *Undue process: The NCAA's injustice for all.* Champaign, IL: Sagamore Publishing.

CHAPTER 9

The European
Sport Club System

Berend Rubingh and Adri Broeke

Key Words: kantine, industrialization, modernization, voluntary associations, sportification, self-organization, federations, traditional association, professional club

INTRODUCTION

An American Experience in the European Sport Club System

As a post-collegian trying to break into the top level of track and field in the United States in the mid-1980s, I worried over the lack of support I was getting after graduation. Using the track could be a struggle, since we had to wait until university practices were finished. Finding a coach was next to impossible, since there were really no coaches available outside of the college system, and if there were, we could not afford one. Discussions with other runners usually came around to how much better off we would be in Europe, where athletes were nurtured for life in the club system. European athletes were valued and had unlimited access to facilities, coaching, and most important, financial resources. The whole club was behind them so the chances for success were much better. In the United States, only those who could go it alone made it to the top.

Now, 15 years later and armed with hindsight and firsthand knowledge about a Dutch track-and-field club, I see that a European-style system would be completely foreign to most Americans in that its function is not to promote superior athletes. I've found that clubs, at least in the Netherlands where I live, fulfill a social function with sport serving as a common interest for the group.

Anyone can join a club, and for a very reasonable fee (around $125 per year) receive the use of good facilities (usually owned and maintained by the local

195

*government) and coaching three or four nights per week. When I first moved to the Netherlands, I decided to begin running again and joined a club, but I quickly discovered that training sessions were much different from training in the United States. Instead of running as hard as possible for an hour or so, and then going your separate ways, Dutch sessions seemed to take forever, with much of the time spent chatting while warming up and stretching, and discussing vacation plans in between bouts of running. Afterward, it was expected that you join your training mates in the **kantine**, the small bar that is part of every Dutch clubhouse, for a couple of drinks and an hour or so of conversation. Training became an evening of intense social interaction. This approach still frustrates me, since it seems athletes stand around and talk more than they run, chatting about the latest movie they've seen or making plans for a teammate's birthday. But friendship is the reason that most of the athletes come at all, with their interest in sport providing a common bond.*

The kantine is the focus of much of Dutch club life. Since most of even the largest clubs in the Netherlands are democratically governed and run by volunteers from within the membership, the kantine and its flourishing social life are where many of the decisions are made. Sitting over a beer after training, members decide which meets the team will run, what events it will put on, who will be hired as the next coach, or how much money will be spent. If you are not involved in the kantine culture, you can forget about getting anything done or having any influence in decision making. In fact, the training session is not a prerequisite for visiting the kantine, since many athletes come on their off nights or on a Sunday morning to have a drink or cup of coffee and enjoy a bit of "home away from home." As a coach, this can be a bit disconcerting when you have a potentially good athlete practicing only two nights a week whom you see another two nights in the kantine wasting (in your opinion) valuable training time.

Kantines also play a financial role in clubs, since they provide a reliable source of income from drink and food sales. Members pay for their drinks, and volunteers staff the bar. But maximizing this income source sometimes raises this question: Is the club's function to sponsor sporting activities or to run a social organization? I am now an overall coordinator and coach at a track-and-field club in the Netherlands and was recently involved in a decision that raised this dilemma. A triathlon group that branched off from the track-and-field club three years ago but was still without its own kantine requested use of the track-and-field bar two nights a week. The triathletes are often at cross-purposes with the track-and-field portion of the club, and their use of the kantine would mean our athletes would be unable to use the kantine or the small weight room attached to it on those nights. However, the triathlon group's request was quickly granted since it had a lot of members who reportedly "bought a lot of beer."

Before moving to the Netherlands, I was a coach and athletics administrator in American colleges and universities for over 10 years, and I can remember no real sports equivalent that has the European club's social emphasis. Club sports in universities come the closest, since they bring together members with a common interest and they often provide a social outlet. Although the club itself is largely student-run, it operates under the auspices of the university, which governs and controls its operation to some extent. There are also some clubs that operate outside of the educational system and there are service organizations such as the YMCA, but I believe their focus is primarily on providing a service, in the form of coaching or access to facilities and competitions.

With its emphasis on social integration, I'm not sure the European club model is the ideal way to develop top athletes. As a coach with a decidedly American attitude, focused on competition, I feel that the social identity attached to a club often discourages potentially good athletes who do not want to stand out from the group or who get caught up in socializing during workouts rather than hard training. However, coaching in a club with the motto "Kwaliteit (equality) en Gezelligheid (a term that has no real English equivalent, but coziness probably comes close)," as I do, makes it difficult to discourage the conversation and joking that is an essential part of training sessions.

On the positive side, members form lifetime attachments to their clubs, and even after they've stopped competing and training, they often become involved in the governance or operation of the organization. Changes can be difficult because of this, since new ideas can upset the club's traditions and there are still plenty of people around to remind you that the same idea did not work 20 years ago and it will not work now. Members value the club, however, and will spend great amounts of time and effort to make it work. An experience of a friend whose 12-year-old son began to play in a tennis club provides a good example of this effort. About a month prior to the beginning of the competitive season my friend was handed a folder by another boy on the team, also only 12 years old but with a few years' experience in the club. In the folder was a travel plan the boy had worked out for all the away matches for the season, designating which parent was to drive on which day and including detailed maps, departure times, and travel times for each trip. This cooperative, responsible attitude is what makes the European club system work.

—Brett Ayers

HISTORY

The Origin of Modern Sport

The Industrial Revolution played an important role in the historic development of sport. In the course of the nineteenth century the "classical sports" of ancient Greece, such as athletics (track and field), weightlifting, and wrestling, transformed into "modern" sport, such as soccer and cricket. Societal changes, such as improved transportation and communication, combined with the emergence of larger cities, allowed people to contact each other faster and more often. Communities previously closed to others now opened up to the outside world. At this time, people were first granted the legal right, regardless of social class, to unite together to form self-governing associations, including sport clubs.

To understand the origin of the sport club system, it is necessary to understand two important concepts—industrialization and modernization. **Industrialization**, hinging on the development of such things as steam engines, electricity, and mechanized equipment, had a great economic impact. Life in industrialized countries and regions changed dramatically for the working population. **Modernization** led to larger urban populations, opportunities for more social interaction, improved work and leisure facilities, and better living conditions in general. Through modernization, working-class citizens achieved higher educational levels and amassed the increased material possessions necessary to enjoy the life, customs, and traditions of the higher socioeconomic classes. Sport participation was one of the aspects of life of the well-educated and upper classes that the lower classes soon began to access. This adoption of facets of upper-class life, often called the "trickle down effect," occurs as people from lower social classes slowly achieve the opportunity to access traditionally upper-class activities such as sport.

In Western Europe, England was the early leader in the development of sport clubs. In the beginning of the nineteenth century, thanks to industrialization, Great Britain became one of Europe's most powerful and thriving countries. People from all walks of life and regions of the country organized meetings that revolved around athletic contests. Teams from various cities competed in local sporting events such as cricket, horse racing, golf, and soccer, leading to the need to standardize rules. These local events eventually led to the rise of several generally accepted types of sport, such as field hockey and soccer. Modern progressive citizens, especially the well-educated youngsters from urban environments, considered these English sports characteristic of "modern" times. Students as well as workers in other Western European countries actively took part in these originally English competitive sports, which were associated with "modern" (higher-status) lifestyles. Sport lovers organized themselves and founded sport clubs, often called **voluntary associations**. Some of these clubs (cricket clubs) had exclusive membership, with members having to be interviewed to see if they were acceptable for membership based on their income, their profession, or their family status. Other clubs (soccer clubs) were more democratic and opened their membership to just about anyone. Whatever the type of club, the members of these voluntary associations created a sport world of their own, setting rules and creating uniforms for their competitive sport activities.

These developing clubs contributed to what is referred to as **sportification**—the transformation of local sport for amusement into regulated competitive sport

(Stokvis, 1989). A similar process also took place in the United States, although the process differed slightly from that in Europe. Early in the industrialized Northeastern United States, English sports were not viewed as "modern" because people in the "former colony" opposed anything remotely resembling English structures. Home-grown American sports like baseball and American football, and later basketball, were held in much higher esteem. Prominent universities such as Harvard and Yale, and ideological youth organizations such as the Young Men's Christian Association (YMCA), nurtured the development, standardization, and growth of these "typically American" sports. Sportification took place, but because of social and economic forces operating in the United States, American "modern" sport did not adopt the traditional Western European sport club model.

The Origin and Development of Internationally Organized Sport Clubs

From the nineteenth century until the beginning of the twentieth century, modernization led to the free movement of larger portions of society. Citizens soon banded together to form a variety of organizations dealing with health care, social welfare, and leisure, including activities involving youth work, charities, and sport. These organizations, of which sport clubs are a subset, shared a number of common characteristics (van Munster, 1996):

1. Place. These associations formed a sort of common ground among families, relatives, the government, and the marketplace.
2. Interest. The members of these associations were drawn together by shared interests. Members gave their all for a common effort that surpassed their individual interests. Voluntary efforts for the common good took place without expectation of financial rewards.
3. Organization. Voluntary associations were initiated by private citizens. A characteristic of voluntary associations is **self-organization**, meaning that goods and services are produced by the group for use by the members.
4. Functions. These associations fulfilled a combination of three basic functions: values (the organization is formed around certain values and norms), interests (the organization is formed around one common issue for the members), and services (the organization is formed around the process of creating services for the members) (see Figure 9–1).

Voluntary associations can be represented by this functional triangle. Sport clubs are found in the middle of the triangle. Service organizations such as "Triple A" (AAA) motor club, witness organizations such as Greenpeace, and lobby organizations such as labor unions are found at the corners of the triangle. The traditional sport club is located in the middle of the triangle and exhibits charac-

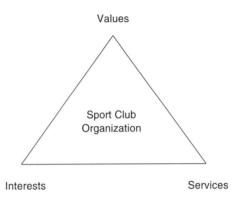

Figure 9–1 The Function Triangle. *Source:* Data from van Munster, O. (1996). *De toekomst van het middenveld.* Den Haag: Delwel, The Netherlands.

teristics of each of these three organizations. The values that underlie industrial society—discipline, a focus on results, standardization, and so on—match the fundamentals on which club sports were eventually based. Industrial society therefore accepted the organized practice of sport as natural.

Over time, a strong foundation of organized competitive sport grew from people's desire to band together and enjoy sport. Often, former athletes took on the administrative job of organizing competitions. On the local level the needs of club members for facilities, competitions, training, and social interactions were well accommodated. Because these local clubs shared common values, they soon began to align with each other, forming **federations**. On the national level these federations took care of arranging and organizing competitions and acted as lobbying organizations, looking out for the interests of the member clubs as a whole. Soon competitive sport was being controlled on the national level by sport federations.

Sport competition occurs on three levels, as shown in Figure 9–2. On the bottom level is the broad base of sport for all. The middle level represents the group of general competitive athletes. The very top of the pyramid is formed by the elite, high-performance athletes (Digel, 1995).

Sport associations create a clearly recognizable and defined system. Clubs develop a mutual bond through regulations and agreements to perform certain tasks and responsibilities. While sport clubs form the basic foundation of sport participation, national sport federations set up appropriate rules and regulations to govern competition. This web of voluntary sport organizations is directed by a voluntary board of national sport federations. Until the 1950s the amateur national sport federations controlled sport. Eventually these organizations grouped together to form international federations, which now control the market for sport

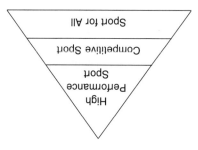

Figure 9-2 The Pyramid Structure of Sport Systems. *Source:* Data from Digel, H. (1995). *Sport in a changing society.* Schorndorf, Germany: Verlag Karl Hoffman.

matches and events. During this time government organizations and the media were dependent upon the cooperation of various voluntary sport associations. Because these organizations controlled national and international competitions, training, rules enforcement, and standards for competitive facilities, they held a competitive advantage over other entities that supplied sport, such as the government or businesses. The relationship among the international federations, national federations, and independent sport clubs is represented by the pyramid in Figure 9-3.

VARIATIONS OF SPORT CLUBS IN VARIOUS SPORT SYSTEMS

The previous two sections explained how the sport club system came into existence and became the dominant sport system in Western Europe and other countries. In addition to the sport club system, there are also other sport systems ("Images of Sport," 1995). The sport systems are the sport club systems, the state

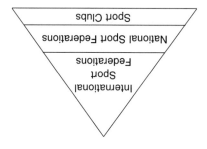

Figure 9-3 The Pyramid Structure of Sport Club Organizations.

sport system, the school sport system, and the commercial sport system, as shown in Table 9-1.

Clubs in each system, influenced by social and economic developments, have developed in their own directions. The term "sport club," therefore, has different meanings in each context. The remainder of this chapter concentrates on the sport club itself and its various manifestations.

In the traditional sport club, the concept of participation, that is, everyone joining in to help the club operate, is important not just for sport, but for the idea of voluntary work as well. Democracy and solidarity play a major part in the governing boards of these organizations. The organizations make optimal use of their members' efforts. Members volunteer to schedule, organize, and manage club events. The clubs, as voluntary organizations, stress the feeling of "we," that is, "Let's make things happen together." These kinds of voluntary associations in Europe developed for three reasons:

1. the role of local government authorities, who saw sport as an instrument for social and welfare development
2. the special character of physical education in the schools, where physical activity was completely different from "competitive sport"
3. the absence of other opportunities in the sport sector

Basically, the entire sport infrastructure of Europe is run by these "self-organizations," as illustrated in Figure 9-3. In a small country like the Netherlands, for example, there are 35,000 associations through which approximately one-third of the country's 4.5 million people participate in sport. This extremely broad base helps explain how large international sport federations (described in Chapter 10, International Sport) derive their power.

Table 9-1 Sport Systems

System	Characteristics	Location
Sport club system	Focus: members, volunteers, and self-organization	Western Europe
State sport system	Focus: state Club is part of state companies.	Eastern Europe Asia
School sport system	Focus: school Organization is part of educational system.	USA, Canada, Great Britain
Commercial sport system	Focus: commercial Organizations and companies are for-profit.	USA, Canada, Japan, Australia, and growing markets in Europe and South America

In North America, where there is hardly any governmental influence in sport and a dominant capitalist economic system reigns, there are far more service organizations to meet the needs of consumers. The members often become clients who pay for the services offered. In addition, the need for voluntary associations in the North American sport system is reduced (as compared with Europe) because of sport's large role in educational institutions.

TRADITIONAL ASSOCIATIONS VERSUS PROFESSIONAL CLUBS

When examining clubs in the various systems, two ideal types of organizations can be distinguished, the traditional association and the professional club. The **traditional association** tries to achieve a balance in accommodating members' interests, values, and requested services. The **professional club**, such as a health and fitness club, on the other hand, focuses on services. The professional club actually has clients as opposed to members, and it utilizes professional management and staff members. This type of club uses the "club" concept to make clear that the client belongs to a certain group to whom special services are offered. The "club" concept here stands for a certain kind of service. In exchange for paying a certain amount of money (a membership fee), one is given a package of services and products for a certain period of time.

The traditional association and the professional club can be placed at two opposite ends of a continuum. A sport club can be placed along this continuum either toward the traditional end or toward the professional end and based on a number of factors. A comparison of these two ideal typical associations on certain factors appears in Table 9-2. Many associations can be found somewhere between these two extremes.

McCarthy (1990) identifies three different segments in the North American athletic and fitness club industry: (1) the old-line, member-owned country clubs,

Table 9-2 Continuum of Differences between Traditional Associations and Professional Clubs

Traditional Associations	Professional Clubs
Based on solidarity	Based on service
Everybody participates in club operation	Professional staff operates club
Many volunteers	No volunteers
Members	Clients
Board and management from among the members	Board and management for the clients
Tasks and responsibilities informally divided and appointed	Tasks and responsibilities formally divided and appointed

(2) the new breed of investor-owned for-profit clubs, and (3) the "quasi-clubs" or community clubs. On the previously mentioned continuum, the "quasi-clubs" would be closer to the traditional end, whereas the old-line member-owned clubs would be closer to the professional end. The investor-owned for-profit "clubs" are actually businesses that use the designation "club" to clarify special services to customers, namely services that are exclusively available to them by virtue of "membership." These "clubs" are examples of purely professional clubs, which bear no resemblance to the traditional club. In North America, most clubs are small businesses and therefore are more on the professional end of the continuum. In Europe, the club system more closely matches the ideal on the traditional end of the continuum, although there is a growing, noticeable trend toward more professional clubs. It is important to understand that in Europe the whole sport system is based on the sport club system, while in North America, sport is mainly organized around educational or commercial systems. These distinct characteristics strongly influence the sport systems on each continent.

MANAGEMENT CONSEQUENCES

The "sport club" is a multifaceted concept. The concept and the organization developed differently depending on context, country, and culture. This is true, too, for the sport club system, which flourishes especially in Western Europe, where it is considered the dominant sport system (the sport club system is less dominant in other parts of the world). The previous section showed how a sport club can be positioned on a continuum ranging from the traditional (participatory) club to the professional (service-providing) club (see Table 9-2). The organization and management of a sport club also depend on the club's location on the continuum between traditional associations and professional clubs. Table 9-3 illustrates how management practices differ between the traditional associations and the professional clubs.

CURRENT TRENDS AND DEVELOPMENTS IN THE SPORT CLUB SYSTEM

The sport club system is currently undergoing change, as the traditional clubs face internal and external problems.

Internal Problems

The interests of members are more diverse than in previous decades because members now have more options for spending their free time. As time becomes

Table 9–3 Differences in Management and Operations between Traditional Associations and Professional Clubs

Traditional Associations	Professional Clubs
Planning and organizing is informal and has many channels, often improvised.	Planning and organizing is formal and clearly divided over a limited number of persons.
Democratic and complex decision making often done through commissions and meetings.	Central decision making is performed by management.
Board executes.	Board supervises.
Board comes up with ideas and decides on them.	Board judges solutions made by management.
Management goals include efficiency, solidarity, and participation.	Management goals include quality and effectiveness.
Everybody knows everything about operations and decisions.	Only board and management know everything about operations and decisions.
Volunteers do most of the work and are motivated by various factors.	Paid staff are motivated by normal work relations, salary, bonuses, leisure time, etc.

Source: Data from Rubingh, B., & Westerbeek, H.M. (1994). De professionele sportvereiniging, kiezen of delen. *Spiel en Sport.*

important, so does the choice of how to spend one's time. Doing volunteer work is not the most popular activity anymore, whereas in the past decades it was one's social duty. Today a member sees him- or herself more as a client who pays for membership (pays fees for a service) rather than as a member whose volunteer work, in addition to dues, is necessary to help the club operate.

External Problems

More than ever before, sport clubs face increased competition from other sport and recreation suppliers. Members have left clubs for other activities that are available at the same price. In addition, as a result of a major political trend in Europe to privatize (that is, to lessen governmental influence and give more initiatives to private business), local governmental authorities have decreased their subsidies for sport clubs. These sport clubs have now become more dependent on consumers and corporate sponsors, who have recognized a growing demand for professionalizing the sport club. A different expertise is now necessary to successfully manage these more "service"-oriented organizations.

The Impact of Television

A final important influence on the club system is television. The growing demand for sport on television has given clubs with first-division teams (the highest skill level) throughout Europe an enormous financial boost. These sport clubs, which were initiated from the traditional club system, now operate as full-scale companies with enormous total income. Today many clubs struggle over the way they should be organized. Many of the European first-division teams in soccer, basketbal., and volleyball are still organized as traditional clubs. They still have voluntary boards utilizing a democratic decision-making process, even though they are structured and managed in a manner comparable to teams in the American professional leagues.

SUMMARY

In the early development of the sport club system, England was the most prominent country, thanks mostly to its early industrialization and modernization. Citizens began to join together to form a large variety of organizations, including sport clubs. Soon these sport clubs, which shared common interests, banded together to form larger groups called federations. These federations began to organize sport competitions on both the national and international levels.

The sport club system is actually part of a larger set of sport systems that operate in Western Europe, including the state sport system, the school sport system, and the commercial sport system. Sport clubs themselves tend to fall on a continuum somewhere between traditional clubs, emphasizing participation by the members in club operation, and professional clubs, focusing on member services. The basic orientations and management structures of sport clubs differ depending on where they are located on this continuum.

As the basic foundations of the sport club system evolve, some parts of the original club system will disappear while other parts remain, perhaps changing somewhat to fit the times. As part of this evolution, the sport club system is experiencing a growing trend toward professionalization (Broeke, Hattink, & Rubingh, 1995). It will be interesting to observe how the sport club system continues to change and develop over the next decades.

REFERENCES

Broeke, A.H., Hattink, B., & Rubingh, B. (1995). To develop management in sport. *Proceedings from the Third European Sport Management Congress.* Budapest, Hungary.

Digel, H. (1995). *Sport in a changing society*. Schorndorf, Germany: Verlag Karl Hoffman.

Images of sport in the world. (1995). *German Sport University Cologne Conference Proceedings*. Cologne, Germany.

McCarthy, J. (1990). Sports club management. In J.B. Parks & B.R.K. Zanger (Eds.), *Sport and fitness management* (pp. 95–101). Champaign, IL: Human Kinetics.

Rubingh, B. & Westerbeek, H.M. (1994). De professionele sportvereiniging, kiezen of delen. *Spiel en Sport*.

Stokvis, R. (1989). *De sportwerold*. Alphen aan den Rijn/Brussels, Belgium: Samson Ditgevery.

van Munster, O. (1996). *De toekomst van het middenveld*. Den Haag, The Netherlands: Delwel.

CHAPTER 10

International Sport

James M. Gladden and Mireia Lizandra

Editor's Note: Since the majority of the world refers to soccer as "football," throughout this international chapter we will do the same. When referring to football as is played in the National Football League (NFL), Canadian Football League (CFL), and World League of American Football (WLAF), we will use the phrase "American football."

Key words: international sport management, distribution, technology, nationalism, International Olympic Committee (IOC), Olympism, global strategy, licensed merchandise, grassroots efforts, National Olympic Committees (NOCs), Organizing Committees for the Olympic Games (OCOGs), International Federations (IFs), National Governing Bodies (NGBs), cultural differences, The Olympic Program (TOP)

INTRODUCTION

The field of **international sport management** arises because sport regularly crosses international boundaries. Defining "international" as having an impact on more than one nation, it is extremely difficult to name sports that are not affected by international influences. Increasingly, there are fewer and fewer boundaries involving athletes playing professionally in foreign countries, people watching sporting events held in other countries, or people purchasing the licensed sport merchandise of foreign teams. Consistent with the overall reduction of trade barriers worldwide, sport managers are increasingly capitalizing on the opportunities to sell their products in overseas markets. Major sport leagues and events are accessed by people in hundreds of countries. The National Football League's (NFL's) Super Bowl is watched by worldwide audiences in over 170 countries in

14 different languages (*NFL International*, 1997). The Summer Olympic Games attract more than 5 million athletes, coaches, spectators, and members of the media. These games are funded in large part by corporate sponsorship agreements, some of which are worth as much as $40 million over four years. As a result of this increasingly global nature of sport, there are abundant career opportunities for sport management students.

The popularity of sport varies from country to country. With the exception of football (soccer in America) and potentially basketball, very few sports have achieved worldwide popularity. It is more common to find a particular sport enjoying regional appeal in several neighboring countries. For example, hockey is very popular in the Scandinavian countries of Sweden, Norway, and Finland, and also the North American countries of Canada and the United States. Meanwhile, baseball is popular throughout Mexico, Central America, and most of the Caribbean, as well as in Japan. Further, the organization of sport in the United States is not typical of the organization of sport throughout the world. As opposed to the school-based (high school or college) organization in the United States, the club system form of sport organization is more common throughout the rest of the world (for a more detailed discussion on sport clubs, see Chapter 9, The European Club Sport System).

Sport is subject to many of the same forces that are increasing the global **distribution** of consumer and entertainment products today. For example, Coca-Cola and the National Basketball Association (NBA) have similar international goals: increasing distribution and sales in foreign markets throughout the world. Both the NBA and Coca-Cola are responding to two forces that are stimulating international development. First, each has a need to find new markets in which to sell its products. Because the NBA wants to continue to grow and increase its revenues, it must look to international markets that have not been saturated with television programming and licensed merchandise. Second, the increased use and availability of **technology** is making international distribution easier. The advancements in technology (e.g., satellite television, the Internet, and video games), coupled with the increased accessibility to such advancements, makes expansion possible.

Given the prevalence of sport in the international marketplace, it is imperative that sport managers understand the issues surrounding the governance and management of international sport. This chapter first examines the historical development of sport in the international marketplace, then takes a look at the factors behind the global expansion of sport, addressing both the growth of sport-related corporate activities and the growth of professional sport. The chapter then examines the Olympic movement, including its organization and its primary responsibilities. Finally, because the international emphasis on sport will continue to grow, meaning an increased number of job opportunities in international sport, this chapter concludes by addressing the variety of potential employment opportunities in international sport today.

HISTORY

Sport has not always had such an international flavor. Sport first spread across international borders through imperialistic efforts. As countries such as Great Britain colonized various areas throughout the world, sport was used to impose the conquerors' culture on the colonized land. For example, cricket and rugby were introduced to Australia by the British when they colonized that continent. Today, cricket and rugby are immensely popular in Australia, and an intense rivalry exists between Australia and Great Britain. In this way, sport has fueled a feeling of pride in one's country, also known as **nationalism.** Nationalistic sentiments have also assisted in the growth of international sport today. The United States' victory over the Soviet Union ice hockey team in 1980 increased nationalistic pride as well as the interest in hockey toward the end of the Cold War.

The Olympic Games have played an important role in the development of international sport. Modern Olympus was conceived by Baron Pierre de Coubertin, on whose initiative the International Athletic Congress of Paris was held in June 1894. It was then, on June 23, 1894, that the **International Olympic Committee (IOC)** was constituted as the supreme authority of the Olympic Movement. Beginning with the inaugural modern Olympic Games in 1896 in Athens, Greece, the IOC has been entrusted with the control and development of the modern Olympic Games. In this capacity, the IOC has been quite successful. The Olympic Games are the largest international sporting event today. At the 1996 Summer Olympic Games in Atlanta, 15,000 athletes and coaches from 197 countries competed in events watched by 8.7 million spectators and 10,000 members of the media (Katz, 1996). In addition, television coverage reached 19.6 billion viewers in 214 countries and territories (International Olympic Committee, 1997).

Olympism is the philosophy behind the Olympic Games. To understand its universality, one must study its definition:

Olympism is a philosophy of life, exalting and combining in a balanced whole the qualities of body, will and mind. Blending sport with culture and education, Olympism seeks to create a way of life based on the joy found in effort, the educational value of good example and respect for universal fundamental ethical principles. (International Olympic Committee, 1993, p. 10)

This description of Olympism makes no mention as to whether the athletes competing should be amateurs or professionals. Prior to the 1980s, a major mission of the Olympic movement was to ensure that only amateurs competed. However, as the Games grew, the cost of financing the Games increased, and thus Games organizers were forced to rely more heavily on commercial enterprises.

The 1984 Summer Olympic Games in Los Angeles marked the turning point for commercial involvement with the Olympic Games, generating a profit of more than $200 million largely due to corporate involvement (Graham, Goldblatt, & Delpy, 1995). However, as they committed significant sums of money, corporations also saw the athletes and individual Olympic teams as opportunities through which to market their products. As such, it became very difficult to maintain amateurism as a standard for Olympic competition. All pretenses of amateurism were dropped in 1992, when professional basketball players from the NBA and other professional leagues around the world competed for their home nations on "Dream Teams" at the 1992 Summer Olympic Games in Barcelona.

Sport has also provided a platform through which different cultures can become more similar. Much of the world shares in the excitement of popular sporting events. For the first time ever, the World Cup of Football was held in the United States in 1994. A record 3 billion viewers watched these games take place in front of sellout crowds. This is incredible given the fact that football had only a minimal presence in the United States 30 years ago.

Concurrent with the growth of the Olympic Games, professional sport leagues and corporations have seized the opportunity to sell their products in international markets. Of the North American professional sport leagues, Major League Baseball has the longest history of attempting to export its product. In 1888, driven by Albert Spalding's desire to sell more sporting goods, a group of professional baseball players traveled overseas to play exhibition games and introduce the sport of baseball through clinics. Such practices were continued following the turn of the century as Babe Ruth and other stars of the time regularly toured Canada, Latin America, and Japan (Field, 1997). Recently, the major North American leagues have begun playing actual league games overseas. In 1986, the NFL became the first American professional sport league to export a contest between two teams (*NFL International,* 1997).

While each of the four major North American professional sport leagues aggressively attacks the international marketplace, the world's most popular sport is still football. In fact, just as American football, basketball, baseball, and hockey are attempting to spread the popularity of their sport overseas, so too is football attempting to spread its popularity. However, in the case of football, recent efforts have focused on increasing the interest and participation in the United States.

Even though football has been played in the United States since before the turn of the twentieth century, its popularity has been limited to the last 30 years. Professional football garnered widespread interest and popularity in the late 1970s and early 1980s with the North American Soccer League (NASL). The presence of foreign talent, such as all-time great Pele, made outdoor football an attractive entertainment option for many Americans. However, due to financial mismanagement and a talent pool devoid of any top North American players, the league folded in 1985. As the 1990s dawned, the hope for outdoor professional football rested with Federation International de Football Association (FIFA), the international federation for football. FIFA awarded the 1994 World Cup to the United States in the hopes of reenergizing interest and participation in football in that country. As part of the agreement to host the World Cup, USA Soccer, the national governing body for football, was to spearhead the efforts to start another professional outdoor football league. The 1994 World Cup was immensely successful, generating sellout crowds and larger-than-expected TV audiences, ultimately resulting in a revenue surplus of $60 million (Gilbert, 1995).

THE GLOBALIZATION OF SPORT

It has never been easier to sell products across international boundaries (Cateora, 1996). Increasingly liberal trade policies have combined with the rapidly developing capabilities of technology to provide companies the ability to reach many countries easily. New agreements between countries that loosen the restrictions on trade, such as the General Agreement on Tariffs and Trade (GATT) and the North American Free Trade Agreement (NAFTA), make exporting products easier. Further, the presence of satellite and digital technology, as well as the popularity of the Internet, have made the transmission of visual images worldwide simple and virtually simultaneous. Corporations have realized they must look outside their boundaries to sell their products. This only makes sense given the fact that only about 300 million of the world's 5 billion people live in North America (Cateora, 1996). Clearly, then, to sell more products corporations must seek to sell their products globally. This is a challenge facing not only mainstream businesses but sport organizations as well.

To capitalize on the global marketplace, corporations have begun to adopt a **global strategy** in selling their products. The premise for a global strategy is basic: create products that have the same appeal and generate the same demand in all corners of the world. Early proponents of this strategy were Coca-Cola, Levi's, and Disney (with theme parks in Tokyo and Paris). However, even these large companies found that in order to create demand, the product or advertising message must be adapted to account for differences in local culture and laws (Miller, 1996). Hundreds of different languages and dialects are spoken throughout the world. In addition, customs and traditions in one country may be disrespectful in another country. For example, the "thumbs up" gesture, viewed as positive in North America, has negative connotations in both the Middle East and Australia ("When in Japan," 1996). Therefore, when selling products overseas, some degree of adaptation to the local or regional culture is necessary. For example, when Disney opened EuroDisney (now called Disneyland Paris), Snow White spoke German (Barnet & Cavanagh, 1994).

Increasingly, sport organizations are eyeing a global strategy. Why does a Nike commercial for the "Air Jordan" running shoe have no spoken or printed words? Why does it only include visual images followed by Nike's trademark symbol, the Swoosh, at the end of the commercial? The answer to these questions is simple: These ads are created so that they can be shown to a global audience. People in America will see the exact same ad as people in Japan. Further, the ad will have the same impact on both American and Japanese consumers. Unfortunately, the exportation of the sport product is not always this easy. As with mainstream consumer products, adaptation based on the cultural preferences often must be made. For example, when the World League (of American football) was restarted in 1995 after a two-year hiatus, several changes were made to appeal to the European audiences. First, the uniforms were made more colorful and flashy, much like the professional football (soccer) uniforms in Europe. Second, the rules were altered to allow for more action and more scoring (Murphy, 1995).

Efforts at globalizing the sport product can be seen on two fronts: (1) corporations are attempting to utilize the sport theme and sport products to enter the international marketplace, and (2) professional sport leagues are attempting to spread the popularity of their leagues and associated products (televised games, licensed sport products, etc.) overseas.

Corporate Involvement with International Sport

As indicated in Chapter 3, Marketing Principles Applied to Sport Management, sport is a form of entertainment. People attend and watch sporting events expecting a good experience. With advances in technology, particularly satellite technology, audiences worldwide now have access to the top sporting events in the world. Realizing that such access exists, corporations increasingly are using sport to sell their products to consumers on other continents. Generally, such activities can be grouped into two categories: efforts by manufacturers of sport-related products, such as athletic shoes, athletic equipment, and sport drinks, and efforts by non–sport-related companies, which sponsor international sporting events, teams, and athletes to gain name recognition and thus sell their products in new global markets.

International Efforts of Sport-Related Products Manufacturers

Similar to many corporations throughout the world, manufacturers of sporting goods and sport-related products are increasingly attempting to capitalize on potential overseas sales. The reason for such efforts is very simple: American markets are becoming saturated. Today, there are many companies competing for the American sporting enthusiast's dollar because Americans are sport-oriented and have money to spend on sport-related items. However, the average American will only purchase a certain amount of sport-related product and merchandise in a given year. In America today, sporting goods manufacturers are reaching a point where they can no longer drastically increase their sales to American consumers. Yet, at the base of most corporate missions is the need to continually grow and expand product sales. As a result, sport-related corporations are attempting to broaden their product distribution. For example, Nike hopes to have better than half of its business come from outside U.S. borders by the year 2000 (Thurow, 1997). To do this, Nike must not only focus on its most popular product lines, such as running and basketball shoes, but it must also look to other products such as football cleats and apparel. Since more people play and watch football than any other sport in the world, it is only logical for Nike to expand its operations and focus on increasing its share of the soccer market. To do so, Nike has created its own events and marketing division called Nike Sports Entertainment (NSE). NSE's mission is to "create events worldwide featuring its stable of sponsored superstars" in an effort to increase the visibility, presence, and sales of Nike products worldwide (Himelstein, 1997, p. 78). To meet this goal, Nike is spending $200 million to sponsor the Brazilian national football team from 1996 to 2006. During this 10-year sponsorship, Nike will create events, for which it will be the title sponsor, featuring the Brazilian national team (perhaps the most popular and famous team in the world) in a series of five matches every year against national teams throughout the world. To support these efforts, Nike will spend $140 million upgrading its overseas distribution and increasing its overseas sales staff to well over 6,100 (Himelstein, 1997).

International Development via Sponsorship of Sporting Events

Non–sport-related corporations are also attempting to use sport to sell products internationally. Primarily, this is done through the sponsorship of international athletes and teams. Generally, such efforts are geared toward increasing awareness and sales overseas. For example, in 1986, Anheuser-Busch became the title sponsor of an American football league in the United Kingdom (UK) called The Budweiser League. Researchers determined that people in the UK did not drink Budweiser because they considered it weak and undesirable in comparison to its English competitors. Therefore, the primary focus of this sponsorship was to utilize a sport with a strong image to overcome Budweiser's image as a weak beer (Wilcox, 1995). By sponsoring prominent international sport efforts, corporations hope to benefit from the increased interest in sport. Coca-Cola is another large American corporation that attempts to increase its popularity worldwide through the sponsorship of international events. Coca-Cola sponsored some of the NBA's international events in an effort to increase sales and distribution of Sprite overseas. In conjunction with exhibition games played in Mexico City, Sprite produced over 1 million cans with the NBA logo in an attempt to increase the sales of Sprite in Mexico (*Global Game*, 1997).

Professional Sport Leagues' International Focus

North American professional sport leagues are aggressively seeking to increase the popularity and consumption of their respective products overseas. International travelers who see people in other countries wearing Chicago Bulls T-shirts or Dallas Cowboys hats witness the potential impact of new distribution channels for the major professional sport leagues. As mentioned earlier, the National Football League's Super Bowl reaches over 170 countries and is broadcast in 14 different languages. Because technology enables people all around the world to watch North American professional sporting events, the champions of the NFL, NBA, National Hockey League (NHL), and Major League Baseball (MLB) are called "World Champions." While this may not currently be an accurate designation given the fact that Japan has a very successful professional baseball league and Italy has a high-caliber professional basketball league, given the potential for increased speed of travel in the future it is certainly not out of the realm of possibility that the North American professional leagues might someday expand to Mexico City, Tokyo, London, and beyond.

Today, North American professional leagues are aggressively attempting to spread the popularity of their leagues internationally. Organizationally, each of the leagues has created an international division to guide such efforts. Within each of these divisions, each of the leagues maintains offices in cities throughout the world. For example, Major League Baseball International Partners has an office in Sydney, Australia, which focuses on improving the popularity of baseball through merchandise sales, game telecasts, and grassroots programs. These divisions and international offices have focused on increasing the popularity of North American professional sport utilizing several common techniques and strategies: broadcasting, licensing and merchandising, playing exhibition and regular season games, and cultivating participation in sport throughout each country (grassroots efforts).

Broadcasting

For many people around the world, their first introduction to North American professional sport comes from television broadcasts of games and highlights. Visual images are an easily exportable commodity. When attempting to export a tangible good such as a Spalding basketball or a Champion basketball jersey, tariffs (fees for selling a foreign product) must often be paid. However, it is nearly impossible to place a tariff on a visual image. Therefore, it is much easier for a professional sport league to reach international markets by first exporting its product in the form of visual images. This strategy is aided by the fact that access to television sets is increasing at a rapid rate. Even in underdeveloped countries, people are increasingly gaining access to visual images. For example, whereas in 1980 only 1% of all Chinese households had television sets, by 1987 35% did (Barnet & Cavanagh, 1994). This growth has also been assisted by the continued mergers occurring in the mass media industry. Major corporations now own major media outlets in numerous countries throughout the world. Perhaps the most notable conglomerate is the series of networks owned by Rupert Murdoch. Murdoch owns media outlets throughout Australia, Asia, Europe, and North America. In this case, MLB games televised by Murdoch's FOX Sports in the United States can also be packaged for overseas viewers on other Murdoch-owned stations such as B-Sky-B and Star-TV. ESPN, which is not part of Murdoch's holdings, has an international division that beams games out in Mandarin Chinese to the Pacific Rim and in Spanish to Latin America (Weisman, 1996).

Professional sport leagues have seized the opportunity to capitalize on such trends. During the 1996–1997 season, the NBA reached over 550 million households in 188 countries worldwide (*Global Game*, 1997). Such broadcasts have begun to produce significant revenue for the NBA. Recently, the NBA received $200,000 from a cable channel in France to broadcast NBA games in French (Wilcox, 1995). The NFL is also very aggressively pursuing distribution of American football games. During the period 1989 to 1996, the number of countries carrying NFL games went from 35 to 175, a 500% increase (*NFL International*, 1997).

In an effort to introduce their respective sports in foreign countries, leagues not only rely on actual game broadcasts but also utilize highlight show formats. For example, the NBA produces a half-hour weekly show entitled "NBA JAM" that is distributed to more than 15 countries throughout the world. The format of the show incorporates highlights in a music video format, attempting to attract the interest of 12- to 17-year-olds. Highlights are used rather than extended action clips in an attempt to attract young people to the sport's excitement. Similarly, when the NFL was introduced to Europe via television in the early 1980s, games were not shown in their entirety. Instead, key plays and highlights were condensed into half-hour and hour formats.

Licensing and Merchandising

Another tactic typically used in attempting to expand a sport to international markets is to sell **licensed merchandise**. Team-logoed merchandise provides people with a means to identify and associate with their favorite teams. However, sales of team-logoed items traditionally were isolated to the country in which the sport team competed. Increasingly, though, sport leagues are utilizing the sales of logoed merchandise as a means to increase league popularity overseas. For example, the NBA sold $5 million worth of NBA Cologne in Europe in 1993 (Wilcox, 1995). The J-League, a Japanese professional football league, greatly enhanced its popularity through Sony Creative Product sales of hats, jackets, and flags (Morris, 1995). Once licensed merchandise is sold, it serves as a promotional vehicle for the respective teams or leagues. People purchasing and wearing Chicago Bulls T-shirts and hats in Beijing serve to increase the awareness of both the NBA and the Chicago Bulls in China.

Exhibition/Regular Season Games

The most obvious step a professional sport league can take in exporting its product is to actually hold games on foreign soil. In this way, people in different countries have the opportunity to witness the sport in person. The NFL has been the most aggressive using this strategy. The NFL has played exhibition games outside the United States since 1986. In almost every case, these games were played before sold-out crowds. Such success led the NFL to create an international professional football league, the World League. Implemented during the 1991–1992 and 1995–1997 seasons thus far, the World League currently consists of six European teams from the Netherlands, Spain, England, Scotland, and Germany ("A Rookie's Guide," 1997). The World League's mission is ultimately twofold: (1) increase the popularity of American football in Europe and (2) develop talent that can later play in the NFL. The World League also attempts to develop home-grown talent, mandating that at least seven players on every roster be from the native country. While this strategy has not produced many European NFL stars, that remains a larger goal (Murphy, 1995).

The other professional sport leagues have also undertaken significant efforts to export their product in game format. In August 1996, the San Diego Padres and New York Mets played a three-game regular season series in Monterrey, Mexico. The NBA began playing exhibition games in 1988, when the Atlanta Hawks traveled to the former Soviet Union. Since then, NBA exhibition games have been played in Spain, the Bahamas, Mexico, France, Germany, the United Kingdom, and Japan. In 1996, the NBA went one step further, having the New Jersey Nets and the Orlando Magic play two regular season games in Tokyo. More than 70,000 tickets were sold for the two games in less than 5 hours, a testament to the popularity of basketball in Japan.

Marketing of Foreign Athletes

In the last 20 years, as trade barriers between countries have decreased, so too have barriers preventing the top players in the world from playing in North American professional sport leagues. The presence of foreign players has enabled the professional leagues to increase their popularity overseas. Thirty percent of all players under contract to professional baseball clubs in the United States (both major league and minor league) are from other countries (Lefton, 1996). By marketing these players in their homelands, the professional leagues are able to increase the popularity of both the players and their respective sports overseas. The rise of satellite television has aided in this venture. Improving technology allows worldwide audiences to see Toni Kukoc play for the Chicago Bulls and increases the popularity of basketball throughout Croatia. Increasingly, exhibition games are being held in foreign countries featuring some of these foreign stars. For example, when Hideo Nomo returned to Japan with a Major League Baseball tour, 56,000 turned out to watch him pitch (Whiteside, 1996). The marketing of foreign players is also a key strategy for the recently created women's professional leagues. For example, the Women's National Basketball Association (WNBA) features the stars of the Australian and Chinese national teams (*Global Game*, 1997).

Grassroots Programs

Grassroots efforts are programs and activities undertaken to increase sport participation and interest in a particular international region. Each professional sport league undertakes significant grassroots efforts, and will continue to do so, thus providing many potential employment opportunities for future sport managers. These efforts are primarily focused in two areas: increasing participation and educating people about the specifics of a particular sport. The theory behind grassroots efforts is that long-term popularity and interest will only be achieved when there is both a knowledgeable fan base and a significant portion of the population participating in the sport.

MLB implements several grassroots programs in its effort to spread the popularity of baseball. The Pitch, Hit, and Run program reaches more than 500,000 boys and girls in Australia, Germany, Japan, Korea, Taiwan, and the United Kingdom (*MLB International*, 1997). The program helps teach baseball fundamentals to school children over a six- to ten-week period, culminating with a competition of throwing, hitting, and base running. In an effort to help the individual schools teach the fundamentals, MBL provides each school with baseball equipment, instructional videos, and manuals (*MLB International*, 1997). To provide expertise in the game, MLB has created the "Envoy Program" in which baseball coaches travel to 24 countries in Europe, Latin America, and the Pacific Rim conducting clinics and teaching baseball skills.

Each of the leagues employs different approaches in implementing its grassroots programs. For example, the NBA employs two common tactics. First, the NBA has sponsored 3-on-3 basketball tournaments overseas since 1992. Such tournaments have achieved widespread success. Tournaments in Madrid, Athens, Paris, and Berlin all draw more than 1,000 teams (*Global Game*, 1997). Secondly, the NBA has created a game called "NBA 2ball" in which players work in teams of two, dribbling, passing, and shooting from various points on the floor in an effort to accumulate the most points for their two-person team. This game has been used to introduce basketball to students in schools throughout the United Kingdom and Mexico (*Global Game*, 1997).

The Importation of Football

Major League Soccer (MLS) debuted in 1996, following the widespread success of the 1994 World Cup. In attempting to establish a foothold for professional football in the United States, MLS is using many of the same strategies the NFL, NHL, NBA, and MLB use in spreading popularity overseas. Of quintessential importance is the televising of league games. Given the better-than-expected success of the 1994 World Cup on television in the United States, MLS was able to obtain contracts with ABC and ESPN.

MLS is also buoyed by a significant grassroots presence in the United States (Gilbert, 1995). Initially stimulated by the North American Soccer League (NASL), youth football programs and organizations have grown significantly over the past 30 years. Today, over 16 million Americans, of which 41% are female, play football (Gilbert, 1995). Besides targeting women, MLS also markets itself to and attracts much interest from the Latino population (Langdon, 1997c). With such significant interest from minority groups, football attracts a more diverse following than do the other four U.S. professional sports.

Its diverse participants make football more appealing to sponsors attempting to reach diverse audiences with their sponsorship programs. Accordingly, many large companies have signed on as MLS sponsors, including MasterCard, Nike, Pepsi, Reebok, and Anheuser-Busch. MLS executives have also attempted to increase league popularity by focusing on increasing the amount of licensed merchandise in the marketplace. They have been so aggressive in this area that they even sold a license to a company to produce action figures (Langdon, 1997b). Finally, because of the popularity of football among women, a women's professional football league is being started. The National Soccer Alliance (NSA) will begin play in the spring of 1998, a nice lead-in to the United States' hosting of the 1999 Women's World Cup of Football (Langdon, 1997a).

ORGANIZATION OF THE OLYMPIC MOVEMENT

For a better understanding of the Olympic structure, see Figure 10–1. At the top is the IOC. The IOC is responsible for overseeing the Olympic Movement throughout the world. Beneath the IOC, the Olympic structure splits into two arms. On one side are the **National Olympic Committees (NOCs) and Organiz-**

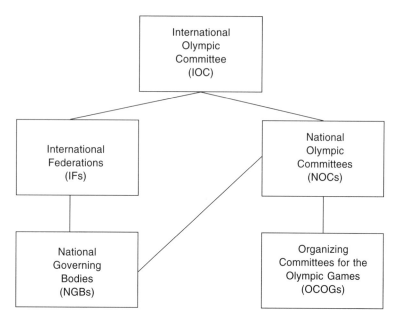

Figure 10–1 Organizational Structure of the Olympic Movement.

ing **Committees of the Olympic Games (OCOGs)**. These organizations are primarily responsible for the operational aspects of the Olympic Games. For example, the United States Olympic Committee (NOC for the United States) and the Salt Lake Organizing Committee (host for the 2002 Olympic Games) will work together to implement the Winter Olympic Games in 2002. On the other side of the Olympic structure are organizations that are responsible for the administration of individual sports. **International Federations (IFs)** are responsible for the administration of individual sport competitions throughout the world. For example, the International Amateur Athletics Federation (IAAF) oversees the World Track and Field championships. **National Governing Bodies (NGBs)** operate within the guidelines set forth by their respective IFs to administer sport in a given part of the world. USA Track and Field is the NGB in the United States that would select athletes to compete in the World Track and Field Championships. Each of the five organizational entities is explored in depth in the following discussion.

The International Olympic Committee

The defined role of the IOC is to promote Olympism in accordance with the Olympic Charter. The IOC is a nongovernmental, nonprofit organization based in

Lausanne, Switzerland. The IOC initially consisted of 14 members, with Demetrius Vikelas (of Greece) as its president. Today it has 111 members. The Olympic Charter is the codification of the fundamental principles, rules and bylaws adopted by the International Olympic Committee. It governs the organization and operation of the Olympic Movement and stipulates the conditions for the celebration of the Olympic Games. As such, the IOC has a key role because it is the final authority on all questions concerning the Olympic Games and the Olympic Movement.

The IOC owns exclusive rights to the Olympic Games, the Olympic symbol (the five rings used alone, in one or in several colors), the Olympic flag (white background with the Olympic symbol in its five colors located in the center), the Olympic anthem, the Olympic motto ("Citius, Altius, Fortius," meaning "swifter, higher, stronger"), the Olympic flame, and the Olympic torch. Corporations wanting to use any of these marks must first pay the IOC a rights fee. For example, IBM provided the IOC with $40 million worth of computers and cash in return for using the interlocking rings in their advertising efforts in 1996.

The IOC is governed by its members, who are self-selected (i.e., there is no outside vote on who is an IOC member). IOC members represent their countries, not their NOCs. IOC members must speak at least one of the languages used at the IOC sessions (French, English, German, Arabic, Spanish, and Russian). There cannot be more than one member elected per country, except in the case of countries that have hosted an Olympic Games. In this case, countries are allowed two members. The IOC Session, the general meeting of IOC members, is held at least once a year and is the supreme operating entity of the IOC. However, the president can call an extraordinary session if necessary. In these general sessions, the IOC members elect one president, three vice-presidents, and seven members to form the Executive Board. This board is ultimately responsible for the administration of the IOC and must report on its activities periodically by submitting proposals to the entire membership for approval. The Executive Board meets several times a year outside the Session in order to fulfill the duties assigned to it by the Olympic Charter. The duties of the Executive Board include supervising the strict observation of the IOC rules, ratifying the agendas for IOC Sessions, and submitting to the IOC the names of persons it recommends for IOC membership. In addition, the president can nominate special commissions to study certain specific subjects and submit recommendations to the Executive Board. Some of these special commissions are joint, meaning they comprise members of the IOC, representatives of the IFs and NOCs, technicians, consultants, and specialists. Examples of these commissions include the IOC Radio and Television Commission, Press Commission, Finance Commission, Medical Commission, and Athletes Commission.

National Olympic Committees

The NOCs are responsible for developing and protecting the Olympic Movement in their respective countries, in accordance with the Olympic Charter. Specifically, NOCs are responsible for:

* supporting the fundamental principles of Olympism in their country
* ensuring the observance of the Olympic Charter in their countries
* encouraging the development of high-performance sport as well as sport for all within their respective countries
* assisting in the training of both athletes and sport administrators
* representing their respective countries at the Olympic Games and at regional, continental, and world multisport competitions patronized by the IOC

In addition, NOCs have the authority to designate cities that may bid to host Olympic Games in their respective countries. For example, the United States Olympic Committee (USOC), through its board of directors, voted not to seek a U.S. candidate city for the 2008 Olympic Games.

The NOCs are organized regionally. The umbrella organization is the Association of National Olympic Committees (ANOC). Underneath ANOC, the NOCs are organized into five regional NOC organizations: the Association of National Olympic Committees of Africa (ANOCA), the Olympic Council of Asia (OCA), the Pan American Sports Organization (PASO), the European Olympic Committees (EOC), and the Oceania National Olympic Committees (ONOC). With the reunification of Germany, the readmittance of South Africa and the Baltic States, and the breakup of the Soviet Union, there are now 197 NOCs recognized by the IOC. Before existing as an NOC and acquiring the right to be designated as such, an organization must be recognized by the IOC. Recognition can be granted only to an NOC, the jurisdiction of which coincides with the limits of the country in which it is established and has its headquarters (International Olympic Committee, 1993). An interesting case in this regard is that of Hong Kong. Until recently, countries that were ruled by other countries, as Lithuania, Estonia, and Latvia were by the former Soviet Union, didn't have recognized NOCs. Consequently, they were prohibited from competing in the Olympic Games with their own teams. However, Hong Kong has been a different case. When the IOC was founded in 1894, Hong Kong was a colony of Great Britain. When Hong Kong's Olympic Committee was founded in 1950, it met all the requirements and was accepted by the IOC in 1951. Since then, Hong Kong has sent a delegation to compete at the Olympic Games. As a consequence of Hong Kong's becoming part of China on July 1, 1997, the IOC president met with distinguished Chinese dignitaries and signed a document guaranteeing the continuity of Hong Kong as an NOC (Merc, 1997).

The United States Olympic Committee

The NOC for the United States of America is the USOC. The USOC is the organization mandated by Congress under the Amateur Sports Act of 1978 to govern activities in the United States related to the Olympics and the Pan American Games. The USOC represents Olympic sport athletes, coaches, administrators, and the American people who support the Olympic Movement. Most important, the USOC is responsible for sending the U.S. Olympic teams to the Olympic Games. The USOC members include Olympic and Pan American sport organizations, athletes' representatives, the Armed Forces, Disabled in Sports, state fund-raising organizations, associate members, and representatives of the public sector, comprising a total of 72 member organizations (United States Olympic Committee, 1996).

The organizational structure of the USOC includes an executive committee and a board of directors. The executive committee meets as often as needed and is responsible for supervising the conduct of the business affairs of the USOC, according to the policy guidelines prescribed by the board of directors. The board of directors carries out the purposes and objectives of the USOC. It meets twice a year, unless otherwise decided by the constituency.

Organizing Committees for the Olympic Games

The honor of hosting the Olympic Games is entrusted by the IOC to the city designated as the host city of the Olympic Games. This honor is given to a city after it has gone through the bidding process. Some cities, such as Salt Lake City before being awarded the 2002 Winter Olympic Games, have bid two and three times before being selected to host the Games. In other cases, a city has been awarded the Games the first time it bids, as was the case with Atlanta and the 1996 Summer Olympic Games. The bidding process has become increasingly complex due to the enhanced interest in hosting the Games. Therefore, the IOC has implemented a preselection process stipulating a number of rules and regulations interested cities must follow. Table 10–1 presents a summary of the areas that Salt Lake City addressed in formulating its bid for the 2002 Winter Olympic Games. In the most recent bid process for the 2004 Summer Olympic Games, there were originally 11 cities vying to host the Games. A selection college appointed by the IOC in March 1997 chose 5 finalists from the 11 original candidates. From these 5 cities, the IOC membership, in September 1997, selected Athens, Greece, as the host city of the 2004 Games.

Once a city has been awarded the Games, it forms an Organizing Committee for the Olympic Games (OCOG). At this time, the IOC enters into a written agreement

Table 10–1 Technical Areas Addressed by Salt Lake City in Bid for 2002 Olympic Games

Specific topic
General facts about city
Demographics
Goals
Support from city
Experience with international events
Commitment to hosting games
Venues
Slalom
Giant slalom
Ski ballet and moguls
Downhill and Super G
Ski jump, bobsled, and luge
Cross country and biathlon
Figure skating
Ice hockey
Speed skating
Athlete's village
Opening and closing ceremonies
Practice facilities
Construction
Facilities for opening and closing ceremonies
Inventory/winter sports facilities
Housing for athletes, coaches, and officials
Medical plan
Press/media considerations
Transportation of athletes, staff, coaches, and media
Financial projections

Source: Reprinted with permission from *Technical Specifications Salt Lake City*, April 14, © 1989, Salt Lake City Winter Games Organizing Committee.

with the host city and the NOC. For example, Atlanta was awarded the Games on September 18, 1990. On January 28, 1991, The Atlanta Committee for the Olympic Games (ACOG) was incorporated. From that moment, the OCOG is responsible for planning, implementing, and staging the Games. The responsibilities of the OCOG are enormous. The OCOG is ultimately responsible for the construction of all the venues, accommodations for the athletes and coaches, accreditation, logistics, host broadcasting, security, medical services, technology, tickets, transportation, communications, finances, risk management, government relations, protocol, volunteer services, operations, and sports competition, among other duties. It must also establish a marketing program and sign sponsorship agreements separate from those implemented by the IOC.

International Federations

IFs are the international governing bodies for individual and team sports throughout the world. They are nongovernmental organizations responsible for developing sport and organizing competitions at the Olympic Games. IFs must petition for formal recognition by the IOC. The IOC then grants two years of provisional recognition during which the IOC observes the federation to determine whether it deserves official recognition. This process has recently been particularly important for some emerging sports, such as snowboarding, that are attempting to become part of the Olympic Games.

After each Olympic Games, the IOC reviews the program and determines whether new sports and/or new events can be added. At this time, IFs that are recognized by the IOC, but not included on the Olympic Program, can petition to be included. In order for a sport to be included on the Summer Olympic Program it must be practiced by men in at least 75 countries on four continents and by women in at least 40 countries on three continents. For Atlanta, there were 26 IFs involved in the Olympic Program. To be included on the Winter Olympic Program, a sport must be practiced in at least 25 countries on three continents. The IFs are organized by type of competition:

- Association of Summer Olympic International Federations (ASOIF)
- Association of International Winter Sports Federations (AIWF)
- Association of IOC Recognized International Sports Federations (ARISF)
- the General Association of International Sports Federations (GAISF)

IFs are run as international organizations, with their staffs determined by financial resources and objectives. Table 10–2 presents a listing of the IFs. Sports such as basketball and football have large international federations, sometimes employing more than 25 people. In contrast, IFs for sports such as field hockey and team handball have very few employees.

In addition to actual Olympic competitions, each IF sanctions international competitions and establishes its own eligibility rules. An IF can have one set of eligibility rules for the Olympic Games, which must be approved by the IOC, and another set of rules for all other international competitions. For example, the International Ice Hockey Federation (IIHF) could decide to use different eligibility standards during the World Cup of Hockey than during the Olympic Games.

National Governing Bodies

National Governing Bodies (NGBs), or National Sports Federations, are the organizations governing a sport within each country. Each IF recognizes a single

Table 10–2 International Sport Federations

Symbol/ Abbreviation	International Federation
AIBA	International Amateur Boxing Federation
FEI	International Equestrian Federation
FIAC	International Amateur Cyclists Federation
FIBA	International Basketball Federation
FIBT	International Bobsled and Tobogganing Federation
FIC	International Canoeing Federation
FIE	International Fencing Federation
FIFA	Fédération Internationale de Football Association
FIG	International Gymnastics Federation
FIH	International Field Hockey Federation
FIL	International Luge Federation
FILA	International Amateur Wrestling Federation
FINA	International Amateur Swimming Federation
FIS	International Ski Federation
FISA	International Rowing Federation
FITA	International Archery Federation
FIVB	International Volleyball Federation
IAAF	International Amateur Athletic Federation
IFWHA	International Federation of Women's Hockey Associations
IHF	International Handball Federation
IIHF	International Ice Hockey Federation
IJF	International Judo Federation
ISU	International Skating Union
IWF	International Weightlifting Federation
IYRU	International Yacht Racing Union
UIPMB	International Union of Modern Pentathlon and Biathlon
UIT	International Shooting Federation

Source: ESSENTIALS OF AMATEUR SPORTS LAW, Glenn M. Wong, Copyright © 1988 by Greenwood Publishing Group, Inc. Reproduced with permission of GREENWOOD PUBLISHING GROUP, INC., Westport, CT.

NGB in each country participating in the sport. For example, in the United States, USA Basketball is the NGB for basketball recognized by Fédération Internationale de Basketball (FIBA), the international federation for basketball. An NGB's membership must be open to all national organizations concerned with promoting the sport. Each NGB is responsible for approving and sanctioning competitions open to all athletes in its country (United States Olympic Committee, 1997). For example, USA Track and Field is responsible for the coordination and administration of the United States Track and Field Championships. In addition, NGBs set the national policies and eligibility standards for participation in their respective sports. Finally, NGBs are responsible for the training, development, and selection of the Olympic teams in their respective sports. USA Track and Field uses the

United States Track and Field Trials to select the Olympic Team for every Summer Olympic Games.

The Paralympic Games

The Paralympic Games, where the world's best athletes with physical disabilities compete, also represents one of the world's largest sporting extravaganzas. In 1996, more that 3,500 athletes from over 120 countries competed at the Atlanta Paralympic Games (Allen, 1996). A wide variety of athletes compete in the Paralympic Games, including amputees, wheelchair athletes, the visually impaired, dwarfs, athletes with cerebral palsy, and athletes with spinal cord injuries. Introduced in Rome in 1960, the Summer Paralympic Games have been held every Olympic year since. The Winter Paralympic competition began in 1976 (Hums, 1996). Starting in 1988 in Seoul, South Korea, the Paralympics immediately followed the competition dates of the Olympic Games and shared common facilities.

Organizers of the Paralympic Games face the same major challenge as organizers of the Olympic Games: raising money to cover operating costs. With the Paralympic Games increasing in size and scope, the Games must generate revenues from corporate sponsorships, licensing agreements, and ticket sales. The Paralympics face an added challenge in that they are not governed by the IOC and thus do not share in the millions generated by the Olympic Movement. Instead, the Paralympics are governed by the International Paralympic Committee (IPC). The Paralympics have an organizational structure similar to that of the Olympics. The IPC oversees National Paralympic Committees (NPCs), and the city hosting the Paralympic Games has a Local Paralympic Organizing Committee (LPOC). In the United States, the USOC serves as the NPC, but this is not the case in all countries. The 1996 Paralympic Games in Atlanta were organized by the Atlanta Paralympic Organizing Committee (APOC).

CAREER OPPORTUNITIES

This chapter examines a wide variety of settings in which sport crosses international boundaries. In addition, it is evident that significant growth is occurring in each of these settings. As a result of such development, a wide variety of career opportunities are potentially available to future sport managers. Before discussing the areas in which job opportunities may exist, it is important to note that two unique competencies are required of most international sport managers. First, with the many different languages spoken throughout the world, sport efforts within other countries require that sport managers be multilingual. Therefore, the future sport manager should take every opportunity to learn a second language. Second, different countries have different customs. Sport managers must not only make themselves aware of these customs but must appreciate and accept the differences that exist (Masteralexis & McDonald, 1997).

Corporate Sport

With corporations throughout the world attempting to extend the markets for their products through sport, there will be increased opportunities for experts in international sport management. Regardless of whether the corporation is sponsoring the 1998 Nagano Winter Olympics or a 3-on-3 basketball tournament in Paris, sport management experts are needed to ensure that a corporation's association with the sporting event is maximized. For example, Coca-Cola had over 100 employees dedicated to overseeing its involvement with the Olympic Games. Thus, corporations (both sport-related and non–sport-related) may have job openings specifically in international sport.

Professional Sport Leagues

Professional sport leagues are aggressively attempting to expand the popularity of their leagues in markets throughout the world. Trained sport managers are needed to help the leagues increase their visibility through broadcasting agreements, licensing agreements, exhibition games, marketing athletes, and grassroots programs. In fact, most professional sport leagues have a number of employees in overseas offices. For example, the Sydney, Australia, office of MLB employs people who focus on increasing the distribution and promotion of MLB in Australia. These efforts include working with local retailers to sell MLB-logoed hats and T-shirts, as well as working with Australian television stations to secure broadcast coverage of MLB in Australia.

Sport Marketing Companies

As highlighted in Chapter 11, Sports Agency, and Chapter 14, Event Management, behind nearly every major event is a sport marketing company. This is also true with respect to international sport. Corporations, Olympic organizations, and professional sport leagues regularly hire sport marketing agencies to coordinate their international efforts. For example, even though the NBA and Nike sponsor the NBA 3-on-3 basketball tour throughout Europe, these street basketball events are organized, marketed, and administered by Streetball Partners, a Dallas-based

Table 10–3 Sport Marketing Agencies Involved with the Olympic Games

Sport Marketing Company
Advantage International
International Marketing Group (IMG)
ISL
Meridian
MBD-IMG (Switzerland)
Real-Marketing (Germany)
RSL Marketing (United Kingdom)
Sorgem (France)
Sponsoring Consultancy Group (Holland)
Sponsorium International Inc. (Canada)
Sports Marketing Surveys (United Kingdom)

Source: Data from M. Carroggio, *Patrocinio Deportivo: Del Patrocinio de Los Juegos Olimpicos al Deporte Local,* © 1996, Ariel Communication.

company specializing in grassroots tournaments. To coordinate the various tournaments they hold throughout Europe, Streetball Partners has a number of employees who travel throughout Europe organizing and managing these tournaments. IMG, the largest sport marketing agency, has 78 offices in 38 countries (Helyar, 1997).

There are numerous sport marketing companies that work integrally with the Olympic Games. Table 10–3 presents a list of sport marketing companies known to work closely with the Olympic Games. Most of these either represent a sponsor and/or an athlete and/or a team. ISL was the sport marketing agency originally hired by the IOC to sell The Olympic Program (TOP) sponsorships (discussed in detail later in this chapter, under the heading The Olympic Program). Recently, however, the IOC has switched to Meridian as the marketing agency for the IOC and TOP program. Meridian was founded in January 1996 and has its headquarters in Lausanne, Switzerland, with a U.S. office in Atlanta. While ISL is no longer the marketing agency for the IOC, it continues to be the marketing agency for other sport governing bodies and international sporting events, such as the World Cup. Advantage International and IMG have Olympic clients, mainly Olympic sponsors and Olympic athletes. In order to support their clients, both of these agencies have offices around the world.

International Olympic Committee

The IOC is an international organization, and most of its staff have international experience. Language skills are mandatory in order to work for the IOC, and most

IOC employees are fluent in either French or English. A sport manager interested in working for the IOC should identify his or her area of interest and contact the appropriate department within the IOC. Some departments offer internship programs. If a sport management student is interested in pursuing this approach, it is important to consider the time and distance factors and also to start the process well in advance.

Organizing Committees for the Olympic Games

Jobs become available with the organizing committees for the Olympic Games from the time the committee is formed (about six years prior to the Games). However, the last three years before the Games are a crucial time for recruiting the right staff. The available jobs can be related to any of the aspects needed to organize the Games, including administration, hospitality, international relations, logistics, protocol, technology, transportation, and ticketing. Usually jobs with OCOGs are temporary, lasting until the Games are over. However, there are some people who work for one organizing committee after another because they have become experts in a specific area and enjoy living in a variety of different settings. The most appealing part of working for an organizing committee is receiving a unique experience. The drawback is that it is temporary and usually there is not much opportunity to grow inside the organization. Most of the time, an employee is hired to perform a specific task, and there is not much room for advancement.

National Olympic Committees

There are different job opportunities within a National Olympic Committee. Depending on its size, an NOC can have from 0 to 100 employees. In the United States, the USOC is a large organization, employing approximately 100 people. This number can increase with temporary jobs during Olympic years. In the case of the USOC, many employees are hired via internships. The USOC offers a formal internship program in which it solicits applications and conducts interviews prior to hiring interns. Job opportunities at the USOC vary, but include positions in athlete development, broadcasting, coaching, corporate sponsorship, fund-raising, government relations, grants, human resources, international games preparation, international relations and protocol, legal aspects, licensing, management information systems, marketing, national events and conferences, public information and media relations, sports medicine, sports science, sports for the disabled, and training centers. In addition, the NOC may also be helpful in securing a position with one of the many NGBs within each country's sport movement. Again, the number of opportunities will vary greatly from country to country and from sport to sport.

CURRENT ISSUES

Cultural Awareness and Sensitivity

In undertaking any international sport management efforts, the sport manager must always be sensitive to **cultural differences**. Nike tailors the presentation of its product to the markets it serves. For example, Nike has always portrayed an antiestablishment image, allying with athletes who were prone to challenge conventional wisdom or accepted traditions. However, as Nike attempts to expand into the global marketplace, it has found that such a brash stance is frowned upon in many countries throughout the world (Thurow, 1997). Rather than attempting to buck established tradition, Nike must instead focus on respecting the cultures of other countries. Thus, in its initial efforts to sell more shoes in Europe, Nike featured a number of popular professional athletes in opera-themed ads. Incorporating into its advertising one of Europe's most popular traditions, the opera, enabled Nike to sell products to Europeans.

A lack of cultural awareness can negatively impact the efforts of American companies sponsoring international sporting events. For example, Anheuser-Busch became an "Official Sponsor of the 1998 World Cup" in an effort to broaden the distribution of its products in conjunction with one of the premier sporting events in the world. A major component of its marketing strategy was to increase brand name awareness via stadium signage where games were played. However, French law prohibits the advertising of alcohol in any spaces that can appear on television (Swardson, 1997). Thus, Anheuser-Busch was faced with a major impediment to successfully implementing its sport marketing strategy.

Foreign Student-Athletes in U.S. Colleges and Universities

In addition to the presence of international players in U.S. professional sport leagues, U.S. colleges and universities have seen an increase in the number of foreign student-athletes competing in intercollegiate athletics. Foreign student-athletes have been participating in intercollegiate athletics since the early 1900s. In the late 1950s and early 1960s, college coaches began recruiting older foreign student-athletes who had several years of experience with international teams from their respective countries. In an effort to curb this practice, the NCAA ultimately implemented a rule whereby a student-athlete loses a year of eligibility for every year any student-athlete competes after his or her twentieth birthday (Barr, 1996). The implementation of this rule has not had a dramatic effect on the recruitment of foreign student-athletes. In fact, participation by foreign student-athletes is on the rise. For example, at the Division I level, 17% of all student-athletes were foreign in 1996, representing an *increase* from 16% in 1993. Foreign student-athletes are most prevalent in tennis, soccer, ice hockey, and track (Barr, 1996). While some people argue that there are too many foreign student-athletes, others suggest that the presence of foreign student-athletes improves the caliber of play in U.S. colleges and universities.

International Special Olympics

In addition to the Olympic Games and Paralympic Games, the Special Olympics also stages large international competitions. The Special Olympic World Games provide a competitive forum for children and adults with mental retardation. Founded in 1968, the Special Olympics strives to provide improved physical fitness and motor skills, positive self-image, and self-confidence. To do so, more than 15,000 games and meets in 22 official sports are conducted every year. A total of 143 countries have accredited Special Olympics programs ("What Is," 1997). These events culminate in the Special Olympics World Games, which alternate between winter and summer Games every two years. Site selection and the sanctioning of events are done through the Special Olympics headquarters in Washington, D.C. Integral to the success of any Special Olympics event is volunteer participation. The Special Olympics relies on 500,000 volunteers worldwide to coordinate the thousands of competitions held annually (Thoma & Chalip, 1996).

Gay Games

The Gay Games were founded in 1980 as a means of educating people about the diversity and scope of the gay and lesbian community (Kennedy, 1997). The inaugural Gay Games were held in San Francisco in 1982, drawing 1,300 athletes from three countries. Since then the Gay Games have grown rapidly. Gay Games IV, held in New York City in 1994, attracted more than 10,000 athletes from 25 countries. In 1989, the Federation of Gay Games (FGG) was formed to oversee the International Gay Games and provide structure to the rapidly developing event (Thoma & Chalip, 1996). In this capacity, the FGG selects the host cities for future Gay Games. For example, the FGG awarded the 1998 Gay Games V to Amsterdam, the Netherlands.

Marketing the Olympic Games

After the success of the Los Angeles Games it was evident that marketing to corporations could provide much-needed financing for the Olympic Movement.

Today, all levels of the Olympic Movement rely heavily on revenues from broadcasting and sponsorship agreements.

Broadcasting Rights

Broadcasting rights fees are significant for the IOC, since the IOC controls the television rights to the Olympic Games. Figures 10–2 and 10–3 depict the growth of U.S. television rights paid in conjunction with the Olympic Games. These rights are sold to broadcasting outlets throughout the world. Table 10–4 provides a list of the countries that purchased broadcasting rights for the 1998 Olympic Games in Nagano, Japan. Thus, while the U.S. television agreements account for the largest portion of rights fees, the IOC receives rights fees from numerous countries throughout the world.

Sponsorship Sales

All levels of the Olympic Movement (IOC, NOCs, OCOGs, IFs, and NGBs) rely on sponsorship sales to finance their operations. Following the IOC principles established in the Olympic Charter, there are three levels of sponsorship for the Olympic Games.

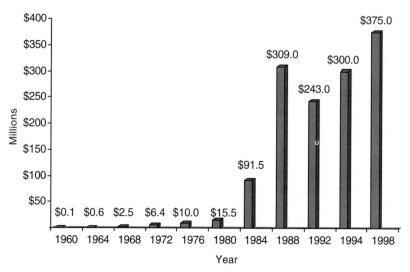

Figure 10–2 U.S. Television Rights for Winter Olympic Games. *Source:* Reprinted with permission from R. Schultz, *Business and Financial Aspects of the Olympic Games,* February 12, © 1996.

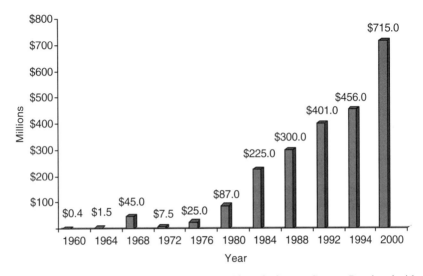

Figure 10–3 U.S. Television Rights for Summer Olympic Games. *Source:* Reprinted with permission from R. Schultz, *Business and Financial Aspects of the Olympic Games,* February 12, © 1996.

The Olympic Program

As touched on previously, the Olympic sponsorships sold by the IOC and its selected agencies are referred to as **The Olympic Program (TOP).** Based on the success of the L.A. Games, in 1985, the IOC established TOP, under which corporations pay millions of dollars for status as an official Olympic sponsor for a four-year period (quadrennium). The idea of TOP started in 1983, but it took two years to negotiate with the NOCs on behalf of the corporations and the IOC.

Table 10–4 Nagano Winter Olympic Broadcast Fees

Territory	Network	Fee ($ millions)
USA	Continental Broadcasting System	$375
Europe	European Broadcasting Union	$72
Canada	Canadian Broadcasting Company	$16
Australia	Channel 7	$6
South Africa	South African Broadcasting Company	$1.25
Japan	Japan Olympic Pool	$135
Asia	Asian Broadcasting Union	$0.54

Source: Clip and save: Nagano winter Olympic broadcast rights. (1997, March 3). *The Sports Business Daily,* p. 13.

The thought behind TOP was to sell a limited number of worldwide sponsorships, thus increasing the benefits received by each of the companies. As such, each TOP sponsor was granted exclusivity in a sponsorship category. This meant that the IOC would not sell any advertising rights to the competitors of TOP sponsors, thus supposedly providing exclusive exposure for the sponsor. For example, because Coca-Cola was the "official soft drink" of TOP I, the IOC prevented Pepsi and 7UP from advertising at the Olympic Games.

The first TOP program, TOP I, was in effect from 1985 to 1988 and included the Calgary Winter Olympics and Seoul Summer Olympics. Nine companies, paying a minimum of $10 million each, participated. For TOP II, covering the 1992 Barcelona Summer Olympics and 1992 Albertville Winter Olympics between 1988 and 1992, 12 companies paid approximately $20 million apiece for worldwide sponsorship rights. For TOP III, which included the 1994 Lillehammer Winter Olympics and 1996 Atlanta Summer Olympics, the sponsorship rights fees rose to $40 million, and 10 companies paid this amount for category exclusivity. The companies and the category in which they received exclusivity are listed in Table 10–5.

NOC Sponsorship Programs

NOCs also have their own sponsorship programs. Within these programs, the NOCs usually target domestic companies in an effort to generate funds for the development and travel of their Olympic Teams. However, before entering into a sponsorship agreement, the NOC must obtain approval from the IOC. The IOC reserves the right of approval so that the TOP sponsor's exclusive rights will be protected. For example, the IOC would prevent the USOC from selling sponsor-

---

Table 10–5 TOP III Sponsors

Sponsor	Categories
Coca-Cola	Soft drinks, juices, juice drinks, and sport drinks
Kodak	Imaging
Sports Illustrated/Time	Publishing
VISA	Payment systems
Bausch & Lomb	Optical products, dental care
Xerox	Document processing equipment
Matsushita/Panasonic	Audio, TV, and video equipment
IBM	Worldwide information systems
UPS	International express mail and package delivery systems
John Hancock	Life insurance

Source: Reprinted with permission from International Olympic Committee Press Release, May 9, 1997, © International Olympic Committee.

ship rights in the soft drink category in an effort to protect the rights of Coca-Cola as a TOP sponsor. The NOCs, in conjunction with the IOC, in turn oversee the sponsorship agreements generated by the OCOGs and NGBs.

OCOG Sponsorship Programs

An OCOG also identifies and targets its own sponsors. However, it needs approval from both the IOC and NOC. In an effort to maximize the revenue potential of these agreements, the Salt Lake Olympic Committee (SLOC) and the USOC have formed a venture to jointly market the properties of the 2002 Olympic Winter Games and the 1998, 2000, 2002, and 2004 U.S. Olympic Teams to sponsors in specific product categories. Sponsors who participate in this program gain the rights to use the 2002 Olympic Winter Games marks, as well as the marks and terminology associated with the USOC and the U.S. Olympic Teams.

SUMMARY

Today more than ever, corporations, sport leagues, and sport governing bodies are attempting to increase their popularity and revenues in international markets. Technology, particularly with respect to the transmission of visual images, greatly enhances the ease with which sport managers can introduce their products to foreign markets. In effect, the world is becoming smaller. Corporations are attempting to capitalize on this trend by sponsoring international sporting events in an effort to increase the distribution channels for their products. Major professional sports worldwide are attempting to utilize the shrinking marketplace to increase exposure for their respective leagues and sports in an effort to expand their revenue bases. This is true for both the popular North American professional sports as well as for the world's most popular sport, football. Ultimately, both corporations and professional sport leagues are attempting to improve the global appeal of their products, and to do so they must hire people with experience in international sport management.

The Olympic Movement also offers career opportunities for sport managers. Whether at the top with the IOC, or with an NOC, NGB, or OCOG, the opportunities within the Olympic Movement continue to increase as the size, proportion, and number of competitions continue to grow. Other international events, such as the Special Olympics World Games and Gay Games, are also experiencing dramatic growth. With such growth, there is also an increased need for revenues. Such financing, most often in the form of sponsorships, is heavily reliant on the corporate sector. Thus, sport managers are needed to sell sponsorships and assist the corporations in implementing their sponsorship programs.

There is clearly a diversity of opportunities for the sport manager interested in international sport. Further, because technology will continue to improve and trade barriers between countries will continue to be reduced, the volume of opportunities in international sport will increase. However, in order to capitalize on these opportunities, the sport management student must become more knowledgeable and sensitive to the cultures of other countries. In addition, the prospective international sport manager should learn new languages because multilingual capabilities are necessary at the highest levels of international sport.

CASE STUDY: PLANNING THE TORCH RELAY

As a recently hired Marketing Coordinator for the Sydney Organizing Committee (SOC), Leon Hinshaw was nervous as he entered Marketing Director Trinda Fisher's office to receive his first assignment. Sitting down across the desk from Fisher, Hinshaw was also ready to put his sport management background to work.

"We are going to see how talented you are right from the start," said Fisher. "As the Marketing Director for the 2000 Sydney Games, I am responsible for the sponsorship solicitation and promotion of the games. Trying to find sponsors is more than a full-time job. Therefore, I am going to rely on you, Leon, to handle the logistical side of some of our biggest promotions. First and foremost, what do you know about the torch relay?"

"Unfortunately, not that much," replied Hinshaw.

This did not seem to bother Fisher. "Well, today begins your education. You have to start somewhere Hinshaw, and from here on out, you are in charge of the Olympic Torch Relay for the Sydney Summer Olympic Games. See my assistant Paul on your way out for all of the background material."

Leaving Fisher's office, Hinshaw was both excited and overwhelmed, for his boss had given him a large assignment. Even though he was not fully aware of the details, he remembered hearing a lot about the Torch Relay conducted in conjunction with the 1996 Atlanta Olympic Games. He soon became overwhelmed reading about the details behind the Torch Relay.

The Olympic Torch, which lights the flame every Olympic year, is housed in Athens, Greece, site of the first Modern Olympic Games. Over the years, a tradition has developed that when the Torch arrives from Athens in the country hosting the games, it is carried around the host country generating spirit and excitement for the upcoming Olympic Games. Given the national pride that host countries derive, the Torch Relay has become the premier event leading up to the Olympic Games. In every city the Torch visits, people stand in the streets as the Torch is carried from one town to the next, passed from carrier to carrier.

The length of the relay is open, to be defined by the Organizing Committee for the Olympic Games, in this case SOC. Further, there are no limits on how far the

Torch travels or by what mode the Torch travels. All that is mandated is that the Torch arrive at the Olympic Stadium prior to the Opening Ceremonies. Prior to the 1996 Atlanta Games, the Torch was transported over 10,000 miles throughout the United States utilizing people on foot, in cars, on trains, in sailboats, and in rowboats.

As Hinshaw mulled this information over, he began to grasp the immensity of his new task. The Torch Relay would require coordination in every location, publicity to pique the Australian citizens' interest, local celebrations, selection criteria for Torch bearers, and more. And then it hit him—a Torch Relay involving the entire country over weeks, maybe even months, would be an extremely expensive proposition. Hinshaw realized that he did not know the budget for the relay. Picking up his phone, he dialed Fisher's extension.

"Good afternoon, Trinda Fisher."

"Miss Fisher, Leon Hinshaw. I have been reading through the background material on the Torch Relay and have begun to make a list of initial considerations. However, I cannot go any further without knowing the budget for this event. Do we have any initial budget for the Torch Relay?"

Hinshaw heard a pause on the other end of the phone. Fisher was apparently leafing through papers on her desk.

"Here it is in my notes from a previous meeting with the president of SOC," Fisher finally answered. "Unfortunately, there is no budget for this event, Leon. Cost overruns on facility construction have eliminated that line item all together. Why don't you mull it over and get back to me with an initial description of the event and potential sources of financing. Is two weeks enough time?"

Hinshaw was overwhelmed. But all he could do was to reply, "Uh, yes, that will be sufficient." Hanging up the phone, Hinshaw immediately realized that this was not a problem but rather an opportunity. If he performed well on this task, it would enable him to impress his superiors and bolster his résumé for future employment opportunities. Employment with SOC ended at the conclusion of the games, after all. Not wanting to waste any more time, Hinshaw began to list the questions he had to get answers for within two weeks.

Questions for Discussion

1. What logistical considerations must be addressed in implementing this event?
2. Can Torch Relay 2000 match the Atlanta Torch Relay in distance covered? Why or why not?
3. Given the logistical considerations coupled with the fact that SOC has not budgeted for the event, how can Hinshaw generate funds to make this event possible?

4. What can SOC do to ensure that the event maximizes the exposure and awareness for the Torch Relay and the parties involved with the Torch Relay?
5. What will the personnel demands be for this event? How should Hinshaw address the staffing needs of this multistop tour?

RESOURCES

Advantage International
1751 Pinnacle Drive, 15th Floor
McLean, VA 22102
703-905-3300

International Management Group (IMG)
One Erieview Plaza, Suite 1300
Cleveland, OH 44114
216-522-1200

International Olympic Committee
Chateau de Vidy
Lausanne CH 1009
Switzerland
011-41-21-612-6111 (phone)

ISL Sports & Company, Inc.
1281 E. Main Street
Stamford, CT 06902
203-324-6800

Major League Baseball International Partners
350 Park Avenue, 22nd Floor
New York, NY 10022
212-350-8304

Major League Soccer
110 E. 42nd Street, Suite 1000
New York, NY 10017
212-687-1400

Nagano Olympic Organizing Committee
KT Building
3109-63 Kawaishinden
Nagano City 380
Japan
011-81-262-25-1898

National Basketball Association
645 Fifth Avenue
New York, NY 10022
212-407-8000

National Football League
410 Park Avenue
New York, NY 10022
212-758-1500

National Hockey League
1251 Avenue of the Americas
New York, NY 10020-1198
212-789-2000

Salt Lake City Organizing Committee
215 South State Street, Suite 2002
Salt Lake City, UT 84111
801-322-2002

Sydney Olympic Organizing Committee
Level 14
The Maritime Center
207 Kent Street
Sydney, New South Wales 2000
Australia
011-61-2-931-2020

United States Olympic Committee
One Olympic Plaza
Colorado Springs, CO 80909
719-578-4654

World League of American Football
410 Park Avenue, 6th Floor
New York, NY 10022
212-758-1500

REFERENCES

Allen, K. (1996, August 10). Olympic family expands. *USA Today*, p. 3C.

Barnet, R.J., & Cavanagh, J. (1994). *Global dreams: Imperial corporations and the new world order*. New York: Simon & Schuster.

Barr, C.A. (1996). Multiculturalism within United States collegiate sport: Recruitment of international student-athletes. *Proceedings from the Fourth European Congress on Sport Management*, Montpellier, France, 465–473.

Carraggio, M. (1996). *Patrocinio deportivo: Del patrocinio de los Juegos Olimpicos al deporte local*. Lausanne, Switzerland: Ariel Communication.

Cateora, P. (1996). *International marketing*. New York: Irwin.

Clip and save: Nagano winter Olympic broadcast rights. (1997, March 3). *The Sports Business Daily*, p. 13.

Field, R. (1997). Play ball: Just whose pastime is it anyway? *Play Ball*, 109–117.

Gilbert, N. (1995, February 14). Kickoff time for soccer: Can U.S. pro soccer turn from bush league to big league? *Financial World*, 79–85.

Global game. (1997). [On-line]. Available: http://www.nba.com

Graham, S., Goldblatt, J.J., & Delpy, L. (1995). *The ultimate guide to sport event management and marketing*. Chicago: Irwin Publishing.

Helyar, J. (1997, September 5). Net losses: How ProServ, legend among sports agents, fell from the top seed. *The Wall Street Journal*, pp. A1, A8.

Himelstein, L. (1997, May 12). The swoosh heard 'round the world. *Business Week*, 76–80.

Hums, M.A. (1996). Marketing the Paralympic Games: Increasing visibility for athletes with disabilities. *Proceedings of the Third European Congress on Sport Management*, Budapest, Hungary, 346–356.

International Olympic Committee. (1993). *Olympic charter*. Lausanne, Switzerland: Author.

International Olympic Committee. (1997). Olympic marketing and the new sources of financing commission. [On-line]. Available: http://www.olympic.org/femkt.html

Katz, D. (1996, January 8). Atlanta brave. *Sports Illustrated*, 72–93.

Kennedy, S. (1997). *The federation of gay games*. [On-line]. Available: http://gaygames.nl

Langdon, J. (1997a, February 14). First women's pro league planning to kick off in '98. *USA Today*, p. 15C.

Langdon, J. (1997b, January 9). MLS devises strategy to help fans get hands on merchandise. *USA Today*, p. 10C.

Langdon, J. (1997c, January 17). Survey: Pro game attracts young, families. *USA Today*, p. 11C.

Lefton, T. (1996, November 4). Tim Brosnan: COO Major League Baseball International. *Brandweek*, 56–58.

Masteralexis, L.P., & McDonald, M.A. (1997). Enhancing sport management education with international dimensions including language and cultural training. *Journal of Sport Management, 11*(1), 97–110.

Merc, A. (1997, July 2). Hong Kon mantendra su Comite Olimpico Nacional. *La Vanguardia*.

Miller, C. (1996, December 2). Chasing a global dream. *Marketing News*, 1–2.

MLB International. (1997). [On-line]. Available: http://www.majorleaguebaseball.com

Morris, K. (1995, February 14). How Japan scored. *Financial World*, 82–85.

Murphy, A. (1995, May 22). As the world turns. *Sports Illustrated*, 62–65.

NFL International. (1997). [On-line]. Available: http://www.nfl.com

A rookie's guide to the World League—The NFL's spring league. (1997). [On-line]. Available: http; www.worldleague.com

Rozin, S. (1995, July 24). Olympic partnership (special advertising section). *Sports Illustrated*, 37–76.

Schultz, R. (1996, February 12). Business and financial aspects of the Olympic Games. Unpublished presentation to the University of Massachusetts, Amherst.

Swardson, A. (1997, April 14). Battle over Bud brewing for French-hosted World Cup soccer. *Washington Post*, p. A12.

Technical specifications Salt Lake City. (1989, April 14). Technical Report prepared by Salt Lake City Winter Games Organizing Committee.

Thoma, J.E., & Chalip, L. (1996). *Sport governance in the global community*. Morgantown, WV: Fitness Information Technology, Inc.

Thurow, R. (1997, May 5). In global drive, Nike finds its brash ways don't always pay off. *The Wall Street Journal*, pp. A1, A10.

United States Olympic Committee. (1996). 1996 Annual Report. Colorado Springs, CO: Author.

United States Olympic Committee. (1997). 1997/1998 Fact Book. Colorado Springs, CO: Author.

Weisman, L. (1996, August 29). Padres, Mets go home happily. *USA Today*, p. 8C.

What is Special Olympics? (1997). *Special Olympics International*. [On-line]. Available: http://www.specialolympics.org

When in Japan don't cross your legs. (1996, March/April). *Business Ethics,* 50.

Whiteside, L. (1996, November 17). The rising son returns to Japan. *The Boston Globe*, p. C12.

Wilcox, R.C. (1995). The American sporting enterprise in contemporary Europe: Capitalist imperialism or cultural homogenization? *Proceedings of the Third European Congress on Sport Management*, Budapest, Hungary, 677–693.

Wong, G.M. (1988). *Essentials of amateur sports law*. Dover, MA: Auburn House Publishing Company.

CHAPTER 11

Sports Agency

Lisa Pike Masteralexis

Key words: sports agent, reserve system, reserve clause, reserve list, collective bargaining agreement, standard/uniform player contract, free-standing sport management firm, law practice only, sport management firm affiliated with a law firm, sports event managers, sports marketing representative, income mismanagement, incompetence, conflicts of interest, charging excessive fees, overly aggressive client recruitment

INTRODUCTION

This chapter focuses on the field of sports agency, examining how athlete management firms operate. Most sports agency firms began with the goal of representing athletes and coaches. The larger, multiservice firms have evolved to also include sports marketing and event management segments. Although these three aspects of the sports agency business will be discussed, the chapter primarily focuses on agents who represent athletes and coaches. A **sports agent** is difficult to define. As Ruxin (1993) points out, the term "sports agent" covers a broad range of relationships with an athlete. In some aspects, a sports agent is similar to a talent agent in the entertainment industry in that both serve as personal managers who find the best outlet for the client's talent (Ruxin, 1993). When an agent acts as a representative of an athlete or coach, the law of agency imposes certain fiduciary duties on the agent. The fiduciary duties that establish the parameters within which the agent must operate are discussed in detail in Chapter 5, Legal Principles Applied to Sport Management.

There are many people holding themselves out as sports agents. The exact number is hard to pinpoint, but there are more people who claim to be agents than there are professional athletes and coaches. In addition, it is estimated that over

80% of professional athletes are represented by approximately 20% of the agents. Thus, many agents either have no clients or are working part time and supplementing their incomes through other professions such as law, marketing, accounting, or financial planning. This chapter discusses in detail some of the challenges to entry in the field of sports agency and also clarifies the role of the sports agent and agency firms in the sport industry and in the lives of the athletes they represent.

HISTORY

Theater promoter C.C. "Cash and Carry" Pyle is often called the first sports agent. In 1925 C.C. Pyle negotiated a deal with George Halas's Chicago Bears for Red Grange to earn $3,000 per game and an additional $300,000 in endorsement and movie rights (Berry, Gould, & Staudohar, 1986). A few years later, New York Yankee George Herman "Babe" Ruth allegedly consulted sports cartoonist Christy Walsh to serve as his financial advisor through the Great Depression (Neff, 1987).

Until the 1970s it was extremely rare for a player to have a sports agent because teams generally refused to deal with agents. Some players even found that having an agent turned out to be a detriment to their contract negotiations. One often-told story involves a Green Bay Packers player, Jim Ringo, who, in 1964, brought his financial advisor (agent) to help him negotiate his contract with legendary coach and general manager Vince Lombardi (Hofmann & Greenberg, 1989). Lombardi immediately excused himself for a minute. When Lombardi returned he told the agent he was negotiating with the wrong team, for he had just traded Ringo to Philadelphia (Hofmann & Greenberg, 1989). This type of treatment and the inability to negotiate on what the players believed was a level playing field led the Dodgers' star pitchers Sandy Koufax and Don Drysdale to hire Hollywood agent Bill Hayes to represent them in 1965. Hayes orchestrated Koufax's and Drysdale's joint holdout in which they each demanded a three-year $1 million contract, up from the $85,000 and $80,000 the Dodgers had paid them the season before (Helyar, 1994). The idea of a joint holdout, the amount of money the two demanded, and the prospect of other players trying the tactic outraged the Dodgers, and Hayes lined up an exhibition tour for Koufax and Drysdale in Japan and threatened to get Drysdale a movie contract. Although the two had talent, they had little bargaining power because the rules in Major League Baseball (MLB) did not allow them to negotiate with other Major League teams. As a result, Koufax and Drysdale ended up settling for $125,000 and $115,000 respectively (Helyar, 1994). It was a great deal less than they sought, but more than they would have received had they bargained individually and without an agent.

Most players in team sports did not have sports agents until the late sixties and early seventies (Ruxin, 1993). In fact, Major League Baseball's Collective Bargaining Agreement with the Players Association did not recognize a player's right to be represented by an agent until 1970 (Ruxin, 1993). In that era, even those who had agents used them more as advisors than as agents. For instance, in 1967 Bob Woolf counseled Detroit Tigers pitcher Earl Wilson (Woolf, 1976). Wilson went to the front office of the Tigers alone while Woolf stayed in Wilson's apartment; whenever Wilson had a question he excused himself from the room and called Woolf for more advice (Woolf, 1976).

Players in individual sports such as golf and tennis have relied on agents for a longer time. C.C. Pyle also made his mark in professional tennis when, in 1926, he guaranteed French tennis star Suzanne Lenglen $50,000 to tour the United States (Berry et al., 1986). At the time people were startled by the sum, but by the end of the tour, Pyle had helped popularize professional tennis, and all involved earned a handsome share of the revenue it generated (Berry et al., 1986). Mark McCormack, founder of the International Management Group (IMG), was one of the first sports agents to represent individual athletes, which he started doing in the 1960s. A golf lover, McCormack became "famous for launching the modern sports-marketing business when he packaged and marketed Arnold Palmer, endorsement king of the pre-Michael Jordan era" (Katz, 1994, p. 231).

Growth of the Sports Agency Business

By 1977 most segments of the sport industry had acknowledged the role that agents play in professional sports (Sobel, 1990). According to Sobel, five factors account for the growth of the sports agency business: the reserve system, the development of competing leagues, the evolution of players associations, players' need for financial advice, and rising product endorsement opportunities. Until the mid-1970s, players in MLB were bound perpetually to their teams by the **reserve system**. Each league used a restrictive system to limit a free and open market, so that the owners would retain the rights to players and depress salaries. Baseball's reserve system was the first and serves as a great example. The system consisted of two parts: the reserve clause and the reserve list. The **reserve clause** in the players' standard contracts gave teams the option to renew players for the following season. Each contract contained a reserve clause and thus a player could be renewed season after season at the team's option. The **reserve list** was a list sent to each team in the league. League rules entitled each team to place its reserved players on a list, and the teams had a "gentlemen's agreement" not to offer contracts to any other teams' players reserved on the list. This two-part system kept players bound to their teams, and thus depressed player salaries and left the players without bargaining rights or power. Free agency in MLB was born in 1976 with agents such as Jerry Kapstein, who represented 60 baseball players, raising salaries by, in essence, holding auctions for talented players (Helyar, 1994). Kapstein played to the owners' lust for talent by driving them into bidding wars for his free agents (Schwarz, 1996). As salaries increased, so too did the players' demand for agents.

The second reason for the growth of the sports agency industry was the development of competing leagues from the 1960s through the 1980s (Sobel, 1990). Competing leagues such as the American Football League (1960–1966), the American Basketball Association (1967–1976), the World Hockey Association (1972–1978), and the United States Football League (1982–1986) offered an alternative to players. These new leagues offered higher salaries to induce players to move from their original teams, and these offers provided leverage during contract negotiations. As players jumped to competing leagues their salaries increased, as did the salaries of players that owners were trying to keep in the dominant leagues. Agents often played a crucial role in finding interested teams in the new leagues and negotiating and sifting through players' offers.

The evolution of the players associations in the late 1960s and early 1970s is Sobel's (1990) third reason for the growth of sports agency. The Major League Baseball Players Association (MLBPA) led the move away from informal, powerless associations to true labor organizations engaging in collective bargaining and willing to fight or strike to convince management to meet their demands. In their negotiations with Major League Baseball's Management Council, the MLBPA achieved the right to labor grievance arbitration. Labor grievance arbitration is a system that allows both players and management to settle work-related conflicts in a hearing before a neutral arbitrator. Both sides agree in advance that the arbitrator's decision shall be final and binding on all parties. The players achieved free agency through such an arbitration award in 1975. Achieving free agency opened the door for sports agents to negotiate better contracts for the players. Players associations opened the door for the agents to have more power. In addition, players associations often monitor agents' negotiations and work with players' agents since both represent the players' interests. The difference between the two is that the union represents the collective interests of all players and an agent represents the individual interests of a particular player. As such, the union will negotiate a contract for all players in the league, called the **collective bargaining agreement,** and the agent will negotiate a contract for the player he or she represents, called the **standard/uniform player contract.** Through collective bargaining the players associations establish league salary minimums, and agents negotiate for salaries above and beyond the minimum, length of contract, bonuses, and guarantees through the players' individual contracts (Berry et al., 1986). This relationship is unique, since in most unions the union represents all interests, terms, and conditions of employment. Players associations also possess a great deal of data and information to help the agent in contract negotiations. This information includes leaguewide salary data, bonus standards, nonsalary contract data, information regarding team needs, league and team revenue, and league and team background information (Yasser, McCurdy, & Goplerud, 1997).

Fourth, as players' salaries increased, the need for tax planning (Sobel, 1990) and other forms of business advice became crucial to a player's financial planning and off-field success. Agents help athletes negotiate more favorable contract clauses for increased income, tax breaks, and postcareer income. According to Shropshire (1990) an agent also provides a level of parity between the athlete and the team, event, or sponsor with which he or she is negotiating. Sports team or event management people have had a great deal of experience negotiating many contracts each year, whereas an athlete may have just one opportunity to negotiate and thus should hire an agent with comparable negotiating experience to level the playing field (Shropshire, 1990). This is particularly important when complex systems such as salary caps are involved. It is highly likely that most athletes have not seen a player's contract before, let alone a collective bargaining agreement. Without an agent's help, an athlete may be at a severe disadvantage. Agents also allow athletes to focus their attention on performing in their sport while the agent acts as a "shield" to outside distractions (Schwarz, 1996). The shield is the transparent bubble that agents build around their clients to protect them from such distractions as tax and insurance forms, payment of bills, travel arrangements, the media, and the emotional struggles of being a professional athlete (Schwarz, 1996).

Finally, as professional sport grew into a nationally televised business and its entertainment value increased, so too did opportunities for athletes to increase their income through product endorsements (Sobel, 1990). Martin Blackman pioneered the negotiation of endorsement contracts for athletes with his deals for retired athletes to star in Miller Lite's television commercial series (Shropshire, 1990). Now, many athletes hire agents with sports marketing expertise to help them create images, market their images and services, and negotiate endorsement deals. Beyond product endorsement, athletes are becoming more involved in parlaying their images into other aspects of the entertainment field. Some, such as Michael Jordan and Shaquille O'Neal, are starring in motion pictures, while Barry Bonds, Bobby Bonilla, and Mike Piazza are finding bit parts on television and the silver screen. Others, such as Shaquille O'Neal and Jeff Juden, are recording music. And still others, such as the All-Star team of Andre Agassi, Wayne Gretzky, Ken Griffey, Jr., Joe Montana, Shaquille O'Neal, Monica Seles, and Tiger Woods, are opening theme restaurants, sports bars, and music clubs. The sports agent often performs a crucial role in helping the athlete make transitions and carrying out business transactions to establish these outside ventures. One agent, David Falk of Falk Associates Management Enterprises (F.A.M.E.), even became one of the producers of *Space Jam*, the Warner Brothers movie starring his client, Michael Jordan.

Representing Individual Athletes

Representing the individual athlete differs significantly from representing the team-sport athlete. Much of what the individual athlete earns is dependent on consistent performance in events, appearance fees from events, and the ability to promote and market his or her image. Therefore, an agent representing an individual athlete often travels with the athlete, tending to daily distractions so the athlete can stay focused on winning. For instance, as Ivan Lendl's agent for seven years, Jerry Solomon of ProServ spent nearly twenty-four hours a day for seven days a week traveling and representing Lendl (Feinstein, 1992). This can take a toll on one's social and personal life, but in some cases it is necessary in order to retain a client. When Solomon eventually pulled away from this relationship with Lendl, Lendl resented it and moved from ProServ to IMG (Feinstein, 1992). An agent of an individual-sport athlete is also more involved in managing the individual player's career, much like the business managers hired by entertainers. The management tasks include booking exhibitions and special competitions to supplement the athlete's winnings from regular tour/circuit events, as well as managing training, travel, lodging, and the athlete's personal life. For the team-sport athlete, the professional team takes care of many of these details. However, this may be changing a bit, for competition in acquiring and retaining clients is causing agents to offer more services. Some agents are taking a more active role in their athletes' training regimens by providing access to trainers and coaches to help get players drafted to a higher position or signed onto a team (Helyar, 1997a). Finally, a task that is similar for agents of both individual and team-sport athletes is marketing.

The three largest sports management companies representing athletes in individual sports are IMG, ProServ, and Advantage International (Feinstein, 1992). While IMG, ProServ, and Advantage International are not currently limited to representing individual-sport athletes, all started with golfers or tennis players. IMG, the largest and most powerful, "is a colossus, running tournaments all over the world in both golf and tennis, even controlling the computer that assigns worldwide rankings to golfers" (Feinstein, 1992, p. 131). IMG currently represents close to 1,000 athletes and has 78 offices in 38 countries (Helyar, 1997b). More recently, IMG, like P.S. Stars (a ProServ spinoff owned by Jerry Solomon and Nancy Kerrigan), have become involved in running figure skating tours. IMG first created Scott Hamilton's America Tour for its client Scott Hamilton (Brennan, 1996). Soon the tour's name was changed to Stars on Ice (so the tour can continue after Hamilton retires), and although Hamilton remains its star, the tour has, like IMG's tennis and golf events, become a moneymaker for IMG's figure skating clients (Brennan, 1996).

The second major sports management firm, ProServ, was created by attorney and former Davis Cup team member Donald Dell and two partners, Lee Fentress and Frank Craighill. Their first clients were Dell's Davis Cup teammates Arthur Ashe and Stan Smith (Brennan, 1996). ProServ is not quite as large as IMG but is very involved in tennis as it "manages players, runs tournaments, produces [television] for tournaments, and sells sponsorship for others" (Feinstein, 1992, p. 131). In fact, Donald Dell may well be doing television commentary for ProServ events, too (Feinstein, 1992). It has been said that in the sports of golf and tennis, agents Mark McCormack (IMG) and Donald Dell (ProServ) are so powerful they virtually run the sports, and they are the reason for the rapid growth of appearance fees at non-PGA golf and non-Grand Slam tennis events (Neff, 1987). IMG has, though, clearly eclipsed ProServ by moving into the global market. ProServ has no international offices; personal problems among partners and CEO Donald Dell have caused many key people to move on, and recently, in the face of mounting losses ProServ was sold to Marquee Group, a holding company for entertainment-oriented businesses (Helyar, 1997b). The sales of ProServ, Advantage International, and Boston-based Bob Woolf and Associates (now named Woolf and Associates) represent a clear recognition of professional sport as entertainment. The sales will likely increase the financial viability by diversifying losses, and it will also increase the power of these firms in the market, making it even more difficult for competitors to survive the drive to recruit and retain clients. The sales may also open more opportunities for the athletes these firms represent to move into the advertising and entertainment businesses.

The third largest firm, Advantage International, was developed by two ProServ partners and 30 ProServ staffers in 1983. Like ProServ, Advantage International was recently sold to an advertising agency holding company, Interpublic Group of Companies (Helyar, 1997b). A key difference between individual athlete representation firms and agency firms primarily representing team-sport athletes is that the firms doing individual representation not only negotiate for the athletes but are intimately involved in all aspects of the sport, from running the sports' tournaments to televising them. Such involvement can create a conflict of interest. As Brennan (1996) points out, though, athletes often decide that the conflict created when their agent becomes their employer is not as trying as the conflict created when their training and traveling bills come due and they have generated no income from their sport. Later in the chapter the duty of loyalty and the concept of conflict of interest are discussed in greater detail.

As the Olympic Movement has moved away from its rigid rules on amateurism, top-level Olympic athletes have increasingly found that they, too, have a greater need for sport agents. In figure skating, for example, new revenues coming into the sport from television rights have increased the athletes' opportunities to earn money. Until recently, Michael Rosenburg, Dick Button, and the management firm IMG had worked to develop professional skating careers for athletes such as Dorothy Hamill, Janet Lynn, and doubles partners Tai Babilonia and Randy Gardner after their Olympic appearances (Brennan, 1996). As figure skating's popularity has increased, so has the money flowing into the sport. The popularity and money have legitimately created an increased need for agents. The United States Figure Skating Association expects young stars Michelle Kwan and Tara Lipinsky to be out participating in promotions, interviews, tours, and various competitions, and as a result these young athletes are now hiring agents to promote them and to protect them from the "blastfurnace media" (Brennan, 1996, p. 126). In previous years a family struggled financially to enable a daughter or son to pursue the Olympic dream, but now with the help of an agent, an athlete may earn money to help pay some of his or her training and traveling expenses (Brennan, 1996).

Representing Coaches

There are a handful of sports agents whose primary clientele are professional and Division I collegiate coaches. Not all coaches have sports agents, but the number who do seek representation is growing. The reasons are varied. One may be the growing income of coaches; for instance, the average salary of National Basketball Association (NBA) coaches in 1997 was $2.2 million (Boeck, 1997). A second reason may be the increased job movement and added pressures on coaches to succeed (Greenberg, 1993). And finally, for many of the same reasons players have sought representation, the increased complexities of the position of head or assistant coach may make having an agent to rely on for advice and counsel almost a necessity. Specific details regarding the nature of coaching contract negotiations are discussed in the Career Opportunities section later in this chapter.

As mentioned at the beginning of the chapter, it is difficult to determine the number of sports agents in North America. Estimates vary widely, from 2,000 to as high as 15,000 (Sobel, 1990). In any case, the number of sports agents exceeds the number of athletes and coaches seeking representation. As a result, many people hold themselves out as sports agents but do not actually represent any clients in the industry. The fact that some athletes have more than one person representing their interests may contribute slightly to the high number of agents. For instance, one agent may be retained for contract negotiations, another employed for public relations and media work, and yet another for marketing. In the past two decades, as a result of the competition for clients, the industry has been jolted by stories of unscrupulous conduct by sports agents recruiting clients—and often those who resort to unethical conduct during the recruiting process do not end up with the clients they were pursuing. Unethical behavior is discussed in greater detail in the Current Issues section of this chapter.

SPORTS AGENCY FIRMS

There is no blueprint for how a sports agency firm should operate. In smaller firms an agent works alone or with one or two others, and work is often subcontracted or referred out to other professionals. In larger firms, the agent may be part of an international conglomerate representing many athletes in a broad range of sports and working on many aspects of an athlete's career.

In a presentation before the American Bar Association's Forum Committee on the Entertainment and Sports Industries, Boston College Law Professor Robert A. Berry stated that there are three models for the sports agency business (Berry, 1986/1990). The first, which he called the most popular model, is the **free-standing sport management firm**. It is established as a full-service firm providing a wide range of services to the athlete. Although each sport management firm may not perform all the services discussed in the Career Opportunities section of this chapter, it is likely that a firm performs several, including contract negotiations, marketing, and some financial planning. These free-standing sport management firms may be further divided into two categories: (1) those that represent athletes only (or possibly some entertainers and athletes), such as David Falk's F.A.M.E. and Leigh Steinberg's Steinberg and Moorad, and (2) those that are combined athlete representation and event management, such as IMG, ProServ, and Advantage International (Berry, 1986/1990).

According to Shropshire (1990) the benefits to a free-standing sport management firm are twofold: (1) the athlete is presumably able to receive the best service without having to shop around for many experts, and (2) the agent retains all aspects of the athlete's business. The firm benefits as the athlete usually pays additional fees for any services provided beyond the contract negotiation. Fees will be discussed in greater detail below.

Berry (1986/1990) identifies a second type of firm as a **law practice only**. In this type of firm "lawyer sports representatives often participate as principals in a sports management firm, but opt to include this as just one aspect of their law practice" (Berry, 1986/1990, p. 4). In this practice, the lawyer performs many legal tasks for the athlete, such as contract negotiation, legal representation in arbitration or other proceedings, legal counseling, dispute resolution, and the preparation of tax forms. Often the lawyers do not undertake financial management, marketing, or investing of the athlete's money; the sports lawyer may, however, oversee the retention of the athlete's other needed professionals to advise the athlete and protect him or her from incompetent service (Berry, 1986/1990).

The third type of firm identified by Berry (1986/1990) is the **sport management firm affiliated with a law firm**. Many sports lawyers who represent athletes originally developed a law practice and as their businesses grew they recognized the advantages of expanding the services they offered the athlete beyond legal services. Some have abolished their law practices in favor of a free-standing sport management firm, but others have retained a law practice and created a sports management subsidiary within the practice to provide those services not traditionally offered by lawyers. In more recent years, an affiliated business has developed where the law firm remains, but the firm creates a working relationship with a free-standing sport management firm, each filling the void by providing the services the other does not offer (Berry, 1986/1990).

Small firms will find greater success by representing athletes in one sport or simply providing one or two services for the athletes. Small firms often subcontract work to other professionals or refer the athlete to experts for such services as tax planning and preparation, financial investing, and public relations. Large firms employ professionals from many disciplines to provide services ranging from negotiating contracts to marketing the athlete's image to financial planning to establishing outside business interests (Ruxin, 1993). Most agents fall somewhere between, though the large multipurpose firm with offices worldwide is becoming an increasingly dominant force in the athlete representation market (Ruxin, 1993).

It is important to realize the different types of firms are market-driven. Some athletes prefer association with a large firm, whereas others prefer the individual attention of the small firms. Those who choose the large firms often do so for the following reasons: (1) a large firm provides "one-stop shopping" by employing many skilled professionals to take care of all services, (2) a large firm may have a more established history and reputation, (3) many athletes prefer representation by firms representing other star players (it's similar to being on the same team), and (4) some athletes believe that being with an agent who represents many players helps their own bargaining position. For instance, David Falk's F.A.M.E. represents more than 30 NBA players, allowing the firm to slot free agent salaries behind those of its star client Michael Jordan. F.A.M.E. has access to information and control over so many players that it can actually influence the signing of players (Burwell, 1996).

Athletes who choose small firms often do so because of the attention they receive from such a firm. At large firms, the attention of the more established agents will often go to their superstar clients. Those professional athletes on the bottom of the priority list may be assigned an assistant to deal with or may have trouble getting telephone calls returned. Even established athletes may have difficulty with the large firms. For example, golfers Greg Norman and Nick Price moved away from the large IMG and formed their own management companies to focus solely on their own needs because they found that calls to IMG often took a couple of days to answer—not because IMG was irresponsible but because it had so many clients to service (Feinstein, 1995). Both golfers also found it more cost-effective to hire their own staff than to pay IMG's 20 to 25% commission on business deals (Feinstein, 1995).

A recent innovation in the agent industry was the launching in 1992 of a Nike-controlled sports agency initiative called Nike Sports Management (NSM) (Katz, 1994). NSM's objective was to create a new kind of endorsement that exchanged the control of the athlete's other marketing opportunities for money in order for Nike to have greater control over the athlete's image. NSM's first client, basketball player Alonzo Mourning, signed a five-year guaranteed contract worth $16 million, apportioned to cover his NBA contract, his shoe contract, and other marketing opportunities (Katz, 1994). When Mourning's earnings reached those assigned apportionments, he would receive all of his remaining NBA money and half of the marketing monies (Katz, 1994). For example, assume NSM had determined that over the five years Mourning would earn $7.5 million from the NBA and $8.5 million for his shoe contract and other endorsements. Once Mourning's NBA income exceeded $7.5 million, he would receive the additional salary and once his marketing income exceeded $8.5 million, Mourning and Nike would split the additional marketing income. NSM's goal of keeping the athlete's image pure and uncluttered far outweighed any ambitions of their earning money representing the athlete (Katz, 1994). By contracting with NSM the athlete relinquishes his or her right to choose sponsors in exchange for a guaranteed, high-income contract up front. This is clearly a detriment to team negotiations, as was evident in Mourning's holdout during contract negotiations with the Charlotte Hornets: Mourning's financial security from the Nike deal removed his incentive to settle with Charlotte until he received what he was looking for ($26 million) (Greenberg, 1995). Nike recently dissolved the Nike Sports Management Division due to lack of interest by professional athletes and the move of its executive director, Terdema Ussery II, to the position of general manager of the Dallas Mavericks.

Fees Charged by Sports Agents

Fees charged by agents vary because such fees are market-driven and depend on whether the athlete is participating in a team sport or an individual sport. Fees are usually based on one of four methods: the flat fee, the percentage of compensation, an hourly rate, or a combination of an hourly rate with a percentage of compensation cap (McAleenan, 1990). The first method, the flat fee arrangement, requires an athlete to pay the agent an amount of money agreed upon before the agent acts for the athlete (McAleenan, 1990).

The second method, the percentage of compensation method, is by far the most popular. Although it is criticized as being inflated, agent Leigh Steinberg defends it. Steinberg "dismisses those who bill by the hour as 'egg-timer agents' and argues that such a fee structure militates against an important aspect of the agenting: developing a personal relationship with clients" (Neff, 1987, p. 83).

There is a drawback to the percentage formula, though. There may be no guarantee that the agent receives his or her expected percentage, in that the agent is paid as the athlete earns the money. An agent may negotiate a contract and the athlete may be cut during training camp, or an athlete who reports to the minor leagues may never make it to the major leagues. This is difficult for the agent because in both cases the agent spent time and money getting the athlete signed or supporting the player through the minor leagues. Until an agent makes it by landing a first rounder as a client, the agent is often left paying his or her dues and investing a great deal of time, energy, and money into clients who may not provide a financial return.

The third method, the hourly rate, is often not used for the reasons stated above by Leigh Steinberg. For a high-round draft pick or a superstar free agent, however, McAleenan (1990) suggests that an hourly rate will provide the lowest fee. For example, assume the agent charges $150 per hour and works 40 hours negotiating a three-year $1 million compensation package. Working on a 4% fee structure, the agent would receive $40,000, but working the hourly rate the agent would receive only $18,000 (McAleenan, 1990).

The fourth method, the hourly rate with a compensation cap, addresses the athlete's concern that the agent may pad the billable hours and inflate the fee. This option provides an hourly rate, the total of which will not exceed a certain percentage of the athlete's compensation (the percentage cap) (McAleenan, 1990).

A key component of the Major League Baseball Players Association (MLBPA), the National Football League Players Association (NFLPA), and the National Basketball Players Association (NBPA) regulations governing agents is the limitation on the fees agents can charge athletes. These players associations have set ceilings for agents' fees at between 4% and 6% (Greenberg, 1993). The fierce competition for clients has driven the average fees down closer to 2% to 4%, although well-established agents, such as F.A.M.E., still charge the maximum 6% (Burwell, 1996). The MLBPA, NFLPA, and NBPA have also set some maximum fees. For instance, MLBPA regulations prohibit agents from charging any fee at all unless the player's salary exceeds the league minimum (Greenberg, 1993), and the fee percentage can only be taken from that amount that exceeds the minimum salary. The NBPA has adopted a similar measure in that agents collecting fees for negotiating rookies' salaries are limited by the rookie salary cap. The NFLPA has a similar measure that limits the agents' fee to 5% of the player's compensation that exceeds the minimum salary for the first three years in the league (Greenberg, 1993). In addition, agents representing players in the minor leagues are prohibited from charging the player any fee. Some agents, though, do take a percentage of the athlete's signing bonus negotiated just after the player is drafted. Other aspects of player association regulation of agents are discussed later in the chapter.

These fee limitations, though, exist only for the fees the agents can charge for negotiating the athlete's standard/uniform player contract. Again due to competition, some agents will charge the same fee percentage for negotiating the athlete's marketing deals as for negotiating the player's contract. This, however, is not the norm, as fees charged by many agents range between 15% and 33% for negotiating marketing deals. While this is much higher than the team contract negotiation compensation, more effort may go into creating an image for an athlete in the media and selling that image to marketers at companies that create a positive fit for the athlete and product. In addition, some agents charge for other services rendered, such as tax planning, financial planning, and investing money. Others, again to compete, include these services at no charge above and beyond the charge for contract negotiations and/or marketing fees.

For athletes in other sports and professional and collegiate coaches, there are no regulations over fees, so the fees tend to be higher. The athlete or coach and the agent negotiate these fees individually, so the fee will depend on market factors and bargaining power. In tennis, for example, the standard fee players pay agents when they first become professionals is 10% of their prize money and 20 to 25% of all other revenue, while superstars usually will have their prize money fee waived and off-court fees cut to 10% or less (Feinstein, 1992). For example, when Ivan Lendl was a ProServ client his contract provided for a flat fee of $25,000 and 7.5% of all earnings (Greenberg, 1993).

CAREER OPPORTUNITIES

Sports Event Manager

Some free-standing sport management firms also control the rights to sporting events. The sport management firms hire **sports event managers** to run these events. Event managers generally have no involvement with the representation of professional athletes. Information about event managers and the skills necessary to work as one is provided in Chapter 14, Event Management.

Sports Marketing Representative

The **sports marketing representative** coordinates all of the marketing and sponsorship activities for sports properties (sports properties are discussed in detail in Chapter 14, Event Management). Such sports properties may be sporting events run by the agency firm or they may be the athletes the agency represents. A sports marketing representative's responsibilities may include conducting market research, selling sponsorships for an event, promoting an event and the athletes participating in it, or making calls to find endorsement opportunities for athletes who are clients of the firm. As free-standing sport management firms face greater competition in the market, more firms are focusing energies on marketing activities and even consulting in marketing. To learn more about sports marketing and the skills necessary for a career in the field, refer to Chapter 3, Marketing Principles Applied to Sport Management.

Sports Agent

Sports agents often refer to themselves as athlete representatives or sports lawyers because the term "sports agent" has a negative connotation to some people. However, many sports agents are not lawyers and need not be lawyers. As Ruxin (1993) points out, the term "agent" covers a broad range of relationships, from family friend and advisor to lawyer, teacher, or coach. In fact, there is no regulating body that defines minimal educational training or that requires a formal degree to represent an athlete. The lack of such requirements has been blamed for the incompetent and sometimes unethical behavior of some sports agents. This issue is discussed in greater detail in the Current Issues section of this chapter.

The functions of sports agents vary more widely than do the types of firms. While this section discusses the functions generally performed by sports agents, keep in mind that some agents perform just one function and others may have more than one employee performing each of these functions for their clients. The ability to offer a broad range of services depends on an agent's education, skills, and training, and the amount of time he or she has to devote to these tasks. The amount of time spent per athlete is dependent on the number of athletes the agent represents. The number of agents or employees in the firm and the variety of skills each has to offer will influence the ability to offer many services. The eight essential functions performed by sports agents are:

1. Negotiating the athlete's or coach's contract
2. Marketing
3. Negotiating the athlete's or coach's marketing and endorsement contracts
4. Financial planning
5. Career and postcareer planning
6. Dispute resolution
7. Legal counseling
8. Personal care

These eight functions are discussed individually below.

Negotiating the Contract

The Athlete's Contract. Contract negotiation varies depending on whether the agent is negotiating a team-sport contract or negotiating a contract for an individual athlete to participate in an exhibition or event. When negotiating a contract for an individual athlete, the agent must be familiar with the sport and the rules, regulations, and common practices of its governing body. When negotiating a contract for a team-sport athlete, the agent must understand the collective bargaining agreement, the standard/uniform player contract, and the league's constitution and bylaws to know what terms are negotiable. Some examples of negotiable terms include:

1. Bonuses: signing, reporting (to training camp), attendance, incentives
2. Deferred income (income paid after the player has retired from the sport)
3. Guaranteed income (income guaranteed to be paid to the player even if he or she has retired)
4. A college scholarship plan (available for MLB players leaving college early)
5. Roster spots (generally not available, but positions on the 40-man roster in baseball are negotiable)

After negotiating the contract, the agent's work continues. Agents must administer the contract. This involves making sure that the club and the player comply with their promises under the contract. If promises are not kept, the agent may be involved in conversations, negotiations, and dispute resolution between the player and the club. The agent may have to resolve unanticipated situations through informal channels, such as renegotiation of some or all of the contract, or through formal ones, such as alternative dispute resolution systems or courts. As the representative of the player and the negotiator of the contract, when problems arise, it is the agent's responsibility to represent the athlete's interests.

The Coach's Contract. Due to the lack of job security for coaches in the Division I college and professional ranks, it has become increasingly important for coaches to have well-drafted contracts and a representative available to administer the deal (Greenberg, 1993). When negotiating a contract for a college coach, an agent must be familiar with the sport, the National Collegiate Athletic Association (NCAA) and conference rules, any applicable state open records laws, and common concerns of collegiate athletic directors and university presidents (Greenberg, 1993). When negotiating a contract for a professional coach, an agent must understand the league's constitution and bylaws, as well as the coaching/management environment of a particular team or league. Unlike for professional athletes, there is no uniform coaching contract, so there is much more flexibility in terms of negotiable terms. Examples of negotiable terms in coaches' contracts include:

1. Duties and responsibilities
2. Term of employment and tenure
3. Compensation clauses (guaranteed, outside/supplemental, endorsement, and deferred income; bonuses; moving expenses; retirement; and fringe benefits)
4. Termination clause
5. Buyout/release of contractual obligations by either side
6. Support of the team by athletic program or ownership
7. Support staff (coaches, other personnel)
8. Confidentiality (to the extent allowable under law, the promise to keep terms confidential)
9. Arbitration of disputes (Greenberg, 1993)

In the past decade, representing coaches has become far more lucrative for sports agents, particularly for those representing Division I college football and basketball coaches and NBA coaches. The trend in the NBA is for coaches' salaries and terms to be higher and longer than those of the athletes on their teams (Boeck, 1997). Agents have also played an important role in negotiating for the coaches to serve as general managers or team presidents. Such clauses give the coach more power in player personnel decisions and presumably more control over their athletes and the direction in which the team is headed in achieving its goals. This trend is a direct reaction to athletes' apparent loss of respect for their coaches and the athletes' temptation to remove the coach due to athletes' leverage and financial clout with the team (Boeck, 1997). It is also a reaction to the coaches' having to take the brunt of the blame for a losing season. These new long-term multimillion dollar deals for coaches may well change the dynamics in the locker rooms and on the basketball courts (Boeck, 1997). Coaches' agents, such as Lonnie Cooper, who represents five head NBA coaches and 17 assistant NBA coaches, are also the beneficiaries of these deals. In the summer of 1997 alone Cooper negotiated a three-year, $15 million package for Chuck Daly with the Orlando Magic; a four-year, $8 million package for Brian Hill with the Vancouver Grizzlies; and for Lenny Wilkins of the Atlanta Hawks and Mike Fratello of the Cleveland Cavaliers, two four-year contract extensions each worth $22.5 million (Boeck, 1997).

Marketing the Athlete

The sports agent should develop a plan in which each endorsement creates an image consistent with the athlete or coach's ambitions and long-range goals (Lester, 1990). At the same time, the agent must keep in mind that the client's career and public persona may be short-lived, and thus, "Every opportunity should be assessed according to its potential to maximize the [client's] earnings and exposure during and after his or her playing [or coaching] career" (Lester, 1990, p. 23-2). The sports agent must also be familiar with restrictions that may limit an athlete or coach's ability to market himself or herself. Restrictions include limitations on compensation as set by National Governing Bodies, professional sports regulations, group licensing programs, and rules prohibiting the endorsement of alcohol or tobacco products (Lester, 1990). Group licensing programs are very popular among professional sports unions, where often a major share of the players association's funding comes from trading card deals or marketing arms, such as the NFLPAs Player's, Inc. Under these group licensing programs the players pool their bargaining power and licensing resources in exchange for a prorated (proportionate) share of any surplus income.

Agents usually seek product endorsements (goods necessary for the athlete to play his or her sport) before nonproduct endorsements because they are easier to obtain (Lester, 1990). Before targeting potential endorsements, the agent should assess the athlete's marketability. The assessment should be realistic and should include:

1. An assessment of the athlete's past and present endorsements, including the athlete's desire for endorsements, willingness to make appearances, likes/ dislikes of product, and his or her strengths and weaknesses.
2. Consideration paid to intangible factors of an athlete's marketability, including his or her image, reputation, geographic appeal, achievements on and off the field, unique skills, personality, public speaking ability, and physical appearance.
3. A determination if factors listed in the previous item can be enhanced by creating and maintaining an image. (Lester, 1990)

The agent should also conduct a market assessment. Some agents have a well-developed network of contacts with sports product and nonproduct endorsement companies. For those who do not, the following four steps are useful:

1. Choose a product category and determine which manufacturers market those products.
2. Compile an exhaustive list of manufacturers of those products.
3. Determine which companies spend money on athlete endorsers.
4. Learn about potential target companies. (Lester, 1990)

Marketing an athlete or coach may include creating or polishing a public image for that person. To assist with image building, some agents are beginning to hire "sports-media coaches" to train athletes or coaches for meeting the press and public. Sports-media coaches offer training sessions that mix lectures, mock interviews, a question-and-answer session, and videotapes of other athletes or coaches to critique (Dunkel, 1997). For instance, Jerry Stackhouse's media coach, Andrea Kirby, began his session with an exercise in which he wrote down a list of his personal positive qualities (Thurow, 1996). Stackhouse's list included "friendly, caring, talkative, athletic, well-dressed . . . good son, good family person, a leader, warm, respectful, generous" (Thurow, 1996, p. A4). Kirby copied the list and told Stackhouse to carry it with him and review it every time he faced fans, the media, or commercial cameras so that he would consistently portray the image he had of himself. Beyond the media coaching, Stackhouse's training also included taking a couple of college drama courses, practicing speaking with a smoother cadence, and shaving his mustache (Thurow, 1996).

Finally, the agent should determine the athlete's market value. Many factors influence an athlete's market value, including the athlete's skill/success in sport, individual characteristics (image, charisma, physical appearance, and personality), how badly the organization wants the athlete, and any negative factors (crimes, drug use, public scandal) (Lester, 1990).

Negotiating the Athlete/Coach's Marketing and Endorsement Contracts

Due to salary caps and rookie wage scales, an agent's ability to supplement a team salary with lucrative endorsement contracts has gained greater importance in athlete representation (Thurow, 1996). As far as the specifics of marketing deals, the agent must first know any limitations the sport places on an athlete's abilities to endorse products. For instance, all major professional sport leagues prohibit the use of team names and logos in endorsements, and most professional sport leagues ban the endorsement of alcoholic beverages and tobacco products (Lester, 1990). Agents representing athletes in individual sports, such as golf, tennis, racquetball, figure skating, and auto racing, should examine the rules and regulations of the sport. Restrictions vary from the simple requirement of the PGA Tour that endorsements be "in good taste" to the specific limitations in tennis and racquetball that limit the number and size of patches displayed on players' clothing and equipment bags (Lester, 1990).

Negotiation of endorsement deals has been a lucrative supplement to Division I college coaches' income, particularly in the sports of football and men's basketball. University athletic departments that are financially strapped, have, however, begun to examine the coaches' outside endorsement deals and to negotiate contracts with athletic shoe, apparel, and equipment companies that benefit the entire athletic department, rather than just the coach of the university's major revenue-producing sport. Good examples of this movement are Nike's shoe, apparel, and equipment contracts with the University of Georgia and the University of Michigan. Under its deal with the University of Georgia, Nike pays the school a large sum, which Georgia's Athletic Association controls; thus, the Georgia Athletic Association decides how its coaches will be compensated from the Nike payment (Greenberg, 1995). The University of Michigan's groundbreaking deal was similar in that it gave Michigan's athletic department control over the shoe, apparel, and equipment contracts ("Michigan-Nike," 1994). In addition, due to Michigan's leverage as an entire department (much greater than that of various coaches getting separate deals), Michigan was able to negotiate for Nike to pay for various athletic scholarships and a new state-of-the-art tennis court ("Michigan-Nike," 1994).

When negotiating an endorsement contract, an agent should be certain to maintain the client's exclusive rights and control over his or her image and other endorsements. The agent must also be familiar with the following terms typically negotiable in athlete endorsement contracts:

1. Endorsed products
2. Contract territory
3. Term (length)
4. Annual base compensation
5. Bonus compensation
6. In-kind compensation
7. Signature products
8. Promotional efforts to be made by company
9. Personal appearances
10. Athlete's approval of company advertising
11. Athlete to use/wear product
12. Company protection of athlete endorsement (Lester, 1990)

Financial Planning

Financial planning covers a wide range of activities, such as banking and cash flow management, tax planning, investment advising, estate planning, and risk management (Grossman, 1995). From this function have arisen many legal cases concerning sports agents' incompetence, fraud, and breaches of fiduciary duties. These cases have exclusively involved athletes and not coaches, so financial planning for athletes will be the focus in this section. Many sports agents have made mistakes because of the complex nature of the financial affairs of athletes. Sports agents often attempt to take on this function without proper skills and training, which can lead to allegations of incompetence and negligence. Also enticing to less scrupulous agents is access to the athlete's money. There are many allegations of agents "double dipping" into athletes' funds, investing money into businesses from which the agent derives benefit, and outright embezzlement of an athlete's money. This behavior is discussed in greater detail later in the chapter.

An athlete earning a multimillion-dollar salary should adopt a budget (Willette & Waggoner, 1996). Without a budget, athletes who earn sudden wealth face risks

(Waggoner, 1996), one of which is the risk of rushing into an investment. Athletes often receive many unsolicited prospectuses and requests for investments, and many athletes have lost money in failed business ventures. Thus, planners often advise athletes to see a written business plan and have the plan analyzed by a professional before investing—and even if an investment seems to be worthy, planners advise an athlete to commit no more than 5 to 20% of the athlete's portfolio to it (Willette & Waggoner, 1996). The second risk is making a radical lifestyle change. Curtis Polk, vice president of finance for F.A.M.E., shares this example: For a client earning $10 million per year he gives the athlete a budget of $1 million per year and invests $4 million, leaving the remaining $5 million for local, state, and federal taxes (Willette & Waggoner, 1996). The third risk is guilt, which often leads athletes to make bad loans to family and friends or to hire them as an entourage; to overcome guilt, advisors suggest that athletes raise money for charities (Waggoner, 1996).

Finally, insurance plays a key role in an athlete's financial planning. Star athletes in the major professional team sports usually invest in disability insurance plans to protect themselves from career-ending injuries. In contract negotiations with a professional team, the agent may negotiate for the team to cover the cost of this policy. Athletes in individual sports also insure against these types of injuries. Many insurance companies, though, will only insure an athlete after that athlete is ensured of achieving a certain level of income.

Career and Postcareer Planning

An agent must help an athlete with the transition to a professional career and again with the transition into retirement from the sport. The average career length varies by sport, but generally it is under five years. Thus, the agent must maximize the athlete's earning potential during and after his or her playing career. Simultaneously, the agent must protect against overexposure of the athlete's image. The agent must balance the need to maximize exposure with doing what is best personally and professionally for the athlete. For instance, in *Inside Edge*, Olympic silver medalist Paul Wylie criticized agent Jerry Solomon's handling of Nancy Kerrigan after the 1994 Olympics, in which she won a silver medal but failed miserably in the poll of public opinion (Brennan, 1996). According to Wylie:

> After seven weeks of pressure, [Kerrigan] needed to go to an island, be deprogrammed, debriefed. What happened was she wasn't allowed to come down off that . . . to normalize . . . to feel good about herself. . . . In fact she was under more and more pressure. *Saturday Night Live*, Disney, missing closing ceremonies, all of a sudden her image had spun out of control because CBS had used a bad quote [Kerrigan criticizing

Oksana Baiul]. . . . At that point . . . Jerry Solomon . . . should take care of his client more for the long-term as opposed to feeling that they have to [pursue and say yes to every opportunity]. They said 'have to' way too much. She's too big a star to 'have to,' at that point." (Brennan, 1996, p. 122).

Career planning may also involve the agent's investing time, energy, and money into a player's career while the player is training in the minor leagues or training toward events, exhibitions, or the Olympics. This often occurs when the agent is trying to break into the business. The agent may reap little financial benefit from this effort, as many of these athletes do not make it to the big leagues or the Olympics.

Another aspect of career planning the agent may take on is the establishment of sports camps or charitable organizations under the athlete's name. Running sports camps and charitable organizations does many positive things for the athlete. Camps provide additional income, but beyond that camps and charities create goodwill for the athlete's name and image; give the athlete contact with his or her community; give something back to children, communities, or a worthy cause; provide a useful outlet for the athlete's energy and time in the off-season; and may provide a hefty tax break. The camps and charitable organizations are also activities the athlete can stay involved with after his or her playing career is finished.

During the career transition out of sport, the agent must address the potential for a financial crisis (Grossman, 1995). Proper financial planning including investing and contracting for deferred income can avert a disaster. Beyond the financial aspect, the athlete needs a sense of purpose. Participation in sport has defined many athletes' lives and self-images, and agents can be helpful in preparing athletes for the psychological difficulties that may accompany retirement. By exploring career and business opportunities for the athlete inside and outside the sport industry, the agent can help the athlete make a more successful transition.

Dispute Resolution

It is the sports agent's responsibility to resolve disputes the athlete or coach may have with his or her league, team, teammates, fans, referees or umpires, press, endorsement companies, and the like. Renowned baseball agent Dennis Gilbert likens the role of the agent to a "shield," stating that it is the agent's task to shield the athlete from the headaches that go along with resolving disputes (Schwarz, 1996). The shield allows the athlete to focus solely on playing or coaching to the best of his or her ability without distractions. (This analogy was also touched on earlier in the chapter, in a less specific application.)

Legal Counseling

If the sports agent is a lawyer, the agent may provide legal counseling. Legal counseling may include contract negotiation, legal representation in court, arbitration or sport-related administrative proceedings, estate planning, dispute resolution, and the preparation of tax and insurance forms. However, the nature of the legal work may dictate that a lawyer specializing in a particular area is better suited for providing the actual legal services. For instance, a given sports agent may be very confident in providing negotiation and contract advice on any matter in his or her client's life, yet that same agent will not likely be the best lawyer to handle the client's divorce proceedings. For such a dispute, the best advice an agent can give is to help the client to find an attorney experienced in high-profile, high-income divorce proceedings.

Personal Care

The tasks required under this function are personal in nature. They include finding and furnishing a house or apartment, arranging transportation, purchasing cars, and helping the athlete's family and friends.

Key Skills Required of Sports Agents

There are currently no established educational standards or degree requirements necessary to become a sports agent. Even so, many sports agents possess professional degrees and credentials. Some are lawyers, some are certified public accountants, and others are investment advisors or financial planners. With the various services demanded of agents by athletes and in light of competition in the field, a professional degree is practically a necessity.

Primarily, the sports agent must have a good working knowledge of the professional sport industry, particularly the specific sector of the industry in which he or she practices. This knowledge includes an understanding of the sport the athlete plays, the documents used in the industry, (e.g., contracts, policies, rules and regulations, constitutions and bylaws, and collective bargaining agreements), and insight into the innner workings of the industry. The sports agent must also possess a good network of industry contacts.

The skills needed by sports agents vary depending on the services provided; however, all agents must possess good listening and counseling skills. The agent works for the athlete and must invest time in getting to know the athlete on a personal level. This builds trust and a stronger relationship between the two. Agents must make decisions according to the athlete's desires and goals. The agent should only act *after* consulting the athlete and must always act in the athlete's best interest.

Excellent oral and written communication skills are also essential, as the agent represents the athlete in many forums. Many of the agent's functions require polished negotiation skills. An agent must also be loyal to the athlete and be strong enough to shield the athlete from the media and even from his or her own general manager. Professional athletes, like entertainers, find their lives scrutinized by the press, and the agent must help the athlete adjust to the pressure that accompanies fame and teach the athlete to properly deal with the media. When the athlete has to negotiate a contract or go into arbitration against his or her team, the relationship is adversarial. This is not always the best situation for professional athletes, for whom psychology plays a key role in their on-field success. The agent must shelter the athlete from the derogatory statements made about him or her in those forums, for often those statements can damage the athlete's confidence.

CURRENT ISSUES

Unethical Behavior

In the 20 or so years that the sports agency field has been active, there has been a great deal of criticism and a public perception that the behavior of those in the profession is excessively unethical. There are, in fact, many ethical agents who run their businesses professionally; however, there have been many high-profile cases of unethical and illegal behavior reported, tainting the image of the profession. In addition, sports agency is a field in which outsiders perceive there is quick and easy money to be made and a field in which clients are scarce. These two factors combine to bring an element of corruption to the profession.

According to Sobel (1990), there are five key problems in the profession: (1) income mismanagement, (2) incompetence, (3) conflicts of interest, (4) charging of excessive fees, and (5) overly aggressive client recruitment. Of the five, **income mismanagement** is probably the most devastating to the athlete. Since the agent is often dealing with the income of a multimillion-dollar athlete, the losses can be great, and it is unlikely the athlete will reclaim the money from the agent or earn back the amount lost. While many reported cases stem from incompetence, others begin with incompetence and further deteriorate to fraud or embezzlement (Sobel, 1990). A good example is the case of agent Joseph Senkovich, Jr. Senkovich and his wife, Karen, operated Sencorp Sports, Inc., a company that would manage players' finances for a fee of 5% of a player's earnings (Greenberg, 1995). They managed the money of about 50 athletes, including Pittsburgh Steeler Dermontti Dawson and Washington Redskin Jamie

Morris. The Senkoviches lost $204,500 of the players' money in a two-month period in 1989 and in addition acquired approximately $314,000 of the athletes' money for their own expenses and falsified players' monthly financial statements to conceal it (Greenberg, 1995). The two pled guilty to charges of mail fraud and wound up with criminal sentences; however, since they were unemployed they were not required to pay restitution to the athletes (Greenberg, 1995).

Agents have also been accused of performing their responsibilities negligently because of sheer **incompetence**. As the industry has become more complex, some agents have run into problems because they are incapable of figuring out their clients' worth, working with complex documents necessary to effectively negotiate, or carrying out the tasks they promise athletes they will do. It is likely this problem has been compounded by the competition in the industry. Agents may make promises they cannot keep for fear of losing a client or may exaggerate when trying to land a client.

Conflicts of interest raise serious questions about the fiduciary duty of loyalty required of all agents under agency law (see Chapter 5, Legal Principles Applied to Sport Management). A conflict of interest occurs if there is a situation in which the agent's own interest may be furthered over that of the athlete's (principal's) interest. Keep in mind that an agent works for an athlete and possesses a fiduciary duty to put the athlete's interest first. It is clear, though, that in business settings there are bound to be conflicts of interest. If the agent fully reveals the conflict and allows the athlete to direct the agent, or in some cases suggests that the athlete hire a neutral party to see the athlete through the conflict, the agent will not have breached his or her fiduciary duties. There are many examples of conflicts of interest in the sports agency business. Earlier in the chapter, conflicts that arise for agency firms that also run events were mentioned. Those firms have a fiduciary duty to fully reveal the extent of the conflict of interest and to allow the athlete to bring in a neutral negotiator to negotiate with that particular event. Some, such as Jerry Solomon, however, argue that these companies operate as diverse entities (athlete representation versus event management), and as a result the two groups have built invisible walls between them that prevent such a conflict from arising (Feinstein, 1992; Solomon, 1995). Another conflict may arise when an agent is representing two players on the same team or two players who may be vying for the same position on a team. Clearly in these situations there may be a tendency for the agent to give greater attention to the athlete who will better serve the agent's own interest. A final example that has come up occasionally in professional sport occurs when an agent, such as Alan Eagleson in hockey or the late Larry Fleischer in basketball, represents the union as its executive director. Clearly, the agent may lead the union to fight for benefits that favor his or her clients over those that favor the interests of the majority of members of the union.

The complaint of **charging excessive fees** occurs when agents charge fees that do not fairly represent their time, effort, and skills. To an extent this complaint has been addressed by players association regulations mentioned earlier and also by competition in the market. Competition for clients has forced some agents in the market to reduce their fees to entice clients. However, while the fees have dropped for the negotiation of team-sport contracts, many agents continue to charge what may be considered excessive fees in the marketing area. Another recent complaint is charging the athlete for every service the agent performs, when the athlete may believe that all services are provided. Such confusion may arise because some agents do not use written contracts and representation agreements. This problem is also being overcome as the players associations are insisting that players use standard-form representation agreements that clearly establish fees and contractual promises.

Overly aggressive client recruitment is a problem that has plagued the amateurism requirement of collegiate athletics. Under NCAA rules, an athlete loses his or her eligibility if he or she signs with a sports agent and/or accepts anything of value from a sports agent. In the competition for clients, many agents have resorted to underhanded tactics such as paying athletes to encourage them to sign with agents early. The difficulty in becoming an agent or obtaining clients has led some to offer inducements. For example, World Sports Entertainment (WSE), an athlete representation firm operated by entertainment agent Norby Walters and partner Lloyd Bloom, spent approximately $800,000 to induce athletes to sign representation agreements with them before their NCAA eligibility expired. Walters argued that what he did broke no laws (just NCAA rules) and was a common practice in the music industry, where entertainers often received financial advances from their agents (Mortensen, 1991). The athletes, too, are to blame, because some encourage this type of activity from the agent, believing that their skills and talent should enable them to make this money for signing. For instance, when football player Ron Harmon signed with WSE while a junior at the University of Iowa, the FBI investigation found that he ran up expenses of over $54,000 in cash, plane and concert tickets, and other entertainment. Clearly Harmon was taking advantage of the situation for his own entertainment and not using the money, as other athletes did, for bills and family expenses (Mortensen, 1991).

Regulation of Sports Agents

Agents representing athletes in MLB, the NFL, the NBA, the NHL, and the Canadian Football League are regulated by players associations. The Major League Soccer Players Association and the Women's Professional Association (a union representing professional soccer and fast-pitch softball players) have just been established and have not yet begun regulating agents. Unions do not yet exist for players in the American Basketball League, the Women's National Basketball Association, or the World League of American Football, and thus, agents for athletes in these leagues are not regulated. The National Hockey League Players' Association (NHLPA) is still in its initial stages of agent registration and has not set as many formal standards as the other unions (Conway, 1995).

Players associations have also created uniform athlete-agent representation agreements that have clauses mandating the arbitration of disputes between players and their agents. The uniform agreements are renewable annually. Each year a copy must be sent to the players associations as evidence of the renewed relationship. This puts the players associations on notice about who is representing the athlete and also allows the agent access to players association assistance.

Twenty-four states regulate sports agents (Roberts, 1995), and three state legislatures have bills to regulate agents pending (Curtis, 1997). The state legislation varies widely, but it all has the common goal of addressing abuses by sports agents, most often overly aggressive client recruitment. Critics of state regulations insist that the various statutes do not encourage agents to abide by the law. For instance, if an agent were to register with every state, posting bonds and paying fees would cost the agent over $30,000. That is a great investment for a new person seeking to break into the field. In addition, critics argue that it is a nationwide business, so having one federal uniform statute would make the most sense. After much prodding by the Sport Lawyers Association and with the promise of backing from the NCAA, the National Conference of Commissioners on State Laws has created a drafting committee with the goal of developing a proposed uniform agent registration law that can be adopted by all states. The committee is in the very initial stages of the process, but one participant, Sports Law professor Gary Roberts, has found the tone of the draft statute to be "decidedly anti-agent, with the underlying assumption that anything that ma[kes] life for agents more difficult and expensive [is] a positive goal" (Roberts, 1997, pp. 1, 6). Finally, there are already criminal, tort, agency, and consumer protection laws that provide recourse for athletes injured by unscrupulous agents.

Race and the Sports Agent Industry

Critics have argued that since the majority of athletes in professional sport are people of color, there should be more opportunity for agents of color in the field (Freeman, 1997; Shropshire, 1996). While no statistics have been formally gathered, Shropshire (1996) estimates that 3% of the 150 agents registered with the MLBPA are African-American and 10 to 12% of the 862 agents registered with the NFLPA are African-American. Freeman (1997) reports that approximately 30% of NBA agents are African-American. No data exist for African-American agents in hockey, soccer, tennis, golf, or other sports.

One reason suggested for the lack of sports representation by agents of color is due to long-held perceptions of those in the African-American community that African-American professionals' skills are somehow inferior to those of other professionals (Freeman, 1997; Shropshire, 1996). In the past five years, influential African-Americans such as actor-comedian Bill Cosby, producer-director Spike Lee, and former professional athletes Kellen Winslow and Len Elmore have publicly encouraged black athletes to hire African-American agents. In that time there have been increases in the numbers of athletes seeking African-American representation. Of the 27 players taken in the 1992 NBA draft, five chose African-American agents, but in 1994's NBA draft of the same number of athletes nine chose African-American agents (Shropshire, 1996). And in the NFL's 1993 draft, 36% of the first two rounds, or 20 of the first 56 athletes drafted, chose African-American agents (Shropshire, 1996).

Finally, high-profile African-American attorney Johnnie Cochran and producer-director Spike Lee have recently developed a partnership to open a sports and entertainment management firm, and Cochran has mentioned that C. Lamont Smith (Detroit Lions' superstar Barry Sander's agent) and many other prominent entertainment attorneys may join the firm (Freeman, 1997). The jury is out on how the firm will do, but from a pure marketing standpoint it may be hard for others to compete against a large firm made up of so many prominent African-American lawyers geared mainly toward the representation of athletes and entertainers of color.

SUMMARY

The field of sports agency can be exciting. Landing a first-round draft pick and negotiating a playing contract or creating an image and negotiating major marketing deals for a Wimbledon champion can bring an incredible thrill for an agent. Servicing their clients' needs can open the agents to the world of these elite athletes, and as a result, it is a highly competitive business. Those seeking an entry-level position face an uphill battle, for there are far more people trying to break into the field than there are athletes seeking representation. As a result, recruiting a client is just part of the struggle because keeping the client in this competitive market is also a battle. Furthermore, it is estimated that over 80% of the athletes are represented by approximately 20% of the agents, so many agents are working part time and supplementing their income through other professions such as law, marketing, accounting, or financial planning. Nevertheless, there are a handful of large, dominant multiservice firms engaged in athlete representation and event management that may provide a good launching point for breaking into this field. On the representation side, many of the entry-level positions at these firms are in client recruitment. In reality, this may mean that if an entry-level agent delivers athletes to the firm he or she will stay employed, but if not, that agent may be looking to move on to another position. This competitive environment may lead new agents to act in an overly aggressive manner while recruiting clients.

CASE STUDY: THE BOSTON BRUINS LOSE THEIR HALL OF FAME DEFENSEMAN

Bobby Orr, a star defenseman in the 1970s for the Boston Bruins, is one of the greatest players in the history of the National Hockey League (NHL). One of the saddest events in Boston sports history occurred at a Montreal press conference on June 9, 1976, when Orr's agent, Alan Eagleson, announced that Orr had signed a guaranteed $3 million contract with the Chicago Blackhawks. He went on to explain that the Bruins had effectively stopped negotiating on December 10, 1975, when Orr had reinjured his left knee.

At the time of the signing, Alan Eagleson was one of the most powerful people in the world of hockey. He operated a sports agency firm representing over 150 hockey players, served as executive director of the National Hockey League Players Association (NHLPA), operated Team Canada, managed the Canada Cup event, and oversaw international hockey exhibitions involving NHL players. In addition, he maintained close friendships with National Hockey League Commissioner John Ziegler and Chicago Blackhawks owner Bill Wirtz, who was also chairman of the NHL's Board of Governors. Among its many duties representing the interests of the NHL owners, the Board of Governors is responsible for negotiating the collective bargaining agreement with the NHLPA. In his capacity as chairman, Wirtz served as chief negotiator for the owners, while Eagleson, as NHLPA Executive Director, was chief negotiator for the union. Wirtz also maintained a friendship with Ross Johnson, CEO of Standard Brands, one of Eagleson's sponsors of international hockey events (Conway, 1995).

Bobby Orr's contract with the Boston Bruins ran through June 1, 1976. During the months leading up to its expiration the Bruins had made offers to Eagleson, as Orr had directed them to do. Orr had been a client of Eagleson's for his entire hockey career and trusted him. Orr did not want to have to be involved in the negotiation process with Bruins management. The Bruins management approached Orr a couple of times at practice to discuss the inability to get anywhere with Eagleson but did not push it with Orr. Each time the managers brought it up, Orr told them that Eagleson was his friend and that he trusted him. At no time did the Bruins give Orr an offer. Orr honestly believed that as his agent Eagleson would look out for his best interests and follow his request to stay in Boston and re-sign with the Bruins (Conway, 1995).

Eagleson reported to Orr that the Bruins did not want to keep him due to his knee injury and fourth surgery and that the Bruins' offers did not represent Orr's worth. Eagleson also reported that Chicago Blackhawks' owner Bill Wirtz had expressed interest and that Eagleson thought he could get a guaranteed contract from Chicago that would make Orr a millionaire. Orr kept telling Eagleson he wanted to stay in Boston and Eagleson kept responding, "Bobby, Chicago's the one that's guaranteeing you $3 million. Boston hasn't made anywhere near that offer" (Conway, 1995, p. 143).

On May 17, 1976, Orr went to Ross Johnson's house to meet with Quebec businessman Roger Baikie about marketing a new skate blade he had developed. Baikie was a friend of both Johnson and Eagleson. Eagleson, Johnson, and Bill Wirtz showed up later and a meeting was held on Orr's contract. On Standard Brands stationery an agreement was signed that read, "'We agree to a three-year contract guaranteed commencing June 1/76 through May 31/79 at $500,000 per annum. In addition Chicago will have options annually for a further seven years on Orr's services at $500,000 per annum. The contract registered with the NHL will be 10 × $300,000. The contract will be for services in hockey and other business activities.' The agreement was signed by William W. Wirtz and Robert G. Orr, and witnessed by F. Ross Johnson" (Conway, 1995, pp. 144–145). The only problem was that the Bruins' contract with Orr had not yet expired and NHL rules prohibited such conduct (tampering). Violators faced a $500,000 fine.

At a Montreal press conference on June 9, 1976, Alan Eagleson made public the details of Orr's contract with the Chicago Blackhawks and told the public that the Bruins had stopped negotiating with Bobby Orr on December 10, 1975. What he failed to mention is that the Bruins had made an offer to Orr, through Eagleson, as late as the night before this official announcement. The offer was for $295,000 per year in salary for five years, plus a payment of $925,000 on June 1, 1980, or 18.5% of the Boston Bruins hockey club in lieu of the lump sum payment (Conway, 1995). Eagleson declined that offer and never told Orr that such an offer existed. Had Orr accepted the offer, the 18.5% alone would have been worth over $16 million in 1984.

Questions for Discussion

1. Under agency law, are there any problems with Alan Eagleson's conduct?
2. What should Eagleson have done differently?
3. What should Bobby Orr have done differently?
4. What should the Bruins' general manager have done differently?

RESOURCES

Professional Associations

American Bar Association Forum Committee on the Entertainment & Sport Industries
750 No. Lakeshore Drive
Chicago, IL 60611
312-988-5580

Sport Lawyers Association
11250-8 Roger Bacon Drive, Suite 8
Reston, VA 22090
703-437-4377; fax: 703-435-4390

Agency Firms

Advantage International Management
1751 Pinnacle Drive, Suite 1500
McLean, VA 22102
703-905-3300; fax: 703-905-4495

Falk Associates Management Enterprises (F.A.M.E.)
5335 Wisconsin Ave, N.W., Suite 850
Washington, DC 20015
202-686-2000; fax: 202-686-5050

International Management Group
One Erieview Plaza, Suite 1300
Cleveland, OH 44114
216-522-1200; fax: 216-522-1145

ProServ, Inc.
1101 Wilson Blvd.
Arlington, VA 22209
703-276-3030; fax: 703-276-3090

Steinberg & Moorad
500 Newport Center Drive, Suite 820
Newport Beach, CA 92660
714-720-8700; fax: 714-720-1331

Woolf & Associates
Prudential Center
Boston, MA 02119
617-437-1212

Players Associations

For a listing of players associations, please see Chapter 12, Professional Sport.

REFERENCES

Berry, R.C. (1990). Representation of the professional athlete. In American Bar Association Forum on the Entertainment and Sports Industries (Ed.), *The law of sports: Doing business in the sports industries* (pp. 1–6). Chicago: ABA Publishing. (Reprinted from Continuing Legal Education Satellite Network, 1988.)

Berry, R.C., Gould, W.B., & Staudohar, P.D. (1986). *Labor relations in professional sports.* Dover, MA: Auburn House Publishing Co.

Boeck, G. (1997, September 25). Cooper cashes in for NBA coaches: Agent snags rewarding deals. *USA Today*, pp. C1–C2.

Brennan, C. (1996). *Inside edge: A revealing journey into the secret world of figure skating.* New York: Doubleday.

Burwell, B. (1996, June 28). David Falk: The most powerful man in the NBA? *USA Today*, pp. C1–C2.

Conway, R. (1995). *Game misconduct: Alan Eagleson and the corruption of hockey.* Toronto: MacFarlane, Walter, & Ross.

Curtis, T. (1997, July/August). Athlete agent legislation and regulation update. *The Sport Lawyer*, 3.

Dunkel, T. (1997, March). Out of the mouths of jocks. *Sky*, 97–103.

Feinstein, J. (1992). *Hard courts.* New York: Villard Books.

Feinstein, J. (1995). *A good walk spoiled: Days and nights on the PGA tour.* Boston: Little, Brown and Co.

Freeman, M. (1997, July 25). Cochran the agent? It could work. *The New York Times*, p. B13.

Greenberg, M.J. (1993). *Sports law practice.* Charlottesville, VA: The Michie Co.

Greenberg, M.J. (1995). *Sports law practice, 1995 Supplement.* Charlottesville, VA: The Michie Co.

Grossman, J.W. (1995). Financial planning for the athlete. In G. Uberstine (Ed.), *The law of professional and amateur sports* (pp. 3-1–3-37). Deerfield, IL: Clark, Boardman, and Callaghan.

Helyar, J. (1994). *Lords of the realm.* New York: Villard Books.

Helyar, J. (1997a, June 25). Net gains? A providence guard leaves college early, hoping for NBA gold. *The Wall Street Journal*, pp. A1, A8.

Helyar, J. (1997b, September 5). Net losses? How ProServ, legend among sports agents, fell from the top seed. *The Wall Street Journal*, pp. A1, A8.

Hofmann, D., & Greenberg, M.J. (1989). *Sport$ biz.* Champaign, IL: Leisure Press.

Katz, D. (1994). *Just do it: The Nike spirit in the corporate world.* New York: Random House.

Lester, P. (1990). Marketing the athlete; endorsement contracts. In G. Uberstine (Ed.), *The law of professional and amateur sports* (pp. 23-1–23-36). Deerfield, IL: Clark, Boardman, and Callaghan.

McAleenan, G. (1990). Agent-player representation agreements. In G. Uberstine (Ed.), *The law of professional and amateur sports* (pp. 2-1–2-85). Deerfield, IL: Clark, Boardman, and Callaghan.

Michigan-Nike endorsement deal includes scholarships, new court. (1994, October 21). *USA Today*, p. 6C.

Mortensen, C. (1991). *Playing for keeps: How one man kept the mob from sinking its hooks into pro football.* New York: Simon & Schuster.

Neff, C. (1987, October 19). Den of vipers. *Sports Illustrated*, 74–104.

Roberts, G.R. (1993, Fall). Editor's note: Agent rules and regulations proliferate. *The Sport Lawyer*, 1, 8.

Roberts, G.R. (1997, May/June). Uniform state agent regulation law efforts are finally underway. *The Sport Lawyer*, 1, 6.

Ruxin, R. (1993). *An athlete's guide to agents* (3rd ed.). Boston: Jones & Bartlett Publishers.

Schwarz, A. (1996, March 4–17). Agents: What's the deal? *Baseball America*, 14–19.

Shropshire, K. (1990). *Agents of opportunity.* Philadelphia: University of Pennsylvania Press.

Shropshire, K. (1996). *In black and white: Race and sports in America.* New York: New York University Press.

Sobel, L. (1990). The regulation of player agents and lawyers. In G. Uberstine (Ed.), *The law of professional and amateur sports* (pp. 1-1–1-107). Deerfield, IL: Clark, Boardman, and Callaghan.

Solomon, J. (1995, April 26). Guest lecture: Professional sports and the law class. University of Massachusetts, Amherst.

Thurow, R. (1996, February 9). The 76ers are lowly, but Jerry Stackhouse scores big in marketing. *The Wall Street Journal*, pp. A1, A4.

Waggoner, J. (1996, July 12). Walk, don't run, after a windfall. *USA Today*, p. 5B.

Willette, A., & Waggoner, J. (1996, July 12). Rich can't afford to dismiss budget: Even superstars need financial coaching. *USA Today*, p. 5B.

Woolf, B. (1976). *Behind closed doors.* New York: The New American Library.

Yasser, R., McCurdy, J., & Goplerud, P. (1997). *Sports law: Cases and materials.* Cincinnati: Anderson Publishing Co.

CHAPTER 12

Professional Sport

Lisa Pike Masteralexis

Key words: gate receipts, corporate governance model, franchise rights, territorial rights, revenue sharing, corporate ownership, public ownership, cross-ownership, commissioner, league think, franchise free agency, impasse

INTRODUCTION

The professional sport industry involves paying athletes who compete on teams or individually in events and exhibitions. Usually the events and exhibitions are live, include a paying audience, and are sponsored by a professional league or professional tour/event. The professional sport industry is a major international business grossing billions of dollars each year (see Chapter 4, Financial Principles Applied to Sport Management). While leagues and events derive revenue from **gate receipts** (ticket sales) and luxury suite sales, they derive the bulk of their revenue from the sale of radio, television, and cable television rights to their events or exhibitions. Improved international communication combined with the increased demand for cable sports programming have moved North American professional sport into markets abroad and brought international sport into the North American market. The international sale of professional sport leagues' licensed products (apparel, videos, books, memorabilia) and the worldwide availability of on-line services further characterize the industry's international growth.

Five preeminent professional leagues are currently based in North America: Major League Baseball (MLB), the National Basketball Association (NBA), the National Football League (NFL), the National Hockey League (NHL), and Major League Soccer (MLS). By the year 2000 the total number of franchises in those five leagues will total 131. In addition, many new leagues are emerging, including the American Basketball League (ABL), the Women's NBA (WNBA), Women's Professional Fastpitch (WPF) (softball), and the National Soccer Alliance (NSA) (women's soccer). The minor leagues in baseball, basketball, soccer, hockey, and football are too numerous to list here. Table 12–1 gives a breakdown of the number of major and minor league sport franchises currently operating in the North American professional sport industry.

There are also numerous professional leagues operating throughout South America, Europe the Middle East, Asia, Australia, and Africa, in the sports of Australian Rules and American Football, rugby and rugby union, cricket, baseball, basketball, American football, soccer, hockey, and volleyball.

Athletes in these leagues are salaried employees whose bargaining power and ability to negotiate salaries varies. In some cases athletes are unionized, enabling them to negotiate collectively for hours, wages, and terms and conditions of employment. (Players associations are discussed in greater detail later in the chapter.) In other cases, such as in minor league baseball or hockey, unless a

---

Table 12–1 Professional Sport Teams in the United States and Canada: Number of Major and Minor League Teams by Sport

Sport	Number of Teams
Baseball/softball:	
Major League (MLB)	30*
Women's Fastpitch	6
Minor Leagues	248
Basketball:	
Major Leagues (NBA)	29
Women's Leagues	17
Minor Leagues	33
Football:	
Major League (NFL)	32*
Canadian (CFL)	9
Arena	14
Ice hockey:	
Major League (NHL)	28*
Minor Leagues	158
Soccer:	
Major Outdoor (MLS)	12*
Minor Outdoor	118
Indoor	27
Lacrosse:	
Major Indoor	6
Roller hockey:	
Major Indoor	18
Team tennis	7
Total	792

*These numbers include upcoming expansion franchises.

player is a high-round draft pick with the leverage to negotiate a high signing bonus, the player must take whatever is offered. In minor league baseball, salaries are uniform across the league and are far below minimum wages. For example, in baseball's Class A and AA minor leagues, players' salaries are set at $850 to $1200 per month. Assuming in an average week a team plays half of its games home and half away, a player works (travel, practice, games, community/fan relations) approximately 60 hours. Players generally have one to two days off per month. Thus, the player is averaging around $4 or $5 per hour of work. Players do, however, receive a small amount of per diem money to cover meals and expenses incurred when on the road. In minor league hockey, conditions are a bit more favorable due to the fact that the players are unionized and have negotiated collective bargaining agreements.

A number of professional sports events are also staged around the world in individual sports, including boxing, fencing, figure skating, golf, tennis, racquetball, and track and field. Individual sports are often organized around a tour, such as the PGA (Professional Golfers' Association of America) and LPGA (Ladies Professional Golf Association of America) Tours, the ATP (Association of Tennis Professionals) and WTA (Women's Tennis Association) Tours, and the International Racquetball Tour. An athlete on a professional tour earns prize money, and a top (seeded) player who is considered a "draw" may earn an appearance fee. The tour will stop at various sites for events and exhibitions. These events and exhibitions are usually sponsored by one named corporation and a number of other sponsors. Some tours have broadcast television, radio, and/or cable contracts. There are also tours or exhibitions that have been created for athletes by sports agency firms. These tours or exhibitions are generally in tennis, golf, and figure skating. They are run by the agency firms and the firms' athletes are paid for their participation. More recently, exhibitions have been created in track and field, such as the challenge involving Michael Johnson vs. Donovan Baily to determine who is the fastest runner in the world, and in other sports, such as aerobics and extreme sports. These tours and exhibitions generate income for athletes and sports management firms primarily from sponsorship, media, and ticket sales. Occasionally, some of the income generated from these events is donated to charity. (See Chapter 11, Sports Agency, and Chapter 14, Event Management, for more information on sports agency firms.)

HISTORY

Professional Sport Leagues

In 1869 the first professional sport team, the Cincinnati Red Stockings, paid players to barnstorm the United States (Jennings, 1989). The 10-player team's payroll totaled $9,300. At the time the average annual salary in the United States was $170, so the average player's salary of $930 shows that even in 1869 professional athletes' incomes exceeded those of average workers (Jennings, 1989).

In 1876 the first professional sport league in North America, the National League, was organized and it included the Cincinnati Reds, the Chicago Cubs, and other teams (Jennings, 1989). Several principles from the National League's Constitution and By-Laws continue as models for professional sports today (Berry, Gould, & Staudohar, 1986). For instance, the first constitution limited franchise movement, provided territorial rights to clubs, and provided a mechanism for expulsion of a club (Berry et al., 1986). These rules all exist in today's professional leagues. Interestingly, these rules also allowed a player to contract with a club for his future services (Berry et al., 1986). It did not take long—just three years—for owners to change that rule.

Following the National League's lead, other professional leagues have organized themselves into a system of self-governance, as opposed to a **corporate governance model** (Lentze, 1995). Under a corporate governance model, owners act as the board of directors and the commissioner acts as the chief executive officer (CEO). While it may appear that leagues have adopted a corporate governance model, Lentze (1995) argues that the commissioner's power over the owners does not place the commissioner under the direct supervision and control of the owners in the manner that a CEO is under the direct supervision and control of a corporate board. This distinction is made because the commissioner in professional sport possesses decision-making power, disciplinary power, and dispute resolution authority (Lentze, 1995). The commissioner's role is discussed in greater detail below.

Franchise Ownership

Historically, professional sport team ownership was seen as a hobby for the wealthy. Many teams were family-owned and operated as "Mom and Pop" businesses. In the NFL there are still a handful of family-owned teams, since owning a team is more feasible in the NFL than in other leagues because the NFL shares a greater portion of revenues among teams than do the other professional leagues. The NFL also maintains the strictest franchise ownership rules of all the professional leagues. Permission to own a sports franchise must be granted by the ownership committee of the league in which one seeks team ownership. The ability to own a professional sports team depends upon the ability to obtain **franchise rights**. Franchise rights are the privileges afforded to owners. These include such rights as **territorial rights**, which limit a competitor franchise from moving into another team's territory without league permission and providing compensation, and **revenue sharing**, which gives a team a portion of various leaguewide revenues (expansion fees, national television revenue, gate receipts, and licensing revenues). Owners also receive the right to serve on ownership committees. Ownership committees exist for such areas as rules (competition/rules of play), franchise ownership, finance, labor relations/negotiations, television, and expansion. The ownership committees make decisions and set policies that the commissioner's office implements.

Ownership Rules. Not just anyone can become a sports franchise owner. It takes a great deal of capital, but even having the financial capacity and the desire to purchase a team does not guarantee eventual ownership of a team. Each league imposes restrictions on ownership, including a limit on the number of franchise rights granted and restrictions on franchise location. Leagues may also impose eligibility criteria for franchise ownership. For instance, MLB has no formal ownership criteria, but it does have key characteristics it looks favorably upon when granting ownership rights (Friedman & Much, 1997). The key considerations include substantial financial resources, a commitment to the local area in which the franchise is located, a commitment to baseball, support from local government, and an ownership structure that does not conflict with the interests of MLB (Friedman & Much, 1997).

The NFL has the strictest ownership rules. It is the only league to prohibit **corporate ownership** of its franchises, which it has done since 1970. The NFL has made just one exception to its rule and that was for the San Francisco 49ers. Their owner, Eddie DeBartolo, Jr., transferred ownership of the team to the Edward J. DeBartolo Co., a shopping mall development corporation, in 1986, and while the NFL fined DeBartolo $500,000 in 1990, it let the corporate ownership remain (Friedman & Much, 1997). The NFL also bans **public ownership**, but here it also has made one exception, in this case for the Green Bay Packers, which were publicly owned prior to the creation of the 1970 rule and thus were exempted from it. A former owner of the New England Patriots, Billy Sullivan, is currently embroiled in an antitrust lawsuit against the NFL, alleging that the public ownership restriction is a restraint of trade. Sullivan had asked the other NFL owners for permission to sell 49% of his team in a public stock offering. The NFL rejected his request. Due to losses he incurred in promoting a Michael Jackson tour he could no longer afford the team and was forced to sell his ownership interest. Until March 1997, the NFL also banned **cross-ownership**, that is, ownership of more than one sport franchise in a particular league (Friedman & Much, 1997). The NFL softened its rule for Wayne Huizenga to purchase the Miami Dolphins. Huizenga is currently majority owner of MLB's Florida Marlins and the NHL's Florida Panthers. The new rule allows an NFL owner to own other sports franchises in the same market or own an NFL franchise in one market and another franchise in another market, provided that market has no NFL team (Friedman & Much, 1997).

The Commissioner

The role of the **commissioner** in professional sport leagues has evolved over the past three-quarters of a century. Prior to 1921, professional baseball was governed by a three-man board called the National Commission. In September 1920 an indictment was issued charging eight Chicago White Sox players with attempting to "fix" World Series games, an incident commonly known as the Black Sox scandal (*Finley v. Kuhn*, 1978). To squelch public discontent, Major League Baseball owners appointed Judge Kennesaw Mountain Landis the first professional sport league commissioner in November 1920. Landis was signed to a seven-year contract and received an annual salary of $50,000 (Graffis, 1975). Landis agreed to take the commissioner's position on the condition that he be granted exclusive authority to act in the best interests of baseball (Helyar, 1994). In his first act, he issued lifetime bans against the eight "Black Sox" players for their involvement in the scandal (Helyar, 1994). In his first decade in office he banned 11 additional players, suspended Babe Ruth, and said no to any attempts to change the game by introducing marketing strategies or opening Major League Baseball to players of color (Helyar, 1994).

In all of the professional sport leagues, the commissioners' powers are derived from the league's constitution and bylaws. Through collective bargaining the players associations have attempted to limit the commissioners' powers. This has mainly been achieved by negotiating for labor grievance arbitration provisions in which a neutral arbitrator (rather than the commissioner) rules on labor disputes between the club and a player or the league/commissioner and a player. In the eyes of the players, the commissioner is an employee of the owners and thus will usually rule in the owners' favor for fear of losing his or her position. For example, many people cite former MLB Commissioner Fay Vincent's intervention in the lockout of 1990, which he did because of his belief that it was in the best interest of baseball and the best interest of the fans, as the beginning of the end of his term as commissioner. Team owners have tried to limit the power of the commissioner through court challenges. Three cases have upheld the baseball commissioner's right to act within the best interests of the game, provided the commissioner follows the rules when levying sanctions. In *Milwaukee American Association v. Landis* (1931), Commissioner Landis's disapproval of an assignment of a player contract from the major league St. Louis Browns to a minor league Milwaukee team was upheld. In *Atlanta National League Baseball Club, Inc. v. Kuhn* (1977) the court upheld Commissioner Kuhn's suspension of Ted Turner for tampering with player contracts but found that the commissioner's removal of the Braves' first-round draft choice exceeded his authority since there was no mention of such a penalty in the MLB Rules. Finally, in *Finley v. Kuhn* (1978), Commissioner Kuhn's disapproval of the sale of the Oakland A's rights to Vida Blue to the New York Yankees for $1.5 million and the rights to Rollie Fingers and Joe Rudi to the Boston Red Sox for $2 million as being contrary to the best interests of baseball was upheld. *Finley v. Kuhn* (1978) is particularly interesting in light of the fact that baseball currently has no permanent commissioner and arguments can be made that some of the moves made by team owners and general managers in the past five years to liquidate talent have been allowed due to the lack of oversight by a permanent commissioner. Good examples of this are the fact that San Diego Padres' 1992 "fire sale" of players and Chicago White Sox owner Jerry Reinsdorf's player moves in August 1997 have gone unquestioned, likely due to the lack of a strong and permanent commissioner.

To this day commissioners do maintain some of the authority created by MLB and Judge Kennesaw Mountain Landis, particularly the authority to investigate and impose penalties when those involved with the sport are suspected of not acting in the best interests of the game. The commissioner generally relies on this clause to penalize gamblers, drug users, and those players or owners involved in behavior that might embarrass the sport. Typically, the commissioner no longer has the power to hear disputes regarding player compensation or player performance but continues to possess discretionary powers in the following areas:

1. Approval of player contracts
2. Resolution of disputes between players and clubs
3. Resolution of disputes between clubs
4. Resolution of disputes between player or club and the league
5. Disciplinary matters involving players clubs, front office personnel, owners, etc.
6. Rule-making authority (Yasser, McCurdy, & Goplerud, 1997).

Commissioners in other professional sports were modeled after baseball's commissioner; however, not all embraced the role of disciplinarian as Landis did. Modern sport commissioners are more concerned with marketing than with discipline. For example, in the 1960s, Pete Rozelle took the NFL to new levels of stability with his revenue-sharing plans. Rozelle introduced NFL Properties, a division of the NFL that markets property rights for the entire NFL instead of allowing each team to market its own property rights. This idea was consistent with the "league think" philosophy he introduced to the NFL (Helyar, 1994). With **league think**, Rozelle preached that owners needed to think about what was best for the NFL as a whole, as opposed to what was best for their own individual franchise (Helyar, 1994).

David Stern, the current and long-reigning NBA Commissioner, followed Rozelle's lead in marketing but has clearly taken it to new levels. Stern's legacy is likely to be that he led the NBA into the "professional sport as entertainment" era and brought the NBA to the world. The NBA introduced exhibition games overseas and sends top players on international goodwill tours to teach basketball. The league encouraged its stars to play in the 1992 Olympics, resulting in the United States "Dream Team" and international NBA stars competing for their home countries. For a while it also appeared that integral to Stern's legacy and success would be his role as a consensus builder among the owners. Unlike in

MLB and the NFL, NBA owners rarely fight publicly or sue the league, and there were few if any labor disputes until the late 1980s. This placid scene changed when the Chicago Bulls and cable superstation WGN sued the NBA to challenge the NBA's limitation on the number of games an NBA team could televise. This litigation, does, however, appear to be more of an isolated incident than a trend of owners' taking issue with league rules and policies. On the other hand, NBA labor disputes are far more serious. The NBA and the National Basketball Players Association (NBPA) have engaged in two lawsuits, a lockout, messy negotiations, and a decertification attempt by the players. The battle is mainly over the continued use of the salary cap. The players argue that it is no longer necessary because the league is now financially viable (the salary cap was put into place in 1983 when the NBA was headed for financial ruin) (Fatsis, 1997). To put it simply, the players cannot seem to wrangle the salary cap out of the collective bargaining agreement at the negotiating table, and if they remain unionized, under labor and antitrust laws the salary cap will remain exempt from a legal challenge on those grounds (Helyar, 1995b). In effect, the only way for the players to legally challenge the salary cap to decertify the union, leaving no one for the owners to negotiate with, and then to file an antitrust suit for the owners' restraining competition in the market by setting a cap on spending rather than paying market value for players' services.

The NBA's former general counsel, Gary Bettman, is ushering in a new era as the NHL Commissioner. Many of his activities in his first few years in the position were undertaken to make the workings of the NHL model those of the NBA. For instance, like the NBA, the NHL has made strides into international markets. The NHL scouts talent internationally, and its athletes will participate on hockey "Dream Teams" at the 1998 Nagano Winter Olympics. The NHL also just announced that its All-Star format will change to include NHL All-Stars competing against a team of international all-stars.

Labor Relations

John Montgomery Ward, a Hall of Fame infielder/pitcher and lawyer, established the Brotherhood of Professional Base Ball Players as the first players association in 1885 (Staudohar, 1996). Although the Brotherhood had chapters on all teams (Staudohar, 1996), it became the first of four failed labor organizing attempts in baseball (Jennings, 1989). Ward fought the reserve system, salary caps of between $1,500 and $2,500 per team (depending on the team's classification), and the practice of selling players without the players' receiving a share of the profits (Jennings, 1989). Under the reserve system, players were bound perpetually to their teams, so owners could retain player rights and depress players' salaries. (The reserve system is discussed in detail in Chapter 11, Sports Agency.) When owners ignored Ward's attempts to negotiate, about 200 players organized a revolt, which led to the organization of the Players League, a rival league that attracted investors and was run like a corporation, with players sharing in the profits (Jennings, 1989). The Players League attracted players by offering three-year contracts under which the salary could be increased, but not decreased. The Players League folded after its first year after the National League spent approximately $4 million to bankrupt it and the media turned on the Brotherhood; most players returned to their National League teams, and collective player actions were nonexistent for about 10 years (Jennings, 1989).

In the six decades following the Players League, three other attempts to organize were unsuccessful due to the owners' ability to defeat the labor movement or the players' own sense that they did not want to belong to a union. The players were somewhat naive in their thinking and they viewed their associations more as fraternal organizations than trade unions (Cruise & Griffiths, 1991). They started the organizations to get information and make some change in their working conditions, but they feared that if they positioned themselves as a trade union their relationship with the owners would automatically be adversarial and in turn it would damage the sport (Cruise & Griffiths, 1991).

The Major League Baseball Players Association (MLBPA), formed in 1952, was initially dominated by the owners, and negotiated agreements were reached only on pensions and insurance (Staudohar, 1996). However, in 1966, things changed when a new executive director with a trade union background came on board. Marvin Miller's success as the executive director of the MLBPA is attributed to, among other things, organizing players by convincing *all* players that *each* of them (regardless of star status) was essential to game revenues and by bargaining for provisions that affected most players (minimum salary, pensions, insurance, salary and grievance arbitration, free agency, etc.) (Miller, 1991). Miller also convinced the players to develop a group promotional campaign in order to raise funds for the players association. The players authorized the association to enter into a group licensing program with Coca-Cola in 1966, which provided $60,000 in licensing fees (Miller, 1991). Miller also encouraged the players to hold out with Topps Trading Card Company. By holding out, the players association doubled the fees for trading cards from $125 to $250 per player and contributed a percentage of royalties to the union (8% on sales up to $4 million and 10% thereafter). Twenty-five years after these agreements were made, the players association brought in approximately $57 million in licensing fees and $50 million in trading card royalties from five card companies (Miller, 1991).

Except for a brief attempt by the NHL players to unionize in 1957, players associations in other leagues generally followed the lead of the MLBPA. In 1957, NHL players Ted Lindsay, Doug Harvey, Bill Gadsby, Fernie Flaman, Gus Mortson, and Jimmy Thomson attempted to organize a players association in order to protect the average hockey player and in particular to establish a strong pension plan (Cruise & Griffiths, 1991). They received authorization from every NHL player but one. After the owners publicly humiliated players, fed false salary information to the press, and traded players (including Lindsay) or sent them to the minors in retaliation for their involvement with the union, the NHL finally broke the players association (Cruise & Griffiths, 1991). Many average players feared for what would happen to them, since the NHL owners seemed to have no problem humiliating, threatening, trading, and/or releasing superstars such as Lindsay for their involvement in the players association (Cruise & Griffiths, 1991).

Among the minor leagues, the only players association is the Professional Hockey Players' Association, which has been representing minor league hockey players in the American, East Coast, and International Hockey Leagues since 1967. The players associations representing major leaguers do not represent minor leaguers because representing minor leaguers could result in a conflict of interest, with the union's having to forsake one group to represent the interests of the other. Additionally, both groups may be negotiating with the same management team, yet they have varying interests. Finally, if the minor league players improved their wages or benefits, it might take away from the revenues available for the major league players.

Individual Professional Sports

Individual professional sports generally exist around a professional tour of events, meets, or matches. This chapter discusses only one of the individual professional tours, the Professional Golfers' Association of America (PGA) Tour, as an example of the history of individual-sport tours and the different issues facing these professional associations.

The first U.S. Open was held in 1895, but the PGA was not born until January 1916, when a New York department store magnate called together a number of area golf professionals and amateur golfers to create a national organization to promote the game of golf and to improve the golf professional's vocation ("A History of the PGA Tour," 1997). Its constitution, bylaws, and rules, which were modeled after those of the British PGA, were completed in April 1916 (Graffis, 1975). The PGA's objectives were:

1. To promote interest in the game of golf.
2. To elevate the standards of the golf professional's vocation.
3. To protect the mutual interest of PGA members.
4. To hold meetings and tournaments for the benefit of members.
5. To establish a Benevolent Relief Fund for PGA members.

6. To accomplish any other objective determined by the PGA. ("The History of the American PGA," 1997).

During the PGA's formative years (1916–1930), much of its energy was focused on developing rules of play; establishing policies for itself; cleaning up jurisdictional problems with manufacturers and the U.S. Golf Association (the leading amateur golf association); standardizing golf equipment; and learning its own administrative needs (Graffis, 1975). In 1921, the PGA hired an administrative assistant and began its search for a commissioner. The PGA was not looking for a disciplinarian, unlike the MLB commissioner hired at the time, but rather an individual with strong administrative capabilities who could organize and operate the PGA on a daily basis (Graffis, 1975). Finally, in 1930 the PGA hired Albert R. Gates, a Chicago lawyer and four-time president of the Western Golf Association, as commissioner for a salary of $20,000 (with a membership of just 1,200, dues had to be raised to pay this sum). Gates's guiding principle was to raise the question "What good will it do golf?" and determine if the answer was satisfactory (Graffis, 1975).

The charging of spectators began at fundraisers. Top male and female golfers put on fundraising exhibitions to benefit the Red Cross during World War I (Graffis, 1975). The PGA later adopted the practice for its tournaments to raise money for the PGA's Benevolent Fund, and soon golfer Walter Hagen, who was earning a decent sum on his exhibition circuit throughout the United States, began to charge for his performances (Graffis, 1975). When the PGA was founded there was no distinction between club and touring professionals. Tournaments remained relatively small and manageable until television began paying for golf programming. Like professional sport all over the United States, the influence of television made golf more of a business than a game.

In the early to mid-1960s a number of factors created a growing tension between the PGA tournament professionals and the local country club professionals, and conflicts arose as the two groups' interests clashed (Graffis, 1975). Questions were raised concerning the mission of the PGA. Was it to operate the PGA Business Schools for local country club professionals, trained in golf business and primarily given the task of promoting interest in golf and golf-related products locally? Or was the mission of the PGA to work with those tournament professionals coming through the Qualifying School (Q-School) for the PGA Tour Circuit? At annual meetings held in 1961 to 1966, the PGA became a house divided over control, power, and which of the two groups was going to represent the PGA (Graffis, 1975). The tournament professionals claimed they had the support of a majority of golf's sponsors and threatened to leave the PGA to form a new association and tour. At the 1966 meeting, through the work of lawyers and skilled negotiators, the PGA came to the realization that there were two different constituencies in professional golf: first, the club professionals who served the amateur players and second, the showcase professionals who provided the entertainment for golf's spectators (Graffis, 1975). Finally, in 1968, the PGA tournament players broke away from the larger membership to form a Tournament Players Division, which in 1975 was renamed the PGA Tour ("The History of the American PGA," 1997). The PGA Tour is headquartered in Ponte Verde, Florida, and operates three tours: the PGA Tour, the PGA Senior Tour, and the NIKE Tour ("A History of the PGA Tour," 1997). Television revenues and corporate sponsorship have increased the purses for players on the PGA Tour ("A History of the PGA Tour," 1997). The PGA Tour runs for the first 10 months of the year, and from January through August purses average over $1.2 million per week, while in September and October they drop to around $1 million per week (Feinstein, 1996).

The PGA of America, the larger association of local club professionals, is also located in Florida, on a multicourse development ("The History of the American PGA," 1997). The facility employs 125 people and is a training ground for course professionals. The PGA of America also runs the second largest golf show and has begun to acquire world-class courses to host the over 30 tournaments held for its members and apprentices ("The History of the American PGA," 1997).

Tours in the various individual sports have their own rules and regulations. In tennis, the 50 top-ranked players are required to submit their tournament schedules for the following year to their respective governing bodies by the conclusion of the U.S. Open "so decisions can be made on designations and fields can be balanced to meet the commitments the WTA and ATP have made to their tournaments" (Feinstein, 1992, p. 392). Throughout Wimbledon and the U.S. Open, players' agents and tournament directors negotiate appearance fees and set schedules for the top-ranked players' upcoming seasons, while the other players are left to make decisions about whether to return to the tour the following year. In golf, every year players must prove themselves to qualify for the PGA Tour (Feinstein, 1996). "There are two ways to avoid the hell of qualifying: winning and earning" (Feinstein, 1996, p. 69). Winning a tournament exempts a player from qualifying for two years, whereas winning one of the four majors (the Masters, U.S. Open, British Open, PGA), the World Series of Golf, the Tour Championship, or the Players Championship exempts a player from qualifying for 10 years (Feinstein, 1996). Therefore, approximately 12 players have long-term exemptions, 30 to 40 have two-year exemptions, and everyone else competes in the Q-School for one of the 40 spots on the next year's PGA Tour. In 1993, for example, there were 800 entries to the PGA's Q-School, and of those, 191 made the final stage of the Q-School tournament (Feinstein, 1996). Players who do not make the PGA Tour usually play on the NIKE Tour for approximately 20% of what they would make on the PGA Tour (Feinstein, 1996).

For information on the management of tour events, see Chapter 14, Event Management, and for information on the sports management firms operating in the golf or other professional sport industries, see Chapter 11, Sports Agency.

KEY CONCEPTS

Franchise Values

Today's franchise costs make family ownership a rarity. Most franchise owners need to diversify their investments to protect against the risk that their sports franchise will lose a great deal of money. Currently many owners purchase teams as a primary business investment, while others purchase teams as an ancillary business to their primary business (i.e., Ted Turner's ownership of sports teams as ancillary businesses which provide sports programming for his television business). Still others are fulfilling a dream with a number of co-owners. Due to rising franchise fees, expansion fees, player salaries, and the leveling off of or decrease in television revenues, there is too much at risk for one owner if that person does not have diverse pools of money to cover team operating costs.

Much and Gotto (1997) note that the two most important factors in determining a sports franchise's value are the degree of revenue sharing and the stability of the league's labor situation. Two current problems confronting professional sport arise when considering the degree to which revenue sharing occurs. The first is specifically a result of MLB's large-market–small-market dichotomy. MLB does not share local broadcast revenues, and thus a large-media-market team such as the New York Yankees derives far more revenues than does a small-market team such as the Seattle Mariners. For instance, the New York Yankees' Madison Square Garden (cable) Network/WPIX-TV contract provides the team with $42 million in rights fees annually ($500 million over 12 years) and WABC-AM provides an additional $4.5 million in radio rights fees annually (Friedman & Much, 1997). Comparison of this figure with the Seattle Mariners' media revenues reveals a disparity of nearly $36 million, as the Mariners receive approximately $10.5 million in media rights fees (Friedman & Much, 1997). This disparity results in an unfair advantage for a large-market team in terms of operating revenue and franchise valuation. Due to this disparity, small-market teams such as the Pittsburgh Pirates and the Montreal Expos are constantly building from their farm systems and losing franchise players to the free market, since they lack revenue to meet players' salary demands.

The second problem arising from a lack of revenue sharing is the disparity in stadium and arena lease arrangements. It is universal in professional sport leagues that stadium and arena revenues are not shared. Thus, teams that play in facilities with luxury boxes, personal seat licenses, and club seating generate additional operating revenues and/or profit for their owners. For example, in 1995 *Financial*

World noted that of the 10 top-ranked franchises, 8 possessed the most lucrative lease agreements (Ozanian et al., 1995). The most notable of these are two small-market franchises, the Baltimore Orioles and Texas Rangers, ranked second and third respectively in franchise values in MLB in 1995 (Ozanian et al., 1995). The Orioles opened Camden Yards in 1992 and the Rangers opened the Ballpark at Arlington in 1994, and in 1994 they ranked second and fifth respectively in stadium revenues, earning $13.4 and $10.3 million during the 1994 strike-shortened season (Ozanian et al., 1995). In 1996 the Orioles again ranked second among MLB teams, behind the large-media-market New York Yankees, in total revenues and in franchise value ("What Franchises," 1996).

A number of team owners have used their leverage to negotiate favorable lease agreements that provide the team with a majority of the revenues generated by the facility, including facility sponsorship (signage and naming rights), concessions, and parking. As a result of the race for these revenues, a strategy called **franchise free agency** has emerged in the 1990s. Under this strategy team owners threaten to move their teams if their demands for new stadiums, renovations to existing stadiums, or better lease agreements are not met. This concept is discussed in further detail in the Current Issues section of this chapter.

League Revenues

Leagues derive revenue from national television and radio contracts, leaguewide licensing, and leaguewide sponsorship programs. Leagues do not derive revenue from local broadcasting, gate receipts, preferred seating sales, or any of the stadium revenues. All of those forms of revenue go to the teams and as a result have caused competitive balance problems among teams, as discussed in the previous section. For detailed information on league revenues see Chapter 4, Financial Principles Applied to Sport Management, and for information on broadcasting revenues see Chapter 16, Sport Broadcasting.

Legal Issues

The key areas of the law impacting the professional sport industry are contract law, antitrust law, and labor law. Historically, most of the cases have developed either when players and owners (current and prospective) have challenged league rules or when competitor leagues have tried to compete against the dominant established league that possesses market power. Over time the majority of contract cases have been resolved, and all players now sign a standard player contract drafted by the league. This does not mean that contractual disputes do not continue to arise. There will occasionally be such cases because the commissioner of a league can refuse to approve a player's contract if he or she believes it violates a league rule or policy. For instance, in the NBA and NFL there are occasionally player contracts in which the commissioner finds an attempt to circumvent the salary cap. The team and player may either go back and renegotiate the contract or else challenge the commissioner's finding. Occasional contract disputes have begun to arise in another area as professional sports have become more global. Disputes may occur over which team retains the rights to a particular player, and such disputes may lead to court battles between teams and players of different countries. To avoid these types of disputes, the NBA, NHL, and MLB and leagues abroad are entering into or revising their player transfer agreements.

Antitrust law is a second area in which many disputes arise. Antitrust laws regulate anticompetitive business practices. At the outset it is necessary to point out that MLB is exempt from antitrust laws as a result of a 1922 Supreme Court case, *Federal Baseball Club of Baltimore v. National League of Professional Baseball Clubs*, which held that baseball was a game and not a business (see Chapter 5, Legal Principles Applied to Sport Management). All professional sport leagues have adopted restrictive practices to provide financial stability and competitive balance between all teams in the league. The game would not be appealing to fans if the same teams dominated the league year after year because they had the money to consistently purchase the best players. Similarly, fans and front office staff would not like to see their teams change player personnel year after year. It is the nature of sport that teams must be built and that players and coaches must develop strong working relationships. However, restrictive practices, such as reserve systems, salary caps, free agent restrictions, and free agent compensation may lead to players' receiving offers that are below their market value and may also keep competitor leagues from getting access to marquee players. Therefore, players and competitor leagues have used antitrust laws to argue that these practices are anticompetitive and either restrain trade or monopolize the market for professional team sports. Additionally, in the past decade, owners have sued their own leagues on antitrust grounds in order to challenge restrictive practices (see Chapter 5, Legal Principles Applied to Sport Management). Antitrust laws carry with them a treble damage provision, so if a league loses an antitrust case and the court triples the amount of damages, it could effectively run into a multimillion-dollar damage award.

Labor relations did not play a major role in the professional sport industry until the late 1960s, but it has become a dominant legal force in recent times. By the early 1970s the professional sport industry had begun its transformation to a more traditional business model (Staudohar, 1996). Growing fan interest and increased revenues from television and sponsorship transformed leagues into lucrative business enterprises that lured more wealthy business owners looking for tax shelters and ego boosters (Staudohar, 1996). New leagues and expansion of existing leagues provided more playing opportunities and, thus, more bargaining power to the players, and the increased bargaining power and financial rewards led players to turn increasingly to player agents and their players associations (Staudohar, 1996). Players associations, once "weak or nonexistent, became a countervailing power to the owners' exclusive interests" (Staudohar, 1996, p. 4). Under labor law, once players have unionized, professional sport league management can no longer unilaterally change hours, wages, or terms and conditions of employment. A collective bargaining agreement covering these items must be negotiated between the league (representing the collective interests of the owners) and the players association (representing the collective interests of the players).

When the collective bargaining process reaches an **impasse** (a breakdown in negotiations), the players will go out on strike or owners will "lock out" the players. Over the three-decade history of labor relations in professional sports, there have been six strikes (involving MLB, NFL, and NHL) and three lockouts (involving MLB, NBA, and NHL). Strikes and lockouts are far more disruptive in professional sports than in other industries, because players possess unique talents and cannot be replaced. Therefore, a strike or lockout effectively shuts the business down. A good example of the difference can be seen in the nationwide UPS strike of 1997. Although the strike severely disrupted UPS's ability to deliver packages, it did not totally close the business because managers could drive the trucks to deliver packages and replacement workers could be hired. In contrast, it would be very difficult to find a replacement for a Ken Griffey, Jr., a Michael Jordan, a Deion Sanders, or a Wayne Gretsky. Fans will not pay to see unknown players on the field, and television networks and sponsors would pull their financial support from such events. In the 1995 baseball strike, the owners attempted to use replacement players and their attempts failed for just those reasons.

The one time that replacement players did make an impact in professional sports was during the NFL strike of 1987. The only reason that the owners were able to break the strike by using replacement players was because there was a labor pool of unemployed, talented, marquee United States Football League (USFL) players who were available since the USFL had disbanded the previous year.

Labor relations in professional sports are unique because it is in the leagues' best interests for players to unionize. In other types of business, management groups usually prefer that unions be either weak or nonexistent. However, with a union in place league management can negotiate restrictive practices with the players associations through the collective bargaining process. Under antitrust law, any restrictive practice that primarily injures the union but is negotiated in a collective bargaining agreement is exempt from an antitrust law challenge. All of the restrictive practices in professional sport—negotiating the draft, salary cap, restrictions on free agency, and the like—included in the collective bargaining process enable management to be free from worry over an antitrust lawsuit by the players.

Race and the Professional Sport Industry

Critics have argued that since the majority of athletes in professional sport are people of color, there should be more opportunity for people of color to move into management positions. Four specific statements and one specific incident in the past decade stand out as having brought the issue of race and professional sport into the public eye. The first statement was Al Campanis's statement made on ABC's *Nightline* on the occasion of the 40th anniversary of Jackie Robinson's integration of MLB. At the time of the appearance Campanis was an executive with the Los Angeles Dodgers. When host Ted Koppel asked why there were no black general managers, managers, or owners, Campanis replied that they did not have the "necessities" to hold the positions (Shropshire, 1996). The second statement involved a 1988 interview with Jimmy "the Greek" Snyder, a CBS football commentator, on Martin Luther King Day. When asked about the role of blacks in football in the context of a Martin Luther King story, Snyder responded that going back to slavery, black players were bred to play sports like football, but they were not in a position to coach (Shropshire, 1996). (Both Campanis and Snyder were fired for their statements.) The third "statement" actually involves a series of occasions on which Marge Schott, owner of the Cincinnati Reds, has made a number of racist and antisemitic comments (Shropshire, 1996). Schott has twice been suspended and sent to diversity counseling by MLB for these statements. The final statement involves PGA Tour player Fuzzy Zoeller's comments to the press in which he referred to golfer Tiger Woods as "a little boy" and stereotyped him as favoring fried chicken and collard greens for the Masters Dinner ("Zoeller's Comments," 1997). Zoeller's comments met with public disfavor and the loss of some of his sponsorship.

The incident that is categorized with these four racial statements involved the 1990 PGA Tour and Hall Thompson, the founder and president of Shoal Creek, a Birmingham, Alabama, country club that was hosting the PGA Tournament for the second time in six years (Feinstein, 1996). When asked publicly about why Shoal Creek had accepted no black members, Thompson responded, "'That's just not done in Birmingham'" and implied that a black would not even be proposed for membership in the club (Feinstein, 1996, p. 422). In the face of public scrutiny, Shoal Creek agreed to admit one black member, and the PGA Tour, the PGA of America, and the United States Golf Association (USGA) all agreed to revise their guidelines for hosting events that required minority membership at host country clubs (Feinstein, 1996). These actions by those prominent in professional sport bring to light the fact that racism still exists in the industry.

Data on Racial Composition in Professional Sports

As 1997 marked the fiftieth anniversary of the integration of MLB by Jackie Robinson, much attention was paid in the press about integration on the business side of baseball. Former major leaguer and current ESPN broadcaster Joe Morgan predicted that until baseball has black ownership or blacks in high positions in the sport, integration will be an uphill battle, for in professional sport many positions are filled by word of mouth, and if blacks and whites do not mix in the same social circles and whites are in the positions with power to hire, they will continue to hire whites whom they know (Morgan, 1996). In 1997, 36% of MLB players are people of color, of which 18% are African-American (Lainson, 1997). Among those working at MLB's central offices in 1996, 28% were people of color, including 21% of the executives and department heads; in individual teams, people of color held 18% of front-office positions (9% were African-American, 7% were Hispanic, and 2% were Asian), which includes people of color who held 11% of the executive and department head positions; and among top managers (chairman of the board, president, CEO, vice president, or general manager of a pro franchise) only 5% were people of color (Lainson, 1997). The Racial Report Card, a study conducted annually by Northeastern University's Center for the Study of Sport in Society, reported that in 1995–1996, 12% of all management positions (business operations, marketing/promotions, public and community relations, finance, game operations) were held by people of color and 67% of all players were people of color (Lapchick, 1997). Of those positions people of color held 18% of management-level positions at the NFL offices but only 6% of front-office positions at the team level (Lainson, 1997). In 1995, 68% of the players, 5% of top management, 11% of administration, and 11% of support staff were people of color (Lainson, 1997). In the NBA, the Racial Report Card found that 80% of the players and 15 to 16% of NBA management were people of color (Lapchick, 1997). Of those positions, it was reported that 21% of professional staff positions in the league offices were held by people of color and at the team level people of color held 17% of the top positions (chairman of the board, president, CEO, vice president, or general manager of a pro franchise) (Lainson, 1997). In 1995, 82% of players, 15% of top management, 13% of administration, and 23% of support staff were people of color (Lainson, 1997). The racial composition of the NHL is difficult to find, presumably because less than 1% of players and front-office staff are people of color. As for the MLS, ABL, and WNBA, the leagues are too new to have data reported. For further information on racial issues in the sports agency industry, see Chapter 11, Sports Agency.

Shropshire (1996) stressed pointedly that integration of people of color into management positions will not happen without a concerted effort by owners, commissioners, and those in positions of power. He suggests that to combat racism in professional sport there must be recognition of what "both America and sport in reality look and act like" as well as what both "should look and act like in that ideal moment in the future [when racism is eliminated]" (Shropshire, 1996, p. 144). He suggests that between these two phases is an intermediate period of transition and that during the transition a number of steps must be taken. First, Shropshire suggests changing the focus of the black community's youth to move athletic success away from being a substitute for other forms of success. Second, he suggests the need for a stronger united action by the athletes to take a stand against racism. Shropshire's third step is leaguewide action evidencing a commitment to address diversity, and his fourth step is continued civil rights action such as that put forth by Jesse Jackson's Rainbow Coalition for Fairness in Athletics. Finally, apart from the political action suggested, Shropshire suggests the need for legal action in the form of lawsuits and government intervention by such organizations as the Department of Justice and the Equal Employment Opportunity Commission. The combination of all of these actions may provide a step toward erasing racism in professional sport. For further information on managing diversity, see Chapter 2, Management Principles Applied to Sport Management.

CAREER OPPORTUNITIES

Commissioner

The role and responsibilities of a league commissioner are fairly well detailed earlier in the chapter. A wide variety of skills are required to be an effective commissioner. They include an understanding of the sport and the various league documents (league constitution, bylaws, rules and regulations, standard player contract, and collective bargaining agreement), negotiating skills, diplomacy, the ability to work well with a variety of people, an ability to delegate, a good public image, an ability to handle pressure and the media, an ability to make sound decisions, and in general, a visionary outlook. These are not skills that are easily taught; for the most part, they evolve over time. While there is not a specific path to this position, it appears that one pattern is to become a lawyer and work as general or outside counsel to the league in which one hopes to become commissioner or to another professional league. Those qualifications are common among the current commissioners in the NBA, NFL, and NHL.

Other League Office Personnel

Each league has an office staff working in a wide variety of positions. While the number of positions varies in league offices, a good example comes from the

NBA, where there are approximately 148 employees in management positions ("Miami Heat," 1993–1994). Of these staff members, 72 work in the Commissioner's Office, 25 work in the NBA Properties Division, 49 work for NBA Entertainment, Inc., and 2 work for NBA Television Ventures. Their titles are too numerous to mention here, but all positions are organized into departments. For instance, departments in the Commissioner's Office include administration, broadcasting, corporate affairs, editorial, finance, legal, operations, player programs, public relations, security, and special events. Departments in the NBA Properties Division include business development, finance, international offices, legal, licensing, marketing, media and sponsor programs, and team services. Departments in NBA Entertainment include administration, accounting, legal, licensing, operations, photography, production, and programming. Thus, there are a wide variety of opportunities in league offices for individuals with degrees in sport management and those who couple their initial degrees with an advanced degree such as a law degree or a masters in business administration (MBA). Skills necessary for working in a league office vary with the position, yet a few universal skills include having a working knowledge of the sport, teams in the league, and the professional sport industry in general; good customer relations skills; and a willingness to work long hours (especially during the season and postseason).

Team General Manager

A team general manager is usually in charge of all player personnel decisions. These include overseeing the scouting and drafting of players, signing free agents, trading or selling players, and negotiating contracts with players and/or their agents. The general manager must understand the sport and be able to assess talent. He or she must also possess a working knowledge of all league documents (constitution, bylaws, rules and regulations, collective bargaining agreement, standard player contract). A career path for the position has traditionally been to move into the position from the playing and/or coaching ranks. As the position has become more complex, individuals with sport management degrees, MBAs, and/ or law degrees have become desirable employees. Some teams will continue to have a general manager who has risen from the playing and/or coaching ranks, but will hire one or more assistant general managers to deal with complex contract negotiations and to decipher league rules and policies.

Other Team Front-Office Personnel

Like league office staffs, team front-office staffs offer a wide variety of positions. A look at the Miami Heat front-office staff provides a glimpse at the variety of positions available. The team possesses 40 full-time employees and four partners and four limited partners. Of the 40 employees, there is one executive vice president and four other vice presidents (finance, broadcasting/ special projects, sponsor relations, community relations), two legal counsels, seven Basketball Operations staff members (scouting, coaching, player personnel), seven directors (public relations, corporate education, marketing/community services, customer relations, community sales development, sales, sponsor relations), two managers (box office, equipment), and 16 assistant managers, assistant directors, or administrative assistants. Finally there are two medical staff members. Entry-level positions tend to be in the sales, marketing, community relations, and media/public relations departments. Salaries tend to be low, because many people would love to work for a professional team and therefore supply always exceeds demand. Most people are hired from within, so completing an internship will help get a "foot in the door." Often in the sales departments, commissions for ticket, corporate, or group sales may be a part of the salary. As for league office positions, skills necessary for working in a front office are knowledge of the sport and the professional sport industry, good customer relations abilities, and a willingness to work long hours (particularly during the season and postseason). As for educational requirements, a sport management degree and, depending on the position, possibly an advanced degree such as a law degree or an MBA are appropriate for someone looking to break into a front-office position.

Tour Personnel

Tours such as the PGA Tour have a number of employees as well. As with league sport the positions vary from commissioner to marketer to special events coordinator. Much of the event management work for the actual site operations for the tour is, however, often left to an outside consultant. Tours and sites contract with event marketing/management agencies to take care of all of the details of putting on the event at a particular country club. For more details on these kinds of positions, see Chapter 14, Event Management.

Agents

Almost all team and individual athletes in the professional sport industry have sports agents representing them and coordinating their business and financial affairs. In addition, a growing number of professional coaches rely on sports agents. For more details on the skills and responsibilities of this career choice, see Chapter 11, Sports Agency.

CURRENT ISSUES

Salary Caps

Salary caps in the NBA and NFL are currently being reevaluated to determine if they are working properly. Salary caps are intended to create parity among league teams by placing a limit on how much a team can spend on its players' salaries. In order to impose a salary cap in a league in which a union exists, owners must negotiate with the players (since the salary cap affects wages). In the negotiation process, the union will inevitably negotiate for some exceptions to the salary cap. These exceptions have in reality created loopholes for creative general managers and agents representing players. For instance, in the NFL, signing bonuses are applied to the cap by prorating them across the life of the contract. Therefore, a team like the Detroit Lions can still offer Barry Sanders a six-year $34.6 million contract despite a 1997 salary cap of $41 million per team (Fatsis, 1997). Of the $34.6 million, $11.5 million is his signing bonus, and under the salary cap provisions just $1.8 million of the signing bonus counts toward the Lions' 1997 salary cap computation (Fatsis, 1997). Another problem with the caps is that they routinely force teams to cut established players or renegotiate their contracts to make room under the cap to sign another player, and a third problem is that all of the caps provide for a team spending minimum, so low-revenue teams are prevented from cutting their payrolls in order to stay competitive (Fatsis, 1997). Despite complaints, the NFL negotiated with the NFLPA to extend its cap through the year 2000 and will vote as to whether to extend it further. There is also a rumor that the NBA may reopen the labor agreement with the NBPA to reconsider the salary cap (Fatsis, 1997).

Franchise Free Agency

A new strategy has emerged among professional sport team owners in which they threaten to move their teams unless the local government meets their demands for a new stadium or arena, makes improvements to their current venue, or renegotiates a better lease agreement. The fiber of the professional sport industry is woven into the political process and the emotional identification of cities. The sport industry is unique in that while it should be viewed as an industry and its contributions judged upon "industry" comparisons, that does not happen. In other words, a city does not treat a major league sport franchise the same way it treats a "major league" paper mill (Euchner, 1993). Although sports franchises are not the dominant industries in any city, they receive the type of attention one would expect a city to bestow on one of its major economic producers and employers (Euchner, 1993). As a result, team owners have become adept at leveraging their power to receive tax breaks, land for stadium development, and the lion's share of the stadium and arena revenues. For this reason in June 1995,

39 of 109 professional teams were threatening to move from their home cities (Crothers, 1995).

It has been argued that a shortage of teams has been built into the current structures of organized baseball and football and has been reinforced by the individual and collective decisions made by franchises (Euchner, 1993). The limited supply of teams and the great demand for them enhances their value to cities. Their leverage and bargaining power make it very difficult for cities to make demands on teams. For every city desiring a pledge of long-term stability or an increase in taxes on ticket sales, there is another city willing to forgo the security or income to lure a franchise. How else can one logically explain the decision of the city of St. Louis to build a $260 million football stadium, agreeing to give the Rams all money generated from the sale of personal seat licenses, concessions, and parking, as well as the majority of stadium advertising revenue? Or the Denver Metropolitan Major League Baseball Stadium District Board's agreement to pay all of the estimated $156 million Coors Field construction costs and to provide 100% of concession, parking, novelties, luxury boxes, stadium naming rights, and all stadium advertising revenue, as well as free rent through the year 1999—after which the district will receive a meager 2.5% of the owners' net taxable income (Whitford, 1993)?

Leagues other than MLB are cautious of limiting franchise relocation for fear of an antitrust lawsuit. Since baseball is exempt from the antitrust laws, it has the strictest franchise relocation guidelines, and teams rarely move. In 1984, NFL owner Al Davis moved his Raiders from Oakland to Los Angeles despite the NFL owners' voting against the move. The NFL lost an antitrust challenge to the rule brought by Davis. As a result, the NFL and other leagues are too threatened by the potential for treble damages to take a strong stand against relocation. Most disputes end with the relocating team's giving some sort of payment back to the league. In a way this payment can be seen as a fee for taking a viable franchise from the other owners, since the owners are losing out on a high expansion fee that would be assessed (and shared among them) for a new team entering that city. Unfortunately for cities, the teams have now begun to factor this into their negotiations with a new city, and now rather than having the fee come out of the budget of the relocating team, the relocating team is assessing its new city for the amount.

The NHL has adopted a policy to stem the movement of teams out of Canada and into the United States (Friedman & Much, 1997). The NHL has adopted a revenue-sharing plan in which funds from league-generated television, licensing, and sponsorship revenue reimburse Canadian teams for the currency imbalance between the two countries. To qualify, a team must be in the bottom half of NHL revenues and have revenues that are at least 80% of the NHL average, or must sell a designated amount of season tickets, luxury suites, or sponsorship (Friedman & Much, 1977).

Women's Professional Sport Leagues

On the heels of the success of women athletes in the Centennial Olympic Games in Atlanta, four women's professional sport leagues have emerged. These are the ABL and WNBA in basketball, the WPF in fastpitch softball, and the NSA in soccer. With the emergence of these leagues is the emergence of labor relations for female professional athletes. The National Basketball Players Association has entered into discussions with the ABL and WNBA players to see if they are interested in forming trade associations to represent the labor interests of the women (Kessler, 1997). Creating trade associations rather than becoming certified as labor unions will allow the women to avoid the labor exemption to antitrust law limiting their ability to bring an antritrust lawsuit against the league. The women in soccer and fastpitch softball have united to create a trade association named the Women's Players Association. One of the Women's Players Association's biggest concerns has been the creation of pregnancy policies for the female athletes ("Baby Talk," 1997). The Women's Players Association negotiated a collective bargaining agreement with the NSA in which they agreed to include a maternity leave clause modeled after the federal Family and Medical Leave Act of 1993 (under which most female professional athletes are not covered). The provision guarantees that NSA players remain under contract and receive a portion of their salary during a leave period of up to 10 months, and then if a player chooses not to return when her leave expires her team may terminate her contract ("Baby Talk,"1997). The WPF, WNBA, and ABL have chosen to deal with each pregnancy as it arises. High-profile WNBA player Sheryl Swoopes missed most of the 1997 season with the birth of her son and was paid her entire $250,000 salary, but without uniform pregnancy policies, teams may choose to treat employees differently than Swoopes was treated and may find themselves fighting discrimination lawsuits ("Baby Talk," 1997).

The creation of professional women's sport leagues may raise another interesting issue: Will women be hired in the key management positions to match the gender composition of the players on the field or on the court? While the leagues are too new to have data available on the gender breakdown among those in management positions, it will be interesting to monitor the leagues on this point. Access to management positions for women in professional sport has traditionally been limited, and these leagues may prove to provide new management opportunities for female sport managers.

SUMMARY

The professional sport industry involves the sale of the entertainment value of sport events and exhibitions. Revenue is generated primarily through media rights fees, licensed product sales, gate receipts, and (recently) stadium revenues. The leagues and tours face a number of challenges, including keeping fans satisfied in light of their perceptions regarding the "highly paid athlete." Directly related to this is finding a means to achieving labor peace in the leagues and methods of keeping a fan base that is representative of society as ticket prices continue to skyrocket. The four dominant major professional leagues (MLB, NBA, NFL, and NHL) also face a challenge in market share from the new upstart leagues for women, the expansion in the minor leagues, the growing interest in soccer, and the growing interest and commercialization of collegiate sport.

The professional sport industry is entering an exciting period. With the innovations in technology professional sport is becoming more global, particularly as leagues struggle to find unsaturated markets and new revenue streams. This exciting environment, coupled with the perception of the glamour of working for a team or league, attracts many job seekers to professional sports. Therefore, landing an entry-level position is competitive, and salaries tend to be lower than in other segments of the industry. Those who are persistent, are willing to intern in the industry, and are committed to keeping abreast of this fast-paced industry will be rewarded. Professional sports are constantly changing and are often addressing challenges. The sport manager who can adapt to change and resolve problems and who possesses a vision for the professional sport industry's entrance into the twenty-first century will find success in this field.

CASE STUDY: THE RAMS MOVE TO ST. LOUIS

The NFL St. Louis Cardinals owner Bill Bidwell attempted to upgrade Busch Stadium a number of times. The outdated stadium held just 51,000 seats (Frei, 1995). Bidwell moved the team to Phoenix after numerous failed attempts to get voters to agree to provide the team with financial support for stadium renovations.

After the Cardinals departed, St. Louis made two unsuccessful attempts at winning an expansion franchise through the NFL expansion process. The city did not succeed, but not for lack of trying. In its most recent attempt (1993), the expansion group brought in Chicago Bears legend and NFL Hall of Fame player Walter Payton as a partner and ran a campaign that culminated with a full-page advertisement in *USA Today*. The advertisement featured a picture of Payton with the heading "St. Louis Congratulates Walter Payton (on his selection to the Hall of Fame and partnership in this team)" ("St. Louis," 1993). The advertisement spoke of Payton's on- and off-the-field persona: his dedication to excellence in football and in the community as well as the grace and dignity with which he carried himself. It went on to say that Payton would bring to St. Louis's NFL Partnership the same dedication to secure a new expansion franchise for St. Louis. Finally, the advertisement promised "a new 70,000 seat domed stadium, corporate and fan support, the largest TV market (of all the NFL expansion bids), a central location, and an ownership group which includes Walter Payton" ("St. Louis," 1993). Despite St. Louis's efforts, the NFL Expansion Committee rejected its bid.

After years without a team, the citizens of St. Louis agreed to put up $720 million in financing to build a new domed stadium in the hopes of luring a franchise unhappy with its city and lease agreement. In the running were many prospective takers. A handful of owners had made their unhappiness with their current agreements known publicly. Among them were Bud Adams, owner of the Houston Oilers; Al Davis, owner of the Los Angeles Raiders; Georgia Frontiere, owner of the Los Angeles Rams; and Art Modell, owner of the Cleveland Browns. Interestingly enough, the Rams and Raiders are both teams situated in the country's second-largest media market.

In the race to move to a viable market, Georgia Frontiere moved out in front in the negotiations and agreed to a deal with St. Louis. The deal provided:

- $180 million for the sale of 40,000 personal seat licenses at $4,500 each for the Trans World Dome
- 100% of concessions revenues from the Trans World Dome
- 100% of the revenue from 120 luxury boxes and from 6,200 club seats in the Trans World Dome
- 75% of stadium advertising sales revenues (Helyar, 1995a)

The Rams used $27 million of the $180 million to pay off the Anaheim Bond Debt, $15 million for a new training facility, and $13 million for relocation costs. The deal produced an estimated yield to the Rams of $20 million per year in stadium revenues. The cost to the taxpayers totaled $720 million, of which $260 million is for stadium construction and $460 million is for interest and lease guarantees. Finally, these same taxpayers may also be responsible for the possible cost for a guarantee of the sale of 85% of the seats (Helyar, 1995a).

Incidentally, the Trans World Dome was part of a city (urban development) plan to lure more conventions and tourists to St. Louis. The plan also included a new arena for the St. Louis Blues NHL team, a new convention center, and a new transportation infrastructure. The city created a rail system to take tourists and conventioneers from the airport to their hotels, the convention center, and the sports facilities.

Finally, the other prospective owners have all moved to new cities and the promise of greater revenues. Bud Adams has moved the Oilers to Nashville, albeit with a two-year stopover in Memphis while waiting for the new stadium to be completed. Al Davis has returned to Oakland for the promise of personal seat license revenues and luxury boxes. He originally moved to Los Angeles because the L.A. Coliseum had promised him the luxury boxes which were not available in Oakland. After a 12-year wait for the luxury boxes, Davis returned home to Oakland. And finally, Art Modell moved the Browns out of their beloved Cleveland to Baltimore, where their name has changed to the Ravens. The NFL did no more than threaten legal action against Frontiere, Adams, and Modell as all three eventually shared a portion of their profits with fellow owners. Davis has refused to share the relocation revenue derived from the personal seat licenses, luxury boxes, and club seating, and as a result, the NFL has filed an antitrust suit against him.

Questions for Discussion

1. If you were the mayor of the city of St. Louis, would you have agreed to this arrangement with the Rams?
2. What benefits does the city of St. Louis derive from this plan?
3. How should NFL Commissioner Paul Tagliabue have responded to the moves by Frontiere, Adams, Davis, and Modell?
4. Should there be a clear league policy in place to govern franchise relocation? Why or why not?
5. Assume you are a consultant for a city seeking a new sports franchise. What advice would you give?

RESOURCES

Professional Sport Leagues

American Basketball League (ABL)
1900 Embarcadero Road, Suite 100
Palo Alto, CA 94303
415-856-3200
http://www.ABLeague.com

American Hockey League (AHL)
425 Union Street
W. Springfield, MA 01069
413-781-2030; fax: 413-733-4767
http://www.canoe.ca/ahl

Continental Basketball League (CBL)
701 Market Street, Suite 140
St. Louis, MO 63101
314-621-7222; fax: 314-621-1202

East Coast Hockey League (ECHL)
125 Village Boulevard, Suite 210

Princeton, NJ 08540
609-452-0770; fax: 609-452-7147
http://www.echl.org

International Hockey League (IHL)
1577 Woodward Ave., Suite 212
Bloomfield Hills, MI 48304
810-258-0580; fax: 810-258-0940
http://www.theihl.com

Major League Baseball (MLB)
350 Park Ave.
New York, NY 10022
212-339-7800; fax: 212-355-0007
http://www.majorleaguebaseball.com

Major League Soccer (MLS)
2029 Century Park E., Suite 400
Los Angeles, CA 90067
310-772-2600; fax: 310-843-4836

National Association of Professional Baseball Leagues
201 Bayshore Drive, S.E.
St. Petersburg, FL 33701
813-822-6937; fax: 813-821-5819

National Basketball Association (NBA)
645 Fifth Ave.
New York, NY 10022
212-407-8000; fax: 212-832-3861
http://www.nba.com

National Football League (NFL)
World League of American Football (WLAF)
410 Park Ave., 6th Floor
New York, NY 10022
212-758-1500; fax: 212-872-7464
http://www.nfl.com

National Hockey League (NHL)
1251 Avenue of the Americas
New York, NY 10020-1198

212-789-2000; fax: 212-789-2020
http://www.nhl.com

United States Interregional Soccer League; W-League Division of USISL
14497 N. Dale Mabry Highway, Suite 211
Grand Plaza, North Bldg.
Tampa, FL 33618
http://www.womensoccer.com

Women's National Basketball Association (WNBA)
645 Fifth Ave.
New York, NY 10022
212-688-9622; fax: 212-750-9622
http://www.nba.com

Women's Professional Fastpitch (WPF)
90 Madison Street, Suite 200
Denver, CO 80206
303-316-7800; fax: 303-316-2779

Professional Sport Tours

Association of Tennis Professionals (ATP) Tour
200 ATP Tour Blvd.
Ponte Vedra Beach, FL 32082
904-285-8000; fax: 904-285-5966
http://www.atptour.com

ATP Tour Europe
Monte Carlo Sun
74 Blvd D'Italie
98000 Monaco
33-93/159565; fax: 33-93/159794

ATP Tour International
Level 23, Grosvenor Place
223 George Street
PO Box N573
Sydney, NSW 2000 Australia
61-2/241-4066; fax: 61-2/247-1125

Ladies Professional Golf Association (LPGA)
100 International Golf Drive
Daytona Beach, FL 32124
904-274-6200; fax: 904-274-1009
http://www.lpga.com

PGA Tour
112 TPC Blvd., S 'wgrass
Ponte Vedra Beach, FL 32082
904-285-3700; fax: 904-285-7913
http://www.pgatour.com

Professional Golfers' Association (PGA) of America
100 Avenue of Champions
PO Box 109601
Palm Gardens, FL 33410
407-624-8400; fax: 407-624-8448
http://www.pga.com

Women's Tennis Association (WTA) Tour
1266 E. Main Street, 4th Floor
Stamford, CT 06902
203-978-1740; fax: 203-978-1702

Players Associations

Canadian Football League Players' Association (CFLPA)
1686 Albert Street
Regina Saskatchewan, Canada S4P 2S6
306-525-2158; fax: 306-525-3008

Major League Baseball Players Association (MLBPA)
12 E. 49th Street
New York, NY 10017
212-826-0808; fax: 212-752-3649

National Basketball Players Association (NBPA)
1775 Broadway, Suite 2401
New York, NY
212-463-7510; fax: 212-956-5687

National Football League Players Association (NFLPA)/Major Indoor Soccer
   League Players Association
Major League Soccer Players Association/Womens Professional Association

2021 L Street, N.W.
Washington, DC 20036
202-436-2200; fax: 202-857-0380

National Hockey League Players Association (NHLPA)
One Dundas Street, W., Suite 2300
Toronto, ON Canada M5G 1Z3
416-408-4040; fax: 416-408-3685

Professional Hockey Players' Association (PHPA)
One St.
St. Catherines, Ontario CANADA
905-682-4800; fax: 905-682-4822
http://www.phpa.com

WTA Tour Players Association
1740 Broadway, 16th Floor
New York, NY 10022
212-399-1165; fax: 212-399-0644

REFERENCES

Atlanta National League Baseball Club, Inc. v. Kuhn, 432 F. Supp. 1213 (N.D. Ga. 1977).

Baby talk. (1997, Fall). *Sports Illustrated Women/Sport*, 20–21.

Berry, R.C., Gould, W.B., & Staudohar, P.D. (1986). *Labor relations in professional sports.* Dover, MA: Auburn House Publishing Co.

A chronology of the PGA Tour. (1997). http://worldgolf.com/wglibrary/main.html

Crothers, T. (1995, June 19). The shakedown. *Sports Illustrated,* 78–82.

Cruise, D., & Griffiths, A. (1991). *Net worth.* Toronto: Viking Penguin Group.

Euchner, C.C. (1993). *Playing the field: Why sports teams move and cities fight to keep them.* Baltimore: The Johns Hopkins University Press.

Fatsis, S. (1997, June 25). Is battle looming over salary caps? *The Wall Street Journal*, p. B9.

Federal Baseball Club of Baltimore v. National League of Professional Baseball Clubs, 259 U.S. 200 (1922).

Feinstein, J. (1992). *Hard courts.* New York: Villard Books.

Feinstein, J. (1996). *A good walk spoiled: Days and nights on the PGA tour.* Boston: Little, Brown and Co.

Finley v. Kuhn, 569 F.2d 527 (7th Cir. 1978).

Frei, T. (1995, March 25). Locking horns. *The Sporting News*, 19–20.

Friedman, A., & Much, P.J. (1997). *1997 inside the ownership of professional sports teams.* Chicago: Team Marketing Report.

Graffis, H. (1975). The PGA: The official history of the Professional Golfers' Association of America.

Helyar, J. (1994). *Lords of the realm.* New York: Villard Books.

Helyar, J. (1995a, January 25). Beat me in St. Louis. *The Wall Street Journal*, p. A1.

Helyar, J. (1995b, August 7). Power plays: Pro basketball loses its "feel good" image in nasty labor dispute. *The Wall Street Journal*, pp. A1, A10.

A history of the American PGA. (1997). http://worldgolf.com/wglibrary/main.html

The history of the PGA Tour. (1997). http://worldgolf.com/wglibrary/main.html

Jennings, K. (1989). *Balls and strikes: The money game in professional baseball.* Greenwich, CT: Praeger Publishing.

Kessler, J. (1997, ⌐ :ober 23). Presentation made at Negotiating Sports Contracts Conference. New York: New York Law Seminars Press.

Lainson, S. (1997). Minorities in sport. *Sports News You Can Use, 24,* 1–2.

Lapchick, R. (1997, March). *The racial report card.* Boston: Northeastern University Center for the Study of Sport in Society.

Lentze, G. (1995). The legal concept of professional sports leagues: The commissioner and an alternative approach from a corporate perspective. *Marquette Sports Law Journal, 6,* 65–94.

Miami Heat media guide (1993–94). Miami, FL: Miami Heat.

Miller, M. (1991). *A whole different ballgame.* New York: Birch Lane Publishing.

Milwaukee American Association v. Landis, 49 F.2d 298 (D.C. Ill. 1931).

Morgan, J. (1996, November 6). Discussion as part of the Jackie Robinson Initiative, University of Massachusetts, Amherst.

Much, P.J., & Gotto, R.M. (1997). Franchise valuation overview. In A. Friedman & P.J. Much (1997), *1997 inside the ownership of professional sports teams* (pp. 6–7). Chicago: Team Marketing Report.

Ozanian, M.K., Ashe, T., Fink, R., Reingold, J., Kimelman, J., Osterland, A., & Sklar, J. (1995, May 9). Suite deals: Why new stadiums are shaking up the pecking order of sports franchises. *Financial World*, 42–56.

Shropshire, K. (1996). *In black and white: Race and sports in America.* New York: New York University Press.

St. Louis congratulates Walter Payton. (1993, February 8). *USA Today*, p. 4C.

Staudohar, P.M. (1996). *Playing for dollars: Labor relations and the sports business.* Ithaca, NY: ILR Press.

What franchises are worth. (1996, May 8–14). *USA Today Baseball Weekly*, p. 8.

Whitford, D. (1993). *Playing hardball: The high stakes battle for baseball's new franchises.* New York: Doubleday.

Yasser, R., McCurdy, J., & Goplerud, P. (1997). *Sports law: Cases and materials.* Cincinnati: Anderson Publishing Co.

Zoeller's comments out of line. (1997, April 18). http://www.espnet.sportszone.com

CHAPTER 13

Facility Management

Michael J. Graney and Kevin Barrett

Key words: arenas, stadiums, International Association of Auditorium Managers (IAAM), convention centers, exposition centers, theater, bonds, marketing director, public relations director, event director, booking director, operations director, box office director, amphitheater, Americans with Disabilities Act

INTRODUCTION

People congregate in large groups for a number of reasons. Public assembly facilities must be large enough to accommodate the large numbers of people who want to be entertained at a sports or entertainment event or who meet together for social or business purposes. The facilities that are designed and built to accommodate these large groups of people include arenas, stadiums, convention (or exposition) centers, theaters (or performing arts facilities), racetracks, and casinos. Generally, only the first four of these are recognized from a facility or sports management perspective. **Arenas** and **stadiums** are the primary venues for professional and amateur sports events. While convention centers and theaters do not typically host sports events, they are often jointly built, owned, managed, or booked with an arena or stadium. Convention and exposition centers do, however, host sports-related conventions such as sporting goods expositions, sports card shows, and league meetings. Management principles are similar for all types of these facilities, and their managers are eligible for membership in the **International Association of Auditorium Managers (IAAM)**, the professional trade association for this field. In this chapter, the discussion of public assembly facilities considers arenas, stadiums, convention (exposition) centers, and theaters.

HISTORY

Public assembly facilities have existed since ancient times. In fact, the word "stadium" is derived from the ancient Greek *stade,* a site for early Olympic-style athletic competition. Many of today's famous facilities bear the names of ancient and medieval facilities—The Forum, The Coliseum, The Globe Theater—or have names with an ancient connotation—The Spectrum, The Centrum. Throughout recorded history. people have gathered to witness sporting competitions and live theater at their era s version of public assembly facilities. From a sports management perspective, today's version of public assembly facilities evolved during the late-nineteenth and early twentieth centuries in America, coinciding with the development of professional and intercollegiate athletics.

Stadiums

As professional baseball and intercollegiate football began to gain widespread popularity, open fields and parks became inadequate to handle the number of spectators who wanted to watch the contests. Baseball team owners and universities began to construct stadiums to accommodate fans. The constraints of urban space limitations dictated the irregular sizes and shapes of the older ballparks (Danielson, 1997). Some of these facilities still exist and are much beloved. How many authors, poets, journalists, and ordinary fans have waxed poetic over Fenway Park and Wrigley Field (Quirk & Fort, 1992)? The question of their financial viability in today's sports market will be addressed later, but their status as cultural sports icons is unquestioned.

In the early twentieth century, baseball was the national pastime. Team owners built stadium facilities for themselves, so teams stayed in the home cities for years. The era of team movement and expansion did not begin until the late fifties and sixties. The National Football League (NFL) was founded in 1923 and slowly grew into the sport marketing powerhouse we know today. As the league gained popularity, its need for larger stadiums grew. Early on, NFL teams typically played in the major league baseball stadium in their cities. These stadiums were designed and built for baseball, resulting in occasional quirks, such as end zones that were a yard short, and generally poor sightlines for football. It was not until the public stadium construction boom in the sixties and early seventies that sightlines for both sports were taken into consideration.

Arenas

In the early twentieth century, indoor team professional sports were in their infancy. The National Hockey League (NHL) started in 1927 but was limited for the first 40 years to teams in four American and two Canadian cities (Boston, New York, Detroit, Chicago, Toronto, and Montreal). Hockey owners followed the lead of baseball owners and built arenas to host their teams. The hockey season then was roughly one-third the length of the baseball season (50 games compared to 154), so hockey owners had more empty nights to fill their arenas with events. Boxing filled some empty nights in both stadiums and arenas. It may surprise boxing aficionados who came of age in the eighties and nineties that championship fights were not always held in casinos. New York in general and Madison Square Garden in particular were to boxing for most of this century what Las Vegas is today. Still, the occasional fight did not by itself satisfy the hockey barons' need for more activity in their facilities, so they pursued other events.

NHL arena owners along with some of their minor league counterparts founded the Ice Capades, the first large-scale annual touring ice show, so they could fill a week or two of their arena schedule with skating fans, creating an additional revenue stream for themselves. The Ice Capades was very successful and lasted for over 50 years as a skating variety show. (It was put out of business by a number of more specialized figure skating shows such as "Disney On Ice," the "Tour of Olympic and World Figure Skating Champions," and "Stars On Ice.") However, even profitable week-long runs of the Ice Capades did not have a significant enough impact on arena profits. Arena owners needed another major sport to limit the number of dark days. Basketball filled this need.

Basketball is the youngest of the four major North American professional sports and the only one with a verifiable birth date and place: December 22, 1891, in Springfield, Massachusetts. The National Basketball Association (NBA) is the youngest of the four major professional sports leagues, having celebrated its 50th birthday during the 1996–1997 season. The original arena owners, though, initially capitalized on college basketball. Colleges and universities built field houses for their basketball teams, but as the sport's popularity grew, it became necessary to host big games and tournaments in the big city arenas. College basketball doubleheaders became a staple of major arena event calendars, particularly Madison Square Garden, which was as much a mecca for college basketball as it was for boxing. The National Invitation Tournament (N.I.T.), which preceded the National Collegiate Athletic Association's (NCAA's) Final Four, has been held in Madison Square Garden for decades.

Professional basketball prior to the NBA was primarily a touring, barnstorming event. Good teams would travel from city to city playing the best the locals had to offer. The NBA and its forerunner, the Basketball Association of America, changed that and established a league structure similar to that of major league baseball (MLB), the NFL, and the NHL. Arena owners then earned revenue from two tenants (hockey and basketball). Given the popularity and marketing scope of the NHL and the NBA today, the historical truth that basketball owners paid rent to hockey owners may be hard to believe. However, that relationship still exists in some cities, such as Boston, where the Celtics rent from the New Boston Garden Corporation, owners of the Bruins and the Fleet Center.

The Modern Era of Stadium and Arena Construction

Basketball and hockey are much more compatible in terms of building design and sightlines than are baseball and football. Stadium quirks and fan annoyance factors were never as critical in developing arenas capable of hosting both indoor sports as they were in stadiums attempting to host both outdoor sports. Still, it is clearly advantageous for sports facility owners (whether indoor or outdoor) to have two prime sport tenants. Baseball-only stadiums that had served their owners and fans for more than 40 years were becoming obsolete during the 1960s. Some were too small, and most lacked "modern" amenities such as wide seats, legroom, easy access to concession stands, and artificial turf. Several new stadiums were built during the 1960s and 1970s, but not by the team owners.

Team owners at this time were beginning to learn a lesson they would use to their advantage in the future—that they could make a great deal of money by having their host city build their stadium rather than building it themselves. Cities, driven by the civic pride that "big league" status endows, built shiny new facilities to keep their teams as enthusiastic about their hometowns as the civic leaders were. It made sense for the cities to build facilities with both their football and baseball tenants in mind because more activity justified the public investment. The result was the so-called "cookie cutter" stadiums like Veterans Stadium in Philadelphia, Three Rivers Stadium in Pittsburgh, and Riverfront Stadium in Cincinnati. They were new, they were modern, they had artificial turf (so field maintenance was easy), and they all looked alike. Arena construction boomed during this era, too. Civic centers and civic arenas sprang up in a number of major and secondary markets as cities competed for major and minor league sport teams by building suitable facilities. This time also marked the dawn of the touring concert industry, and concerts became an extremely lucrative addition to a facility's schedule. City leaders generally believed that a publicly built stadium with both baseball and football tenants or a publicly built arena with both basketball and hockey tenants, along with the concert and family show tours, were good investments. They contributed to the city's quality of life by providing sports and entertainment for the citizens and spinoff benefits for the local economy.

Eventually, team owners, and many of their fans, decided that multipurpose facilities were not quite good enough. Stadiums designed to be *acceptable* for both baseball and football ended up being *desirable* for neither. The trend over the past decade favors single-purpose stadiums. Financing these facilities has become an interesting dilemma, particularly given team owners' desire to use facility revenue to compete for free-agent players and to boost their own profits. Some cities have constructed (or promised to construct) facilities that will provide team owners the design and revenue streams they need to be successful. Team owners are now seeking lucrative stadium leases that provide revenue from four sources: preferred seating (luxury suites, club seating, and personal seat licenses), parking, concessions, and stadium sponsorship (signage and naming rights) (Greenberg & Gray, 1993). As a result, franchise free agency has developed. Team owners flee their traditional locations for greener pastures not because of market size and growth but because of more profitable facility deals. In fact, the facility in which a professional sport team plays has the most significant impact on its profitability and is often its primary consideration in choosing to remain or move to a new location. For more information see Chapter 4, Financial Principles Applied to Sport Management, and Chapter 12, Professional Sport.

TYPES OF PUBLIC ASSEMBLY FACILITIES

Arenas

Arenas are indoor facilities that host sporting and entertainment events. They are usually built to accommodate one (or more) prime sports tenant(s) or to lure a prime tenant to the facility. Colleges and universities typically build an arena for their basketball teams and occasionally their hockey teams. These arenas may also be used for volleyball and gymnastics, as well as concerts and other touring shows. Intercollegiate facilities are financed by private donations, endowments, student fees, fundraising campaigns, and, in the case of public institutions, public grants.

Some NBA and NHL teams have built their own arenas. In other cases, municipalities, state governments, or public authorities have built them. Sometimes the public owner manages its facility and sometimes it contracts out for private management. The public or private manager then negotiates a lease with the prime sports tenant. If the arena is privately built, commercial lenders issue loans to the team, which pledges facility revenue streams as collateral. Public financing typically involves issuing bonds that can be tied to direct or indirect facility revenue but more often are a general obligation of the governmental entity.

Basketball and hockey teams can generally peacefully coexist in the same arena without either being forced into unacceptable compromises. Arenas also host indoor soccer leagues, arena football, concerts, ice shows, family shows, graduations, other civic events, and some types of conventions. Maximizing bookings (confirming events) is an arena manager's primary responsibility.

Stadiums

Stadiums are similar to arenas, but they are outdoor or domed facilities. Stadiums provide sites for baseball, football, and outdoor soccer teams. The ownership, financing, and management issues discussed in the arena section also apply to stadiums. Like their arena counterparts, stadium managers try to maximize bookings, but it is more difficult. First, baseball and football teams do not coexist as easily as basketball and hockey teams do. Second, there are far fewer nonsport events that can play stadiums, primarily because stadiums are significantly larger than other venues and most other events cannot attract stadium-sized crowds. The main nonsport events for stadiums are outdoor concerts given by performers who have the drawing power to fill a stadium.

Convention Centers

Convention centers are almost always built and owned by a public entity, with the exception of some exposition centers. Convention centers are built to lure conventions and business meetings to a particular municipality. They are publicly financed because the rents and fees they charge do not always cover costs. However, the municipality they serve benefits in other ways, namely through the economic impact the convention or business meeting has on the municipality. Convention centers are typically located near the downtown districts of large cities. The convention business is extremely competitive, and municipalities (and states) offer significant financial inducements to convention and meeting planners for the opportunity to host visitors. The conventioneers and meeting attendees stay in local hotels, eat in local restaurants, shop in local stores, and patronize local tourist attractions, all of which support business and employment in the region. Conventioneers are also typically taxed, so the state and municipality receive indirect revenue from the events. The increased business, employment opportunities, and indirect fiscal revenue justify the public entity's construction and continued subsidy of convention centers.

Exposition centers can be privately financed because they do not have a responsibility to host events at rates below cost to support the local hospitality industry. Exposition centers host gate shows such as car, boat, camping, and home shows. They receive revenue from the dealers who rent space or booths to display their products and from patrons who purchase tickets to enter the event. Expo centers (and convention centers) can also host trade shows. Trade shows are events operated for a specific company or industry trade group. Attendance is usually limited to employees or customers of the company or members of the trade group and its suppliers. Their purpose is to display new products or industry technology to enhance sales. A great example of a sport industry trade show is The

Super Show™, held annually in Atlanta (see Chapter 17, The Sporting Goods Industry and the Sale of Licensed Products).

Theaters

Theaters are public assembly facilities that are primarily utilized for the presentation of live artistic entertainment. Universities, public entities, and private (usually not-for-profit) groups construct them. Like stadiums and arenas, theaters often house prime tenants such as symphony orchestras, opera and dance companies, and resident theater groups. Theaters attract an active touring market of popular and classical concerts, Broadway musicals and plays, dance troupes, lecture series, and children's and family theater. Theater managers base their schedules around the needs of their prime tenant(s) and then try to book as many touring events as possible.

The arts are heavily subsidized by governmental and corporate entities. Revenue earned by most arts organizations does not cover their costs. Public or private nonprofit theater owners typically subsidize their arts tenants' rents and try to generate revenue from touring shows. Profits are rare, but the spinoff business from theater attractions (hotel stays for touring artists and restaurant business from theater patrons) again justifies public subsidy. Theater performances also provide culture and entertainment for a community, enhancing its quality of life much as its sport teams do.

FACILITY FINANCING

There are a variety of ways to finance public assembly facilities, but the specific financing decision is always preceded by a single fundamental question: Will the facility be financed publicly or privately? The answer depends on a number of factors, including the type of facility being constructed. Convention centers are almost always financed publicly because they are not intended to make money. Convention centers do not book events to make a profit for themselves; rather, they book events that maximize the impact on the local economy, particularly the hospitality industry. Because of their "public" focus, the public sector pays for them, often by initiating or raising taxes on the state or local hospitality industry (e.g., hotel room taxes, restaurant meal taxes, and rental car fees).

Arena and stadium financing is not as clear-cut, particularly when a major league professional sport team is a prime tenant. Professional sport teams are in business to make money, sometimes enormous amounts of money. There are those who argue that any for-profit enterprise should build its own facility where it conducts its business. On the other hand, some studies show that sports facilities provide significant economic benefits to their host communities, and teams are undeniable sources of civic pride and community spirit. Attracting a sport team can provide a public relations boost to a city, too, particularly one attempting to prove it is "major league."

The discussion of how to finance stadiums/arenas financing has fluctuated between public and private methods over the years. In the early years of the current major professional sport leagues, team owners generally built their own facilities. A public building boom, generally of multipurpose facilities, ensued during the 1960s and 1970s as the original facilities were approaching obsolescence. Over the past 20 years, as free agency has increased player salaries, team owners have had to look for additional revenue to compete for, and pay, their players while maintaining profitability. Controlling stadium revenue streams such as concessions, advertising, sponsorship, premium seating and suites, and seat licenses has become the primary means to the owners' ends. Single-purpose facilities with one team as primary tenant designed to the specifications of a particular sport are desirable to team owners because revenue streams do not have to be shared.

For the cities, states, stadium authorities, and other representatives of the public sector, these issues became increasingly problematic. The public benefits justifying stadium construction remained, but the costs were going up, particularly if two teams were each looking for their own stadium or arena. Cities in particular faced hard choices because most had stable or declining tax revenue and increasing municipal government costs. Building public assembly facilities meant other services had to be neglected. In many locations the question of publicly financing a stadium was put to a vote.

In the early 1980s, Joe Robbie, owner of the NFL Miami Dolphins, became disenchanted with the Orange Bowl, a facility the Dolphins shared with the University of Miami. He proposed a new stadium, but the voters in south Florida did not approve public funding. Robbie proposed a novel solution. He pledged stadium revenues from suites and specialty seating, secured by multiple-year contracts from their users, as collateral to his bankers and *privately* financed his stadium. The NBA Detroit Pistons followed suit and privately constructed The Palace of Auburn Hills, apparently ushering in a new era of private facility construction financed by anticipated stadium or arena revenue.

Still, this was not a perfect world for a team owner. Pledging facility revenue streams to pay for debt service or mortgage expenses takes revenue away from profits. If a team owner could find a city or state willing to build a new facility and let the *team* control the stadium revenue streams, the owner could maximize revenue without heavy debt service expenses. Two interesting case studies are Baltimore and Cleveland. Both cities decided to construct new facilities in their downtowns to maintain or attract sport teams while simultaneously revitalizing decaying sections of their cities. Their strategies have proven successful. Baltimore, through the Maryland Stadium Authority, agreed to build a new baseball stadium, Oriole Park at Camden Yards, for the Orioles and a football stadium for an NFL expansion team or any existing team willing to move there. Baltimore had previously lost its football team, the Colts, to a better stadium deal in Indianapolis. Cleveland built a new baseball stadium, Jacobs Field, for the Indians and a new arena, Gund Arena, for the NBA Cavaliers. The new stadiums fostered tremendous spinoff economic benefit in both cities and a host of new businesses have started up in the vicinity of the facilities. All of the facilities received excellent marks for design and for their ability to mesh into the urban fabric while providing great ballpark ambience. Camden Yards and Jacobs Field in particular were enthusiastically supported by baseball fans, as each has the charm of Fenway Park or Wrigley Field combined with the modern fan comforts and revenue opportunities of Joe Robbie Stadium or The Palace.

The Orioles and Indians took advantage of their new facilities, rocketing from the middle of the pack to close to the top of Major League Baseball in attendance and revenue. Each team used its newfound financial strength to sign free-agent players and to keep its own stars, guaranteeing winning teams that keep fans coming and provide more revenue. MLB teams from around the country are trying to emulate Baltimore and Cleveland by convincing public officials and voters to build new stadiums like Camden Yards and Jacobs Field. If they get turned down, team owners threaten to move to cities that *will* build the facilities they want.

As mentioned above, there was also a role for football in Baltimore's building equation. Cleveland had built a new baseball stadium and basketball arena, but not a new football stadium, a fact not lost on Art Modell, the Browns owner. Baltimore was marketing its new stadium to any NFL franchise willing to move and found a taker, the Cleveland Browns, who are now the Baltimore Ravens. Baltimore made Modell an offer he could not refuse, and he moved a team that had arguably the most loyal fans in America. In today's revenue-hungry major league sports, huge markets and loyal fans pale in comparison to the profitability of new stadiums and arenas. Not one but *two* NFL teams have vacated Los Angeles, the second-largest media market in the United States, because of more lucrative stadium offers. Oakland, which lost its Raiders to Los Angeles a decade earlier, enticed them back by upgrading their former home, the Coliseum, and guaranteeing stadium revenue streams. St. Louis, which had lost the Cardinals to Arizona, built a new facility, the Trans World Dome, to entice a new team and convinced the Rams to forsake Los Angeles, too. For further information, see the case study and franchise free-agency sections in Chapter 12, Professional Sport.

Facility Financing Mechanisms

Facility construction and renovation are expensive undertakings. In order for a construction project to begin, funding must be sought from different sources, both public and private. This section provides a brief overview of the different types of financing available for facility construction or renovation.

Bonds

The money to build facilities is usually obtained by issuing **bonds**. According to Howard and Crompton (1995), "Bonds are formally defined as a promise by the borrower (bond issuer) to pay back the lender (bond holder) a specified amount of money, with interest, within a specified period of time" (p. 98). Bonds may be issued by local authorities (cities, counties, or states) to underwrite the cost of sport facility construction. Bonds usually fall into one of two categories: general obligation bonds or revenue bonds. General obligation bonds, backed by the local government's ability to raise taxes to pay off the debt, are considered relatively safe investments. Revenue bonds, backed specifically by the facility's ability to generate revenues, are somewhat riskier as the facility has to generate sufficient funds to meet both the annual operating costs of the arena *and* the annual debt payments (Howard & Crompton, 1995). If the facility has a down year financially, there may not be enough money left after covering the annual operating costs to make the debt payments.

Taxes

A number of different taxes can be used to generate money to fund sports facilities, each of which has advantages and disadvantages. The first of these taxes is property taxes. These taxes are paid by homeowners, who are often long-term residents of a city. It makes sense to tax these people, as they live in the location where the facility is being constructed and would be most likely to receive its full benefit. However, in order for a property tax to be imposed, people must be given the chance to vote. In terms of facility financing, this is an especially problematic aspect of property taxes because long-term residents, who most likely are property owners whose taxes will go up, tend to vote regularly, and are not inclined to vote to raise their own taxes. A second option is an occupational tax, which taxes anyone who works in the community, regardless of whether that person actually resides in the community. This tax must also be voted on, but in many instances it has been more likely to pass than a property tax (Mahony, 1997).

All of these taxes are imposed on local residents, but there are other taxes that pass the burden onto out-of-town visitors instead. Most notable among these is a hospitality tax, such as the one used in Atlanta to help build the Georgia Dome and in Chicago to construct new Comiskey Park. This tax forces visitors to pay directly for the facility, but a locality must be careful not to make the tax so high that it becomes a barrier to people visiting the location or to organizations deciding to hold business meetings or conventions there. Rental car taxes meet this same description. Local residents often prefer these types of taxes, since the local residents receive the benefit of the facility without shouldering so much of the construction costs (Mahony, 1997).

Some tax plans affect both local residents and visitors. The first of these is the general sales tax, which is imposed on nearly all transactions, although the sales of food for at-home consumption and prescription drugs are typically exempted (Howard & Crompton, 1995). A sales tax was used to help fund the Fargo Dome. The "sin tax," which taxes only alcohol and tobacco products, was used in the construction of the MetroDome in Minneapolis. Other options include a meals tax placed on people who dine out or a transportation tax on bus and taxi travel (Mahony, 1997).

Corporate Investment

In addition to public sources of funding, there are a number of private sources a sport facility could tap to cover construction costs. One source is corporate sponsorship. As mentioned in Chapter 4, Financial Principles Applied to Sport Management, the sale of naming rights for stadiums and arenas is a current trend. Facilities such as Coors Field in Denver, Miller Field in Milwaukee, the Trans World Dome in St. Louis, the United Center in Chicago, and the Papa John's Cardinal Stadium at the University of Louisville all received millions of dollars from naming rights. Soft drink companies like Coca-Cola or Pepsi, and beer companies such as Anheuser-Busch or Miller, will also pay considerable sums for facility pouring rights, which means being the facility's exclusive soft drink or beer distributor. In addition, corporations may also make outright donations to defray costs in exchange for the publicity and public relations benefits that may result from such a donation (Mahony, 1997).

Facility Revenues

Finally, money for construction may come directly from facility revenues. As mentioned in Chapter 4, Financial Principles Applied to Sport Management, the sale of personal seat licenses (PSLs) as well as luxury suites and club seating make up a considerable source of revenue for stadium construction. This money, paid "up front," can be used to offset facility costs. A ticket tax may also be imposed on the sale of tickets to events at already existing facilities. An organization may also use other facility revenues, such as rent from tenants, concessions, and parking, to pay for the cost of the facility. As mentioned earlier, depending on these revenue sources is riskier because they are not earmarked specifically for the facility and are not guaranteed in any way (Mahony, 1997).

CAREER OPPORTUNITIES

College graduates seeking career opportunities in the facility management industry will be pleasantly surprised at the wide variety of options available in arenas, convention and exposition centers, stadiums, and performing arts centers. The career opportunity areas in facility management are shown in Exhibit 13–1 and discussed in the paragraphs that follow.

Marketing Director

Being the **marketing director** for an arena, performing arts center, or other venue is one of the more exciting careers in facility management. It is a fast-paced, highly stressful, enormously challenging career track that can lead a successful individual all the way to the executive suite.

Facility marketing directors act primarily as in-house advertising agents for the various events booked into facilities. Buying media (TV, radio, print, billboards, etc.), coordinating promotions, and designing marketing materials (TV commercials, brochures, flyers, newspaper advertisements, etc.) are some of a marketing director's primary responsibilities. A typical day in the life of a facility marketing director may include creating a marketing plan and ad budget for "Sesame Street Live," meeting with radio and TV sales staff to discuss cross-promotions with McDonald's for the Harlem Globetrotters, and designing a print ad for Sunday's newspaper.

The more successful marketing directors are multi-skilled performers who possess excellent people skills, sales ability, and written and oral communication skills. Most important, a successful marketing director possesses an almost uncanny ability to consistently make money for facilities or promoters. The quickest way to become a facility general manager or executive director is to showcase the talents and skills it takes to improve the bottom line. Moneymakers are few and far between, so proven producers will get noticed—and promoted.

Exhibit 13–1 Career Opportunity Areas in Facility Management

Marketing
Public relations
Event management
Booking
Operations
Advertising/signage/sponsorship sales
Group ticket sales
Box office

Public Relations Director

A good **public relations (PR) director** is essential for facilities as they deal with the media on a wide variety of issues. A talented PR director can "spin" the news, good or bad, and position a facility in the best possible light. This is a very important skill to have when the media are banging on the door wanting to know why the arena's $2 million scoreboard just came crashing down on the ice, why attendance is down 20%, or why the box office is missing $25,000 and the director has just left for a long trip to Mexico.

One of the primary goals for a facility PR department is to forge solid working relationships with TV and radio news directors, newspaper editors, and reporters so that when bad news hits, the media report a balanced story. Good rapport with local media helps a great deal when seeking publicity for positive stories and at times it can mean the difference between receiving front-page coverage or being buried next to the obituaries.

A typical day in the life of a facility PR director may include coordinating a live TV broadcast from the arena with the local sports anchor to publicize that evening's basketball game, writing a press release announcing tickets are going on sale that weekend for a Garth Brooks concert, and arranging a publicity stunt for Bert and Ernie to visit the local children's hospital while they are in town for an upcoming "Sesame Street Live" tour. The most important attributes of a good PR director are a strong writing ability, a creative mind, and an ability to respond rationally while under pressure. Excellent training grounds for facility PR people are college and daily newspapers, TV stations, and internships in corporate PR departments.

Event Director

Events are the lifeblood for all types of facilities. Hundreds of events may be booked at a facility in the course of a year. With thousands of people in the venue at any given time, it is imperative that there be excellent crowd control and exceptional customer service provided at all times. The **event director** acts as the point person for the facility during each show. Supervising a full staff of ushers, police officers, firefighters, emergency medical technicians, and private concert security forces, the event director manages the show from start to finish.

The event director must be able to think and react quickly to any problems arising during the event and must be able to deal with show promoters, angry customers, lost children, intoxicated patrons, and other situations calmly, but forcefully. He or she must handle all this pressure while thousands of guests are in their seats enjoying the show. Being in charge of the safety and satisfaction of so many people is an immense responsibility, and for this reason the event director's position is not for everyone.

A typical day in the life of an event director might begin as early as 8:00 AM, with six tractor-trailer trucks pulling up to the facility to begin the load-in for a major concert. The event director supervises and schedules traffic, parking, and security personnel to help ensure that the concert load-in runs as smoothly as possible. Later that day, he or she meets with the band road manager and reviews all security requirements for that evening's show. As the concert time draws near, the event director will meet with all ushers, police, and private security staff, giving instructions on how to handle that evening's event. During the concert, he or she will likely deal with customers, emergency situations, intoxicated patrons, and perhaps an altercation or two. By the end of the night, he or she will have been at the facility for 18 long hours. Then it's get in the car, go home, and get a little sleep—because "Disney On Ice" is rolling into town tomorrow.

Booking Director

Events in smaller facilities are booked by the general manager or executive director. In larger venues, however, there is usually a separate position devoted to booking events. This person works in tandem with the general manager or executive director to land as many events as possible. This is an exciting career path involving much time spent talking on the telephone to agents and promoters and attending conventions to solicit events.

A facility **booking director** can land events in several different ways. Most concerts and Broadway shows are booked by dealing directly with agents who represent the acts or by negotiating with promoters who rent the facility and deal directly with agents on their own. The booking director may choose to rent the facility to a promoter, to co-promote an event, or to purchase the show directly from an agent. There are advantages and disadvantages associated with all three methods. Renting the facility to a promoter is a risk-free way to increase events; however, it limits the amount of income a building may receive from an event. For some events with limited income potential or risky track records (conventions, trade shows, etc.), this method is the smartest way to do business. For potentially highly lucrative events (concerts, family shows, Broadway), partnering with a promoter in a share of the profits or purchasing the event directly from an agent may be the more profitable strategy—albeit also the one with the greatest risk to lose money if the show is not successful.

A typical day in the life of a booking director might begin at 8:00 AM with telephone calls to local radio program directors gauging the current popularity of a specific concert act. At 10:00 AM the constant phone calls back and forth with Broadway agents in New York begin as the booking director tries to fill up next year's Broadway lineup for the performing arts center. Lunch with a local concert promoter cutting a rental deal for an upcoming show will be followed by telephone tag the rest of the day with other agents and promoters. Negotiating contracts and getting them out in the mail completes a typical facility booking director's day.

Operations Director

Facility operations departments are the heart and soul of this industry. The **operations director** supervises facility preparation for all types of events. He or she typically spends the lion's share of a facility's annual expense budget on labor, maintaining and repairing all equipment, and purchasing all necessary supplies (toilet paper, cleaning materials, etc.) that the events require on a weekly basis.

Perhaps the most important part of an operations director's job is coordinating, scheduling, and supervising the numerous changeovers that take place each year as one show moves in and another moves out. An operations director faces logistical problems daily as the facility may change over from hockey to basketball, then to a concert, then to a Broadway show, all in one week. The job requires a mechanical knowledge of a facility's inner workings. A good operations director must be an expert on heating, ventilation, and air conditioning equipment, ice making, and structural issues such as how many pounds of pressure can be rigged to the roof without its collapsing. An operations director must also possess superior people skills, as he or she is directly in charge of the majority of the facility's staff, including foremen, mechanics, laborers, stagehands, and the 50 to 200 part-time workers required to set up and clean up after events.

A typical day in the life of an operations director likely begins early in the morning with a check of the previous night's changeover from basketball to hockey. Inspecting the overnight cleanup and the temperature and condition of the ice surface and discussing any problems with assistants will keep the operations director busy most of the morning. Then it will be time to plan ahead for next week when the circus rolls into town with 30 elephants, 14 tigers, and other assorted animals and equipment. The circus will take over the entire facility and two square blocks in the downtown business district for six days. Meetings with circus managers and city officials to plan for the event, as well as scheduling, will complete the day for the person with his or her hand constantly on the pulse of the facility operation.

Advertising/Sponsorship/Signage Salesperson

Advertising and sponsorship revenue represent a significant total of a facility's annual revenue. Most facilities, depending on size, designate a staff person or an entire department to sell signage and event sponsorships to corporations. College graduates who perform well in high-pressure sales environments can make a substantial amount of money selling signage and sponsorships. This area offers good entry-level positions. Most facilities hire sales staff on a commission-only basis. Commissions can range from 5 to 20% depending on the size of the deal. Salespeople must possess excellent interpersonal and presentation skills. They also must be able to handle plenty of rejection on a daily basis. For every 100 telephone calls a salesperson makes to corporations, an average of only 5 or 10 will result in actual business. Sales is a numbers game, and only strong, thick-skinned personalities are successful in such an environment. Successful sales-people generate money for themselves and the facility—and that will turn heads at the executive level. It is not uncommon for good salespeople to ultimately end up in the general manager's or executive director's chair.

A typical day in the life of an aggressive signage and sponsorship salesperson will include at least 25 cold calls to corporate decision makers, two to four face-to-face sales presentations, and plenty of writing. A good salesperson must have strong writing skills as he or she must create outstanding sales proposals, follow meetings up with thank-you letters, and draft contracts once deals have been finalized.

Group Ticket Salesperson

Many college graduates begin their facility management careers in the group sales department. Entry-level opportunities are numerous as there is a fairly high turnover rate in this facility management segment. Group salespeople are prima-rily responsible for selling large blocks of tickets for various events to corpora-tions, charity organizations, schools, Boy Scout and Girl Scout troops, and other parties. Group sales for certain types of shows ("Sesame Street Live," "Disney On Ice," Ringling Bros. and Barnum & Bailey Circus, the Harlem Globetrotters, professional sport teams, etc.) contribute significantly to an event's success. Similar to the successful signage and sponsorship staff person, a good group salesperson is tenacious and excels on the telephone and in face-to-face presenta-tions. Usually paid on a commission basis (typically 10 to 15%), group sales is also a numbers game. However, renewal business is usually strong, and solid personal relationships with key decision makers at area corporations and other organizations can result in excellent sales year after year. A good group salesper-son is an important asset to a facility.

Box Office Director

This facility position is responsible for the sale of all tickets to events as well as the collection of all ticket revenue. The facility box office is typically the first impression patrons have of the venue, making good customer service critical. The **box office director** must be a patient, understanding individual with a great mind for numbers. He or she must also have good supervisory skills. Within most venues the box office is usually the second largest department, after operations. Made up of a combination of full- and part-time help, the box office personnel must be completely trustworthy as millions of dollars and thousands of credit card numbers flow through the department each year.

A typical day for a box office director begins at 9:00 AM. On any given day, events may be going on sale and the telephones and lobby windows are generally extremely busy. Meetings with promoters to set up scaling of shows and filling ticket orders for advertisers and VIPs takes up a good portion of the day. Scheduling staff for all of the shows and daytime hours is also a time-consuming job. The box office director will be in his or her office for most of the day, but the real work begins when the event starts.

Dealing with customers who have lost their tickets, are unhappy with their seats, or have other concerns will occupy the box office director's time during the event. The box office will usually close halfway through the event so the staff can begin their paperwork. Counting all the money, preparing settlement documents for the promoter's review, and other tasks take up the rest of the evening. By the time all is said and done, the box office director will have worked 12 to 18 hours.

CURRENT ISSUES

Amphitheaters

A segment of the theater market that has seen dramatic growth over the last decade is the **amphitheater**. Amphitheaters, which are outdoor concert venues, have virtually taken over the touring concert business. Unlike other theaters, amphitheaters are usually privately built and owned and are operated on a for-profit basis. Until the late 1980s, arenas were the venue of choice for most touring concert acts. The biggest stars can fill stadiums, but stars of that level are rare. Concert promoters rented arenas and booked acts to play them. The various revenue streams were divided between the artists (who receive, and deserve, the largest share), promoters, and arenas. The promoters took the risk that show revenue would cover costs and they could pay the arena and the artist.

Promoters eventually realized that they could build amphitheaters and deal directly with the artists without involving another party (the arenas) with whom they would have to share revenue. Armed with revenue from tickets, concessions, merchandise, VIP/luxury suites, and parking, promoters could make more lucrative offers to artists to play their amphitheaters (rather than in arenas), while simultaneously making more money for themselves. The public responded positively to the amphitheater movement, attending concerts in larger numbers in the outdoor amphitheaters than in the indoor arenas, further increasing the disparity in revenue for promoters and artists in favor of the amphitheater. Amphitheaters multiplied. Arenas lost 70 to 80% of their concert business virtually overnight, further increasing their dependency on their sports tenants. At the same time, amphitheaters have changed the touring concert business in a way the public endorsed.

Americans with Disabilities Act

The **Americans with Disabilities Act** (ADA) has had a profound effect on the building and renovation of public assembly facilities. The ADA requires new facilities to be accessible to people with disabilities so they can enjoy equal access to entertainment and leisure (Department of Justice, 1997). A common misconception over the ADA and renovations is that if a facility renovates, the whole facility must be brought into compliance (Huggins, 1997). However, the ADA only requires that when a facility is renovated, the renovations must comply with the Act. In addition, if a primary function area is renovated, 20% of the total cost must be spent to improve access for those with disabilities (Huggins, 1997). Finally, for facilities not being renovated, the ADA guidelines encourage the facilities to implement "readily achievable barrier removal," such as the lowering of a paper towel dispenser, replacing a step with a curb cut and/or ramp, or installing a grab bar in the restroom (Huggins, 1997).

A key accessibility requirement is seating. Under the ADA, at least 1% of seating must be wheelchair accessible, a companion seat must be provided next to each wheelchair seat, and whenever more than 300 seats are provided, wheelchair seating must be dispersed throughout all seating areas and price ranges (Department of Justice, 1997). In addition, wheelchair seating must be on an accessible route from parking areas to public areas (restrooms, concessions, etc.) and to stage, performing, and playing areas. Finally, wheelchair seating locations must provide sightlines comparable to those provided to spectators without disabilities (Department of Justice, 1997). Other accessible features include concession areas, public telephones, restrooms, parking areas, drop-off and pick-up areas, entrances and exits, water coolers, visual alarms, and signs. Assisted listening systems must also be provided when audible communications are integral to the use of the facility. The law requires that a facility adapt, but only to the extent that the reasonable accommodation does not cause an undue burden on the facility. A good example of this was the case of *Cortez v. NBA*, in which a group of disabled fans sought to have the San Antonio Spurs provide "live-time captioning" at games. To provide "live-time captioning" the Spurs would have had to provide a court reporter typing all that is announced in the arena onto the scoreboard. Since the Spurs' scoreboard did not provide the technology for such captioning, providing an interpreter for fans was selected as a fair alternative (Department of Justice, 1997).

SUMMARY

Public assembly facilities provide a site for people to congregate for entertainment, social, and business purposes. The many types of facilities range from stadiums and arenas to convention centers and exposition centers to theaters and amphitheaters. The key challenges facing facilities involve financing new facilities or renovations, retaining the revenue generated by the facility (as professional teams seek to retain more of the revenues under their leases), retaining tenants, and addressing the ADA. Facility management provides a career field that is fast-paced and exciting, though filled with long hours and, at times, pressure and stress.

CASE STUDY: WHAT DO YOU DO WHEN YOUR PRIME TENANT THREATENS TO RELOCATE?

It was a raw November morning in 1996 when Bob Hodgen, the Civic Center General Manager, picked up the telephone. He probably wished he hadn't. On the other end was Bart Smith, majority owner of the Rockets, and the Civic Center's prime tenant. The American Hockey League expansion team had been struggling financially since it began operations two years ago.

"Bob, we just crunched the numbers for the first 10 games, and I'm afraid we've reached a critical point," said Smith. "Last year we lost $300,000, and if things keep going the way we're going this season, we could lose $500,000. If we don't do something quickly to keep us afloat, I'm afraid I will have no choice but to recommend to the rest of our ownership group that we move the team to Nashville. We just can't survive another year given our current rental deal and attendance figures."

Hodgen was stunned. But he recognized the urgency in Smith's voice. He had heard it before.

"What can we do?" he responded. Smith got right to the point.

"We need to restructure our building rental and concessions deal as soon as possible. We're bleeding and the other team owners are drooling over Nashville's offer. They just will not tolerate another $500,000 loss this year. I don't want to leave. I think we can make hockey work in this city. But the deal's gotta change or . . ."

Smith didn't have to finish the sentence. "I understand what's at stake," said Hodgen. "Outline a proposal, get it to me quickly, and I'll go see the mayor."

Within 24 hours, the Rockets delivered their proposal to Hodgen. They requested a response within one week. The Rockets were currently paying a rental fee of $4,500 per game for 40 home games. They also received 15% of all concession revenue during their games. The new proposal slashed rent to $1,000 per game and asked for an increase in concession percentages to 25% for all games. The Rockets also requested a 10-year deal retroactive to the beginning of the season. The bottom line for Hodgen, the Civic Center, the mayor and the city's taxpayers? A net loss of $7.5 million during the next 10 years if they agreed to the Rockets' terms, a major financial setback for a city that was already in debt up to its ears. Currently, the Civic Center was operating at a loss of $1 million annually.

Questions for Discussion

1. Assume you are Bob Hodgen, the Civic Center General Manager. What should you do?
2. Assume you are the mayor. What should you do? What if it was an election year?
3. Is there any way to create a win-win situation for the city and the team? If so, discuss the key components necessary to have a compromise.

RESOURCES

Amusement Business Magazine
49 Music Square West
Nashville, TN 37203
615-321-4250; fax: 615-327-1575
home page: http://www.billboard-online.com

ARAMARK Corporation
1101 Market Street
Philadelphia, PA 19107
215-238-3000; fax: 215-238-4099

Centre Management
One Harry S. Truman Drive
Landover, MD 20785
301-499-6300; fax: 301-499-3FAX

Facilities Magazine
650 First Avenue, 7th Floor
New York, NY 10157-1467
212-532-4150; fax: 212-213-6382

International Association of Auditorium Managers (IAAM)
4425 Airport Freeway, Suite 590
Irving, TX 75062-5835
214-255-8020; fax: 214-255-9582
home page: http://www.iaam.org

Ogden Entertainment Services
2 Penn Plaza, 25th Floor
New York, NY 10121
212-868-6211; fax: 212-868-8108

Panstadia International
Stadium House #12
Harrow, Middlesex HA1 2JR, England
44 81 424-8554; fax: 44 81 424-0918

Spectacor Management Group (SMG)
701 Market Street
Independence Center, 4th Floor
Philadelphia, PA 19106
215-592-4100; fax: 215-592-6699

REFERENCES

Danielson, M.N. (1997). *Home team: Professional sports and the American metropolis.* Princeton, NJ: Princeton University Press.

Department of Justice, Civil Rights Division, Disability Rights Section. (1997). *Accessible stadiums.* http://www.usdoj.org

Greenberg, M.J., & Gray, J.T. (1993, April/May). The stadium game. *For the Record*, 2–3.

Howard, D.R., & Crompton, J.L. (1995). *Financing sport.* Morgantown, WV: Fitness Information Technology.

Huggins, S. (1997, Spring). Sports facilities and the Americans with Disabilities Act. *The Sports Lawyer, 2*, 9–11.

Mahony, D. (1997). *Facility funding.* Reading packet provided to SPAD 390, Current Trends and Issues in Sport Administration, undergraduate course, The University of Louisville.

Quirk, J., & Fort, R.D. (1992). *Pay dirt.* Princeton, NJ: Princeton University Press.

CHAPTER 14

Event Management

James M. Gladden, Mark A. Mcdonald, and Carol A. Barr

Key words: barnstorming tours, sport management/marketing agencies, sport property, full-service agencies, specialized agencies, in-house agencies, grassroots programs, budgeting, cash-flow budgeting, zero-base budgeting, risk management, D.I.M. Process, tournament operations, script, volunteer management, integrated marketing, hospitality, licensed merchandise, not-for-profit, cause-related marketing efforts, business development, vertical integration, made-for-TV events

INTRODUCTION

Sport event management is one of the fastest-growing segments in the sport management field. Graham, Goldblatt, and Delpy (1995) define sport event management as "the administration, coordination, and evaluation of any type of event related to sport" (p. x). Although events range in size and scope from running local basketball tournaments to staging the Olympic Games, they all share one common element—the need for educated and trained managers and marketers to ensure success.

A number of different special events exist, such as parades, fairs, and other community activities. Sport events are a subset of special events, so the two share many characteristics. Two notable shared characteristics are the need for several levels of professional management and the importance of customer service (Graham et al., 1995). Areas requiring professional management include, but are not limited to, personnel, marketing, public relations, vendor relations, concessions, tickets, and finance. As with all service industries, the success of sport events hinges on attracting and retaining customers, with superior customer service being crucial.

This chapter presents an overview of the event management segment of the sport industry. First, the historical evolution of event management is discussed. Then, since many large and small events are managed and marketed by sport management/marketing agencies, the types and roles played by these unique sport organizations are explored. Successful event management requires the appropriate application of all the management functions, so this chapter reviews finance/budgeting, risk management, marketing, tournament operations, hospitality, and volunteer management within the context of event management. The next-to-last section explores career opportunities in event management, including information on educational backgrounds appropriate for those in sport event management. Finally, current issues surrounding the management of events are discussed.

HISTORY

The management of sporting events has been necessary since the first events took place in ancient Greece, Egypt, and China (Graham et al., 1995). However, it was not until the late-1800s that the focus turned to the professional aspects of managing sport events. A desire to increase profits was the catalyst for such an emphasis. Following his retirement as a professional baseball player in the 1870s, Albert Spalding organized tours throughout North America to promote baseball in order to create a larger market for his products. Spalding's tours were an early example of what were called **barnstorming tours** or the touring of star athletes and teams to promote the popularity of a particular sport soon became exercises in event management. George Halas, longtime owner of the Chicago Bears, used his star player, Red Grange, to increase the popularity of professional football in the early 1900s (Schaaf, 1995). Professional boxing also provided a platform for professional event management. With the stakes of boxing events reaching more than $1 million by the turn of the twentieth century, boxing event promoters were forced to attend to the business aspects of managing an event.

Just as the need for a business focus prompted the creation of the sport management discipline, profit motives spurred the creation of professional event managers in the 1960s and 1970s. The growth of sport event management led to the emergence of multifaceted companies called **sport management/marketing agencies**. A sport management/marketing agency is defined as a business that acts on behalf of a **sport property**. A sport property can be a person, company, event, team, or place. Sport management/marketing agencies were initially established to represent the legal and marketing interests of athletes. As the sport industry evolved, agencies expanded to incorporate a myriad of functions beyond representing athletes. International Management Group (IMG), for example, was founded in 1960 by Mark McCormack to locate endorsement opportunities for professional golfer Arnold Palmer. As IMG signed more athletes as clients, its business soon expanded to include managing and promoting events in which its athletes competed. Agencies capitalized on the concurrent growth and interest of televised sporting events to rapidly increase the revenues generated through events of all sizes. Today, there are hundreds of sport management/marketing agencies, which are intricately involved with the creation and promotion of most events.

TYPES OF SPORT MANAGEMENT/MARKETING AGENCIES

Sport management/marketing agencies vary widely in terms of numbers of employees, revenue generation, scope of services provided, and types of target clients. Sport agencies can be categorized as full service agencies, specialized agencies, or in-house agencies. These types of agencies are briefly described below. (For more detailed information, see Chapter 11, Sports Agency.)

Full-Service Agencies

Full-service agencies perform the complete set of agency functions discussed in the section of this chapter called Sport Management/Marketing Agency Functions. These firms represent the interests of professional athletes, develop and manage events, produce television shows, and solicit and service corporate sponsors. While a number of firms fall into this category, the largest are IMG, ProServ, and Advantage International. IMG, for example, has 68 offices in 38 cities throughout the world, with headquarters located in Cleveland, Ohio (Helyar, 1997). With operating divisions for athlete management services, event management services, and marketing and consulting services, this firm covers the entire gamut of sport event and athlete functions (Myers, 1997). IMG clients include athletes such as Pete Sampras (tennis) and Nancy Lopez (golf) and events such as the World Professional Figure Skating Championships and the ITT Automotive Detroit Grand Prix (Team Marketing Report, 1996).

Specialized Agencies

Specialized agencies limit either the scope of services performed or the type of clients serviced. For example, Collegiate Advantage, Inc., based in Boston, specializes in sport event promotions directed to the college market. This company works with companies seeking sport sponsorship opportunities. Another firm that specializes functionally is Ticketmaster. Operating out of Dallas, Texas,

Ticketmaster works with professional and college sport teams to expand ticket sales via new marketing ideas and strategies.

In-House Agencies

A trend to be discussed later is the formation within major corporations of separate departments or divisions dealing with event management, typically called **in-house agencies**. For example, Chase Manhattan Bank employs 22 people in its event marketing department (Lainson, 1997). These agencies perform functions on behalf of the products or divisions of the company. These in-house agencies review sponsorship opportunities and create and/or implement sport programming in conjunction with brand managers, the advertising department, and community relations department.

SPORT MANAGEMENT/MARKETING AGENCY FUNCTIONS

Table 14–1 provides a list of the various roles sport management/marketing agencies play. It should be noted that while some agencies perform all of the functions on this list, many of the over 700 sport agencies specialize in only one or a few of these functions (Myers, 1997). The first function listed, client representation, refers to acting on behalf of a client in contract negotiations. Contract negotiations could take place with any type of sport property, such as a franchise, an event, the media, or a licensee. Detailed information regarding this agency function is included in Chapter 11, Sports Agency. The function of client marketing is closely related to client representation. Marketing includes locating appropriate endorsement opportunities, booking personal appearances, and developing entertainment extensions. With his trade to the Los Angeles Lakers, for

---

Table 14–1 Sport Management/Marketing Agencies' Roles

Client representation
Client marketing
Event development
Event management
Television production
Sponsorship solicitation
Hospitality services
Grassroots programs
Market research
Financial planning

example, Shaquille O'Neal has developed from a mere basketball superstar into an entertainment mogul. This has been well orchestrated via recording music, creating music videos, acting in motion pictures, and developing video games.

In addition to representing the interests of individuals, agencies are also involved in event development and management. Creating and marketing new events has become financially lucrative with the introduction of Direct TV and the continued proliferation of sport networks (Crespo, 1995). The creation of the Extreme Games (summer and winter) and the Bikes, Blades, and Boards Tour by ESPN are a direct result of the growth in sports television. Interestingly, while ESPN has elected to manage the two Extreme Games in-house, management of the Bikes, Blades, and Boards Tour has been contracted out to one of the largest event management/marketing firms, Advantage International. (The term "in-house" refers to producing a product or service within the organization.)

While one result of the growth in televised sports has been the creation of new events, another impact has been increasing demand for television production and development work. Two agencies, Raycom and Host Communications, for example, have been involved for years in producing college basketball and football games. These games are then sold to major over-the-air and cable networks, such as ABC, ESPN, and TBS. Potential revenue streams from television have led to the creation of television production divisions within some of the larger agencies. IMG developed Trans World International (TWI) to allow for in-house development, production, and dissemination of televised sports events.

Soliciting corporate sponsorships is a role the majority of sport agencies play. With corporations spending upward of $3 billion annually to partner with sport properties (Schreiber, 1994), a viable market has been created for organizations skilled in identifying and acquiring sponsors. Likewise, corporations often hire sport management/marketing agencies to locate and negotiate sponsorship agreements with teams and events with customers matching their target markets. In each of these cases, the sport agency is paid a set percentage of the sponsorship fee. To facilitate matching corporations with sport properties, Team Marketing Report annually publishes the *Sports Sponsor Fact Book* (Team Marketing Report, 1996). This publication lists and provides detailed information on the activities of sport sponsors and also reviews sponsored sport properties. In addition, IEG, Inc., publishes the *IEG Sponsorship Report,* a newsletter covering sponsorship of sports, music, festivals, the arts, and causes, and the *IEG Sponsorship Sourcebook,* which lists over 3,000 major sports events and properties available for sponsorship (Myers, 1997).

Another function of sport management/marketing agencies is to develop and market **grassroots programs**. These programs are targeted at individuals at the most basic level of involvement, typically emphasizing sport participation and not spectatorship. These smaller events, marketed at the local level, are often not profitable in the short term. However, these programs have the potential to expand consumption of the sport product or service in the long term. The National Hockey

League (NHL), for example, has made large up-front investments in grassroots roller hockey events. As part of its sport spectatorship pyramid, the league counts on the consumer moving from participation in roller hockey to ice hockey. Furthermore, this long-term investment in roller hockey ultimately pays off when a percentage of these roller hockey participants also watch the NHL live or on television. One of the most successful grassroots sport event management companies is Hoop-It-Up. In 1986, Terry Murphy staged a 3-on-3 street basketball tournament in Dallas to raise money for charity. This event drew 450 teams the first year, growing to over 1,400 teams the following year. Murphy's Hoop-It-Up basketball events in 1992 attracted more than 150,000 players and more than one million fans (Lainson, 1997).

Sport organizations require market research to evaluate the success of events and initiatives. By implementing mail surveys, focus groups, on-site surveys, and sponsorship/economic impact surveys, sport management/marketing agencies assist sport properties in documenting the relative success or failure of programs and pinpointing areas needing improvement. Market research is particularly crucial for corporations wanting to know the impact of their sponsorship activities. While this valuable service is provided by many of the agencies, the agency of Joyce Julius and Associates is perhaps best known for measuring sponsorship impact. Joyce Julius quantifies the value of sponsorships by computing the amount of media exposure afforded a company's logos, displays, and signage. Media exposure for a company can be derived from television, radio, or print advertising. A value is placed on this exposure based on the traditional advertising costs per 30 seconds for the particular media vehicle.

One of the least likely functions for a sport management/marketing agency to perform is financial planning. This role is usually contracted out to financial institutions and investment specialists who, while not involved full-time in the sport industry, can apply their expertise to guiding professional athletes. One notable exception to this pattern is IMG, which has an internal department devoted to this function.

CRITICAL EVENT MANAGEMENT FUNCTIONS

Finance/Budgeting

The complexity of managing events, coupled with the need to constantly monitor financial conditions, places the functions of **budgeting** and finance at the forefront of successful sport event management. Budgeting is the process of developing a written plan of revenues and expenses for the next accounting cycle. For events, an accounting cycle is usually the time period necessary to plan, organize, and operate the upcoming event. This cycle can be as short as a month, or in the case of an organization such as the United States Olympic Committee

(USOC), budgeting can attempt to predict revenues and expenses for the following four years of activity. While there are a number of different types of budgets and budgeting processes, two that are particularly important for events are **zero-base budgeting** and **cash-flow budgeting**. Zero-base budgeting requires a review of all activities and related costs of an event as if it were the first time. Previous budgets and actual revenues and expenses are ignored. All projected revenues and expenses have to be justified prior to becoming part of the overall budget. This type of budget process forces managers to view their event from a fresh perspective, never taking elements for granted and always searching for ways to become more efficient and effective. Cash-flow budgeting refers to accounting for the receipt and timing of all sources and expenditures of cash. Cash-flow budgeting informs the manager of the cash amount needed to pay expenses at predetermined times throughout the accounting cycle. Events often expend sizable amounts of cash during the planning and organizing phases, while only receiving cash just prior to the actual execution of the event; therefore, planning carefully to avoid cash shortfalls is critical.

Risk Management/Insurance

In staging an event, event organizers strive to eliminate—or at least minimize—any activities or occurrences that could injure a participant, worker, or spectator. If an injury does occur, event organizers want to ensure the injured party is attended to in a responsible and medically proper manner. Event organizers also want to be aware of any problems that may affect the financial aspects of the event. The person in charge of **risk management** for an event is responsible for identifying and determining which methods to employ against potential threats that may negatively affect the sport event (Graham et al., 1995). In sport, the risk management approach combines the traditional corporate interest of limiting financial risk with the interest of the sport industry—providing for increased safety (Ammon, 1997). The management of risks associated with an event includes two approaches: development and implementation of a risk management plan, and purchasing appropriate insurance coverage. The risk management plan covers the health and safety issues of the event, while also identifying potential financial losses. Purchasing insurance not only covers health and safety liability issues but also addresses financial concerns such as corporate sponsorship investments and participant fees in case the event is canceled.

Fully ensuring the safety and security of individuals is a difficult task that is possible only through the development and utilization of a comprehensive risk management plan (Ammon, 1997). It is critical when dealing with risk management that the sport event manager is attentive to details and thorough in communicating this information. Ammon (1997) suggests the usage of the **D.I.M. Process** as a tool to construct a practical and effective risk management plan. The D.I.M. Process involves three steps: (1) *d*eveloping the risk management plan, (2) *i*mplementing the risk management plan, and (3) *m*anaging the risk management plan. A more thorough discussion of the D.I.M. Process can be found in Chapter 5, Legal Principles Applied to Sport Management.

A common tool used for events is the waiver and release of liability. This is a form signed by participants and volunteers that releases the venue and event organizers from a negligence action in case of accident or injury. Waivers and releases of liability are enforceable against competent adult participants unless the waivers and releases violate public policy or unless the party getting the waiver was unfairly dominant in the bargaining process (Berry & Wong, 1993). If the participant is a minor, the signature of a parent is suggested. The validity of a waiver is determined by the law in each state; consequently, the validity of waivers will vary across state lines (Cotten, 1997). Event organizers must remember that a waiver and release of liability does not exonerate them from all responsibility and liability regarding the event. Waivers and releases of liability can only be used to waive or release a defendant from negligence claims. Event organizers are still responsible for running an event in a responsible, safe manner or they may be found liable for any injuries or problems that may occur. Exhibit 14–1 contains an example of a waiver and release of liability form for an outdoor 3-on-3 basketball tournament.

Another approach necessary when handling risk factors associated with an event is purchasing insurance. Insurance can be purchased not only to cover safety concerns, but also to provide security to an event regarding potential financial losses. For example, an outdoor event which collects sponsorship dollars and registration fees from participants in advance may need to refund a portion if not all of this revenue if the event is cancelled due to inclement weather. The event organizers, though, still incurred expenses in getting ready to host the event. Purchasing cancellation insurance can help to offset some of these expenses. Most venues require that the promoter, sponsor, or organizer of the event maintain a minimum level of insurance. The premiums for these types of insurance are based on the level of risk.

There are also a variety of insurance premiums that can be purchased, including:

- comprehensive general liability—provides protection against fire, theft, and injury;
- cancellation or contingency—provides protection against cancellation of the event;
- prize indemnity—protects sponsors against loss of money due to contest awards; and

Exhibit 14–1 Waiver and Release Form

Waiver and Release

I, _____, the undersigned Participant, for myself, my heirs, executors, administrators, successors and assigns; and I/we, the under-signed, individually, and/or as mother and father and/or as next friend and/or as natural guardian of said participant, IN CONSIDERATION of permission granted to the undersigned participant by the _____ to participant in an event entitl ' "_____" which will be held in the area of _____ at the _____ from Saturday, _____ through Sunday, _____ (including the appropriate rain dates of _____ and _____) and to participate in basketball tournaments and related activities which are a part of said event, do hereby remise, release and forever discharge the _____ its _____ officers, employees and agents hereinafter "_____" both in their individual capacity and by reason of their relationship to said _____, and their heirs, executors, administrators, successors and assigns of and from all liabilities whatsoever including but not limited to all debts, demands, actions, claims, causes of action and lawsuits, in law, equity and otherwise, which I/we the undersigned, as above described, have or may have against said "_____" by reason of injury or bodily harm, including but not limited to death, and loss of, including but not limited to destruction of property, arising or resulting directly or indirectly from the undersigned participant's participation in the said "_____" event.

Further, the undersigned warrants that he/she has medical insurance and assumes full responsibility for any medical expenses that may result from participation in "_____" and thereby remises, releases and forever discharges the "_____" from any said medical expenses. Further, the under-signed participant understands that basketball is a strenuous contact sport and that serious injuries may result from his/her participation in said event.

By signing this waiver the participant understands that _____ will be videotaping the events of _____ . The Participant understands that this videotape will be used for cablecasting on _____, and may be distributed to local cable access operators and community television stations, and/or sold to the general public.

In Witness Whereof, the undersigned has/have set his/her/their hand(s) and seal(s) this _____ day of _____, 1997.

Participant   Witness
_____   _____
Signature   Signature

---

continues

Exhibit 14–1 continued

<table>
<tr><td>_____
Print Name</td><td>_____
Print Name</td></tr>
</table>

Individually and/or as father and/or
mother and/or next friend and/or natural
guardian of the minor Participant.*

_____
Witness

_____
Signature

_____
Signature

_____
Print Name

_____
Print Name

*Parent or legal guardian must sign if Participant is under 18 years of age.

Courtesy of Sports Management Department, University of Massachusetts, Amherst.

- participant accident coverage—provides protection against accidental death or dismemberment of an event participant (Graham et al., 1995).

Risk management and insurance are of primary importance to event organizers and should never be overlooked when running an event. Appropriate advance planning in these areas can help alleviate problems when the event actually takes place. In addition, event organizers should realize the importance of addressing risk management and insurance concerns surrounding an event in order to limit the legal liability of the event.

Tournament Operations

Tournament operations can be described as the nuts and bolts of an event. The tournament operations staff stage the event, meet facility and equipment needs, and provide any operational items for the event. Tournament operations can be divided into pre-event, actual event, and postevent activities. Pre-event tournament operations require appropriate planning and information collection to ensure all aspects and details surrounding the actual event are identified. Depending on the size and scope of the event, pre-event tournament operations planning may start four months prior to an event, common for local events such as bike races or basketball tournaments, or eight to ten years prior to an event, as is common with large events such as the Olympic Games. During the pre-event planning stages it is important for the tournament operations staff to be clear as to the type of event being planned and the event's goals. This information is critical in determining how the tournament will be organized and run—components central to the responsibilities and concerns of the tournament operations staff. Items that should be addressed in the pre-event planning stages include:

- venue plan and layout
- equipment and facility needs
- schedule of activities
- sponsorship needs
- signage con. .nitments and locations
- food and beverage
- merchandise sales
- media concerns
- promotional activities and needs
- transportation concerns
- housing of athletes
- staff communication
- personnel responsibilities
- lines of authority
- security issues
- Americans with Disabilities Act requirements
- policies to address other legal concerns such as alcohol use
- crowd control

This list is not all-inclusive, as the items handled by the tournament operations staff will vary depending upon the type, goals, size, and scope of the event.

During the actual event the tournament operations staff are responsible for ensuring the event takes place as planned. This includes attending to the activities and needs relating to participants, sponsors, and spectators. To help in this area, many events utilize a script of activities. The **script** is a specific, detailed, minute-by-minute (or even second-by-second) schedule of activities throughout the day, including information on the tournament operations responsibilities for each activity. This script provides information relative to: (1) the time of day and what is taking place, (2) the operational needs (equipment and setup) surrounding each activity, and (3) the event person(s) in charge of the various activities. During the actual event the tournament operations staff implement the tournament script while also troubleshooting as needed. Advance preparation and planning can certainly assist in running an event, but the tournament operations staff must also be prepared to troubleshoot and to be flexible and adaptable to change when an unforeseen problem arises.

The postevent stage of an event consists of the activities surrounding the completion of an event. Areas covered during the postevent stage include:

- tear-down of the venue
- storage of equipment and supplies
- trash pickup and disposal
- return of borrowed equipment, sponsorship signage, etc.
- final financial accounting regarding expenses relative to the operations portion of the event
- thank-you notes sent to appropriate constituencies assisting in the tournament operations area

It is important for the tournament operations staff to realize that the completion of the actual event does not signal the end of their responsibilities. Numerous items such as those just listed still need to be addressed before the event is wrapped up.

Registration

Registering participants for an event is of utmost importance as this is the first time event staff members come into contact with participants. An efficient registration system is crucial for making a good first impression on the event's clientele. Appropriate advance planning and attention to information needed from participants guide the development of a registration system that is appropriate for the event and convenient for participants. In developing a registration system, event managers must consider:

- number of participants who will be registering
- information that needs to be collected from or disseminated to the participants (e.g., waiver forms, codes for sportsmanship conduct, inclement weather policy, event schedule)
- registration fees that must be collected
- whether identification is needed (e.g., regarding age limitations)
- whether information is collected manually or via a computer system
- whether the event involves minors, who require the signature of a parent or guardian on a waiver form

This list is not all-inclusive as the event will dictate the items that need to be covered during the registration process. Different systems can be used to accommodate the participants and alleviate congestion during the registration process while still collecting or disseminating appropriate information. Examples of such registration systems include using a staggered schedule that provides times when certain divisions of participants for an event should register or using different registration sites for different categories of participation. Note that it is important to create or establish security measures if registration fees are being collected.

Volunteer Management

The importance of volunteers to an event cannot be emphasized enough. Events from the smallest local bike race to those as large and complex as the Olympic Games rely on volunteer help. **Volunteer management** staff supervise the volunteers involved with an event. Volunteer management can be divided into two areas:(1) working with event organizers and staff to determine the areas and quantity of volunteers that are needed, and (2) soliciting, training, and managing the volunteers. Once again, advance planning and preparation are critical in determining how many volunteers are needed and in what capacities they will serve. The volunteer management staff must communicate with every division or area within an event to determine its volunteer needs. Information must include the number of volunteers a particular area may need, qualifications of volunteers, and also the type of work to be performed. This information is important when scheduling volunteers as the volunteer management staff would not want to assign a volunteer to work moving heavy equipment, for example, if the volunteer were not physically capable.

Once the volunteer management staff have calculated or estimated the number of and areas of work where volunteers are needed, the staff can make sure that recruitment efforts are appropriate to solicit that number of volunteers. Volunteer recruitment should begin well in advance of the event to ensure that the appropriate number of volunteers are recruited. In addition, the volunteer management staff should be aware of the method in which volunteers are being recruited. (For example, if adult volunteers are needed, the recruitment efforts obviously should not be aimed at area middle schools.)

After the recruitment of volunteers takes place, appropriate training sessions must be held. Training sessions typically include a basic educational component followed by specific department training (Graham et al., 1995). Items covered in the basic educational component training session may include how the volunteers should dress or obtain their volunteer uniforms, how they can obtain food and beverages during the event, and the communication system that will be used so they know whom to contact in case of a problem; in addition, all volunteers should be trained concerning risk management and what procedures they should follow in case of an injury or accident. Specific department training will include a description of volunteer duties, how to carry out these duties, when and where volunteers should check in, the name of their direct supervisor, and any other information specific to the volunteer work they will be performing.

Finally, event organizers must understand the importance of volunteers to the continual operation and success of an event. It is important for the volunteer management staff and event organizers to make sure certain things are done in order to keep the volunteers happy so they will keep coming back year after year. First, volunteers should not be scheduled into too many time slots so they do not become tired. The schedule should also include appropriate food and bathroom breaks. Second, volunteers need to be recognizable to participants and spectators. Uniforms can help the volunteers be more recognizable while also increasing the professional perception of the event. Finally, volunteers need to be recognized for their assistance and contribution to the event. This can be done in a number of different ways, including constant recognition during the event, holding a volunteer party after the event is over, and running volunteer raffles where the volunteers have a chance to win prizes or receive some benefits in exchange for volunteering.

Event Marketing

Sport and special events cannot be successful without carefully planned marketing programs. There are eight areas on which event marketers must focus:

- sales of corporate sponsorship
- advertising efforts
- public relations activities
- hospitality
- ticket sales
- broadcasting
- licensing/merchandising
- fundraising

These eight areas are intricately linked. Efforts toward soliciting corporate sponsors will impact advertising strategies, and broadcasting agreements will influence ticket sales. Because these areas are so interrelated, the event marketer must employ an **integrated marketing** approach. Integrated marketing entails long-term strategic planning to manage functions in a consistent manner. For example, ticket sales strategies should be formulated considering the potential sales promotion efforts of sponsors. With this in mind, each of the eight event marketing areas will now be explored.

Corporate Sponsorship

Many events could not happen without the infusion of corporate sponsorship dollars (Schaaf, 1995). As the corporate commitment to sports and special events continues to grow, so does the reliance of events on corporate funding. This is true even with respect to the largest global events. Nearly one-fourth of all revenues from the Atlanta Olympic Games came from corporate sponsorships. In professional tennis, Wimbledon, the French Open, and the U.S. Open are the only three tournaments that do not have title sponsors. The fourth "major" tournament, the Australian Open, receives nearly $2 million annually from a title sponsor (Feinstein, 1992). As the size of the event decreases, event promoters typically become even more reliant on sponsorship fees. For example, corporate sponsor dollars are often the difference between making money or losing money for a local 3-on-3 basketball event. Estimated sponsorship fees for selected events are presented in Table 14–2.

Typically, corporate sponsorships are either sold by the event (in-house) or by an outside sport marketing agency. Sport marketing agencies are hired by a sport property because the property does not have sufficient personnel or expertise in selling sponsorships. In the early 1980s, the International Olympic Committee (IOC) decided the Games were becoming too reliant on broadcasting fees for funding. In response, it decided to sell worldwide sponsorships for the Olympic Games. However, it did not have the expertise or personnel to approach global companies asking for multimillion-dollar sponsorship commitments. Therefore, in 1983 the IOC turned to ISL Marketing, which raised $100 million for the 1988 Olympic Games (Simson & Jennings, 1992).

Advertising

Most events operate on very tight budgets. As a result, many events are not able to allocate significant expenditures for advertising through the traditional forms of media. Most often advertising expenditures are a very minor portion of an event's expenses. However, this does not mean that events do not expend energy devising alternative means for mass media advertising. Events typically seek advertising through one of two means: (1) media sponsors or (2) attachment to corporate sponsor advertisements.

Table 14–2 Estimated Costs of Event Sponsorships

Event	Type of Sponsorship	Estimated Cost
Twin Cities Marathon	Presenting sponsor	$150,000
Gus Macker 3-on-3 Basketball	National sponsorship	$250,000–
Tournament		$500,000
Los Angeles Lakers	Team sponsorship	$625,000
ATP (tennis) event	Title sponsorship	$750,000
PGA (golf) event	Title sponsorship	$1–3 million
Fiesta Bowl	Title sponsorship	$2.85 million
World Cup of Soccer	Worldwide sponsorship	$40 million

Source: Reprinted with permission from 1996 *Sports Sponsorship Cost Study,* © 1996, Team Marketing Report.

In addition to selling corporate sponsorships, nearly all successful events sell sponsorships to media outlets. Such sponsorships rarely involve a cash exchange. Instead, an event provides the typical sponsorship benefits to a newspaper, magazine, radio station, or television station in exchange for a specified number of free advertising spots or space. For example, *Sports Illustrated* included a 40-page special advertising section in one of its issues prior to the 1996 Olympic Games as part of its Olympic sponsorship. Event promoters will also work with sponsors to promote their events through traditional forms of mass media. Most often, such advertising is geared around promotions. For example, in conjunction with their title sponsorship of the 7Up Shootout, a college basketball double-header, 7Up ran basketball-themed advertisements in both newspapers and on television.

Public Relations

Because events are so constrained in their advertising efforts, generating free publicity is extremely important. Most important to attaining publicity is developing a good working relationship with the members of the media. Hospitality efforts can greatly assist in this endeavor and will be discussed later in this section. In addition, regular communication with media outlets helps enhance the publicity an event receives. However, because members of the media seek stories of interest to the masses, the event must be creative. Graham et al. (1995) suggest contests such as "design the logo" or "name the mascot" as creative ways to generate publicity. Athletes participating in events can be used to generate publicity. For example, in an effort to promote its Ladies Professional Golf Association (LPGA) event, the 1994 Heartland Classic received publicity surrounding golfer Michelle McGann's visit to a local children's hospital.

Hospitality

Hospitality represents "a management plan that satisfies the needs and expectations of guests" (Graham et al., 1995, p. 79). The sport manager must strive to provide an enjoyable experience to all parties associated with an event: participants, spectators, media, and sponsors. Most events occur on a regular basis, and providing good hospitality is one way of improving event loyalty. The sport manager should take strides to ensure that prominent event participants receive private housing, meals, changing areas, and warm-up space. If the participants are also celebrities, the sport manager must ensure that extra security is available to shield them from the masses. If hospitality is not successfully implemented, the participants are less likely to return to the event. With respect to spectators, hospitality entails attempting to ensure that people attending the event have an enjoyable time. This includes clear signage directing participants to their seats, to restrooms, and to concession stands. In addition, training all support staff personnel is imperative so that interpersonal interactions with event staff are always positive. In sum, event managers should plan hospitality based on how they believe each spectator would like to be treated (Graham et al., 1995).

The event manager will often expend the most energy providing hospitality to members of the media, to corporate sponsors, and to other VIPs. Because the event manager is seeking positive publicity from the media, there should always be a separate, prime seating location for the media. In addition, members of the media are accustomed to having private meals and accessibility to a private room where they can complete work. Increased spending on corporate sponsorships has led to growing awareness and interest in hospitality services. Sport sponsors utilize hospitality to interest targeted individuals in their product or strengthen ties with their existing customer base (Howard & Crompton, 1995). For this reason, hospitality has become one of the 10 most common functions of a sport agency (as presented in Table 14–1). Most sponsors will seek some sort of entertainment area where they can host selected guests. For example, as part of its sponsorship of the Senior PGA Golf Tour, Cadillac has a hospitality tent at every Senior PGA event where it invites current Cadillac owners to enjoy food and beverages at the company's expense.

Ticket Sales

Sporting events rely on ticket sales to varying degrees. For larger events, such as the Olympic Games, which sold 8.3 million tickets in 1996, ticket sales are a very important revenue stream. However, for medium-sized and smaller events, ticket sales are a less effective way to generate revenues. Much of the ability to charge admission for these events is dependent on where the event occurs and how easily the event manager can control entry to the event. For example, many professional golf tournaments experience difficulty generating revenues through ticket sales because it is hard to control entry to the course and because so many tickets are given away to corporate sponsors. In these cases, the event is more reliant on sponsorship revenues. However, event managers have discovered creative ways to increase revenues tied to ticket sales. In exchange for a higher monetary outlay, golf tournaments have begun offering preferred viewing lanes whereby spectators receive preferred seating in front of the typical gallery areas. Luxury suites have also become popular revenue-generating vehicles. Golf promoters sell luxury suites around the 18th hole in an effort to increase their ticket sales revenues (Klein, 1997). Renovations at the Foro Italico Complex, home of the Italian Open tennis tournament, were partially funded by luxury suite sales (Feinstein, 1992).

Broadcasting

Radio and television broadcasts of an event add credibility to the event and provide increased exposure benefits to sponsors. There is a wide variety of broadcast outlets for sporting events, including:

- national network television (ABC, NBC, CBS, and FOX)
- national sports networks (ESPN, ESPN II)
- national cable outlets (TNT, TBS, The Nashville Network, The Golf Channel)
- local television stations
- regional sports networks (SportsChannel, Fox Sports, Prime, Sunshine, New England Sports Network)
- national radio (CBS, ESPN)
- local radio stations

While the increased number of sport mediums has increased the demand for sport event programming, a sport property must still meet certain criteria in order to interest a radio or television broadcast outlet. In fact, only the most valuable sport properties, such as the Super Bowl, the Olympic Games, Wimbledon, the Masters, professional sports, and Division I college athletics, are able to secure direct rights fees payments from broadcasting affiliates. It is important to remember that television and radio stations are funded by advertising sales. Advertisers purchase advertising time during programs that will attract large viewing or listening audiences. Therefore, if a broadcast outlet does not feel a property will be attractive to a large audience, which limits the ability to sell advertising time, then the outlet will not be willing to pay a rights fee to televise or broadcast an event. If a sport property is unable to secure a direct rights fee payment, there are two other options for receiving broadcast time. First, the event promoter can solicit a revenue-sharing agreement with the broadcast outlet. In this case, the event promoter can offer to cover production costs or provide the event free of charge in exchange for a share of advertising sales revenues. This is the means employed by IMG to televise many of its events. For example, an IMG event can be produced by its Trans World International (TWI) television production unit and then provided to broadcast outlets. IMG and the broadcast outlet then share the revenues generated through advertising sales during the event. If a revenue-sharing partnership cannot be arranged, then the least attractive option is to purchase airtime directly from a broadcast outlet. This is the least attractive option because it is the most expensive to the event promoter (Graham et al., 1995).

Licensing/Merchandising

The sale of **licensed merchandise**, that is, items that display an event's name or logo, is usually only beneficial for large, televised, multi-day events. Merchandise sales are ultimately an indicator of popularity (Schaaf, 1995). Therefore, for popular events such as the Olympic Games and the Super Bowl, there will be significant demand for logoed merchandise. However, for smaller, less recognizable events, such as a high school football game or a 10K road race, the effort and expense needed to sell merchandise may be higher than the revenue generated from such events. In order to cover the costs of inventory, staffing, and space allocation, significant sales must be achieved for the event to make a profit. Typically, selling tens or even hundreds of pieces of merchandise will not allow the event promoter to record a profit from merchandise sales. Careful research of the potential event audience can help the event manager determine whether or not to sell licensed merchandise (Graham et al., 1995).

Fundraising

When the operating motive of an event is **not-for-profit**, another marketing tool is fund-raising. Fund-raising differs from sponsorship in that it does not offer advertising benefits associated with a donation. When deciding to donate money to a not-for-profit event, altruistic motivations are typically more important than commercial motivations (Howard & Crompton, 1995). Most often, not-for-profit events center around raising money for some charitable enterprise. The Race for the Cure and the March of Dimes Walk-a-Thon are good examples of not-for-profit events (Graham et al., 1995). **Cause-related marketing efforts** by corporations are another instance in which fundraising may be appropriate. For example, the CVS Charity Classic is a professional golf tournament sponsored by CVS, a drugstore chain, for the purpose of generating money for charity.

CAREER OPPORTUNITIES

Event management offers a diverse array of career possibilities. Any event, from the local 3-on-3 basketball tournament to the Olympic Games, requires event management expertise. As a result, the event management field offers one of the most fertile areas for career opportunities. However, in order to successfully implement any sporting event, the event manager's day often begins before dawn and concludes late at night. In addition, because events are usually held on weekends, employment in event management often requires extensive travel and work over weekends. Thus, to be successful in event management, one must be prepared to work long and typically inconvenient hours.

Career opportunities in event management center around working with one of three types of organizations: sport management/sport marketing agencies, events, and charities.

Sport Management/Sport Marketing Agencies

Because of the wide variety of tasks carried out by agencies, job responsibilities within agencies vary. Typically, an entry-level position with a sport marketing agency will require a person to implement programs on behalf of corporate clients. These programs can include any combination of the key event management functions already discussed. While an entry-level person is usually not responsible for recruiting corporate clients, he or she is required to successfully manage events and programs created for specific sponsors. For example, an account manager might be responsible for ensuring that a corporation's signs are properly placed throughout an event site, or the account manager might be responsible for supervising hospitality at an event. To move beyond the entry level within an agency, a person is usually required to accept more business development responsibilities. For example, most vice-presidents of sport management/sport marketing agencies are responsible for attracting new clients for the agency. This function is typically called **business development**.

Events

While sport management/sport marketing agencies are typically involved with any sport event, many events have their own offices of full-time employees. This is most often true for events to which a corporation or sport management/sport marketing agency does not own the rights. Instead, the rights to the event may be owned locally. In this case, the management team for the event would not be from an agency or corporation. However, because most events are seasonal in nature, the full-time year-round staffs for such events are not very large. For example, an LPGA event held every summer might have two full-time employees, one to handle the sales of sponsorship packages and another to address the remaining operational issues. At the other end of the spectrum, some agencies may have hundreds of employees each working on multiple events.

Charities

Many charities view events as a way to increase revenues. For example, Race for the Cure is a road-race series staged by the Susan G. Komen Foundation for breast cancer research. However, rarely do such charities possess personnel with event management experience. Therefore, there are a number of event management positions with charities that implement a series of events. In the case of the Race for the Cure, multiple positions are needed to assist in managing this national series of races.

Key Skills

Any sport event requires management and marketing expertise to achieve financial success. Further, as the previous section illustrates, an event manager assumes a variety of responsibilities. In order to successfully execute these responsibilities, the sport manager must first have the necessary skills and experience. First, the sport manager must possess the proper educational background. Therefore, students interested in event management should seek a sport management program or business school that will provide them with coursework in sport marketing, event management, sport management, business, and finance. Many events are created by one person and begin as a small business, so classes in entrepreneurship and accounting are also important for the prospective event manager.

In terms of experience, an internship is almost always required prior to being hired for an entry-level position in event management. In many cases, sport management/sport marketing agencies will turn to their most effective interns when seeking to fill full-time entry-level positions. Because agencies are charged with supporting corporate clients, new accounts often mean agencies will need to hire additional personnel. Therefore, students must put themselves in a position to be hired when new accounts are acquired. In addition, it is never too early to begin working for events. A number of volunteer and paid opportunities exist in any university community: athletic department, intramural department, community recreation programs, charity events, and so on. Nearly all of these activities can help improve a student's background in event management, making him or her more marketable.

CURRENT ISSUES

Vertical Integration

Vertical integration refers to the efforts of a sport management/sport marketing agency to control all aspects of an event. This is a tactic commonly employed by the three largest sport management/sport marketing agencies (IMG, ProServ, and Advantage International). For example, ProServ represents players, runs the tournaments in which they play, produces television coverage of the tournament, and sells sponsorships associated with the tournament (Feinstein, 1992). From a business perspective, this allows the agencies to maximize their revenues. Collectively, these agents represent the best players in professional tennis. Due to their relationship, an agency can guarantee its star athletes will appear in its own events, thus enhancing attendance. The ability to guarantee the appearance of talent also can enhance the agency's ability to arrange for broadcasting outlets to carry the event. By producing the telecast through its own television unit, the agency can also ensure that its sponsors' signs will be displayed prominently in certain camera vantage points, thus allowing the agency to charge higher sponsorship fees.

While vertical integration exists and helps agencies maximize revenues, it also raises a significant ethical dilemma. Basically, there is no other organization or entity in place to ensure the ethical operation of an event. To illustrate this problem, consider professional golf and tennis. There are a limited number of spots available in any professional golf or tennis tournament. Therefore, the sport management/sport marketing agencies such as IMG, ProServ, and Advantage International have used their control over openings in high-profile tournaments to attract new clients. In another case, IMG used its control over the Sony Rankings of professional golfers to disproportionately reward winners of IMG events, thus helping clients of IMG who were guaranteed spots in IMG events (Feinstein, 1992).

Consolidation of Sport Management/Sport Marketing Agencies

The prevalence of vertical integration is likely to increase in the face of the consolidations by sport management/sport marketing agencies occurring in the late 1990s. Larger, more diversified sport and entertainment companies have begun purchasing sport management/sport marketing agencies. For example, Interpublic, a company that also owns numerous advertising agencies, purchased Advantage International (Lombardo, 1997), and Marquee Group, an entertainment company, purchased ProServ (Helyar, 1997). Such transactions only broaden the scope of vertical integration in event management. Advertising agencies owned by Interpublic now have another viable medium for their clients' advertisements—Advantage International–owned events.

Made-for-TV Events

The 1973 "Battle of the Sexes," in which Billie Jean King defeated Bobby Riggs in a professional tennis match played before 35,000 fans at the Houston Astrodome and a national television audience, demonstrated the ability of an event promoter to create an event specifically for mass consumption (Davies, 1994; Helitzer, 1996). **Made-for-TV events** are created solely to generate a profit by appealing to a large television audience. With the increased number of outlets providing sports programming, there is a continual need for programming that will attract large television audiences. For example, several months following the 1996 Atlanta Summer Olympics, Donovan Baily, who won the 100-meter gold medal, and Michael Johnson, who won the 200- and 400-meter gold medals, raced each other on national television for the right to be called the "fastest man in the world." This event was a made-for-TV creation, an event invented to appeal to a large audience and generate large sponsorship fees. Another example of made-for-TV programming is the Extreme Games, in which athletes compete in "extreme sports" such as skateboarding, in-line skating, and street luge.

In creating made-for-TV events, agencies have been focusing on events that appeal to women, who are watching more televised sporting events than they used to. With more women participating in sport than ever before, television outlets are recognizing the interest and providing more sports programming (Grabarek, 1995). One event particularly popular among female audiences is figure skating. Sport management/sport marketing agencies have attempted to capitalize on this popularity by creating made-for-TV figure skating events. For example, "Ice Wars," reprising the 1994 Olympic rivalry between Nancy Kerrigan and Oksana Baiul, was created to appeal to a national television audience (Brennan, 1996).

SUMMARY

By virtue of the continued increase in sporting events, sport event management offers a wide variety of career opportunities for young sport managers. Most of these opportunities exist within sport management/sport marketing agencies, the entities that most often organize, manage, and market sport events. Due to the variety of event management functions, it is possible for multiple agencies to work together on a sporting event. For example, a professional golf tournament may have one sport agency responsible for the operational aspects of the event and another sport agency responsible for the sponsorship sales, public relations, and hospitality of sponsors and VIPs. Yet another agency could be financially and legally responsible for the event and thus would be in charge of implementing budgeting and risk management practices. In some cases, one large agency will handle all of these aspects and perhaps even produce a television broadcast of the event. Regardless of how these functions are delegated, each one is crucial to the sporting event's success. With the proliferation of made-for-TV events, opportunities for sport managers in event management will continue to grow. In order to enter the event management field, however, a student must obtain a strong background in sport management, entrepreneurship, finance, and accounting. The good news is that the student can begin immediately by seeking both volunteer and paid opportunities with sporting events on campus and in the local community.

CASE STUDY: PLANNING FOR A NEW EVENT: 3-ON-3 BASKETBALL TOURNAMENTS

Paul Evers sat in his third floor office contemplating the new challenge dropped in his lap by his employer, Excellent Events, Inc. Having played and coached soccer at the collegiate level, Paul was quite comfortable with his role as Regional Director of indoor soccer tournaments. Now, however, a new wrinkle had been added to his promising career. Paul had just been assigned the responsibility of developing four 3-on-3 outdoor basketball tournaments within the coming year.

Within the southern region of the United States, Excellent Events was the largest organizer of grassroots sports events. With an inventory of events ranging from indoor soccer to beach volleyball, Excellent Events was known in the sports community for operating safe and entertaining events. Because of liability concerns and large equipment requirements, the company had delayed entrance into the lucrative outdoor basketball market. Now, the company was placing its faith and reputation in Paul to replicate its history of success in this new area.

Raised in California, Paul had never played competitive basketball. But, through conversations with colleagues, Paul had gathered some rudimentary information about outdoor basketball and how it could be presented by Excellent Events. First, everyone he spoke to mentioned the physical nature of the game. While traditionally categorized as a noncontact sport, all serious competitors realized that playing on small outdoor courts results in high levels of player contact. Second, as he was attempting to manage and market his first basketball tournaments he had to keep in mind that the competitive advantage enjoyed by Excellent Events was its ability to create a festival atmosphere at sporting events. Lastly, the financial success of these events was contingent on a combination of team registration fees and corporate sponsorships.

Paul had never felt so challenged in his life. While he considered himself a great event manager, he was not sure how much of his success at running indoor soccer tournaments would transfer to this new venture. However, one thing he had learned in his four years as an event manager was that attention to details sprinkled with creativity could carry an event manager far.

Questions for Discussion

1. How can Paul Evers transform his events from basketball tournaments into basketball festivals?
2. While Paul is well aware of the equipment and supplies necessary to run an indoor soccer tournament, he lacks familiarity with the sport of basketball. Provide a comprehensive list of all equipment required to successfully operate a 3-on-3 outdoor basketball festival.
3. Given the demographics and psychographics (see Chapter 3, Marketing Principles Applied to Sport Management) of basketball participants and spectators, what type of corporations should be targeted by Paul for sponsorship solicitation?

RESOURCES

Advantage International
1751 Pinnacle Drive, 15th Floor
McLean, VA 22102
703-905-3300

Edelman Sports Marketing
200 E. Randolph Drive, 63rd Floor
Chicago, IL 60601
312-240-3000

Golden Bear Sports Management
11780 U.S. Highway #1
North Palm Beach, FL 33408
407-626-3900

Integrated Sports International (ISI)
One Meadowlands Plaza, Suite 1501
East Rutherford, NJ 07073
201-507-1122

International Events Group (IEG)
640 North LaSalle, Suite 600
Chicago, IL 60610-3777
800-834-4850

International Management Group (IMG)
One Erieview Plaza, Suite 1300
Cleveland, OH 44114
216-522-1145

Millsport Inc.
Stamford Towers
750 Washington Boulevard
Stamford, CT 06901
203-977-0500

ProServ, Inc.
1101 Wilson Blvd., Suite 1800
Arlington, VA 22209
703-276-3090

Regency Productions
225 W. Washington Street, Suite 1550
Chicago, IL 60606
312-641-1234

Streetball Partners International
4006 Belt Line Road, Suite 230
Dallas, TX, 75244
214-991-1110

Triple Crown Sports
253 Linden Street, Suite 201
Fort Collins, CO 80524
303-224-2502

REFERENCES

Ammon, R. (1997). Risk management process. In D.J. Cotten & T.J. Wilde (Eds.), *Sport law for sport managers* (pp. 174–180). Dubuque, Iowa: Kendall/Hunt Publishing Company.

Berry, R.C., & Wong, G.W. (1993). *Law and business of the sports industries*, Vol. II (2d ed.). Westport, CT: Greenwood Publishing Group, Inc.

Brennan, C. (1996). *Inside edge: A revealing journey into the secret world of figure skating.* New York: Doubleday Books.

Cotten, D. (1997). Exculpatory agreements or waivers. In D.J. Cotten & T.J. Wilde (Eds.), *Sport law for sport managers* (pp. 63–69). Dubuque, Iowa: Kendall/Hunt Publishing Co.

Crespo, M. (1995, February 14). You get more eyeballs: Satellite television sports. *Financial World, 164*(4), 94–98.

Davies, R.O. (1994). *America's obsession: Sports and society since 1945.* Fort Worth, TX: Harcourt Brace College Publishers.

Feinstein, J. (1992). *Hard courts: Real life on the professional tennis tours.* New York: Villard Books.

Feinstein, J. (1996) *A good walk spoiled.* Days.

Grabarek, B. (1995, February 14). Ladies, don't touch that dial. *Financial World*, 99–102.

Graham, S., Goldblatt, J.J., & Delpy, L. (1995). *The ultimate guide to sport event management & marketing.* Chicago: Irwin Publishing Group.

Helitzer, M. (1996). *The dream job in sports: Publicity, promotion and marketing.* Athens, OH: University Sports Press.

Helyar, J. (1997, September 5). Net losses: How ProServ, legend among sports agents, fell from the top seed. *The Wall Street Journal*, pp. A1, A8.

Howard, D.R., & Crompton, J.L. (1995). *Financing sport.* Morgantown, WV: Fitness Information Technology, Inc.

Klein, F.C. (1997, February 21). Down in front! Golf experiments with choice seats. *The Wall Street Journal*, p. B9.

Lainson, S. (1997). *Sports news you can use* (electronic newsletter). Boulder, CO: SportsTrust.

Lombardo, J. (1997, August 29–September 4). Sports marketer closes its doors. *Washington Business Journal, 1*, 70.

Myers, K.J. (Ed.). (1997). *Sports market place.* Phoenix, AZ: Franklin Quest.

Schaaf, P. (1995). *Sports marketing: It's not just a game anymore.* New York: Prometheus Books.

Schreiber, A.L. (1994). *Lifestyle & event marketing.* New York: McGraw-Hill.

Simson, V., & Jennings, A. (1992). *Dishonored games: Corruption, money & greed at the Olympics.* New York: S.P.I. Books.

Team Marketing Report (1996). *1996 sponsorship cost study.* Chicago: Author.

CHAPTER 15

Media Relations

Howard M. Davis

Key words: College Sports Information Directors of America (CoSIDA), beat writers, camera-ready, general news release, inverted pyramid, five Ws, fact sheet, pregame notes, contact sheet, retainer system, media guide, game program, press conference, media relations contest management, one-call system, fax on demand, fax back

INTRODUCTION

Media relations is a fast-paced, multifaceted job. An individual will be able to succeed in media relations if he or she possesses such skills as writing ability, literacy in computer and electronic communications, publications competency, statistical expertise, more than a basic knowledge of sports, and the ability to work well with diverse populations. Certainly, a college media relations specialist must be able to relate to coaches, athletes, administrators, alumni, politicians, and that most complex entity, the media. A media relations person in professional sport has to possess the ability and flexibility to appease all kinds, from the wealthy owner or conglomerate, to the well-paid athlete, to the media member with the ever-present investigative mind. Although the media relations person may not have an abundance of extra time, if an athlete requests a meeting with the media relations director, be it business or social, time should be made available. While the general manager, athletic director, or coach may control the future of the media relations director, a positive rapport with the athletes is equally important. The increasing use of such technological advancements as e-mail and the Internet does not eliminate the necessity for interpersonal communications. Only the ability to work well with people under all situations will lead to success in media relations.

356

HISTORY

The birth of the sports media relations profession can be traced to the decade of the 1950s when professional clubs and college athletic departments realized that a coach, a secretary, or any other designee could no longer produce game programs, compile statistics, and answer requests from the media by themselves while still performing their other functions. The amount of requests and the intensity of the work created a need for a full-time professional. During the 1950s the Sports Division of the American College Public Relations Association (ACPRA) formed its own group, the **College Sports Information Directors of America (CoSIDA)**, an organization with a current membership of over 1,700 that continues to be extremely active and influential today. Currently, every professional team and college athletic department on any level has specialists involved in the area of media relations. Professional teams will more than likely have two full-time people working with the media on a day-to-day basis. These professionals answer media requests, arrange for credentials, prepare notes and/or fact sheets, update statistics, coordinate photography sessions, moderate player/staff interviews, and facilitate pregame and postgame operations. In addition, the media relations staff of the late 1990s may have a publications specialist who produces event programs and media guides using computer software.

It is very important for the media relations director to be aware of the philosophy of the general manager and head coach in professional sports or the athletic director and head coaches in college sports. Do these people wish to have daily contact with **beat writers**, journalists assigned to cover the day-to-day activities of a team? Will they set aside two hours each day in which they will attempt to return phone calls? Will they have a weekly or biweekly teleconference call in which they speak to the media? Although some of this may be mandated by leagues and conferences, it is very important for the media relations director to understand the organizational policies.

On the college level, are all sports treated equally? Do all sports have a representative of the media relations office present at every event, home and away? Do all sports have preseason media guides? Do all sports report their scores to the media? Again, policies must be in place for these situations, and the media relations director must understand what is expected.

DAILY OPERATIONS

Office Location and Organization

If at all possible, the media relations office should be located "where the action is." The media relations office for a professional sport team should be located close to the head coach and all front-office personnel in decision-making capacities. An office in close proximity to those people who are constantly needed by the media makes everyone's life easier. If the head coach, general manager, and director of player personnel are in one building and the media relations director is in another, the media will tend to bypass the media relations director.

College media relations is similar. It may be impossible to have all coaches and athletic administrators housed in the same building, but it is extremely inefficient if the media relations director is located with other university news bureau personnel, a distance from the athletic director.

As far as staffing is concerned, access to a full-time administrative assistant is a major plus. On the collegiate level, Division I college media relations staffs may have up to six full-time people to work with men's and women's teams. Smaller colleges may have an information specialist specifically assigned to athletics or one who splits his or her responsibilities between general media work and athletic media relations. On the professional level, major league teams have approximately three to five employees working in media, public, and community relations. In addition, professional teams and colleges will hire interns, graduate assistants, or undergraduates to work with their media relations staff. Interns are usually treated as full-time staffers, although an expected inequity exists in terms of pay and benefits. Additional people can also be hired for game day operations, including press box attendants, statisticians, and runners.

The media relations director should not be asked to "compete" against other teams/schools in the league without a full complement of workers and electronic technology, including such staples as high-speed copy machines, fax machines, and several computers (both desktop and laptop). In addition, it is imperative to have software that communicates instantaneously and generates and distributes **camera-ready** statistical reports (i.e., reports in final form that can be sent directly to the printer). These are not luxuries; they are necessities.

Written Materials

Prior to each season a college athlete completes a "Publicity Form" that includes such valuable data as height, weight, age, hometown, high school, college major, year in college, and hometown newspapers. These publicity forms are used to generate rosters and to give the media relations staff the material needed to include in general news releases, fact sheets, or hometown features. At the professional level, the media relations staff need to have a publicity form completed for all first-year and newly acquired players.

The General News Release

A **general news release (GNR)** is always positive and always refers to the future. It announces upcoming contests and appointments and should be written in a manner that follows the basic journalist style of the "inverted pyramid" with a lead that includes the **five Ws**. Should an editor have a need to fill space, the GNR would be able to be used without any, or only slight, modification. The **inverted pyramid** style of composing a GNR places the most important parts of the subject matter early in the release. Therefore, should an editor not need all the material, the release can be cut from the bottom without eliminating critical data. The lead paragraph of the GNR should actually be a single lead sentence. That lead sentence should include as many of the five Ws—Who, What, Where, Why, and When—as possible. The GNR *never* details a recently completed event or contest. Even the use of modern technology deems that type of release "old news" by the time it is retrieved. The GNR should mention outstanding performances by several athletes, but play-by-play descriptions of these performances is inappropriate. The GNR is a well-written document conveying a message in perfect English and does not exceed a page and a half. It is rarely used on the professional level or Division I collegiate level unless an announcement needs to be made.

Fact Sheets

Day-to-day general data take the form of a **fact sheet**. Again, only positive data are written by a media relations office. If a football team is 0–7 or a field hockey team is 1–13, the media relations professional still needs to find and disseminate positive material. While this may become a difficult chore, the media relations person must meet with coaches and find that proverbial "silver lining." A negative fact sheet or GNR, even in jest, could lead to the unemployment line. After a fact sheet has been prepared for distribution, either electronically or through the mail, the fact sheet will be reformatted and distributed to the media as pregame notes. The fact sheet covers a wide variety of topics, stated in the form of phrases and with each separate thought preceded by elipses, a series of dots or periods (. . .).

A fact sheet could be produced on a weekly basis for "Olympic (or non-revenue) sports" on the collegiate level. Such a fact sheet would give a brief synopsis of the progress of each team to date and would list outstanding performances, records, achievements, and notes of future contests. It might also include a more detailed sheet of statistics for each sport. For example, a football fact sheet could break down data in terms of offensive unit, defensive unit, special teams, team tendencies, outstanding players, injuries, lineup changes, records, standings, success (or lack of it) against the next opponent, and any other note deemed significant by the media relations professional.

Pregame Notes

As mentioned earlier, the **pregame notes** do not vary drastically from the fact sheet. The notes include starting lineups, confirm injuries, indicate the event officials, and give any late-breaking material such as additions to the roster or injuries. Copies of positive newspaper stories that may have been printed about the team and/or players from different cities around the country may also be included to give the journalists a sense of what others are writing about the team. The pregame notes, fact sheets, and GNR always include detailed statistics for the team and individuals.

Hometown Features

When a GNR or fact sheet is produced on the college level, the hometown of each athlete should be mentioned in parentheses—for example, "Josephine Smyth (E. Overshoe, IN)"—and highlighted. A copy of this document is then sent to Ms. Smyth's hometown newspaper. An additional copy of the hometown feature, in addition to any GNR or fact sheet mentioning the athlete's name, should be placed in the athlete's file in the media relations office. All pictures (head and shoulders and action) are also included in the athlete's personal file. Should a situation develop in which an athlete's picture or notes about the athlete are needed, the personal folder of the athlete is the place to look.

Professional teams have little need for the hometown feature, but it is one of the most valuable publicity tools used by a college media relations office. A "hometowner" is a feature of one to one-and-a-half pages about a student-athlete and is mailed to one (and only one) newspaper in the hometown area of the student-athlete. The smaller the town and the smaller the newspaper, the better the chances are of seeing the hometown feature actually appear in print. If an athlete lists the hometown paper as *The New York Times*, it would be a waste of time to send a hometown feature; however, if there is a "shopper's weekly" that is sent free of charge to every family in the Bronx, there is a good possibility that the hometown athlete's story would be published. The heading should read: "Special to the East Overshoe Gazette." It follows the same journalistic style as a GNR, but it states the hometown of the student-athlete, the college or university, and the individual's name in the lead sentence/paragraph. Other important material includes athletic accomplishments, the athlete's academic major and any awards he or she has received, the college coach's name, quotes from the college coach, the high school attended, and the high school coach for that sport. The parents' name and address should be mentioned at the end.

A hometowner should only be written about outstanding athletes. Smaller colleges utilize the hometown feature for every sport, whereas larger universities may not need such features for sports that constantly keep the athlete's name in the public eye. The hometown feature is mailed with a head-and-shoulder photo and/ or an action shot. Often the paper will print the picture with a cutline (caption) and no story, which is equally effective for hometown visibility.

One copy of the hometowner is retained for the individual's folder and another is sent to the parents with a form letter requesting the parents to mail the media relations office a copy of the story when it appears in the paper. The latter copy achieves two purposes: It lets the parents know that the university has an interest in their child, and if the story does not appear in the paper by the regular route, it is possible that a parent will have a contact to make sure the story is printed.

Hometown electronic media are a valuable tool for added publicity. Most radio and television stations will contact the media relations office of a professional team for updates on a hometown athlete. For athletes who are not in the major sports, a college media relations office must take the initiative. If a student-athlete resides in a small town with only one or two radio stations, the media relations director could arrange for the sports director of the radio station to tape an interview with the athlete and the coach. If there is no sports director or that individual does not have enough time, the media relations director could conduct an interview and send the tape.

Hometown television is another asset. A video, produced on 3/4″ tape (the standard home video is 1/2″), that shows highlights of a local athlete and is still timely when it arrives at the television station, may well be shown. It would be wise for the media relations director to communicate with the sports director ahead of time to see if the station is receptive to accepting such a tape or if the hometown TV station will merely contact an affiliate in the area of the college to transmit action footage of the athlete over the satellite. Note that it would be unreasonable to send a videotape of an athlete from a small college to a Chicago television station and expect to have it used, even if the athlete is outstanding; however, if a student-athlete lives in an area that is not considered a "major" metropolitan market, sending a highlight tape would be worthwhile.

Many large universities now have their own satellite dishes capable of transmitting material to any TV station in the country. This has become an area in which talented individuals involved in mass communications can earn jobs or internships. Many professional teams have their own video departments and are in need of competent workers. These video departments gather footage of potential draft choices for viewing by coaches and front-office personnel. In addition, they splice actual in-season contest footage of future opponents to be used as a scouting tool by the coaching staff.

Statistics, Statistics, Statistics

Statistics are necessary items in media relations. All sports have statistics to varying degrees. The media can dwell on statistics. While statistics certainly are not the most important aspect of the profession, a media relations person cannot live without them. The media must have a statistics sheet handed to them at the end of each time period and a complete packet of statistics available shortly after each game; therefore, high-speed copy machines are a must.

In the late 1980s, computer specialists developed software to make compiling statistics in different sports "easier." While software can truly make this task less time-consuming, most software has so many capabilities that some media relations people spend an unreasonable amount of time generating reams and reams of statistical data. Some of the more widely used software packages are StatMan, Hoop Stat, Grid Stat, and Base/Soft Stat. Professional football and basketball teams and most Division I college teams utilize computerized statistics. The media relations director therefore needs to find people who not only know the intricacies of the sport, but are also computer-literate. Smaller colleges may not have the personnel, hardware, or software to allow the statistics to be computer-driven. In these situations, reliable individuals who know the sport are a must. These people are essential game-day personnel. Baseball and softball, sports with volumes of statistics, only need one person, the official scorer, to compile statistics. Basketball should have a crew of three to four people to accomplish all necessary statistics, while football stat crews can involve up to 10 people.

Photography

A media relations office on either the professional or collegiate level cannot exist without quality photography. Pictures of individual coaches and athletes, team pictures, and videotape are a must. Colleges and pro teams will hire photographers on a permanent basis or utilize the literally scores of people who are classified as freelance photographers. A photographer can supply the media relations person with contact sheets of photograph negatives and allow the media relations person to pick and choose what is needed. (A **contact sheet** is one 8 × 10 piece of photographic paper on which all the negatives appear.) A "positive" print is then made from each of the selected negatives. If the shoot is done in color, these "negatives" can be "filed" on a CD-ROM, which allows for the storage of thousands of photographs.

Large colleges and universities often have the luxury of having their own photo centers. If a professional photographer is not a part of the university's full-time staff, a freelancer or private studio must be hired per event or placed on a **retainer system**. A retainer system is used when a media relations person has a precise budget. A photographer is hired and told that there is, say, $2,000 available for game action. In this case the photographer must "budget" the amount of photographs delivered per sport or per season and not exceed the $2,000.

Photographs, either black-and-white or color, fall into two main categories: posed action and action. The posed action picture is the head and shoulder shot of the athlete in uniform, used for guides, programs, and autographs. More prints of star athletes need to be produced than of the average team member. Team pictures are also considered to be "posed action." These pictures are generally shot during a team photo day held early in the preseason when media are invited to attend to take pictures and do several interviews with team members. Also during a photo day for a high media interest sport, a 3/4" videotape is produced of head-and-shoulder shots of each athlete and coach. The individual sits on a chair and holds a sign waist level indicating name and uniform number. The technician starts the video at a wide angle in order to include the sign and then gradually zooms in to make a tight head-and-shoulder shot. The media relations person can then produce duplicate tapes and send them to each television affiliate intending to telecast an event. In addition, the media relations person always carries a spare video of the head shots on each road trip. This process eliminates the inconvenience of a television crew's reporting to practice the day before or the morning of an event to shoot video head shots.

Team or group shots vary from team to team. In football, a team picture is often taken in the bleachers, for example, and can include nearly 100 people, while tennis teams, which are much smaller, prefer to have their pictures taken with the athletes holding racquets or at the net. Regardless, if a group picture is shot and the head of each individual is smaller than a dime, the individuals will be difficult to identify. Teams sitting in bleachers should sit in every other row and between the shoulders of two people in front of them; otherwise, the picture will appear squashed. If a football team has its team picture taken in an elevated bleacher, the photographer should be on a ladder or in a cherry picker. If the photographer remains ground level and shoots at an upward angle, athletes in the lower rows will have larger head shots than those in the top rows.

All athletes should be presented in a professional manner. Good action pictures, in both color and black-and-white, can make or break a publication. There are some photographers who specialize in studio shoots, while others make a living on the field or court. Rarely does a photographer excel in both areas. An action photographer must have a feel for the game so he or she knows where to point the lens at all times. Pictures of the back of an athlete are ordinarily not good. A total frontal view is best, and a side view is acceptable. In addition to in-house publications, several national media outlets may request action pictures of the athletes.

Publications

The Media Guide

A **media guide** is usually a massive (and often expensive) undertaking by both professional teams and colleges that must be completed and distributed before a season begins. A media guide should be utilized by the media as a preseason tool to allow the journalists to write features on players and coaches and generate stories about the team. It is also handy throughout the season as a resource for the media and thus should include *everything* a journalist would need to know about the team and its athletes.

Such valuable items as a team directory (administration) and phone numbers; biographies of key front-office personnel (administrators); a preseason forecast of strengths and weaknesses (perhaps broken down position by position); a schedule located in an area of the guide that is easily accessible (front, back cover, page 1); biographies and statistical breakdowns of each player and coach; coach's thoughts on each player; game, season, and career records; playoff history; and year-by-year results are all appropriate material for a media guide. A professional team may want to list every player whoever played for the organization. Head-and-shoulder pictures of current players, coaches, and administrators are usually included. College guides, which also serve as recruiting guides, tend to be flashier and generally include several action pictures.

In addition, college teams may want to list the following information: directions to campus, All-Americans, professional players, game-by-game results from the previous year, letter winners, and individual and team success within a league or conference. Also, many universities include such information as famous nonathletic alumni, athletic facilities, academic support, training and medical staff, weight-training resources, and a capsule of each opponent with that team's schedule.

Most professional leagues dictate the size of the media guide; for example, Major League Baseball's team guides must be 4 1/4″ × 9″. That is actually a size that has become standard throughout professional sport. College sports, on the other hand, usually produce a slick, 8 1/2″ × 11″ guide that is also used as a recruiting guide for each team. In the mid-1980s, the National Collegiate Athletic Association (NCAA) stepped in and determined that a college or university could not send both a media guide and recruiting guide to a prospective student-athlete. Therefore, the media guide became the sole glamour piece for coaches to use in the recruiting process. The NCAA also mandated that athletic publications could only be printed in one color, except on the inside and outside covers. This eliminated competition among the larger, wealthier schools, which had started to print color pictures of all players, coaches, and support personnel.

These guides are not only valuable to the media (their originally intended audience) and college coaches, but also to alumni, legislators, fans, and collectors, who have shown an increasing interest in recent years. Since these guides can cost in excess of $25,000 to produce each year, many professional and college teams have started to charge for nonmedia requests.

The Postseason Media Guide

If a team has done well and has advanced to postseason play, an expanded set of pregame notes will not suffice. Instead, a postseason media guide is in order. This guide will have a cover different from the preseason guide and may include action photographs of key athletes taken during the season. The guide will include updated game-by-game season and career statistics with notes and honors that may have occurred during the recently concluded regular season. Depending upon space, it could also include game-by-game reports, newspaper articles, and roster changes. On the collegiate level, attention could be given to national rankings.

A postseason guide cannot be produced in one or two days. If a postseason guide is needed for a particular volleyball team, for example, the media relations director should have realized early in the season that the team had a good chance to participate in the postseason. Every week, single-game data, that is, stat sheets and newspaper stories, should have been mass-reproduced and stored, awaiting the end of the season. At that point, a major section of the guide, the game-by-game results, would have been copied, and the media relations director would have a jump on the postseason media guide.

Game Programs

Everyone's been to a game and heard the hawker yell, "Programs here! You can't tell the players without a program!" How true, how true. A **game program** must be available for the fan and media for every event in which the individual athlete is identifiable, that is, has a uniform number or a specific order of competition. Football, basketball, baseball, softball, and volleyball, for example, all supply uniforms with numbers. There must be some means for the fan and the media to identify who is in competition. If other sports, such as wrestling or gymnastics, have a specific order of competition, a program is useful. Some sports (professional golf and tennis) produce a "yearbook" that is sold under the guise of a program. Flashy and magnificently printed with pictures, biographical data, and statistical reports of the players, these are great souvenirs for the fans—but they are not actually game programs.

The scope of a game program varies among professional sport and college teams. Certainly, a numerical roster from both teams is a must; in fact, it is the only absolute necessity in the program. Everything else—feature stories on players, administrators, former greats, support staff, and national coverage—adds to the breadth and glamour of the publication. Many teams reprint material from their media guide. Items such as alphabetical rosters; future schedules; and location of restrooms, first aid stations, disability services, and lost and found areas are extremely important to fans and media and should be included if possible.

Some professional sport leagues have contracted game programs to large national companies that publish these mammoth books for every team in the league. However, in nearly every college and university in the nation, the responsibility for the game program falls under the job description of media relations. The advent of desktop publishing has allowed much of the work to be done in-house. A¹ ·o, national firms have emerged that, at a cost, will supply each college or university with an attractive, full-color supplement that is stapled into the game program, expanding the game program by as many as 64 pages. These include national features and advertisements that make interesting reading. A small college that could only afford to print a 12-page program would thus be able to add a glamorous 64-page insert at a minimal cost, giving it a very presentable game program for fans.

Local advertising must be sold in order to offset the cost of production. The advertisements, ordinarily solicited by the media relations office on the college level, can be systematically scattered throughout each program or else can be located in a special advertising section. Although very few professional sport teams or large colleges sell advertising in their media guides, it is unusual to see a game program that does *not* include advertising.

Promoting the Special Athlete

Professional athletes become known to the media as a result of constant national exposure. From the time a professional athlete is a rookie, he or she is covered by national television and newspapers on a daily basis. Most college athletes, on the other hand, rarely have the daily exposure of the professional athlete and consequently require an additional "push" to make them known to the people who vote for postseason awards. Although additional promotion is advisable in professional sport, college sports really requires the extra effort by the media relations staff in order for an athlete to achieve such awards as Player of the Year. To be sure, professional media relations people must prepare reams of literature if they are to promote one of their athletes as a Most Valuable Player, Rookie of the Year, or All-Star; however, most of the people who vote see all of the athletes in the league, live or on television, a number of times, so the athlete is already a known commodity.

The college athlete, however, can be a virtual unknown to many voters and *must* be promoted to have a chance at such awards as All-American. First and foremost, the athlete must be more than a "press player," that is, an individual who receives all kinds of publicity, is inconsistent in competition, and offers excuses for poor performances. Just because a coach wants an athlete to be named an All-American does not mean the athlete is worthy of all of the additional work that must be done by the media relations staff.

The media relations director must keep the athlete in front of all voters throughout the season. The "campaign" for All-American must begin preseason. If a media relations director decides to start an All-American promotion two-thirds of the way through the season, the effort will be wasted. During the preseason the media relations staff must try to get the athlete mentioned in national preseason magazines. If the athlete is a candidate for Player of the Year, it is beneficial to have that athlete's picture appear on the cover of one of these publications. Also during the preseason the media relations staff must acquire a list of the names and addresses of the voters for all of the postseason awards. Of course, the candidate must be highlighted in his or her school's own media guide.

Each week of the season, the athlete should be nominated for weekly all-star teams organized by the conference office. Weekly news releases highlighting exceptional efforts and admiring quotes from other coaches and reporters should be generated and mailed, faxed, or e-mailed to the voters. There will obviously be some voters who have never had the opportunity to see the athlete in action. Budget permitting, produce a highlight video of the star to send to these voters. Also, desktop publishing will enable a media relations staff to print personalized flyers highlighting the successes of the athlete. Most of the voting is completed a week or so before the season has ended, so *the final, major push should be completed with a month remaining in the season.*

It is much easier to promote an athlete for postseason honors in sports in which committees of coaches have postseason teleconference calls to make selections. Mailing weekly material to the voting coaches should suffice in such cases. The fairest manner of All-American selection occurs in such sports as track and field, swimming, and gymnastics, in which designated top finishers at a national championship are named to an All-American team.

The One-on-One Interview

Most professional leagues have specific stipulations regarding athletes and how they communicate with the media. Even some professional athletes have been known to have problems conducting themselves in an appropriate manner with members of the media, so each athlete should be schooled in terms of proper behavior when meeting the media. Sport agents and professional teams, such as the Dallas Cowboys, have also begun to hire media coaches (consultants) to work with their athletes and coaches (Dunkel, 1997). Often these media coaches are called in to assist an athlete or a team to properly address the press after a crisis, but more and more they are being used to help players work with the media to create a positive image for marketing purposes (Thurow, 1996).

Most Division I colleges require the media relations director to meet with teams to educate the athletes on what is appropriate or inappropriate when communicating with the media. First, not one person involved in media relations should ever give a member of the media an athlete's home/apartment/residence hall phone number. If a media member desires an interview with an athlete, the college's media relations professional should arrange a time and a place where the athlete and journalist will meet. Many coaches set aside a time period prior to practice for media interviews. Otherwise, the athlete could call the media person (collect) after hours at a time convenient to the athlete. If all athletes are aware of this policy, they will know that an unexpected phone call from a stranger who claims to be a journalist is not legitimate.

The athlete should be told that everything that is said to a journalist should be positive. Athletes must not be negative about their teammates or coaches and, most important, must never say anything negative about an opponent. (Negative comments about an opposing team become what is known in the business as "bulletin board material" and can be used by opposing coaches to create psychological warfare.) Also, athletes should never discuss injuries with the media.

The Press Conference

There are occasions when a general news release—mailed, faxed or e-mailed—will not do justice to the magnitude of an announcement, such as when a new coach, general manager, or president is being named to a professional team or an athletic director or head coach is being named to a marquis sport for a college or university. This is the time for a **press conference**. Once a decision has been made on a major hiring—for example, a professional sport head coach—the organization should not procrastinate, but should make the announcement as quickly as possible to keep the media from reporting incorrect data or rumors. For example, if a decision is made at 11:00 AM on Monday to hire a new women's basketball coach, it would be foolish to wait and hold the press conference on Thursday or Friday. When all involved parties are in place—that is, the new coach and the top administrators for the organization—announce the press conference. In the example, late Monday or early Tuesday would be the most desirable.

After the exact time and venue are determined, a fax should be sent to all media indicating the specifics in terms of day, time, and location. A follow-up call to media close to the organization would be a courtesy. The organization should then determine who will speak and whether to make food available. Media should have access to phone lines and fax machines. A fact sheet or general news release detailing the involved individuals, their backgrounds, and quotes from high-ranking individuals within the organization is a must. Also, it is wise to have a photographer present representing the organization.

Ethics

Every media relations person on the college level should be aware of the Buckley Amendment (the Family Educational Rights and Privacy Act of 1974). Indeed, every athlete, every year, on every level of competition should be asked to sign a disclaimer, which should be printed on each publicity form, so the media relations director is free to disseminate material pertinent to the athletic accomplishments of that athlete. Should an athlete choose not to sign the waiver, the media relations director will not be allowed to mention the athlete in any news release or publication produced by the media relations office. However, any time the athlete steps on the field, the court, the track, or the mat and is in the public eye, the media is allowed to write what they see and feel. Even if an athlete signs the waiver, which is the norm rather than the exception, it is still *not* permissible for a media relations professional to divulge such items as grades or personal history. If an athlete is an exceptionally high-calibre student and is the recipient of academic awards, that data may be released only with the consent of the athlete, even though the data are positive material for both the individual and the institution. An example from the negative side: If an athlete who is considered a professional prospect with a future worth of several millions of dollars is injured but decides that the injury should not be made public, that request must be honored.

Crisis Management

The degree to which the media relations specialist becomes involved with crisis management will vary. Professional sport general managers and college athletic directors should include the media relations person in all meetings related to problems occurring within the organization. The front office will eventually inform media relations of the need for a press conference or news release, but it is most advantageous to keep the media relations staff aware of any problems from the outset.

On the professional level, the media relations person has to deal with the high-salaried athlete and his or her willingness to meet with the media. College athletes may refuse to meet with certain media, which forces the head coach to become involved. Both college and professional organizations have become more aware of legal rights of the individuals and have referred any statements regarding legal matters to the university news bureau or legal counsel. On the professional level, many teams, lawyers, and agents are now using media coaches (consultants) to work with those involved in a crisis to formulate the best response to the media and the public (Dunkel, 1997).

Should a problem arise, the media relations specialist can best serve his or her organization by being available for any meetings, producing an organized press conference, and being aware of the "party line" in terms of what to say or not to say to the media.

CONTEST MANAGEMENT

The Home Game

Unlike professionals in other areas of athletic administration, a media relations specialist does not arrange for site preparation, towels, or security. The media relations professional is only concerned with the activities of the media before, during, and after a game. Most colleges or universities will treat **media relations contest management** for their major teams differently than they would for those followed by fewer people. In many cases football and men's and women's basketball are the sports that command the major media coverage, but at some universities the major sports may include baseball or ice hockey. The attention given to an event before, during, and after the contest will place that event into either a "formal" or "informal" category. All professional sports, as well as Division I college football and men's and women's basketball games, are considered formal. Much of the information regarding the responsibilities of a media relations person for football or men's and women's basketball can be applied to other sports, so this section will concentrate on these three areas since they traditionally receive the majority of attention from the media.

The working press room for basketball should be in an area that does not allow access to the general public. Most football press boxes have restricted entry. However, not all indoor arenas were designed to give the media adequate working conditions. A working press room should be an area where the media can congregate before the contest. All game notes, statistics, programs, and announcements should be available in this area. Additionally, a working press room should have an adequate number of telephones available for postgame calls and filing via computer or fax machine. A high-speed copy machine should also be located in this area.

Many members of the media travel a distance to attend an event and will remain at the venue for several hours. Budgets notwithstanding, some kind of food should be provided. The food can be as simple as coffee, soft drinks, and sandwiches or as fancy as a hot buffet.

All events, either formal or informal, will have some source to identify the athletes, such as a program or roster sheet. A roster sheet could suffice for most informal events, but a major publication is needed for a formal event (see the section of this chapter called Publications). Press passes, usually color-coded by event, season, or personnel, must be distributed prior to the event or left at the designated "Press Will Call" area. There will be distinct passes for writers, photographers, television people, and those people running the event. Some passes may specify press box only, field access, or all access. The media relations director should have some way to communicate with the person in "Press Will Call" in the event a problem arises. If phone lines are impossible, the walkie-talkie is a perfect stand-in. If at all possible, press parking should also be available so the media do not worry about parking conditions. A separate parking pass, a stub attached to the press pass, or a list left with the parking attendant at a specified lot is critical. The media should also have a separate entry area to the venue rather than that used by the general public.

A press box for a football game or a press row for a basketball game takes time and care to orchestrate. Phone lines must be ordered for radio and television. If there are multiple radio stations involved in live play-by-play, the seats of these stations need to be spaced apart from each other. Seat location for television talent is fairly simple: Basketball announcers should be at center court, while football talent should have a private area in the press box. Media relations personnel should be located in an area that allows for easy access. Name tags must be placed at all seats, and a seating chart needs to be formulated and placed in various locations of the working press room. Statisticians should be located in an area allowing them to perform their task smoothly. They should be located at the scorer's table for a basketball game and in a prime viewing area of a football press box. Statistics should be provided to the media at normal breaks in the action: at halftime, after a quarter or period, or at a TV time out. Statistics compiled via computer will allow quicker distribution than those compiled manually. In addition to his or her other responsibilities, the media relations director is usually in charge of hiring such important day-of-game employees as the public address announcer, the official scorer, the television time out coordinator, statistics runners for live electronic media, and cable pullers for television camera people.

The head media relations person *should not have a specific responsibility during a contest*. That individual should be available to anybody, for anything. The individual should act as a troubleshooter and not be tied to any one specific task. A seat close to center court for a basketball game or in the middle of the press box for football is desirable.

Postgame interviews must be coordinated by a media relations person. Most media relations people will poll the media near the end of a game to determine which athletes need to be interviewed. It has become common practice to allow a short "cooling off" period of usually 10 minutes from the time the team and coaching staff enter the locker room and close the door. After that time period has elapsed, the athletes are brought to a formal interview room where they address questions from the media. Some professional organizations and universities also allow members of the media to enter the locker room after the formal interview room process has been completed. Training rooms are off limits to members of the media, and some athletes may "hide" in the training room in order to avoid the questions of the media. Many organizations will have a media relations professional moderate the postgame press conference. Another member of the media relations staff could be present at the postevent press conference to compile, type, collate, and distribute notes.

The Road Contest

When a team travels, the media relations director should only be concerned with meeting with the media in the road city to acquaint them with the visiting team. The media relations directors communicate ahead of time to ensure the host director had all of the game notes, statistics, and a list of the traveling media. The host media relations director should prepare a packet that includes a press pass for the game, reports on recent games, current cumulative statistics, a team media guide, pregame notes, rosters, and a game program. The packet should include material for both teams. To make sure they are received, the host media relations director could have an intern deliver these packets to the hotel in which the media will stay. This information allows the media to prepare advance stories and may eliminate time-consuming, unproductive phone calls. If the courtesy of hotel delivery is impossible, this material should be available in the host media relations office or in the working press room well ahead of game time.

Once the contest begins, everything should go smoothly, all the details having been arranged by the host director (see The Home Game section, above). At game's end the visiting director may have to escort coaches and athletes into the interview room, but everything else should be done by the host director and the director's staff.

When a media relations professional travels with an "Olympic" sport, that is, soccer, field hockey, or gymnastics, the media attention is less intense and the workload for the traveling media relations person is more involved. (The media relations person should bring game notes and media guides to the contest in the event that a member of the media is present.) The media relations person may have to take notes of the contest, make postevent calls to the hometown electronic media, write a story on a computer and transmit it via modem to various newspapers, and fax a summary back to the home office, where students may be waiting to update statistics and/or notes. If at all possible, calls to the local media should come from someone who is at the event site, allowing the reporter at home to get data from an individual who witnessed the event. In a bind, the traveling representative of the media relations office may transmit the story to the home office and have interns or assistants then notify all local media of the contest outcome, but this "relay" system is undesirable since the results are being reported in a secondhand fashion. If a journalist has a question not covered in the transmission, it will be impossible to get an answer from the "relay" person. This is referred to as the **"one-call system,"** and it is not as effective as having all calls originate from the venue of the contest.

There will be many road trips for which no representative of the media relations office accompanies a team. In such cases a coach, assistant coach, manager, or athlete will be asked to report results back to the media. Prior to each season, coaches should receive a list of local media that need to be called (collect) with road results. This sheet should include the name of the media, the phone number, and the deadline. If there are several calls to be made (more than four or five), the one-call system is acceptable. And coaches must remember to make the calls— *win or lose!*

Hosting a Postseason Championship

A professional team can be involved in a playoff series, forcing anywhere from 3 to 12 additional games onto the plate of the media relations staff. Ordinarily, little has to be done in terms of promotion for these playoff or championship games, but game-day personnel, photographers, credentials, seating charts, postseason guides and notes, and working press rooms must be organized. The league is usually responsible for the production of game programs, eliminating a major undertaking from the workload of the media relations staff.

On the college level, when the university's athletic department has bid a high enough financial figure to win the rights to host a postseason championship, the media relations office must promote and publicize this event. News releases should be transmitted and mailed to all media announcing the dates, times, participants, and ticket prices. A pre-event press conference or luncheon should be conducted to publicize the event. Local coaches involved with the sport should attend, in addition to the administrators from the host institution. Media relations personnel from competing institutions need to be contacted to determine rosters, availability of photographs, and lists of attending media. Credentials need to be printed for media, photographers, and administrators. A media area must be designated with telephones, extra phone lines, and copy and fax machines. Food and drink should be ordered and should be available throughout the championship in a media hospitality area. Game-day personnel, including a photographer, must be assigned. Seating charts also need to be established.

If an institution has known for nearly a year that it will be hosting a postseason championship, a sufficient amount of time is available for preparation. However, if a regional or even national event is given to a college with two or three weeks' notice, the media relations office must act quickly. Aside from all of the items mentioned above, some kind of an event program, suitable for distribution/sale to the public, must be printed. This could vary from a simple roster sheet with statistics, results, and game notes, to a rather extensive publication with advertising, pictures, and the history of the event. Fortunately for individual institutions, in the early 1990s the NCAA hired Host Communications of Lexington, Kentucky, to produce championship programs for all major national events. Host Communications compiles rosters; biographies and photographs of players, coaches, and administrators; statistics; and results. Any university that is a contender for postseason play is contacted by Host midway through a season. The material is gathered, placed on disk, and is ready for print when the teams are determined. Keep in mind, this service is *not* available for regional events in every sport. Similar to the professional league office's assuming this responsibility for professional sports, the assignment of event programs to an organization such as Host Communications eliminates a considerable amount of work for the media relations staff.

The Game's on TV!

Contest management differs when a game is being televised. Space must be provided for one or two television trucks, each the size of an 18-wheeler. This space must be close enough to the venue to allow for the massive amount of television cable to be hauled into the venue. Additional credentials must be provided for all television personnel. The seating chart must accommodate the talent (announcers) and, in most instances, a stage manager and statistician. An additional seat near the regular game stat crew must be provided for a TV statistician. That person relays statistics to the TV truck. The TV outlet will also ask the media relations office to supply cable pullers for the camera operators and, most important of all, a TV time out coordinator for those sports that work on a time clock. This individual must know the sport and must know the television business. The TV time out coordinator controls the flow of the game and is as important to contest management as the referees.

A pregame format (Exhibit 15–1) that details the start of the pregame clock, when teams start practice, when they return to the locker room, when the anthem is played, and when the starting lineups are announced is distributed to both teams, all contest personnel, and the media. The scoreboard operator and PA announcer are critical if the pregame format is to be followed. This format is usually broken down into hundredths of a second and is done in coordination with the TV clock.

If there is extra time at the end of the televised contest, the affiliate may decide it needs to speak to the winning coach before the coach goes to the locker room with the team. Assuming this possibility was communicated to the coach before the game and he or she agreed to it, a member of the media relations staff should

Exhibit 15–1 Example of a Pregame Format

UNIVERSITY OF MASSACHUSETTS VS. DUQUESNE
MEN'S BASKETBALL
FEBRUARY 6, 1997

Television: Atlantic 10 Network
Radio: UMass Network, UMass Student Station
National Anthem: Robert Lord
Halftime: Court Club Shootout; SNET Game Sponsor Recognition;
                      Field Hockey Team Recognition

SCRIPT

ACTUAL TIME	CLOCK TIME	DESCRIPTION
7:02PM	30:00	Floor Available
7:22PM	10:00	Teams Leave Floor
7:23PM	9:00	National Anthem
7:28PM	4:00	Team Return to Floor
7:32PM	0:00	Sound Horn/Clear Floor
7:33PM	0:00	Introduction of Starters
7:34PM	20:00	Pregame Huddle
7:35PM	20:00	TIPOFF

(Electronic media timeouts will take place at the 16-, 12-, 8-, and 4-minute marks of each half.)

---

escort the coach to the area on the court in which the informal interview will take place.

CAREER OPPORTUNITIES

Anyone interested in media relations, either on the college level or professional sport level, needs to get involved in media relations early in his or her college life. Volunteering in a media relations or sports information office as a college freshman is a wise first step. Being able to list four years of undergraduate experience on a resume is critical. Although an individual may have to volunteer in the first year, student funds may become available as responsibilities are increased.

With four years of undergraduate work on the resume, the aspiring media relations professional may be able to land an assistant's position at either the college or professional level. However, it is more likely that the person would have to become involved with either a graduate assistantship or full-time internship before landing a full-time position. Most colleges cannot afford to hire all of the full-time media relations staff they need; therefore, they will hire interns and pay these interns as well, if not better, than other internships in the sport industry. Professional teams will usually take interns, but most professional teams do not believe that they have an obligation to pay the intern.

The field of media relations is wide open. It is a profession that continues to employ as many women as men. People entering sports media relations should understand that this is not a five-day, 40-hour-per-week profession. In fact, it is not unusual for a media relations professional to be either in the office or at an event for six to seven months without a day off. People should be aware of the time commitment prior to entering the field, as such hours clearly can impact on both social life and family life.

CURRENT ISSUES

Technology

E-mail, the World Wide Web, home pages, **fax on demand**, and **fax back** are examples of modern technology that have allowed media relations professionals to inform their constituencies almost instantaneously of the progress of their team or college. Fax on demand and fax back allow a reporter to dial a specific phone number and have material electronically downloaded to his or her fax machine. All media are able to dial a number that will return to their own fax machines lists of statistical data or fact sheets. Home pages must be updated on a daily basis to guarantee that the media have current material. Some professional teams and NCAA Division I colleges will hire a professional with computer expertise who will update these items with pertinent material. To be sure, many of these organizations have eliminated the costly and time-consuming process of printing, folding, stuffing, and mailing general news releases. Instead, after a news release has been constructed it is added to the organization's website and made available through fax on demand. When statistical reports are computer-generated they are made available to the media via fax on demand or fax back. Again, interns or full-time assistants with computer knowledge are extremely valuable for this constant updating.

SUMMARY

In terms of specific skills, the media relations professional needs to have the ability to create news releases and publications. In addition, the individual should have an above-average knowledge of the sport or sports in which he or she is involved, and the knowledge of computer programs for statistical packages, word processing, e-mail, and desktop publishing is imperative. As far as "soft" skills are concerned, the media relations person must be able to retain positive relationships with athletes, coaches, administrators, fans, and most important, the media. During various times of the year, the media relations professional should be prepared to work seven days a week, 70 hours a week.

Several years ago, a well-regarded media relations director at an NCAA Division I institution was asked what he did the most. The answer? "Get interrupted!" The media relations director may be in the middle of producing a major publication when a reporter calls to ask a question. The response cannot be, "Call back. I'm busy."

CASE STUDY: ATHLETES INVOLVED IN AN OFF-CAMPUS INCIDENT: AN APPROPRIATE RESPONSE?

As director of media relations for an NCAA Division I hockey institution, you wake up one morning and hear a radio report that two of your star players and a recruit were arrested the night before for driving the wrong way down a one-way street. In addition, they could not convince the police that standard equipment in their vehicle included a microwave oven and expensive stereo components!

As it turns out, the two hockey players had taken the recruit to an off-campus party. They left the party and went to the apartment of a former girlfriend of one of the players. After words were exchanged, the players removed some of her appliances. The former girlfriend called the local police, who apprehended the hockey players.

How did this story get to the media before the University's Director of Media Relations was informed? A local newspaper, in making its normal rounds for the "Police Blotter," called the local police station and received this report. Inasmuch as the names of the hockey players were recognizable, the newspaper treated this with more weight than an ordinary college town incident. After the report appeared in the local paper, it was picked up by Associated Press, which meant that every affiliate, print and electronic, had the story.

The hockey coach and athletic director were notified early in the morning, but the athletic director's decision was to consider this a nonathletic university affair of no concern to the athletic department. Hence, the university's news bureau would handle all inquiries from the media, and no one from the athletic department would be available to the media. Nothing would be addressed by the athletic media relations office.

QUESTIONS FOR DISCUSSION

1. Is the athletic director correct in assuming that this is a nonathletic university affair and of no concern to the athletic department?
2. Should the media relations director have been consulted before the athletic director made the decision to have the university's news bureau handle all inquiries? Why or why not?
3. What are the benefits in having the university news bureau handle this incident? What are the detriments?

RESOURCES

Baseball Writers Association of America
78 Olive Street
Lake Grove, NY 11755
516-981-7938

College Sports Information Directors Association (CoSIDA)
Campus Box 114A
Kingsville, TX 78363
512-593-3908; fax: 512-592-0389

Football Writers Association of America
PO Box 909
Bloomington, IN 47402
812-332-4401; fax: 812-331-4383

National Association of Collegiate Directors of Athletics (NACDA)
24651 Detroit Road
Westlake, OH 44145
216-892-4000; fax: 216-892-4007

National College Baseball Writers Association
University of Florida
PO Box 14485
Gainesville, FL 32604
352-375-4683; fax: 352-375-4809

Professional Basketball Writers Association of America
30 Oakland Park Blvd.
Pleasant Ridge, MI 48069
313-222-2260

Professional Hockey Writers Association
Buffalo News
1 News Plaza
Buffalo, NY 14240
716-849-4461; fax: 716-856-5150

For the address of the U.S. Olympic Committee see Chapter 10, International Sport, and for the addresses of professional league offices see Chapter 12, Professional Sport.

REFERENCES

Dunkel, T. (March, 1997). Out of the mouths of jocks. *Sky*, 97–103.

Thurow, R. (1996, February 9). The 76ers are lowly, but Jerry Stackhouse scores big in marketing. *The Wall Street Journal*, pp. A1, A4.

CHAPTER 16

Sport Broadcasting

Tim Ashwell

Key words: broadcast rights, Alvin "Pete" Rozelle, Roone Arledge, cost per thousand (CPM), audience research, designated market areas (DMAs), rating, share, cume, demographic segments, total return, ESPN, Internet

INTRODUCTION

The electronic media—television, radio, and digital computer technology— have utterly transformed the sport industry and its relationship with the public. Until the development of radio broadcasting in the 1920s and television broadcasting in the 1930s, the only people who could witness a game as it was being played were the fans who paid their way into the ballpark. If the event was important enough, say, a heavyweight championship boxing match or the baseball World Series, the most eager nonattending fans gathered outside newspaper offices or in hotel ballrooms to monitor the Western Union telegraph circuit for the latest bulletins from the stadium. The rest of the public waited for the story in the morning paper to find out who won and what happened.

Today, sports fans can watch events unfold around the world as they happen. Images and sounds of every major event—and many not so major ones—flash into our homes at the speed of light, and we have come to expect the instant replays, dazzling computerized graphics, and expert commentary that accompany the games. When Donovan Bailey crossed the finish line in Atlanta's Olympic Stadium in the summer of 1996 to win the gold medal in the 100-meter dash, viewers in Canada saw it as it happened. So, too, did vast audiences watching in Africa, Europe, Asia, and the Americas. Thanks to advanced video technology, fans not only saw the race and Bailey's triumphant victory lap in lifelike color, they saw it replayed in slow motion, from several different camera angles, and in extreme close-up. The view at home was, in fact, far superior to that of any fan in the stadium. Most of the fans in attendance watched the race replayed on television, too, on giant video screens showing the details they could not see in real life.

If broadcasting has changed the way fans experience sport, it has also profoundly altered the business of sport. Television and radio organizations around the world pay billions of dollars for the **broadcast rights** to sporting events, and sports organizations gain priceless exposure, publicity, and status by being showcased by the electronic media. Broadcast revenues have fueled the explosive growth of spectator sports since World War II, and the search for new audiences and new revenues has spurred professional league expansion, college conference realignment, and the era of franchise relocation. Major League Baseball's fractious battle between large-market and small-market clubs is largely due to differences in local television revenue paid to teams in major metropolitan areas and those in smaller cities. The financial success of the National Football League (NFL) can be traced to the league's decision to pool and divide equally its network television revenue, ensuring financial stability of teams in cities as huge as New York and as small as Green Bay, Wisconsin.

The sport industry and the broadcasting business are closely allied in a symbiotic relationship. While sport organizations rely on broadcasters for revenue and publicity, the electronic media know that sporting events are a sure-fire means of attracting the audiences that advertisers will pay to reach. Popular sporting events also lend prestige to the radio and television organizations associated with them. The FOX television network used its contract with the NFL to prove to advertisers, station operators, and the public that it was a major network. In small towns across the country, local radio stations air hometown college and high school games to prove they care about their communities. Broadcasters also know sports programming is a proven way to convince consumers to invest in new technology or purchase additional services from existing media. For more than 75 years, promoters of new communications systems, from radio in the 1920s to direct satellite television broadcasting and the Internet today, have understood that the lure of sport, the opportunity to get more information faster about more games and events, could convince hundreds of millions of consumers to spend tens of billions of dollars on new equipment.

The Electronic Media

All electronic media—radio, television, computer data transmitted on the Internet—function in fundamentally the same manner (Head, Sterling, & Schofield, 1994). Sound and images are captured by electronic devices (microphones and cameras) and electronically encoded. The information is then transmitted at the speed of light via land lines such as fiber-optic and coaxial cable or through the air by broadcast transmitters or satellites to a receiver, where it is decoded and transformed back to sound and images that can be heard through speakers or seen on a video screen. A local radio broadcast of a high school football game might involve a single announcer speaking into one microphone linked by telephone lines to equipment at the radio station and then transmitted to receivers within range of the station. A Super Bowl telecast involves dozens of cameras and microphones augmented by videotape recorders, computerized graphics, and special effects units operated by hundreds of skilled engineers and technicians. The signal is then flashed from the game site to a communications satellite orbiting nearly 23,000 miles over the earth and relayed to network headquarters in New York or California. The game broadcast, augmented by commercials, promotional announcements, and material presented live in studios at network headquarters, is then distributed via satellite to local stations across the country, which add their own commercial announcements and transmit the complete program to viewers in their area. If people subscribe to cable television, the local station's signal is received by the cable company—which may add its own local commercials to the mix—and transmitted to their homes through a network of wires. The entire process takes less than a second.

All that electronic information can also be recorded for use at a later time. Electromagnetic impulses depicting the sound and images of a sporting event can be embedded on audio- and videotape or transformed into computer language of bits and bytes and preserved on computer disks. This allows broadcasters to replay highlights or entire games at any time in the future. It also allows fans to search the Internet and summon recordings of crucial plays or postgame interviews. Computer programs also allow the images to be manipulated in countless ways. Images created by computer can be inserted to allow Michael Jordan to play basketball with Bugs Bunny, as in the movie *Space Jam*. Electronic media technology has advanced to the point that if someone can imagine a sound or sight he or she would like to hear or see, it can be created.

THE HISTORY OF SPORT BROADCASTING

Electronic communications began with the telegraph and the telephone. The first operational telegraph, a 40-mile circuit between Washington, D.C., and Baltimore, was opened in 1844 by Samuel F.B. Morse (Head et al., 1994). Morse sent messages along a wire by opening and closing an electrical circuit in a series of dots and dashes representing letters and numbers. In 1876, Alexander Graham Bell demonstrated his telephone, using a simple microphone to transmit sound along wires (Head et al., 1994). Both inventions relied on electricity and conductive wires, and since scientists knew that electricity could also travel through the atmosphere without wires, many inventors around the world set to work to develop wireless communications. In 1888, German physicist Heinrich Hertz published the results of an experiment proving that radio waves could be generated, transmitted, and detected. While Hertz failed to understand the implications of his work, many others did not. Within a decade, several wireless transmission systems had been devised, the most famous by Guglielmo Marconi, who patented his device in 1896 (Head et al., 1994).

By World War I the "wireless" (radio) was a well-established fact of life, a standard method of communication for business and government as well as a valuable military asset. Thanks to the new invention, messages could be sent across the ocean and over inaccessible terrain beyond the reach of telephone or telegraph wires. Major corporations, including General Electric and American Telephone & Telegraph, as well as American Marconi, a subsidiary of Marconi's British company, developed improved transmitters and receivers, and soon messages were flashing around the world at the speed of light. Unfortunately, the corporations agreed, there was one problem with the wireless: Once a message was transmitted, anyone within range who had a receiver tuned to the proper frequency could hear the message. It seemed to be an insurmountable problem. Why would anyone want to send a message through the air that thousands, perhaps millions, of people could listen to?

A few visionaries understood that the perceived weakness of the wireless would prove to be its greatest virtue (Douglas, 1987). One was a Westinghouse Electric Company executive named Harry Davis, whose company had a warehouse full of World War I surplus radio receivers. Perhaps, he reasoned, if a wireless station broadcast entertainment and news programs every day on a fixed schedule, people would buy his receivers and listen. On November 2, 1920, the evening of the presidential election, radio station KDKA signed on from studios at the Westinghouse plant in Pittsburgh to broadcast the returns as well as some musical entertainment, and the radio boom of the 1920s was under way (Barnouw, 1966–1970).

Radio broadcasting took the United States, and much of the rest of the world, by storm. For the first time, listeners could hear events as they happened, and some of the most important early broadcasts involved sporting events. KDKA broadcast the first baseball game on August 5, 1921, an 8–5 Pirates victory over the Philadelphia Phillies at Forbes Field in Pittsburgh. WJZ in Newark, New Jersey, broadcast the heavyweight title fight between Jack Dempsey and George Carpentier and the Yankees–Giants World Series later that same year. By the end of the 1920s, virtually every major baseball and football game and boxing match as well as dozens of other lesser events were broadcast locally or across the country on networks of radio stations linked by telephone lines. Network radio—or "chain broadcasting" as it was called in the early days—allowed many local stations across the country to broadcast the same event. This had the obvious advantage of allowing listeners across the country to hear a game or news event, but it also allowed advertisers to reach an audience far greater than any single station could reach.

Broadcasters understood that sports sold radios. One industry analyst estimated that $14 million was spent on radio receivers across the country in the days leading up to the second Dempsey–Gene Tunney heavyweight title fight in 1927. "The broadcast of a heavyweight title fight is the biggest boon that the industry can have," the *Boston Globe* reported following the fight. "In second place . . . the World Series baseball championship, then the more important football games, and then events of national importance such as national political conventions . . . and Presidential speeches" ("Fight Booms," 1927, p. 19). Sports were also among the first radio programs to attract sponsors willing to pay handsomely to have their products promoted in connection with the event. The Royal Typewriter Company paid a reported $30,000 to sponsor the first Dempsey–Tunney fight on a national network in 1926 ("The Dempsey–Tunney Fight," 1926).

At first, few teams profited directly from radio coverage. Gradually, however, sport managers began to understand the value of their product. Dempsey's promoter, Tex Rickard, was among the first to demand payments in exchange for the right to broadcast fights, but others quickly followed. By the 1930s, many colleges sold exclusive rights to their football games to a sponsor who in turn purchased radio time from broadcasters to air the games. Some baseball teams worried that radio broadcasts of home games would hurt attendance, but most agreed that radio games increased fan support and were a valuable publicity and promotional tool. Additionally, in the Depression era, cash payments from sponsors were always welcome. In 1938, the Pittsburgh Pirates sued a local radio station for broadcasting the team's games without permission and won (*Pittsburgh Athletic Co. v. KQV Broadcasting Co.*, 1938). It was a landmark case, establishing the right of sports organizations to control the broadcast rights to their events.

When television arrived on the scene following World War II, the pattern was similar. Broadcasters used sports to convince men to purchase televisions, which in turn created the male audiences advertisers desired (Rader, 1984). Set manufacturers supplied free televisions to bars, and retailers left televisions on in store windows to show consumers that they could now both hear and see their heroes in action. Advertisers such as Gillette, with its long-running series of Friday night boxing matches, as well as the leading auto makers and breweries, quickly jumped on board the sports television bandwagon. Two men dominated the growth of sport broadcasting in the 1960s and beyond: NFL commissioner **Alvin "Pete" Rozelle** and ABC executive **Roone Arledge**. Rozelle was only 33 years old when he became NFL commissioner in 1959; Arledge was 29 years old when he joined ABC in 1960. Each played a vital role in shaping the sport broadcasting industry.

Rozelle had been a publicist for the Los Angeles Rams prior to becoming commissioner. He knew both the broadcasting and advertising industries and sensed that the NFL was on the brink of cashing in on a coming sport broadcasting boom. Because he understood that television was driven by ratings and demographics, he knew the appeal of football. He also understood that large-market teams such as the New York Giants and Chicago Bears would soon be rolling in television revenues that teams in small cities such as the Green Bay Packers could never match. This, he feared, would create a competitive imbalance and might destroy the league. Throughout the 1950s, NFL teams had signed individual contracts with broadcasters with each team keeping the revenue it earned. Soon after taking office, Rozelle proposed a new idea: The NFL would pool its regular season and playoff television rights and sell them to the highest bidder. The revenue would then be divided equally among the teams. The first pooled network contract was signed in 1960 and promptly ruled in violation of antitrust laws by a federal judge. Rozelle was unfazed. Calling on his contacts in the television business as well as mobilizing the nation's professional sport teams and their fans, he pushed Congress to pass the Sports Broadcasting Act of 1961. The Act explicitly granted professional football, baseball, hockey, and basketball immunity from antitrust actions regarding the pooled sale of broadcast rights. The NFL immediately re-signed its contract with CBS, and today, thanks to the immunity granted by the 1961 law, NFL teams share annual television revenues of more than a billion dollars. And the small-market Green Bay Packers, who receive a share equal to the major-market teams, won the 1997 Super Bowl.

Arledge was an award-winning producer of children's programs at NBC when he jumped to ABC. His new network was by far the weakest of the three national chains, but Arledge wanted to produce sports and ABC gave him the opportunity. Television technology was evolving rapidly. Innovations such as color broadcasting and videotape recording as well as better cameras and more sensitive microphones were opening the door to new ideas, and Arledge had one. "Television has done a remarkable job of bringing the game to the viewer," he wrote in a famous memo to his new employers in 1960. "Now, we are going to take the viewer to the game" (Gunther, 1994, p. 17). Arledge proposed using television technology to capture the experience of sports—the color, the excitement, "the thrill of victory and the agony of defeat." Instead of simply showing the game, ABC cameras would show the fans in the stands, the exhausted players on the bench, the cheerleaders, the mascots. The idea, he explained, was to bring the viewer "up close and personal," to involve them emotionally with the contest. "In short," Arledge explained, "we are going to add show business to sports!" (Gunther, 1994, p. 18). Arledge understood that sports television could reach new heights if it broadened its appeal beyond the hard-core fan to the casual viewer. To reach that new audience, sports would have to feature drama, humor, character development, emotion, and, always, state-of-the-art production values. Sports, in other words, should be entertainment for those who might not care for the game but would enjoy the show.

Together, Rozelle and Arledge created one of the enduring hits of sports television: *ABC Monday Night Football*. When it debuted in 1970, *Monday Night Football* was a revolutionary concept. Pro football belonged on Sunday afternoons. Monday nights were for entertainment programs. Rozelle, however, saw an opportunity. CBS and NBC were already broadcasting NFL games on Sundays. Monday games would give the league an opportunity to forge a new broadcast partnership and open a new revenue channel. Arledge saw the chance to prove that football, in his hands, could be successful mass entertainment, and he was eager to break the CBS–NBC stranglehold on what was rapidly becoming the nation's favorite sport. Arledge turned *Monday Night Football* into a television extravaganza, using more cameras, more videotape machines, more announcers than ever before. In an inspired decision, he chose to use two color analysts: Don Meredith, the laid-back former Dallas Cowboy quarterback from Mount Vernon, Texas, and Howard Cosell, the abrasive and opinionated lawyer-turned-broadcaster from New York City. The unlikely pair of Dandy Don and Humble Howard was an immediate sensation, and *Monday Night Football* rocketed into the Nielsen Top Ten, where it remains today, the longest-running hit show on network television.

The huge ratings garnered by popular sport programming such as *Monday Night Football* and the Olympic Games led broadcasters to pursue the rights to additional sporting events. Many sport managers assumed rights fees would continue to spiral upward and eagerly sought television contracts. From the 1950s until the 1970s, the National Collegiate Athletic Association (NCAA) operated a television cartel, tightly controlling the broadcast rights to every game played by member schools. College games were rationed as the NCAA limited the number of times any one university could appear on television and distributed television revenue among its members. The Saturday game of the week, however, was a smash hit. People who were college football fans watched the game. It might not always be the game they wanted to watch, but it was the only game in town. By 1982, the NCAA football contract was worth $280 million, and major college football powers, realizing they were the principal attraction and hoping they could make that much or more themselves, sued the NCAA for the right to sell their broadcast rights themselves and keep all the money. The antitrust case went all the way to the U.S. Supreme Court, and the colleges won their freedom (*National Collegiate Athletic Association v. Board of Regents of the University of Oklahoma*, 1983). The NCAA television contract was dissolved, and colleges and conferences from coast to coast rushed to make their own deals.

Today, instead of a single game of the week, college fans can choose from literally dozens of broadcasts every Saturday. That is good news for fans, but the news for many colleges has been bad. Notre Dame, the most popular college football team of them all, was a big winner, signing a five-year, $75 million deal with NBC. Major conferences such as the Big 10 and Southeastern Conference also fared well, signing lucrative network pacts for broadcast rights to their games. Many smaller schools, however, found the brave new world of free market competition a harsh and unprofitable place. Teams from the Mid-American Conference and the Ivy League, for example, had been guaranteed occasional network appearances under the NCAA contract, but now they were on their own. As the number of games on television climbed, the football audience fragmented. Smaller audiences for each game meant less advertising revenue and lower rights fees for many colleges. By the 1990s, member schools of the Eastern Collegiate Athletic Conference were forced to pay $10,000 a week in production subsidies in order to televise a game of the week on a regional cable channel.

THE BUSINESS OF BROADCASTING

Technological wizardry makes sport broadcasting possible, but it is the economics of broadcasting that make sport broadcasting a reality. Broadcasting in the United States, and increasingly in countries around the world, is a business. Broadcasters, whether they are national television networks such as NBC or local radio stations with signals covering a single city, survive by attracting audiences and selling time to advertisers who want to sell those listeners and viewers—us— their wares. The bigger the audience, the more valuable the commercial time. The Super Bowl, which nets the largest television audience of the year, also features the most expensive advertising time: more than $1 million for a single 30-second announcement, or "spot." A 30-second commercial on a local radio station in a small town might retail for $10 or less. Advertisers, always seeking the most exposure for their money, measure advertising efficiency by calculating an advertisement's **cost per thousand**, or **CPM** ("M" symbolizes 1,000 in Roman numerals). This allows advertisers to gauge the relative efficiency of a high-cost advertisement that reaches a large audience and a less expensive spot that reaches a smaller audience. If an advertisement on a local television station costs $100 and reaches 10,000 viewers, the CPM is $10. A $250,000 spot on a network program reaching 25 million viewers also has a CPM of $10. While the size of the audience is vital, the demographic make-up of the audience is even more important. An advertiser who sells products to older women would not want to pay to advertise on a program that attracts an audience made up of young men. Every advertiser yearns to deliver the right message to the right audience at the right time for the best price. And broadcasters do their best to provide the programming that produces the audiences advertisers crave.

Because the broadcasting business is so closely tied to the advertising industry, **audience research** plays a vital role in deciding what sports get on the air. The leading broadcast media research firm in the United States today is the A.C. Nielsen Company (Nielsen Media Research, 1997). Founded in 1923, Nielsen first began measuring nationwide radio audiences in 1942 by attaching a device called an "Audimeter" to radio sets in a sample of 800 homes across the country. The Audimeter, developed in the 1930s by researchers at the Massachusetts Institute of Technology, mechanically recorded when the radio was turned on and off and noted where the dial was set. Today, Nielsen monitors television sets in approximately 5,000 homes across the country chosen to represent a statistical model of the nation with a computer-age version of the Audimeter called the "People Meter." The People Meter monitors what channel the set is tuned to, but it also measures who is watching. Each member of every "Nielsen family" is assigned a code number to punch in to the meter when he or she is watching television. Early every morning, the data collected by each People Meter is downloaded via telephone lines to computers at Nielsen's research center in Dunedin, Florida. By mid-morning, broadcast executives and advertising agencies who subscribe to Nielsen's service receive detailed breakdowns of who watched what the night before.

Nielsen divides the nation's nearly 97 million television households into 211 discrete units called **designated market areas,** or **DMAs**. The largest, New York City, encompasses over 6.7 million households in New York, New Jersey, Connecticut, and Pennsylvania. The smallest, Glendive, Montana, includes just 4,700 homes in rural eastern Montana. Nielsen defines each DMA by determining which local stations residents most often watch, a system that reflects the technical limitations of television. Because television signals, like FM radio signals, travel in a straight line, the coverage area of a station can be calculated by factoring its channel number or frequency, power, and the height of its transmitting tower above average terrain with topography and the curvature of the earth. The most powerful television stations—very high frequency (VHF) channels 2 through 6—can be seen about 65 miles from their transmitter. Stations at the upper end of the ultra high frequency (UHF) band—channels 41 through 69—can only reach about 30 miles. Currently, over 1,500 television stations are on the air in the United States, nearly 700 VHF stations and over 800 UHF broadcasters, all operating on assigned frequencies under licenses granted by the Federal Communications Commission (FCC). The FCC, established as an independent agency by the Communications Act of 1934, regulates the communications industry. In addition to broadcast television, it licenses 12,000 AM and FM radio stations and also regulates other communication media, including both wired and cellular telephone service. It replaced the Federal Radio Commission (FRC), which had been established by the Radio Act of 1927. The FRC was created after both the radio industry and the listening public complained that the radio dial was being choked with static and interference as new stations went on the air and interfered with existing broadcast signals. The commission's role was likened to that of a traffic officer. Today, television and radio stations are licensed to avoid interference with one another's signals and to create a mosaic of clear broadcast signals for viewers and listeners across the country.

Nielsen uses its People Meter data supplemented by viewer diaries and other research tools to measure national audiences as well as audiences in each DMA. Audience size is most often discussed in terms of ratings and shares. A program's **rating** represents the percentage of television households in the survey universe—whether the entire nation, a particular DMA, or a selection of DMAs—that is tuned into the program. A program with a national 22 rating, therefore, was watched by 22% of the nation's television homes. Each rating point represents 1% of the nation's television households, about 970,000 homes. Thus, a 22 rating means the program was viewed in 21.3 million homes (22 × 970,000). A program's **share** represents the percentage of the television households watching television at the time that are tuned in to the program. Obviously, not every television is on all the time. Viewing peaks during the prime time evening hours and is significantly lower during the day. While ratings and shares are the most often discussed audience measurements, Nielsen data also allows broadcasters to calculate their cumulative audience over time, a figure usually referred to as the **"cume."** This is an important number in sport broadcasting. A single telecast of a baseball game, for instance, may garner a small audience because only the most devoted fans watch every game. When the cumulative audience over the course of the season is calculated, however, the total numbers can be impressive. In radio, the weekly cume, the total number of people who tune in during a week, is the standard audience measurement. In addition to providing national and local audience counts, Neilsen and similar market research firms conduct surveys, focus groups, and other studies to further break down audiences by **demographic segments** along age, gender, and ethnic lines, as well as according to income, purchasing habits, and other lifestyle factors.

If audience research is science, the interpretation of data produced by Nielsen and other market research firms is an art. Broadcasters and advertising agencies constantly spar with Nielsen over the accuracy of its information and comb through the data to find the most positive information. Sport broadcasting has been an important programming feature of broadcasting largely because audience research confirms a widely held stereotype: Men love sports. While the audience for prime time television entertainment shows is typically 60% women, sports broadcasts routinely attract audiences that are 60% or 70% men. The sports audience is on average wealthier, better educated, and older than the typical television audience. While sports audiences in general do tend to be older, game broadcasts attract a disproportionate number of younger men in the important 18 to 34 age group, a group that is notoriously difficult to reach through most mass media. Sports audiences are also intensely loyal and predictable. If an NFL game is on, pro football fans will watch it. The audience for sports such as basketball, soccer, and football also includes a far higher percentage of young African-American and Hispanic males than virtually anything else on television. For advertisers in search of those key demographics, sports broadcasts are just the ticket.

The economics of the sport broadcasting industry are based on advertising. The value of a program, whether it is a football game or a situation comedy, is determined by the size and composition of the audience it attracts because that determines the amount of advertising revenue that can be generated. Broadcasters must calculate how much it will cost to purchase broadcast rights and pay for the personnel and facilities needed to promote and produce the program and balance that figure against the amount of advertising revenue they can expect to raise. Sport managers must determine what broadcast rights to their games are worth in the marketplace in order to gain top dollar. While both broadcasters and sport managers are in business to make a profit, in the competitive environment of the two industries, profit is not always easily defined. Both broadcasters and sport managers must look beyond the bottom line. Each side should consider benefits that do not immediately appear on the balance sheet.

Klatell and Marcus (1996) describe these benefits as **"total return."** For broadcasters, this could include gaining a competitive edge over a rival station or network, generating goodwill and favorable public relations, or building good relations with a team, league, or conference to gain the inside track when additional, more profitable events are up for bid. For sports producers, total return from broadcast exposure might include promotional opportunities to stimulate additional ticket or licensed merchandise sales or favorable publicity to introduce a new team or sport to a market. College athletic directors should also consider how broadcasts of a school's games generate new applications from high school students or raise the spirit of alumni who might be inspired to make donations. Televised games also provide a significant recruiting edge. Many star high school athletes want to play on television and would never consider signing with a school that is not on ESPN. From the beginning of the electronics age, both broadcasters and sports producers have sought to maximize total return.

CAREER OPPORTUNITIES

As sports organizations become increasingly involved in producing their own game broadcasts, career opportunities in sport organizations multiply. Most major colleges and professional teams now employ an associate athletic director or vice-president in charge of broadcasting who serves as a liaison with the team's broadcasters. Many sport organizations also sell broadcast advertising as part of their overall corporate sponsorship and marketing strategy, so knowledge of the broadcasting industry and how it works is an important qualification for anyone interested in a sales and marketing career. A growing number of colleges and minor league professional teams produce their own game broadcasts and utilize employees, frequently former players or coaches now employed in public relations or development, as announcers. In most cases, the actual nuts-and-bolts production of the broadcast is handled by employees of the flagship radio or television station or by a professional production firm that supplies the necessary equipment and personnel on a contract basis. By producing its own games, however, a sport organization maintains total control of the broadcast and its content and can present its product in the most favorable light.

The men and women who appear on camera to broadcast major sporting events are usually employed by the broadcaster, although it is common for a club or organization to include the right to approve the announcers as a condition of the contract. On-the-air performers in the radio and television industries are often referred to as the "talent," but because sport broadcasting is fundamentally show business, success in the crowded field requires not only talent but also hard work and plenty of good luck. Veteran football announcer Pat Summerall was the place-kicker for the New York Giants when he got his first broadcasting job in the 1950s. As Summerall tells the story, a New York radio station wanted to hire Giants quarterback Charley Connerly, Summerall's roommate at the time, but Connerly was taking a shower when the station manager called. Summerall answered the phone, and by the time Connerly got out of the shower, Summerall had the job. Baseball announcers Joe Buck and Skip Carey are the sons of established announcers and literally grew up in the business. Chip Carey became the third generation of the family to break into the business when he became the voice of the Orlando Magic. Most play-by-play announcers, however, got their jobs the old-fashioned way. They started out in college radio or as part-time announcers for local events and gradually worked their way up the ladder.

Students pursuing a career on the air should explore courses in radio and television production and performance as well as journalism courses, which will provide them with necessary reporting skills. Courses in public speaking and theater are also valuable. Experience, however, is the best teacher. College radio and campus television stations provide excellent opportunities to develop on-the-air techniques, and many radio and television stations offer internship opportunities. Entry-level sports broadcasting positions frequently require budding announcers to wear several hats. In addition to broadcasting the local high school or college's games, for example, an announcer might be expected to sell advertising time, cover local news, or be responsible for administrative duties behind the scenes. Color commentators, hired to add their insights and personality to the broadcast, are often former players or coaches chosen because they are recognizable to the audience. The best way to become the next Terry Bradshaw or Phil Simms is to quarterback a winning team in the Super Bowl.

CURRENT ISSUES

The sport broadcasting industry today is still coming to terms with trends that began to develop soon after the debut of *Monday Night Football*. In 1970, most Americans with television sets chose from among five or six stations. Cable television with its vast array of choices was still in the future. Only 7% of the nation's homes subscribed to cable at this time, most of them in rural areas where small systems picked distant network stations off the air and sent the re-amplified signal to their customers. In 1975, Time Incorporated announced it would distribute Home Box Office, its new premium entertainment channel, to cable systems around the country. Soon, more programmers realized they could distribute television programming coast-to-coast via satellite, and cable operators realized that once they provided unique programming that was not available over the air, they could move into the densely populated suburban and urban areas.

Not surprisingly, sports again played a key role. On September 7, 1979, a new cable service was launched: **ESPN**, the world's first all-sports channel. ESPN's satellite signal was delivered to cable systems across the country, providing sports coverage beyond anything available over the air. The all-sports channel had the time to cover at length events ranging from the America's Cup yacht races to the NFL player draft. The audience was small but intensely loyal, and since viewers could only watch ESPN if they subscribed to cable, the new service helped promote the new medium. In 1980, only 18% of television homes subscribed to cable, but by 1985 the figure had soared to 43%. By 1990, nearly 60% were hooked up, and today more than two-thirds are. ESPN and similar specialty services—HBO, CNN, MTV, The Nashville Network, and dozens more—gave television viewers a reason to buy cable television and thus changed the broadcast industry radically.

Today, most television viewers can choose from dozens of programming alternatives, not just five or six. In the 1960s, at any given time, more than 90% of all televisions were tuned to one of the three major commercial networks. Today, there are four major networks, but their share of the audience has dropped to about 60%. As the television dial has grown more diverse, the television audience has divided into ever-smaller chunks. Audience fragmentation has changed the economics of the industry and created a new programming philosophy. While the networks continue to vie for the mass audience, hoping to appeal to all of the people some of the time, ESPN and other specialty services pursue niche programming, hoping to reach some of the people all of the time. CNN pursues news addicts around the clock. For those who want to track the hurricane swirling in the

Atlantic, The Weather Channel offers constant updates. Care for some country music? The Nashville Network is there. ESPN and its competitors offer wall-to-wall sports and take direct aim at the sports audience.

Cable television, the simultaneous growth of FM radio stations in the 1970s and 1980s, the introduction of videocassette recorders, and, in the 1990s, the increasing popularity of the **Internet** and the World Wide Web have turned the electronic mass media into something entirely new. Thanks to digital technology, people around the world can listen to or watch a game, concert, or other event simply by logging on to their computers. No longer do consumers all watch or listen to the same broadcasts; today, thanks to the choices offered by new technology, each member of the audience can choose to watch or listen to any program he or she desires at his or her convenience. The economic rules of the media, however, remain the same: Financial success depends on creating an audience that is either large enough to attract advertisers who will pay the bills or eager enough to purchase information and entertainment in numbers great enough to cover the cost of production.

Where Do We Go from Here?

For sport managers, the new electronic environment presents both opportunities and challenges. Major sports such as the NFL and National Basketball Association (NBA) will continue to prosper because they offer broadcasters readily identifiable entertainment with a proven track record. Their loyal fans will seek out the games and watch. There is only one Super Bowl and only one NBA Finals. These events will continue to dominate the ratings because they stand out from the crowd, and the major networks will continue to pay dearly for the right to broadcast the games. The new environment also offers bright opportunities to less well-known sports. Sports can provide hours of exciting, live programming to broadcast and cable television and radio stations. In the wake of ESPN's success, regional cable sports channels have developed across the country. To attract subscribers and advertisers, they need hours and hours of programming. Sports that in the past received little or no attention are now on television.

Women's sports have benefited greatly from the multichannel television environment. A generation of women has grown up since the passage of Title IX in 1972, and they are now adult consumers and mothers whose daughters are playing organized sports. Broadcasters and advertisers see women's sports as a way to reach "soccer moms," the archetypical upper-middle-income working women and mothers market researchers believe determine how a large portion of the nation's consumer dollar is spent. Televised women's sport, once limited to Olympic events such as figure skating and gymnastics and major women's golf and tennis tournaments, now includes team sports such as college and professional basketball and volleyball. The success of women's basketball on television, especially that of the Women's National Basketball Association (WNBA) in the summer of 1997, indicates that women, like traditional male sports viewers, will watch games they once played themselves or watched as youngsters. With girls' basketball a staple in high school athletic programs across the country, the audience for the professional and college versions of the game will likely expand.

The combination of a potentially valuable audience and available broadcast time may also offer an opportunity for international sports such as soccer, rugby, and cricket. Soccer, despite the best efforts of its promoters, has yet to attract a significant television audience in the United States, but the game remains a passion for European and Latin American immigrants. Broadcast stations and cable services serving the immigrant community, such as the Spanish-language networks Telemundo and Univision, have found soccer a successful means of reaching ethnic communities. Rugby, a major spectator sport in Europe and Australia, has also begun to appear on U.S. cable systems. Cricket is rarely seen, but the sport is avidly followed in India, Pakistan, and Sri Lanka, and edited highlights of international matches could prove an effective means of reaching those communities.

Because specific audiences are smaller than in the past, however, advertising revenue is less and the cash rewards for playing on television have diminished. Many broadcasters are eager to air sports programs that will associate them with local franchises and college teams and set them apart from their competition. They may be unwilling, however, to guarantee significant rights fees in advance. This trend is already apparent. The NBA's current contract with NBC, the National Hockey League's (NHL's) television deal with Fox, and a growing number of team contracts around the country incorporate revenue sharing as an alternative to guaranteed rights. Among Major League Baseball teams, for example, a few successful franchises in the largest markets can command rich guaranteed contracts. The New York Yankees signed a 12-year television deal in 1989 that pays the team an average of $42 million a year. The majority of small-market clubs, however, retain the rights to their own games, sell advertising time, and then buy time on local stations to air the broadcasts. The Detroit Tigers, for example, air 60 games a year on a five-station television network. The club pays to produce the games, sells commercials, and buys air time on the stations (McClellan, 1995). The NBA–NBC pact calls for the network and the league to share advertising revenue, while Fox's contract with the NHL, which includes guaranteed rights payments of $155 million over five years, was based on the fact that Anheuser-Busch and Nike had already agreed to purchase 10 spots, eight for Anheuser-Busch and two for Nike, valued at an estimated $230,000 per spot during each game (Schmuckler, 1995). Revenue sharing, broadcasters say, is a favorable development both because it frees them from financial burdens and because it forces teams and leagues to become active partners with a vested interest in marketing and promoting the games.

Sports organizations and broadcasters have always been partners, each with a serious stake in the success of the other. No team wants its games broadcast in a less-than-professional manner. A haphazard broadcast reflects on the team and alienates the audience, resulting in less advertising revenue and lower rights fees. Broadcasters, on the other hand, know that even the most creative and entertaining broadcast can only partially offset a lackluster game. A winning, exciting team will attract more viewers and more advertising revenue. Ultimately, broadcast contracts are like any other business agreement: Both sides must benefit if the partnership is to survive and prosper.

Sport managers must understand how the media work and keep in mind the total return principal. Television and radio rights fees can become an important source of revenue, but sport managers must be able to fairly assess the value of their product in the marketplace. If a team has not established a record of commercial success in the broadcast marketplace, revenue sharing may be a possible solution. Teams can also package radio and television advertising with stadium signage, program advertisements, and other promotional opportunities when recruiting corporate sponsors. Many colleges help ease the financial burden of their broadcast partners by underwriting production costs or travel expenses. Many colleges and professional teams also produce their own game broadcasts, purchasing or renting the necessary equipment, hiring the personnel, and selling advertising. Complete game broadcasts are then placed on local stations or cable systems, sometimes with advertising time left available for the station to sell, sometimes with the team paying the station to carry the broadcast. Most radio and many television stations will sell blocks of air time to organizations seeking exposure. Ideally, advertising sales will offset the costs of productions, but sport managers must consider the promotional and marketing benefits of having their games on the air.

Broadcasting games may not always net a cash windfall, but broadcasting remains an important part of establishing a team's status and promoting its goals. The cost of producing a game broadcast is difficult to estimate because it involves many variables such as location, transmission costs, and the cost of assembling equipment and crews. A two-hour basketball game telecast, however, could be professionally produced and delivered complete to a local broadcasting station for as little as $10,000. A college athletic department could cut costs further by utilizing teleproduction equipment owned by the campus audiovisual or distance learning department and relying on salaried employees and student volunteers. Ideally, advertising sales would offset the cost, but should a broadcast fail to make money, is that actually a loss? Two hours of television time can provide important promotional and marketing opportunities for an athletic program and the campus at large. How much is the opportunity to spread the good news about the college worth? Will it result in increased ticket sales, alumni donations, or freshman applications? Major colleges today routinely spend tens of thousands of dollars to publish and distribute promotional literature. A two-hour telecast with six or eight minutes of commercial time devoted to selling team-related products and a halftime feature devoted to praising the college's new science center could be considered an investment well worth several thousand dollars. Many teams and most colleges today have home pages on the World Wide Web. Few directly profit from them, but a presence on the Internet is deemed a worthy promotional tool. In the future, perhaps, fans will routinely buy their tickets and T-shirts simply by clicking a computer mouse and charging the cost to a credit card or debit account. That day has not yet arrived, but the relatively modest cost of a web page can be justified as increasing the team or college's total return on its media investment.

SUMMARY

The electronic media are changing at the speed of light. New technology emerges nearly every month, and the future becomes more exciting and uncertain every day. The fundamentals, however, hold. The electronic media remain a powerful tool for getting the word out about sport. A team that is featured on radio, television, and the Internet can appeal to fans both old and new who in the future will buy tickets and merchandise. The economics of broadcasting also remain the same: Sport managers must either assemble an audience valuable enough to attract advertisers or else provide a service individual fans are willing to pay to receive. Thanks to the proven loyalty of sports fans, sport managers are in position to cash in on the dynamics of the emerging media environment.

Sport managers must keep up with new technical and competitive developments in the field. They must also be able to honestly assess the comparative value of their games or events in the eyes of broadcasters and advertisers. While broadcast rights fees can provide an important revenue stream for sports organizations, sport managers must also keep the idea of total return in mind. Promotional opportunities, favorable publicity, the status of having an organization's games broadcast to fans in the widest possible area, and other nonmonetary factors are important and have long-lasting implications for the success of any sports organization.

There is a place in the electronic media for virtually every sports organization. Those with a national audience can command lucrative network contracts. Local organizations may find homes on hometown radio or television outlets or local cable television. While local contracts may require a sports organization to share the cost of production or produce the games itself, sport managers may still discover that the total return factors of exposing their products to the public through the electronic media are well worth the time, effort, and expense.

CASE STUDY: NEGOTIATING A TELEVISION CONTRACT

The NCAA negotiating team assembled for one last meeting prior to the start of talks to nail down a new network television contract for the Division I men's basketball tournament. "I think we're in good shape," the chair said. "We've done our homework. Our market research tells us what kind of audience the tournament attracts. We've compared the projected ratings with all the other major sporting events on television. We know from our other telecasts about how much it will cost CBS to produce the games, and our friends in the advertising agencies have told us how much CBS can expect to gross from selling the ads. We know as much about the economics of this business as CBS does! It took some solid research, but I think we're ready to go get 'em. Anyone have any questions?"

"Only one," said the Midwestern athletic director as he collected his documents, "How much do you think CBS will pay for all this? But I suppose if we knew that, it would take all the fun out of the bargaining. I love taking money from the networks!" Everyone in the room laughed and started to head out the door, until the student intern who had done most of the research spoke up.

"I have a question—well, a suggestion, really," she said. "I don't think we want to take their last dollar. I think we'd be better off if we left some money on the table and asked CBS for some other considerations."

There was total silence for a moment, then a West Coast conference commissioner said, "The network knows what this event is worth and what they can make from it. We count on this money to run our organization. And rest assured CBS has the money to spend."

"Oh, I understand that," the intern said, "but what do you think about this? The organization can benefit from this deal in several ways. Let's tell CBS that in order to get the tournament, they have to broadcast some of our other championships, maybe even women's sports such as basketball and softball."

"But there's no demand for that! You've looked at the audience projections," the commissioner said. "Why would CBS want to do those events, and why would we want them to? Let's just take the money."

"I can give you several reasons. First, you're right. The events, especially women's sports, don't have a big audience right now, but given television exposure, they might develop an audience. In any case, wouldn't this show that the organization really does support athletic equality for women? CBS just might go for it, too, since it would give them a chance to showcase women's sports. Plus, if we tell them it's a condition for getting the Final Four, what can they say? And we should tell CBS we want to take back a couple of minutes of advertising time every game for us to use to tell our story and promote some of the good things about college sports."

"They'll never go for that," the chair said, " If we take back time, they won't make as much and we'll get less."

"But we get positive network exposure," the intern countered. "And speaking of ads, we should write into the contract some restrictions on what kind of ads they sell. No gambling casinos, no booze—well, maybe one or two beer spots, but no hard liquor—and no ads for the NBA. No reason to promote the competition."

"You know, she may be on to something here," offered a second commissioner, "We may be able 'o get more than money out of this deal. We can get some good PR, and maybe some in-kind services, too. Maybe we can get CBS to provide some production help, satellite feeds of postgame press conferences, highlight packages, and the like. My schools tell me their local stations would love to have that kind of thing. Some of these things she's talking about," he said as he nodded to the intern, "may cost us a little money up front, but we could get some real benefit out of them down the road."

Questions for Discussion

1. As a sport manager, how would you balance the need to maximize revenue with longer term, less quantifiable benefits such as those mentioned by the intern?
2. If you were representing CBS in the negotiations, how would you respond to the intern's suggestions? What would you want in return?
3. It is vital to do your homework before entering into any kind of contract negotiation. What kind of information should the NCAA have in hand before meeting with CBS?
4. CBS wanted exclusive rights to the tournament. What factors might influence CBS—or any network—to make an all-out effort to secure rights to a major sporting event?
5. Can you think of any other conditions the NCAA might want to include in a contract awarding tournament rights? Why would those conditions be important?

RESOURCES

Because the sport broadcasting industry changes so rapidly, it is important for sport managers to keep abreast of the latest news of the industry. While many of the details of the broadcasting business are in theory "confidential," the trade press has cultivated sources in the broadcasting, production, and advertising businesses who are often glad to share the news about the latest contracts, advertising packages, and demographic trends. The best single source of industry news is *Broadcasting & Cable* magazine, published weekly in Washington, D.C., and available in many college and larger municipal libraries, as well as on the

World Wide Web. Other trade journals, including *MediaWeek, AdWeek,* and *Advertising Age,* are also valuable. The annual *Broadcasting & Cable Yearbook* includes listings for every radio and television station in the country, hundreds of broadcast service companies, and trade organizations.

The major television broadcast organizations maintain World Wide Web sites that contain useful information. For a listing of what's available on-line, check http://www.ultimatetv.com. Often the most up-to-date information on the industry can be obtained from local television and radio stations and cable systems throughout the country.

Network and cable public relations offices are often helpful if contacted directly:

ABC Sports
47 W. 66th Street
New York, NY 10023
212-456-7777

CBS Sports
51 W. 52nd Street, 25th Floor
New York, NY 10019
212-975-5230

ESPN
ESPN Plaza
935 Middle Street
Bristol, CT 06010
860-585-2000

Fox Sports Net
1211 Ave. of the Americas, 2nd Floor
New York, NY 10019
212-556-2400

NBC Sports Division
30 Rockefeller Plaza
New York, NY 10112
212-664-3930

REFERENCES

Barnouw, E. (1966–1970). *A history of broadcasting in the United States* (Vols. 1–3). New York: Oxford University Press.

The Dempsey-Tunney Fight. (1926, December). *Radio Broadcast*, 161–162.

Douglas, S. (1987). *Inventing American broadcasting: 1899–1922*. Baltimore: Johns Hopkins University Press.

Fight booms sales of radio equipment. (1927, September 23). *Boston Globe*, 19.

Gunther, M. (1994). *The house that Roone built: The inside story of ABC news*. Boston: Little, Brown and Co.

Head, S., Sterling, C., & Schofield, L. (1994). *Broadcasting in America* (7th ed.). Boston: Houghton Miff'in.

Klatell, D., & Marcus, N. (1996). *Inside big time sports: Television, money & the fans*. New York: MasterMedia.

McClellan, S. (1995, March 27). Broadcasters balk at admission price. *Broadcasting & Cable*, 34–35.

National Collegiate Athletic Association v. Board of Regents of the University of Oklahoma, 104 S. Ct. 1 (1983).

Nielsen Media Research. (1997). *Company history*. http://www.nielsen.com

Pittsburgh Athletic Co. v. KQV Broadcasting Co., 24 F. Supp. 490 (W.D. Pa. 1938).

Rader, B. (1984). *In its own image: How television has transformed sports*. New York: Free Press.

Schmuckler, E. (1995, March 6). Bucks fly for NHL pucks. *Mediaweek*, 6.

CHAPTER 17

The Sporting Goods Industry and the Sale of Licensed Products

Mary A. Hums and Dan Covell

Key words: sporting goods equipment, athletic footwear, sports apparel, trade associations, entrepreneurs, licensed products, licensees, licensors, trademarks, royalty, properties division, branded products

INTRODUCTION

This chapter presents information on two related, yet different segments of the sport industry: sporting goods and licensed products. The sporting goods industry has a long history and is a broad industry segment, encompassing equipment, apparel, and footwear. Licensed products, on the other hand, have been around for a relatively short period of time and comprise a specialized subset of the sporting goods industry. Both of these areas continue to grow and produce revenues in the billions of dollars worldwide. Since these areas are intertwined yet distinct, this chapter deals with each separately. The first part of this chapter focuses on the sporting goods industry, and the remainder of the chapter focuses on the specialized area of licensed merchandise.

SPORTING GOODS

History of Sporting Goods

In 1996, sales of sporting goods equipment totaled $15.18 billion. Sports apparel sales equaled $17.28 billion and sales of athletic footwear totaled $9.03 billion. Sales of licensed sports products reached $13.8 billion (Riddle, 1997). This industry has come a long way since the time Dr. James Naismith first nailed peach baskets on the wall for basketball and since the days when football players didn't wear helmets! How is it the sporting goods industry has become so large? This section presents a brief history of the industry, examines where the industry is now, and discusses where it could be headed in the future.

The sporting goods industry in the United States can be traced back to the early 1800s. As early as 1811, George Tryon, a gunsmith, began to carve out a niche with people interested in sport. After expanding into the fishing tackle business, Tryon's compan⌐ became a major wholesaler of sporting goods east of the Mississippi River ₍Hardy, 1995). In the late 1840s and 1850s Michael Phelan and John Brunswick each had established production of billiards equipment. Hillerich and Bradsby began in 1859 as a wood-turning shop in Louisville and expanded to baseball bat production in 1884 (Hardy, 1995). Former professional baseball player George Wright, along with partner H.A. Ditson, operated Wright and Ditson beginning in the late 1880s, until they were eventually bought out by Albert Spalding. In 1888, Rawlings began operations in St. Louis, promoting itself as offering a "full-line emporium" of all sporting goods (Hardy, 1995).

Perhaps the best known person in the early sporting goods industry was Albert G. Spalding, the former professional baseball player, whose influence began in the late 1800s and extended past the turn of the century. Among Spalding's contributions was providing different product quality levels so that people of all economic classes could afford sporting goods. He also created instructional materials (Spalding Official Guides) for different sports. Within these guidebooks Spalding advertised his company's products, which broadened distribution and sales of his products (Sutton, 1991).

Each of the decades of the twentieth century saw different trends in the sporting goods industry. The Sporting Goods Manufacturers Association (SGMA) was founded around the same time as the National Collegiate Athletic Association (NCAA) in 1905. This was no coincidence, as the NCAA was working to make sport, specifically football, safer. This resulted in modifications in football equipment. In the 1920s a number of famous sport personalities began to endorse sporting goods products, including Knute Rockne, Honus Wagner, and Nap Lajoie. In the 1940s there was a retrenchment in spending on sporting goods, but after the Korean War in the 1950s, as prosperity returned to the country, spending on sporting goods increased. In the 1960s imported products arrived in greater numbers in the American market, especially Japanese baseball products. In the 1970s the industry began to make a big impression on the global scene. In 1976 the first meeting to explore the possibility of forming a world SGMA took place in Cologne, Germany. In 1977 the SGMA organized a meeting in Chicago that laid the foundation for creating the World Federation of the Sporting Goods Industry (WFSGI). The 1970s also brought increased recognition of product liability and the injuries associated with sports equipment. This recognition engendered in teachers, coaches, and administrators increased concern for risk management. As the industry has moved through the 1980s and 1990s there has been continuing growth as products and consumer demographics have become more diverse (Sporting Goods Manufacturers Association, 1995).

In the 1980s and 1990s the industry experienced the emergence of several industry giants, most notably Nike and Reebok. Nike, the brainchild of Phil Knight, began as an offshoot of Knight's original Blue Ribbon Sports company. The Nike name came from one of Knight's colleagues in 1971 (Katz, 1993). By 1980, Nike had pulled in $269 million and replaced adidas as the United States' top sneaker. Although Nike temporarily lost its top ranking to Reebok in 1986, the advent of the "Air Jordan" and "Bo Knows" marketing campaigns in the late 1980s propelled Nike back to the top, and Nike was a $2 billion company by 1990 (Katz, 1993). For the fiscal year ending May 31, 1997, Nike reported record worldwide revenues of $9.19 billion (Nike, 1997b). Nike has branched out far beyond shoes, now selling apparel and headwear, and is rapidly expanding its reach into sports where it has not been strong before, specifically soccer and hockey.

Key Industry Segments

The SGMA defines the sporting goods industry as comprising manufacturers of sporting goods equipment, athletic footwear, and sports apparel, as well as manufacturers of accessory items to the sport and recreation market (Riddle, 1997). **Sporting goods equipment** includes fitness products as well as sport-specific products for golf, soccer, tennis, in-line skating, and so on. Participation rates in sport and physical activities are on the rise, accompanied by related increases in sales of sporting goods equipment. Stair-climbing machines, in-line skating, treadmills, mountain biking, and snowboarding indicated the largest percentage growth in participation from 1987 to 1996 (Sporting Goods Manufacturers Association, 1997g). Sales of traditional team sports equipment for basketball, soccer, and baseball have remained solid.

In the fitness equipment area, the SGMA (1997f) identifies several key trends, including the following:

1. Treadmills remain the best-selling major item for the home.
2. Cross-trainers appear to be the next big trend in exercise equipment.
3. Recumbent stationary bikes are increasingly available at lower prices for the home.
4. Weight resistance machines are being refined to accommodate smaller bodies and permit a greater range of motion.

The second segment is **athletic footwear**. Athletic footwear is defined as branded and unbranded athletic shoes for casual wear or active usage, outdoor/

hiking sports boots, and sports sandals (Riddle, 1997). As of 1995, athletic footwear made up 37% of the sales in the total footwear market. In 1995, sales of athletic shoes for women equaled $148 billion, for men $116 billion, and for children $85.6 billion (Sporting Goods Manufacturers Association, 1997b). Currently, basketball is the dominant category, and walking and hiking/outdoor shoes are a "hot" market. Hiking, hunting, and fishing boots, as a group, totaled $1.45 billion in retail sales in 1995. The reason athletic footwear is so popular is its versatility. Peopl᷉ are now wearing athletic footwear as much for fashion as function. Informaῖion from the SGMA indicates that 35% of people use athletic footwear for school wear, 28% for sport or exercise, 22% for casual wear, and 15% for work (Sporting Goods Manufacturers Association, 1997d).

What characteristics do consumers look for in athletic footwear? Most important to buyers of athletic footwear are comfort, style, and fit; shoes that fit their active lifestyles; shoes offering performance advantages; or shoes having fashion advantages (Sporting Goods Manufacturers Association, 1997h). Approximately 40% of consumers buy athletic footwear at either discount stores or self-service stores, both of which sell shoes at the lowest prices. Athletic shoe stores account for around 11% of sales, while sporting goods stores and pro shops account for around 8% of sales (Sporting Goods Manufacturers Association, 1997h).

The third segment is **sports apparel**. Broadly defined, sports apparel encompasses garments that are designed for, or could be used in, active sports (Riddle, 1997). The sports apparel market accounts for 22% of the total apparel market. Interestingly, only 17% of sports apparel is actually purchased for active sport use, which also reinforces the idea that people wear sports apparel for fashion rather than for function (Sporting Goods Manufacturers Association, 1997c). Information reported by the SGMA indicates similar trends in selected countries. For example, 70% of people in Japan, 89% of people in Germany, and 55% of people in the United Kingdom indicated they use sports apparel for recreation, and 38% of people in Japan, 6% of people in Germany, and 27% of people in the United Kingdom indicated they use sports apparel for everyday wear (Sporting Goods Manufacturers Association, 1997e). When it comes to decision making for purchasing sports apparel, women dominate. In 1995, 40% of all sports apparel dollars were spent on women's apparel, 36% on men's apparel, and 24% on children's apparel (Sporting Goods Manufacturers Association, 1997a). The major reasons people purchase sports apparel include comfortable fit, quality, durability, easy care, and good value. Approximately 42% of consumers purchase sports apparel at either discount stores or sporting goods stores.

Sporting Goods Trade Associations

Within the industry there are a number of **trade associations** for sporting goods professionals. One of these is the previously mentioned Sporting Goods Manufacturers Association. The SGMA is the trade association for North American manufacturers, producers, and distributors of sports apparel, athletic footwear, and sporting goods equipment. The mission of the SGMA is "to increase participation in sports and foster industry growth and vitality" (Sporting Goods Manufacturers Association, 1996). Founded in 1906, the SGMA provides a variety of business services to its members, and states as a goal the preservation and advancement of recreational sport in North America. The SGMA also owns The Super Show®, the world's largest trade show for sporting goods equipment, apparel, and accessories, The Super Show®, held annually in Atlanta, showcases the upcoming year's new industry product lines, attracting thousands of sporting goods representatives from around the world. The National Sporting Goods Association (NSGA) is another trade association that represents retailer/dealer outlets and product manufacturers, suppliers, and sales agents (National Sporting Goods Association, 1997). The NSGA sponsors the annual World Sports Expo™ (National Sporting Goods Association, 1997). The Association of Black Sporting Goods Professionals (ABSG) was founded in 1990 with the mission to "further the interests and development of ethnically diverse professionals in all facets of the sports/sporting goods industry." ABSG members benefit from industry research, a career awareness program, a job information system, and a partners in progress program (Association of Black Sporting Goods Professionals, 1997). The World Federation of the Sporting Goods Industry (WFSGI) has members from Europe, America, and Asia. Its aims are (1) promoting fair trade of sporting goods in the international trade market; (2) improving the standard of quality of sporting goods; (3) standardizing the sizing of equipment and the rules of sports; and (4) promoting the world's sporting activities (World Federation of the Sporting Goods Industry, 1997).

Career Opportunities

A number of career opportunities exist in the sporting goods industry, ranging from entrepreneurs with an idea for a specific product or store to employment with major firms such as Rawlings, Spalding, Rossignol, Cannondale, Nike, or Reebok. Also there are sporting goods stores, which include locally owned single unit stores, large chains such as Champs or Sports Authority, and team stores like the Orlando Magic's FanAttic, which is discussed in the Licensing section of this chapter.

There are always opportunities for people with creative ideas to develop those ideas independently as **entrepreneurs**. An example of an entrepreneurial approach is Title 9 Sports. Title 9 Sports, started in California by Missy Park, is a catalog-based sporting goods firm specializing in sports equipment, apparel, and footwear specifically for women. Park, an athlete herself, knew that women wanted products made specifically for them, not just downsized men's athletic gear. She established her business based on that mission, and it has proven to be successful (Baker, Doti, & Tulloch, 1997).

The opportunities in larger corporations vary by type of company. Within large companies such as Rawlings there are sport divisions, such as baseball, basketball, and football. Other companies may have product divisions, such as Titleist/ Footjoy, which produces golf equipment as well as golf shoes, or Burton Snowboards, which produces snowboards and apparel. Some companies may be single-product companies such as the New Era hat company, which manufactures only headwear and supplies the official hats of all Major League Baseball (MLB) teams. There are also companies making products for athletes with disabilities, such as Quickie Wheelchair, which makes racing wheelchairs; Flex-Foot, which produces prosthetic legs and feet for runners with disabilities; and Cannondale bicycles, which recently released its new Seated Sports Technology (SST) line of road racing chairs.

Sporting goods stores operate on many levels. Locally owned independent retailers operate sporting goods stores that often have been traditionally family owned and operated for a number of years in the same town and offer a somewhat limited variety of different types of sporting goods depending on geographic location. The larger chain stores tend to offer a wider selection of products. Some of these stores, like a Champs or Foot Locker, are usually located in malls, where people stop in if they go to the mall to shop. Others, like Sports Authority, are free-standing "big box" stores considered a final destination for shoppers. As opposed to the mall stores, where people stop in if they are shopping at the mall, people go to a Sports Authority with the intention of buying sporting goods and nothing else. Each of these stores needs sales staff, as well as managers who oversee the financial, marketing, and personnel aspects of the store. Larger chains need store managers as well as people to work on the corporate level. Depending on the size of a store, buyers may be needed to make decisions on what products to stock in the upcoming seasons. Buyers, the people who deal directly with the sporting goods companies, often attend events such as The Super Show® or the World Sports Expo™ to see what new products will be on the market in the approaching year and place their store orders accordingly. In general, the larger the store, the greater the variety of positions available.

In addition to jobs with sporting goods stores, there are opportunities with large firms such as Nike, Reebok, adidas, Umbro, and Spalding. Many people start with these firms as sales representatives, or "sales reps." These sales positions vary depending on the type of sporting goods company. A sales rep could be responsible for checking in with clients within a specific geographic region. Nike, for example, hires a large number of shoe experts (called "EKINs"—"Nike" spelled backward), often in their mid-20s, who travel from store to store to talk with retailers about Nike shoes (Katz, 1993). From there, one may move upward into an assistant director or director of sales position, overseeing a group of sales reps. Sporting goods firms are always looking for creative people in their product design departments. These employees generate the ideas and create the designs for state-of-the-art equipment, ranging from titanium shaft golf clubs, to lighter mountain bikes, to Air Jordans. Getting the public excited about these products is the responsibility of the marketing department employees. Think of the slogans some of the more popular companies use to market themselves: Nike's "Just Do It," Reebok's "Planet Reebok," Champion's "It Takes a Little More To Make a Champion." Sporting goods companies need employees in marketing to get their product message out to consumers. Similar to other sport organizations, sporting goods companies need people in finance or human resources positions as well. These are just a sampling of the types of jobs in the sporting goods industry.

Current Issues

In his 1997 State of the Industry Report, SGMA President John Riddle highlighted a number of current and future concerns for the sporting goods industry, some of which are discussed in the following section.

International Influences

There is an incredible international influence in the sporting goods market. In a survey of manufacturers, approximately 25% of those queried indicated they were looking to offshore production, specifically in Asia, China, or Mexico. Currently almost 25% of all sporting goods come out of China. Sales of U.S. products continue to grow overseas, with Japan, Germany, and the rest of Europe the main consumers of U.S. exports (Riddle, 1997). Consumers all around the globe are spending more and more on sporting goods. In a survey of the buying habits of sporting goods shoppers conducted for the WFSGI and the SGMA, the Japanese were discovered to lead in spending per person on sporting goods in 1995, at $888 per year. Per-person spending per year for Germans was $790, for United States citizens $695, and for United Kingdom consumers $443 (World Federation of the Sporting Goods Industry, 1997). The reasons for continued globalization in the sporting goods industry were:

1. implementation of high-tech computer systems in manufacturing and com-munications
2. favorable wage rates
3. improved accessibility to raw materials
4. investment in state-of-the-art manufacturing processes
5. easing of tariffs and freer trading policies (Riddle, 1997)

Recently, Nike has come under fire for paying unfairly low wages and having unsafe working conditions in its overseas operations, particularly in Asian nations. Reports indicated, for example, that Nike was paying workers in Indonesian plants $1.35 per day (Katz, 1993). Nike answered these charges with a report issued by Andrew Young, spokesperson for GoodWorks International. After six months of visiting 12 Asian factories and interviewing workers in Indonesia, China, and Vietnam about labor practices, Young concluded, "It is my sincere belief that Nike is doing a good job . . . but can and should do better" (Nike, 1997a). The report was met with mixed reviews by Nike critics, and so the debate in this area continues. Another issue a number of sporting goods manufacturers are facing is the outcry over use of child labor to produce sporting goods in certain countries. After learning that as many as 20% of soccer ball stitchers in Pakistan may be children, Reebok was determined to build a soccer ball factory in Pakistan where child labor could be eliminated (Reebok, 1997). In addition, 54 soccer manufacturers signed a pledge to eliminate child labor (Sporting Goods Manufacturers Association, 1997i). Labor practices in general, but specifically those involving children in the workplace, will continually need to be addressed on a global scale.

Impact of Technology

The impact of technology on the sporting goods industry is immeasurable. Computerized technology, eliminating many formerly manual tasks, has reduced labor costs and increased manufacturing efficiency. Technology also links retailers and manufacturers as never before, allowing manufacturers to adjust production based on items that are "hot" sellers and items that are slow sellers. Perhaps the hottest technology of all is the Internet. The Internet is opening up new marketing opportunities for the sporting goods industry. In a survey about Internet use, 73% of SGMA respondents indicated they use the Internet primarily to exchange information with consumers, 12% use it to exchange information with retailers, and 5% are selling directly to consumers. The amount of Internet purchasing has been predicted to increase given the development of security code systems, lower computer prices for consumers, increased computer literacy by consumers, and the development of more "user friendly" computer equipment and programs (Riddle, 1997).

Product Delivery

The way products are delivered and to whom products are delivered are always evolving. Customers are now less enthralled by mass marketing and more demanding of custom products and delivery. One approach to this trend is to customize products and services to specific groups of consumers. For example, women's participation in both fitness activities and school team sports continues to rise rapidly, and as mentioned previously, women are beginning to demand products that are not just scaled-down versions of men's products but products designed specifically for women. Baby boomers, who have high levels of disposable income, continue to be prime consumers of fitness equipment. The Latino/Latina market represents about $230 billion in buying power and is a strong market for soccer and basketball. The sporting goods industry needs to continue to be responsive to the constantly changing interests of these demographic segments (Riddle, 1997).

Women's Market

Women are participating in sport in increasing numbers. As pointed out throughout this chapter, not only are women participating—they are purchasing sporting goods in record amounts. These trends are making sporting goods manufacturers recognize the importance of strategically planning to capture as much as possible of this burgeoning market. Manufacturers need to better determine women's needs and design products that can truly increase women's performance while making the sport experience more enjoyable. Manufacturers are discovering that merely having smaller or lighter products originally made for men and then tagged for women is not a correct strategy. Retailers need to concentrate on enhanced product merchandising aimed specifically at women (Riddle, 1997). Stores such as Lady Foot Locker are pursuing women's dollars by selling both American Basketball League (ABL) and Women's National Basketball Association (WNBA) merchandise made for women. Women athletes such as basketball stars Rebecca Lobo and Dawn Staley endorse Reebok and Nike products for women. Some sporting goods companies have responded on the executive level as well; for example, Spalding recently created a Director of Women's Marketing position.

LICENSING

A quick glance at the crowd at a sporting event, or shoppers at the mall, or students in a classroom, will reveal that many are wearing an item of clothing bearing the name or logo of a popular collegiate or professional sport team. In addition, it is likely that most of these fans own a pen, notebook, poster, or pennant also displaying the name and colors of their favorite sport teams. These are all **licensed products**. The manufacturers of these products, the **licensees**, include well-known sport-product companies such as Nike, Champion, and Reebok; prominent electronics manufacturers Nintendo, Sega, and Sony; and smaller firms such as Artcarved (jewelry), Mead (stationery), Pinnacle (trading cards and memorabilia), and Rah Rah Sales (apparel). Licensees pay teams and leagues, the **licensors**, for the right to manufacture products bearing team and school names, nicknames, colors, and logos. If these names and logos are registered with the U.S. Patent and Trademark Office, they are referred to as **trademarks**. A trademark is defined under the Federal Trademark Act of 1946, commonly referred to as the Lanham Act, as "any word, name, symbol, or device or combination thereof adopted and used by a manufacturer or merchant to identify his goods and distinguish them from those manufactured or sold by others" (Federal Trademark Act of 1946). The law defines trademark infringement as the reproduction, counterfeiting, copying, or imitation, in commerce of a registered mark, and bars companies that do not pay for the right to use these trademarks from manufacturing products bearing those marks (Berry & Wong, 1993).

Those who own such items are among the millions of consumers who purchase licensed product items to show support for and demonstrate affiliation with sport entities. Revenues from licensed product sales have become a big part of the sport industry in a relatively short period of time. Consider the following statistics:

- A 1996 marketing survey of 25,000 youths (ages 15 to 18) from 41 countries found that the Chicago Bulls logo ranked among the top 10 corporate logos recognized by the survey group (Watanabe, 1997).
- In 1990, U.S. retail sales of licensed products were $5.3 billion. By 1994, they had nearly doubled, reaching $10.6 billion ("Licensed Sport Products," 1997).
- $10.9 billion was spent on collegiate, National Football League (NFL), MLB, National Basketball Association (NBA), and National Hockey League (NHL) items in 1996, a 4.8% increase over 1995 ("Licensed Sport Products," 1997).
- Collegiate licensed product sales totaled $100 million in the early 1980s. In 1995, sales reached $2.5 billion.
- Retail sales for National Association of Stock Car Auto Racing (NASCAR) licensed products totaled $600 million in 1995 ("TLB 1996 Annual Industry Report," 1996).
- Major League Soccer retail sales hit $20 million in 1996, the league's inaugural season.
- 1995–1996 U.S. retail sales of merchandise licensed by the Atlanta Committee for the Olympic Games were estimated at $1 billion.
- More than 600 companies have licensing arrangements with professional sport leagues; 2,000 companies have such arrangements with individual colleges and collegiate licensing organizations.
- 20% of Division I-A schools earned over $1 million from licensed product sales in 1995.

- The University of Michigan, annually at or near the top in apparel sales, earned nearly $6 million on these sales in 1994, and $4 million in 1995.
- The retail sales of all licensed products for the five-college University of Massachusetts system, including products not related to sport, exceeded $20 million in 1996.

Licensing enables schools and teams to generate brand recognition and interest and to increase revenues with very little financial risk. For example, NBA licensees sold 3 million recreational-use backboards with NBA team and league logos in 1996. Such sales enable the NBA to establish team and league awareness with consumers with a strong interest in basketball (Lefton, 1996). The licensees assume the risk by manufacturing the product, then pay a fee to the licensor, called a **royalty**, for the use of specific trademarks on specific products. Royalty fees generally range from 6 to 10% and are based on gross sales at wholesale costs (Van Meter, 1995). Wholesale costs are those paid by the retailer, not the price paid by consumers. Licensees use the established images and popularity of sport teams to boost their sales. Other sport organizations, such as the United States Olympic Committee (USOC) and the United States Tennis Association, also act as licensors. The USOC returns 82.7% of proceeds from sales of Olympic merchandise back to athletes through the funding of training programs and athlete grants and services. USOC licensees include Champion, Starter, and Mattel. Cross-licensing agreements, defined by Van Meter (1995) as the use of more than one licensed mark on the same product, with a split of subsequent royalties, exist with the USOC and Warner Bros. for merchandise bearing the Looney Tunes characters (Bullington, 1995a).

History of Licensing Programs

Professional Sport

The licensing programs in professional sport leagues are administered by a for-profit branch of the league, generally referred to as a **properties division**. Properties divisions approve licensees, police trademark infringement, and distribute licensing revenues equally among league franchises. Properties divisions usually handle marketing and sponsorship efforts as well. The NFL was the first professional league to develop a properties component in 1963, under the leadership of Pete Rozelle, the commissioner at the time. The first license was granted to Sport Specialties. David Warsaw, the founder of the company, had worked with Chicago Bears owner George Halas in the 1930s in selling Bears merchandise and later developed licensing agreements with the Los Angeles Dodgers and what were then the Los Angeles Rams ("Sports Merchandising," 1996). Sport Specialties, now a subsidiary of Nike, provides player sideline headwear for several NFL teams. By the late 1970s, each NFL team's licensing share was believed to be nearly half a million dollars annually. MLB followed with the creation of its properties division (MLB Properties) in 1966, although many teams who had strong local sales were reluctant to give up their licensing rights to the league. NHL Enterprises began formal league-governed licensing in 1969, and NBA Properties initiated activities in 1982 (Lipsey, 1996).

Player unions also administer licensing programs, such as the National Football League Players Association's (NFLPA's) Players Inc., which represents agreements with nearly 3,000 current and former NFL players. Union properties divisions such as this establish separate licensee agreements, and also jointly license and share revenue with leagues, for trading cards, electronics and video games, and associated memorabilia sales. The Major League Baseball Players Association (MLBPA) was the first to enter into such an agreement in the late 1960s when then-Executive Director Marvin Miller entered into a two-year, $120,000 pact with Coca-Cola to permit the beverage manufacturer to put players' likenesses on bottle caps. Such royalties helped fund the emerging union's organizing activities. Miller also negotiated a comprehensive agreement with trading card manufacturer Topps Company in 1968. Topps was permitted to continue manufacturing trading cards bearing player likenesses for double the players' previous yearly fees (from $125 to $250), and it paid the union 8% on annual sales up to $4 million and 10% on all subsequent sales. The first year the contract earned the MLBPA $320,000 (Helyar, 1994). Licensees also negotiate separate endorsement agreements with players to wear their products and appear in ads, such as the $200,000 deal between Logo Athletic and Dallas Cowboys quarterback Troy Aikman (Horovitz, 1997). MLB also handles associated licensing duties for minor league and Negro League properties. "Professional Baseball—The Minor Leagues" is MLB Properties' licensing program for 156 minor league clubs, with minor league retail sales reaching over $50 million annually (Jones, 1995). "Professional Baseball—The Negro Leagues" is handled pro bono by MLB, with royalties distributed to surviving Negro League players, the Negro League Baseball Museum in Kansas City, and the nonprofit Jackie Robinson Foundation.

Some smaller professional leagues hire independent companies to run their licensing operations. Brian P. Hakan & Associates runs licensing operations for the Arena Football League, the Major Indoor Lacrosse League, the United States Figure Skating Association, and the East Coast Hockey League. Sony Signatures works on behalf of the International Hockey League, which garners retail sales in excess of $20 million annually, and on behalf of World Cup '98. Battle Enterprises serves as the licensing agent for Goodyear Racing, the Bass Anglers Sportsman Society, the PGA Tour, and the Senior PGA Tour. These firms serve as "middle persons" for smaller leagues lacking the resources to maintain effective licensing operations, and work for a percentage (as high as 35%) of gross revenues from retail sales.

An examination of NBA Properties' licensing component provides insight into the structure of a league's licensing operations. The NBA has approximately 150 licensees, half of which are apparel manufacturers. Licensing operations are coordinated by a vice-president and general manager of consumer products, who is responsible for overseeing four departments: sales, marketing programs, apparel licensing, and nonapparel licensing. A separate quality control department has final approval powers over all products and graphics. The league also serves as licensing agent for NBC Sports and USA Basketball. Exhibit 17–1 outlines the general mission of each segment of NBA Properties.

There is no set fee for royalty payments for NBA licensees. The scale ranges from 6% for low-margin sporting goods to 20% for certain apparel items. NBA Properties retains a portion of these royalties to be reinvested in the licensing operations but forwards most of the funds to the clubs (W. Marshall, personal communication, May 27, 1997).

The strengths of league-based licensing programs are the ability to coordinate efforts among many licensees, the ability for increased quality control over approved merchandise, the ability for easier national distribution of product, and an increased and effectively coordinated enforcement of trademark infringement by nonlicensed manufacturers. The ownership of team trademarks by the league also provides greater value to licensees, who need only go to one source to access all league marks (Burton, 1996), and provides potential product licensing exclusivity. League programs also effectively segment the national market for licensed

---

Exhibit 17–1 Components of NBA Properties Licensing Operations

Sales: Responsible for acting as liaison with retailers for sales and retail promotions; oversees shipment of products.

Marketing programs: Oversees development and implementation of retail promotions, produces merchandise catalogs, and coordinates trade show activities (including a 15,000-square-foot booth at the annual SuperShow® in Atlanta).

Apparel Licensing: Coordinates licensing agreements and designs for the following product lines: on-court and courtside authentics, headwear, youth clothing, adult clothing, activewear, outerwear.

Nonapparel Licensing: Coordinates licensing agreements and designs for nonclothing product lines, including school supplies, home furnishings, electronics and video games, sporting goods, toys and games, publishing, collectibles, and trading cards.

Source: Marshall, W. (1997). Personal conversation.

sport products by emphasizing the varied colors, logos, and uniforms of league teams in specific local markets. The major weakness of league-based programs, as underscored by recent multimillion-dollar sponsorship deals inked by Dallas Cowboys owner Jerry Jones and Pepsi and Nike, and a similar pact formed by New York Yankees owner George Steinbrenner with adidas, is that popular and successful clubs such as the Cowboys and Yankees have the leverage to strike up their own deals and are loathe to share any revenues with other clubs. The same holds true for merchandise sales. Jones and Steinbrenner argue that they should be able to make full use of their respective clubs' earning potential. If they sell more merchandise, these two owners feel they should be entitled to keep their teams' percentage of the sales revenue in proportion to unit sales and should not be forced to subsidize less desirable properties through the equal division of sales revenues.

Collegiate Sport

In December 1908 the University of Pittsburgh became the first football team to wear jerseys with numerals in Pitt's 14–0 loss to Washington and Jefferson (NCAA, 1995). In 1947 University of Oregon Athletic Director Leo Harris and Walt Disney agreed to allow Oregon to use Disney's Donald Duck image for the university's mascot (Plata, 1996). While these were some early steps toward the development of licensable properties, the University of California—Los Angeles (UCLA) is generally credited with being the first school to enter into a licensing agreement with a manufacturer when its school bookstore granted a license to a watch manufacturer in 1973. The NCAA formed its properties division to license championship merchandise in 1975, but it does not administer licensing programs for member schools. The NCAA earned $13.9 million in royalties in 1996–1997 (NCAA, 1996).

Following UCLA's lead, many schools began to register their trademarks. This prevented companies from using them without paying royalties. Several schools challenged the notion that school marks belonged in the public domain (available for use by any company without payment of royalties). In one such case, the University of Pittsburgh, Ohio State University, DePaul University, and UCLA sued Champion Products in 1983 for using their marks without permission, winning an eventual out-of-court settlement and royalty agreements. The first Canadian school to establish a licensing program was the University of Calgary in 1988 (Van Meter, 1995). Significant revenue growth began in the late 1980s. For example, the University of Notre Dame, which began its licensing program in 1983, experienced growth of 375% from 1988 to 1989 (Nichols, 1995). Today, nearly 300 schools have established licensing programs (Van Meter, 1995).

According to Mazzeo, Cuneen, and Claussen (1997), 41% of NCAA Division I-A schools administer their own licensing programs. The benefit of self-mainte-nance is that schools can retain a greater portion of sales revenues. The remainder of Division I-A schools, like the smaller pro leagues, enlist the services of independent licensing companies to manage their programs.

Two major organizations administer programs for conferences, bowl games, and over 75% of schools that choose independent companies: the Collegiate Licensing Company (CLC), acting on behalf of 160 colleges, universities, bowls, and conferences, and the Licensing Resource Group (LRG). These companies are paid a portion of the royalties (usually 50%) as their administrative fee. In addition, The Black College Licensing Company (BCLC), founded in 1991 as a subsidiary of the Drew Pearson Companies, assists traditionally African-American colleges with their licensing programs. Exhibit 17–2 lists some schools that administer their own licensing programs and others that use licensing companies.

Using licensing companies affords schools a greater opportunity for national distribution, exposure to a greater number of licensees, increased expertise in sales and design, and broader trademark enforcement protection, while keeping departmental expenses low. Except in certain circumstances, institutional licensing revenue is retained in institutional general funds. The strengths of collegiate licensed product sales to retailers are a longer selling season and greater regional product diversification and coverage (meaning more local schools and conferences). Exact numbers for sales of collegiate licensed products are sometimes difficult to gather, but the schools considered the top sellers as estimated by the Association of Collegiate Licensing Administrators (ACLA) are listed in Exhibit 17–3.

Branded Apparel

Many sport fans also wear apparel items bearing only the logo, mark, or name of the manufacturer, such as the Nike "swoosh" or the Reebok "Vector." Items

---

Exhibit 17–2 University Licensing Programs

Independent schools:	California–Berkeley, Colorado, Grambling, Harvard, Massachusetts, Miami, Notre Dame, Ohio State, Southern California, Syracuse, Texas, UCLA
CLC clients:	Alabama, Arkansas, Brigham Young, Clemson, Duke, Illinois, Maryland, Penn State, St. John's, Tulane, Conference USA, FedEx Orange Bowl, NCAA Championships
LRG clients:	Arizona State, Kansas, Northwestern, Providence, U.S. Naval Academy, Washington State

Source: Reprinted with permission from University Licensing Programs, *Team Licensing Business*, Vol. 8, No. 7, pp. 18–19, © 1996.

Exhibit 17–3 Top-Selling Colleges and Universities, 1996

1. Notre Dame	6. Kentucky
2. Michigan	7. North Carolina
3. Nebraska	8. Tennessee
4. Ohio State	9. Florida State
5. Penn State	10. Florida

Source: ACLA top 25 poll. (1997). *Team Licensing Business,* 9(4), 40.

that carry only the logo and marks of the manufacturer are referred to as **branded products.** The popularity of branded merchandise is a relatively recent phenomenon, as manufacturers who established their brand awareness as licensees have now established their own brand identity independent of professional or college team marks.

Companies such as Champion, Starter, and Reebok have strong ties to the licensed market but have significant independent brand identity as well. Branded marketing has become a significant focus for these companies. Companies such as Nike and adidas have strong independent brand identities and are now leveraging this strength and breaking into the licensed product market. Nike, after a long history of independence, recently became a licensee of the NFL, NHL, and the NBA, with the obligation to provide league uniforms in exchange for the right to manufacture authentic and replica uniforms and other apparel lines; this deal is part of Nike's effort to increase overall annual corporate sales to $12 billion by 2000 (Lefton, 1996). Leagues are also interested in the considerable marketing clout of these companies.

Established branded nonsport apparel manufacturers have also begun to enter the sport market. Fashion apparel companies with strong label recognition, including Tommy Hilfiger, Donna Karan, and Ralph Lauren, have delved into the licensing and sporting goods market to further entrench their brand awareness. Donna Karan is slated to create warm-ups for the 1997 U.S. Figure Skating Association and to release its own brand of running shoe (Keller, 1997). In addition, new companies are forming with the intent to create branded lines with associated licensed tie-ins. An example of this is Rival, a hockey apparel manufacturer, which produces several lines categorized as Performance, Lifestyle, and Sport. Performance will create items for NHL's "Center Ice" line of authentic team uniform apparel, while Lifestyle is a branded line meant to capitalize on casual wear for those interested in hockey-style clothing. The Sport line will contain some licensed products, but it will not base its merchandise on existing team designs or uniforms (Nichols, 1997).

As discussed in Chapter 3, Marketing Principles Applied to Sport Management, branded companies have made their mark in the collegiate world as well, with the recent increase in collegiate institution-wide shoe and apparel contracts with major suppliers such as Nike, Reebok, and Converse. An example of such an agreement is Reebok's five-year, $9.1 million deal with the University of Wisconsin. The deal, which expires in 2001, stipulates that Reebok will provide Wisconsin with uniforms, warm-ups, and footwear for all 22 varsity sports, as well as $2.3 million for scholarships and payments to coaches. In exchange, Reebok gains the right to exclusively market Wisconsin licensed athletic apparel (Naughton, 1996). Exhibit 17–4 gives a number of examples of such agreements.

The State of Licensing Today

The sport licensing industry has enjoyed robust growth over the past decade, with sales nearly doubling since 1980, as illustrated in Table 17–1. Manufacturers, particularly of apparel, found they could increase earnings by expanding and diversifying merchandise offerings. The increase in retail stores selling only licensed merchandise (estimated at 450 stores in 1997) and collectibles have added to this growth. Up until the early 1980s, roughly 80% of collegiate sales took place in college bookstores. Today, that figure has dropped to 20% (Nichols, 1995). The high growth trend has slowed in recent years, however. Licensed sports product retail sales increased by only 1.5% in 1994, fell slightly in 1995, and recovered in 1996 to post a modest gain over 1994 figures (see Table 17–2). One reason for the plateau in sales of licensed products for professional teams is recent and continued professional league labor strife. The 1994 MLB player strike and subsequent cancellation of postseason play, the threatened NBA union decertification in 1995, and the 1995 player lockout by NHL management all served to dampen fan enthusiasm about professional sports. The extended period of growth led to an oversupply of product, with too many licensed vendors

---

Exhibit 17–4 Exclusive Collegiate Athletic Departmental Shoe and Apparel Agreements

Company	Schools
Nike	Alabama, Colorado, Florida State, Illinois, Miami, Michigan, North Carolina, Ohio State, Oregon, Penn State, Southern California
Reebok	Georgia Tech, Wisconsin, Texas, UCLA
adidas	Northwestern, Tennessee

Source: Naughton, J. (1996, September 6). Exclusive deal with Reebok brings U. of Wisconsin millions of dollars and unexpected criticism. *The Chronicle of Higher Education, XLIII*(2), A65.

Table 17–1 Retail Sales of Licensed Products

Year	$ (in Billions)	Year	$ (in Billions)
1980	9.9	1988	59.8
1981	13.7	1989	64.5
1982	20.6	1990	66.5
1983	26.7	1991	63.5
1984	40.1	1992	62.2
1985	50.1	1993	66.6
1986	54.3	1994	70.0
1987	55.9	1995	69.9
		1996	72.3

Source: Retail sales of all licensed merchandise. (1997). *Team Licensing Business, 8*(4), 2.

pushing too much merchandise on too many retail outlets. This led to an oversupply of inventory, resulting in smaller restocking purchases by retailers.

In response to this oversupply, subsequent retail price wars ensued, fueled in part by large chains like JCPenney, Sears, Kmart, and regional department stores, which bought in bulk and undercut specialty retailers such as Champs, Foot Locker, Modell's, the Pro Image, and Lids. The increased competition for retail sales and floor space from major branded products manufacturers, as well as smaller fashion manufacturers such as No Fear, Mossimo, and Stussy, have also cut into licensed sales. Other concerns of retailers include the similarity in distribution of products among retail outlets and the perceived tendency of licensees to meet the orders of large retailers before those of smaller specialty stores.

Table 17–2 Licensed Sports Products Retail Sales—U.S. (Major Sports Leagues and Colleges/Universities, in Millions of Dollars)

	1990	1991	1992	1993	1994	1995	1996
NFL	$1,500	$1,700	$2,000	$2,600	$3,000	$3,150	$3,300
MLB	1,500	2,000	2,400	2,500	2,100	1,500	1,800
NBA	750	1,000	1,400	2,100	2,500	2,650	2,700
NHL	150	275	600	800	1,000	1,000	1,000
Collegiate	1,450	1,750	1,835	1,950	2,000	2,100	2,100
TOTAL	5,350	6,725	8,235	9,950	10,600	10,400	10,900

Source: Reprinted with permission from Licensed Product Retail Sales by League Since 1990, *Team Licensing Business,* Vol. 8, No. 4, p. 21, © 1997.

Career Opportunities

As with the sporting goods industry, a number of potential career opportunities exist in the licensing industry. They include employment with league licensing departments, collegiate licensing offices, and licensees, as well as with the retail sales outlets and product manufacturers described earlier in this chapter. Given the demand for new products and looks, there are always opportunities for innovative products and services related to licensing.

Two companies that have found innovative niches in the business are Blue Marlin and Sean Michael Edwards, Inc. Blue Marlin, owned and founded (in 1995) by San Francisco entrepreneur Erik Stuebe, specializes in selling baseball caps with logos of defunct Negro League baseball teams such as the Baltimore Black Sox and Kansas City Monarchs. The firm has capitalized on the renewed interest in the pre-integration era of baseball by using special techniques to make the caps look older, such as boiling white wool felt logos in tea. The caps retail for around $30, and Blue Marlin sold 200,000 in 1996, with posted wholesale sales of $1.7 million (Givhan, 1997).

Sean Michael Edwards (SME), a New York City design firm, has made a name for itself by specializing in working with professional and collegiate sport entities to create new and innovative logos and trademarks. As most sport organizations have little expertise in the area of visual design, they look to such companies to create and render logos and marks for them. As the licensed product market has expanded and diversified, sport entities now look to utilize numerous logos and marks, referred to as a "family." Companies like SME charge between $40,000 and $100,000 to create a comprehensive family of primary and secondary marks and logos. This emerging logo redesign trend is discussed in more detail later in the chapter.

Current Issues

Trademark Infringement

Although the unauthorized use of a mark is illegal, international counterfeit merchandise sales total $200 billion annually ("Baseball Gets Tough," 1997). Licensors spend substantial resources in policing the marketplace to stop the sale of unauthorized merchandise, and leagues and independent companies use internal legal departments and publicity campaigns in the mainstream media. There is also cooperation between these entities, as demonstrated by the formation of CAPS (the Coalition to Advance the Protection of Sports Logos). The coalition was formed in 1992 to conduct criminal and civil seizures of counterfeit merchandise and campaigns for stricter anticounterfeiting legislation. Members include

CLC and Starter, as well as the properties divisions of the NBA, NHL, NFL, and MLB. Through 1995, this organization had confiscated unauthorized merchandise and equipment valued in excess of $22 million ("CAPS Seizes," 1995). In 1997, golf phenom Tiger Woods sued and successfully barred the Franklin Mint Company, a manufacturer of commemorative coins and other collectibles, from selling a sterling silver medallion commemorating Woods' Masters tournament victory that year. The company had not been given permission from Woods for the use of his likeness (O'Brien & Hersch, 1997). According to William Edwards, an assistant U.S. attorney, the maximum penalty for violating trademark rights via the sales of counterfeit merchandise is a 10-year prison term ("Baseball Gets Tough," 1997).

Ambush Marketing

As described in Chapter 3, Marketing Principles Applied to Sport Management, the techniques of ambush marketing have also been applied to licensing. Nonlicensed manufacturers can realize the same brand awareness as licensees by entering into endorsement deals with individual athletes. Nonapparel companies can also benefit from ambush marketing techniques. One such company is Bill Goff, Inc. (BGI) of Kent, Connecticut, an art dealership that specializes in original paintings and print reproductions with baseball themes. BGI's paintings and prints that include depictions of former stars and player uniforms are officially licensed through MLB's "Cooperstown Collection," the line of official merchandise that celebrates baseball's history. But the company also does significant business in the selling of works of art that depict current and former ballparks. Such works need not be licensed through MLB, as they are works based on artistic interpretations, but they have come under fire from architecture firms that claim the design of parks is their property and should not be used without permission. The association between MLB and the manufacturers is implied, but not formally exhibited.

International Sales

As growth diminishes in the domestic market, licensors and licensees alike are looking toward international markets to boost sales. Licensees are purchasing foreign companies not only to market U.S. products overseas but also to capitalize on the growth of indigenous sales as well. Russell Corporation's purchase of several Dutch and British firms allowed Russell to make use of established product distribution lines, to produce products to capitalize on locally popular sports, and to cultivate relationships with European retailers ("Russell Extends," 1995). Nike has committed to cracking the world soccer market and set a deadline of the 2002 World Cup to become the top international supplier for soccer shoes, equipment, and apparel. In 1997, the Brazilian National Soccer Team agreed to a 10-year, $200 million deal to wear Nike shoes and apparel and to appear in Nike-produced exhibition matches and community events. Nike has also spent over $140 million in upgrading distribution operations in Europe, Japan, Korea, and Australia (Himmelstein, 1997).

Leagues see foreign markets as ripe for sales expansion as well. Foreign exhibition and regular season games have been used successfully to prompt local interest in league games and merchandise, and the NFL has used the World League and arrangements with the Canadian Football League to further their sales and brand awareness in Europe and Canada. The NHL, with its large percentage of European players and a two-week mid-season break to allow league players to participate in Olympic competition, seeks to leverage this in combination with the USOC, the NHL Players Association, and USA Hockey for the 1998 Nagano Winter Olympics. Adapting the league's "Coolest Game" theme through the "Coolest Game in Nagano" program, NHL Enterprises has gained permission from the USOC to use the Olympic rings in sales and promotions and will market the program to both domestic and international consumers ("NHL Establishes," 1997).

Manufacturer and Licensee Conduct

Although licensors demonstrate quality control over the images on licensed products, they do not control all operations of the licensees. Licensees are independent businesses, and as such conduct their businesses as they see fit. Nike has received significant negative publicity for its business practices in Vietnam, where local production managers treated workers harshly and punished them if they did not wear Nike products. Sometimes, however, the business practices of licensees reflect back on the licensors. When the University of Wisconsin made public its licensing agreement with Reebok, certain personnel at the university questioned Reebok's business practices and labor relations with Southeast Asian manufacturers, claiming that shoe assemblers in Indonesia received only $2.45 per day. A petition circulated by professors stated: "If the University of Wisconsin advertises a firm like Reebok, it accepts the conditions under which Reebok profits" (Naughton, 1996, p. A65). The licensing agreement originally contained a clause stating that university employees would not disparage Reebok, but after campus outcry the clause was omitted from the contract (Naughton, 1996).

In response to these concerns, some schools have published a code of conduct for licensees. Notre Dame has composed a code stating the school is "committed to conducting its business affairs in a socially responsible manner consistent with its religious and educational mission" and stipulating that licensees must meet the university's stated standards for legal and environmental compliance, ethical principles, and employment practices (University of Notre Dame, 1997).

Logos: Expansion and Redesign

In 1991, the NHL's San Jose Sharks topped the league's licensed product sale chart—before the team had played a single game. The black-and-teal logo depicting a shark biting through a hockey stick represented a watershed for the industry. Although teams that win tend to sell the most merchandise, teams, leagues, colleges, and manufacturers realized that sales could be increased through logo introduction and redesign, as well as through uniform redesign and diversification and secondary and commemorative logos and marks. In a 30-month period spanning 1995 to 1997, over 20 major league teams unveiled significantly redesigned logos and uniforms, including the Philadelphia Eagles, Houston Rockets, and Anaheim Angels. Minor league baseball teams such as the Portland Sea Dogs (Marlins AA affiliate) and the Carolina Mudcats (Pirates AA affiliate) enjoy high national sales and distribution due to innovative logos and color schemes. The introduction of alternate logos and uniform components, such as jerseys, hats, and patches, have also served to increase sales. For example, teams such as the Seattle Mariners and Florida Marlins have more than one official game hat. Also, in 1997 all MLB teams wore patches commemorating the 50th anniversary of Jackie Robinson's breaking into the Major Leagues.

Many colleges and universities have also undergone image changes and sales increases through uniform redesign. Iowa State, Maryland, UCLA, St. John's, Virginia, and Villanova are among the schools that have seen licensing revenues jump after recent significant logo redesigns, with accompanying uniform changes for high-visibility sports like football and men's and women's basketball. After the release of its redesigned logo in 1994, Villanova saw its licensing profits jump to $200,000 annually. However, some schools that redesign logos suffer student, alumni, and consumer backlash when a new logo and/or mascot is introduced, as was the case in 1996 when Lehigh University in Pennsylvania changed from the Engineers (a tribute to the school's strong engineering and science programs) to the Mountain Hawks (Nicklin, 1996).

Another motivation for some logo redesigns has been public criticism over the inappropriate use and depiction of women or minority groups through school and team mascots and logos. Although many professional teams, such as the Cleveland Indians (named in honor of former player Louis Sockalexis, a Native American from Old Town, Maine), Atlanta Braves, and Washington Redskins, have withstood periodic outcries for demeaning Native Americans (including protests directed at the Cleveland Indians at the 1997 MLB All-Star Game), some professional teams and colleges have responded to these calls and altered their mascots and nicknames. Both Stanford University and Dartmouth College dropped Indians as a moniker in the early 1970s, and Eastern Michigan University changed from Hurons (a local indigenous people) to Eagles in 1991 after the Michigan Department of Civil Rights issued a report suggesting that all state schools drop logos and mascots that promoted racial stereotypes (Donovan, 1997). In 1996, the Syracuse Chiefs, the Toronto Blue Jays' affiliate in the AAA International League, were renamed the Skychiefs and adopted a flying baseball bat logo.

Retail Trends

Retailers are looking to keep sales from lagging in the coming years by fine-tuning their selling efforts. Here are a few things retailers, licensors, and licensees will be working on together to ensure continued growth:

- Popular product segments such as children's apparel (gearing associated promotional efforts to coincide with holiday and back-to-school purchase windows), electronics and video games, authentics and sideline/courtside merchandise, including alternate uniforms.
- Continued product expansion, such as commemorative "throwback" items that celebrate tradition and history, casual-wear lines (as many older fans want a more understated look and won't buy authentics or replicas), and items specifically for women (such as the Detroit Pistons' "Fit for Style" line).
- A continued development of specialty stores and purchasing areas. Such outlets and space allocations are used to reinforce brand awareness and affiliation for licensees, licensors, and retailers. The following are examples of the breadth of this trend:
  - PGA Tour Shops, operated as a joint venture between the PGA and mall retail operator Paradies.
  - NASCAR Thunder Stores, the first of which opened in the Gwinnett Place Mall in Atlanta in May 1996. The opening drew a crowd of 15,000, which prompted Donna Capilla, group marketing manager for mall operator Urban Retail Shopping Centers, Inc., to comment: "This is the largest response I have ever seen for a store opening" ("NASCAR Retail Store," 1996).
  - Team-operated off-venue retail stores, such as the two FanAttic stores run by the Orlando Magic, and the three Denver Nuggets Sport Gallery stores (two in Denver, one in Colorado Springs).
  - Independent concept shops, in-store theme areas, and point-of-purchase displays that help to focus customer attention and draw in potential buyers. Firms such as Jon Greenberg and Associates serve as design consultants to assist retailers in constructing such areas for retailers like Bradley's Major League Clubhouse Stores, Bob's Stores, and Finish Line (Bullington, 1995b).
  - The University of Massachusetts' recently initiated cooperative plan with key retailers such as JCPenney and Sears to recognize them as "Official Licensed UMass Shops," effectively creating team stores throughout the region ("UMass Promotes," 1997).

Taxation

As licensed product sales become more prominent in the sport industry, they have also become a target for potential taxation. In 1997, legislators and political action groups in the state of Washington proposed a 1.2% sales tax on retail licensed merchandise to help fund a new venue for the NFL's Seattle Seahawks. A similar tax was examined by state legislators in Minnesota ("Washington State," 1997).

Sponsorship and Licensing Synergy

As relationships between sport entities become more fully integrated, the lines that formerly separated sponsors and licensees have begun to blur. Licensees with significant marketing clout and experience are looking to use sport as a promotional vehicle in many ways, including advertising at contests, at venues, during broadcasts, and at associated events. Leagues, teams, and colleges no longer restrict licensing agreements to merchandise production but look to create marketing partnerships with licensees to increase not only merchandise sales but also sponsorship revenues and overall brand awareness.

SUMMARY

This chapter considers two growing and expanding segments of the sport industry: sporting goods and licensed products. The sporting goods industry is categorized by three segments: sporting goods equipment, athletic footwear, and apparel. Several trade associations assist sporting goods professionals, including the Sporting Goods Manufacturers Association (SGMA), the National Sporting Goods Association (NSGA), the Association of Black Sporting Goods Professionals (ABSG), and the World Federation of the Sporting Goods Industry (WFSGI). To be successful, sporting goods professionals today need to be aware of international influences, the impact of technology, product delivery, and the growing women's market.

The licensed product industry continues to grow. Teams and leagues earn a certain percentage of sales, called royalties, on items bearing logos. Leagues and players associations administer licensing programs on the professional level. Colleges may administer their own licensing programs or may enlist the services of organizations such as the Collegiate Licensing Company (CLC). In addition to team- or league-logoed merchandise, branded apparel is also becoming popular, with companies such as Nike and adidas having strong independent brand identities. Several important issues are facing the licensed product industry, including trademark infringement, ambush marketing, international sales, manufacturer and licensee conduct, logo redesign, and retail trends.

People are needed to work many capacities in both the sporting goods and licensed products industries. These areas cut across many other segments of the sport industry, including professional sport, intercollegiate athletics, recreational sport, and the health and fitness industry. Wherever there is a need for equipment to play a sport or a need for the right clothing to announce that a person is a fan of a particular team, the sporting goods industry and the licensed product industry become pivotal.

CASE STUDY: THE DEVELOPMENT OF AN "EXTREME" PRODUCT

"Here's the background file. I need your proposal a week from today. I'll be out of town until then. Good luck, kid."

New Products Manager Kay Seymour dropped the thick binder onto Bronwen Douglass's desk and then left the office. Bronwen opened the binder and started to sift through the information as she prepared for her first assignment in the marketing department of Liberty, Inc. She read the "Company History" section first:

"Liberty is one of the most venerated sport product manufacturers in the world. Eighty years ago, Liberty introduced the "Stan Becker MVPs," the prototypical canvas ankle-length basketball shoe named for Hall of Famer Stan Becker, a cage standout from New Paris, Indiana, who eschewed the collegiate ranks and played for a number of famous barnstorming squads. The MVP and related products became the staple footwear of hoopsters for the next six decades, and by the mid-1960s Liberty owned 80% of the basketball shoe market."

"In the 1970s, Liberty continued its success with updated leather basketball shoes and marketed them through endorsements by contemporary NBA hoop luminaries. However, in the 1980s Liberty began to lose its market share to the emerging twin shoe giants Nike and Reebok. Our current market share of the athletic footwear market, which has diversified significantly in the last three decades, is now somewhere between 4% and 5%. Basketball shoes still account for just over 40% of total sales."

Bronwen put down the binder. She knew the rest. She knew what had been going on in the company in the last few years, as she had monitored the market while working for JunoKrash, a small manufacturer of street shoes popular with the so-called "extreme" set. She had seen Liberty's athletic footwear market share shrink due to pressures from not only Nike and Reebok but also Fila and adidas. Liberty now controlled only 3% of the $7.5 billion-a-year basketball shoe market. In 1995, an effort to bolster its plummeting sales and earnings and to boost its apparel division ended in disaster. Liberty presented shareholders with a $70 million loss that year.

Bronwen took the job with Liberty because she felt that while the company had hit rock bottom, it had the potential to regain its place in the athletic footwear market. Sales were already turning around; they had increased 48% in the first quarter of 1997. Liberty has price competitiveness, a strong history, and shoe and apparel contracts with several major men's collegiate programs, Bronwen thought, and it had introduced new products into the basketball shoe market. But the company was also looking to attract other segments of the market, and that is where Bronwen came in. She had been hired away from JunoKrash and given the task to determine how Liberty should market a new street/skateboard shoe, "the Beckster," to the "extreme" segment (alternative males, ages 13 to 18). But as she thought about how to take on this challenge, she had many concerns: What is the perception of Liberty now? The company was putting a lot of effort and millions of dollars into research, design, and marketing for the new "MVP 2000," the shoe to be hawked by several NBA stars with appeal to younger consumers. The company was already taking to the streets in major metropolitan areas to "seed" the shoe in the urban market, including giveaways to gang members. As Bronwen knew, control of the "extreme" market changes frequently because the wants and needs of the customers are so volatile. Could such a big company tap into this and stay on top of it? She took a pair of black suede Becksters out of the day-glo orange shoebox sitting on her desk, looked it over, and started to think.

Questions for Discussion

1. Is this the correct way for Liberty to attempt to regain market share?
2. Are the company's efforts to court gang members ethical?
3. How does this approach mesh with this street/extreme product?
4. How will that impact the company's current strengths and consumer perceptions?
5. Should the company look to increase licensing revenues instead of releasing an extreme product?

RESOURCES

Association of Black Sporting Goods Professionals (ABSG)
55 Marietta Street, Suite 2000
Atlanta, GA 30303
404-588-1104; fax: 404-588-1601
home page: www.sportlink.com/nonprofits/absg/index.html

Association of Collegiate Licensing Administrators (ACLA)
638 Prospect Avenue
Hartford, CT 06105-4250
860-586-7524; fax: 860-586-7550

Collegiate Licensing Company (CLC)
320 Interstate North, Suite 102
Atlanta, GA 30339
770-956-0520; fax: 770-955-4491

Licensing Resource Group (LRG)
515 Kirkwood Avenue
Iowa City, IA 52244
319-351-1776; fax: 319-351-1978

National Sporting Goods Association (NSGA)
1699 Wall Street
Mt. Prospect, IL 60056
847-439-4000; fax: 847-439-0111
e-mail: NSGA@aol.com
home page: http://www.nsga.org

Sporting Goods Manufacturers Association (SGMA)
200 Castlewood Drive
N. Palm Beach, FL 33408
561-842-4100; fax: 561-842-8984
home page: http://www.sportlink.com/sport

Team Licensing Business (TLB)
Virgo Publishing
3300 North Central Avenue, Suite 2500
Phoenix, AZ 85012
602-990-1101; fax: 602-990-0819
e-mail: tlbmag@vpico.com

World Federation of the Sporting Goods Industry (WFSGI)
200 Castlewood Drive
N. Palm Beach, FL 33408
561-842-4100
home page: www.sportlink.com/international/general/wfgen-3.html

REFERENCES

Association of Black Sporting Goods Professionals. (1997). *ABSG.* www.sportlink.com/ nonprofits/absg/index.html

Baker, S., Doti, M., & Tulloch, T. (1997). *Business plan project for Title 9 Sports.* Unpublished document.

Baseball gets tough on All-Star goods. (1977, July 1). *USA Today*, 5C.

Berry, R.C., & Wong, G.M. (1993). *Law and business of the sports industries: Common issues in amateur and professional sports* (Vol. 2, 2nd ed.). Westport, CT: Praeger Publishers.

Bullington, T. (1995a, July). USOC licensing program. *Team Licensing Business, 7*(7), 36.

Bullington, T. (1995b, October). What a concept! *Team Licensing Business, 7*(10), 22.

Burton, R. (1996). A case study on sports property servicing excellence: National Football League Properties. *Sport Marketing Quarterly, V*(3), 23.

CAPS seizes more than 70,000 in pogs raid. (1995, April). *Team Licensing Business, 7*(4), 16.

Donovan, M.L. (1977). *The Name Game.* Toronto: Warwick Publishing.

Givhan, R. (1997, June 15). Flipping for lids. *The Washington Post*, F3.

Hardy, S. (1995). Adopted by all the leading clubs: Sporting goods and the shaping of leisure. In D.K. Wiggins (Ed.), *Sport in America* (pp. 133–150). Champaign, IL: Human Kinetics.

Helyar, J. (1994). *Lords of the Realm.* New York: Random House.

Himmelstein, L. (1997, May 12). The Swoosh heard 'round the world. *Business Week*, p. 13.

Horovitz, B. (1997, January 3). Jocks don pay apparel. *USA Today*, p. 1C.

Jones, T. (1995, September). Fashion forward. *Team Licensing Business, 7*(9), 18.

Katz, D. (1993, August 16). Triumph of the Swoosh. *Sports Illustrated*, 54–73.

Keller, K. (1997, June). Designer watch. *Self, 19*(6), 116.

Lahham Act, 15 U.S.C. § 1051–1127 (1946).

Lefton, T. (1996a, October 28). At age 50, Stern looks ahead. *Brandweek, XXXVII*(41), 35.

Lefton, T. (1996b, December 9). Category wars: Nike uber alles. *Brandweek, XXXVII*(47), 25.

Licensed sport products expect moderate growth. (1997, March/April). *Team Licensing Business, 9*(3), 20.

Lipsey, R. (Ed.). (1996). *Sports market place.* Princeton, NJ: Sportsguide.

Mazzeo, M.E., Cuneen, J., & Claussen, C.L. (1997). Retail licensing procedures used by selected NCAA Division I institutions: Implications for licensees of collegiate memorabilia. *Sport Marketing Quarterly, V*(1), 41.

NASCAR retail store opens to thunderous response. (1996, July/August). *Team Licensing Business, 8*(5), 18.

National Sporting Goods Association. (1997). *Welcome to the National Sporting Goods Association.* http://www.nsga.org

Naughton, J. (1996, September 6). Exclusive deal with Reebok brings U. of Wisconsin millions of dollars and unexpected criticism. *The Chronicle of Higher Education, XLIII*(2), A65.

NCAA. (1995). *NCAA day by day calendar*. Overland Park, KS: Author.

NCAA. (1996a). Direct distribution up 9.2 percent (1996, September 2). *The NCAA News, 33*(31), 9.

NCAA. (1996b). 1996–97 General operating budget. *The NCAA News*.

NHL establishes partnerships with Nagano in mind. (1997, May/June). *Team Licensing Business, 9*(4), 12.

Nichols, M.A. (1995, April). A look at some of the issues affecting collegiate licensing. *Team Licensing Business, 7*(4), 18.

Nichols, M.A. (1997, May/June). Tapping the subculture. *Team Licensing Business, 9*(4), 20.

Nicklin, J.L. (1996, March 22). Marketing by design. *The Chronicle of Higher Education, XLII* (28), A33.

Nike. (1997a). *Frequently asked questions*. http://info.nike.com

Nike. (1997b). *Nike reports record fourth quarter and fiscal 1997 earnings: Worldwide futures orders increase 18 percent*. http://info.nike.com/earnings/4q1997.html

O'Brien, R. & Hersch, H. (Eds.). (1997, July 7). Scorecard: Go figure. *Sports Illustrated* 87(1) 16.

Plata, C. (1996, September/October). Ducks & dollars. *Team Licensing Business, 8*(6), 38.

Reebok. (1997). *Reebok human rights*. http://www.reebok.com/humanrights/index.html

Riddle, J.D. (1997). *1997 state of the industry report*. North Palm Beach, FL: Sporting Goods Manufacturers Association.

Russell extends licensing concept to Europe. (1995, April). *Team Licensing Business, 7*(4), 16.

Sporting Goods Manufacturers Association. (1995). *The Sporting Goods Manufacturers Association (SGMA): A commemorative report*. North Palm Beach, FL: Author.

Sporting Goods Manufacturers Association. (1996). *Sports participation trends report 1996*. North Palm Beach, FL: Author.

Sporting Goods Manufacturers Association. (1997a). *About sports apparel consumers*. www.sportlink.com/apparel/market/monitor96/about.html

Sporting Goods Manufacturers Association. (1997b). *Athletic pairs purchased*. http://www.sportlink.com/footwear/market/footwearmarket96/afmt_consumer_segs.html

Sporting Goods Manufacturers Association. (1997c). *An outline of the U.S. sports apparel market*. www.sportlink.com/apparel/market/monitor96/outlines.html

Sporting Goods Manufacturers Association. (1997d). *The primary uses of athletic footwear, 1995*. www.sportlink.com/footwear/market/footwearmarket96/afmt_how_used.html

Sporting Goods Manufacturers Association. (1997e). *Special report: A look at global consumers*. www.sportlink.com/apparel/market/monitor96/special_report.html

Sporting Goods Manufacturers Association. (1997f). *Trends in fitness equipment and participation*. http://www.sportlink.com/individualsports/market/fitness/fitnesstrends/fit_trend_97html

Sporting Goods Manufacturers Association. (1997g). *"What's hot and what's not—in sports."* Press release, April 28.

Sporting Goods Manufacturers Association. (1997h). *Where athletic shoes are purchased.* www.sportlink.com/footwear/market/footwearmarket96/afmt_decisions_infl.html

Sporting Goods Manufacturers Association. (1997i). Soccer manufacturers pledge to eliminate child labor. http://www.sportlink.com/teamsports/media/sica97-2.html

Sports merchandising industry loses its creator, David Warsaw. (1996, July/August). *Team Licensing Business, 8*(5), 18.

Sutton, W. (1991). Sport marketing. In B.L. Parkhouse (Ed.), *The management of sport: Its foundation and application* (pp. 149–174). St. Louis: Mosby.

TLB 1996 annual industry report. (1996, May/June). *Team Licensing Business, 8*(3), 20.

UMass promotes local retailers. (1997, May/June). *Team Licensing Business, 9*(4), 34.

University of Notre Dame. (1997, February 19). *Code of Conduct for University of Notre Dame Licensees.* Notre Dame, IN.

Van Meter, D. (1995). Sales of licensed products and services. In D.R. Howard & J.L. Crompton (Eds.), *Financing sport* (pp. 171–185). Morgantown, WV: Fitness Information Technology.

Washington state tax targets sports licensed merchandise. (1997, May/June). *Team Licensing Business, 9*(4), 16.

Watanabe, T. (1997, June 14). Far east youth embrace Jordan, Bulls. *Boston Globe*, 62.

World Federation of the Sporting Goods Industry. (1997). *WSGFI general media information.* www.sportlink.com/international/general/wfgen-3.html

CHAPTER 18

Health and Fitness Industry

Mark A. McDonald and William Howland

Key words: commercial clubs, wellness programs, deconditioned market, quick-fix market, Generation X, profit centers, risk management plan

INTRODUCTION

The health, fitness, and sports club industry experienced tremendous growth in the 1970s, leading many observers to label the fitness movement as a fad that would pass. Current evidence, however, suggests that this movement has evolved into a major lifestyle choice among consumers. Harvey Lauer, President of American Sports Data, Inc., projects increasing numbers of fitness enthusiasts. "What we are experiencing is a dramatic shift in the social consciousness of the American population with regard to health and fitness. In just a few decades, society has literally transformed its self image of life-style behavior to an active and healthy use of leisure time. The health and fitness revolution, one of the most profound value changes of this century, continues unabated as more Americans become health conscious" (IHRSA, 1995, p. 4).

This trend toward health consciousness is reflected in U.S. club membership. In the past 10 years, memberships have grown by 51% (see Table 18–1). Additionally, the number of Americans participating in sport or fitness activities at least 100 days per year reached 43.9 million in 1993. While the fitness movement in the 1970s was driven by the 18- to 34-year-old singles, the most notable demographic trend today is the growth of members ages 35 to 54. Participation by this age group has grown by 55% since 1987, while for the 18- to 34-year-olds it grew by only 20% during the same period (American Sports Data, Inc., 1995). Where do all these fitness enthusiasts exercise? Currently there are approximately 48,000 fitness facilities in the United States. Table 18–2 provides a breakdown of the

Table 18–1 U.S. Club Memberships

Year	Members (in Millions)
1987	13.8
1988	15.2
1989	16.6
1990	16.4
1991	16.7
992	16.5
1993	18.2
1994	20.0
1995	19.1
1996	20.8

Source: IHRSA/American Sports Data, Inc. (1997). *IHRSA/American Sports Data health club trend report.* Boston: IHRSA Publications.

numbers of each type of club. The types of facilities vary greatly, from small 500-square-foot hotel clubs that are simply an amenity for the hotel guest to the 100,000-square-foot mega clubs with thousands of members.

Dominating the health club industry are the approximately 13,300 **commercial clubs** that serve over 11 million of the 20.8 million Americans who belong to health clubs. Commercial clubs are investor- or member-owned fitness, racquet, and athletic facilities that pay property taxes and do not accept tax-deductible contributions for capital or operating costs. The vast majority of these clubs, about 70%, fall into the pure fitness (fitness-only) category, and such a club typically offer members aerobics programs, a fitness center, a cardiovascular equipment area, and some limited amenities such as a snack bar and a pro shop. The larger,

Table 18–2 Types of Clubs

Club Type	Number of Clubs
Health and sport clubs	12,000
Hotel/resort/spa facilities	10,000
Member-owned clubs	5,000
Apartment/condo facilities	4,000
College/university facilities	4,000
Racquet clubs	3,000
Charitable/religious facilities	3,000
Public facilities	3,000
Corporate facilities	3,000
Military/penal facilities	1,000
Hospital facilities	250

Source: IHRSA. (1995). *The 1995 IHRSA report on the state of the health club industry.* Boston: Author.

multipurpose clubs generally offer the same fitness components as the fitness-only clubs, but in addition they offer members racquet sports like tennis and are more likely to have pools, basketball or volleyball courts, restaurants, physical therapy centers, and other such services.

Typically, the hotel/resort/spa, apartment/condo, corporate, and military facilities are smaller in size and limit access to hotel guests, apartment residents, company employees, or military base personnel. However, these facilities are growing in size and sophistication as a greater percentage of the American public embraces an active lifestyle and expects to be able to work out while traveling on business or vacation. Corporations have also begun to invest more of their resources in corporate fitness centers and **wellness programs** for their employees as a means of recruiting and retaining qualified employees, improving morale, reducing absenteeism due to illness, and reducing health insurance costs. Wellness is a holistic approach to preventive health care, providing services that address a person's unique health needs at each stage of life. While still a very small percentage of the total number of clubs, hospital-owned facilities have already made their mark on the industry. Combining fitness and medical expertise, hospital-owned clubs have successfully taken advantage of the good reputations of their parent hospitals within their communities to differentiate themselves from competitor clubs.

The number of commercial health/fitness centers in the United States grew steadily throughout the 1980s as illustrated in Figure 18–1. Specifically, there were about 13,000 clubs in 1989, more than double the 6,211 commercial clubs in 1982. The growth pattern, however, began to change dramatically when the industry entered the 1990s. The number of commercial clubs in the United States peaked in 1990 and then declined throughout the early 1990s. A national recession resulted in stalled demand for club memberships due to reduced participation by frequent fitness enthusiasts.

This downturn in demand resulted in fierce competition between clubs for remaining potential members, ultimately leading to a shakeout of marginally operated clubs and a slowdown in new club development. This was actually a positive trend for remaining clubs, which learned to survive using sound operating and managerial concepts. This trend, however, led to the demise of many small "Mom and Pop" operations and the rise of big club chains.

Figure 18–2 depicts the steady reduction in the pool of owners in the club industry. While single-club ("Mom and Pop") operations still dominate the market, they are losing market share. In 1989, 14% of clubs were part of a multiple operation or chain. This percentage increased to almost 50% by 1996. While major chains and franchise groups are a driving force, budding management companies are fueling this trend. Specifically, clubs that were single operations a couple of years ago have expanded to include several more clubs under a common umbrella.

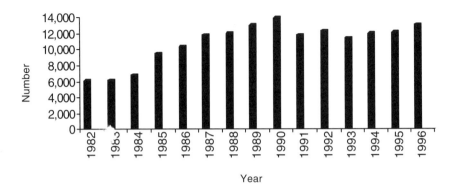

Figure 18–1 Number of U.S. Commercial Health Clubs/Fitness Centers. *Source:* Reprinted with permission from *1997 Profiles of Success*, p. 12, © 1997, IHRSA.

Table 18–3 gives a breakdown of the major players in the health/fitness market. Five of these club chains are headquartered internationally: Central Sports Co., Ltd. (Japan), G&P Gockel, Paul & Partner (Germany, Switzerland, Austria), Clark Hatch Fitness Centers (Asia/Pacific rim), Archer Leisure Limited (England), and Health & Racquet Club Limited (South Africa).

There is a clear cutoff point between the first five club chains on this list and the remaining club chains. American Club Systems, Gold's Gym, Bally's, World Gym, and Club Corporation of America, with more than 200 clubs each, are the dominant chains in the marketplace.

HISTORY

Prior to the 1960s, health and fitness clubs were mainly small, sport-specific facilities such as boxing gyms and weightlifting clubs. These facilities catered to

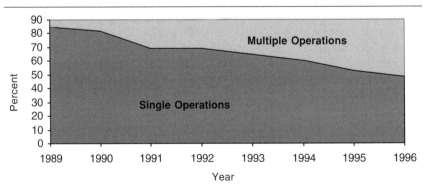

Figure 18–2 Single Operations vs. Multiple Operations. *Source:* Adapted with permission from *The 1995 Profiles of Success*, p. 18, © 1995, IHRSA.

Table 18–3 The Industry's Big Players

	Number of Clubs						
	1990	*1991*	*1992*	*1993*	*1994*	*1995*	*1996*
American Club Systems	2	10	15	15	42	53	661
Gold's Gym Enterprises	330	350	375	400	467	500	503
Bally's Health & Tennis Corp.	N/A	307	310	336	339	N/A	320
World Gym Licensing, Ltd.	88	120	145	175	194	253	255
Club Corporation of America	N/A	200	220	230	240	250	250+
Central Sports Co., Ltd.	137	143	151	157	159	152	159
Fitness Holdings, Inc.	N/A	N/A	76	89	101	110	140
Health Fitness Physical Therapy	N/A	N/A	30	31	35	85	120
G&P Gockel, Paul & Partner	19	24	37	54	84	92	98
Compagnie Gymnase Club	N/A	N/A	N/A	N/A	75	94	94
Family Fitness	48	54	60	65	72	77	N/A
The Fitness Company	N/A	N/A	30	38	50	55	68
Clark Hatch Fitness Centers	43	46	50	53	57	58	60
American Leisure Corporation	32	35	46	51	55	57	61
Living Well Health Clubs	N/A	N/A	7	12	32	33	55
WTS International, Inc.	N/A	N/A	12	21	25	28	49
DIC Renaissance, Inc.	N/A	N/A	28	33	39	42	44
TCA	N/A	N/A	N/A	N/A	41	42	43
Archer Leisure Limited	16	18	22	26	38	40	N/A
Organizacion Britania	N/A	N/A	36	38	39	40	40
Good Life Fitness Clubs	N/A	N/A	27	33	33	36	39
Club Sports International	25	25	26	26	33	37	N/A
#1 Nautilus Fitness Center	26	27	27	33	33	36	N/A
Town Sports International	16	17	18	20	24	30	34
24 Hr Nautilus Fitness Centers	12	13	16	24	32	33	N/A

Source: IHRSA. (1997a). *The IHRSA report on the state of the health club industry.* Boston: Author.

a very small percentage of the U.S. population. Beginning in the 1960s, the dramatic growth in the popularity of both tennis and racquetball fueled the construction of thousands of racquet clubs around the country. Interest in tennis and racquetball continued throughout the 1970s. At this time, the beginnings of the aerobics movement and the advent of more sophisticated and durable cardiovascular equipment, such as stationary bikes and treadmills, led to fitness centers offering aerobics classes, strength training areas, and cardiovascular equipment. Expanded programs and facilities began to attract members interested in more than racquet sports and body building. In particular, women began to join clubs, leading to an explosion in the popularity of aerobics classes during the 1980s. During the 1970s and 1980s, the health club industry unfortunately developed a reputation for engaging in poor business practices. Free of legal and regulatory constraints, many clubs engaged in high-volume, high-pressure sales tactics and deceptive advertising, which significantly eroded consumer confidence in the industry, translating into high membership attrition rates. In addition, facility safety standards were neglected as clubs vigorously pursued new members. Beginning in the early 1980s and continuing into the 1990s, consumer participation in tennis and racquetball declined, damaging the racquet club segment of the industry. Faced with slumping demand for their courts, many racquet clubs went bankrupt. Some owners, however, converted court space into fitness, aerobics, and cardiovascular equipment areas and expanded their locker rooms, becoming multip' 'rpose clubs offering both racquet sports and fitness. At this time, regional chains began to grow as successful club companies expanded their operations to run multiple locations. Typically, these chains comprised three to five facilities in one regional market, with a few pioneers managing multiple locations in several states.

Along with the expansion of regional club chains, a trend toward consolidation started as larger companies absorbed stand-alone clubs into their operations. Industry consolidation has accelerated during the 1990s. Today, the club industry is still made up largely of companies operating fewer than three locations. However, several larger chains have taken advantage of their size and sophistication to attract investment from financial institutions such as banks and venture capital firms, providing the capital necessary to continue their expansions. The emergence of large club chains, coupled with overall industry growth, has expanded career opportunities.

BUSINESS PRINCIPLES

The highly competitive environment, resulting from the emergence of multiple operations and the entrance of new competitors such as hospitals and hotels into the industry, has directly impacted the marketing strategies undertaken by clubs. When the industry was in a high growth phase during the 1970s, consumer demand (prospective members) far outstripped supply (club facilities). Under these conditions, mass untargeted marketing was sufficient to drive customers into clubs. As the industry became more competitive, however, and supply caught up with and eventually surpassed demand, new and more sophisticated marketing strategies were needed.

Target Marketing

One of the first changes was the move from mass marketing to target marketing, which entailed dividing the market into smaller segments based on demographics (age, income, gender, and so forth), lifestyles, and motivations for participation. Exhibit 18–1 presents some of the segments that have been successfully targeted. Three of these target markets require further explanation. The **deconditioned market** refers to the segment of the population that is either completely physically

Exhibit 18–1 Fitness Consumer Segments

Deconditioned market
Family market
Corporate market
Children's market
Senior's market
Women's-only market
Minority market
Generation X
Rehabilitation market
Quick-fix market

inactive or active for less than 60 days a year. Individuals classified as deconditioned are the most difficult to get to join health and fitness centers. Individuals constituting the **quick-fix market**, in contrast, readily join clubs but only for short periods of time. These consumers join specifically to satisfy short-term fitness needs. Once their goals are met, they discontinue club usage. Lastly, **Generation X** refers to the segment of the population between the ages of 18 and 34. Currently, 38 million people in the United States make up this segment.

In order to successfully target different segments within the health club consumer base, club operators develop facilities and programs, and train staff to meet the needs of particular demographic groups. A good example is a club catering exclusively to women, with fitness equipment and weights designed specifically for the anatomical needs of a woman's body and programs addressing issues like exercise and pregnancy, menopause, and breast cancer. These women-only clubs promote themselves as offering a single-sex environment committed to women's health and exercise needs, and as a result, often attract members who would not seriously consider joining a coed club.

Another example of a targeted market is the corporate market. Historically, health club membership was reserved as a perk for a company's executives. Today, many health clubs develop arrangements with local employers to give a company's entire work force, and their families, access to the club. In addition, many clubs help their corporate clients implement employee wellness programs by organizing health education classes at the work site, offering nutritional counseling to employees, running stress management workshops, and providing physical therapy services to injured employees.

Targeting Generation X

Some health clubs, such as Crunch, are beginning to actively pursue the Generation X market. The four Crunch fitness centers in Manhattan have been highly successful where many other clubs have failed. Crunch has created an environment attractive to young adults. Founded by Doug Levine, a former investment banker, in 1989, Crunch has the following mission statement: "Crunch is not competitive, it is nonjudgmental, it is not elitist, it does not represent a kind of person" (Hildreth, 1996, p. 35).

Crunch aims to provide an environment of unconditional acceptance. One advertisement, espousing this theme, has the following tag line: "Why bother working out? You're beautiful just the way you are." When patrons work out in the clubs, the emphasis is on entertainment. Some pieces of equipment come with Sony PlayStations, and the programming is always innovative and adventuresome (e.g., roller aerobics and CYKED, which is yoga class taught using stationary bikes in a candlelit room). One new innovation, a Hypoxic Training Center, is particularly interesting. This, says Levine, is a "depressurized Plexiglas room that simulates the air conditions at 9,000 feet above sea level. If you're conditioning your cardiovascular system in this environment, think of what your performance will be at sea level" (IHRSA, 1997b, p. 19).

Eighty percent of Crunch's membership is between the ages of 20 and 35. According to the chief operating officer, Roger Harvey, "The health club industry has become fixated on the baby boomers, but I think that more and more owners are recognizing that the 18- to 35-year-old market is a large and profitable one" (Hildreth, 1996, p. 36). While the club business is going well, Crunch receives over 50% of its profits from other sources. Through hair-care and skin-care products, CDs, books, videos, and nationally syndicated exercise shows, Crunch has been able to build a major brand. Levine notes, "We are, in fact, a marketing company; we use our gyms as the engine for our brand, and when we license our name or engage in joint ventures, we pick our partners wisely" (Keeny, 1997, p. 42).

Clubs have traditionally relied heavily upon membership sales to fuel revenue growth. This overreliance on dues revenue, however, is beginning to change. Fitness-only clubs, which are typically the most dependent upon membership sales for growth, generated about 27% of their revenues in 1995 from non-dues sources such as tennis lesson fees, personal training fees, and pro shop merchandise sales, up from 20% in 1994.

Program Offerings

To survive in a competitive marketplace, clubs are learning the importance of providing "one-stop shopping" for their customers. By offering a diverse range of innovative services, clubs discourage current members from checking out the competition. Additionally, a variety of programs and **profit centers** also enhance the value of memberships and improve retention. Profit centers are strategic operating areas within a club for which distinct operating revenues and expenses can be determined. While club operators in the past have attempted to house the most expensive new equipment, the competition has shifted to providing services that foster a healthy lifestyle.

The list of popular club programming shown in Table 18–4 is a good indication of the breadth of services being provided by clubs. Almost two-thirds of clubs, for example, offer some form of child care, and 38% offer members the opportunity to learn yoga or martial arts. Clearly, club programming is no longer limited to traditional fitness activities. Nutritional counseling, weight management, wellness education, and the like are now prevalent in the health club setting.

Clubs have found they can increase sales of current products and services by developing programming and profit centers that attract new members from outside the traditional club market. Some clubs have discovered, for example, that by raising the water temperature of their pools, they can offer a diverse range of aquatics classes suitable for deconditioned, mature adults and physical-therapy patients. Special programs are being developed for children and seniors. Additionally, the connection between mind and body is increasingly being empha-

---

Table 18–4 The Top 20 Club Programs

Program	% of Clubs Offering Program
Fitness evaluation	87
Step/bench aerobics	84
Personal training	81
Strength training	78
Child care	66
Cross-training	62
Weight control	61
Nutritional counseling	61
Massage	60
Corporate programming	56
Exercise prescriptions	51
Seniors' programming	46
Aquatic exercise	45
Special programs, diabetes	43
Juniors' programming	40
Competitive sports	40
Martial arts	38
Yoga	38
Health-education programs	34
Children's programming	31

Source: IHRSA. (1996). *Annual IHRSA member census.* Internal Association Member Database. Boston: Author.

sized. With a changing population interested in a holistic approach to health, this programming trend is likely to continue. According to Kevin Hood, Director of Fitness at Denver's International Wellness Club:

Combining mind, body, and spiritual fitness is important, because the whole is always greater than the sum of its parts. Most clubs focus on the body. People who go to them walk out having exercised, but still not feeling great. We need to position ourselves as health care providers in the future, part of the continuum of health care. We don't deal with acute cases, like hospitals do, but we do deal with the next step down. We can administer physical, mental, and spiritual treatment at that level to help individuals maintain a healthy lifestyle. (IHRSA, 1995)

All of these developments point to superior programming fast becoming the key competitive advantage in this industry.

Facility Types

The average club has approximately 45,000 square feet of indoor space and about the same amount of usable outdoor space (IHRSA, 1997a). While clubs are competing more and more in the realm of programming, they still offer a wide variety of facilities for their members. Some of the most commonly offered facilities are listed in Table 18–5. The three facilities that are considered the heart of clubs—cardiovascular, free weights, and fitness center—are being provided by more than 90% of fitness clubs. Saunas continue to grow in popularity among club owners. Resistance machines lead the way in terms of the most popular equipment in clubs, with 9.3 million active users. Other popular equipment with increasing usage includes treadmills and free weights. The utilization of stair climbers, a hot item in the early 1990s, has leveled off and is experiencing zero growth (Table 18–6).

LEGAL AND ETHICAL ISSUES

Currently, the health club industry remains largely unregulated in the United States. With club revenues driven by membership fees, operators have traditionally focused on member sales, rather than customer service. Minimal government regulation, combined with this sales orientation, has led to the development of a number of pressing ethical and legal issues, which tend to erode consumer confidence in the industry.

Table 18–5 Most Commonly Offered Facilities

Facility	% of Clubs Offering Facility
Cardiovascular	93
Aerobics	91
Fitness center	91
Free weights	89
Variable resistance	82
Sauna	71
Pro shop	58
Nursery	57
Snack/juice bar	52
Whirlpool	50
Steam room	45
Indoor pool	42
Vending machines	41
Racquetball	37
Basketball	32
Bar/lounge	26
Restaurant	23
Squash	22
Outdoor tennis	20
Outdoor pool	20

Source: IHRSA. (1996). *Annual IHRSA member census.* Internal Association Member Database. Boston: Author.

Good examples of the dangers inherent in the sales orientation are high-pressure sales tactics and the coercing of potential members to sign lifetime contracts. The drive for membership revenues—some clubs set monthly quotas as high as 200 to 300 new members—has led to the use of manipulative sales tactics that force consumers to sign contracts they do not fully comprehend. Additionally, given the high attrition rates in this industry, some clubs encourage individuals to sign long-term or lifetime contracts, which result in clubs' continuing to

Table 18–6 "Top 5" Club Activities

Activity	Number of Participants
Resistance machines	9.3 million
Treadmills	7.4 million
Free weights	7.7 million
Stationary bikes	7.4 million
Stairclimbers	6.4 million

Source: IHRSA/American Sports Data, Inc. (1997). *IHRSA/American Sports Data health club trend report.* Boston: IHRSA Publications.

receive member dues long after a member has stopped utilizing the service. In response to these abuses, most states have developed some form of consumer protection legislation governing the nature of membership contracts clubs can utilize with their customers. In those states regulating membership agreements, most limit the length of a membership contract, prohibit lifetime contracts, and require that the consumer have certain rights of contract cancellation. In many cases, the rights to cancellation include a "cooling-off" period, typically three business days after joining a club, during which a new member has the right to cancel the membership for any reason.

Operators are not required to obtain licenses to open clubs. As a result, the image of the industry has further been tarnished by the abrupt closing of clubs. With the ability to pre-sell membership contracts, a club developer can sell high-priced memberships prior to opening. With the money in hand, an unscrupulous developer can then leave town, leaving the customers "holding the bag." Additionally, health clubs have also been known to switch locations or change their names to confuse creditors (Mooney, 1982). To combat these problems, some states require developers to post bonds prior to pre-selling memberships and/or opening a new facility.

Given that club membership involves participation in physical activities, all clubs must contend with injury liability issues. These issues fall into four categories: (1) maintaining safe conditions in areas such as parking lots, locker rooms, courts, exercise areas, and pool areas; (2) providing exercise programs appropriate to members' physical conditions and abilities; (3) instructing and supervising members during exercise sessions; and (4) responding appropriately to accidents and medical emergencies (Adams, 1996). Given the constant risk of injury posed by the sport club environment, all facilities should develop and implement a **risk management plan**. A risk management plan provides a systematic approach incorporating all actions that can reduce or eliminate the potential for injury to club members (Walker & Stotlar, 1997). (For more information about risk management, see Chapter 5, Legal Principles Applied to Sport Management.)

The importance of liability issues has increased with the passage of the Americans with Disabilities Act (ADA). To accommodate the needs of people with disabilities, this law requires club managers to make certain modifications when building new facilities or renovating existing facilities. The ADA requires clubs to eliminate "architectural barriers that are structural in nature, when it is readily achievable to do so" (Department of Justice, 1992, p. 258). Architectural barriers are elements such as steps, curbs, mirrors, and equipment that impede or prevent access or use by the participant with a disability (Miller, 1997). In a health club setting, for example, a four-foot partition that stops an individual in a wheelchair from speaking with a health club worker on the other side would be classified as a communication barrier (Miller, 1997). The ADA raises ethical considerations because it gives managers the choice of merely meeting the minimum legal requirements or exceeding the guidelines in order to provide maximum opportunities for people with disabilities to participate in club offerings.

Historically, tort and contract liability, consumer protection, and other legal issues relevant to running a health club have not served as a barrier to entry into the industry. It is much more likely for access to sufficient financial funding to be an entrepreneur's greatest challenge when attempting to launch a new club.

CAREER OPPORTUNITIES

Working for a club is not like working for IBM, where one can work an entire career within one company. Very few clear career paths exist for advancement within the industry. The recent trend of club ownership and/or management consolidation, however, has created a number of larger companies overseeing multiple facilities and offering employees potential career paths into well-paying management positions.

Careers in this industry usually begin with part-time or summer work. People gain entrance by helping out at the front desk, in the sales department, or as athletic instructors. Hourly pay for some typical part-time positions is provided in Table 18–7. Upon graduating from college, these individuals are then placed in positions such as pro-shop, front-desk, or service manager. Salaries for entry-level positions in this industry range from $12,000 to $22,000. Not surprisingly, these positions are usually held by young men and women. Table 18–8 displays average salaries for entry-level positions.

While entry-level salaries are low in the health, fitness, and sport club industry, people in such entry-level positions have the opportunity to take on numerous responsibilities their first couple years on the job and thus prove themselves as workers while they learn a variety of tasks. Demand for managerial talent still far outstrips supply, providing ample room for talented individuals to move quickly

---

Table 18–7 Hourly Wages for Part-Time Positions

Position	Hourly Wage
Aerobics instructor	$16.88
Fitness center personnel	$7.17
Front-desk personnel	$6.20
Child-care staff	$5.85
Summer camp staff	$6.25

Source: IHRSA. (1997). *The 1997 IHRSA profiles of success report.* Boston: Author.

Table 18–8 Annual Salaries for Entry-Level Positions

Position	Annual Salary
Children's program manager	$19,231
Food and beverage manager	$23,599
Summer camp director	$14,729
Service manager	$21,591
Aquatics director	$22,453

Source: IHRSA. (1997). The 1997 IHRSA profiles of success report. Boston: Author.

up the ladder to managerial positions and better pay. The typical club general manager earns between $30,000 and $40,000, with pay differentials corresponding to club size and total revenues.

Working conditions in this industry are comparable to those in the hotel and restaurant industries. Clubs are often open 18 hours a day, seven days a week, 12 months a year. Staffing these open hours requires three 40-hour shifts per week. Managers should be prepared for 50+ hours in an average workweek. Club staff members are required to work weekend, early morning, and/or evening shifts.

There is, however, an upside to working in this industry. In addition to the free membership that customarily comes with employment at a club, forward-thinking employers often work with staff on schedules that meet both the club's and employees' needs. In addition, because of the small financial rewards associated with entry-level positions, the fitness industry is dominated by people motivated to maintain their own active lifestyle as well as helping others live healthy and productive lives. This industry is definitely for people who like being surrounded by high-energy, like-minded people.

What skills and knowledge base does a person need to develop before entering the health, fitness, and sport club industry? Success in this industry requires a combination of sport/fitness expertise and business skills. Club professionals need to be able to do what is expected of managers in general: read an income statement and balance sheet, prepare budgets, develop and implement a marketing plan, manage employees, and use excellent customer service skills. Additionally, since people in these positions guide the sport and fitness activities of members, knowledge and expertise in specific sport or fitness activities increases the attractiveness of candidates.

Educational preparation for careers in sport club management is derived from two major sources: collegiate programs and professional associations. Since success in this field requires an understanding of business and fitness concepts, degree programs in sport management and/or exercise science are particularly relevant. These two areas of study should be viewed as complementary. Understanding and responding to the fitness and wellness needs of club members requires specific knowledge in exercise science. Coursework in human anatomy and physiology, kinesiology, and nutrition is particularly helpful for those seeking to break into this industry. In addition, a background in sport management can prepare a person with club management aspirations to face the myriad of legal, marketing, accounting, and financial issues involved in successfully operating a health and fitness club.

Beyond earning a college degree in exercise science and/or sport managment, a person on the sport/fitness club career track can connect with several organizations that offer advanced educational opportunities and certification programs. The International Health, Racquet and Sportsclub Association (IHRSA), the largest association in the health and fitness area, offers two major conferences annually, as well as sponsoring executive education courses and a large trade show held in conjunction with its December conference. These events present great networking opportunities for both new entrants and established professionals in the field.

Professional associations also provide certification in activity areas. Examples of these associations include the American College of Sports Medicine (ACSM), United States Professional Tennis Association (USPTA), and the International Dance-Exercise Association (IDEA). Individuals with expertise in specific sport or fitness activities who aspire to be instructors should seek certification from the appropriate governing organization.

CURRENT ISSUES

The health, fitness, and sport club industry is moving toward maturity. After experiencing tremendous growth in the 1970s and consolidation in the late 1980s and early 1990s, the industry is stabilizing. Students planning on entering this industry should be aware of a number of trends that will impact the industry in coming years.

Health Care Affiliations

The industry is currently repositioning itself as the normative institutional setting for "upstream" health promotion—the promotion of health and the prevention of illness and injury. Traditional health care providers now realize that the public understands the relationship between regular exercise and health. Thus, health maintenance organizations and health insurance companies are beginning to provide incentives for their subscribers to participate in health promotion programs at clubs.

Currently, almost one-half of clubs have established relationships with organizations, businesses, or professionals within the health care industry. As more and more consumers become aware of the relationship between exercise and health, and more medical providers recognize the benefits of affiliating with health clubs, this number is bound to rise (IHRSA, 1997a).

Commercial versus Nonprofit Clubs

One issue continuing to impact the industry is unfair competition. Tax-exempt companies, such as YMCAs, YWCAs, and hospitals with lower cost structures, often compete directly with commercial clubs, offering many of the same services. Eighty-six percent of IHRSA clubs report being threatened by such competition (IHRSA, 1997b). The YMCA, for example, has increased its building and expansion activities in recent years. And on the heels of the health care community's becoming more and more interested in exercise as a preventive measure, hospitals are starting to enter the fitness market. The good news, however, is that even with this increased competition from nonprofits, commercial clubs are claiming a growing share of total memberships. A decade ago, 46% of all club members worked out in commercial clubs. This share has now risen to 61% (IHRSA, 1997b). YMCAs are now marketing their programs heavily, and utilizing the additional revenues to increase their market share (Miller & Fielding, 1995).

Home Fitness

Approximately 70% of Americans over the age of 40 are now more concerned about their health than they were in the past. Additionally, 46% of sedentary Americans indicate they would like to initiate regular exercise programs. As a result of these attitudes, the home fitness market, currently estimated at $2.5 billion, is growing. Millions subscribe to fitness and health publications and spend more than $200 million on exercise videos (IHRSA, 1997b).

Does the home fitness market compete with club fitness? Two-thirds of health club users also own and use home exercise equipment. Thus, club owners tend to view home fitness as a complement to club fitness. IHRSA's Executive Director John McCarthy concurs: "It's a little like the video market vs. movie theaters. People enjoy both for different reasons. They may exercise at home to be with family members. But they continue to come to clubs because they enjoy the choices of equipment and programs, the service and instruction from club staff, the camaraderie with other exercisers, and the amenities. It's time people take for themselves" (IHRSA, 1995, p. 20). Club operators will need to leverage home fitness in the future. Home fitness offers a natural opportunity for clubs to sell equipment and provide consultation to their members on how to maximize the combination of home and club fitness.

Going Public

Investors have historically been hesitant regarding the $7.75 billion heath club industry, making it difficult for club operators to obtain the capital required to expand or acquire clubs. Slowly, this is starting to change. There were no public, stand-alone health club companies five years ago. Currently, there are six publicly traded health and fitness clubs: Bally Total Fitness, Main Street Athletic Clubs, Health Fitness Physical Therapy, Health Tech International, The Sports Club Company, and Ultrafit Centers.

In 1995, The Sports Club Company, owner of high-end clubs in Southern California, raised $42 million in capital for expansion through a public stock offering. David Alan Lloyd took his United Kingdom company, David Lloyd Leisure PLC, public in March 1993. In McLean, Virginia, Sport and Health Company, L.C. has successfully completed a financial capitalization involving $21 million in debt and $11 million in equity (Keeny, 1997).

Going public can offer a company the benefits of improved cash flow and increased availability of financial resources. It is likely that over the next decade many companies will go public or be coerced through the forces of consolidation to join another public entity. Companies such as Bally and The Sports Club Company have begun to gain acceptance by Wall Street, and additional companies are likely to follow.

This industry has changed in the past decade from being made up primarily of "Mom and Pop" clubs to being an increasingly integrated and professionally managed industry. This evolution coincides with rapidly expanding career opportunities. Leadership of the club business is now dominated by people who believe quality is the key to long-term profitability. This quality initiative has been a call to upgrade club facilities, equipment, and most important, services.

SUMMARY

The fitness craze of the 1970s has evolved into a lifestyle choice for consumers of every age, race, and ability level. Currently, over 20.8 million Americans belong to health clubs, with the vast majority joining fitness-only facilities. During the 1990s, fierce competition in this industry led to the demise of many "Mom and Pop" operations and the subsequent increase in the numbers of big club chains such as Gold's Gym. The emergence of this franchise aspect of the industry has created new and expanded career opportunities. Entry-level salaries are low, but the potential for talented individuals to assume responsibility and rapidly move through the ranks is high. Success in this industry depends on a combination of sport or fitness expertise and business skills.

Revenue growth has traditionally been a function of membership fees. A competitive marketplace, however, has forced clubs to provide "one-stop shopping" for their customers. A wide variety of programming options are now being provided by innovative operators, including nutritional counseling, martial arts, and wellness education. As this industry moves toward maturity, a number of trends will impact managers attempting to succeed in this fluid environment. Some of these trends are the establishing of business relationships with health care providers, the unfair competitive advantage enjoyed by nonprofit clubs, emergence of home fitness as an exercise option, and the increasing numbers of health clubs going public in order to obtain the capital required to expand or acquire clubs. Additionally, the search for new revenue sources and growth opportunities has led to clubs targeting very specific markets such as the Generation X, the deconditioned, and the mature markets. These same pressures have resulted in a number of ethical and legal issues. Specifically, club operators have sometimes resorted to high-pressure sales tactics and coerced members into signing lifetime contracts. Clubs are also facing legal challenges arising out of tort liability concerns and the ADA. Concerning the health and fitness industry, one thing is certain—this will continue to be an exciting and dynamic environment in which to build a career.

CASE STUDY: THE RACQUET CLUB FACES A CHALLENGE

Established in 1971 as a large indoor tennis facility with 10 courts, The Racquet Club, like many other indoor tennis clubs facing dramatically declining demand for tennis in the 1980s, converted two of its tennis courts to build a 10,000-square-foot fitness center and cardiovascular area, a 1,000-square-foot aerobics studio, and expanded locker rooms for both men and women.

At first the conversion to a multipurpose club went well. The Racquet Club was able to recruit enough new fitness members to justify the conversion to a multipurpose facility. During the past five years, however, business has limped along at barely a break-even pace. Presently, the club has about 2,500 members and generates approximately $2 million in yearly total revenues.

Still the place in town to play tennis, The Racquet Club has developed a reputation for running the best junior tennis program in the state. However, the restaurant continues to lose about $10,000 a year, and the personal training program generated just $45,000, with the six independent contractor trainers refusing to work together to grow the program. The trainers, instead, focus entirely on developing their individual client lists. This frustrates the owners, who know of similar clubs that report operating training programs generating $300,000 a year in revenues.

The Racquet Club currently faces challenges from two new fitness-only clubs that have opened within the past 18 months. One of these is a well-known licensed/franchised "gym" that appears to be properly run and is successfully leveraging its recognized name, brand-new facilities, and well-equipped center to lure members away from The Racquet Club. The other new facility is a fitness-only club, which has declared that it will be the low-cost fitness center in town, offering memberships for as little as $19 a month, compared to the $55 per month Racquet Club fitness members pay and the $75 monthly charge for tennis/fitness members.

The Racquet Club's sales staff increasingly report that prospective members are shopping the competitor, that some of the eight-year-old equipment in the fitness center does not impress prospective members, and that they want to be able to offer special, discount prices to combat the price objections they insist have become a problem since the low-cost competitor recently opened.

On a positive note, The Racquet Club's 25-year-plus history with the community, its ownership of its own land, and the business' relatively debt-free status all combine to make obtaining a loan for renovations or equipment upgrades easy. The Racquet Club's reputation in the community has resulted in the local hospital approaching it first about a potential partnership. However, it is unlikely that any formal arrangement would be signed during the upcoming 12 to 18 months.

Intrigued by the potential of the hospital partnership, the owners have expressed a willingness to obtain loans for a major renovation. Before they move ahead, though, they need to see dramatic improvements in profitability for the coming year.

Questions for Discussion

1. As The Racquet Club's general manager responsible for increasing profitability this year, what would be the two facets of the business that you would select first for improvement? Why?
2. How would you resolve the personnel problems in the personal training area? How would your solution lead to increased personal training growth?
3. The sales staff are pushing to discount membership rates. What are two advantages of allowing prices to be discounted and two disadvantages of such a practice?
4. How could advertising be utilized to leverage The Racquet Club's good reputation within the community to help compete effectively with the two new competitor clubs?

RESOURCES

Professional Organizations

Aerobics and Fitness Association of America (AFAA)
15250 Ventura Blvd., No. 200
Sherman Oaks, CA 91403
818-905-0040; fax: 800-446-2322

The International Association of Fitness Professionals (IDEA)
6190 Cornerstone Court E., Suite 204
San Diego, CA 92121
619-535-8979

International Health, Racquet and Sportsclub Association (IHRSA)
263 Summer St.
Boston, MA 02210
617-951-0055
www.ihrsa.org

National Athletic Trainers' Association
2952 Stemmons Freeway
Dallas, TX 75247
214-637-6282

National Strength & Conditioning Association
530 Communications Circle, Suite 204
Colorado Springs, CO 80905
719-632-NSCA
e-mail: NSCA@USA.net

Professional Publications

Club Business International
263 Summer St.
Boston, MA 02210
617-951-0055; fax: 800-228-4772

Club Industry
1300 Virginia Drive, Suite 400
Ft. Washington, PA 19034
215-643-8081

Fitness Management
3923 W. 6th St.
Los Angeles, CA 90020
213-385-3920
e-mail: fitmgt@cts.com

IDEA Today
6190 Cornerstone Court E., Suite 204
San Diego, CA 92121
619-535-8979

REFERENCES

Adams, K. (1996). Injury liability: How to protect your club. *IHRSA government relations briefing paper*. Boston: IHRSA Publications.

American Sports Data, Inc. (1995). *Health club trend report*. Boston: Author.

Hildreth, S. (1996, January). Crunch has decoded the niche that confounds other clubs. *Club Business International*, 35–39.

IHRSA. (1995). *The 1995 IHRSA report on the state of the health club industry*. Boston: Author.

IHRSA (1997a). *The 1997 IHRSA profiles of success report*. Boston: Author.

IHRSA (1997b). *The 1997 IHRSA report on the state of the health club industry*. Boston: Author.

Keeny, B.A. (1997, February). The pure-play players: Bally total fitness and Mike Talla's sports club have made an impression on Wall Street. *Club Business International*, 32–45.

Miller, L.K. (1997). *Sport business management*. Gaithersburg, MD: Aspen Publishers, Inc.

Miller, L.K., & Fielding, L.W. (1995, February). The battle between the for profit health club and the "commercial" YMCA. *Journal of Sport and Social Issues*, 76–107.

Mooney, C. (1982, September 10). Keeping track of health clubs is a workout for consumers. *Miami Herald*, p. 12.

Walker, M.L., & Stotlar, D.K. (1997). *Sport facility management*. Sudbury, MA: Jones and Bartlett Publishers.

CHAPTER 19

Recreational Sport

Laurie Gullion

Key words: direct participation, indirect participation, parks movement, community-based recreation, public recreation, military recreation, outdoor recreation, university outdoor programs, therapeutic recreation, public sector, private sector, environmental awareness, cultural awareness, Americans with Disabilities Act, risk management, informed participant consent

INTRODUCTION

An interest in recreation is integral to most American's lives from childhood through adulthood. Whether the arena is indoors or outdoors, people seek to be involved directly or indirectly with recreational activities for a variety of reasons: fun, excitement, relaxation, social interaction, challenge, and lifestyle enhancement.

The roots of involvement with organized recreation may begin in childhood with Little League baseball and Lassie League softball. It can be nurtured through involvement in YMCA aquatics programs and summer camp experiences. In adulthood people explore enjoyable activities such as the thrill of whitewater kayaking and summer vacations with families in national parks. Through retirement a person can embrace a range of "masters" activities like "70 plus" ski clubs that encourage lifelong participation in an activity.

The recreation industry in the United States is extensive and diverse, although the various segments usually share a common mission. Organizations strive to create structured activities that provide personal and social benefits to individuals during their leisure time. A characteristic of recreation that sets it apart from other segments of the sport industry is that there is often **direct participation** by people through active performance in an activity, such as aerobics classes, a mountain bike race, or fishing with a certified guide. However, **indirect participation** by spectators may also occur in recreation and still contribute to the economic base, a strategy effective in the tourism industry, which seeks to promote recreation-based events that draw people to a particular region.

HISTORY: THE MODERN RECREATION MOVEMENT

Leisure time in the nineteenth century emerged as a result of the urbanization and industrialization of American society. Technological innovations in factories made work more monotonous and prompted citizens to seek diversions. The recreation movement sought to address social issues affecting a population faced with a 66-hour workweek (six days a week, 11 hours a day). Public attitudes toward work and leisure changed from a more Puritan ethic, which valued work over play, to a perception of recreation as important to the growth and health of the individual and also as a means to improve community well-being.

By mid-century, a number of developments helped to expand and formalize recreation. In reaction to accelerating urban development, the **parks movement** resulted in the establishment of public lands, like Central Park in New York City, open free of charge to all people. Boston's famous "Emerald Necklace" of parkways began to surround and provide an escape from its urban center. Technology also brought innovations like the bicycle and golf ball to the American public, and the moderate price of sporting goods such as canoes and rowboats opened these activities to all economic classes. Social and religious institutions like the Young Men's and Young Women's Christian Associations (YMCA, YWCA) organized in local cities.

An increasing fascination with the American wilderness prompted an interest in outdoor travel and construction of the famous mountain houses and wilderness camps of the Northeast, most popularly in the Adirondacks of New York. Only the most daring ventured to the uncivilized West, yet Theodore Roosevelt was able to convince the federal government to establish Yellowstone as the first national park in 1872. This act established America's commitment to the preservation of public lands, a unique philosophy later exported to European countries.

By the end of the century, the recreation movement had created formal organizations in the form of local clubs and national associations devoted to recreation and committed to developing standards for activities (Braden, 1988). Organizations such as the American Canoe Association, established in 1880, began to shape not only recreational participation through the development of instructional guidelines but also rules for competition in races and regattas. Early in the twentieth century, the interest in recreation continued to accelerate with the establishment of well-known organizations like the Boy Scouts in 1910 and the Girl Scouts in 1912.

A phenomenon unique to the United States also emerged during this time. According to Eells (1986), organized summer camps for children began to proliferate, largely in New England. In the previous century the camping movement had often focused on gatherings of a religious nature for adults. Concerned about the effect of urbanization on children, advocates developed the first "Fresh Air" camps in the latter half of the century to allow urban children to travel to the country. By the early 1900s, the camping movement had gained momentum in attracting children to these popular outdoor experiences. Now specialty camps for sports and recreational activities have been added to the mix. The American Camping Association reported in 1996 that 8,500 camps existed nationwide and served 6 million children (Coutellier, 1997).

Following World War II, an expanding American economy broadened the scope of the recreation industry. It led to the creation of local parks and recreation departments, the establishment of armed forces recreation to improve the morale of individuals and families, and the emergence of commercial recreation enterprises such as the skiing industry. In 1996 the United States had 15,390 golf courses, 69% of which were open to the public (National Golf Foundation, 1996b). Technological improvements continue to develop new sporting goods that generate interest in activities such as snowboarding, in-line skating, and roller hockey.

TRENDS IN PARTICIPATION

An appreciation of the outdoors is central to the American lifestyle, and recent trends in participation support the enduring value of outdoor recreation. The National Survey on Recreation and the Environment (U.S.D.A., Bureau of Land Management, U.S. Army Corps of Engineering, & National Park Service, 1995) shows the top 15 outdoor recreation activities for people 16 years and older (see Table 19–1). A comparison of participation rates from 1982 to 1995 from the National Survey on Recreation and the Environment shows significant growth in a number of specific outdoor activities (see Table 19–2) and a decline in others (see Table 19–3).

As the American population ages and the 81 million people in the "baby boomer" generation approach retirement, the recreation industry must be aware of changes in age among its participants (Riddle, 1997). The age distribution among the population is shifting from younger to older. In 1900, the median age was 23 years, but it is expected to reach 41 by 2025 (Dwyer, 1994). The largest segment of the population will be middle-aged or older, most likely with diverse interests and a range of fitness levels, and recreation professionals will need to respond to the needs of these participants.

Table 19–1 Top 15 Outdoor Recreation Opportunities for People 16 Years and Older

Activity	Number in 1994–1995 (Millions)
Walking	133.6
Sightseeing	113.4
Picnicking	98.4
Attending a sports event	95.2
Swimming (pool)	88.5
Swimming (nonpool)	78.1
Boating (motorized and nonmotorized)	60.1
Fishing	58.3
Bicycling	57.3
Camping	53.7
Bird-watching	54.1
Running/jogging	52.5
Outdoor team sports	49.5
Hiking	47.7

Source: U.S.D.A., Bureau of Land Management, U.S. Army Corps of Engineering, & National Park Service. (1995). *National Survey on Recreation and the Environment.*

Increased racial and ethnic diversity is anticipated with related growth in urban areas. Between 1990 and 2025, the U.S. population is expected to increase by 50 million, of which 81% is expected among minority groups, particularly Latino/Latina Americans (Dwyer, 1994). Not only will the recreation industry need to respond to the needs of a more diverse population, it must also address the impact on recreation areas near cities. In examining recreation visits by population centers, the National Park Service's *1996 Statistical Abstract* showed that 37% of

Table 19–2 Fastest-Growing Activities

Activity	Percentage Increase 1994–1995
Hiking	93.0
Backpacking	72.7
Camping (primitive area)	58.2
Walking	42.7
Sightseeing	39.5
Camping (developed area)	38.3
Swimming (nonpool)	38.2

Source: U.S.D.A., Bureau of Land Management, U.S. Army Corps of Engineering, & National Park Service. (1995). *National Survey on Recreation and the Environment.*

Table 19–3 Declining Activities

Activity	Percentage Decrease 1994–1995
Tennis	29.3
Hunting	11.4
Horseback riding	10.7
Sailing	9.4
Fishing	3.0
Ice skating	1.9

Source: U.S.D.A., Bureau of Land Management, U.S. Army Corps of Engineering, & National Park Service. (1995). *National Survey on Recreation and the Environment.*

total visits were to rural facilities, the highest category. However, the next highest category was urban facilities with 31% of total visits, a 2% increase from the previous year. For instance, Angeles National Forest near Los Angeles attracts 30 million visitors a year, and 90,000 vehicles can enter the park on a summer weekend (Sullivan, 1997).

A challenge for the recreation industry will be to continue to attract younger ages to activities to sustain growth. For instance, young and old are significant participants in the game of golf, but the industry is aware that it needs to develop strategies to increase retention rates of beginners and especially women, who are increasingly attracted to the sport. According to the National Golf Foundation (1996a), almost half (48%) of all golfers are between the ages of 18 and 39 and play 12.6 rounds a year. Senior golfers (over age 50) make up 25% of the golf population and constitute the category the foundation describes as "avid" golfers. They play 36.7 rounds of golf a year. While women total only 21.5% of all golfers, they represent 38.3% of new players and are a target population for a sport that is seeing flat rates of growth after a boom in the early 1980s.

Women are participating increasingly in a variety of outdoor activities. According to a 1994 U.S. Bureau of the Census study of participation in selected recreational activities, women outnumbered men 51.5% to 48.5%. By 1997 the Sporting Goods Manufacturers Association said 53% of fitness participants were women, a 33% increase since 1987 (Riddle, 1997). This increased participation is evident in the emergence of women's-only programming such as the popular "Becoming an Outdoorswoman" series run by state fish and wildlife divisions.

Participation rates vary greatly by activity, and a newcomer to the recreation field would be wise to examine the demographic trends in each area. As the demographics shift, managers will be faced with the difficult task of changing recreation facilities and programs to meet participants' needs. Overall, participants will be older, more racially and ethnically diverse, and urban, and there will be a greater involvement of women. These factors will shape the industry in the coming years as recreation managers modify strategies for designing facilities, marketing programs, and hiring staff to deliver recreational opportunities responsive to this changing population.

SEGMENTS OF THE RECREATION INDUSTRY

Today the recreation industry offers people a wealth of opportunities for participation across its many segments, and consumers can find many intriguing activities to suit their needs. Competent recreational professionals are needed to staff the industry, and interested people are wise to explore a variety of options in what has become a very competitive job market. The industry is so diverse that it can appear very fragmented because it is divided into a myriad of professional associations specific to certain activities. The categories presented in the next few sections were selected as a means to explore major segments, but a prospective employee must realize that a particular recreation business may fit into two or three of the basic segments.

Community-Based Recreation

The term **community-based recreation** implies that participants are united by a common interest in recreation at the local level. General services are offered by local parks and recreation departments and such community agencies as the YMCA, the YWCA, the Girls and Boys Clubs, and the Scouts. Some agencies may target specific ages through youth centers and senior centers.

Parks and recreation departments are supported through a mix of local property tax monies and user fees from participants. No longer are these programs free to the public, given the increased competition for budgetary support among all town services (for example, fire and police departments). As a result, recreation managers are becoming increasingly creative in soliciting private sponsorships from local companies to sponsor special programs to keep program costs low to the public. To support their programs, agencies like the YMCA and the Boys and Girls Clubs often rely on a greater mix of funding sources, including user fees and memberships, private donations (such as United Way), grant programs from public and private sources, and in-house fund-raising events.

Public Recreation

Public recreation reaches beyond the local level to state and federal agencies. Recreational opportunities on public lands are managed by state forest and parks departments, the National Park Service (a division of the U.S. Department of the

Interior), and the National Forest Service (a division of the U.S. Department of Agriculture).

Interest in the national forests and parks remains high, with an explosion of visits to the 374 areas in the national park system and the 119 national forests. The National Park Service (1997) recorded more than 265 million visits to national parks, seashores, monuments, and historic sites in 1996. However, high use is impacting a system beleaguered by federal budget constraints, and repairs needed at national parks exceed $4 billion (Miller, 1997). As a result, the park service is considering new private–public partnerships to help defray the costs of running the national system. Under this proposed initiative, corporations could donate private funds to sponsor a particular park or battlefield and use a national park logo in their promotions.

The National Forest Service employs 30,000 permanent employees and a temporary force of 15,000 at more than 900 separate work locations (Martin, 1996). Traditionally, available positions focused on resource management, but the agency has added recreation employees in the last decade even while cutting the total number of employees in other areas, and this trend is expected to continue.

Military Recreation

The U.S. Department of Defense also maintains extensive **military recreation** programs through branches of the armed services. While an overriding mission is the fitness and military readiness of personnel, the armed services also seek to provide an array of recreational opportunities for families on bases in the United States and abroad as a means of improving overall morale and a sense of community. Facilities include but are not limited to ski areas, marinas, recreation centers, fitness centers, youth centers, golf courses, and bowling centers. Since 1948 the armed services have also supported the training of athletes for Olympic and other major international competitions, and more than 500 active-duty personnel have achieved Olympic status as a result (Rice, 1996).

Military recreation organizations face the same challenges as other government-funded recreation programs. Recent decreases in appropriated funds have challenged the armed services to maintain program quality and to improve their economic performance. The majority of recreation employees at military facilities are civilians rather than military personnel, which creates job opportunities for trained people from the local communities.

Outdoor Recreation

Outdoor recreation attracts people who enjoy natural environments in different seasons, and the increasing American passion for the outdoors continues to expand this already large segment of the industry. The Outdoor Recreation Coalition of America (ORCA) reported that retail sales for outdoor industry equipment, apparel, and accessories rose 9.3% in 1996 to $4.7 billion (1997). It is important to realize that ORCA's analysis does not include the dollar value of recreation programming during that same period, such as user fees paid for instruction, rental equipment, or facility use, which would increase the total substantially.

The outdoor industry is highly diverse, with a mix of for-profit and not-for-profit ventures in each subcategory. Segments include but are not limited to skiing and snowboarding, paddlesports (rafting, canoeing, and kayaking), golf, summer camps, backpacking and camping, natural resource management, and tourist travel. Adventurous programs modeled after Outward Bound are also popular among people seeking high degrees of challenge in the outdoors.

University Outdoor Programs

Extracurricular **university outdoor programs** and clubs provide excellent opportunities for students to participate in a variety of outdoor activities and develop instructional and leadership skills through instructor training programs. They are an excellent vehicle for obtaining experience prior to seeking a job and for beginning to create a network in the recreation industry. The most popular activities at the 180 university programs in the United States include rafting, ropes courses, backpacking, indoor and outdoor rock climbing, downhill skiing, and canoeing and kayaking (Webb, 1996). Fifty-five percent of the programs generated more than $100,000 each in gross income in 1993, with four programs tallying between $500,000 and $800,000 (Webb, 1996). These formal college programs are larger than many commercial recreation centers and offer excellent training to students in management areas such as marketing, accounting, and finance, as well as experience in instruction and leadership.

Therapeutic Recreation

The **therapeutic recreation** field uses recreational activities as a means to improve a participant's physical, emotional, and mental health. The activities can be offered as part of an overall treatment or rehabilitation program that may have evolved from medical care at a hospital, psychiatric facility, or nursing home. Therapeutic recreation services are also offered through park and recreation departments, independent living centers, schools, community mental health agencies, specialty recreation organizations, and social service agencies. Such services may also include programs for individuals who may be at risk of entering or are already in the judicial system.

The programs vary widely, from hospital-based cardiac rehabilitation, for which recreation is used to improve physical fitness, to a wilderness camp sponsored by a state division of youth services, which seeks to change the behaviors of court-referred youth. Therapeutic recreation organizations often seek personnel with experience in recreation, counseling, or social work. Most important, they need employees whose specific skills and experience match the needs of a specific population, such as trained chemical dependency counselors. Therapists who do not have specialized training in recreational activities such as ropes/challenge courses or watersports work in conjunction with other recreation professionals who can offer that leadership. As the American population ages, prospective employees should explore the opportunities available in adult day care, outpatient programs, psychiatric rehabilitation, and physical rehabilitation, especially services for people with disabilities.

CAREER OPPORTUNITIES

The recreation field offers individuals an excellent opportunity to work indoors and outdoors in pleasant surroundings, to enjoy a healthy lifestyle, and to introduce others to the benefits of participation at any age and any ability level. A number of common positions exist at recreation organizations, whether public or private, for-profit or not-for-profit (see Exhibit 19–1).

Recreation consumers, particularly those ready to pay a fee for participation, are increasingly savvy customers who expect a high degree of professional service in instruction and in overall service delivery. From the moment they telephone an organization to inquire about recreation programs and services, customers often seek to be reassured that they will obtain an educational, enjoyable, and safe experience. Some recreational activities can be very exciting, with higher degrees of risk than are present in other activities. After all, the challenging nature of outdoor sports like whitewater kayaking or rock climbing is the very element that intrigues participants. Recreation professionals have a responsibility to deliver these programs with a high degree of skill and manage them with an eye toward safety.

Job Search Strategies

Recreation managers are always seeking effective instructors, leaders, or guides who can create and execute programs, deliver excellent instruction tailored to the participants' needs, and provide leadership in challenging situations. A recreation manager wants people-oriented employees who know how to commu-

Exhibit 19–1 Typical Recreation Positions

Activity director (cruise ships, senior centers)
Aquatics director
Aquatics specialist (town summer programs, YMCAs, YWCAs)
Armed forces recreation leader
Camp counselor
Camp director
Facilities manager (bowling, marinas, rafting)
Guide (river, fishing, hunting)
Instructor (skiing, swimming, canoeing, kayaking, scuba, wilderness, etc.)
Naturalist
Outdoor travel/tour leader
Park ranger
Park superintendent
"Pro" (golf, tennis)
Program director
Recreation director (town, community center)
Recreation therapist
Retail manager
Youth coordinator

nicate well with the public, who work well with a variety of customers and staff, and who are responsible individuals committed to delivering quality programs and services. A recreation agency is often a small, lean operation that also needs employees who bring business skills to the operation. As recreation professionals move into managerial positions, particularly with larger agencies, they may need to supervise programs and staff, monitor risk management concerns in recreation, create innovative marketing campaigns, develop and administer budgets, be a liaison with public and private agencies, and develop alternative sources of funding beyond user fees.

Finding a recreation job requires a general understanding of all segments of the industry and a sense of where expansion in this highly competitive industry is occurring or is likely to occur. A prospective employee should analyze the specialized instructional and managerial skills necessary in specific areas of interest. A multifaceted approach should be adopted to successfully obtain a recreation position (see Exhibit 19–2).

Professional Preparation

Two different approaches to professional preparation exist in the recreation field. There is the recreation *skills* approach, which provides shorter, more

Exhibit 19–2 A Four-Step Strategy

Step 1.   *Participate in a variety of activities.* Explore both popular and relatively uncommon activities (such as backpacking, scuba diving, sailing, or rock climbing). Employers and clients want to see staff with active experience in a variety of interesting undertakings.

Step 2.   *Develop general instructional/programming skills.* Working with a wide variety of ages, sexes, abilities, and types of programming is help ıl, particularly for those who aspire to an administrative position as a coordinator or director. Recreation managers are seeking employees with tangible skills, and a useful strategy is to obtain training and hands-on experience through internships, cooperative education, summer employment, and volunteer opportunities.

Step 3.   *Refine skills in several specific programming areas.* Recreation is becoming increasingly specialized, and prospective employers may want an employee with a set of skills unique to a specific activity. Obtaining specific training and certification from a designated national governing body such as Professional Ski Instructors of America, the American Red Cross, or the American Canoe Association is necessary. First aid and emergency preparedness skills are essential part of this training.

Step 4.   *Consider associated skills that can strengthen a resume.* A versatile candidate also offers a base of knowledge and skills useful to a business office, including marketing, accounting, public relations, business computer applications, writing, knowledge of legal issues, and computer-aided promotional design. Academic programs enable a prospective candidate to develop this more extensive background.

intensive preparation in a particular area, often resulting in certification. The other approach is to select an *academic* program of one, two, or three years' duration at a college or university, which provides a broader knowledge base. It is important to realize that not every prospective employee has a recreation or outdoor recreation degree. Other related, useful degrees include forestry, social work, sport management, business, early childhood education, criminal justice, environmental education, and public administration.

The skills approach enables a person to obtain training and experience through organizations like the National Outdoor Leadership School (NOLS) or Outward Bound, two of the largest outdoor organizations that provide specialized leadership development. A person might also participate in the certification processes offered by national governing bodies such as the American Canoe Association or Professional Ski Instructors of America. Other nationally recognized agencies also provide training. Project Adventure, for example, teaches people to use structured activities on challenge/obstacle courses in environments ranging from summer camps to corporate training and development. Project Adventure provides a short-term, focused program at a lower cost (than other training avenues) that develops an individual's instructional and leadership skills in one specific activity.

Academic programs at colleges and universities offer a broader base of knowledge through expanded curricula for bachelor's and master's degrees. Individuals who seek to advance to managerial positions in program development or general administration are wise to seek a master's degree. These programs vary in their alignments within the institution, and such alignments may flavor the curriculum. For instance, they may be housed in schools of health, physical education, recreation, or education as well as departments of sport management, forestry and natural resources, or travel and tourism.

Interested students are wise to establish a foundation of knowledge through general courses and select a focus in a particular segment that provides deeper knowledge and skills. Exhibit 19–3 provides an overview of some basic courses that can be useful in the recreation field. Because industry segments overlap, it is difficult to strictly divide academic courses into the various segments. A blend of courses from those listed for specific segments is useful preparation for the field.

CURRENT ISSUES

The traditional roots of the recreation industry continue to shape the modern profession. The worth of recreation programming is still judged in terms of its ability to build better human beings and enhance community life. Today recreation professionals are faced with additional challenges in fulfilling their missions because of changing factors in our society. Managers will need to monitor shifting demographic trends to adequately handle the impact of continuing financial constraints facing the recreation industry.

A fundamental shift in the financing of recreation has occurred in an era in which federal, state, and local governments have reduced their proportionate share of recreation budgets. Public recreation now competes for funding in an economic climate shadowed by a rising federal deficit, the emergence of state tax reform initiatives, and constrained local budgets. The recreation professional is often faced with the task of finding alternatives to government funding or user fees to support recreation services.

Park and recreation officials at local, state, and federal levels are faced with challenges that include deteriorating park and recreation infrastructures, increasing crime, and declining federal, state, and local tax resources. Professionals must determine creative methods for capital development while simultaneously controlling operating expenses and establishing spending priorities in light of increasingly reduced budgets. Recreation managers must also strategize how to make parks safe from vandalism, crime, gangs, and substance abuse so that parks don't have an image that prevents citizens from enjoying them. They must compete

Exhibit 19–3 Academic Course Preparation for the Recreation Industry

General Recreation Courses Useful for Any Industry Segment
Introduction to Recreation and Leisure Services
History of Recreation
Recreation and Society
Program Planning and Organization
Group Leadership and Supervision
Risk Managen: t in Recreation
Recreation Facilities Planning and Design
Internship/Cooperative Education placement

General Business Courses Useful for Any Industry Segment
Financial Accounting
Introduction to Marketing
Fundamentals of Finance
Management Principles
Personnel Management
Public Relations
Computer Business Applications

Courses for Public Recreation
Park and Recreation Administration
Public Administration
Recreation Resource Management
Conservation Law and Enforcement

Courses for Outdoor Recreation
Introduction to Outdoor Recreation
Commercial Recreation
Travel and Tourism
Environmental Education and Interpretation

Courses for Therapeutic Recreation
Introduction to Therapeutic Recreation
Recreation and Rehabilitation
Special Populations in Therapeutic Recreation

effectively at the community, state, and federal level for funding as well as position themselves politically to shape government policies affecting their governance (Russell, 1996).

The role of public recreation at the local level is increasingly one of human service, and it often involves collaboration between recreation agencies and other departments, such as police, housing authorities, school departments, and social service agencies. In 1994 the National Recreation and Park Association (NRPA) stated that the perception of public recreation must move "'beyond fun and games' to the status of an essential service" that directly addresses social problems (National Recreation and Park Association, 1994, p. iv). Further, NRPA case studies of successful programs (National Recreation and Park Association, 1996) show that recreation programs can help to combat gang problems, revitalize families and communities, prevent substance abuse, enhance academic development, and provide employment training.

For instance, in 1989 the Dallas Park and Recreation Department created a cooperative gang prevention program with police and other community agencies in an effort to combat gang-related violent crime. The program, which had 3,000 participants by 1990, was designed to provide education programs, counseling, recreation, and job training and placement. In 1993 police stated the program played "a significant role" in reducing juvenile arrests by 26% (National Recreation and Park Association, 1994, p. 33). To monitor the program's success, park and recreation staff continue to track the significant numbers of youth gaining general equivalency diplomas, staying in school, and obtaining jobs and promotions.

Public and Private Sectors

At the state and federal level, a recreation manager must have an understanding of the unique interaction between public and private sectors (Sem, Clements, & Bloomquist, 1996). The **public sector**, or government, owns and manages the trails, beaches, information centers, and wildlife that attract people to a particular region. The **private sector**, or non-government, often provides the jobs and services that enable people to enjoy their experience while they are there. The relationship may be quite formal, as when concessionaires are contracted by the government to provide food services or run hotels in national parks or when ski areas use national forest land for their operations. The effects of this interaction can be far-reaching; for instance, proposals by ski areas to expand their snow-making capacity on federal lands require review by a host of government agencies, including federal, state, and local and environmental protection divisions. To be successful, a commercial operator must have a knowledge of public laws, policies, and practices.

Many private or nonprofit businesses that are not recreation-related also use public lands, as in the case of ranchers who graze cattle on public lands or logging companies that cut timber in national forests. Effective government coordination is needed between all interested parties to promote a viable recreation and tourism industry. While an awareness of public policy is essential at every government level, it is particularly crucial for managers grappling with controversial issues. Proposed resource management plans, particularly a change in forest practices, often attract the attention of diverse groups, including logging interests, recreational users, and environmental or conservation agencies. Today's park managers need to be politically savvy to balance a variety of constituents' interests in public lands and handle the public scrutiny inherent in their positions.

Commercial outdoor recreation organizations grapple with continuing challenges in achieving financial security. As segments of the industry expand rapidly, they may face a shakedown similar to that occurring in the maturing ski industry. Recent mergers have combined seven or more mid-sized ski areas under one owner in an effort to increase financial efficiency (Gilpin, 1996). However, an unanswered question is whether "bigger is better," because the impact on skier ticket prices has yet to be felt, and an analysis of improvements in skier services must occur in the future ("Skiing in the Land," 1997). Anticipating and planning for the adverse effects of unfavorable weather is necessary in outdoor recreation and affects financial stability; for instance, snow-making costs at ski areas have increased to cover fluctuations in snow conditions, and rising insurance premiums have also contributed to contractions in the industry. Vermont Ski Areas Association (1990) noted there were 81 ski areas in Vermont in 1970; in 1997 there were 24.

As visitors to public lands increase, recreation professionals have a responsibility to monitor and control use to prevent destruction of natural resources and enhance participant safety. Improved **environmental awareness** is necessary as instructors and guides need to abide by the increasingly strict regulations that control public use and also to educate their participants about those guidelines. Users must understand recommended environmental practices for minimizing impact upon trails, rivers, and camping areas, particularly in high-traffic areas, and abide by the restrictions in group numbers that federal and state agencies have levied. Leaders need to minimize conflicts between diverse users, such as hikers and mountain bikers, skiers, and snowmobilers. They also need to conduct activities in accordance with recognized safe practices in the activity to minimize accidents and rescues. While client safety itself is an issue, cost is a concern as well. The public cannot afford to underwrite the costs of rescues, which are increasing as the total number of visitors escalates in the outdoors.

Beyond increased environmental awareness, recreation professionals also need to develop **cultural awareness** in an industry that has become more global. Travel companies now attract customers to trekking in Nepal, sea kayaking in New Zealand, bird watching in Central America, and skiing in Scandinavia, among many other opportunities. For recreational professionals who do their work abroad, understanding local customs, laws, and the environment is important in providing successful experiences. For instance, Norway has a heritage of land use for recreation that allows a visitor to camp on private lands as long as the camping is unobtrusive, but this practice would not be advisable in a place like the province of Quebec, where certain rivers are strictly regulated and reserved for private salmon fishing and guiding.

Americans with Disabilities Act

Access to recreational facilities and services is being examined in light of the **Americans with Disabilities Act** (ADA) of 1990, which creates a unique set of challenges to the industry. The rugged terrain, remote wilderness environments, and necessary safety equipment inherent in outdoor activities require that a manager be creative and practical in developing programs accessible to people with disabilities. America Outdoors, Wilderness Inquiry, and the United States Department of Agriculture Forest Service (U.S.D.A., 1997) have noted that ADA implementation is slow as the full implications of the legislation are being interpreted. Park managers, outdoor outfitters, and guides must keep abreast of developments in this area as they create frameworks for improved access to programs and activities, such as rafting, canoeing, hiking, and horseback riding. The legislation will benefit our aging population as well as people with severe physical limitations.

Initially some people questioned whether the Wilderness Act of 1964, which prohibits mechanized transport in wilderness areas, also prevented the use of wheelchairs in these areas. But Section 507(c) of the ADA clearly states that nothing in the Wilderness Act prevents wheelchair use in a wilderness area. Section 507(c) also directed the National Council on Disability to examine the use of national wilderness areas by persons with disabilities. One major finding was that federal managers need training and assistance in making consistent decisions regarding ADA compliance (U.S.D.A., 1997). As a result, the Forest Service's *Wilderness Access Decision Tool* (U.S.D.A., 1997) was devised to provide a resource for managers to help them make decisions about physical modifications to trails and facilities, accommodate assistive devices including service dogs, and review visitor use regulations and policies for inadvertent discrimination against people with disabilities, such as group size restrictions.

Therapeutic recreation professionals need to study the economic restructuring of the health care system and understand how a shift from institutional care to home-based care will affect delivery of services. As the American population ages and the number of people with disabilities increases, the demand for services is likely to increase. The therapeutic recreation professional may be asked to integrate recreation services as a part of a comprehensive home health care plan. He or she might also explore respite care, wherein caregivers provide for older citizens at a central facility during the day, providing stimulating programs that involve and challenge participants.

In therapeutic recreation, staff also need specialized training to effectively meet the needs of a particular population. A professional may need to understand substance abusers, eating disorders, attention deficit and hyperactivity disorders, mental health issues such as depression and post-traumatic stress syndrome, and physical health issues such as cardiac problems and disability challenges. Understanding the range of medications and their side effects in combination with exercise is also important. Developing an accurate and positive portrait of each participant's capability is necessary, and recreation staff must work with agency personnel prior to programs to develop program goals that meet participants' needs.

Risk Management

Understanding the role of **risk management** in recreation is integral to all segments of the industry. Employees have a responsibility to develop safe, enjoyable programming at appropriate sites and conduct it prudently without eliminating the challenge and excitement that originally attracted people to the activity. Administrators and staff who understand the laws affecting recreation and are familiar with the elements of risk management can combat the increase in lawsuits against recreational professionals and in out-of-court settlements by insurance companies.

Recreation programs need well-defined, written risk management plans to establish guidelines for equipment and facility use, program development and operation, management of changing environmental conditions, and emergency preparedness. The recommended practices of an organization should be reflected in its risk management plan, and an ongoing review of the plan is necessary to ensure that employees are abiding by the guidelines and that the guidelines are still appropriate in light of current standards in the field. Many larger, nationwide programs have designated national safety committees that review procedures and accidents and use outside evaluators to help target areas for improvement. Smaller businesses conduct internal reviews among staff and administrators to improve their practices.

Elements of a risk management program include but are not limited to the following: participant health screening prior to participation to determine the appropriate level of involvement, if any; pre-program information to inform participants about an activity; equipment and facility safety checks; criteria for staff hiring, including necessary activity certifications or experience and first aid credentials; recommended progressions of activities that meet current national standards; adequate staff–student ratios and protocols for general and specific supervision of groups; emergency response protocols, including first aid response, evacuation, and search and rescue; and critical accident protocols, including those covering interaction with families and the press.

Informed participant consent is an important legal issue in recreation programming. Participants must be made aware of the potential risks inherent in activities before they begin so they can make informed decisions about the nature of their participation. Organizations often provide pre-program activity information, recommended clothing and equipment lists, and an assumption-of-risk/ waiver-of-liability form in an effort to inform people about the upcoming experience. Safety education is an integral part of a program plan, and individual and group responses in emergency situations are sometimes practiced in recreational activities as a part of a participant's education. As the popularity of adventurous activities increases, professionals have a responsibility to train participants in rescue so that they do not rely on agencies to execute rescues on their behalf.

Greater degrees of risk are inherent in some recreational activities, which make them exciting, but organizations have a responsibility to use this element wisely. Leaders have a legal responsibility to develop programs that do not involve unreasonable risks, and they should only ask participants to perform activities that have a clear benefit. Pushing people into risk without an educational purpose is an unsound practice; risk should be in the environment, not in the program (Hunt, 1994). (For more information on risk management, refer to Chapter 5, Legal Principles Applied to Sport Management.)

SUMMARY

The complexity of modern life is likely to promote a continuing need for enjoyable, safe, and challenging recreational activities as a diversion for the American public and also as a partial solution to social problems in our society. Just as American lifestyles have become more complex, so has the nature of the recreation profession. The industry faces numerous challenges as it seeks to provide quality recreational experiences for diverse participants.

Technological changes in equipment and communications require that employees understand their impact upon recreation businesses. Such things as cellular phones on wilderness trips and marketing through the Internet have changed the face of the industry. The ease of international travel and the emergence of popular eco-vacations overseas prompts professionals to understand different cultures and physical environments. Increasing government regulation, particularly in the area of safety, means professionals must be aware of and comply with new laws, policies, and procedures. As specific industry segments mature, employees will be held to higher and higher standards of training and performance.

These challenges require that employees bring a broad range of skills to their positions and that they continue their education to deliver quality experiences that meet current standards in the field. The reward is involvement in enriching experiences that enhance the recreation employee's life and that can effect social change.

CASE STUDY: TRAGEDY ON MT. EVEREST

On Mt. Everest, climbers call the dangerous area above 24,000 feet the "Death Zone" because the lack of oxygen literally begins to kill a person's brain and alters his or her perceptions. But the Zone might have earned its name for another reason. One in four people who reach the summit of Mt. Everest die on the descent. At 29,028 feet, the mountain is the highest in the world, and it has killed more than 130 people since British expeditions first explored it in 1921.

American climber Jon Krakauer (1997a), who reached the summit of Mt. Everest on the afternoon of May 10, 1996, has said a person has to be "clinically delusional" to climb the mountain against such odds. He was one of 23 who reached the top of the world that day, before ferocious winds and triple-digit windchill from a fast-moving snowstorm trapped teams on the exposed ridges. Eight lost their lives, including his expedition leader and the head of a competing guide service. One frost-bitten survivor, who lost his nose, also had to have his hand amputated after a dangerous evacuation from the mountain.

"Let's not mince words: Everest doesn't attract a whole lot of well-balanced folks," said Krakauer (1997a), in the May 1997 issue of *Outside* magazine. "The self-selection process tends to weed out the cautious and the sensible in favor of those who are single-minded and incredibly driven."

However, the $65,000 paid to one guide service doesn't weed out the inexperienced and the unprepared. Even Krakauer, a superb technical rock climber with more than 25 years of experience, had never climbed as high as the Everest base camp, which rests at 17,000 feet. The sizable fee for guide service can place enormous pressure on the guides to get their clients to the top. Yet the guides must be aware of their clients' safety in an environment that induces a numbing hypoxia, a condition that arises from a lack of oxygen, that invites hallucinations and can prevent a guide from being able to take care of himself or herself.

When Krakauer began his descent, he passed 20 other climbers who were still ascending and faced a traffic jam at the Hillary Step, a narrow, technical section near the summit where only one person can pass at a time. He waited more than an hour to continue downward, running out of bottled oxygen before reaching his re-supply, as others, including some of the guides, ignored the predetermined turnaround time and trudged slowly upward to reach the summit. More than 135 people from 16 different teams were on the mountain at various camps during this time.

One native Sherpa guide, who should have been fixing ropes in place on one ascent, was tending to a struggling New York socialite who had planned to transmit news bulletins via satellite from one of the high camps. His failure to establish these rope guides delayed advancing members from reaching the summit in a timely fashion. Then quick, blinding snow struck various team members trying to descend a 3,000-foot stretch to the first tent camp below the summit.

Krakauer wrote that commercial ventures prevent customers from coalescing as a team, because Sherpa guides perform the majority of chores and decisions are made by the highly skilled expedition leaders. Unlike a self-guided trip, participants are not called upon to cooperate or support each other. As a result, the guides are expected to take care of anyone in trouble, which Krakauer believes contributed to the Everest tragedy. Some of the guides could not assist with the emergencies because, Krakauer told *Outside*, "They were dead or dying, and there wasn't enough of them" (Krakauer, 1997a).

By the end of the 1996 season, 12 people had perished on Everest, the largest body count in the mountain's history. Even if people had overlooked the dangers in recent years as more guided clients made the summit, they could not ignore Everest's reality after the 1996 season. Superior skill does not necessarily guarantee success on the mountain, as shown by the deaths of some experienced leaders. Sometimes only sheer luck gets an individual off the mountain's face. Nevertheless, commercial parties continued to flock to Everest in 1997, and eight more people died.

Now the Nepali and Chinese governments, which control access to the peak, must face numerous international suggestions concerning changes in policies and procedures for Everest. The poverty of both nations makes them desperate for the hard currency from the $10,000 permit per individual, and they will probably not want to limit their revenues. The risk is well-known to the climbing community, yet the lure of Everest continues to capture the imaginations of not only mountaineers but also an international audience drawn to the world's tallest mountain.

Questions for Discussion

1. Should a guide-to-client ratio of one-to-one be established to enhance safety?
2. Should the Nepali and Chinese governments be pressured to limit numbers when wealthy outsiders, aware of the risks, are willing to pay the fee and risk death?
3. Should criteria for guides be established by countries whose bewildering bureaucratic structure might limit enforcement? Or should the criteria be established by an international guiding association?
4. Should governments impose a "no oxygen" rule, which would in essence force marginally qualified climbers to turn back when faced with their physical limitations? This policy would also help to reduce the growing volume of trash from empty canisters and would reduce the overall number of climbers, since many would not attempt the climb without supplemental oxygen.

5. How should the international climbing community police itself? Should it endorse guidelines which outfitters would voluntarily adopt? Which guidelines might be appropriate?

RESOURCES

American Alliance for Health, Physical Education, Recreation and Dance (AAHPERD)
1900 Association Drive
Reston, VA 22091
703-476-3400
http://www.aahperd.org/

American Camping Association (ACA)
5000 State Road, 67 North
Martinsville, IN 46151
765-342-8456
general information: http://www.aca-camps.org/
job information: http://www.greatsummerjobs.com

Association for Experiential Education
2305 Canyon Boulevard, Suite 100
Boulder, CO 80302-5651
303-440-8844
e-mail: info@aee.org

National Golf Foundation
1150 South U.S. Highway One, Suite 401
Jupiter, FL 33477
407-744-6006
http://www.ngf.org

National Park Service
1100 Ohio Dr., S.W.
Washington, DC 20242
202-619-7256
general information: http://nps.gov/
job information: http://www.nps.gov/pub-aff/jobs.htm

National Recreation and Park Association (NRPA)
American Park and Recreation Society
Armed Forces Recreation Society
National Therapeutic Recreation Society
2775 S. Quincy St., Suite 300
Arlington, VA 22206-2236
703-820-4940
http://www.nrpa.org/

Outdoor Recreation Coalition of America
P.O. Box 1319
Boulder, CO 80306
303-444-3353
http://www.orca.org/

Resort and Commercial Recreation Association
P.O. Box 1209
Port Richey, FL 34656-1208
813-845-7373
http://www.rcra.org

U.S.D.A. Forest Service
U.S.D.A.
Auditors Building
201 14th St., S.W.
Washington, DC 20250
202-205-1661

U.S. Golf Association
P.O. Box 708
Far Hills, NJ 07931
908-234-2300

Young Men's Christian Association of the USA
101 N. Wacker Drive
Chicago, IL 60606
800-USA-YMCA

Young Women's Christian Association of the USA
726 Broadway
New York, NY 10003
212-614-2700

REFERENCES

Braden, D. (1988). *Leisure and entertainment in America.* Detroit: Wayne State University Press.

Coutellier, C. (1997). *Today's camps.* Martinsville; IN: American Camping Association, 1.

Dwyer, J. (1994). *Customer diversity and the future demand for outdoor recreation* (General Technical Report RM-252). Fort Collins, CO: U.S. Department of Agriculture, Forest Service.

Eells, E. (1986). *History of organized camping: The first 100 years.* Martinsville, IN: American Camping Association.

Gilpin, K. (1996, November 29). Seven ski resorts merge. *The New York Times*, p. D13.

Hunt, J. (1994). *Ethical issues in experiential education.* Dubuque, IA: Kendall/Hunt Publishing Co.

Krakauer, J. (1997a, May). Everest: A year later. False summit. *Outside*, 57–62.

Krakauer, J. (1997b). *Into thin air.* New York: Villard.

Martin, T. (1996). *Employment in the USDA forest service.* U.S. Department of Agriculture, Forest Service. www.fs.fed.us/people/employ.html#nfsoverview

Miller, L. (1997). *Sport business management.* Gaithersburg, MD: Aspen Publishers, Inc.

National Golf Foundation. (1996a). *Overview: Golf in the U.S.—1996.* Jupiter, FL: Author.

National Golf Foundation. (1996b). *Trends in the golf industry 1986–1995.* Jupiter, FL: Author.

National Park Service. (1996). *1996 Statistical abstract.* Washington, DC: Author.

National Park Service. (1997). *1997 Visitation statistics.* www.nps.gov/pub-aff/faqs.html

National Recreation and Park Association. (1994). *Beyond fun and games: Emerging roles of public recreation.* Arlington, VA: Author.

National Recreation and Park Association. (1996). *Public recreation in high risk environments: Programs that work.* Arlington, VA: Author.

Outdoor Recreation Coalition of America and Sporting Goods Manufacturers Association. (1997). *1997 State of the industry report.* Boulder, CO: Author.

Rice, H. (1996, September). Taking recreational sports to the limits: Military athletes go for gold. *Park and Recreation*, 40.

Riddle, J. (1997, February). 1997 State of the industry report. Report presented at The Super Show, Atlanta, GA.

Russell, R. (1996). *Public park and recreation trends: A status report.* ezinfo.ucs.indiana.edu.dmclean

Sem, J., Clements, C., & Bloomquist, P. (1996, September). Tourism and recreation management. *Park and Recreation*, 94–95.

Skiing in the land of the giants. (1997, March/April). *Ski*, 30.

Sullivan, L. (1997, July). Dark behind it rose the forest. *Outside*, 66.

U.S. Bureau of the Census. (1994). 1994 Statistical abstracts. Washington, DC: Author.

U.S.D.A., Bureau of Land Management, U.S. Army Corps of Engineering, & National Park Service. (1995). *National Survey on Recreation and the Environment*. Washington, DC: Author.

U.S.D.A. Forest Service. (1997). *Wilderness access decision tool*. Washington, DC: Author.

Vermont Ski Areas Association. (1990). *Ski area quiz*, 15.

Webb, D. (1996). *Outdoor recreation program directory and data/resource guide*. Boulder, CO: Outdoor Network.

Wilderness Inquiry, America Outdoors, & U.S.D.A. Forest Service. (1995). *Universal access: Guidelines for outfitters operating on public lands*. Washington, DC: Author.

CHAPTER 20

Strategies for Career Success

Mary A. Hums and Virginia R. Goldsbury

Key words: network, internships, informational interviewing, resume, cover letter, interview, professional qualities

INTRODUCTION

What is *your* dream job in sport management? General Manager of the Atlanta Braves? Director of Stadium Operations at Jacobs Field? Athletic Director at the University of North Carolina? How do you begin to climb the sport industry ladder? What are the realities of trying to break in to the sport industry? This chapter deals with these questions and gives you suggestions on how to market your most valuable resource—*You!*

MYTHS OF CAREERS IN SPORT MANAGEMENT: A REALITY CHECK

People are drawn to the sport management profession for a great number of reasons. The reason most often given is a love of sport. To be very honest, many people love sport, but a love of sport is simply not enough to land a job in the industry. As a matter of fact if you gave that as your answer to a prospective sport employer in an interview, it would be a very short interview! What prospective employers look for is a person who wants to work in the *business* of sport. An often used expression is, "It's nice that you love sports, but can you put people in seats?" In other words, sport employers look for people who are business people first and sports enthusiasts second.

476

People who seek careers in the sport industry often have misperceptions about what working in the industry will be like, and there are a number of common myths about working in the sport industry. This section is not meant to discourage students from going into the industry but rather is intended to present a realistic picture of what the job market is like for people trying to break in.

Myth #1: A Sport Management Degree Is a Ticket to Success

As pointed out in Chapter 1, History of Sport Management, the number of sport management programs in the country is growing, with approximately 200 colleges and universities currently offering sport management as a major on either the undergraduate or graduate levels. All of these graduates are seeking employment in the sport industry. In addition, some students graduating with degrees in management, marketing, advertising, communications, or exercise science, as well as many from MBA programs and law schools, are vying to land a job in the field. A couple of examples illustrate the demand for jobs in the industry. At the 1996 Winter Baseball Meetings there were more than 600 attendees at the Career Seminar conducted by Sports Careers and Professional Baseball Employment Opportunities (Lyons, 1997). In 1994, ESPN received approximately 35,000 resumes, and Nike received approximately 23,000 in the same year. Professional major league teams receive anywhere from 25 to 75 resumes a week (Sports Careers, 1994). What this means is that the competition for jobs is intense, and a sport management degree does not guarantee getting a job in the industry. It is important to note, however, that the sport industry is broader than just professional sport. A myriad of employment opportunities exist in health and fitness, facility management, colleges and youth sports segments, and the other areas mentioned throughout this book. Also, the more willing a person is to relocate, the better chance there is of finding employment.

What then are the advantages to earning a degree in sport management? First of all, one learns about the application of business principles to the sport industry. Taking a marketing class, for example, provides a groundwork in basic marketing concepts. As we know from Chapter 3, Marketing Principles Applied to Sport Management, sport marketing is inherently different from traditional marketing because the sport product is unpredictable and perishable, and the sport marketer has very little, if any, control over the core product. A sport management major will have a solid understanding of this difference. A sport management degree also gives a student working knowledge of the industry. Because classes are geared specifically toward sport, students are immersed in industry happenings in the classroom, constantly learning about current issues and current events. Many sport management degree programs allow for access to the industry via internship opportunities with sport organizations. These hands-on learning experiences give students the chance to live the sport industry firsthand, gaining valuable work experience. Beyond this, the internship allows students to meet people working in the industry and begin to establish a professional **network**. In addition, a good number of sport management academic programs have professors who have come to academia after working in the industry and who actively maintain industry ties, which gives students another way to access a network of sport industry people. The importance of networking is discussed later in this chapter. Finally, when working on a sport management degree, students find out about opportunities to build their resumes. Remember all those resumes sport organizations receive? What will make your resume stand out from all the others? Being involved in as many sport management–related opportunities as possible! Sport management programs often stage campus events such as 3-on-3 basketball tournaments and golf tournaments. Sport management programs often receive requests from sport organizations for event volunteers. Students are wise to take advantage of these opportunities and get involved. Having these experiences on a resume makes a difference. People who do not major in sport management do not necessarily have access to these advantages.

Myth #2: It's Not Who You Know, It's What You Know

The truth is, "It's not what you know, it's who you know." Actually, we could take this a step further and say, "It's not who you know, *it's who knows you.*" Having a degree is simply not enough. In the sport industry, as much or perhaps more than in just about any other industry, people hire someone because of a personal recommendation from someone else. The importance of networking cannot be overstated.

Sport managers have to actively work to expand their networks to include all kinds of people. It's easy and comfortable for people to build networks with other people who are like themselves, but for the sport industry to continue to thrive and to serve all constituents, sport managers must broaden their networks so that opportunities will be available to all.

Myth #3: Most Employment Opportunities Are in Professional or College Sport

When people hear the term "sport management," the jobs that most often come to mind are in professional sport or college athletics. To the question, "What do you want to do with your sport management degree?" a common answer is, "I want to be the general manager of the (fill in name of the nearest major professional sport franchise)." The fact is, the number of jobs in professional sport is limited. For example, at present there are only 30 Major League Baseball (MLB) general managers, and while that number may rise slightly via expansion, it will never be very high. The same is true for the other major league professional sports. Professional sport front offices tend to be relatively small. An MLB team may only have as many as 30 people in the front office, while a National Basketball Association (NBA) team may have 20. Also, there tends to be a relatively low turnover rate in these positions. People who get jobs in professional sport tend to stay in their jobs. Also, people already in the industry tend to get "recycled" when positions come open.

In college athletics, many colleges and universities are currently dealing with financial setbacks or concerns unrelated to sport that in turn affect the amount of money spent on athletic programs. If funding is not available to athletic departments, those departments are unable to hire staff people. State universities are especially susceptible to this problem, as lawmakers for the states make decisions about where state funding will go. If the state legislature cuts the amount of dollars available to a university, the cutbacks are felt throughout all areas of the institution, including athletics. This makes it difficult for college and university athletic departments to create new positions. In order to make up for this shortfall in personnel, however, a number of college and university athletic departments are offering more assistantships and internships. These positions offer an opportunity for those trying to enter the field to gain experience.

As this textbook has pointed out throughout the other chapters, someone entering the sport industry needs to look beyond professional and college sport for job opportunities. The multibillion-dollar segments of the industry include sporting goods, recreational sport, and the health and fitness area, to name a few. For example, in 1994, 41% of health and fitness clubs hired additional full-time personnel and 44% hired additional part-time personnel (International Health, Racquet and Sportsclub Association, 1995). The purpose of a book such as this is to help students broaden their horizons to see the vast opportunities that lie in front of them in all different segments of the industry.

Myth #4: Sport Management Jobs Are Glamorous and Exciting

Many people have the impression that sport management jobs are glamorous and exciting. They have visions of "hanging out" with famous athletes, driving around in chauffeured limousines, and being in the glare of the spotlight. However, when it comes to working in the sport industry, nothing could be further from the truth. No one goes to a Notre Dame football game to watch the ticket systems manager do his or her job. People do not go to a Spurs game in the AlamoDome to watch the event coordinator organize the details of the game. The bottom line is that sport managers labor in the background so others can enjoy the spotlight. A typical workweek for that event coordinator is 50 to 60 hours per week, including lots of late nights and long weekends. Remember, when other people are going out to be entertained they are coming to the place where the sport manager is hard at work. While it is exciting to work at games or events, a sport manager very seldom, if ever, gets to see any of the action of the game or event itself. There are too many behind-the-scenes details to take care of to be a spectator.

To a large degree, the jobs that sport managers do are similar to jobs in the corporate world, but they are unique in that they require industry-specific knowledge. Someone who is an accountant for the Brisbane Broncos professional rugby team in Australia, for example, is basically doing the same job as someone who is an accountant for any large business, but the sport accountant needs to understand player salary concerns such as deferred compensation. A sport lawyer works with the same issues as a regular lawyer, but the sport lawyer has to understand salary caps and luxury taxes. General business knowledge is important, but specific knowledge of the sport industry is essential. Another distinction is the affiliation with a team or league. People just feel different about working in sport. It's more fun to say "I work in the business office for the East Coast Hockey League" than it is to say "I work in the business office for Artisan Steel Fabrication." There's just something special about going to your office when your office is in a stadium.

Myth #5: Sport Management Jobs Pay Well

The expression "You have to pay your dues" is as true in the sport industry as in other parts of the business world. In general, salaries, especially starting salaries, tend to be low in the sport industry. There is such a high number of applicants for these jobs that salaries can stay low and people are thankful for the opportunity when they do get jobs. How many times have you heard someone say something like "I'd work for the Atlanta Braves for free!" Cylkowski (1996) gives these examples of starting salaries:

Equipment manager, college: $12,000
Equipment manager, pro: $18,000
Business manager, pro: $30,000
Athletic director, Division III: $30,000
Associate athletic director: $25,000
High school athletic director: $25,000
Assistant sports information director: $14,000

Despite these low figures, it is still possible to work one's way up the ladder to earn a more respectable salary after a few years' experience. For example, Team

Marketing Report (1994) reports these salaries:

Vice-president of marketing, major league level: $114,444
Director of marketing, major league level: $76,785
General manager, minor league: $62,500
Assistant general manager, minor league: $35,166

So now that you are aware of some of the barriers you may encounter on the way to finding your place in the sport industry, how do you go about starting down the road to your sport management career? How do you begin undertaking a success-ful job search? The remainder of the chapter gives you some tools to work with—tools such as informational interviews, job interview skills, and resume writing. Good luck!

FINDING A JOB

Finding a job, any job, is a difficult, time-consuming, and personally challeng-ing process, with the emphasis on *process*. As mentioned earlier, finding work in the sport industry is particularly challenging. Assuming you want a job that will be personally satisfying, your best strategy is to follow a defined course of action.

Steps To Finding a Satisfying First Job

Step 1. Self-Analysis

Analyze your skills, abilities, and interests and your preferred workplace environment. Before you know anything else, you have to know yourself. You may know you want to work in the world of sport, but it's important to find your place in that world. Your goal is to find a job that utilizes your strengths, challenges you where you want to be challenged, and minimizes your frustrations. There are a variety of instruments available to help you with this exercise, such as computer-based systems like *Discover, Sigi-plus,* or *Focus* and professionally administered instruments such as *The Myers-Briggs Type Indicator, Strong-Campbell,* or *Holland's Self-Directed Search.* You may discover that a pen and pencil (noncomputer) instrument may work as well for you. The career center at your college or university can help you discover which instrument or instruments will be most helpful for you.

One means of assessing your skills and accomplishments is through a "personal inventory." Personal inventories serve three purposes. First, they help you iden-tify your skills and accomplishments. Second, they serve as a start for designing your resume. Finally, they help you to define the value of your work experience. A sample personal inventory is provided in Exhibit 20–1.

Exhibit 20–1 Personal Inventory

Experience	Accomplishments	Skills Used	Learning
Court monitor 3-on-3 basketball tournament	Ensured games played fairly	Observation Decision making Communication	Difficult to monitor peers To pay attention in the midst of activity
Ticket clerk, athletic office	Customers received fair and equitable treatment	Communication Detail orientation Decision making Responsibility	Being polite, fair, and honest limits the number of problems
Marketing intern, Pawtucket Red Sox	Solicited corporate sponsors for game-day fan events Coordinated special Kids' Day contests	Communication Writing Organization Persuasion Responsibility Planning	Professionalism How to be clear and concise on the tele- phone and on paper Planning decreases stress

Step 2. Career Exploration

Exploring various career jobs, while time-consuming, can prove to be very interesting. Now that you have been exposed to all aspects of the sport industry by reading this book, select those segments of the industry you think would be most interesting to you and begin your research. The first step is to learn as much as you can about each area. Read books, professional journals, magazines, newspapers, and computerized databases (available in some career centers). The next step is informational interviewing, that is, talking to people who are in positions or organizations that interest you. This is a wonderful way to utilize and expand your network while gaining valuable insight into a variety of career paths. Informa-tional interviewing is explained in more detail later in the chapter.

Step 3. Gaining Experience

"Sorry, we're looking for someone with experience."
"How can I get experience if no one will hire me without it?"
The answer: **internships.** As a student you have the opportunity to gain valuable experience while earning college credit and exploring your career

interests. Professional sport franchises, marketing agencies, health clubs, facilities, and your own athletic department are examples of organizations offering internships. The work is demanding and the pay often nonexistent, but you will gain that sought-after experience, get an inside look at a portion of the industry, and expand that ever-valuable networking pool. An internship can occasionally lead directly to an employment opportunity, but even if it doesn't, in sport management the more you have been involved in the industry, the more interesting you are to any employer.

Take advantage of every opportunity you may have to participate. Many sport organizations need volunteers to help with events such as State Games or Special Olympics. Get involved early and often! Take the initiative and create your own volunteer opportunities even if none currently exist. Each experience will help define your long-term goals and in the long run make you more employable.

Step 4. Job Search Strategy

Once you have completed the above steps, you will have the information necessary to write an effective resume and cover letter. These documents should reflect the energy you have expended in preparing for a sport management career, and in them you can articulate your long- and short-term goals.

So, now what? It's often said, "Looking for a job is a full-time job." Although you may not be able to spend 40 hours per week on your job search, you must set up a schedule that works for you and stick to it. Decide to make a certain number of phone calls per week or mail a certain number of cover letters and resumes per week. Keep a well-documented journal of your job search activities. Follow up each application submitted with a phone call a week or two later. There's a fine line between being persistent and being aggressive, but you want your prospective employers to know you are interested in working with them.

NETWORKING

What is a network? How do networks operate? Everyone has networks, whether they are circles of friends or professional colleagues. Networking means building and maintaining relationships with people who do things that interest you. Networking gives you information and advice about jobs and careers (Smith College, 1993). It is not to be confused with self-promotion or expecting others to find a job for you (Smith College, 1993). Rather, networks help people grow and develop both personally and professionally.

How do networks function? Here's an easy way to remember:

N = Nurture
E = Experience

T = Teamwork
W = Worldview
O = Opportunities
R = Reach up, around, and down
K = Knowledge sharing

Networks operate to *nurture* people who are in them. They allow someone who has questions to safely ask them. Mentors help people grow and develop as individuals both professionally and personally. College coaching ranks provide good examples of how the mentoring relationship operates. For example, football coaches such as Alabama's Paul "Bear" Bryant have mentored other coaches, in his case people such as Gene Stallings at Alabama and Danny Ford at Clemson. Basketball's Dean Smith at the University of North Carolina mentored Kansas's Roy Williams. Famous sports agent Bob Woolf mentored current agent and his former professional football player client, Randy Vataha. Professional baseball's Mike Veeck most certainly learned from one of the best—his father, Bill Veeck.

Networks offer people the chance to gain *experience*. Someone within your network may know of an opportunity to get involved in an event or with a sport organization. A student who found out about an internship with a major league sports franchise through his network worked 10 months as an intern. Because of the experience he gained, when a job opened up with the organization, it was his! Experience also means you benefit from the experiences of those within your network. Even successful sport managers realize they do not know everything about the industry and thus are always open to listening to those with more experience in a particular area.

Networks are inherently about *teamwork* and working together to solve problems or generate ideas. Look around the room at your classmates. There are two ways of looking at them. Yes, you could say that all of you are trying to get into this intensely competitive industry, so they are your competition and you must squash them to succeed. Or you could see them as your *future colleagues*. These are the people who, when you are out working and you have a problem or need to bounce ideas off someone, you will pick up the phone and call for help. This is how networks work as teams, and the people around you are your current and *future* teammates. Be a team player now, and it will benefit everyone in the long run. Probably everyone has had an experience with an uncooperative group member. In a real-life group project example, a class was given a set of potential test questions to prepare in advance. Each group member was responsible to prepare and share the answer to a given test question, and the group scheduled a meeting to exchange answers. One student came to the group meeting, took everyone else's answers without sharing his information, and left. The group was incensed because this member had acted selfishly by thinking he would take advantage of and gain advantage over his classmates. When this same student could not find a job in the sport industry, he called upon his former classmates for help. Needless to say, he had "burned those bridges," and having no network, was unsuccessful gaining access to the industry.

Networks help people gain a *worldview*. The sport marketplace today is truly global in scope. It is impossible for an individual alone to know about cultures all over the world. However, by building networks inclusive of people from different countries, we come to learn and appreciate not just sport in other cultures but also the very cultures themselves. This knowledge is essential for success in today's global economy. We can no longer think in terms of national issues—we must think internationally. Networks can provide you with access to this worldview. A sport manager working for USA Basketball or for an event firm that organizes world-class soccer events in different countries has the chance to meet people from all over the world and the opportunity to benefit from the expertise of sport managers from all over the world.

Networks are all about *opportunities*. By developing your networks now, you will open the doors to valuable opportunities. A good example of this is a student who utilized her network to secure a job with the Atlanta Committee for the Olympic Games. This student, Lisa, got involved early, as a volunteer for the Georgia State Games. She started as simply a volunteer but so impressed her supervisors that when an internship position opened up, she was given the opportunity to assist in game operations. When the Summer Olympic Games came to Atlanta, Lisa's supervisor from the Georgia State Games was in charge of a major Olympic venue, the Georgia World Congress Center. Because of her previous experience, Lisa was given the opportunity to become an assistant venue logistics director. After only five months on that job, she was promoted to venue logistics manager. Because of the network she started building as an undergraduate who volunteered at an event, this opportunity opened up for her.

Networks also work to create opportunities for those who have been denied access to the sport industry in the past. Women, racial/ethnic minorities, and people with disabilities have not traditionally had access to management positions in the sport industry. Expanding personal and professional networks can help change this trend.

Networks *reach up, around, and down*. What this means is that networks are three-dimensional and you will find yourself in different positions within your network as you progress through your sport management career. Right now, as students wanting to break into the industry, in your network you are *reaching up* to those already in the industry who can help you. Your network now also reaches around you to your classmates. Remember, you never know who knows the person sitting next to you! When you are actually in the industry, your network will *reach around* to your professional colleagues and peers at your workplace and other sport organizations. Also when you are working in the industry, you will have the opportunity to *reach down* to help someone who is sitting where you are now. As the saying goes, "No one stands taller than the person who reaches down to help another person up."

Finally, networks are about *knowledge sharing*. When looking back at how networks nurture, offer experience, promote teamwork, build worldviews, create opportunities, and reach up, down, and around, one realizes that the whole networking process is based on knowledge sharing. It could be knowledge about solving a problem, knowledge about international opportunities, or knowledge shared with new professionals. Whatever the situation, networks are about knowledge sharing so that individuals within the industry grow, making the industry stronger.

INFORMATIONAL INTERVIEWING

An important way to expand your understanding of a career, an industry, or a particular organization is to talk to someone who is already there. The information you glean from **informational interviewing** serves as a foundation for making your own career decisions, while simultaneously building a valuable network of professional connections. You may choose to interview relatives, friends, acquaintances, alumni of your school, or someone you don't know personally. Alumni are often an overlooked resource; however, if they have remained in contact with their school, they may be very willing to help you with your process. Check with the career center at your college or university, which may maintain a database of alumni who have offered their services for just this purpose. Your sport management program may also maintain such a list.

Be prepared before you make your call. Have your questions written down. Everyone is busy, and although a person may want to talk to you, you do not want to waste anyone's time. You have 20 minutes or so to talk with a person who has a job *you* would like to have. What is it you really want to know?

How Do I Proceed? What Do I Ask?

Some suggestions to consider are:

- Please describe briefly what you do. What tasks take most of your time? How would you describe your working conditions, including hours, pressure, pace, and so on. How does your position relate to the rest of the organization?
- What particular character and personality traits would you suggest one have to be successful in your position in this industry?
- What experiences, education, and other training would prepare me to enter this field?

- What kind of lifestyle choices have you had to make because of your job and how do you feel about them?
- What about your job do you find most satisfying? What is the most challenging or frustrating?
- I know that the sport industry is very difficult to break into. What advice would you give to help me successfully enter this world?
- Can you recommend two or three other people who would be worthwhile for me to talk to? May I use your name when writing or calling them?

Keep accurate notes of your interviews. You may want to refer back to them at a later date.

Other Information To Obtain

Professional journals, relevant books, and publications are valuable sources of career information. They provide current trends and plans for the future. Many of these have been discussed in previous chapters. Know what they are for your particular area of interest, whether it be college athletics, professional sports, event management, facility management, marketing, health and fitness, or recreation.

Almost all professions have an association that provides support for the profession. Such associations provide valuable information, job listings, and a means of maintaining a network of professional contacts. Some have student memberships, which is a convenient way to begin your professional affiliations. A number of these have also been discussed in previous chapters.

Final Hints on the Informational Interview Process

If possible, conduct your interview at your interviewee's place of work and dress appropriately. Dressing appropriately means to dress as if you were going to a job interview—after all, you will be making an impression on the person you are interviewing as well as gathering information. Be professional and articulate in your personal presentation. Observe the setting and the overall culture of the organization. Observe the relationships among the employees. Bring copies of your resume and business cards (if you have them) just in case someone at the organization asks for these materials. While you are there, ask yourself, would I be comfortable working in this environment?

Get business cards from everyone you speak with, and write thank-you notes to each immediately upon returning home. Remember that each person you met may become part of your personal and professional network, so you want to leave a positive impression.

WRITING RESUMES

What Is a Resume?

A **resume** is a marketing tool, and, as with any marketing tool, it is geared toward a particular segment of the sport industry. Remember, most organizations receive hundreds of resumes for every potential opening. The reader quickly scans each resume, looking for a reason to consider the applicant further. The purpose of a resume is *not* to get the applicant a job, but rather an interview.

What Makes an Effective Resume?

Use impact statements. When writing about your experiences think in terms of your accomplishments, what you brought to the organization, and any positive changes resulting from your experience there. Begin each statement with an action verb or skill and do not just restate your job description.

Quantify your work if possible. How many participants were in an event you organized? How many additional corporate sponsors participated this year as a result of your efforts? How much money was raised? Figures give the reader a clearer picture of the depth and breadth of your experience.

Use the professional jargon of the industry when appropriate. Use acronyms and abbreviations (e.g., NCAA or IHRSA) only if they are easily recognizable or the complete name has been used previously on your resume.

A stated "objective" is valuable if you are looking for something specific, such as a specific department or job. Otherwise, you might want to identify the skills you want to use on the job and consider a "skills summary" or a "profile" instead. This gives you the opportunity to restate your short- and long-term goals and to highlight your particular abilities. Especially in the sport industry, you will want to capitalize on your strengths and not a specific job title.

Think in terms of the accomplishments you identified in your personal inventory. Think, too, of what makes you unique. Have you held leadership positions on-campus or off-campus ? Do you speak/read/write another language? Have you studied abroad? Did you assume the responsibility for the majority of your educational expenses? Write with confidence, *not* arrogance. When putting together your resume remember one simple rule: If you can't back it up, don't write it down.

Two sample resumes are included in Exhibits 20–2 and 20–3.

Exhibit 20–2 Sample Resume #1

Paul L. Santini
55 North Elm Street
Northhampton, PA 18003-4444
815-462-8257

EDUCATION: University of Massachusetts, Amherst
Bachelor of Science, May 1997
Major: Sport Management   GPA: 3.26
Minor: Spanish

Select Coursework: Accounting, Sport Marketing, Media Relations in Sport, Sport Broadcasting, Sport Management Policy, Sport Event Sponsorship.

EXPERIENCE: **Marketing Intern, January-July 1997**
Boston Celtics, Boston, MA

Coordinated the New England Regional basketball event for boys and girls. Generated promotional materials; solicited corporate prizes and sponsorship; coordinated registration and event-day procedures. Participants numbered approximately 500. Assisted the Client Services Coordinator with planning, coordinating, and executing other major events, e.g., Celtics practice parties for corporate sponsors, game-day festivities for fans, and Draft Day [blow-out] for clients and fans.

Ticket Clerk, Athletic Ticket Office, September 1995-December 1996
University of Massachusetts, Amherst

Sold tickets for athletic events (basketball, football, hockey) to the general public. Resolved customer concerns and complaints when necessary. Balanced cash drawer at the end of shift.

Assistant Coach, Boys Lacrosse, September 1994-December 1996
Amherst Regional Junior High School

Taught proper lacrosse techniques to students 12 to 14 years old. Encouraged fair play and good sporting conduct.

ACTIVITIES: Bay State Games, Volunteer
Special Olympics, Track Timer
President and Founding Member, Sport Management Club
Lacrosse Club Team
Boltwood Project

SKILLS: Microsoft Word, WordPerfect, dBase, Excel, Adobe Pagemaker, Pascal

Exhibit 20–3 Sample Resume #2

Erica G. Walker
605 S. Lynn St.
Warwick, MA 01361
508-555-6011
e-mail: egwalker@umassd.edu

EDUCATION:	**University of Massachusetts, Amherst** B.S., May 1998 Major: Sport Management
EXPERIENCE:	**Assistant Membership Coordinator,** September 1997-present Winners' Athletic Club, Sunderland, MA • Participate in the design and implementation of marketing strategies • Write, edit, and do layout for monthly newsletter, using Adobe Pagemaker • Sell all individual memberships
	Chairperson, Third College Council, September 1996-May 1997 University of Massachusetts, Amherst • Spokesperson for college government, and liaison between student body and administration • Presided over $20,000 operating and programming budgets • Scheduled and facilitated all Council meetings • Planned and conducted student elections • Wrote regular articles for the campus newspaper
	Special Projects Intern, June 1996-September 1996 New Students Program, University of Massachusetts, Amherst • Solicited corporate sponsorships of events • Wrote and edited majority of welcoming materials for new students • Addressed groups of incoming students and their parents • Performed various administrative functions
COMPUTER SKILLS:	Microsoft Word, WordPerfect, Access, Excel, Adobe Pagemaker

continues

Exhibit 20–3 continued

ACTIVITIES:	Bay State Games Media Relations
	Assistant Coach, Girls Tennis, Amherst Regional High School
	Linesperson, High School Regional and State Championships
	USTA Team Tennis
	Volunteer, Haigis Hoopla, 3-on-3 Basketball Tournament

COVER LETTERS

A resume is *never* mailed without a **cover letter**, which should *always* be addressed to a particular person. If all else fails, call the organization to get the name and title of the appropriate person. Better still, use your network. Write to someone you've met or use his or her name in the letter. Remember all those resumes sport organizations receive? You want to set yourself apart—you want your resume to be read!

Use the cover letter to *enhance* your resume, not restate it. Cover letters should include examples. Instead of saying, "I possess leadership skills," give a specific example of a time you used those leadership skills. The cover letter is an integral part of your marketing campaign, and you are the product. Unlike the sport product, you are nonperishable, you want to be positively predictable, and you do have total control over the product. Show this in your application package by making it professional and confident.

THE JOB INTERVIEW—SUCCESSFULLY MARKETING YOURSELF

The job **interview** is your golden opportunity to show off all your positive traits and characteristics and to demonstrate to the prospective employer that you are the best candidate for the position. It is also your golden opportunity to find out more about the organization, the position, the opportunities for advancement—in short, to determine if you are interested in continuing to pursue employment with the organization. The keys to an effective interview are threefold: preparation, the interview, and follow up.

Preparation

The preparation phase is critical and should be given the same respect the actual interview receives. It will take much more energy and time than either of the other two phases. To be effective in the interview you must be very well-prepared. A football team practices for hours each day of the week for Saturday's three-hour game. The harder the players practice, the better they will be able to play in the game. The better they play, the greater the chance of a win. The same principle holds true for the interview. The more time you spend in preparation, the more comfortable you will be in the interview and the better chance you'll have to make a good impression.

In order to present a clear picture of who you are and what you have to offer, you must take time to assess yourself. Be honest with yourself. Evaluate the person you *are*, not the person you would like to be. Refer to your personal inventory and the section in this chapter titled What Makes an Effective Resume? Assess your strengths and weaknesses. We all have them. You should be able to discuss your strengths with confidence and your weaknesses with a plan for improvement. In assessing the appropriate industry, organization, and job for yourself, ask questions such as:

- Do I prefer working independently or with a group?
- How do I deal with stress and frustration?
- What kind of supervision works best for me?
- Do I like to write? Am I good at it?
- Am I energetic and good-humored?
- Am I really happy in competitive, fast-paced situations?
- Am I persuasive and able to motivate others?
- Is salary a top priority for me?
- Am I flexible, able to work long hours or on changeable projects?

The interviewer will assume you know something about his or her organization. Don't disappoint; learn as much as you can. Here are some potential information sources:

- Make use of the Internet, which is one of the prime information sources for almost every industry. Most organizations have their own home page. It's also possible to use the Internet to gather valuable information regarding the competition.
- Call the public relations office of the sport organization for written information.
- Read newspapers and professional journals.
- Talk to someone who currently works for the organization. Perhaps that person had the job for which you are applying or worked with the person who did.
- Speak to clients, customers, and competitors.

The Interview

Interviews are limited in time, therefore it is important to start off appropriately. Remember, you only get one chance to make a first impression. As in any new relationship, the first goal is to *establish rapport.*

- Dress appropriately.
- Be early—it is better to be ten minutes early than one minute late!
- Shake hands firmly (man or woman) and smile.
- Engage in conversation.
- Be friendly, warm, and interested.

Once the actual interview begins, concentrate on communicating effectively:

- Listen attentively. Restate the question if you are unsure what the interviewer is actually asking.
- Answer questions directly, providing examples.
- Talk openly about yourself, your accomplishments, and your goals.
- Maintain a positive, interested demeanor.
- Always ask appropriate questions.
- Be sure the interviewer has a fairly clear picture of who you are by the end of the session.
- Make certain you have a clear idea of what position they are hiring for.
- Always get a business card or a means of connecting with the interviewer at a later time before you conclude.

Follow-Up

The follow-up of an interview is an indication of your interest and maturity. As part of the follow-up, do the following:

- Assess the interview. Were all your questions answered? Was there anything you could have presented more clearly?
- Write a thank-you note immediately, reinforcing your interest and qualifications for the position.
- Call the interviewer if you have something to add or if you have additional questions. This shows you to be enthusiastic, persistent, and interested.
- Call the sport organization if you have not heard from the organization in the designated amount of time.

If you are well-prepared, aware of your competencies and areas for development, understand the type of work environment you would be most comfortable in, and feel you have the necessary skills and abilities, you will be successful. When qualifications of competing candidates are relatively equal, interviewers are inclined to hire people they like, who they feel have been honest and straightforward. Be yourself—that is the person the organization is hiring. If you are hired being someone else, that is the person you will have to be in order to succeed in that job.

What Makes a Successful Candidate?

Regardless of the skills a particular job requires, there are other **professional qualities** that the majority of employers seem to want (University Career Center, 1996):

- Preparation—knowledge of and interest in the employer and the job that is available.
- Personal or soft skills—confidence, adaptability, flexibility, maturity, energy, drive, enthusiasm, and empathy.
- Goal orientation—ability to set short- and long-term goals.
- Communication skills—written and oral, including listening and nonverbal communication skills.
- Organizational skills—teamwork, leadership, problem identification and solving, and time management.
- Experience—ability to articulate the relevance of previous experience to the position for which you are interviewing.
- Professional appearance—business suits for men and women alike, although women should stick with skirt suits. Since some people have allergic reactions to perfumes and colognes, it is best to not use them prior to your interview.
- Cross-cultural awareness—multiple language, international, or intercultural experience.
- Computer skills—word processing, database management systems, spreadsheets, statistical packages.

When answering interview questions, honesty is the best policy. An interviewer can always tell when a candidate is being less than honest. It is not only what you say that impresses an interviewer but also how you conduct yourself. "Behavioral interviewing" is a current style whereby the interviewer can gain information in a manner that allows him or her to predict future behavior based upon your past behaviors. The key to your successful interview is for you to provide real-life examples and document them with details. Discuss the situation, the task at hand, what action you took, and the results. Look at the above list of what employers typically look for and, using this model, prepare an anecdote demonstrating each trait. For example, when working on a group project, how did *you* react to a group member who was uncooperative? Or, how did you respond when you had to make a decision without having all the information you needed? Write your examples down and practice discussing them out loud. (As the entire interview may only take 30 minutes, you need to be prepared and succinct.) If you do this, it's unlikely you will be caught off guard.

In addition to questions you can answer using the behavioral format, be ready for some of the old standards: "Tell me about yourself," "How would your friends describe you?" "What are your three greatest strengths and weaknesses?" Again be honest. The recruiter is trying to find out how well you know yourself and how comfortable you are with who you are. The discussion of weaknesses is always disconcerting; however, whom do you know that does not have a single weakness? No one. You have put in hours assessing your skills and strengths. During that process you must have come across some things you wish you could do better. Choose three things you are either working on or have a plan to improve upon and discuss them while stressing your strategies for improvement.

Illegal Questions

There are laws regulating the questions employers may ask in an interview situation. Interviewers must limit themselves to gathering information that will help them decide whether a person can perform the functions of a particular job. Therefore, questions seeking more personal information—for example, marital status, sexual orientation, national origin or citizenship, age, disability, or arrest record—do not have to be answered. The decision to answer or not is the interviewee's. Although most interviewers will not ask these questions, you should think about how you will respond if the situation arises. If you feel particularly uncomfortable, discuss this issue with a counselor in your career center before your first interview.

SUMMARY

Finding a job in the sport industry is an arduous task, but the results can be rewarding. Incorporating the techniques included in this chapter, such as personal inventories, networking, informational interviewing, resume and cover letter writing, and interviewing skills, will help increase your marketability in the sport industry. Here's hoping all the hard work you do during your job search results in your dream job someday!

REFERENCES

Cylkowski, G.J. (1ᵒ ᵪ6). *Developing a lifelong contract in the sports marketplace* (3rd ed.). Little Canada, мN: Athletic Achievements.

International Health, Racquet and Sportsclub Association. (1995). *IHRSA's industry data survey*. Boston: Author.

Lyons, C. (1997, January 1). Baseball's payoff pitch. *The Insider*, pp. 1, 3.

Smith College. (1993). Materials from Smith College Career Development Office. Northampton, MA: Author.

Sports Careers. (1994, October 28–30). Sports careers conference. Miami, FL.

1997 Sports Marketing Salary Survey. (1997, May). *Team Marketing Report*, 7.

Team Marketing Report. (1994, January). *Team marketing report*.

University Career Center. (1996). *The career highway guide*. Amherst, MA: University of Massachusetts.

INDEX

497

ABOUT THE AUTHORS

Lisa Pike Masteralexis, JD

Lisa Pike Masteralexis is an Associate Professor in the Sport Management Program at the University of Massachusetts, Amherst. She holds a JD from Suffolk University School of Law and a BS in Sport Management from the University of Massachusetts, Amherst. She teaches courses in Amateur and Professional Sport Law and in Labor Relations in Professional Sport on both the graduate and undergraduate levels. Her primary research interests are in legal and ethical issues in the sport industry.

Her scholarly work includes contributions to *The Journal of Sport Management, The Journal of Sport and Social Issues, The European Journal for Sport Management,* and *The Women's Sport and Physical Activity Journal,* in addition to numerous book chapters in *Sport Law for Sport Managers, Management for Athletic/Sport Administration,* and *Sport in the Global Village.* She is also an occasional contributor to *Athletic Business.* Professor Masteralexis has made over 30 presentations in the United States and abroad before the American Bar Association, the Society for the Study of Legal Aspects of Sport and Physical Activity, the North American Society for Sport Management, the European Association for Sport Management, and numerous law schools.

Professor Masteralexis received an Outstanding Teacher Award from the University of Massachusetts and completed a year as an Eli Lilly Foundation Teaching Fellow. She serves on the Women's Sports Foundation's Athlete Protection Committee, is a member of the Massachusetts Bar, and serves in a pro bono capacity addressing Title IX issues in the state. Over the past five years Professor Masteralexis has also served as a consultant to a professional athlete management firm.

Carol A. Barr, PhD

Dr. Carol A. Barr is an Assistant Professor in the Sport Management Program at the University of Massachusetts, Amherst. She received her BS in Athletic Administration from the University of Iowa and an MS and PhD in Sport Management from the University of Massachusetts, Amherst. Dr. Barr teaches undergraduate and graduate courses in the areas of College Athletics, Sport Management Policy, Event Management, and Sport Enterprise (a graduate management course). She has published numerous articles in the area of sports law and has conducted research regarding the management of college athletic departments. She has also performed consulting work with the National Collegiate Athletic Association (NCAA) on faculty athletic representative involvement in the governance of intercollegiate athletics.

Dr. Barr is involved in the area of gender equity within interscholastic and intercollegiate athletics. She serves as the Title IX consultant to the Athletic Department at the University of Massachusetts, Amherst and has served as a Title IX consultant to high schools and athletic conferences. She has also spoken on gender equity to the Ontario University Athletics Association.

Dr. Barr was a Division I field hockey athlete at the University of Iowa. She has also served as Director of National Teams for the United States Field Hockey Association (USFHA) and as Volunteer Coordinator for the U.S. Olympic Field Hockey Team's Road to Atlanta Tour, and she currently serves on the USFHA's Events Committee.

Dr. Barr is a member of the North American Society for Sport Management, the Women's Sports Foundation, and the USFHA. She has presented papers at numerous conferences and general meetings, including North American Society for Sport Management (NASSM), National Association of Collegiate Marketing Administrators (NACMA), the Society for the Study of Legal Aspects of Sport and Physical Activity (SSLASPA), and the European Association for Sport Management (EASM).

Mary A. Hums, PhD

Mary A. Hums is an Associate Professor in the Sport Administration Program at the University of Louisville. She holds a PhD in Sport Management from the Ohio State University, an MA in Athletic Administration, an MBA from the University of Iowa, and a BBA in Management from the University of Notre Dame. In addition to being President of the Society for the Study of Legal Aspects of Sport and Physical Activity (SSLASPA), she is an active member of NASSM and the American Alliance for Health, Physical Education, Recreation and Dance (AAHPERD). Prior to coming to the University of Louisville, Professor Hums served on the Sport Management faculty at the University of Massachusetts, Amherst, directed the Sport Management Program at Kennesaw State University in Atlanta, and was Athletic Director at St. Mary-of-the-Woods College in Terre Haute, Indiana.

Her scholarly work includes contributions to *The Journal of Sport Management, The Journal of Legal Aspects of Sport, The Journal of the International Council of Health, Physical Education, and Recreation*, and *The Women's Sport and Physical Activity Journal*, in addition to book chapters in *Sport Law for Sport Managers* and *HIV/AIDS in Sports: Impacts, Issues and Challenges*. Her main research interest is policy development in sport organizations, especially in regards to racial/ethnic minorities and people with disabilities.

She was a 1993 recipient of a Georgia AAHPERD Research Award, and in 1997 was named Outstanding Teacher in the College of Food and Natural Resources while at the University of Massachusetts, Amherst.

She is a 1996 inductee in the Indiana Softball Hall of Fame.

Tim Ashwell, PhD

Tim Ashwell is an Assistant Professor of Sport Management and Sport History in the Department of Health and Human Performance at Iowa State University in Ames. He earned his PhD in history from the University of Massachusetts, Amherst, in 1994 and taught the broadcasting business class in the University of Massachusetts Sport Management Program from 1990 to 1997. Dr. Ashwell was a radio and television broadcaster in Massachusetts and Virginia for 20 years before turning to teaching. He was the play-by-play radio voice of University of Massachusetts basketball and football for more than a decade and organized the statewide radio football network. While teaching at the University of Massachusetts he was also actively involved in local cable television regulation as chair of the Amherst Cable Television Advisory Committee. His current research interests include sport and media history.

Kevin Barrett

Kevin Barrett is a 1990 graduate of the Sport Management Program of the University of Massachusetts. He is currently the general manager of the Springfield Civic Center and Symphony Hall in Springfield, Massachusetts. Prior to that he served as Public Relations Director and Marketing Director for both facilities.

Adri H. Broeke, PhD

Adri H. Broeke is the Director of Hanze Service Gamma of the Hanzchogeschool Groningen. He is also a staff member of the Free University of Brussels,

Belgium, and a staff member of the Sport Management Institute of the University of Groningen, the Netherlands.

Stephen Bromage, MS

Stephen Bromage worked as a literary agent and is currently a graduate student in the History Department at the University of Massachusetts, Amherst. He studies the relationship between mass culture and identity in the United States. He is also working on several documentary film and radio projects.

Dan Covell, MS

Dan Covell is a doctoral student in the Sport Management Program of the University of Massachusetts, Amherst. He has been involved in the administration and study of sport since graduating from Bowdoin College in 1986, having served as a high school coach and athletic director and as administrative intern in the Harvard University Athletic Department. He received his MS in sport management from the University of Massachusetts, Amherst in 1995.

Todd W. Crosset, PhD

Todd W. Crosset received a BA from the University of Texas—Austin and an MA and PhD in sociology from Brandeis University. Dr. Crosset is an Assistant Professor in the Sport Management Program at the University of Massachusetts, where he teaches sociology, history, and ethics to sport management majors. A sociologist trained in qualitative methods, his research focus is the social world of athletes and social problems in sport. He has published articles in the *Journal of Sport and Social Issues* and the *Sport Marketing Quarterly*. His book, *Outsiders in the Clubhouse: The World of Professional Women's Golf*, won Book of the Year honors from the North American Society for the Sociology of Sport in 1995. Dr. Crosset is a recognized authority on the problem of sexual assault in athletics, and he has served as a consultant to the Center for Study of Sport in Society and the Women's Sports Foundation.

Howard M. Davis

Howard M. Davis is a recipient of the Arch Award, the highest award given by the College Sports Information Directors of America (CoSIDA). Mr. Davis was inducted into the CoSIDA Hall of Fame in 1989. He has been a sports information director (SID) at Division I–III schools during his 27 years as an SID. After serving as a sports editor of the Attleboro (Massachusetts) *Daily Sun*, he accepted his first SID position at Kenyon College in Ohio and remained there until returning to his native Massachusetts as the SID at Springfield College in 1968. In 1980, Davis became the SID at the University of Massachusetts, Amherst. A 1966 graduate of the University of Massachusetts, Amherst, in 1993 Davis accepted the position as the assistant department head for external affairs and the director of internships in the Sport Management Program of the University of Massachusetts, Amherst.

James M. Gladden, PhD

James M. Gladden is an Assistant Professor of Sport Management at the University of Massachusetts, Amherst. Dr. Gladden holds a BA from DePauw University, an MA in Sport Administration from The Ohio State University, and a PhD in Sport Management from the University of Massachusetts, Amherst.

Dr. Gladden's research interests lie in the areas of sport marketing, event management, and international sport management. Specifically, Dr. Gladden has published research examining brand equity in the team sport setting. Prior to arriving at the University of Massachusetts, Gladden was a Project Manager for Del Wilber & Associates, where he conducted market research and wrote strategic market plans for a variety of sport and event clients, including the Los Angeles Dodgers, Iowa State University, Anheuser-Busch, and the Ladies Professional Golf Association.

Virginia R. Goldsbury, MEd

Virginia R. Goldsbury has been associated with the field of career development for the past 17 years. She is currently the Director of Career Planning for the College of Food and Natural Resources at the University of Massachusetts, Amherst. Ms. Goldsbury has been working closely with the Department of Sport Studies for eight years. She is also highly involved with her professional association, the Eastern Association of Colleges and Employers, having served on the executive board for over two years. Ms. Goldbury holds a bachelor's degree from the Pennsylvania State University and a master's degree in Education from the University of Massachusetts, Amherst.

Michael J. Graney

Michael J. Graney is a 1977 graduate of Northwestern University. He is currently President of the Springfield Business Development Corporation (SBDC), a private, nonprofit corporation responsible for business and economic development initiatives in the city of Springfield, Massachusetts. SBDC's major projects include the expansion of the Naismith Memorial Basketball Hall of Fame, renovations to the Springfield Civic Center and expansion for a new convention center, development of a baseball stadium and acquisition of a minor league team as a prime tenant, and the creation and management of a business improvement district for downtown Springfield.

Prior to joining SBDC, Mr. Graney was the General Manager of the Meadows Music Theater, an amphitheater in Hartford, Connecticut. He also served a lengthy tenure as General Manager of the Springfield Civic Center and Symphony Hall. He previously taught a course in Facility Management at the University of Massachusetts, Amherst.

Laurie Gullion, MS

Laurie Gullion, the former Undergraduate Program Director in Sport Management at the University of Massachusetts, Amherst, is currently an outdoor recreation specialist in the Outdoor Leadership Program at Greenfield Community College in Massachusetts. She has published six books on recreational sport, including the national instructional text for the American Canoe Association. An outdoor writer, she also leads wilderness expeditions in whitewater canoeing and skiing around the globe. She is currently writing a book on women in canoeing from the late nineteenth century to today. Ms. Gullion holds an MS in Sport Management and a BA in Communications from the University of Massachusetts, Amherst.

Dennis R. Howard, PhD

Dennis R. Howard is a Professor of Sport Marketing in the Charles H. Lundquist College of Business at the University of Oregon, where he has major responsibility for providing instructional and industry-service support to the Warsaw Center for Sport Marketing. Prior to joining the faculty at Oregon, Dr. Howard served as Head of the Graduate Program in Sport Management at The Ohio State University. He has authored or coauthored numerous books and articles on the topics of marketing and financing sport, including a text entitled *Financing Sport*. He currently serves on the editorial board of the *Journal of Sport Management*. A native of the San Francisco Bay Area, Dr. Howard earned degrees at the University of Oregon, University of Illinois, and Oregon State University.

William C. Howland, Jr.

Bill Howland earned a B.A. in psychology from Trinity College in Hartford, CT. For the past five years, he has worked for the International Health, Racquet &

Sportsclub Association (IHRSA) as Publications and Research Manager, directing the development of educational products for the association's member clubs, and supervising the association's consumer and industry research. Among his research responsibilities, he serves as the project manager for IHRSA's annual Industry Data Survey and is the principle author of the study's report, *Profiles of Success*. Prior to arriving at IHRSA, he worked as a tennis instructor and in membership sales for the Weston Racquet Club, and coached tennis and squash at an independent school in the Boston area, and directed the tennis program for a Boston area summer camp.

Mireia Lizandra, PhD

Mireia Lizandra holds an MS and a PhD in Sports Administration from Temple University, and a JD and a BS in Physical Education from the University of Barcelona. Dr. Lizandra is currently a sport management consultant. She has extensive international sport experience, having served as the program director for the National Relations Department at the Atlanta Committee for the Olympic Games (ACOG). In that capacity she orchestrated communications between ACOG and the 197 National Olympic Committees. Prior to her involvement with the Centennial Games, Dr. Lizandra worked for the United States Olympic Committee as an International Relations Coordinator. In that position, she was involved with the 1991 Pan American Games in Cuba, the 1992 Winter Olympic Games in Albertville, and the 1992 Summer Olympic Games in Barcelona. She has taught international sport management classes at Georgia State University and other universities.

Mark McDonald, PhD

Mark A. McDonald holds a PhD in Sport Management from the University of Massachusetts, Amherst, an MBA from Tulane University, and a BS from Warren Wilson College. Dr. McDonald is currently an Assistant Professor in the Sport Management Program at the University of Massachusetts, Amherst. He has published numerous articles in such journals as the *Journal of Sport Management*, *Sport Marketing Quarterly*, and the *Journal of Sport and Social Issues*. He recently served as coeditor for a special *Sport Marketing Quarterly* issue on "Relationship Marketing in Sport." He has given over 25 presentations in the United States and abroad.

Over the past five years Dr. McDonald has consulted with sport organizations throughout the United States, such as the NBA, NHL, Orlando Magic, Cleveland Cavaliers, and Hoop-It-Up. Most notably, he has worked with the International Health, Racquet and Sportsclub Association (IHRSA) for the past six years to produce the annual industry report "Profiles of Success."

Berend Rubingh, PhD

Berend Rubingh is the Director of Manage to Manage, the Sport Management Consultancy. He is also a staff member of the University of Nothumbria, Newcastle, England, and of the Free University of Brussels, Belgium. Most notably, he was the cofounder and served as the first President of the European Association for Sport Management.

William A. Sutton, PhD

William A. Sutton is an Associate Professor in the Sport Management Program at the University of Massachusetts, Amherst. Prior to assuming his present position, Dr. Sutton served as Vice-President for Information Services for Del Wilber & Associates, a sport and lifestyle marketing agency; served as Coordinator of the Sport Management Program at The Ohio State University; and was a member of the faculty at Robert Morris College. A past president of NASSM and coeditor of *Sport Marketing Quarterly*, Dr. Sutton is also a principal in the consulting firm Audience Analysts and has worked for such clients as the LPGA, Hoop-It-Up, IBM, Mazda, the Cleveland Cavaliers, the Pittsburgh Pirates, the Indiana Pacers, and the Philadelphia 76ers. Dr. Sutton, a coauthor of *Sport Marketing*, is widely published in the field of sport marketing and has made over 50 national and international presentations.

Glenn M. Wong, JD

Glenn M. Wong is a Professor and Department Head of the Sport Management Program at the University of Massachusetts, Amherst, where he teaches Sports Law. A lawyer, he is the author of *Essentials of Amateur Sports Law*. He has coauthored *Law and Business of the Sports Industries*, Volumes I and II, and *The Sport Lawyer's Guide to Legal Periodicals*. He has also written several book chapters and articles. Professor Wong writes a monthly column entitled the "Sports Law Report" for *Athletic Business* magazine. He is a member of the Arbitration Panel of the International Council of Arbitration for Sport and has served as a salary arbitrator for Major League Baseball. Professor Wong serves as the Faculty Athletics Representative to the National Collegiate Athletic Association (NCAA) and served as Interim Director of Athletics for the University of Massachusetts. He has also served as Acting Dean of the School of Physical Education. Professor Wong received his BS in Economics from Brandeis University and a JD from Boston College Law School.